P9-CDC-803

A HISTORY
OF UNITED STATES
FOREIGN POLICY

A HISTORY OF UNITED STATES FOREIGN POLICY

Fourth Edition

JULIUS W. PRATT
Professor Emeritus, The University of Buffalo
(State University of New York at Buffalo)

VINCENT P. DE SANTIS
University of Notre Dame

JOSEPH M. SIRACUSA
University of Queensland

Prentice-Hall, Inc., Englewood Cliffs, N.J. 07632

81- 167766

Library of Congress Cataloging in Publication Data

PRATT, JULIUS WILLIAM
    A history of United States foreign policy.

    Includes bibliographies and index.
        1. United States—Foreign relations.
I. De Santis, Vincent P., joint author.
II. Siracusa, Joseph M., joint author.   III. Title.
E183.7.P73 1980   327.73   79-10026
ISBN   0-13-392282-0

© 1980, 1972, 1965, 1955 by Prentice-Hall, Inc., Englewood Cliffs, N.J. 07632

*All rights reserved. No part of this book
may be reproduced in any form or
by any means without permission in writing
from the publisher.*

Printed in the United States of America

10   9   8   7   6   5   4   3   2   1

Editorial/production supervision by Joyce Turner
Cover design by Michael Clane Graves
Manufacturing buyer: Ray Keating

Prentice-Hall International, Inc., *London*
Prentice-Hall of Australia Pty. Limited, *Sydney*
Prentice-Hall of Canada, Ltd., *Toronto*
Prentice-Hall of India Private Limited, *New Delhi*
Prentice-Hall of Japan, Inc., *Tokyo*
Prentice-Hall of Southeast Asia Pte. Ltd., *Singapore*
Whitehall Books Limited, *Wellington, New Zealand*

To the Memory
of Samuel Flagg Bemis

Contents

MAPS   xv

PREFACE   xvii

1 INSTRUMENTS AND PROCEDURES OF FOREIGN POLICY   1

*The Department of State, 1.   The Foreign Service, 2.   History of the Foreign Service, 3.
Integration of State Department and Foreign Service, 4.   Other Agencies of Foreign Policy, 5.
The Channels of Diplomacy, 5.   How Treaties are Made and Ratified, 6.
Other Forms of International Agreement, 8.   The Growing Power of Congress and of the President, 9.
Additional Readings, 10.*

2 THE DIPLOMACY OF THE REVOLUTION   11

*The Quest for Foreign Aid, 12.   The French Alliance, 12.   Spain and the Revolution, 14.
A Pawn in the European Chess Game, 15   Great Britain in Difficulty, 15.
The Stakes of Diplomacy, 16.   The Peace Negotiations, 17.   The Treaty, 19.
Problems of Independence, 21.   Independence Disrupts Trade, 21.   Problems of the West, 22.
A New Government for the United States, 25.   Additional Readings, 26.*

3 WAR IN EUROPE RAISES NEW AND SETTLES OLD PROBLEMS   27

*The First Struggle for Neutrality, 28.   A Crisis with England, 30.   Jay's Treaty, 32.
Pinckney's Treaty with Spain, 34.   Hostilities with France—and a New Treaty, 35.
The Louisiana Purchase and its Sequel, 38.   The Retrocession of Louisiana, 38.
Jefferson and the Retrocession, 40.   The Purchase, 41.   Making the Most of a Noble Bargain, 42.
Additional Readings, 44.*

4 IN DEFENSE OF PEACEFUL TRADE—THE WAR OF 1812 AND ITS AFTERMATH   45

The Impressment Question, 45.   A Blow at American Commerce, 46.
A Competition in Paper Blockades, 47.   Jefferson's "Peaceable Coercion", 48.   Drifting into War, 49.
An Indecisive War, 50.   The Treaty of Ghent, 51.   The Beginning of the "Unguarded Frontier", 53.
Arbitration Becomes a Habit, 53.   The Northern Boundary and Oregon, 54.
The Boundary Treaty of 1818, 55.   The Transcontinental Treaty with Spain, 56.
Additional Readings, 59.

5 THE MONROE DOCTRINE, LATIN AMERICAN INDEPENDENCE, AND OTHER MATTERS   61

What Monroe Said, 62.   The Origin of Noncolonization, 62.   The Origin of Noninterference, 64.
The Problem of Recognizing Spain's Colonies in Revolt, 65.
Canning and Monroe Warn the European Allies, 67.   Effects of the Message in Europe, 69.
The Reception of the Message in America, 71.   A Diplomatic Miscellany, 71.
The Northeastern Boundary Dispute, 71.   The Webster–Ashburton Treaty, 72.
The African Slave Trade and the Right of Search, 76.   The <u>Caroline</u> and Alexander McLeod, 78.
Additional Readings, 80.

6 OREGON, TEXAS, AND THE DIPLOMACY OF ANNEXATION—PART I   81

Americans Colonize Oregon, 81.   The Oregon Question in Politics, 83.
President Polk Looks John Bull in the Eye, 84.   John Bull Will Not Be Bluffed, 85.
Moderation Wins in Congress, 86.   The Controversy is Settled, 87.   Texas, 89.
Texans Win Their Independence, 89.   The United States and the Texan Revolution, 90.
The Texas Question in Party Politics, 90.   Invitation by Joint Resolution, 92.
Texas Accepts Annexation, 93.   Additional Readings, 95.

7 WAR AND PEACE WITH MEXICO AND THE DIPLOMACY OF ANNEXATION—PART II   96

Subjects of Contention with Mexico, 96.   Polk's California Policy, 98.
Polk Reasserts the Monroe Doctrine, 101.   John Slidell's Mission, 102.   Polk Ponders War, 103.
The Clash of Arms, 104.   Initiating the Peace, 105.   Defining the Objects of the War, 105.
The War in Northern Mexico, 106.   The Occupation of California, 106.
A Blow at the Heart of Mexico, 107.   The Mission of Nicholas P. Trist, 108.   Manifest Destiny, 109.
Mr. Trist Makes a Treaty, 111.   Additional Readings, 114.

8 OPEN DOORS, FRUSTRATION, AND OTHER ASPECTS OF PRE-CIVIL WAR DIPLOMACY 115

Agents of Commerce in the Far East, 115. *The "Middle Kingdom" and Its Neighbors, 115.*
American Far Eastern Policy, 116. *The "Old China Trade", 117.* *The First Treaties with China, 117.*
The United States Takes an Interest in Japan, 119.
The United States Defines Its Policy in the Far East, 121. *The Tientsin Treaties, 121.*
The United States Opposes Partition of China, 122. *Townsend Harris and Japan, 122.*
The End of Japanese Isolation, 123. *A Decade of Frustration, 124.*
Canada—Annexation or Reciprocity?, 124. *The Pacific, 125.*
Approaches to the Pacific: Railroad Schemes, 126. *The Gadsden Purchase, 126.*
The Search for a Canal Route: The Clayton–Bulwer Treaty, 127.
Approaches to the Isthmus: The Cuban Question, 130. *The Pierce Administration and Cuba, 131.*
Additional Readings, 133.

9 THE DIPLOMACY OF THE CIVIL WAR 134

The Downfall of King Cotton, 134. *The War and Belligerent Rights, 135.*
Blockading the Confederacy, 137. *A Crisis with Great Britain: The* Trent *Affair, 138.*
The War and Neutral Obligations: The Confederate Cruisers, 140.
The Alabama Claims and the Geneva Arbitration, 141. *Additional Readings, 144.*

10 FROM THE CIVIL WAR TO THE SPANISH AMERICAN WAR 145

The Purchase of Alaska, 146. *Midway Island—and the End of an Era, 147.*
The Isthmian Canal Question, 147. *International Rivalry in Samoa, 148.*
Toward Hawaiian Annexation, 149. *The Monroe Doctrine and Pan Americanism, 152.*
Napoleon III and Mexico, 153. *The Beginning of the Pan American Movement, 156.*
Great Britain and Venezuela, 158. *Chinese Immigration Presents a Problem, 162.*
Japan and China Fight over Korea, 163. *The Open Door is Threatened, 164.*
The Chinese Market and the American Surplus, 165. *Additional Readings, 167.*

11 THE COMING OF WAR WITH SPAIN 168

The New Manifest Destiny, 168. *Expansion Becomes Republican Policy, 171.*
Hawaiian Annexation Revived, 172. *Civil War in Cuba, 172.* *The United States Intervenes, 174.*
The Collapse of Spanish Power, 178. *McKinley and the Philippines, 180.*
Spain Surrenders Her Colonial Empire, 182. *The Senate Debates Imperialism, 184.*
Hawaii, Wake, and Tutuila, 186. *The People's Verdict, 187.* *Additional Readings, 188.*

12 THE PROBLEMS OF A WORLD POWER   190

*Acquiring the Panama Canal Zone, 191.   Protectorates in the Caribbean, 194.
Cuba and the Platt Amendment, 195.   The Roosevelt Corollary of the Monroe Doctrine, 196.
The Dominican Receivership, 197.   "Dollar Diplomacy" in Nicaragua, 198.
Wilsonian Intervention, 200.   Haiti—The Fifth Protectorate, 200.
The Navy Governs the Dominican Republic, 201.   Wilson and Mexico, 202.
A Policy of Contradictions, 206.   The United States and the Far East, 1898–1914, 207.
John Hay and the Open Door in China, 208.   John Hay and the Boxer Rebellion, 209.
What Did Hay Accomplish?, 211.   The Russo–Japanese War, 212.   Roosevelt the Peacemaker, 214.
Japanese Immigration and the "Gentlemen's Agreement", 215.
A Naval Demonstration and a Seeming Diplomatic Victory, 216.   "Dollar Diplomacy" in the Far East, 218.
Additional Readings, 220.*

13 THE ROAD TO WORLD WAR I   221

*Prosperity of the Peace Societies, 221.   The Hague Peace Conferences, 222.
The Root Arbitration Treaties, 223.   President Taft's Abortive Arbitration Treaties, 223.
The Bryan Conciliation Treaties, 224.   Putting the Hague Court to Work, 224.
The Alaska Boundary Controversy, 224.   Arbitration of the Northeast Fisheries Dispute, 226.
The Panama Canal Tolls Question, 228.   Europe Drifts Toward War, 228.
Theodore Roosevelt and the Moroccan Question, 230.   Last-Minute Efforts to Prevent War, 231.
American Opinion and the War, 232.   The American Economy and the War, 234.
The British Navy Revives Old Issues, 235.   The German Submarine Raises New Problems, 237.
The United States Objects, 238.   The Lusitania Crisis, 239.   Germany Retreats, 239.
The British Try Wilson's Patience, 240.   A Peace by Compromise or a "Knockout Blow"?, 241.
The Germans Abandon Moderation, 242.   Additional Readings, 244.*

14 PEACE AND ITS AFTERMATH   245

*Wilson's Peace Program: The Fourteen Points, 246.   The Armistice, 248.   Wilson Goes to Paris, 249.
Could Wilson Put Over His Program?, 250.   Treaty of Versailles, 252.   The Problem of Russia, 252.
Wilson's Great Victory—The League of Nations, 253.   The Peace and the Fourteen Points, 255.
Self-Determination—for Friends but Not Always for Foes, 256.   Reparations, 258.
Germany Accepts, 259.   The League of Nations and the Senate, 260.
An Unsympathetic Committee, 262.   An Appeal to the People, 263.
Senator Lodge's Fourteen Points, 263.   The First Defeat, 265.   The Last Chance, 266.
Who Was Responsible?, 267.   Additional Readings, 268.*

15 THE UNITED STATES RENOUNCES WAR BUT SPURNS PEACE MACHINERY

The League of Nations in the Campaign of 1920, 269.
Relations of the United States and the League of Nations, 270.
The World Court Fulfills an American Dream, 271.
Isolationists Block American Participation in the World Court, 272.   *The Kellogg–Briand Pact, 274.*
The Washington Conference and its Sequel, 277.   *The Lansing–Ishii Agreement, 278.*
The Japanese Mandate and Yap, 278.   *Japanese Imperialism in Siberia, 280.*
Three-Cornered Naval Rivalry, 280.   *The Anglo–Japanese Alliance, 281.*
Limiting the World's Navies, 282.   *The Nine-Power Treaty on Policy in China, 283.*
Ending the Anglo–Japanese Alliance: The Four-Power Treaty, 284.
Other Treaties and Understandings, 284.   *Work of the Conference Appraised, 285.*
The Sequel to Washington, 286.   *The London Conference of 1930, 286.*
The End of Naval Limitation, 287.   *Economic Foreign Policy During the Interwar Period, 288.*
Settling the War Debts, 288.   *The Reparations Problem, 289.*   *Emigrant Dollars, 291.*
Adjusting the Tariff—in the Wrong Direction, 292.   *President Hoover's Moratorium, 294.*
The End of Reparations —and of War Debts, 295.
President Roosevelt Torpedoes the World Economic Conference, 296.
The Hull Reciprocal Trade Agreements Program, 297.   *Additional Readings, 299.*

16 THE MANCHURIAN CRISIS AND THE RISE OF THE EUROPEAN DICTATORS

Sino–Japanese Rivalry in Manchuria, 300.   *The September Eighteenth Incident, 302.*
The United States Joins Hands with the League, 302.   *The Hoover–Stimson Doctrine, 304.*
Manchuria Becomes "Manchukuo", 305.   *The League and the Lytton Report, 306.*
A More Cautious Policy, 307.   *Closing the Open Door, 307.*
European Dictators and American Neutralism, 309.   *The General Disarmament Conference Fails, 310.*
Hitler Repudiates Versailles, 311.   *The United States is Warned of Hitler's Purposes, 312.*
The United States Chooses Neutrality, 313.   *Congress Legislates Neutrality, 314.*
The Italo–Ethiopian War and American Neutrality, 315.
The Spanish Civil War and American Neutrality, 317.   *Making Neutrality "Permanent", 318.*
Additional Readings, 319.

17 A GOOD NEIGHBOR POLICY FOR THE NEW WORLD

First Withdrawals from the Caribbean, 320.   *The End of the Roosevelt Corollary, 321.*
Changing American Opinion, 322.   *A Policy "Opposed to Armed Intervention", 323.*
Nonintervention in Practice, 324.   *"Continentalizing" the Monroe Doctrine, 325.*
Mexico Tests the Good Neighbor Policy, 327.   *The Mexican Settlement of 1941, 330.*
Additional Readings, 331.

18 THE COMING OF WORLD WAR II 332

Beginning of the "China Incident", 332.   The United States and the China Incident, 333.
The Brussels Conference, 334.   The Panay Bombing, 335.   The "New Order" in East Asia, 335.
Hitler Opens His Drang nach Osten, 336.   Chamberlain Goes to Berchtesgaden, 337.
The United States Has a Finger in Appeasement, 338.   The Threat to Poland, 338.
The United States Tries to Shake Off its Fetters, 339.   Hitler Precipitates War, 340.
The United States as a Nonbelligerent, 340.   From Neutrality to "Shooting War", 342.
Hitler Declines a Challenge, 347.   The Road to Pearl Harbor, 348.   The Tripartite Pact, 349.
The United States Applies Pressure, 350.   Deadlocked Negotiations, 351.
Japan Moves South and Is Rebuked, 352.   Konoye Seeks a Meeting with Roosevelt, 353.
Final Negotiations, 354.   Would the United States Fight if Not Attacked?, 356.
Post-Mortem on Pearl Harbor, 357.   Additional Readings, 360.

19 THE GRAND ALLIANCE AND THE ENDING OF THE WAR 361

The United States and Great Britain, 362.   Wartime Relations with Russia: The Background, 364.
Wartime Relations with Russia: Strains and Stresses, 365.   China as an Ally, 367.
Good Neighborliness is Reciprocated, 368.   The European Neutrals and the War, 369.
Ending the War, 371.   "Unconditional Surrender", 373.
The Foreign Ministers' Conference at Moscow, 374.   "While Six Million Died", 375.
Cairo and Teheran, 375.   Churchill at Moscow, 376.
Europe at the Yalta Conference, 377.   The Far East at the Yalta Conference, 378.
Criticism of the Yalta Agreements, 379.   The German Collapse, 381.   Japan Surrenders, 381.
Additional Readings, 383.

20 THE UNITED NATIONS, THE UNITED STATES, AND THE ONSET OF THE COLD WAR 384

The Dumbarton Oaks Conference, 385.   The Yalta Decisions, 386.
The San Francisco Conference, 387.   The United Nations Charter, 388.
The United States Accepts the U.N., 390.   Beginnings of a Rift, 390.   Europe and the Cold War, 391.
Alternative Theories, 391.   The Future of Germany, 393.   The Potsdam Conference, 394.
The Satellite Treaties, 396.   Austria Regains its Independence, 397.   Deadlock in Germany, 397.
The Policy of Containment: The Truman Doctrine, 399.   The Marshall Plan, 400.   Point Four, 401.
The West German Republic, 401.   Divided Germany, 402.   Collective Self-Defense, 403.
The North Atlantic Treaty Organization, 404.   Beginnings of an Arms Race, 406.
Additional Readings, 408.

21 FROM PEACEFUL COEXISTENCE TO DÉTENTE 410

*Tragedy in Hungary, 411.   Berlin and Camp David, 412.   Expulsion at the Summit, 413.
Khrushchev and Kennedy, 414.   The Quest for a Détente with the Soviet Union, 415.
NATO in Trouble, 419.   DeGaulle Sabotages NATO, 419.   The Road to Helsinki, 421.
Additional Readings, 424.*

22 THE POSTWAR FAR EAST, I: BEGINNINGS—THE KOREAN WAR 425

*Toward a Democratic and Peaceful Japan, 426.   First Postwar Steps in China, 427.
The Marshall Mission, 428.   The Downfall of Chiang Kai-Shek, 429.
The People's Republic of China, 429.   The Two Koreas, 430.   Hot War in Korea, 430.
General MacArthur Comes Home, 433.   The Korean Armistice, 433.
No War, No Peace, in Korea, 135.   Additional Readings, 439.*

23 THE POSTWAR FAR EAST, II: JAPAN AND COMMUNIST CHINA 440

*Japan as an Ally, 440.   United States Troops and Bases in Japan, 442.
Return of the Bonins and Ryukyus, 443.   Cold War with Peking, 446.   The Two Chinas, 449.
The Sino–Soviet Quarrel, 451.   The United States Has Second Thoughts, 451.
A Two-Chinas Policy?, 452.   "Ping Pong Diplomacy", 452.   Additional Readings, 455.*

24 THE POSTWAR FAR EAST, III: SOUTHEAST ASIA—THE WAR IN INDOCHINA 457

*The French in Indochina, 457.   The French Fight a Losing War, 458.
The Geneva Conference of 1954, 459.   The SEATO Alliance, 460.   Compromise in Laos, 462.
Diem Faces Guerrilla War, 464.   The United States to the Rescue, 465.   The Fall of Diem, 466.
Escalating the War, 468.   Hawks versus Doves, 469.   The War a Stalemate, 471.
The Search for Peace, 472.   Negotiations Begin, 473.   "Vietnamizing" the War, 476.
The Cambodian Adventure, 477.   The Longest War, 478.   "Peace with Honor", 479.
The Collapse of American Policy, 480.   Additional Readings, 480.*

25 AMERICAN POLICY IN THE MIDDLE EAST   481

*Aims of the United States, 482.   The Baghdad Pact, 484.   The Suez Canal Crisis, 485.
The Eisenhower Doctrine, 489.   Rifts in the Arab World, 490.   American Preferences, 491.
The Six-Day War, 492.   The Search for a Settlement, 493.   The Yom Kippur War of 1973, 497.
The Search for Peace, 499.   Additional Readings, 501.*

26 THE WESTERN HEMISPHERE, FROM TRUMAN TO CARTER   502

*Formalizing the Inter-American System, 502.   Rifts Between Good Neighbors, 503.
The Communist Threat Comes Nearer, 505.   Fidel Castro's Revolution, 506.
A "New Deal" for Latin America, 507.   The Alliance for Progress, 508.   The Bay of Pigs, 509.
Russian Missiles in Cuba, 511.   A New Crisis in Panama, 513.
Intervention in the Dominican Republic, 514.   What Policy for the Future?, 517.
Cuba After the Missile Crisis, 518.   Storm Over the Panama Canal, 520.
The Canadian Partner, 521.   Additional Readings, 525.*

27 NEW DIRECTIONS: THE FOREIGN POLICY OF JIMMY CARTER   526

*The Soviet Union and the Arms Race, 526.   Western Europe and Japan–Trilateralism, 528.
Latin America, 529.   The Middle East, 531.   Asia and Africa, 532.   Additional Readings, 535.*

INDEX   537

Maps

Boundaries of the U.S. under Treaty of Paris, with Alternative U.S. Proposals *20*

The Northwest and the Southwest, 1783–1798 *24*

Acquisition of Florida, 1803–1819 *43*

Louisiana and the Boundary Treaties of 1818 and 1819 *58*

Maine Boundary Controversy *74*

Disputed Boundary, Lake Superior to Lake of the Woods *75*

Oregon Boundary Controversy, 1818–1846 *82*

Territory Acquired from Mexico, 1845–1853 *113*

China Coast and Japan *118*

U.S. Interests in Mexico, Central America, and the Caribbean, 1853–1871 *128*

U.S. Interests in the Pacific, 1867–1898 *149*

Panama Canal Zone *192*

U.S. Possessions and Protectorates in the Caribbean *204*

Alaska Boundary Dispute *225*

Northeast Fisheries Controversy *227*

Japanese Mandate and Yap *279*

Allied Occupation in Germany and Austria *395*

Conflict in Korea *436*

Taiwan Strait   *446*

U.S. Treaty Commitments in East Asia   *461*

Scene of Conflict in Southeast Asia   *467*

Israel and Adjacent Arab States   *483*

The Middle East   *487*

A Note on Documentation

In general, bibliographical data for every book cited in the footnotes are given as part of its first citation in any chapter. The following works, however, are cited so frequently that it seems best to give full citations once and for all and to cite them hereafter only by the short forms indicated:

Bemis, *Latin American Policy*—Samuel F. Bemis, *The Latin American Policy of the United States: An Historical Interpretation* (New York: Harcourt Brace Jovanovich, Inc., 1943).

Documents on American Foreign Relations—29 vols. to 1970. Vols. 1–6, Boston: World Peace Foundation, 1939–1945; Vols. 7–13, Princeton: Princeton University Press, for World Peace Foundation, 1947–1953; Vols. for 1952–1966, Harper & Row Publishers, for Council on Foreign Relations; Vol. for 1967, Simon & Schuster, Inc., for Council on Foreign Relations, New York, 1968.

U.S. in World Affairs—*The United States in World Affairs,* one volume for 1945–1947 and annual volumes thereafter, published for Council on Foreign Relations (New York: Harper & Row Publishers, 1947–67; Simon & Schuster, Inc., 1968). (Note that this and the preceding collection have been replaced by a new single-volume series entitled *American Foreign Relations* published for the first time in 1971 by New York University Press for the Council on Foreign Relations.)

Foreign Relations—*Foreign Relations of the United States: Diplomatic Papers* (Washington: Government Printing Office, 1861–).

Hull, *Memoirs*—*The Memoirs of Cordell Hull,* 2 vols. (New York: Macmillan Company, 1948).

Perkins, *History of the Monroe Doctrine*—Dexter Perkins, *A History of the Monroe Doctrine* (Boston: Little, Brown & Company, 1955).

Pratt, *Cordell Hull*—Julius W. Pratt, *Cordell Hull,* Vols. 12 and 13 of *The American Secretaries of State and Their Diplomacy,* edited by Robert H. Ferrell and Samuel F. Bemis (New York: Cooper Square Publishers, Inc., 1964).

Preface

The principal aim of this revision has been to recount the course of United States foreign policy during the 1970s, from the withdrawal of American troops from Vietnam, to the conclusion of the new Middle East treaties. The volume ends with an assessment of the diplomatic initiatives of the administration of President Jimmy Carter.

In order to restrict its length, substantial condensation, as well as minor revisions, have been effected in the earlier parts of the text, and the total number of chapters has been reduced from fifty to fewer than thirty. Other revisions take cognizance of the results of recent scholarship. For the sake of convenience, the bibliographical essay has been replaced by lists of additional readings at the conclusion of each chapter.

The authors wish to record their intellectual debt to the scholars whose works are recognized in the text, footnotes, and readings. Without their contributions, a book such as this would be impossible.

1. Instruments and Procedures of Foreign Policy

In George Washington's day no less than in Jimmy Carter's, the conduct of foreign relations required a twofold organization, a directing office at home and agents of that office abroad. Today these branches are known respectively as the Department of State and the Foreign Service.

The Department of State

The Department of State (or State Department, as it is popularly called) was a creation of the First Congress under the Constitution in 1789. It had been preceded by a Department of Foreign Affairs (1781–1789), a Committee (of Congress) of Foreign Affairs (1777–1781), and a Committee (also of Congress) of Secret Correspondence (1775–1777). From the opening of the American Revolution in 1775 to the inauguration of the new government under the Constitution fourteen years later, Congress[1] alone exercised authority in the name of the United States. There was no separate executive branch, and the Committee, or Department, of Foreign Affairs served as an agent of Congress, which gave directions and made final decisions. The Constitution, which provided for the executive and judicial branches of the government, placed the direction of foreign

relations in the hands of the President as head of the executive branch. The President was empowered to make appointments, to receive foreign ambassadors and ministers, and to conclude treaties with foreign governments. Congress, however, as the legislative branch of the new government, retained important checks upon the President's direction of foreign affairs. The President's appointments to office, diplomatic or other, had to be confirmed by the Senate. The same body, by a two-thirds vote of the members present, had to approve treaties before they could become effective. Congress as a whole held the purse strings and thus could give or withhold the funds necessary to the execution of a foreign policy. To Congress belonged the power to declare war, though the President was made commander in chief of the armed forces. Congress, through its committees, could also investigate the activities of the executive, though it was early established that in the field of foreign relations the President might withhold from Congress documents whose publication would be "incompatible with the public interest."

Since no one expected the President himself to be able to give adequate time to the management of foreign policy, the First Congress provided by law for a department under the President to have charge of that branch of executive business. Called at first, like its predecessor under the old government, a Department of Foreign Affairs, it was soon renamed the Department of State, a name held to be more suitable because of

---

[1]The Second Continental Congress until 1781; thereafter, the Congress under the Articles of Confederation.

1

the assignment to the department of certain domestic functions, such as relations with the states, the keeping and publication of laws of Congress, and the like.

Under President Washington, the Department of State consisted of the Secretary of State, a chief clerk, three ordinary clerks, and a translator—a total of six persons. For a century or more, the department grew slowly in size and complexity. A reorganization in 1833 apportioned the work of the department among eight divisions or bureaus, topped by a chief clerk and the Secretary. In 1870 the number of bureaus was increased to 13; two assistant secretaries had meanwhile been added, but even then the entire personnel of the department numbered only 53. This modest number of employees had grown to 202 by 1909. Rapid expansion accompanied both world wars. State Department personnel numbered 963 in 1938; 2,755 in 1943; and 5,905 in 1948. In 1963 the figure fell to 5,522, and in 1977 was up to 22,412.*

The Foreign Service

The formation and direction of foreign policy, under the President, are functions of the State Department. The implementation of that policy is shared between the State Department and the Foreign Service, the body of officers who represent the United States in foreign countries. Such officers also contribute to the formation of foreign policy through the information they convey in regard to situations and attitudes in the countries to which they are accredited.

The Foreign Service comprises diplomatic and consular personnel. The diplomatic mission of one government in the

*Source: Federal Budget for the fiscal year ending September 30, 1979, p. 434.

capital of another country is the agency through which the two governments conduct business. The chief of the mission is the direct representative of his government to that of the foreign country. Since early in the nineteenth century, the grades of chiefs of mission have been standardized by international agreement. The officer of highest rank is an ambassador. In a day when most governments were headed by kings or queens, an ambassador was the representative of the sovereign. In the United States, he is the representative of the President. An ambassador's place of residence and official business is called an embassy.

Ranking below an ambassador is—or was—a minister, who, in the days alluded to, represented the foreign office rather than the sovereign. A minister's official residence was called a legation.

Whether a particular diplomatic mission was given the rank of an embassy or a legation—whether its chief was an ambassador or a minister—formerly depended upon the importance that the two governments attached to their mutual relations. During the first century of its existence, the United States maintained only legations abroad, and, reciprocally, foreign governments kept only legations in the American capital. In 1893, Congress provided for the elevation of several of the more important legations to embassies on a reciprocal basis. Thereafter, embassies gradually replaced legations until 1966, when the last American legations (those in Bulgaria and Hungary) became embassies. The change was indicative of the growing importance that the United States attached to its foreign relations. (The rank of career minister—close to the top in the Foreign Service—was still retained, but if such an officer became a chief of mission he was designated an ambassador.)

A chargé d'affaires ad interim is a diplomatic officer of lower rank left in charge of an embassy or legation in the absence of the ambassador or minister and acting for the time being as chief of mission. Below chiefs of mission are lesser diplomatic officers and employers—counselors, secretaries, political and economic officers, attachés, and so forth—the number in each case depending upon the importance of the mission and the volume of the business that it transacts.

The diplomatic officer is the spokesman for his government in its intercourse with the government of the foreign country. The consular officer, or consul, to use the simplest term,[2] is an official guardian in foreign ports of the welfare and interests of the citizens of the country he represents. It is to the nearest United States consul that Americans in trouble in foreign lands normally make their first appeal for aid. It is from consuls that reports on business openings in foreign countries are expected. The consul performs a multitude of duties with reference to trade, shipping, execution of legal documents, the granting of immigration visas, and the like. "In him," writes one authority, "are amalgamated the functions of the secretary of a chamber of commerce, a justice of the peace, a notary public, a commissioner of immigration and naturalization, a Veteran's Administration official, a reporter and information analyst, a local negotiator, a shipping official, a postmaster, and a treasury agent."[3]

History of the Foreign Service

The United States instituted both its diplomatic and consular services very early. Informal diplomatic representation began in 1776 when Benjamin Franklin reached Paris in his quest for French recognition of the United States. That representation became formal upon the granting of recognition in 1778. Other Americans represented the United States diplomatically in the Netherlands, Prussia, Spain, and England during the Revolution or the period of the Confederation. Consular representation, too, began as early as 1780, when Congress sent a consul to France. Under the Constitution, Congress provided for the establishment of a diplomatic service in 1790 and a separate consular service in 1792.

Although possession of suitable qualifications was perhaps never completely lost sight of in the making of diplomatic and consular appointments, for many years after the rise of the spoils system in American politics, such appointments were customarily distributed as political plums to deserving members of the party in power. Occasionally they were used to recognize or reward distinguished literary achievement, as in the cases of Nathaniel Hawthorne (consul at Liverpool, 1853–1857), Washington Irving (secretary of legation at London, 1829–1832, minister to Spain, 1842–1846), and James Russell Lowell (minister to Spain and to Great Britain, 1877–1885). Between 1885 and 1915, however, the consular service and positions in the diplomatic service below the grade of minister were gradually removed from the "spoils system" and placed on a merit basis as to appointments, promotion, and tenure.

The Rogers Act of 1924 combined the diplomatic and consular services into a single Foreign Service, the members of which might be called upon to serve in either diplomatic or consular posts. It classified Foreign Service officers into nine classes, with career ministers at the top, and reaffirmed the requirement that appointments and promotions be based upon merit. Under the Rogers Act as amended in

[2]The grades of consular officers are consul general, consul, vice consul (a grade now discontinued by the United States), and consular agent.

[3]Elmer Plischke, *Conduct of American Diplomacy* (New York: D. Van Nostrand Company, 1950), p. 243.

1969, Foreign Service officers were graded in ten classes. Appointment to Class VIII (the lowest class) after written and oral examinations was probationary. Thereafter promotion was dependent upon the quality of the officer's record as judged by an impartial board. An officer who advanced to Class I was eligible for appointment as counselor of embassy or as consul general. Above Class I were the grades of career minister and (since 1955) career ambassador. A career minister was eligible for appointment as chief of mission with rank of minister or ambassador. Promotion to the grade of career ambassador came only as recognition of long and "exceptionally distinguished service to the Government." The President was left free to select chiefs of mission from among distinguished Foreign Service officers or to base such appointments, as in earlier days, upon political service or distinction outside the field of diplomacy. An ambassador in an important post, such as London, was often burdened with expenses that exceeded his salary and allowances; hence these posts were often assigned to men with substantial private incomes.

As reorganized by legislation subsequent to the Rogers Act (notably the Foreign Service Act of 1946), the Foreign Service included three categories in addition to chiefs of mission and Foreign Service officers. Foreign Service Reserve officers were specialists in other fields (economics, for example) given temporary appointments in the Foreign Service. Since 1968, such appointments may be made permanent in selected cases. Foreign Service Staff officers and employees embraced accountants, clerks, typists, translators, guards, couriers, and the like; they were American citizens and were appointed by the Secretary of State without examination. Alien employees, performing many of the same services as members of the staff group, constituted the third category.

Integration of State Department and Foreign Service

State Department and Foreign Service were manned by distinct and noninterchangeable corps of employees. Permanent members of the State Department staff were members of the Classified Civil Service, administered by the Civil Service Commission. Foreign Service officers and employees were under a separate system with its own examinations and rules of promotion. State Department officers and employees served, as a rule, only in the United States. Foreign Service officers from time to time occupied responsible posts in the State Department but never lost their identity as Foreign Service personnel. This dualism promoted friction and jealousy. It produced, so critics maintained, a State Department personnel ill-informed about foreign countries and a Foreign Service personnel that had lost touch with America.

One of the important proposals of the Commission on Organization of the Executive Branch of the Government (Hoover Commission) in 1949 called for the amalgamation of the two bodies of personnel, "over a short period of years into a single foreign affairs service obligated to serve at home or overseas and constituting a safeguarded career group administered separately from the general Civil Service." The proposed amalgamation would include all State Department personnel below the rank of assistant secretary and all Foreign Service personnel below the rank of minister, with the exception of aliens, unskilled labor categories, and certain technical personnel needed only in Washington.

The proposal for amalgamation, though approved by the administration, encountered foot-dragging, chiefly on the part of the Foreign Service, and not until further study and recommendation by another committee, headed by President Henry M. Wriston of Brown University, was amalgamation—now termed "integration"—actually achieved.

Other Agencies of Foreign Policy

If it were true in the early years of the Republic that the State Department alone, under the President, was responsible for the country's foreign relations, that simple situation has long since ceased to exist. The task force that studied the administration of foreign relations for the Hoover Commission found within the executive branch of the government at least forty-six "departments, agencies, commissions, boards, and interdepartmental councils," the work of which "involves some aspects of the conduct of foreign affairs." The integration of the work of these numerous agencies into a unified foreign policy had become a major problem. Ultimately the President must make decisions on questions of first importance, but most interagency conflicts or contradictions must be resolved at lower levels. The most important and widely used device for such coordination was the interdepartmental committee. The task force found thirty-three such committees operating in the field of foreign affairs, some created by law, others by executive order or interdepartmental agreement.

Of special importance among such committees was the National Security Council, created by the National Security Act of 1947. As later modified (up to 1978), it comprised the President, the Vice President, and the Secretaries of State and Defense.* A Special Assistant to the President for National Security Affairs (who in some instances rivaled or even exceeded the Sec-

*Source—U.S. Government Manual, 1977/78, p. 95.

retary of State in influence) and an Executive Secretary served as officials of the Council; the Joint Chiefs of Staff (the military heads of Army, Navy, and Air Force) were the principal military advisers to the President and the National Security Council. Other members of the President's administration might also be asked to join the Council's deliberations.

It is obvious from the composition of the National Security Council that it is designed to promote harmony between foreign policy on the one hand and the military and material means to support that policy on the other. The Council has advisory powers only; the President must make the decisions.

The act that created the National Security Council also created and placed under its direction the Central Intelligence Agency (CIA). This top-secret agency had as its stated purpose "coordinating the intelligence activities of the several Government departments and agencies in the interest of national security," but, rightly or wrongly, its name came to be increasingly associated with undercover anti-Communist operations, both military and subversive, in many parts of the world.[4]

The Channels of Diplomacy

Although much influence over American foreign policy has found its way into other hands, the State Department still remains the normal channel for communications and negotiations between the government of the United States and other governments. In times of crisis, it is true, the President himself may communicate directly with the heads of other governments in person, by letter or telegram, or by tele-

[4]David Wise and Thomas B. Ross, *The Invisible Government* (New York: Random House, Inc., 1964).

phone. The most notable modern instance of this type of diplomacy is found in the relations of Franklin D. Roosevelt and Winston Churchill, who made frequent use of all the means of communication enumerated. The two of them also met twice with Stalin and once with Chiang Kai-shek, the heads of other allied governments in World War II. In earlier years, President Herbert Hoover had conferred with Prime Minister Ramsay MacDonald "on a log by the Rapidan," and Woodrow Wilson had met with the British, French, and Italian Premiers at the Paris Peace Conference. Other instances of presidential diplomacy were Franklin Roosevelt's plea for peace to the Japanese Emperor on the eve of Pearl Harbor and an appeal by President Taft to the Prince Regent of China in behalf of American would-be investors in Chinese railroads. Usually, however, official communications from one head of state or government to another have been limited to such ceremonial messages as letters of condolence and congratulation or appointments of ambassadors. A President may occasionally hold an important conference with the minister or ambassador of another country or may himself draft diplomatic notes to be signed by the Secretary of State, as Wilson sometimes did; but a President who trusts his Secretary of State customarily leaves such responsibilities to him.

The Secretary of State can follow any one of three courses in communicating with his opposite number, the Foreign Minister of another government. He may confer with him directly, in person, or by other means. Such direct exchanges were almost unknown until very recent times. He may communicate through an "instruction"[5] to the American chief of mission at the foreign capital, who then calls upon the Foreign Minister and either leaves with him a copy of the "instruction" or informs him

[5]Outgoing communications from the State Department to its missions abroad are called "instructions"; those incoming are "dispatches."

of its substance. Thirdly, he may confer in person or by letter with the chief of mission of the foreign government in Washington, who then reports to the Foreign Minister at home. Which of these last two channels is followed in any given case depends upon the subject of discussion and the personalities and personal relationships of the people concerned.

It follows from what has just been said that important negotiations, often resulting in treaties, may be carried on equally well in Washington or in the foreign capital. Thus, to take a few instances, the Jay Treaty with Great Britain of 1794 was drawn up in London; the Clayton-Bulwer Treaty of 1850, in Washington; the Louisiana Purchase was negotiated in Paris; the Florida and Alaska Purchases, in Washington; and the Mexican cessions of 1848 and 1853, in or near Mexico City.

Important negotiations are occasionally conducted not through any of the regular official channels that have been described, but through confidential agents of the President, serving without diplomatic commissions and often bypassing the State Department. Presidents Wilson and Franklin D. Roosevelt were addicted more than others to the employment of such special agents. Thus, Colonel Edward M. House went to Europe on several delicate missions for Wilson, and Harry Hopkins performed similar services for Roosevelt. After Roosevelt's death, President Truman sent Hopkins on a final mission to Moscow, where he secured from Stalin, what seemed then, important concessions in regard to the proposed United Nations Charter and the government of Poland.

How Treaties Are Made and Ratified

Agreements between states may take the form of treaties (or conventions), executive agreements, or simple legislation (acts or joint resolutions of Congress).

The time-honored form of international agreement, legally binding upon all parties, is the treaty or convention. The distinction between the two is one in name only, though agreements on matters of prime importance, such as the making of peace or the transfer of territory, are almost always called treaties. What is said here about treaties applies equally to conventions. Before a treaty becomes effective, five steps must be achieved: (1) negotiation and signing by agents (such as the Secretary of State and the ambassador of the other country) duly commissioned by their governments to perform that function; (2) legislative approval; (3) ratification; (4) exchange of ratifications; (5) proclamation.

Several of these steps require some clarification. Legislative approval, in the United States, means the giving by the Senate of its "advice and consent" by a vote of at least two-thirds of the senators present. The Senate may give its advice and consent in a simple affirmative vote; it may amend the treaty before doing so; or it may attach interpretations or reservations to the treaty, giving its understanding of what the treaty means or of the limits of the obligations assumed under it by the United States. If the Senate amends the treaty, the consent of the other party to the amendment must be secured. If the Senate attaches reservations or interpretations, it may or may not require that the other party agree to these before the treaty becomes binding on the United States. Ordinarily it does not make this requirement.

It is to be emphasized here that, popular opinion and phraseology to the contrary notwithstanding, the Senate does not "ratify" treaties. It merely gives its advice and consent in favor of the treaty. Ratification is an executive act, performed by the President after the Senate has consented. The President, however, is not required to ratify a treaty that the Senate has approved. If he objects to an amendment or reservation made by the Senate, or if he has merely changed his mind about the desirability of the treaty or the need for it, he is under no obligation to ratify. If he fails to do so, the treaty simply dies. To take one hypothetical illustration, if the Senate, in March 1920, had given its advice and consent to the Treaty of Versailles with the Lodge Reservations attached, it seems almost certain that President Wilson would have refused to ratify it, so strong was his disapproval of the reservations.

When a treaty has been ratified by the executives of both governments, following whatever form of legislative approval their constitutions require, copies of the instruments of ratification are exchanged by the two governments, and the heads of states (in the United States, the President) then proclaim the treaty to be in effect.

Treaties may be multilateral instead of bilateral. In that event, the treaty will specify whether ratification by all or by a certain number of the parties shall be necessary to make it binding on those that have ratified. It will also designate the capital at which ratifications are to be deposited. A treaty may be perpetual—that is, without any time limit for its duration or stipulation of procedure for its abrogation. Such a treaty, ideally speaking, can be set aside only by the consent of all parties to it. Only after intermittent negotiations over a twenty-year period did the United States secure British consent to the abrogation of the Clayton-Bulwer Treaty, which blocked American ambitions for an American-controlled isthmian canal. Unilateral abrogation is always possible but is analogous to breaking a contract and may present the other party with a valid grievance. On the other hand, a treaty may be limited to a specified period, or it may provide that either party may terminate it by giving notice, usually six months or a year in advance, of its intention to do so. Thus, the treaty of 1818 for joint occupation of Oregon by Great Britain and the United States set a ten-year limit on that arrangement;

the treaty of 1827, continuing the joint occupation, permitted either government to terminate it by giving a year's notice. Treaties ceding territory are, by their nature, perpetual.

Other Forms of International Agreement

The required two-thirds majority in the Senate has, in a number of important instances, proved an insurmountable obstacle to the approval of treaties desired by the executive. Two means of circumventing this requirement have been utilized more and more frequently in recent times. These two means are the executive agreement and legislation.

Executive agreements, between the President and the executive head of another government, may be made with or without prior authorization by Congress. The Reciprocal Trade Agreements Act of 1934 empowered the President to make executive agreements with other governments providing reciprocally for the lowering of duties (within limits set by Congress) on the products of each country when imported into the other. This was a means of avoiding not only the two-thirds rule but the log-rolling that had always obstructed attempts to lower duties by treaty or legislation. Over forty reciprocal trade agreements were made under the authority conferred by this act and extended by subsequent enactments. Since Congress had authorized them in advance, their legality was assured.

Of a quite different character were certain executive agreements made by the President upon his own responsibility, in circumstances when Senate approval was doubtful or when prolonged debate in Senate or Congress might defeat the objectives of the agreements. Notable among

such agreements was FDR's destroyer-bases trade of September 2, 1940—a transaction far more important than many treaties—by which the United States turned over to Great Britain fifty old destroyers in exchange for the right to establish bases on British territory in the Western Hemisphere. Of similar character were the later agreements with the Danish minister in Washington and the Icelandic government by which the United States in 1941 undertook to garrison and defend Greenland and Iceland for the duration of the war. All of these agreements, unlike certain of those later made at Yalta, were promptly reported to Congress by President Roosevelt. Senate approval was not requested. Whether it could have been obtained is doubtful. In any event, an attempt to secure it would have resulted in long delay at a time when immediate action was deemed necessary. When a president acts in this way, he of course runs the risk that Congress may repudiate his action.

Criticism of certain of President Roosevelt's executive agreements, especially those made at Yalta, led to an attempt to limit the power of the President in this respect. A proposed amendment to the Constitution, sponsored by Senator John W. Bricker of Ohio, would have subjected all such agreements to regulation by Congress and would also have placed restrictions on the treaty-making power, specifying that the Federal government could not exercise through treaties powers not clearly assigned to it in the Constitution. The Bricker Amendment and proposed substitutes for it were defeated in the Senate in February 1954.

Legislation by act or joint resolution of Congress is another substitute for treaty-making, the advantage being that such legislation requires a bare majority in each house of Congress instead of the two-thirds majority in the Senate required for treaties. Such legislation presupposes some parallel action by the other party to the agreement. Early instances of such action by joint resolution were the annexations of Texas and Hawaii. In each of these cases, action by treaty had first been tried and laid aside when the two-thirds majority in the Senate proved unattainable. In 1911 President Taft made an executive agreement with Canada for reciprocal lowering of tariffs, to be carried out by concurrent legislation by Congress and the Canadian Parliament. Congress passed the necessary legislation, but the agreement failed to receive Canadian approval. A more modern instance was the passage by Congress, April 3, 1948, of the Foreign Assistance Act, which set in motion the Marshall Plan for aid to Western Europe in the rehabilitation of its war-shattered economy.

The Growing Power of Congress— and of the President

Mention of the Foreign Assistance Act calls attention to the growing authority exercised by Congress over American foreign policy. Since passage of the Lend-Lease Act in 1941, American foreign policy has included a large element of material assistance to allies and friends—first, aid in winning the war; then aid in economic recovery; still later, aid in rearming to resist the march of Russian Communism, and aid in promoting the economic development of backward nations. In whatever form such aid is agreed upon—treaty, law, or executive agreement—eventually it costs money, and money must be appropriated by Congress. Without the support of Congress, therefore, many aspects of current foreign policy simply cannot be carried out. In the words of one authority: "When money talks as loudly and as often as it does in United States foreign relations since 1940, Con-

gress is an ever-present participant in the making of foreign policy."[6]

But if Congress can tie the hands of the President in many foreign policy programs, Presidents of the post-World War II era were charged repeatedly with assuming powers that rightly belonged to Congress. Indeed, there was growing concern, in Congress and out, over the assertion by the President, in the nuclear age, of the "inherent power" to take the country into war in defiance of the constitutional grant to Congress of the exclusive power to "declare war."[7] Criticism of what seemed to many a dangerous presidential encroachment on the power of Congress began when President Truman decided, on his own responsibility, to send American troops to fight in Korea. It heightened, especially in the Senate Committee on Foreign Relations, when President Johnson sent American troops into the war in Vietnam, after securing the loosely worded Tonkin Gulf Resolution from Congress. The criticism reached a climax when President Nixon ordered the invasion of Cambodia by United States ground forces on April 30, 1970. To concede to one man the power to make such fateful decisions was, said the critics, both plainly contrary to the Constitution and perilous to the nation's existence. What the nation needed and got was the War Powers Act of 1973. Henceforth the President would be required to report to Congress within 48 hours after committing troops to foreign hostilities or, alternatively, after "substantially" increasing combat troops in a foreign country. Moreover, the President would have to cease hostilities

[6]J. L. McCamy, *The Administration of American Foreign Affairs* (New York: Alfred A. Knopf, Inc., 1950), p. 336.

[7]The case for the President's right to make war as commander in chief of the armed forces is presented by L. C. Meeker in "The Legality of United States Participation in the Defense of Viet-Nam," *Department of State Bulletin,* 54 (March 28, 1966), 474–89.

after 60 days unless so authorized by Congress. The 60-day deadline, however, could be extended an additional 30 days if the President could certify the necessity. Even here though Congress could compel an immediate withdrawal within the 60 to 90 day period by passing a concurrent resolution that would not be subject to presidential veto. Such was, for Congress, the "lesson" of Vietnam.

ADDITIONAL READINGS ·

BAILEY, THOMAS A., *The Art of Diplomacy*. New York: Appleton-Century-Crofts, 1968.

BLANCKÉ, W. W., *The Foreign Service of the United States*. New York: Frederick A. Praeger, Inc. 1969.

ILCHMAN, WARREN F., *Professional Diplomacy in the United States 1778–1939*. Chicago: The University of Chicago Press, 1961.

SCHLESINGER, ARTHUR M., JR., *The Imperial Presidency*. Boston: Houghton Mifflin Company, 1973.

SPANIER, JOHN and ERIC M. USLANER, *How American Foreign Policy Is Made*. New York: Praeger Publishers, 1974.

STUART, GRAHAM H., *The Department of State: A History of Its Organization, Procedure and Personnel*. New York: The Macmillan Company, 1949.

2. The Diplomacy of the Revolution

The disruption of the British Empire in the 1770s was one of the fateful events of modern history. Had British statesmanship then been capable of the levels of wisdom it attained in the next century, a British-American, or American-British, Commonwealth of Nations might have guided the world along paths of peaceful development with little to fear from a Wilhelm II, a Hitler, or a Stalin. Such a might-have-been is a fascinating subject of speculation. The student of history, however, must deal with facts.

The facts of the American Revolution are that a shortsighted British policy, bent upon holding the colonies in subordination, drove them instead to complete independence. New taxes, new assertions of imperial authority, new devices for enforcing old commercial restrictions, new interferences with the acquisition of western lands, harsh measures of punishment when the new exactions were resisted—all combined to provoke the colonial population to revolt. The measures undertaken were not ill-intentioned. They were designed, with some degree of justice, to require the colonies to share the cost of imperial defense and imperial administration. But the colonies had come to think of themselves as self-governing entities, as having "dominion status," to use a term of later origin, and they refused to have their duties prescribed for them by Parliament and King. Parliament and King were unwilling to accept such a novel theory of empire. Great Britain, consequently, found herself involved in war not only with her colonies but even-

tually with most of Europe, too. The war, though not wholly disastrous to British arms, deprived Great Britain of the most valuable of her colonial possessions and cast her down from the pinnacle of power that she had attained by the Peace of Paris of 1763.

The initial aim of armed revolt was not independence but a restoration and recognition of what the colonials held to be their rights as British subjects. They professed to have been content with their status under British policy prior to 1763. That the colonies turned to independence in the second year of the struggle was the consequence partly of the British government's spurning of compromise and its adoption, instead, of severe repressive measures; and partly of a dawning realization of the advantages that might accrue from independence. No one set forth the arguments for independence so persuasively as a recent immigrant from England named Thomas Paine, who published the pamphlet *Common Sense* in Philadelphia in January 1776. Among Paine's arguments, two were significant for the future foreign policy of the United States. Independence, said Paine, would free the former colonies from being dragged at the heels of England into European wars in which they had no concern.[1] A

[1]Of the four intercolonial wars, the European origin of the first three was attested by the names given them in America: King William's War, Queen Anne's War, King George's War. The fourth, on the other hand, was of colonial origin, as its name in America—the French and Indian War—suggests.

declaration of independence would improve their chances of securing foreign aid.

The Quest for Foreign Aid

Greatly inferior to the mother country in numbers, in wealth, in industry, in military and naval power, the colonies, as their wiser leaders saw from the beginning, could hardly hope for decisive military success unless aided by one of the major European powers. Months before deciding upon independence, Congress had set up a secret committee to make contact with friends abroad, and this committee had sent to Paris a secret agent in the guise of a merchant to seek supplies and credit. The agent, Silas Deane of Connecticut, arriving in Paris in July 1776, soon found that the French government was disposed to give secret assistance to England's revolting colonies. French ministers, in fact, had been on the lookout since 1763 for an opportunity to weaken and humiliate France's victorious rival, Great Britain. That opportunity had now arrived. So thought the celebrated French playwright and amateur diplomat, Caron de Beaumarchais, who had already been in contact with another colonial agent, Arthur Lee, in London; and so too believed the Comte de Vergennes, French Foreign Minister. Vergennes and Beaumarchais were able to persuade King Louis XVI that aid to the colonies was in the French interest.

As yet, however, France was not willing to avow openly her friendship for the colonies or to give material aid except in secret. This was managed through the creation by Beaumarchais of a fictitious commercial firm, Rodrigue Hortalez et Compagnie, through which were channeled gunpowder and other essential supplies from the French arsenals to the armies of George Washington. Spain, too, was persuaded by France to give aid through this channel and by other means. All in all, measured in the dollars of that day, France contributed to the American cause nearly $2,000,000 in subsidies and over $6,350,000 in loans; Spain, approximately $400,000 and $250,000 in subsidies and loans respectively.[2]

The French Alliance

These arrangements for secret "lend-lease" had been instituted before Deane's arrival in Paris. After the Declaration of Independence, Congress sent to France the most widely known, most admired, and most persuasive American of his day, Benjamin Franklin. In Paris he joined Deane and also Arthur Lee, who had come from London, to form a three-man American commission. As secretary, the commission employed a Dr. Edward Bancroft, a native of Massachusetts and a friend of Franklin. Bancroft was secretly in the pay of the British government, to which he faithfully reported the work of the commission and its relations with the French ministers. Arthur Lee was convinced of Bancroft's treachery but could not shake Franklin's and Deane's faith in their employee.

The principal purpose of Franklin's mission was to secure from the French government official recognition of the United States as an independent nation. Recognition could be accomplished by the signing of a treaty between France and the United States, and Franklin brought with him to Paris a draft of a proposed treaty of amity and commerce, which had been prepared by a committee of Congress and which embodied the liberal commercial principles that Congress hoped to see adopted not only by France but by the entire trading

[2]These figures are slightly simplified from those given in S. F. Bemis, *The Diplomacy of the American Revolution* (New York: Appleton-Century-Crofts, 1935), p. 93.

world. This "Plan of 1776," as it has been called, was to serve for many years as the goal of American commercial policy.

Though friendly to the United States, Vergennes was unwilling to grant formal recognition, thus risking war with England, until the Americans could offer some evidence of their ability to do their share in winning the war. Quite understandably, he did not wish to involve France in a war for a losing cause. Such evidence was not forthcoming until December 1777, when news arrived that General Burgoyne's British army, thrusting down from Montreal into New York, had been forced to surrender to General Gates at Saratoga. This was what Vergennes had been waiting for; he tried to enlist Spain in the cause and when Spain procrastinated, resolved that France should proceed without her. On December 17, the American commissioners were informed that France would grant recognition and make a treaty with the United States, and on February 6, 1778, a treaty of amity and commerce and a treaty of alliance were signed in Paris, the latter to take effect if Great Britain went to war with France because of the former.

Vergennes had hastened to take this action because of fear that if he did not, England would effect a reconciliation with her former colonies. Burgoyne's surrender had produced a sensation in England and led the ministry to offer liberal terms of settlement to the Americans. In March, Parliament passed a series of bills repealing all the legislation enacted since 1763 of which the colonists had complained. In April, a commission headed by the Earl of Carlisle was dispatched to America, empowered to offer to Congress virtually everything it had claimed, independence alone excepted, if the former colonies would lay down their arms and resume their allegiance to the British Crown. The right to control their own taxation, to elect their governors and other officials formerly appointed, to be represented in Parliament if they so desired, to continue Congress as an American legislature; release from quitrents, assurance that their colonial characters would not be altered without their consent, full pardon for all who had engaged in rebellion—these terms of the offer indicate how far Great Britain was willing to go to save her empire from disruption. In effect she was offering "dominion status" to America.[3]

Had such an offer been made at any time prior to the Declaration of Independence, perhaps at any time prior to Burgoyne's surrender, it would have no doubt been accepted, and the thirteen states would have become the first British dominion. Now the offer came too late. With recognition and the promise of an alliance and open aid from France, independence seemed assured, and there was no turning back. Congress ratified the treaties with France without even stopping to parley with the Carlisle Commission.

The treaty of amity and commerce placed each nation on a most-favored-nation basis with reference to the other and embodied, practically unaltered, the liberal principles of the "Plan of 1776"—principles which would protect the interest of either signatory that might chance to be neutral when the other was at war. The treaty of alliance was to go into effect if France should become embroiled in the existing war against Great Britain. Its object was "to maintain effectually the liberty, Sovereignty, and independence absolute and unlimited" of the United States. France renounced forever any designs upon Bermuda or upon any parts of the continent of North America which before the Treaty of Paris of 1763 or by virtue of that treaty had belonged to Great Britain or the former British colonies. She reserved the right to

[3]The Royal Instructions to the Peace Commission of 1778 are conveniently printed in S. E. Morison, ed., *Sources and Documents Illustrating the American Revolution, 1764–1788* (Oxford: The Clarendon Press, 1923), pp. 186–203.

possess herself of any of the British West Indian colonies. The United States, on the other hand, was free to conquer and hold Bermuda or any of Great Britain's mainland possessions. Neither party was to make a separate peace with Great Britain nor lay down its arms until American independence was won. Each signatory guaranteed to the other the American possessions which it then held and with which it might emerge from the war. France, in addition, undertook to guarantee the liberty, sovereignty, and independence of the United States.

The treaty just described constituted the only "entangling alliance" in which the United States participated until the middle of the twentieth century. It was to cause serious embarrassment before it was set aside in 1800, but in the winning of independence, it was indispensable. A French army under General Rochambeau was sent to America, and French fleets under Admirals d'Estaing and de Grasse operated off the American coast. The importance of French aid is pointed up by the reflection that in the final scene of the Revolution, at Yorktown, Cornwallis' British army was caught between a French fleet and an allied army, of which two-thirds were also French.

Spain and the Revolution

Spain, though bound to France by a dynastic alliance, the "Family Compact," and though giving secret aid to the United States, hung back from entering the war for over a year after France had become a belligerent. There were advantages that Spain might gain from a successful war with England: the recovery of Gilbraltar (lost in 1713) and of Florida (lost in 1763). Gibraltar, the more valuable of these, the Spanish court hoped to regain peaceably, as a reward for mediating between Great Britain

and France. Only when Great Britain declined the proffered service did Spain sign a definite alliance with France (Convention of Aranjuez, April 12, 1779) and declare war against Great Britain (June 21, 1779). The Franco-American treaty of alliance had reserved for Spain the right to become a member, but Spain declined to sign it or to make any kind of treaty with the United States. A colonial power herself, Spain naturally hesitated to give formal acknowledgment to a rebellion of the colonies of Great Britain. John Jay spent many bitter months in Madrid asking in vain for recognition. Even an offer to waive the American claim of right to navigate the Mississippi River could not persuade the Spanish government to recognize the young republic. By the Convention of Aranjuez, France and Spain agreed that neither would make peace till Spain had recovered Gibraltar. Since the United States had promised not to make peace without France, it could not, if all treaty engagements were observed, make peace till Gibraltar was restored to Spain.

In America, Spanish interests ran counter to those of the United States. The United States desired the Mississippi River as its western boundary and the right of navigating the river through Spanish territory to the Gulf of Mexico. Spain, anxious to monopolize as far as might be the navigation and commerce of both river and gulf, was unwilling to concede to the Americans either the use of the river or a foothold on its eastern bank. If the Spanish had their way, the western boundary of the United States would be fixed as near as possible to the summit of the Appalachians.

The bargaining position of Spain was strengthened by the daring and vigor of Bernardo de Galvez, the young governor of Louisiana. Less than two years after Spain's entry into the war, he had routed the British out of all of West Florida, from Natchez on the north, to Pensacola on the east. He had established Spain's claim to a cession of Florida at the end of the war and to full control of the lower Mississippi.

A Pawn in the European Chess Game

In order to win independence, the United States had found it necessary to involve itself in the international rivalries and politics of Europe. Those same rivalries and politics, however, threatened to terminate the war with American independence still unwon. Spain, having entered the war reluctantly, soon grew tired of it. In 1780 the Spanish government received a British mission, come to discuss peace terms. For America, the Spanish ministers proposed a long truce between Great Britain and her "colonies," without specific recognition of independence and with a division of territory on the basis of *uti possidetis,* or retention by each party of the areas then occupied. This would have left the British in control of Maine, the northern frontier, New York City, Long Island, and the principal seaports south of Virginia.

Vergennes disapproved these Anglo-Spanish conversations, which violated the Convention of Aranjuez. He was willing to listen, however, to proposals for mediation from the Czarina Catherine II of Russia and the Austrian Emperor, Joseph II, which would have had much the same effect in America. John Adams, who had been named American peace commissioner and came from the Hague to Paris at Vergennes' behest, rejected the proposal out of hand when Vergennes laid it before him. No truce, he said, till all British troops were withdrawn from the United States; no negotiation with England without guarantees that American sovereignty and independence would be respected. But in America, Congress was more easily persuaded than was Adams. Under pressure (and in some instances monetary persuasion) from La Luzerne, the French minis-

ter, Congress on June 15, 1781, drew up new instructions to its prospective peace commissioners in Europe. Not only were they directed to accept the mediation of the Czarina and the Emperor; they were to place themselves in the hands of the French ministers, "to undertake nothing in the negotiations for peace or truce without their knowledge and concurrence," and ultimately to be governed "by their advice and opinion." It was perhaps fortunate for the United States that the British government rejected the proposal for mediation.[4]

Great Britain in Difficulty

The surrender of Cornwallis to Washington and Rochambeau at Yorktown, October 19, 1781, was the climax of Great Britain's misfortunes. She was now at war, or on the verge of war, with most of the western world. To the list of her open enemies she herself had added the Netherlands, forcing them into war rather than permit continuance of their neutral trade with France. The Baltic countries, Russia, Denmark, and Sweden, had in 1780 organized themselves into a League of Armed Neutrality for the purpose of protecting their commerce against what they considered the illegitimate exactions of the British Navy; and they had been joined by Prussia, the Emperor (of the Holy Roman Empire), the Kingdom of the Two Sicilies, and even Portugal, Great Britain's traditional ally. There was little that the British could hope to gain by prolonging the war.

In February 1782, following receipt of the news of the disaster at Yorktown, the British House of Commons resolved that

[4]In the subsequent peace negotiations in Paris, the offer of mediation was accepted as a matter of form by the European belligerents. The representatives of the Czarina and the Emperor signed the treaties, nothing more. In the negotiations between the United States and Great Britain they took not even a nominal part.

the war ought to be terminated. In March, the ministry of Lord North, whose policies had precipitated the American conflict, resigned, and a new ministry headed by the Marquis of Rockingham took office. The Earl of Shelburne, as Secretary of State for the Southern Department, initiated peace talks by sending Richard Oswald, a Scot, to confer with the American representatives in Paris. After Rockingham's death in July 1782, Shelburne became Prime Minister but continued to guide negotiations with the United States. This was fortunate, for Shelburne was an advocate of a generous peace, which might result in recapturing for Great Britain the bulk of American trade and at some future day, perhaps, tempt the United States back into some sort of imperial federation.

The American Congress named five peace commissioners, of whom three actually handled the negotiations. Franklin was in Paris when the talks began. John Jay, who had been vainly seeking recognition and a treaty in Madrid, arrived in June 1782. John Adams, who had secured recognition and a loan from the Netherlands, reached Paris in October. Henry Laurens was on hand in time to sign the treaty. Thomas Jefferson, the fifth of those named by Congress, declined to serve. Most of the work was done by Franklin and Jay, with Adams giving valuable aid toward the close of the negotiations.

The Stakes of Diplomacy

The American commissioners had three principal objectives: (1) recognition of independence, which was now assured; (2) the widest boundaries obtainable; (3) retention of the inshore fishing privileges on the coasts of British North America which the colonials had enjoyed as British subjects. The British government was ready to recognize American independence and to act generously on the other American demands. It hoped in turn to secure from the United States: (1) provision for the payment of the pre-Revolutionary debts of American planters and others to British creditors, and (2) an agreement to compensate the Loyalists (Americans who had sided with Great Britain in the struggle) for the lands and other property that had been seized by the states in which they lived.

Of the American demands the most controversial was that concerning boundaries, for American claims on this point involved not only adjustments with Great Britain but disputes with Spain—disputes in which Vergennes chose to support his Spanish rather than his American ally.

In their more sanguine moments, Benjamin Franklin and other American leaders dreamed of including in their confederacy the whole of British North America and certain of the outlying islands. Such hopes had no chance of fulfillment. What the United States Congress laid claim to as a matter of right was the entire western country between the Appalachian Mountains and the Mississippi River, extending from the thirty-first parallel on the south to a northern line drawn from the St. Lawrence River at north latitude 45° to Lake Nipissing (the southwestern boundary of Quebec before 1774) and thence to the source of the Mississippi. These claims, based chiefly upon the sea-to-sea clauses in certain colonial charters, had never been taken seriously by the British government, which in the years since 1763 had acted upon the theory that the western lands still belonged to the Crown. The campaigns of George Rogers Clark during the war had, in fact, done little to strengthen American claims to the country north of the Ohio River.[5]

[5] J. A. James, in his *Life of George Rogers Clark* (Chicago: University of Chicago Press, 1928), maintains that Clark's military exploits played an important part in inducing the British to surrender the Northwest to the United States. This thesis has not been

South of the Ohio River, American settlements in central Kentucky and eastern and central Tennessee gave the United States a solid basis for claiming those areas, but farther south it was the Spanish, not the Americans, who had driven the British out. The Spanish held the east bank of the Mississippi as far north as Natchez; they hoped, as was previously noted, to deny the Americans access to the Mississippi and to draw the boundary as near as possible to the Appalachian watershed. In this endeavor they had French support.

In the summer of 1779, Congress had taken the first step toward peace negotiations by naming John Adams commissioner for that purpose. In instructions prepared for him (August 14, 1779), it had proposed boundaries including the entire area claimed by the states from the mountains to the Mississippi. It had added that although it was "of the utmost importance to the peace and Commerce of the United States that Canada and Nova Scotia should be ceded" and that equal rights in the fisheries should be guaranteed, a desire to terminate the war had led Congress to refrain from making the acquisition of these objects an ultimatum. Subsequently, under stress of military necessity and pressure from the French minister, Congress had modified those demands. In the new instructions of June 15, 1781, it insisted only upon independence and the preservation of the treaties with France as indispensable conditions. With regard to boundaries, the commissioners were to regard the earlier instructions as indicating "the desires and expectations of Congress," but were not to adhere to them if they presented an obstacle to peace. The task of the commissioners was to get as much as they could of the

terms proposed two years earlier. In this they did very well.

The Peace Negotiations

The first obstacles encountered by the Americans were erected by the Spanish and French, not by the British. When John Jay arrived in Paris, suspicious of both Spain and France after his futile mission in Madrid, he found disturbing confirmation of his distrust. Conversations with the Spanish ambassador in Paris and with a spokesman for Vergennes showed that the Spanish, with French support, were bent upon excluding the United States from the Mississippi Valley.

French support of Spanish claims impaired the confidential relations between Vergennes and the American commissioners. Vergennes had previously agreed that the American and French negotiations should proceed separately but at equal pace and with the understanding that neither settlement should become effective without the other. Franklin and Jay now proceeded to negotiate their own preliminary terms with the British, neglecting, with considerable justification, to make those "most candid and confidential communications" to the French ministers enjoined upon them by their instructions of June 15, 1781. In negotiating their settlement with Great Britain, they simply disregarded Spanish claims in the western country north of the 31st parallel, assuming (as did the British) that that country was still Great Britain's to dispose of.

In informal talks with Oswald, Franklin had already sketched what, as an American, he considered the "necessary" and the "advisable" terms of a lasting peace. Among "necessary" terms he included, after independence and withdrawl of troops, "a confinement of the boundaries of Canada" to what they had been before the Quebec Act

widely accepted. On the other side see C. W. Alvord, "Virginia and the West; an Interpretation," *Mississippi Valley Historical Review,* 3 (1916), 19–38; R. C. Downes, "Indian War on the Upper Ohio, 1779–1782," *Western Pennsylvania Historical Magazine,* 17 (1934), 93–115.

(that is, the St. Lawrence-Nipissing line), "if not to a still more contracted state," and the retention of fishing privileges. Among "advisable" terms which might be expected to contribute to a permanent reconciliation, he mentioned indemnification by Great Britain of those persons who had been ruined through the devastations of war, acknowledgment of error expressed in an act of Parliament or in some other public document, admission of American ships and trade to British and Irish ports upon the same terms as those of Britain, and "giving up every part of Canada."

A delay in the negotiations now ensued, first because Oswald had no formal commission as an agent of the British government, and after his commission arrived, August 8, because it failed to authorize him to recognize the independence of the United States as preliminary to negotiation but, on the contrary, empowered him to treat with representatives of "colonies" of Great Britain. It did, however, authorize him to make recognition of independence the first article of the proposed treaty. Franklin and Jay were at first inclined to insist upon formal recognition of independence as a condition precedent to negotiation; but, becoming alarmed lest France use any further delay to their disadvantage, they agreed to accept as recognition a new commission that authorized Oswald to treat with commissioners of the United States of America. Time had been consumed; nevertheless, in this meticulous stickling for matters of form, and with the passage of time, the situation was modified to the disadvantage of the United States.

On September 1, instructions were sent to Oswald to agree to terms of peace on the basis of the "necessary" terms proposed by Franklin, conceding to the United States the western country as far north as the Nipissing line, and making no stipulation for the payment of prewar debts or the restitution of property confiscated from the Loyalists. A draft of a treaty on these terms was actually initialed by the commissioners on October 5 and referred to London. The unfortunate results of delay now became apparent. News had arrived in Lodon of the failure of a major assault upon Gibraltar, which had been besieged for three years by Spanish and French land and sea forces. With this victory in hand, Shelburne took a firmer tone toward the United States. He not only insisted that something be done for creditors and Loyalists but made a last moment attempt to hold the Northwest, though this latter move may have been merely a gesture designed to secure concessions on the other points. "They wanted," Franklin reported, "to bring their boundary down to the Ohio and to settle the loyalists in the Illinois country. We did not choose such neighbors."

The Americans, now reinforced by Adams, insisted upon retention of the Northwest but were ready to make concessions on this and other points. They agreed to inclusion in the treaty of articles in the interest of the Loyalists and the British creditors. They accepted the St. Croix River instead of the St. John, which Congress had originally proposed, as the northeastern boundary, thereby laying the basis of a controversy which took sixty years to settle. In the West, they dropped the Nipissing line proposal, agreeing to accept instead either of two alternatives: a line drawn due west along the 45th parallel from the St. Lawrence to the Mississippi, or a line through the middle of the St. Lawrence and the Great Lakes and thence via the Lake of the Woods to the Mississippi. The British accepted the second alternative. The preliminary treaty was signed at Paris on November 30, 1782, not to become effective until France also made peace with England.

The treaty thus signed and, in due course, ratified by the parties was less favorable to the United States in three respects than the draft initialed on October 5.

It contained troublesome provisions for Loyalists and for British creditors, and the northern boundary followed the river and lake line instead of that by way of Lake Nipissing. By the latter change, the United States lost the greater and the most valuable part of the modern province of Ontario. Had Jay and Franklin been willing to treat with Oswald on the basis of his first commission, it is at least possible that they might have agreed upon Franklin's "necessary terms" early in September, instead of a month later, and that Shelburne might have accepted these terms before he received news of the victory at Gibraltar.

But this is another might-have-been. What is remarkable about the treaty is that the United States got as much as it did, especially that the British surrendered title to all territory east of the Mississippi between the Great Lakes and the 31st parallel. For the explanation of this surrender, one must look neither to the legal weight of the colonial charters nor to the military victories of George Rogers Clark but to the enlightened policy of the Earl of Shelburne. Desirous of a peace of reconciliation, he saw a means of achieving it at small cost to the Empire. The Northwest, demanded by the Americans, appeared to him to be of slight value to Great Britain. The regulation of the fur trade in that area was proving ruinously expensive to the royal treasury, and experience had seemed to show that the region was of little value without control of the mouth of the Mississippi, now more firmly than ever in the hands of Spain. Why not buy American good will at so cheap a price?

The Treaty

In detail, the principal provisions of the preliminary treaty signed on November 30, 1782, were as follows: The boundary of the United States began at the mouth of the St. Croix River on the Maine frontier, followed that river to its source, and thence ran due north to the highlands dividing the St. Lawrence from the Atlantic watershed, along those highlands to the northwesternmost head of the Connecticut River, and down that river to the 45th parallel, which it followed to the St. Lawrence. It then followed the middle of the St. Lawrence and of Lakes Ontario, Erie, and Huron and connecting waters to Lake Superior; through that lake to Long Lake and then through certain small lakes and streams to the Lake of the Woods, from the northwesternmost point of which it was to be drawn due west to the Mississippi—an impossible line, since the Mississippi rose well to the southward. It followed the Mississippi down to the 31st parallel, ran due east along that parallel to the Chattahoochee, descended that stream to its junction with the Flint, leaped thence straight to the head of the St. Mary's River, which it followed to the Atlantic. A secret article, introduced by the British but not incorporated in the final treaty, stipulated that if Great Britain retained West Florida, the northern line of that province should be, as it had been since 1764, not the 31st parallel but a line drawn east from the junction of the Yazoo with the Mississippi. The navigation of the Mississippi was to remain forever "free and open to the subjects of Great Britain, and the citizens of the United States."

Great Britain acknowledged the independence and sovereignty of the thirteen states individually, promised to withdraw all its armies, garrisons, and fleets from their soil and waters "with all convenient speed," and conceded to American fishermen the "liberty" to ply their trade much as before in the territorial waters of British North America. The United States, on its part, made certain promises in the interest of Loyalists and British creditors. The parties agreed that creditors on either side should "meet with no lawful impediment"

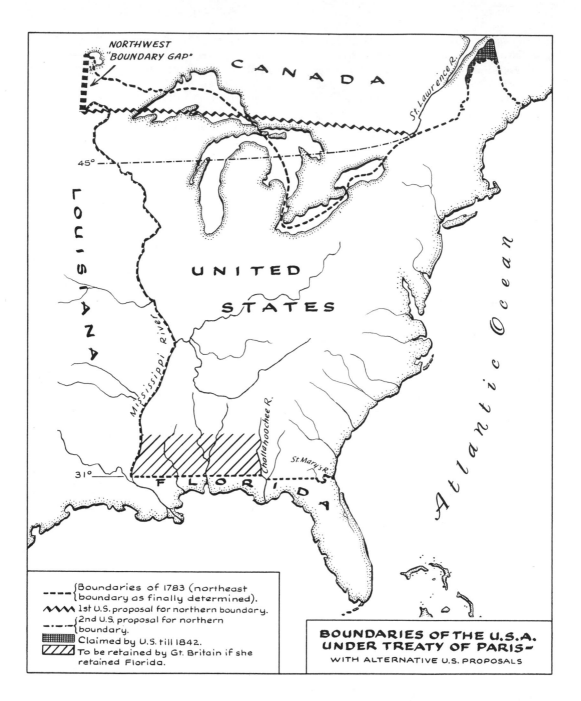

NORTHWEST "BOUNDARY GAP"

C A N A D A

St. Lawrence R.

45°

L O U I S I A N A

U N I T E D

S T A T E S

Mississippi River

Chattahoochee R.

St. Mary's R.

31°

F L O R I D A

Atlantic Ocean

- - - - {Boundaries of 1783 (northeast boundary as finally determined).
∧∧∧∧ 1st U.S. proposal for northern boundary.
-·-·- {2nd U.S. proposal for northern boundary.
▓▓▓ Claimed by U.S. till 1842.
▨▨▨ To be retained by Gt. Britain if she retained Florida.

**BOUNDARIES OF THE U.S.A.
UNDER TREATY OF PARIS—**
WITH ALTERNATIVE U.S. PROPOSALS

in the recovery of the full value of bona fide debts previously contracted. The United States agreed that there should be no further prosecutions or confiscations of property against any persons for the parts they had taken in the war, and promised that it would "earnestly recommend" to the legislatures of the states that, with certain exceptions, rights and properties of Loyalists be restored.

This preliminary treaty, minus the secret article, became the definitive treaty, signed September 3, 1783, at the same time that Great Britain made peace with her other enemies. The Floridas, with limits undefined, Great Britain ceded to Spain. Spain was not a party to the treaty between Great Britain and the United States, and hence did not consider herself bound by its provisions with respect to the navigation of the Mississippi and the southern boundary of the United States. With both Spain and Great Britain, the United States had still many difficulties to overcome before the paper stipulations of the treaty could be converted into reality.

Problems of Independence.

Americans soon learned that independence was no bed of roses. When the war officially ended in 1783, the new government had been recognized by France, Great Britain, the Netherlands, and Sweden. Inexperienced diplomats from the United States had wandered over Europe in vain efforts to secure recognition from Russia, Prussia, Austria, Spain, and the Grand Duke of Tuscany. In all these courts they had been coldly received. Few monarchs cared to imitate the indiscretion of Louis XVI of France, by countenancing rebellion and the institution of republican government.

A few other recognitions followed independence. In 1784 Spain finally gave in, sending Don Diego de Gardoqui as her first minister to the United States. Prussia made a treaty in 1785; Morocco, in 1786. By 1787, then, the United States had commercial treaties with those two powers and with France (1778), the Netherlands (1782), and Sweden (1783). It had no commercial treaty

with Great Britain until 1794, no treaty at all with Spain till 1795. The British government thought so little of the importance of the United States that though it received John Adams as minister in 1785 and maintained consular or other agents in American ports, it did not send a full-fledged minister to Philadelphia until 1791.

There were reasons for this temporary "underprivileged" status of the United States. It was an upstart nation, the product of revolution, an experiment in democracy, small in population, poor in fluid resources. But it also, under the Articles of Confederation, had a government that no foreign power need respect—a government without dependable revenue, without an army or navy, without power to coerce the governments of the thirteen individual states. Such a government was unable to fulfill its obligations under the treaty of peace. Such a government could not make promises with assurance that they would be observed or threats with any expectation that they would be carried out. Such a government was incapable of securing equality of commercial treatment abroad. It was incapable of enforcing its sovereignty in the area assigned to it by the treaty of peace or of putting an end, by either diplomacy or force, to foreign occupation of its soil. Not until after it was replaced by the more effective government provided for by the Constitution of 1787 were any of the pressing national problems solved. Even then, their solution owed much to the involvement of France, Spain, and Great Britain in the wars of the French Revolution. Then, to quote the familiar aphorism of Professor Samuel F. Bemis, "Europe's distress became America's advantage."

Independence Disrupts Trade

Particularly inconvenient for the young nation was the lack of a commercial treaty with Great Britain. The thirteen original states of the American Union had, while they existed as colonies under the British flag, developed a flourishing merchant marine and a large and profitable commerce. Colonial shipyards turned out ships more cheaply than the British. Ships built and owned in the colonies shared equally with English ships the privileges of Empire trade and protection by the Royal Navy. American tobacco, rice, indigo, wheat, flour, meat, fish, rum, furs, and lumber found markets in England, on the continent of Europe, in Africa, and in the West Indies; they were exchanged for manufactured goods, sugar and molasses, coffee, rum, slaves, and specie. The Revolution, while it lasted, disrupted large segments of this thriving commercial activity. American ships, with their cargoes, were excluded from British Empire ports and could roam the seas only at the risk of capture by British cruisers or privateers. Many American shipowners took to privateering themselves and harried British commerce even in the English Channel and the Irish Sea. The coming of peace in 1783 put an end to such warlike employment. It compelled the United States, in the exercise of its newly won independence, to seek markets for its produce, cargoes and foreign ports for its merchantmen, and protection for ships and cargoes against the piracies of North African freebooters.

Trade with the various portions of the British Empire might have gone on as before the war if the British had been willing. The American peace commissioners of 1782 were instructed to secure, if possible, for citizens of the United States, "a direct commerce to all parts of the British dominions and possessions" in return for the admission of British subjects to trade with all parts of the United States. The British government declined, at that time, to make a commercial treaty, and the House of Commons defeated a bill, introduced by William Pitt the younger, that would have admitted American ships and American

commodities to British Empire ports on the same terms as British vessels and products. The British Parliament was in no mood to be generous to its former colonies—least of all to encourage a rival in the American merchant marine. American ships carrying American products were admitted to ports in the British Isles on fairly liberal terms, but, in harmony with prevalent mercantile theory, American ships, like other foreign ships, were excluded from trading with the British colonies. New England merchants missed particularly what had once been a profitable trade with the British West Indies; only gradually, and at considerable risk, did they succeed in reopening this trade through clandestine and illegal channels. To varying degrees, and with some exceptions, other colonial powers adhered to the same mercantilist policy of reserving trade with their colonies to their own ships.

Problems of the West

Even more serious in the long view, than the problem of commerce was that of controlling the great region between the mountains and the Mississippi. The treaty of peace had assigned spacious boundaries to the United States, but American sovereignty within the boundaries was largely a legal fiction. American settlement beyond the mountains took the form of a narrow wedge with its base stretching from Pittsburgh to the Watauga settlements in eastern Tennessee and its apex at Nashville on the Cumberland River. Within it lay the villages in the Kentucky bluegrass region and at the Falls of the Ohio (Louisville). To these should be added the old French villages on the Wabash and in the Illinois country. All told, there were perhaps 25,000 settlers between the crest of the mountains and the Mississippi. Beyond these limits, to the north, west, and south, was the country of unfriendly Indians, and the explorer or trader who penetrated the Indian barrier was likely to find himself facing garrisons of British or Spanish troops upon land within the treaty boundaries of the United States. The British army still occupied every strategic point on the Great Lakes, and Spanish soldiers held the Mississippi at Natchez and (a little later) at the sites of the future Vicksburg and Memphis; and both British and Spanish were in alliance or understanding with the Indians for the purpose of preventing the United States from taking possession of the territory assigned to it by the treaty of peace.

There was, furthermore, no assurance that the frontier settlers themselves would be firm in their allegiance to the state governments in the East or to the weak Congress that symbolized their Union. A do-nothing government could not command a vital patriotism. The frontier found its natural outlets through the Mississippi and the St. Lawrence Rivers, and the nations that controlled those watercourses exerted a powerful attraction upon the settlements on their upper waters. Frontier leaders were not always above bartering their allegiance in return for special favors from the British and Spanish governments.

Before the United States could make its actual sovereignty coextensive with its treaty boundaries, it had to accomplish three difficult tasks. It had to make sure of its hold upon the allegiance of the frontiersmen. It had to bring the Indian tribes under its control. It had to secure from England and Spain, respectively, the execution and the recognition of the terms of the Treaty of Paris. These tasks were interrelated. Only through ousting the British and Spanish from their footholds upon its soil could the United States hope to control the Indians, and only by dealing effectively with both Indians and Europeans could it bind to itself the "men of the western waters."

None of these problems proved capable of solution during the period of the Articles of Confederation. The British held seven fortified posts on United States soil, strung out from the foot of Lake Champlain to Michilimackinac at the junction of Lakes Huron and Michigan. The British excused this violation of the peace treaty by asserting that the United States had not fulfilled its obligations under the same instrument. In reality, the decision to hold the posts had been taken before the treaty was formally proclaimed, obviously before the nature of the American performance under it could be known. Retention of the posts served to keep a valuable trade in furs in the hands of Canadian traders and enabled the British government to meet its obligations to Indian tribes which had been its allies during the recent war. British authorities did not hesitate to encourage these tribes, living south of the Canadian border, to resist American attempts to purchase and settle their lands. The British also showed an interest in the dissatisfaction of American frontier communities in Vermont and Kentucky, which might perhaps be willing to detach themselves from the Confederation.

The treaty of 1783 between Great Britain and the United States had fixed the southern boundary of the latter, from the Chattahoochee to the Mississippi, at the 31st parallel, had made the middle of the Mississippi the western boundary, and had declared: "The navigation of the river Mississippi, from its source to the ocean, shall forever remain free and open to the subjects of Great Britain, and the citizens of the United States." In the contemporaneous settlement with Spain, Great Britain had ceded to that nation East and West Florida without defining their boundaries. Louisiana, embracing the region west of the Mississippi and New Orleans east of that river, had been ceded by France to Spain in 1762. After 1783, therefore, Spain hemmed in the United States on both the west and the south.

Spain was not a signatory to the treaty

NORTHWEST BOUNDARY GAP →

St. Lawrence R.

Pointe au Fer
Oswegatchie
Dutchman's Point

Michilimackinac

Oswego
Niagara

Detroit

Pittsburgh

Cincinnati
Marietta

Louisville
Ohio R.
Lexington

Nashville
Knoxville

Tennessee R.
Hiwassee R.

San Fernando
Tombigbee R.
Flint R.

Ft. Confederacion

Los Nogales
Natchez

WEST FLORIDA   EAST FLORIDA

Mississippi River

L O U I S I A N A

Atlantic Ocean

Gulf of Mexico

Indian barrier state proposed by British and Indians
Extreme Spanish territorial claims

U.S. settlements
---- U.S., Treaty of 1783
++++ Greenville Treaty line, 1795
☐ British posts until 1796
◉ Spanish posts until 1798
● U.S. frontier towns

THE NORTHWEST AND SOUTHWEST, 1783-1798

between Great Britain and the United States and refused to consider herself bound by its terms, either as to the southern boundary of the United States or as to the free navigation of the Mississippi. As a result of the successful campaign under Galvez in 1779–1781, Spain claimed a large area in the Southwest by right of conquest and denied the right of Great Britain to cede it to the United States. Holding both banks of the Mississippi from its mouth to far above New Orleans, Spain likewise denied the right of Great Britain to guarantee to citizens of the United States its free navigation. Spanish policy after 1783 comprised the assertion of title to a region as far north as the Tennessee and Ohio Rivers, the denial to the Americans of the use of the lower Mississippi except as a privilege granted by Spain, and the cultivation of the friendship and trade of the powerful Indian nations of the Southwest with a view to using them as a barrier against the Americans. From time to time, also, Spain intrigued with shifty leaders in the American frontier communities who appeared ready to barter their allegiance for privileges or bounties conferred by the Spanish crown.

The extreme boundary claims of Spain were apparently set up chiefly for bargaining purposes. Diego de Gardoqui, who came to New York at 1784 as the first Spanish minister to the United States, was empowered to make liberal boundary concessions and to offer substantial trading privileges in return for the consent of the United States to waive its claim to the navigation of the Mississippi. John Jay of New York, serving as Secretary for Foreign Affairs under the direction of Congress, thought the trade offer advantageous and the navigation of the Mississippi of little immediate importance. He asked Congress for authority to consent to closure of the river for a period of twenty-five or thirty years. The vote on his proposal showed a sectional cleavage. Virginia, the Carolinas, and Georgia, all with land claims extending to the Mississippi, voted against Jay's pro-

posal. Maryland voted with her southern sisters. The seven states to the north (Delaware having no delegate in Congress) supported Jay. The majority of seven to five was sufficient to alter Jay's instructions, but any treaty that he might make would require the vote of nine states for ratification. Jay and Gardoqui continued their conversations, but there was no point in making a treaty which Congress would not approve.

Failure of the Jay-Gardoqui negotiations left matters *in statu quo*. In the next year (1787), however, the Spanish authorities opened the river at the behest of Americans from the Kentucky settlements. One of these, James Wilkinson, a veteran of the Revolution, paid for the privilege by taking a secret oath of allegiance to the Spanish Crown. He also undertook to advise the Spanish upon the best means of winning over other Kentuckians. Spain made no permanent converts among the frontiersmen—Wilkinson himself was soon to don a United States brigadier general's uniform—and her alternative policy of building anti-American alliances with the southern Indians won no victories. But the establishment of satisfactory relations with Spain, as well as with Britain, awaited the formation of a more efficient American government.

A New Government for the United States

While Britishers and Spaniards flirted with American frontiersmen and dabbled in alliances with the Indians in their respective spheres of influence, the United States was setting up a new government that effectually overcame the deficiencies of the Articles of Confederation and soon gave the country a respectable standing among the nations of the world. The Constitution written at Philadelphia in 1787 went into effect two years later. Under it, the new government had bargaining power that the old had lacked. It could control commerce, raise revenue, create and maintain armies and navies. Treaties, both those already made and those to be made in the future, were declared to be "the supreme law of the land," overriding state enactments and even state constitutions. Separate executive and judicial departments provided all the machinery necessary for enforcement. No longer could foreign governments scorn the promises or scoff at the threats of the United States. The adoption of the Constitution inaugurated a new era in American diplomacy.

ADDITIONAL READINGS

CORWIN, EDWARD S., *French Policy and the American Alliance of 1778*. Princeton: Princeton University Press, 1916.

HUTSON, JAMES H., "The Partition Treaty and the Declaration of American Independence," *Journal of American History*, 58 (March, 1972), 877–96.

MORRIS, RICHARD B., *The Peacemakers: The Great Powers and American Independence*. New York: Harper & Row, Publishers, 1965.

SAVELLE, MAX., *The Origins of American Diplomacy: The International History of Anglo-America, 1492–1763*. New York: The Macmillan Company, 1967.

STINCHCOMBE, WILLIAM C., *The American Revolution and the French Alliance*. Syracuse: Syracuse University Press, 1969.

VAN ALSTYNE, RICHARD W., *Empire and Independence: The International History of the American Revolution*. New York: John Wiley & Sons, Inc., 1965.

3. War in Europe Raises New and Settles Old Problems

In its exertions to secure essential French aid in the Revolution, the United States departed in some degree from John Adams' advice against an alliance with France "which should entangle us in any future wars in Europe." The treaty of alliance of February 6, 1778, looking beyond the war then in progress, bound each of the allies to guarantee to the other the American possessions that it might hold at the end of the war. To that extent only was the United States obligated to assist France in any future war. Should an enemy of France attempt to seize the French islands in the West Indies, France might justly claim the support of the United States.

The other treaty signed on the same date, the treaty of amity and commerce, embodied definitions of neutral rights as proposed by Congress in its treaty plan of 1776, which in turn followed almost word for word a commercial treaty between England and France signed at Utrecht in 1713.[1] The treaty of 1778 between the United States and France defined the privileges to be enjoyed by the ships and commerce of either during a war in which it was neutral while the other was belligerent. The ships

of the neutral should be free to carry non-contraband merchandise not only to the unblockaded ports of an enemy but from one enemy port to another. Free ships were to make free goods; in other words, enemy property, noncontraband, carried on a neutral ship, was not to be liable to capture. The same was true of enemy nationals traveling on a neutral ship unless they were soldiers in enemy service. On the other hand, neutral property on an enemy ship took on the character of enemy property and was subject to confiscation. Contraband goods were defined so narrowly as to consist almost exclusively of arms and ammunition. All else was noncontraband; the noncontraband list mentioned specifically fabrics, wearing apparel, metals, food, provisions, tobacco, and naval stores. All such goods the neutral might carry freely to enemy ports, with the exception of such ports "as are at that time besieged, blocked up or invested." There was no definition of what constituted a legal blockade.

Other articles of the treaty, also contained in the proposals of 1776, allowed special privileges in the ports of the neutral to the armed ships, public and private, of the belligerent ally, while denying them to the ships of the opposing belligerent. Ships-of-war and privateers of the belligerent ally were to be free to bring their prizes into the ports of the neutral (nothing was said of any right to sell prizes or to fit out armed vessels in such ports) and to depart with them at their pleasure and without interference; but such privileges were ex-

[1] The treaties with France are in the usual official collections of treaties. For the "Plan of 1776," see W. C. Ford et al., eds., *Journals of the Continental Congress,* 34 vols. (Washington, D.C.: Government Printing Office, 1904–1937), 5: 768–78. Relevant portions of these documents and of the Utrecht treaty are printed in Department of State, *Policy of the United States toward Maritime Commerce in War,* prepared by Carlton Savage, 2 vols. (Washington, D.C.: Government Printing Office, 1934–1936), 1: 132–40.

pressly denied to the armed vessels of the opposing belligerent, which, furthermore, should not be permitted to fit out ships-of-war or privateers in the ports of the neutral.

It had been the hope of Congress, when it adopted the "Plan of 1776," to have its principles with regard to the privileges of neutral commerce incorporated in treaties with all the maritime powers. Those principles were embodied in treaties with the Netherlands (1782), Sweden (1783), Prussia (1785), and Morocco (1786).

There was one conspicuous exception to the rather general willingness of the European powers to make liberal commercial treaties with the United States. Great Britain refused to incorporate in the treaty of peace (1783) any provision for the protection of neutral trade or even to make a commercial treaty of any kind until the mission of John Jay in 1794. Great Britain, therefore, was under no obligation to observe the principles of 1776 when she and France again went to war.[2]

The First Struggle for Neutrality

In February 1793, following the execution by the French of their King, Louis XVI, and the withdrawal from Paris of the British ambassador, the French Republic declared war upon Great Britain. France was already at war with her neighbors on the continent. The opening of the English phase of the war launched the conflict upon the sea and brought it to the shores of the United States.

Could the United States remain neutral? American popular sympathy was strong for France—the ally in the recent war and now the exemplar of republicanism and de-

[2]Russia also declined to make a treaty with the United States at this time, but in a declaration of 1780, the Russian government had adopted the main principles of the plan of 1776.

mocracy in monarchical and aristocratic Europe. "Jacobin Clubs," patterned after those in France, were organized among the American populace, and their members addressed one another as "citizen" and "citizeness" after the current French fashion. But, aside from popular sentiment, the United States had treaty obligations to France—an obligation under certain circumstances to protect French possessions in America, an obligation to allow French naval vessels and privateers privileges denied to the ships of Great Britain. To these forces pulling the United States toward France was added a British policy of ruthless interference with American trade at sea and consistent opposition to American interests on the frontier. To drift into war with England would be easy, and a war with England, when the United States was barely getting on its feet under the new Constitution, was certain to be disastrous economically and disruptive politically.

President Washington and his advisers were fully aware of the perils of the situation. Anticipating the arrival of the first minister of the French Republic, the young and exuberant Edmond Genêt, Washington submitted a group of thirteen questions to the members of his cabinet—Thomas Jefferson, Secretary of State; Alexander Hamilton, Secretary of the Treasury; Henry Knox, Secretary of War; and Edmund Randolph, Attorney General—and requested their opinions. The essence of the questions can be summarized in three: (1) Shall the President issue a proclamation of neutrality as between France and her enemies? (2) Are the treaties made with the French government of Louis XVI still binding upon the United States, now that that government has been overthrown and the King sent to the guillotine? (3) Shall Genêt be received as the minister of the French Republic?

Of historic importance were the answers to these questions returned by Jefferson and Hamilton—Knox siding with Hamilton and Randolph with Jefferson. To the first question—should there be a proclamation of neutrality?—Hamilton answered yes; Jefferson, no. Jefferson argued, first, that the question of neutrality (like that of war) was one for Congress to determine; second, that neutrality, a boon to Great Britain, should be used to bargain with, not freely given. Jefferson agreed, however, that the President should warn American citizens against giving aid to either party to the conflict.

To the second question—were the treaties binding?—Hamilton answered no, since, among other reasons, the government with which they were made had been destroyed. Even if the treaties were still in force, Hamilton added, the treaty of alliance was expressly a "defensive" one, and France, having declared war against England, was here the aggressor. Jefferson opposed Hamilton's reasoning, arguing that treaties were made by the government of Louis XVI acting as the agent of the French people, and that a mere change of agents did not invalidate the agreements. On this point, Jefferson's position was that now universally accepted in the conduct of international relations. A treaty is made with a nation and is not abrogated by a change in government. But while Jefferson would not repudiate the French treaties, neither would he so interpret them as to involve the United States in the war on the side of France. France, he said, had not yet asked the United States to fulfill its guarantee under the treaty of alliance. Should it do so, the United States could excuse itself on the ground that France, which had similarly undertaken to guarantee the sovereignty and territorial possessions of the United States, had given no aid in ending British occupation of the northwest posts. Thus Jefferson, though considered the head of the pro-French faction, was little less anxious than pro-British Hamilton to preserve American neutrality.

To the third question—should Genêt be received?—both Hamilton and Jefferson answered yes; but whereas Jefferson would receive him unconditionally, Hamilton would give him notice that the United States did not consider itself bound by the treaties of 1778.

Washington, thus finding his advisers divided on every question, was under the necessity of choosing between them. For the most part, he followed Jefferson. Genêt was received, upon his arrival at Philadelphia, without condition. His unconditional reception was a tacit acknowledgment that the treaties were still in effect. A proclamation of neutrality was issued (April 22, 1793), but out of regard for Jefferson's attitude, Washington avoided the use of the word "neutrality." He declared it to be the intention of the United States to "pursue a conduct friendly and impartial toward the belligerent Powers," called upon all citizens of the United States to avoid acts contrary to such a course, and warned them that, far from receiving the protection of the United States against the consequences of committing acts of hostility against any of the belligerents, they must expect prosecution for any violation of "the law of nations" committed "within the cognizance of the courts of the United States."

The arrival of Citizen Genêt and his impertinent attempts to exploit the United States for French purposes in defiance of the government in Philadelphia led before long to a request for his recall and to the passage by Congress of the first neutrality legislation in the history of the United States. Genêt obviously expected to find in the United States, if not an ally, at least a "nonbelligerent"—if we may borrow from the mid-twentieth century a term signifying a state that gives active assistance to one side without engaging in actual warfare. He made no demand for activation of the guarantees of the alliance, but he at once engaged in activities which were unwarranted by any provisions in the treaty of amity and commerce and which, if persisted in, would have compromised the neutrality of the United States. Specifically, he fitted out and commissioned in American ports privateers to cruise under the French flag and to prey upon British commerce. He set up in American ports French prize courts to condemn prizes brought in by French privateers or cruisers.[3] He attempted to organize in the United States military expeditions to attack Florida and Louisiana, both at that time possessions of France's enemy, Spain. To enable him to finance these activities, he demanded that the United States pay before they were due installments of the debt owed to the French government for loans during and after the American Revolution—a demand that the American government refused. In all these ways, Genêt attempted to make the United States a base of French operations—by sea against Great Britain, by land against Spain. When Washington sought to interfere with these brash proceedings, Genêt appealed to the public over the President's head through letters to pro-French journals.

All this misbehavior, which even Jefferson could not condone, led after a few months to a request for Genêt's recall, which was complied with by the French government.[4] More important, the unfortunate experience with Genêt was largely responsible for the enactment by Congress of the neutrality law of June 5, 1794. A glance at this act will show that it forbade precisely those things that Genêt had been

doing or trying to do—the arming or equipping of ships-of-war for a belligerent government in United States ports; the recruiting within American jurisdiction of persons to serve in the armed forces of a belligerent government; the setting on foot within the American jurisdiction of any armed expedition against a friendly power.

The law of 1794 is a landmark in the history of neutrality. Other nations had not been backward about laying claim to their neutral rights. The United States led the way in assuming responsibility for the carrying out of its neutral duties.

A Crisis with England

The termination of Genêt's mission temporarily eased relations with France but did little to help those with England, which was persistently violating what the United States held to be its neutral rights. Never having accepted the principles of the plan of 1776, the British government, in dealing with neutral commerce, was bound only by what it chose to recognize as the generally accepted law of nations; and this, as interpreted by the British, contravened the principles of 1776 in several respects. In violation of the dictum "free ships make free goods," British prize courts condemned enemy (French) property found in American ships. In partial disregard, at least, of the exclusion of provisions from the contraband categories of 1776, the British seized cargoes of American wheat, corn, and flour en route to France—not for confiscation, indeed, but for preemptive purchase, presumably to the injury of the shipper. Against the stipulation of 1776 that neutral ships should be free to trade to and between enemy ports, the British invoked their own so-called "Rule of the War of 1756," or simply the rule of 1756, which stated that trade illegal in peace was illegal in war. What this meant in practice was that

---

[3] It was Genêt's contention that the treaty of amity and commerce, in denying these privileges to the enemies of France, allowed them to France by implication.

[4] Genêt did not return to France. The Girondist faction in the French National Convention, which had sent him to America, had fallen from power and its leaders were being sent to the guillotine. Not liking the prospects at home, Genêt asked and received permission to remain in the United States as a private citizen. He married the daughter of Governor George Clinton of New York and became the progenitor of an American family.

France, which in peace confined trade between herself and her colonies to French ships, was not permitted in wartime to open that trade to neutral shipping, as she had done in the Seven Years' War and was again doing now. Neutral ships admitted to such trade, the British declared, would be considered as incorporated in the French merchant marine and hence subject to confiscation like French property. Toward United States shipping, the British went even beyond the rule of 1756, seizing not only American ships trading between France and her colonies, but also those trading between the colonies and the United States—a trade that France had permitted in time of peace. The British also, in this period, began the practice of stopping American merchant vessels on the high seas and "impressing" members of their crews, presumed to be British subjects, for service in the Royal Navy.

These were the principal maritime grievances which, in conjunction with border troubles and nonfulfillment by both parties of the terms of the treaty of 1783, produced a crisis with Great Britain in 1794. On the frontier, British garrisons still held the border posts on American soil, and British agents continued to encourage the Indians in their resistance to American land claims. Neither Congress nor the new government had attempted to oust the British by force from the posts. Viewing the Indian treaties of 1784 and later years as valid, Congress had provided for the government of the Northwest Territory in the Ordinance of 1787 and had sold large tracts of land north of the Ohio River to companies of prospective settlers and speculators, two of which planned settlements at Marietta and Cincinnati. When General Washington was inaugurated as first President of the United States in the spring of 1789, the settlement of the Northwest had begun, but it had become apparent that the Indians would not honor the land treaties until compelled by force to do so.

Two expeditions against the recalcitrant Indians in 1789 and 1791, led by General Joseph Harmar and Governor Arthur St. Clair, resulted respectively in an inconclusive campaign and a disastrous defeat for the Americans. Washington appointed "Mad" Anthony Wayne, an officer with a fine record in the Revolution, to command a third expedition. In the fall of 1793, with a thoroughly drilled army, Wayne advanced from Fort Washington at Cincinnati into the Indian country, went into winter quarters at Fort Greenville, and prepared for a decisive campaign during the following summer.

When Wayne moved into the Indian country in the fall of 1793, the United States and Great Britain were already engaged in a warm argument over the rights of neutrals. Congress had enacted a temporary embargo on American shipping, and bills were introduced for the sequestration of British debts and other measures of retaliation. Lord Dorchester, Canadian Governor General, at this point lost his head. Apparently assuming that war was inevitable and that Wayne, if successful against the Indians, would press on and attack Detroit, he sent orders to Governor John Graves Simcoe in Upper Canada to seize and fortify a strategic point at the Rapids of the Maumee River. As a result, the British flag flew at Fort Miami, many miles within the boundaries of the United States. In February 1794, Dorchester was visited at Quebec by a delegation of western Indians. In his "talk" to them he asserted that the United States had no desire for peace, that it had violated its treaty with Great Britain, and that war was certain within a year. Then, he said, the Indians could recover what was rightly theirs. This was little short of incitement to war.

Such was the ominous atmosphere in which Wayne began the second phase of his campaign in the spring of 1794. Slowly he advanced until on August 18 he was but two miles from the British fort on the Mau-

mee. Here, in a mass of fallen timber —which gave a name to the battle—he came upon the assembled Indian warriors, re-enforced, it must be added, by numerous Canadian volunteers. Scattering at a determined charge by Wayne's men, the Indians fell back under the guns of the British fort. "Inside the fort," wrote Professor Samuel F. Bemis, "torches hovered above the breeches of loaded cannon trained on the American cavalry."[5] Would some rash British soldier discharge a cannon? Would Wayne attack? On these questions might hang peace or war, perhaps the fate of the American nation. Fortunately, "Mad" Anthony's actions belied his nickname. Campbell, the British commander, showed equal coolness, and the dangerous moment passed. Wayne left the vicinity of the fort. He had beaten the Indians soundly, and now turned to laying waste their villages and fields as the best means of bringing them to terms.

Jay's Treaty

While this crisis was passing on the frontier, another was passing in England. In April 1794, Washington had resolved to send to London John Jay, Chief Justice of the Supreme Court, in a final attempt to reach an agreement with England over the several matters in dispute. Jay was well chosen for such a mission of conciliation. A distinguished member of the Federalist party, he shared the desire of Hamilton, the party's head, for continued peace with Great Britain.[6] He was, furthermore, an experienced

diplomat. He had represented the United States (albeit unrecognized) at the court of Spain (1779–1782), had been one of the American peace commissioners at Paris (1782–1783), and after his return to the United States had served as Secretary for Foreign Affairs for Congress under the Articles of Confederation. His policy in that office had rendered him acceptable to England; he had, in fact, condoned the British retention of the posts as justified by American infractions of the treaty. This fact, had it been generally known, together with his willingness at the same time to surrender the American demand upon Spain for the free navigation of the Mississippi, might have led a westerner to fear that Jay would not be zealous in defense of western interests.

Jay was instructed, nevertheless, to secure fulfillment of the treaty of 1783, meaning among other things the surrender of the northwest posts. In the matter of neutral rights, he was to urge the British government to accept the principles of 1776 and was to seek compensation for seizures of American ships and cargoes in violation of those principles. His instructions, written by Randolph but shaped by Hamilton, were elastic, and it was probably not expected that Great Britain would yield much in principle. The dominant Federalist party, led by Hamilton, placed the maintenance of peace with Great Britain at the head of their list of desirables.

---

[5]S. F. Bemis, *Jay's Treaty, a Study in Commerce and Diplomacy* (New Haven: Yale University Press, 1962), p. 247.

[6]Alexander Hamilton, Secretary of the Treasury under Washington, was keenly interested in the success of the financial measures of which he was the father. He had funded the national debt, assumed the

revolutionary debts of the states, and provided for the payment of interest and the gradual retirement of the principal of this debt. He had created the first Bank of the United States, the chief capital of which consisted of United States bonds. The success of his plans depended upon a steady flow of revenue into the Federal treasury, without which government credit would collapse. The principal source of this revenue was duty collected upon imports. War with England would mean the ruin of this trade and would thus end Hamilton's whole financial structure. See C. A. *Economic Origins of Jeffersonian Democracy* (New York: The Macmillan Company, 1915), chap. 10.

In the last resort [observed Professor Bemis], to preserve peace and national credit, which depended for its revenues on commerce, they were willing, in the face of British sea power, to acquiesce in a complete reversion or suspension of the liberal principles incorporated in the American treaties with France, Sweden, Holland and Prussia.[7]

Negotiating in this spirit and faced by a Foreign Minister, Lord Grenville, who was secretly informed that the United States would not ally itself with the European neutrals for a joint defense of their interests,[8] Jay got nothing at all in the way of concessions in principle. On the contrary, in the treaty signed on November 19, 1794, the United States agreed that enemy goods might be taken from neutral ships, that naval stores should be contraband, that provisions bound for an enemy might be taken from neutral ships if paid for. The rule of 1756 was left intact, and there was no definition of legal blockade—another point on which Jay had been told to seek clarification.

Under the treaty of amity and commerce of 1778 with France, French ships-of-war or privateers with prizes taken from the enemies of France were admitted freely to American ports, but enemy ships that had taken French prizes were excluded. The Jay treaty gave the same privilege to British ships-of-war and privateers and excluded those of Britain's enemies. This direct contradiction of the French treaty was partly nullified, however, by the inclusion of a clause declaring that nothing in the treaty should "operate contrary to former and existing public treaties with other sovereigns or States."

[7]Bemis, *Jay's Treaty*, p. 298.

[8]Jay's bargaining position was weakened when George Hammond, British minister to the United States, relayed to Grenville some indiscreet confidences of Alexander Hamilton, who had informed the minister that the United States would never ally itself with the European neutrals for the defense of its rights against Great Britain.

The West, which might have expected little from John Jay, fared rather better than other sections in the treaty. The document contained a promise, on the part of the British, that the posts would be evacuated not later than June 1, 1796. British traders at the posts might remain there if they chose, and the subjects or citizens of either country should be privileged "freely to pass and repass by land or inland navigation, into the respective territories and countries of the two parties, on the continent of America, . . . and to navigate all the lakes, rivers and waters thereof, and freely to carry on trade and commerce with each other,"—with the reservation that such privileges should not extend to the territories of the Hudson's Bay Company. The Mississippi River was, as under the treaty of peace, to be open to the use of both parties. A joint survey of the upper portion of that river was to be made, and if this survey should show that the river would not be intersected by a line drawn westward from the Lake of the Woods, the boundary in that quarter should be fixed by amicable negotiation. A joint commission should determine the identity of the St. Croix River, which formed part of the northeastern boundary.[9]

From the point of view of the West, the great advantage of the treaty was the liberation of United States soil from British troops. For this gain, Jay deserves no great credit, since Grenville had resolved on this concession before the negotiations opened.[10] The accompanying provision for

[9]A commission appointed under the terms of the treaty fixed upon the Schoodiac River as the eastern boundary of Maine—the St. Croix River of the Treaty of Paris. No survey of the upper Mississippi was made, however, and the line between that river and the Lake of the Woods remained undetermined.

[10]Grenville disapproved strongly of Lord Dorchester's speech to the Indians and of his authorization of the occupation of Fort Miami, and rebuked that official so strongly that he resigned. Bemis, *Jay's Treaty*, p. 320.

mutual freedom of travel and trade across the border enabled the British and Canadian traders to continue their profitable commerce and their Indian connections in United States territory, although it had little practical value for citizens of the United States. Jay had attempted unsuccessfully to secure disarmament on the lakes and an agreement that neither party would employ Indian allies in war against the other, supply the Indians with arms for war against the whites, or enter into political relations with Indian tribes upon the other's territory. These proposals Grenville had refused. On the other hand, Jay had resisted Grenville's attempt to secure for Great Britain a slice of territory reaching down the Mississippi River to navigable water in the vicinity of modern Minneapolis.

Jay's treaty also settled, after a fashion, a number of the other matters in controversy between the two countries. It provided for the adjudication and payment, on the one side, of pre-Revolutionary debts owed by Americans to British subjects and of British claims for damages resulting from Genêt's irregular proceedings; and, on the other, of claims arising from illegal seizures by British cruisers of American ships and cargoes. On these scores the United States paid $2,664,000 for debts and $143,428 for the Genêt claims and received $11,656,000 for injuries to its commerce. British claims for compensation of the Loyalists were dropped, as were American claims for compensation for Negro slaves carried away by departing British troops in 1783. The commercial clauses of the treaty placed the United States on a most-favored-nation basis with reference to trade with the British Isles, opened the East Indian trade to Americans on fairly liberal terms, and also opened the more important West Indian trade but on terms so unsatisfactory that the Senate struck out that article in approving the treaty. The treaty was approved by the Senate and ratified by the President and the necessary appropriations were made by Congress but only after stormy sessions in both houses and widespread popular condemnation of John Jay.

Unsatisfactory though it was in some respects, the Jay treaty not only kept the peace at a critical time, it brought about the full execution by Great Britain of the peace treaty of 1783 and thus the acceptance by her of the United States as an equal and wholly sovereign state. This favorable result must be attributed in part to Great Britain's involvement in the European war and her reluctance to take on additional enemies. Freeing the northern frontier from British garrisons, the treaty was conducive to a settlement with the Indians. General Wayne followed up his victory at Fallen Timbers by a year of desultory campaigning in the Indian country. Deprived of the hope of British support, the tribes at length came to terms. At Fort Greenville on August 3, 1795, their deputies ceded to the United States all of the future state of Ohio except the northwest corner and a strip running thence along the shore of Lake Erie to the Cuyahoga River. With the signing of Jay's and Wayne's treaties, the control of the Northwest for the first time passed to the United States.

Pinckney's Treaty with Spain

Less than a year after the signing of the Jay treaty with Great Britain, Thomas Pinckney, at Madrid, signed a treaty with Spain that accomplished for the Southwest even greater things than Jay's treaty had achieved for the Northwest. Spain, which had been an ally of Great Britain in the coalition against France, was drifting toward a peace with France that would eventually involve her in war against England, and the ministry regarded with apprehension the possibility of a joint Anglo-American attack upon the Spanish colonies. This fear was heightened when Godoy, the Prime Minister, learned (in July 1794) of Jay's mission to England. Friendly relations with the United States, even at the cost of large concessions, seemed the only safe policy for Spain.

At a hint from Madrid that the Spanish government was ready to form an alliance with the United States and to concede the American claims as to the boundary line and the navigation of the Mississippi, President Washington, in November 1794, appointed Thomas Pinckney as minister to Spain. Godoy was now really anxious for a settlement with the United States, and by the time that Pinckney reached Madrid, toward the end of June 1795, circumstances were most propitious for a successful negotiation. Peace negotiations between Spain and France were proceeding rapidly to a conclusion at Bâle, where a treaty was actually signed on July 22, 1795. The news that Jay had signed a treaty with Great Britain had also reached Madrid. Under these circumstances, the Council of State resolved, on August 14, 1795, to yield to the United States its principal demands without insisting upon a treaty of alliance in return. Haggling over details prolonged the negotiations, but on October 27, Pinckney and Godoy signed at the royal palace of San Lorenzo a treaty which for the time being settled the problem of the Southwest.

By the treaty of San Lorenzo, Spain accepted the 31st parallel of latitude from the Mississippi to the Chattahoochee as the southern boundary of the United States, agreed to the free navigation of the Mississippi from source to mouth by citizens of the United States, and consented that the latter might enjoy for three years the privilege of landing and storing their goods at New Orleans without other charge than a fair price for storage. This was the "right of deposit," which Pinckney with considerable difficulty had wrung from Godoy. It was important for the westerners, who brought most of their cargoes down the river in flatboats and must have a place to store them while awaiting suitable oceangoing vessels. After three years, the privilege should be either renewed at New Orleans or provided at another suitable spot on the lower Mississippi. Each party to the treaty agreed to prevent its Indian inhabitants from molesting either whites or Indians in the territory of the other, and there were sections defining neutral rights and duties and providing for the establishment of consulates and the settlement of claims.

The Spanish displayed their usual procrastination in carrying out the terms of the treaty. Their frontier posts north of 31° were not evacuated until 1798. By the end of that year, however, all Spanish garrisons within the United States had been withdrawn, the long-disputed territory was in American hands, and the men of the western waters were freely navigating the great river and utilizing the storage facilities of New Orleans. In the Southwest as in the Northwest, the United States had at length made its sovereignty coextensive with the treaty boundaries of 1783.

Hostilities with France— and a New Treaty

A backward step in the promotion of neutral rights, Jay's treaty, with its gains in other matters, postponed a break with Great Britain to a period in which the United States was better able to endure it. In fact, it ushered in a decade of generally cordial relations with the British.[11] In American relations with France, however, it raised a storm that ended in undeclared hostilities.

When Jay was sent to England in 1794, James Monroe was sent to France to replace

[11]Bradford Perkins, *The First Rapprochement: England and the United States, 1795–1805* (Philadelphia: University of Pennsylvania Press, 1955).

the Federalist minister, Gouverneur Morris, whose recall the French government had requested in return for Genêt's. Monroe, a follower of Jefferson and a sympathizer with France, ingratiated himself with the National Convention, which then served as the French government, but when he learned of Jay's treaty, which was contrary both to the spirit and the letter of American engagements with France, he joined the French in privately condemning it instead of defending it, as became the representative of the United States government. Consequently, he was recalled, and the South Carolina Federalist, C. C. Pinckney, was appointed to succeed him.

France was now (1796) under the rule of the unscrupulous group of politicians known as the Directory. Elated by a series of military victories in Europe, they were reducing the smaller neighbors of France to the role of satellites and tributaries. They proposed to do the same with the United States. Angered by Jay's treaty, they refused to receive Pinckney, suspended the functions of the French minister in Philadelphia, thereby severing diplomatic relations, ordered French cruisers and privateers to seize American ships (on the theory that what the British could do the French could do), and dabbled in American politics with a view to swinging the election of 1796 in favor of Jefferson and his Republicans and against the Federalist John Adams.[12]

Adams (elected nevertheless) named a commission of three—John Marshall, Elbridge Gerry of Massachusetts (a Republican), and the rejected Pinckney—to seek a restoration of diplomatic relations and a promise to respect American rights. Upon their arrival in Paris the commissioners were approached by intermediaries—designated by X, Y, and Z in the printed dispatches—who offered, on behalf of Foreign Minister Talleyrand, recognition by the Directory at the price of a loan to France, a substantial bribe to the Directors, and an apology for some unfriendly references to France in President Adams' recent message to Congress.

The commissioners spurned the proposal. Their report, submitted to Congress by President Adams, with the recommendation that the nation arm itself for defense, stimulated Congress to vigorous action. The lawmakers authorized the President to raise a "provisional army" of 10,000 men in addition to the Regular Army and called George Washington back from retirement to command it. They created a Navy Department (the small Navy that the United States possessed had hitherto been administered by the Secretary of War) and authorized United States naval vessels and armed merchantmen to attack and capture armed French vessels in the western Atlantic and the Caribbean. And they declared the treaties of 1778 with France abrogated. The Army was not used, though Alexander Hamilton, as senior major general under Washington, would have liked to lead it against Florida and Lousiana, the possessions of Spain, formerly an enemy of France but now her ally. The little Navy, with considerable cooperation from the British,[13] gave a good account of itself, cap-

---

[12] It was, in part, this French interference in American politics that inspired the warnings in Washington's Farewell Address of September 17, 1796. He cautioned his fellow countrymen against "inveterate antipathies against particular nations and passionate attachments for others." The current difficulties of relations with France also suggested the declaration that "it is our true policy to steer clear of permanent alliances with any portion of the foreign world." Often overlooked is the qualifying statement that "we may safely trust to temporary alliances for extraordinary emergencies." For a full discussion of the Farewell Address, see S. F. Bemis, "Washington's Farewell Address: A Foreign Policy of Independence," *American Historical Review,* 39 (1934), 250–68. On the partisan character of the "Farewell Address," see Alexander DeConde, *Entangling Alliance: Politics and Diplomacy under George Washington* (Durham, N.C.: Duke University Press, 1958), pp. 463–71, 503.

[13] Bradford Perkins, *The First Rapprochement,* chap. 8.

turing between eighty and ninety armed French vessels.

This was the "quasi-war" with France of 1798 to 1800.[14] That it should become a full-scale war was not the desire of President Adams, or of Talleyrand, or of General Napoleon Bonaparte, who in November 1799 overthrew the Directory and, as First Consul, became the head of the French government. Adams, besides being a man of peace, had no wish to see military laurels gathered by his rival, Hamilton. Bonaparte and Talleyrand, now intent upon securing Louisiana, for that reason desired peace with both the United States and Great Britain. Adams, in one of his messages to Congress, had declared that he would never send another minister to France without assurance that he would be "received, respected, and honored as the representative of a great, free, powerful, and independent nation." Talleyrand sent word that a new minister would be thus received and treated. Adams, against the wishes of Secretary of State Timothy Pickering and other members of his cabinet, who wished the undeclared war to continue, named a new commission of three men, William Vans Murray, Oliver Ellsworth, and William R. Davie, to undertake a new negotiation with France.

The American negotiators were received in Paris with all proper respect. They found that Talleyrand, in his desire for a settlement, had already ordered an end to the seizure of American ships and was arranging for the release of captured American sailors. A commission headed by Joseph Bonaparte, the First Consul's brother, was

[14]In the first year of this undeclared war, a Pennsylvania Quaker, George Logan, went to France on his own responsibility to reassure French officials of the friendly attitude of the people of the United States. This adventure in private diplomacy led Congress to pass the "Logan Act," of January 30, 1799. The act prohibited any unauthorized negotiation by a citizen of the United States for the purpose of influencing the course of action of a foreign government in relation to any controversy with the United States.

appointed to negotiate with the Americans. Murray and his colleagues asked indemnity for French depredations upon American commerce and bilateral abrogation of the treaties of 1778—already abrogated insofar as an act of Congress could perform that function. The French commissioners pointed out that the claims for indemnity rested upon alleged French violations of the treaty of amity and commerce and said to the American commissioners in effect, "If you wish the indemnity, you must keep the treaties; if you insist upon cancelling the treaties, you must forgo the indemnity." No agreement proving possible on this choice of alternatives, the negotiators signed on September 30, 1800, a treaty of which the second article suspended the operation of the treaties of 1778 and left the question of indemnities undetermined, both to be the subject of further negotiation "at a convenient time." As amended by the Senate and further qualified by Bonaparte before ratification, the treaty nullified the earlier treaties and cancelled the claims for indemnity. Thus the United States escaped from its "entangling alliance" with France —so indispensable during the Revolution, so inconsistent with American interest thereafter.

The treaty of 1800 restated almost intact the principles of 1776 with regard to neutral shipping and neutral trade. The ships-of-war and privateers of each nation, with their prizes, were to enjoy in the ports of the other the same treatment "as those of the nation the most favoured; and in general," the text continued, "the two parties shall enjoy in the ports of each other, in regard to commerce, and navigation, the privileges of the most favoured nation. . . ." Thus French privileges in American ports were placed on an equal footing, and no more, with those of England. As a measure toward liquidating the results of the hostilities terminated by the treaty, the document provided for the restoration to each party of all public ships taken by the other.

The chief importance of the treaty of 1800 with France lay in its termination of the treaty of alliance and of the special privileges enjoyed by France under the other treaty of 1778. Thus the United States was released from all obligations that compromised its neutral position in relation to the European belligerents. The restatement of the principles of 1776 was little more than a gesture. Napoleon Bonaparte's promises were kept only as long as they suited his convenience, and in any event, a statement of neutral rights without the concurrence of Great Britain had small practical importance.

The Louisiana Purchase and Its Sequel

The treaties negotiated by John Jay and Thomas Pinckney in 1794 and 1795 validated the boundary provisions of the peace treaty of 1783. A vigorous young nation, however, was likely to overstep these boundaries wherever they proved weak and the land beyond them attractive. This was notably the case with the Spanish territories to the west and south. Settlers from the United States threatened to dominate Upper Louisiana and the eastern bank of the Mississippi in West Florida. At New Orleans, where the right of deposit was proving a boon to the growing settlements up river, American sailing ships far outnumbered all others. Eastward from New Orleans along the Gulf coast lay West and East Florida, sparsely inhabited but commanding the mouths of rivers that would become important to the United States as Georgia and Mississippi Territory filled with people and farms. The East Florida peninsula commanded the principal entrance to the Gulf of Mexico.

Clearly the United States would one day need New Orleans and the Floridas. But Thomas Jefferson, who took the oath of office as President on March 4, 1801, was content to let them remain for the present in the hands of Spain. With Spain, all serious controversies had been settled; Spanish rule in New Orleans and the Floridas had ceased to be a menace to the United States. "We consider [Spain's] possession of the adjacent country as most favorable to our interests," Jefferson wrote in July 1801, "and should see with an extreme pain any other nation substituted for them." Five months after writing this letter, Jefferson received evidence from the United States minister in London that such a substitution was in process of being made. By a secret treaty of October 1, 1800, Spain had retroceded Louisiana to the French Republic, then headed by Napoleon Bonaparte as First Consul.[15]

Louisiana, originally a French colony, had been ceded by France to Spain in 1762, at the close of the French and Indian (or Seven Years') War. French interest in recovering it appeared on the eve of the French Revolution, and on several occasions during the 1790's French diplomats sounded the Spanish government on the possibility of a retrocession. Although Spain had found Louisiana unprofitable and impossible to defend against intrusions from the United States and Canada, the Spanish court resisted French approaches until the summer of 1800. Negotiations were then begun which culminated in the signing of the Treaty of San Ildefonso, October 1, 1800.

The Retrocession of Louisiana

By the terms of the treaty, Spain agreed to "retrocede" to France the colony of Louisiana and to turn over six ships-of-war

[15]General Bonaparte became First Consul and, in reality, dictatorial head of the French government as a result of the *coup d'état* of November 9–10, 1799. On August 1, 1802, he had himself proclaimed Consul for Life, and thereafter chose to be known by his Christian name of Napoleon, after the fashion of other monarchs. In December 1804, he assumed the title, Emperor of the French.

for the French navy. In return, Bonaparte promised to create for the Prince of Parma, nephew of the King of Spain, an Italian kingdom, to be known as Tuscany or Etruria, with at least a million subjects. Bonaparte's efforts to have the Floridas included with Louisiana in the cession were unavailing. Louisiana had formerly been French, but Florida was traditionally Spanish, and sentiment and pride forbade its surrender.

The treaty had been signed, but over two years elapsed before Spain was convinced that Bonaparte was carrying out his part of the bargain. The King of Etruria found his royalty a shadow, unrecognized by any major power save France. Spain, furthermore, insisted upon a promise that France would never alienate Louisiana to another power. The promise was solemnly given on July 22, 1802, and Bonaparte also undertook to induce Austria, Great Britain, and the dethroned Grand Duke of Tuscany to recognize the King of Etruria. Professing satisfaction with these assurances, the Spanish government on October 15, 1802, issued orders for the transfer of Louisiana to France. Still another year was to go by before the transfer actually took place.

It seems clear that Bonaparte, or Napoleon as he now called himself—using his first name after the style of other sovereigns—valued Louisiana as part of a balanced colonial empire, the heart of which would be the sugar island of Santo Domingo.[16] By the treaty of Bâle (1795) France had acquired title to the eastern or Spanish portion of the island and now nominally possessed the whole. But at the time of the retrocession of Louisiana, French authority in Santo Domingo had been reduced to a cipher by a violent slave revolt. Most of the whites had been killed or driven

into exile, and control of the island had fallen into the hands of the Negro ex-slave Toussaint L'Ouverture. Nominally acknowledging allegiance to France, Toussaint had actually established a military despotism and was making himself an independent sovereign.

The overthrow of Toussaint, the reestablishment of French authority in Santo Domingo, and the restoration of slavery were necessary preliminary steps in the building of the colonial empire of which Louisiana was to be a part. The opportunity for these measures came only upon the making of peace with England, for in the face of a hostile British navy, overseas ventures were not to be thought of. The preliminary peace terms of October 1, 1801, were followed by the Peace of Amiens, March 27, 1802. Without waiting for the latter, Bonaparte, in November 1801, dispatched his ill-fated brother-in-law, General Leclerc, with an army of twenty thousand men, to restore French rule in Santo Domingo. This expedition which witnessed the death of Leclerc and the virtual annihilation of his army there because of a combination of yellow fever and renewed Negro insurrection, was to be followed by another to take possession of Louisiana.

Though the Louisiana expedition never sailed, instructions were prepared for the two French officers who were designated to head the civil and military branches of administration in that colony. These instructions suggest the kind of neighbor France would have been in Louisiana. The French officials were instructed to express "sentiments of great benevolence" for the United States. But these benevolent sentiments were not to prevent the French from doing everything in their power to supplant the American trade in the colonies, from maintaining "sources of information"—in other words, spies—in the western states, or from making alliances with the Indian nations of the American Southwest. In fact, the French agents were expressly instructed to do all of these things. The substitution of

---

[16]Custom has attached to the island the Spanish name of Santo Domingo. To the French, it was Saint Dominique. Embracing today the states of Haiti and the Dominican Republic, the entire island is known by its early Spanish name, Hispaniola.

French energy for Spanish lethargy in Louisiana boded no good for the United States.

Jefferson and the Retrocession

The prospect of seeing a decadent Spain replaced in New Orleans by a vigorous and powerful France was alarming to Thomas Jefferson. In a letter to United States Minister Robert R. Livingston in Paris—the substance of which was to be made known to Bonaparte—Jefferson remarked that New Orleans, the outlet for the produce of three-eighths of the national territory, was the one spot on the globe "the possessor of which is our natural and habitual enemy." French possession of New Orleans, the President continued, would seal "the union of two countries who in conjunction can maintain exclusive possession of the ocean. From that moment we must marry ourselves to the British fleet and nation."

Friends in Paris, however, advised the President that Bonaparte could perhaps be more easily swayed by offers of money than by the threat of an Anglo-American alliance. Accordingly, through a letter from the Secretary of State, May 1, 1802, Livingston was instructed to ascertain the price for which France would sell New Orleans and the Floridas, if, as was commonly assumed in the United States, she had acquired the latter provinces in the same transaction with Louisiana.

In November ominous news reached Washington. It was learned that King Charles IV of Spain had actually issued orders for the transfer of Louisiana to France. At almost the same time came information that Morales, Spanish intendant at New Orleans, had on October 16 withdrawn the right of deposit guaranteed by Pinckney's treaty.

Though Morales acted on a secret order from the Spanish government, he maintained, in accordance with his instructions, that he was closing the deposit on his own responsibility. The reasons that he assigned were unimpressive. In reality, the change of policy resulted from the smuggling activities of certain Americans who had abused their privileges at New Orleans. It is difficult to explain, however, why Spain should have risked a breach with the United States over a situation in which her interest would cease within a few months by a transfer of Louisiana to France. The contemporary American belief that Spain was acting at the behest of France was reasonable but almost certainly unfounded.

To the American West, the closing of the deposit at New Orleans was an inconvenience rather than a disaster. The Mississippi remained open, and there was no obstacle to the transfer of cargoes directly from the river flatboats to oceangoing vessels, which at this season were present in adequate numbers. The Spanish action, nevertheless, was an undeniable violation of American treaty rights and, what was most alarming, seemed a foretaste of the policy of the new masters of Louisiana, whose advent was not imminent.

Westerners, for the most part, were willing to leave the solution of the Mississippi question to Jefferson's diplomacy, but eastern Federalists were bellicose. Their strategy was to force Jefferson to choose between war with France and surrender of western interests—either choice contrary to his principles and dangerous to his political supremacy. The strategy failed. Federalist resolutions calling for seizure of New Orleans were defeated in the Senate. From Paris came advice from Jefferson's friend, Pierre Samuel DuPont de Nemours, that New Orleans and the Floridas could probably be purchased for six million dollars. Jefferson resolved to send a special commissioner to Paris to follow up DuPont's suggestion. Successful or not, such a gesture would convince the West that its interests were not forgotten and might put a stop to Federalist talk.

On January 11, 1803, Jefferson sent to

the Senate the nomination of James Monroe as minister extraordinary to France and Spain to assist the regular ministers there in "enlarging and more effectually securing our rights and interests in the river Mississippi and in the territories eastward thereof." Monroe was popular in the West, and his appointment was reassuring to that section. The Senate promptly confirmed Monroe's nomination, and Congress appropriated two million dollars for use in his negotiations. The committee of the House of Representatives that recommended this appropriation dwelt in its report upon the importance to the United States of the free navigation not only of the Mississippi but also of the Florida rivers to the eastward and concluded that

> the possession of New Orleans and the Floridas will not only be required for the convenience of the United States, but will be demanded by their most imperious necessities. . . . If we look forward to the free use of the Mississippi, the Mobile, the Apalachicola, and the other rivers of the West, by ourselves and our posterity, New Orleans and the Floridas must become a part of the United States, either by purchase or by conquest.

Monroe's instructions were not signed until March 2, nor were they drastic in tone. Should the French be willing to sell New Orleans and the Floridas, Monroe and Livingston were authorized to offer as much as $10,000,000 rather than lose the opportunity of obtaining them. Should France refuse to cede any territory, the commissioners were to do what they could to secure and improve the right of deposit guaranteed by the Spanish treaty of 1795. If France refused even the right of deposit, they were to refer the matter to Washington and await the decision of Congress. Only if they learned that France meditated hostilities against the United States or proposed to close the Mississippi entirely to American commerce, were the commissioners authorized to cross the channel and invite England to an alliance.

Thus the marriage "to the British fleet and nation," of which Jefferson had warned DuPont, was to be resorted to only in a remote contingency.

The Purchase

Of the territories which Monroe and Livingston were directed to purchase if they could, France possessed only New Orleans, for Spain had refused to sell the Floridas. Before Monroe arrived in Paris, Napoleon had decided to offer not only New Orleans but all of Louisiana to the United States. On Easter Sunday, April 10, he called two of his ministers into conference and invited their advice on the proposal. On the next day he informed Barbé-Marbois, his Finance Minister, of his decision to sell and instructed him to open negotiations with Livingston.

The new proposal, however, came to Livingston not through Barbé-Marbois but through Talleyrand, who saw him on this same day (April 11) and inquired whether the United States would care to buy all Louisiana. As Monroe's arrival was expected within a day or two, Livingston properly deferred giving a definite answer until he could confer with his colleague.

The commissioners' instructions authorized them to purchase New Orleans and the Floridas. They were offered Louisiana, including the all-important town and island of New Orleans. In the mind of neither was there any serious doubt of the propriety of accepting the offer, and the twenty days that elapsed from Monroe's arrival (April 12) to the signature of the treaty (May 2) were spent in haggling over terms. Napoleon had told Barbé-Marbois to sell for fifty million livres; the thrifty minister asked one hundred million. Since this price considerably exceeded the outside figure in their instructions, Monroe and Livingston attempted to lower it. The negotiators finally agreed on eighty million livres ($15,000,000), of which three-fourths were to be paid to France, the remainder to Americans holding damage claims against the French government. Virtual agreement was reached April 29, the treaty signed May 2, and it and the accompanying documents antedated as of April 30, 1803.

Quoting the language of the Franco-Spanish treaty of San Ildefonso, France by the new treaty ceded to the United States "the colony or province of Louisiana, with the same extent that it now has in the hands of Spain, and that it had when France possessed it; and such as it should be after the treaties subsequently entered into between Spain and other states." Other articles of the treaty promised the incorporation of the inhabitants of Louisiana in the Union of the United States with all the rights of citizens thereof, protected them in the meantime in the enjoyment of their liberty, property, and religion, and permitted French and Spanish ships laden with the produce of those countries or their colonies to enter and use the ports of Louisiana for twelve years upon the same terms as American ships.

Jefferson and his two ministers had achieved an impressive diplomatic success. It is apparent, however, that the only credit they deserve for it is the credit for being willing to accept a bargain when offered. Neither Jefferson nor Monroe nor Livingston—though the last had written a pamphlet to prove that France had nothing to gain from holding Louisiana—could justly claim to have persuaded Napoleon to sell the territory. The decision, which will always be open to speculation, was Napoleon's own.

Making the Most of a Noble Bargain

But of what did Louisiana consist? To this question the treaty gave no answer. Instead of defining the boundaries of the territory, it described it, in language borrowed from the treaty of San Ildefonso, as having "the same extent that it now has in the hands of Spain, and that it had when France possessed it." To requests from the American commissioners for a more specific definition of limits, Talleyrand replied: "I can give you no direction. You have made a noble bargain for yourselves, and I suppose you will make the most of it."

Livingston was quick to discover that the two clauses describing the colony had different meanings: that Louisiana "when France possessed it" had a greater area than when "in the hands of Spain." French Louisiana (before 1762) had extended eastward along the Gulf coast to the Perdido River, thus including the town and bay of Mobile. Spain, on the other hand, had received from France only that portion of the colony bounded on the east by the Mississippi and a line from the Mississippi to the Gulf by way of the Iberville River and Lakes Maurepas and Pontchartrain. The area between the Iberville and the Perdido, ceded to Great Britain in 1763, became part of West Florida and remained so when Spain recovered the Floridas 20 years later. Hence Spanish Louisiana was bounded on the east by the Mississippi-Iberville line.

Of the two conflicting descriptions, Livingston, with Monroe's backing, urged the President to adopt the one more favorable to the United States and to take possession of all Spanish territory between the Mississippi and the Perdido as included in the purchase. Jefferson and James Madison, his Secretary of State, accepted Livingston's interpretation (though not at this time his proposal to use force), and the claim that all of West Florida west of the Perdido, was part of Louisiana henceforth became official American doctrine.

Spain, on the other hand, adhered consistently to the other interpretation of the treaty, insisting that Louisiana was bounded on the east by the Mississippi and the Iberville. This, indeed, was also the French interpretation. Napoleon had

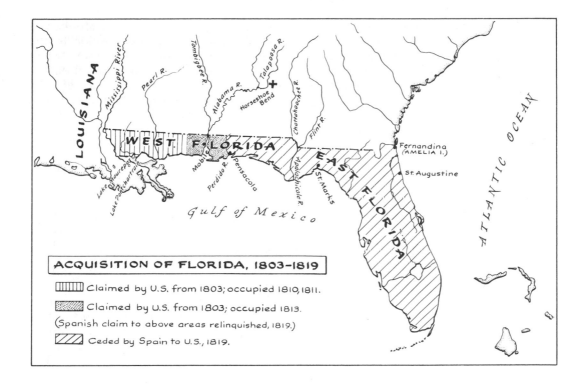

ACQUISITION OF FLORIDA, 1803–1819

|||||||| Claimed by U.S. from 1803; occupied 1810, 1811.

▒▒▒ Claimed by U.S. from 1803; occupied 1813.

(Spanish claim to above areas relinquished, 1819.)

//// Ceded by Spain to U.S., 1819.

sought in vain to secure the Floridas from Spain and had finally accepted Louisiana with the Iberville as its eastern limit. France, therefore, supported Spain in her rejection of an American claim which had little basis in law or history.

Weak though the claim was, the disputed strip of Gulf coast was of such potential value to the United States that Jefferson made repeated efforts to secure it by devious methods that add up to one of the least creditable chapters in the history of American diplomacy. Jefferson tried first to bluff Spain into yielding possession of the territory. When Spain called his bluff, he tried the persuasions of diplomacy. When these proved unavailing, he offered Napoleon a large cash consideration if he would coerce his ally, Spain, into humoring the United States. Napoleon was not above such a deal, but after placing his brother Joseph on the throne of Spain in 1808, he quickly became a defender of Spanish interests.

It remained for Jefferson's successor, James Madison (1809–1817), to make good the American claim to the disputed portion of West Florida. The imposition of a French king upon the Spanish people was the signal not only for revolt in Spain against French domination but also for rebellion in Spain's American colonies. The rebellion in West Florida was of a special character, for there the population was predominantly American in blood, speech, and loyalty. In the autumn of 1810, when revolts had begun in other Spanish colonies, the settlers along the Mississippi at the western extremity of West Florida seized the Spanish fort at Baton Rouge, proclaimed their independence, and invited the United States to annex them. President Madison acted promptly. In a proclamation of October 27, he stated anew the American claim to Florida west of the Perdido as a part of Louisiana and directed Governor W. C. C. Claiborne of Louisiana

Territory to take possession of it in the name of the United States, so far as that could be done without employing force against Spanish troops. The United States took formal possession of Baton Rouge on December 10, 1810, and American authority was extended eastward to the Perdido with the exception of the bay and town of Mobile. A Spanish garrison at Mobile was the sole obstacle to the acquisition by the United States of Louisiana as it was "when France possessed it." The removal of that garrison in 1813 was to be an incident of a conflict with England over frontier rivalries and neutral rights.

ADDITIONAL READINGS

BEMIS, SAMUEL F., *Pinckney's Treaty* (rev. ed.). New Haven: Yale University Press, 1960.

BOWMAN, ALBERT H., *The Struggle for Neutrality: Franco-American Diplomacy during the Federalist Era.* Knoxville, Tenn.: University of Tennessee Press, 1974.

COMBS, JERALD A., *The Jay Treaty: Political Battleground of the Founding Fathers.* Berkeley, Calif.: University of California Press, 1970.

DARLING, ARTHUR B., *Our Rising Empire, 1763–1803.* New Haven: Yale University Press, 1940.

DECONDE, ALEXANDER, *Entangling Alliance: Politics and Diplomacy under George Washington.* Durham, N.C.: Duke University Press, 1958.

———, *The Quasi War: The Politics and Diplomacy of the Undeclared War with France, 1791–1801.* New York: Charles Scribner's Sons, 1966.

———, *This Affair of Louisiana.* New York: Charles Scribner's Sons, 1976.

GIRAUD, MARCEL, *A History of French Louisiana.* Vol. I of *The Reign of Louis XVI, 1698–1715*, trans. J. C. Lambert. Baton Rouge, La.: Louisiana State University Press, 1974.

STINCHCOMBE, WILLIAM, "Talleyrand and the American Negotiations of 1797–1798," *Journal of American History,* 62 (1975), 575–90.

WHITAKER, A. P., *The Mississippi Question, 1795–1803.* New York: Appleton-Century-Crofts, 1934.

———, *The Spanish-American Frontier, 1783–1795.* Boston: Houghton Mifflin Company, 1927.

4. In Defense of Peaceful Trade— The War of 1812 and Its Aftermath

Great Britain and France had signed a preliminary treaty of peace on October 1, 1801, and the formal treaty of Amiens on March 27, 1802. The unstable peace was broken in May 1803. The war then renewed raged unabated between France and England, with other powers participating from time to time, until Napoleon's abdication in April 1814, and flared up again briefly the next year in the Hundred Days' fighting following the imperial exile's return from Elba. In the life-and-death struggle of these giants, the rights of small neutrals got short shrift.

The Peace of Amiens gave a brief respite to neutrals from the exactions of the belligerents. The renewal of the war revived their difficulties. For the United States it meant new controversies over neutral rights with both belligerents. Though both were equally ruthless in their disregard of neutral interests, the offenses of Great Britain, being more varied and brought closer to home by the ubiquity of the Royal Navy, proved in the end more offensive to the party in power in the United States— traditionally the pro-French party. The British, furthermore, also gave offense by their relations with the Indians of the Northwest. Defense of neutral rights, coupled with certain grievances and ambitions of the American frontier, led to the abandonment of neutrality and the declaration of war against England in 1812.

In the realm of neutral rights, the chief belligerent practices of which Americans complained were the impressment of seamen from American ships, of which England alone was guilty, and sweeping "paper blockades," which each belligerent sought to impose upon the ports and coasts of the other.

The Impressment Question

Impressment was a rough-and-ready species of "selective service," by which His Majesty's Navy was kept manned in times of stress. From time immemorial, British naval officers had exercised the right of recruiting their personnel by seizing British subjects (experienced seamen preferred), afloat or ashore, and pressing them into service, willy-nilly. The impressment of British subjects, on British shores or from British ships, was no concern of the United States, but when the practice was applied, on the high seas, to members of the crews of American merchant vessels, it roused American resentment. Such practice was, as the Americans saw it, in direct violation of the sovereignty of the United States; the American flag should protect the crews of American ships.

This the British were unwilling to admit. In support of their position, they advanced the unquestioned facts that thousands of deserters from their Navy found employment in the American merchant marine, where the service was both pleasanter and safer, and that great numbers of these, through small bribes to American consuls or by other means, obtained false certificates of United States citizenship. To forgo the right of recovering such deserters forcibly from American ships would, as the British Admiralty viewed the matter, imperil the efficiency of the naval service in the struggle for existence against Napoleonic France.

If the British had exercised impressment with proper care to see that no injustice was done and that only deserters, or even only British subjects, were seized from American decks, perhaps the United States would have condoned the practice. But impressment was carried out, not by judicially-minded officials, but by naval officers who needed seamen and were apt to resolve any doubt of a promising sailor's nationality in favor of themselves. From the arbitrary decisions of such naval commanders, there was no appeal except through time-consuming diplomatic channels. When the British Foreign Office could be convinced that bona fide American citizens had been impressed, they were released—if still living—with regrets but without indemnification for the injury.

The controversy was further complicated by a contradiction between British and American law on allegiance. The United States practiced naturalization on a large scale. Great Britain adhered to the principle of indelible allegiance—"Once an Englishman always an Englishman." The same man, therefore, might be at the same time an American citizen under American law and a British subject under British law. Hence even genuine evidence of American citizenship was not necessarily adequate protection against forced service in the British fleet.

All attempts to settle the controversy by diplomacy failed. The United States offered, in 1807, to take measures to exclude British deserters from American ships in wartime in return for British renunciation of the right of impressment, but the British Admiralty refused to forgo a valuable current practice for what it regarded as a dubious promise.

The impressment controversy reached a tragic climax in the *Chesapeake-Leopard* incident of June 1807. Ordinarily the British did not venture to interfere with American naval vessels, but in this instance the British frigate *Leopard* fired upon and boarded the American frigate *Chesapeake* and removed four members of the crew, alleged to be British deserters. The American vessel, unprepared for battle, put up only token resistance and suffered over twenty casualties in the melee. This time the British government realized that its naval agents had gone too far. It disavowed the action of the *Leopard's* captain and made tardy amends for the injuries inflicted. Meanwhile the impressment question, still unsettled, dropped somewhat into the background as new controversies held the stage. It was revived as a major issue on the eve of the War of 1812.

A Blow at American Commerce

In spite of impressments and in spite of restrictions placed upon neutral trade by both belligerents, American commerce flourished mightily, at least until 1807. The tonnage of American shipping employed in foreign trade grew from 363,100 in 1791 to 848,300 in 1807. Exports, with adjustments for changing price levels, increased nearly fourfold in the same years; imports grew by 75 percent.[1] This prosperity was in

[1]W. A. Phillips and A. H. Reede, *The Napoleonic Period*, Vol. 2 of *Neutrality: Its History, Economics and Law*, 4 vols. (New York: Columbia University Press, 1935–1936), pp. 226–30, 234.

part a direct consequence of the war. American ships could trade with both belligerents. A form of activity that their owners found particularly profitable was the carrying of goods between France and Spain on the one hand and the French and Spanish Caribbean colonies on the other. French and Spanish ships, which in peacetime monopolized the colonial trade of their respective mother countries, were kept in port by the dominant British navy, and the two governments opened to neutrals a trade from which foreign ships were normally excluded. Of this, American shipping took the lion's share.

Such trade was, of course, contrary to the British rule of 1756, but for some years American shipowners had been able to circumvent that rule by the device of the "broken voyage." An American ship would take on a cargo of sugar, for example, at the French island of Martinique and would proceed to an American port, where the sugar would be entered as an import, probably without being removed from the ship, and either the import duty would be paid or the owner would give bond for its payment. The ship would then be supplied with new papers, showing the sugar as an export from the United States. Most of the duty would be refunded as a drawback, and the ship would proceed on its way to a French port, where the cargo would be finally disposed of. Since neither segment of the voyage alone was forbidden by the rule of 1756 or otherwise, British admiralty courts at first declined to interfere with this species of transaction. But in the case of the ship *Essex* (1805) they held that the voyage—in this instance from Barcelona to Havana with an interruption at Salem, Massachusetts—was to be considered "continuous" and hence prohibited by the rule of 1756.

The *Essex* decision was a serious matter for the American carrying trade, a turning point for the worse in Anglo-American relations. Congress retaliated by an act (April 18, 1806) prohibiting the importation of certain English manufactures but suspended its operation pending the outcome of an attempt to reach agreement by diplomacy. For the latter purpose, Jefferson sent William Pinkney, a Maryland lawyer, to assist James Monroe, the regular minister in London. It was Jefferson's hope that the two envoys might secure satisfactory settlement of the whole complex of issues involving neutral rights—blockade, contraband, the rule of 1756, the continuous voyage interpretation, and impressment. Negotiating with friendly British commissioners, Monroe and Pinkney succeeded in getting a relaxation of the rule of 1756 and the doctrine of continuous voyage, but little else. Of the right of impressment, particularly, the British would yield nothing more than a promise to remedy abuses in exercising it. The treaty that Monroe and Pinkney signed, nevertheless, on December 31, 1806, was not well received in Washington. Jefferson refused to send it to the Senate. He instructed the envoys to try again but to make no treaty without a provision against impressment. Monroe and Pinkney found the new British Foreign Secretary, George Canning, even less conciliatory than his predecessors. Their mission had failed.

A Competition in Paper Blockades

In the meantime, the two major belligerents had embarked upon a course of economic warfare which added measurably to the hardships of neutrals. Napoleon launched his "Continental System," designed to ruin England economically and thus destroy her power to make war. Embodied in his Berlin and Milan decrees (November 21, 1806, and December 17, 1807), it sought to bar continental Europe to British ships and British trade. Neutral ships which had called at British ports or submitted to search by British naval vessels were declared liable to confiscation. The

British retaliated through a series of orders-in-council (especially those of January 7, 1807, and November 11, 1807), which forbade trade with France and her allies, in Europe and the colonies, and threatened with confiscation all neutral vessels attempting to trade with those areas. An important exception was made for neutral ships in the provision that they might trade with enemy ports if they first put in at British ports and paid certain duties on their merchandise. It is evident that the British blockade of France was not designed to cut off trade with the continent: its purpose was to compel such trade, carried in neutral bottoms, to pay tribute to Great Britain.

The combination of decrees and orders-in-council—both of them, in American eyes, constituting illegal "paper blockades"—placed neutral shipping in a truly precarious situation. If an American sea captain obeyed the British orders, touching at an English port on the way to the continent, he exposed his vessel and cargo to confiscation by the French. If he sought to conform to the French decrees by avoiding contact with British ships or shores, he stood little chance of escaping confiscation by the British.

Jefferson's "Peaceable Coercion"

Jefferson was unwilling to submit to the "paper blockades" and other—in American eyes—illegal infringements upon American maritime rights; he was equally unwilling to go to war to defend those rights. He undertook instead to bring the belligerents to terms through economic weapons. It was his belief that trade with the United States was of such vital importance to both France and Britain that exclusion from it could be used to coerce them into respecting American rights. At his suggestion, Congress

passed (December 22, 1807) an embargo act which closed American ports to all foreign shipping and forbade American ships to leave port except to engage in the coastwise trade. When the embargo, while subjecting the American economy to serious hardship, produced no change in French or British policy, it was replaced by a series of milder measures. The last of these—known as Macon's Bill No. 2 (May 1, 1810)—opened American ports to the commercial vessels of all nations, but provided that if either England or France should revoke its orders-in-council or decrees so far as they infringed American neutral rights, and if the other belligerent failed to do likewise within three months, ships and trade of the latter should be barred from American ports.

By signing Macon's Bill No. 2, President James Madison put himself in the hands of a completely unscrupulous French government. Napoleon's Foreign Minister promptly informed the American minister in Paris that the Berlin and Milan decrees, in so far as they affected American ships, would cease to operate on November 1, 1810, upon the understanding that England would thereupon repeal its orders or else that the United States should "cause their rights to be respected by the English." In reality, Napoleon continued to enforce the decrees against American ships. Madison apparently accepted the repeal as genuine and reimposed nonimportation restrictions upon Great Britain (February 2, 1811).

The British government, seeing through Napoleon's subterfuge, refused to revoke or modify the orders-in-council. Though a new Secretary of State, James Monroe, made a genuine effort to reach agreement with a new British minister, A. J. Foster, it was evident by July 1811 that an impasse had been reached. Monroe insisted that the repeal of the French decrees was genuine and demanded that England revoke her orders-in-council. Foster denied that the French decrees were really repealed and demanded therefore that the United States give up its nonimportation policy against Great Britain. This Monroe refused until the orders-in-council were revoked. It was a vicious circle, from which, as it turned out, the only exit was war.

According to Madison's biographer, Irving Brant, Madison had believed from the beginning of his presidency that if England continued to violate American rights, America must fight. He now called Congress to meet in November, a month before the usual time. In his message, he complained of the unfriendly conduct of both belligerents, but he reserved his most wrathful comments for the British, whose practices, he said, "have the character as well as the effect of war on our lawful commerce." To resist their "hostile inflexibility in trampling on rights which no independent nation can relinquish," he asked Congress to put the United States "into an armor and an attitude demanded by the crisis."

Drifting into War

This Congress failed to do, even under the whiplash of the "war hawks," a group of newly elected representatives, most of them young men from western and southern states. Outstanding among them were Henry Clay of Kentucky—elected Speaker in his first session in the House—John C. Calhoun of South Carolina, John A. Harper of New Hampshire, and Peter B. Porter of western New York. Such men were infuriated at seeing their country treated year after year as a second-class power. Insults and injuries, they felt, must be avenged by force of arms. Continued submission to humiliation and wrong, some

believed, would endanger the very existence of the Republic.[2]

To most of the war hawks, in all probability, the principal grievance was the British interference with American seaborne trade. Such interference touched the pocketbook nerve as well as the sense of national honor. The British, at any rate, were widely blamed for a serious decline in the prices of western products which had recently been observed. Some of the war hawks had still another grievance. They blamed the British and their agents in Canada for an epidemic of Indian hostilities in the Northwest. Stimulated by the able Shawnee chieftain, Tecumseh, the Indians of the area from the Ohio to the Mississippi had undertaken to unite in resistance to the surrender of further Indian lands to agents of the United States government. Sporadic attacks on frontier settlers were followed by a dramatic clash between Indians and an army commanded by General William Henry Harrison near the shores of Tippecanoe Creek in Indiana, on November 7, 1811.

The British in Canada were well known to be friendly to Tecumseh and his plans, and when British arms were found among weapons left by the Indians at Tippecanoe, many westerners were confirmed in their belief that expulsion of the British from Canada was essential to peace with the Indians of the Northwest. The conquest of Canada became a secondary motive for war with England. If the annexation of Canada threatened to upset the sectional balance of the Union in favor of the North, there was the further possibility of enlarging the

[2]Roger H. Brown, *The Republic in Peril: 1812* (New York: Columbia University Press, 1964). On the identity and motives of the war hawks (if their existence as a class was not "an historical myth"), see articles by Roger H. Brown and Reginald Horsman, with comments by Alexander De Conde and Norman K. Risjord, in *Indiana Magazine of History,* 60 (June 1964), 121 ff.

southern boundaries by the acquisition of that part of Florida still remaining in the hands of Spain. An attempt to acquire East Florida by subversion met with a well deserved failure in the spring of 1812. But Spain was now an ally of England, and not a few southerners foresaw in a war with England a justification of completing the conquest of the Floridas. It was, in fact, charged with some plausibility by Federalist opponents of the war that northern and southern expansionists had made a deal on the anticipated spoils of war: Canada for the North, Florida for the South.[3]

As one accomplished student of the period has remarked of the causes of the War of 1812, the British orders-in-council were "the central structure"; others—impressments, Indian troubles, expansionist ambitions—were mere "flying buttresses."[4] It was ironic, therefore, that the central structure was being dismantled at the very time that Congress was declaring war. Congress had dillydallied all winter and spring. It had provided neither men nor ships nor money adequate for a war with England. It had at one point almost voted itself into a recess—a sure path to inaction. Urged on by the war hawks, by Monroe, and by Madison, who sent in a final war message on June 1, 1812, it finally declared war on June 18, with large minorities opposing in both houses (79 to 49 in the House, 19 to 13 in the Senate).

Two days earlier the British government had announced its intention of repealing the orders-in-council, and they were actually repealed on June 23. The repeal was—too late—a victory for Jefferson's policy of peaceable coercion. British merchants and manufacturers had been hard hit by the loss of the American market, and it was

pressure from this source that achieved what neither American diplomacy nor the threat of an American war had availed to bring about.[5] Had the United States been competently represented in London, it could have foreseen the repeal of the orders, but Minister Pinkney had taken an "inamicable leave" in February 1811, leaving only a chargé d'affaires at the legation, and the latter failed to see or report what was in the wind.[6]

The British expected this major concession to stop the war if it did not prevent it, but the news of repeal reached America weeks after war had begun and proved insufficient to halt it. Officially, the war went on because the British had not renounced the right of impressment. Other factors, presumably, were the West's aroused appetite for Canada and a feeling that a war begun in defense of the national honor should not be adjourned without some bloodletting.

An Indecisive War

The War of 1812 began on June 18, 1812, and was ended by the Treaty of Ghent, signed on Christmas Eve, 1814. The failure of the United States to achieve any of the maritime concessions or territorial gains

---

[3]J. W. Pratt, *Expansionists of 1812* (New York: The Macmillan Company, 1925).

[4]Bradford Perkins, *Prologue to War: England and the United States, 1805–1812* (Berkeley: University of California Press, 1961), p. 431.

[5]The British government had discounted the chances of the United States going to war. It had been assured by the Federalists and the British minister in Washington that Mr. Madison "couldn't be kicked into a war."

[6]The British had sworn that they would not repeal the orders till they had evidence that Napoleon had revoked the decrees. They were enabled to save face when Joel Barlow, the United States minister in Paris, forwarded a spurious "decree of St. Cloud," antedated April 28, 1811, purportedly declaring the Berlin and Milan decrees revoked with respect to American vessels. This appears to have been produced on the spur of the moment by the French Foreign Minister in response to Barlow's plea for an "authentic act" giving evidence of the repeal of the decrees.

which the war hawks had contemplated was the result of inadequate preparation, incompetent administrative and military leadership, and internal dissensions.

Though Congress had authorized a Regular Army of 35,000 men, fewer than 10,000 had been raised; a large portion of these were raw recruits, and when the war began, they were scattered about the country in small garrisons, unavailable for prompt or vigorous action. The state militia were poorly trained, poorly officered, and many of them were ready to take advantage of their supposed exemption from duty on foreign soil. The higher officers, who commanded the Regular Army at the beginning of the war, were without exception, incompetent. Under these circumstances, it is not surprising that the early attempts to invade and conquer Canada resulted in dismal failures. By the summer of 1814, when able officers—notably Generals Jacob Brown and Winfield Scott—had risen to high command and had instilled discipline and courage into their little army, the chance of conquering Canada had vanished. Napoleon was at Elba, and Wellington's veterans were pouring into Canada. The problem was not how to conquer Canada, but how to defend the United States.

While military incompetence and unreadiness were frustrating northern hopes of winning Canada, southern designs on Florida were frustrated by northern opposition. Two attempts to empower the President to take possession of East Florida were defeated in the Senate by the votes of Federalists, who opposed the war *in toto*, and northern Republicans, who disliked the administration's Florida policy. The only gain on that front was the occupation of Mobile, to which the United States had long laid claims as part of Louisiana.

On the high seas, where the United States in 1812 had some seventeen naval vessels, none of the first class, to oppose the thousand ships of the British navy, American naval commanders put up a gallant but hopeless fight. A few brilliant victories in single-ship actions could not shake British control of the seas. Before the fighting ended, virtually all units of the American navy had been either captured or bottled up in port, and American commerce was excluded from the seas by a tight blockade. The only American naval victories that counted strategically were those on Lake Erie and Lake Champlain. The former (September 10, 1813) enabled the United States to recover Detroit, lost in the first weeks of the war, but did not prevent British occupation of most of Michigan and the Wisconsin-Minnesota area. The latter (September 11, 1814) turned back a formidable British army intent upon invading New York.

All things considered, the United States was fortunate in being able—except in the region of Lake Michigan and the upper Mississippi—to defend its own territory. The battle of Lake Champlain saved New York from serious trouble. Another British army—having taken Washington and burned the public buildings—was repulsed before Baltimore. At New Orleans, two weeks after the signing of the peace treaty, Andrew Jackson inflicted upon a third British force the most crushing defeat of the war.

The Treaty of Ghent

The defensive character that the war had assumed was evident in the final instructions to the American peace commissioners, who opened negotiations with the British at Ghent in August 1814.[7] Earlier drafts had proposed abandonment of impressments as an indispensable condition

[7]The American commissioners were John Quincy Adams, Albert Gallatin, Henry Clay, Jonathan Russell, and James A. Bayard (a Federalist senator from Delaware).

of peace and had expressed a hope also for a definition of legal blockade and abandonment of the rule of 1756. But by the summer of 1814, military failure and the defeat of England's other antagonist, Napoleon, had so weakened the American bargaining position that all these proposals were dropped, and the commissioners were told to ask only a return to the *status quo ante bellum.*

The British commissioners had come to Ghent with more ambitious demands—cessions of territory in Maine, New York, and between Lake Superior and the Mississippi, and the creation of a permanent Indian territory embracing a great area in the American Northwest. The American commissioners rejected these demands at once. While the British hesitated, came news of the American victories at Lake Champlain and Baltimore. The Duke of Wellington, Napoleon's conqueror, advised the Cabinet to accept the American terms, unless it were prepared for an expensive prolongation of the war in America—a burden that the hard-pressed British taxpayer would be reluctant to carry. The British accepted the American terms. The treaty, signed December 24, 1814, provided for restoration of all territory that had been occupied by the forces of either party. Such of Britain's Indian allies as were still at war with the United States were to recover their land holdings of 1811. Finally, joint commissions were to settle certain boundary disputes between the United States and Canada. The United States had won not a single concession in the matter of maritime rights, not a foot of Canadian soil. Yet the treaty was joyously greeted by the American public and on February 16, 1815, was unanimously approved by the United States Senate.

The Treaty of Ghent did not register all the results of the war, and an awareness of some of the unregistered results may partly explain the general satisfaction with the treaty. In the Northwest, the Indian menace that had contributed to the war fever was removed or greatly reduced. Tecumseh died in battle in 1813; his confederacy dissolved; and the Indians who had taken the British side made peace with the United States, the nearer tribes during the war, the others soon afterwards. British support of the Indians ceased. There was no further serious trouble about acquiring or settling Indian lands.

A somewhat similar development had marked the war in the South. There the powerful Creek confederacy, perhaps under British influence, had gone on the warpath in 1813. Its power was broken by Andrew Jackson's Tennessee troops at the battle of Horseshoe Bend, March 27, 1814, and the Creek chieftains were forced to cede a great area of some 23 million acres in southern Georgia and the future state of Alabama. The occupation of Mobile has been mentioned. These gains were direct consequences of the war. Indirectly, Indian troubles growing out of Jackson's treaty with the Creeks were to lead to the acquisition of the remainder of Florida in 1819.

If the war brought gains to both northern and southern frontiers, it did nothing to establish the American position on neutral maritime rights. That the United States had for many years no further occasion to defend its rights as a neutral was the consequence not of its prowess in the War of 1812 but of the fact that for a century after Waterloo, there was no great war among the maritime states of Europe. An attempt by John Quincy Adams as Secretary of State in 1823 to secure international acceptance of a comprehensive code for the regulation of maritime war was abandoned when the British government refused even to discuss the impressment question. Not until the Declaration of Paris of 1856 was any progress made in the definition of neutral rights. That famous declaration embodied most of the principles for which the United States had long contended.[8]

The Beginning of the "Unguarded Frontier"

One of the earliest achievements of peace-minded Americans was the agreement with Great Britain in 1817 to dismantle existing naval forces on the Great Lakes and Lake Champlain and to maintain only such trifling naval armament as would be needed there to enforce the customs and revenue laws. These Americans reflected the strivings of the organized peace movement in the United States, in the wake of the bloody Napoleonic Wars, of which their own with Great Britain was in a real sense a by-product. When the War of 1812 ended, the two governments were engaged in a costly competition for naval supremacy on Lake Ontario; both recognized the dangers inherent in such a contest. Negotiations in London and Washington terminated in an exchange of notes (April 28 and 29, 1817) between Richard Rush, acting Secretary of State, and Charles Bagot, British minister in Washington. By the agreement (later approved by the Senate and thus given the authority of a treaty), the two governments consented to limit their naval armament on the lakes to vessels not exceeding 100 tons in burden nor carrying more than one 18-pound gun each. Of these each party should maintain not more than one on Lake Champlain, one on Lake Ontario, and two on the upper lakes. Either government might terminate the agreement by giving six months' notice.

[8]The British government never formally abandoned the right of impressment, but never again practiced it against American ships. By a convention of 1870, however, it abandoned the principle of indelible allegiance, thus recognizing the right of British subjects to change their allegiance under American naturalization laws.

The Rush-Bagot agreement, subject to some technical violations and to occasional modifications or interpretations, continued in effect from 1817 to the present day. The common belief that the agreement inaugurated an era of an "unguarded frontier" is, however, without justification. Not for over half a century did Anglo-American peace seem sufficiently secure to warrant either party's disarming the frontier. The existing naval forces on the lakes were dismantled but not destroyed. Navy yards on the lakes were maintained for several years. Land fortifications were maintained and were strengthened at times of crisis in Anglo-American relations. Not until 1871, with settlement of the *Alabama* claims assured, did the two governments by tacit consent gradually permit their land fortifications to fall into a state of decay. The "unguarded frontier" dates from 1871, not 1817.[9]

Arbitration Becomes a Habit

It was not an accident that both the Rush-Bagot agreement and the later demilitarization of the frontier followed agreements to submit troublesome Anglo-American controversies to arbitration. No feature of Anglo-American relations in the nineteenth century is more striking than the growing realization that there were better methods than war for settling any disputes that were likely to arise between the two countries.

A good beginning had already been made under the terms of the Jay Treaty in 1794. That instrument had provided for arbitration of four controversies: (1) the identiy of the St. Croix River, designated by the treaty of peace as the boundary between

[9]C. P. Stacey, "The Myth of the Unguarded Frontier, 1815–1871," *American Historical Review,* 56 (1950), 1–18.

Maine and Nova Scotia; (2) the amount to be paid by the United States to British creditors in satisfaction of debts that they had been unable to collect by reason of "lawful impediments" imposed by the states in contravention of the treaty of peace; (3) the compensation to be paid by Great Britain to American claimants for illegal seizures of vessels and other property in the current Anglo-French war; (4) the compensation to be paid by the United States to British claimants for losses resulting from violations of American neutrality by French armed vessels. Arbitration by mixed commissions adjudicated all of these controversies except the second, which in the end was settled by negotiation. The commission on the St. Croix River concluded that of several rivers which had been known by that name, the treaty-makers had meant to designate the Schoodiac, as claimed by Great Britain, not the Maguadavic, as claimed by the United States. Under the third and fourth headings, American and British claimants were awarded $11,656,000 and $143,428.14 respectively. Payment to British creditors under the second heading, as determined by a negotiated convention, was in the amount of $2,664,000.

The Treay of Ghent provided for arbitration of four boundary controversies between the United States and British Canada, embracing certain islands off the coast of Maine and the overland boundary from the head of the St. Croix (Schoodiac) River to the Lake of the Woods. Possession of the islands and the fixing of the boundary line through the St. Lawrence River and other waters to the head of Lake Huron presented no great difficulty. On the segments of the boundary from the St. Croix to the St. Lawrence and from Lake Huron to the Lake of the Woods, agreement at this time proved impossible. On the line from Lake Huron to the Lake of the Woods, the arbitrators failed to make a report. The line from the St. Croix to the St. Lawrence was submitted to the King of the Netherlands as

arbitrator. Instead of deciding in favor of one of the contestants, he recommended a compromise line, which the United States rejected. Both questions were settled in the Webster-Ashburton Treaty of 1842.

The Northern Boundary and Oregon

The Treaty of Ghent made no provision for determining the boundary between the Lake of the Woods and the Rocky Mountains or for adjusting conflicting British and American claims to the Pacific coast region that was coming to be known as Oregon.

The treaty of 1783 had described the boundary line as running from the northwesternmost point of the Lake of the Woods due west to the Mississippi—an impossible line since the Mississippi rose far to the south of the Lake of the Woods. No substitute line had been agreed upon when the United States acquired Louisiana with an undefined northern boundary. Monroe and Pinkney in 1806 tentatively agreed with their British fellow negotiators to fix the boundary at the 49th parallel from the Lake of the Woods to the Rocky Mountains, but the convention embodying the agreement was never signed. The American commissioners at Ghent proposed this same solution but dropped it when the British insisted upon coupling with it a stipulation giving them access to the upper Mississippi and free navigation of that river.

Agreement on a boundary line to the Rocky Mountains, if that were achieved, would still leave unsettled conflicting American and British (as well as Spanish and Russian) claims to the Oregon country. To such American claims as could be founded upon the discovery and naming of the Columbia River in 1792 by Captain Robert Gray of Boston and the explorations of Lewis and Clark (1804–1806), there was now added one based upon actual settlement. In May 1811, representatives of the fur merchant, John Jacob Astor, had established a fort and trading post, which they named Astoria, at the mouth of the Columbia on its southern shore. Their occupancy was brief, however. News of the outbreak of war and the danger that their post and stores might be captured by the British induced them to sell out, in October 1813, to local representatives of the North West Company of Montreal. Two months later a British sloop of war, the *Raccoon*, arrived on the scene; her commander took formal possession of the fort and surrounding country in the name of the British King and renamed the fort Fort George.

The injection of military conquest into what had hitherto been a commercial transaction gave the United States ground for claiming that Astoria should be restored to the United States under the terms of the Treaty of Ghent. The British government did not contest the claim, and on October 6, 1818, the British flag was lowered and the stars and stripes raised over Fort George. The British Foreign Secretary, Lord Castlereagh, emphasized the point that he was not recognizing the American claim to sovereignty at the mouth of the Columbia; he was merely acknowledging that that claim had as much, or as little, force in 1818 as it had had in 1813. It soon became apparent, however, that the British were willing to concede priority of rights south of the Columbia to the United States.

The Boundary Treaty of 1818

Just two weeks after the "restoration" of Astoria, Richard Rush and Albert Gallatin, American commissioners in London, signed a treaty fixing the boundary line from the Lake of the Woods to the Rockies and establishing a temporary *modus vivendi* for the Oregon country. The British were now ready to accept the 49th parallel as the boundary from the Lake of the Woods[10] to the Rocky Mountains, without insisting upon the renewal of their right to navigate the Mississippi. When the Americans proposed extending the same line to the Pacific, the British intimated that they would accept instead the Columbia River from its mouth to its intersection with the 49th parallel, with the understanding that the river and the harbor at its mouth should be open to both British and American shipping. When neither party would accept the other's proposal, a compromise was agreed upon by which all territory on the northwest coast claimed by either Great Britain or the United States should be equally open during a ten-year period to the vessels, citizens, and subjects of the two powers, without prejudice to the claims of other governments (Spain and Russia). This arrangement—the so-called "joint occupation"—was embodied, with the fixing of the boundary east of the Rocky Mountains, in the treaty signed on October 20, 1818.

The same treaty settled another question of considerable importance, especially to New England. The treaty of 1783 had granted to United States citizens the "liberty" of inshore fishing along the coasts of British North America. The British asserted that this "liberty" had been canceled by the War of 1812. Americans were anxious to see it restored. The British now offered a compromise which the American negotiators accepted. In return for the perpetual "liberty" to take fish inside the three-mile limit on the west coast and part of the south coast of Newfoundland, on the coast of Labrador, and in the waters about the Magdalen Islands, the United States renounced its claim to the inshore fisheries on all other parts of the coasts of British

[10]More precisely, from a line drawn due north or south—south as it turned out to be—from the most northwestern point of the Lake of the Woods to its intersection with the 49th parallel.

North America. American fishermen were also allowed to land and cure their fish in the unsettled bays and harbors of Labrador and that portion of the south coast of Newfoundland where inshore fishing was permitted.

With the signing of the treaty of 1818 and the creation of the arbitration commissions provided for in the Treaty of Ghent, it was hoped that most of the troublesome issues between the United States and Great Britain had been disposed of, at least temporarily. Certainly there was an easing in Anglo-American tensions. But the West Indies trade problem had not been solved; the Oregon controversy had been merely postponed; and two questions that had been submitted to the arbitral process—the northeast boundary and the Lake Superior-Lake of the Woods boundary questions had proved incapable of being settled in that manner. Much work remained to be done before Anglo-American relations could be viewed with entire satisfaction.

The Transcontinental Treaty with Spain

While Gallatin and Rush, in London, were fixing the northern boundary of Louisiana and holding the British to a draw in the diplomatic sparring over Oregon, Secretary of State John Quincy Adams, in Washington, was engaged in negotiations that eventually settled the longstanding controversies with Spain. Spain had never accepted the American claim to the Perdido River as the eastern boundary of Louisiana, and American occupation of the strip of land between the Perdido and the Iberville, before and during the War of 1812, had been without Spain's consent. The United States desired an acknowledgment of its title to this area; it desired also to acquire Florida east of the Perdido, to which it had

no similar claim. The western boundary of Louisiana had never been defined. The United States, with little justification, claimed to the Rio Grande. Spain placed the boundary well to the eastward of the Sabine. Thus Texas and part of the state of Louisiana were in dispute.

Added to the boundary controversies were certain damage claims which each country held against the other. The United States claimed compensation for allegedly unneutral conduct on Spain's part during American hostilities with France in 1798–1800 and for damages suffered by American commerce from the withdrawal of the right of deposit at New Orleans in 1802. Spain claimed damages for American incursions into Florida before and during the War of 1812 and for hospitality accorded in United States ports to privateers sailing under the flags of Spain's revolting colonies. The United States paid little heed to Spain's damage claims. In satisfaction of its own, it was willing to accept all of Florida, East and West, of which Spain still held possession. Secretary Adams and Spanish Minister Don Luis de Onis were exchanging ideas about the boundary and damage claims in the spring of 1818, when they were interrupted by warlike noises from Spanish Florida.

Florida, after the War of 1812, was in a state of near anarchy, which Spanish governors at St. Augustine and Pensacola were powerless to remedy. Amelia Island, on the Atlantic coast just south of the United States border, became a haven of freebooters, who claimed to operate under letters of marque from one or another of Spain's revolting colonies. When one of them, Luis Aury, claimed East Florida as part of Mexico, President Monroe sent in United States troops to take possession.

Farther west, Creek warriors, fugitives from Jackson's campaign of 1814, had taken refuge with their kinsmen, the Florida Seminoles. In their hostility to the United States, they were abetted by several

British adventurers who had remained in Florida after the British defeat at New Orleans. When the Creeks undertook to interfere by force with the surveying and settling of their former lands in Georgia and Mississippi Territory, the United States resolved to punish and subdue them, even if that meant pursuing them across the border into Florida—a right which the United States claimed under the 1795 treaty with Spain. This task was handed to General Andrew Jackson, commanding a small army of regulars and militia.

Jackson acted upon the theory that he was expected not only to chastise the Indians, but to take possession of Florida for the United States. For this assumption he later claimed to have had verbal authority from Monroe through an intermediary—a claim that Monroe firmly denied. With or without the President's secret assent, Jackson seized and occupied the Spanish town and fort of St. Marks and after burning a hostile Indian town from which the warriors escaped, turned his attention to Pensacola, seat of government of the Spanish remnant of West Florida. On the excuse that the Spanish were harboring hostile savages, Jackson took possession of the town and fortifications, deposed the governor, seized the archives, appointed one of his officers civil and military governor of West Florida, and directed him to enforce the revenue laws of the United States at the port of Pensacola. As if this affront to Spain were not enough, he had executed—after court-martial—two British subjects, Robert Ambrister and Alexander Arbuthnot, who had fallen into his hands at St. Marks, and whom he charged with being in conspiracy with the hostile Indians.

Well satisfied with his work, the happy warrior returned to Tennessee. In his report to the Secretary of War (John C. Calhoun), he justified his actions on the ground of "the immutable principles . . . of self defence" and urged that in the interest of security the United States hold the Gulf coast in preference to an indefensible "imaginary line"—the 31st parallel.

Reports of Jackson's aggressive course in Florida, accompnied by violent protests from Onis, the Spanish minister, created consternation in Monroe's cabinet. Fortunately for Jackson, he found a warm supporter in the Secretary of State. In opposition to Calhoun and others, Adams insisted that Jackson's acts must be sustained. Rejecting Spain's demands that Jackson be punished or disavowed, Adams took the offensive. He justified Jackson's actions as necessitated by self-defense. He denounced as unfriendly the conduct of the governor of West Florida and the commandant of St. Marks and demanded that those officials instead of Jackson be punished. Pensacola, he said, would be turned over to a proper Spanish official; St. Marks, to a force competent to hold it against Indian attack. In a later note, Adams presented Spain with an ultimatum: let her either place in Florida a force sufficient for the maintenance of order and the fulfillment of her obligations, or cede the province to the United States.

Even before perusing this forceful argument, the Spanish government had resolved to make whatever concessions were necessary to reach an understanding with the United States. Fear of war with the United States, failure of efforts to get assurances of support from England, France, or Russia, and a desire to keep its hands free to put down rebellion in its American colonies induced Spain to give in.

In October 1818 the Spanish consented to reopen the boundary negotiations, which they had broken off upon news of Jackson's exploits. They were willing to cede the Floridas if the United States would agree to a satisfactory western boundary for Louisiana. This was achieved, after months of negotiation, in an agreement by which the United States surrendered whatever claim it had to Texas in exchange for Spanish claims on the Pacific coast, north of

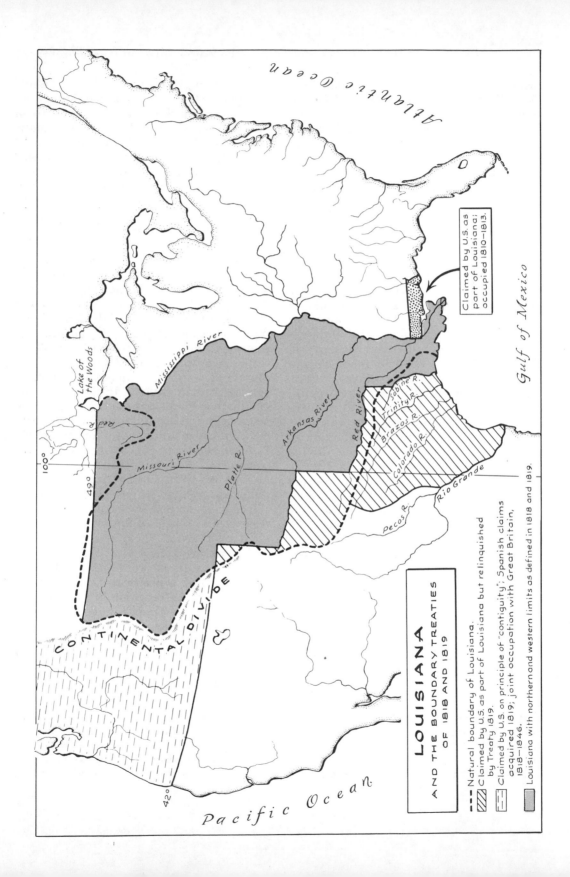

Atlantic Ocean

Gulf of Mexico

Claimed by U.S. as
part of Louisiana;
occupied 1810–1813.

Lake of
the Woods

Mississippi River

Red R.

Missouri River

Platte R.

Arkansas River

Red River

Sabine R.

Trinity R.

Brazos R.

Colorado R.

Pecos R.

Rio Grande

49°

100°

42°

CONTINENTAL DIVIDE

Pacific Ocean

LOUISIANA
AND THE BOUNDARY TREATIES
OF 1818 AND 1819

- - - Natural boundary of Louisiana.

///// Claimed by U.S. as part of Louisiana but relinquished
by Treaty 1819.

||||| Claimed by U.S. on principle of "contiguity"; Spanish claims
acquired 1819; joint occupation with Great Britain,
1818–1846.

▦ Louisiana with northern and western limits as defined in 1818 and 1819.

California. The "transcontinental treaty," as it has been called, was signed on February 22, 1819. By its terms the King of Spain ceded to the United States "all the territories which belong to him, situated to the eastward of the Mississippi, known by the name of East and West Florida." This wording was so devised as to permit each party to adhere to its opinion as to whether Florida west of the Perdido had been included in the Louisiana purchase. Each government renounced its damage claims and those of its citizens or subjects, against the other, and the United States agreed to satisfy the claims of its citizens against Spain to an amount not to exceed five million dollars.

On the west, the international boundary followed the western bank of the Sabine from the Gulf to the 32nd parallel; thence it ran due north to the southern bank of the Red, which it followed to the meridian of 100° west longitude, thence by that meridian to the south bank of the Arkansas and along that bank to the source of the river; from the source of the Arkansas it ran north to the 42nd parallel, which it followed to the Pacific.

Despite some mutterings over the sur-render of Texas, the United States Senate gave its prompt and unanimous approval to the treaty, and Monroe ratified it on February 25. The Spanish King, Ferdinand VII, however, delayed ratification not only beyond the period of six months specified in the treaty, but for a full year and a half. A dispute had arisen over the validity of certain Spanish land grants in Florida which, if recognized, would have absorbed all the vacant land in the ceded territory. This difficulty was settled to the satisfaction of the United States, but only over the resistance of influential individuals at the Spanish court. More serious was the attempt of Spain to exact from the United States, as a condition of ratification, a promise not to recognize the independence of Spain's revolting colonies. Such a pledge was firmly refused. A revolution in Spain early in 1820 compelled Ferdinand to accept a liberal constitution, which added a new hurdle to the treaty's course: approval by the legislative body, or Cortes. This was finally given, and in October 1820 the King ratified the treaty. The Senate again consented, and ratifications were exchanged in Washington on February 22, 1821, exactly two years from the date of signature.

ADDITIONAL READINGS

ADAMS, HENRY, *History of the United States during the Administrations of Jefferson and Madison.* 9 vols. New York: Charles Scribner's Sons, 1889–1891.

BEMIS, SAMUEL F., *John Quincy Adams and the Foundations of American Foreign Policy.* New York: Alfred A. Knopf, Inc. 1949.

BROWN, ROGER, *The Republic in Peril: 1812.* New York: Columbia University Press, 1964.

BURT, A. L., *The United States, Great Britain, and British North America from the Revolution to the Establishment of Peace after the War of 1812.* New Haven: Yale University Press, 1940.

HATZENBUEHLER, RONALD L., "Party Unity and the Decision for War in the House of Representatives in 1812," *William and Mary Quarterly,* 29 (1972), 367–90.

HORSMAN, REGINALD, *The Causes of the War of 1812.* Philadelphia: University of Pennsylvania Press, 1962.

————, *The War of 1812*. New York: Alfred A. Knopf, Inc. 1969.

KAPLAN, LAWRENCE S., "France and the War of 1812," *Journal of American History,* 57 (1970), 36–47.

PERKINS, BRADFORD, *Castlereagh and Adams: England and America, 1812–1823*. Berkeley: University of California Press, 1964.

————, *Prologue to War: England and the United States, 1805–1812*. Berkeley: University of California Press, 1961.

————, *The First Rapprochement: England and the United States, 1795–1805*. Philadelphia: University of Pennsylvania Press, 1955.

SMELSER, MARSHALL, *The Democratic Republic, 1801–1815*. New York: Harper & Row, Publishers, 1968.

ZIMMERMAN, J. F., *Impressment of American Seamen*. New York: Columbia University Press, 1925.

5. The Monroe Doctrine, Latin American Independence, and Other Matters

Of all Presidents of the United States from 1789 to the 1970s, James Monroe alone was honored by having his name attached to a sacred national dogma—the Monroe Doctrine. There is no Washington, Jefferson, Jackson, Lincoln, or Wilson Doctrine, and the so-called Truman, Eisenhower, and Nixon Doctrines of 1947, 1957, and 1969 failed to capture the imagination or affection of the American people. The Monroe Doctrine, therefore, stands alone. Rarely, during the last one hundred years, has any American admitted doubt concerning this article of faith. It has been invoked by isolationists on the one hand and internationalists on the other. In the famous fight over American participation in the League of Nations, opponents denounced such participation as contrary to the Monroe Doctrine, while Woodrow Wilson praised the League as providing a "Monroe Doctrine for the world." Neither side ventured to repudiate the doctrine or to question its relevance to American policy decisions a century after its enunciation.

It seems safe to say then, that the Monroe Doctrine owes its long-continued popularity to the circumstance that it was the first official public pronouncement of a deep-seated American belief—the belief that the Atlantic and Pacific Oceans divide the world so effectively into distinct hemispheres that the nations of the New World should be able to insulate themselves from the quarrels, the interferences, and the colonizing ambitions of the Old World powers. From this belief stem both the neutrality policy of the United States and the Monroe Doctrine. Insofar as the belief meant American abstention from European quarrels, it spelled neutrality. Insofar as it meant exclusion from the Americas of the political interference and the colonizing activity of Europe, it was set forth in President Monroe's message to Congress of December 2, 1823.

The "doctrine" expounded by Monroe on that occasion was not his spontaneous invention. On an earlier occasion, President Washington had declared in his Farewell Address (1796): "Europe has a set of primary interests, which to us have none or a very remote relation." Thomas Jefferson, writing in 1813 of the independence movement in the American colonies of Spain, observed:

> But in whatever government they end, they will be *American* governments, no longer to be involved in the never-ceasing broils of Europe. The European nations constitute a separate division of the globe; their localities make them a part of a distinct system; they have a set of interests of their own in which it is our business never to engage ourselves. America has a hemisphere to itself. It must have its separate system of interests; which must not be subordinated to those of Europe. . . .

President Monroe's ideas were similar to those of Washington and Jefferson. He was led to state them as he did by specific situations that confronted him in 1823. Perhaps it will be best to see first just what he said in his celebrated message, and then to look at the circumstances that called forth his pronouncements.

What Monroe Said

After describing recent negotiations with Russia concerning her claims to territory on the Pacific coast of North America, the President said:

> . . . In the discussions to which this interest has given rise . . . the occasion has been judged proper for asserting, as a principle in which the rights and interests of the United States are involved, that the American continents, by the free and independent condition which they have assumed and maintain, are henceforth not to be considered as subjects for future colonization by any European powers. . . .

This statement embodies what is generally called the "noncolonization" principle.

Later in the message, after alluding to the recent suppression of liberal movements in Spain and Italy, Monroe stated what has since been called the "noninterference" principle.

> . . . Of events in that quarter of the globe [he said], with which we have so much intercourse and from which we derive our origin, we have always been anxious and interested spectators. The citizens of the United States cherish sentiments the most friendly in favor of the liberty and happiness of their fellowmen on that side of the Atlantic. In the wars of the European powers in matters relating to themselves we have never taken any part, nor does it comport with our policy so to do. It is only when our rights are invaded or seriously menaced that we resent injuries or make preparation for our defense. With the movements in this hemisphere we are of necessity more immediately connected, and by causes which must be obvious to all enlightened and impartial observers. The political system of the allied powers is essentially different in this respect from that of America. This difference proceeds from that which exists in their respective Governments; and to the defense of our own, which has been achieved by the loss of so much blood and treasure, and matured by the wisdom of their most enlightened citizens, and under which we have enjoyed unexampled felicity, this whole nation is devoted. We owe it, therefore, to candor and to the amicable relations existing between the United States and those powers to declare that we should consider any attempt on their part to extend their system to any portion of this hemisphere as dangerous to our peace and safety. With the existing colonies or dependencies of any European power we have not interfered and shall not interfere. But with the Governments who have declared their independence and maintained it, and whose independence we have, on great consideration and on just principles, acknowledged, we could not view any interposition for the purpose of oppressing them, or controlling in any other manner their destiny, by any European power in any other light than as the manifestation of an unfriendly disposition toward the United States. In the war between those new Governments and Spain we declared our neutrality at the time of their recognition, and to this we have adhered, and shall continue to adhere, provided no change shall occur which, in the judgment of the competent authorities of this Government, shall make a corresponding change on the part of the United States indispensable to their security.

The Origin of Noncolonization

The noncolonization principle was the brainchild of John Quincy Adams, Monroe's Secretary of State. Adams had a strong distaste for the presence of European colonial establishments in the neighborhood of the United States. He disliked the commercial exclusiveness with which colonizing powers still surrounded their dependencies, distrusted monarchical neighbors, and desired, in the words of a recent authority, to "keep North America open as a preserve for the republic of the United States to expand over at leisure." Thus noncolonization was "a principle of territorial containment."[1]

The ostensible occasion for putting forth the noncolonization principle at this time was an inclination on the part of Russia to enlarge her holdings upon the Pacific Coast of North America. Russian traders had found lodgment on the northwest coast since the voyages of Vitus Bering between 1727 and 1741, but not until 1799 was the Russian American Company chartered, with exclusive trading rights and jurisdiction along the coast as far south as 55° north latitude. The company not only planted settlements north of that line, but in 1812 set up the trading post of Fort Ross on Bodega Bay only a few miles north of San Francisco Bay. The American government seems never to have been seriously concerned about Fort Ross. It was alarmed, however, by an imperial ukase of September 1821, by which the Russian government extended its exclusive claims down the coast to 51° and forbade all non-Russian ships to come within one hundred Italian miles* of the American coast north of that latitude. Discussion of this new claim with Baron Tuyll, the Russian minister in Washington, gave Adams an opportunity to state the idea that he had been turning over in his mind for several years. The United States, he told Tuyll in July 1823, would assert the principle "that the American continents are no longer subjects for *any* new European colonial establishments." A few days later he embodied the same idea in instructions to

the United States ministers in both Russia and Great Britain, stating it even more emphatically to Richard Rush in London than to Henry Middleton in St. Petersburg.

Thus, though the Russian ukase provided the occasion for the launching of the noncolonization principle, the statement was perhaps aimed less directly at Russia than at Great Britain, whose rivalry in territorial expansion Adams feared more than he feared Russia's. It seems likely, furthermore, that Adams was here indulging in an early instance of the game of twisting the British lion's tail for political purposes. Adams was an active candidate for succession to the presidency in the impending contest of 1824. Political enemies were charging him with having betrayed American, and especially western, interests to Great Britain and Spain in the treaties of 1818 and 1819. A forthright statement forbidding further European colonization, not only in North America, but in "the American continents" might be useful in silencing such criticism.[2]

That Adams, or the government that he represented, had any *right* to veto further colonial enterprises in the great areas of North America that still remained unoccupied and unexplored can hardly be maintained. Nor was Adams himself consistent in his position. Two years before, he had asserted to the British minister that Great Britain had no rights on the northwest coast; and only the arguments of his cabinet colleagues had restrained him from telling Tuyll that Russia had no right to *any* territory in North America. Yet in the treaty of 1818, he had, in effect, acknowledged the equality of British with American rights in the Oregon country; he was willing, in 1824 and later, to divide that region with the British at the 49th parallel; and in 1824 he accepted the Russian claim to exclusive sovereignty north of 54° 40′. Thus Adams himself did not attempt to enforce

---

[1] Frederick Merk, *Albert Gallatin and the Oregon Problem, A Study in Anglo-American Diplomacy* (Cambridge: Harvard University Press, 1950), p. 28.
*One Italian mile = 6,085.2′.
  One American mile = 5,280′.

[2] Merk, *Gallatin and Oregon*, pp. 28–34.

the noncolonization dogma. No European government ever recognized it. "There is room to doubt its wisdom as a diplomatic move," noted Dexter Perkins, "and a harsh critic might even go so far as to describe it as a barren gesture."[3]

A summary of the negotiations with Russia, supplied by Adams and using almost the exact language of his statement to Tuyll, was incorporated verbatim by Monroe in this message of December 2, 1823, and thus took its place as an integral part of the Monroe Doctrine.

The Origin of Noninterference

The second fundamental principle of the Doctrine—the announced opposition of the United States to European interference with the independent nations of the New World—has a more complicated origin. Immediately, it was the American answer to a British proposal for a joint Anglo-American declaration of such opposition. The situation that produced the British proposal was itself the product of two separate trains of events, one in Europe, the other in America.

The destinies of Europe, after the overthrow of Napoleon in 1815, were guided for some years by an alliance of the four powers that had made the chief contribution to his defeat—Russia, Prussia, Austria, and Great Britain. At Vienna in 1815, the four agreed to use their joint efforts to prevent France from again becoming the plaything of "revolutionary principles" and also to hold further meetings from time to time to consider measures that might prove "most salutary for the repose and prosperity of Nations and for the maintenance of the Peace of Europe." The members of the Quadruple Alliance, thus formed, met in a series of congresses for the purpose

[3]Perkins, *History of the Monroe Doctrine*, p. 32.

stated—at Aix-la-Chappelle (1818), Troppau (1820), Laibach (1821), and Verona (1822). At all except the first, they found serious work to do, for the liberal spirit, suppressed by the settlement at Vienna, was again raising its head. Liberal revolutions in the kingdoms of Naples, Piedmont, and Spain compelled the sovereigns of those states to accept constitutions that rigidly limited their prerogatives. It was this liberal spirit that the Quadruple Alliance, under the leadership of Prince Metternich, Austrian Foreign Minister and Chancellor, was resolved to crush. At the congresses of Troppau and Laibach the powers commissioned Austria to send troops into Italy to suppress the uprisings there; at Verona they sent French armies into Spain and thereby suppressed the liberal constitution of 1820 and restored Ferdinand VII to his former status as an absolute monarch.

During these proceedings, the composition of the Quadruple Alliance had suffered an unannounced change. France under the restored Bourbon sovereign, Louis XVIII, had shown such a strong disposition to reliable behavior that it had been virtually accepted into the alliance. England, on the other hand, though under a conservative Tory government, had protested repeatedly against the armed interventions practiced in Italy and Spain. She thus, in effect, drifted out of the alliance, and France took her place. When, having restored Ferdinand to power in Spain, the continental statesmen began to talk of restoring his authority also in Spain's former American colonies, England went completely into opposition and sought cooperation from the United States.[4]

[4]The work of the Quadruple Alliance is often attributed to the Holy Alliance as if the two were synonymous. The Holy Alliance treaty, which originated in the brain of Czar Alexander I of Russia, was a harmless declaration to the general effect that the signatory sovereigns would be guided by Christian principles in their relations with one another and with their subjects. It was signed by all the sovereigns of Europe except the Pope, the Sultan of Turkey, and the

The Spanish colonies that Ferdinand would have liked to recover had been in the process of establishing their independence since 1810. Napoleon's attempt (1808) to set a French king on the throne of Spain had, in their eyes, absolved them from any allegiance to that throne. The restoration of Ferdinand had done nothing to tempt them back, and by 1822 Spanish rule had been effectively overthrown in all the mainland colonies from Mexico to Argentina and Chile. The elimination of Spain's monopoly of the trade of her colonies had been economically beneficial to Great Britain and, to a minor extent, to the United States. For that reason, neither of them wished to see Spanish rule restored. Both had other reasons, however, for frowning upon any such intervention as rumor was forecasting. Great Britain feared that France might take advantage of Spain's necessity to appropriate some of the colonies for herself. Americans felt a natural sympathy for colonial populations who had won the fight for independence as they themselves had done a scant forty years earlier. They rejoiced at the success of the Spanish Americans and would have resented any attempt by the reactionary powers of Europe to restore the despotic rule of Spain.

The Problem of Recognizing Spain's Colonies in Revolt

The United States, moreover, had just recognized the independence of Colombia, Mexico, the United Provinces of Rio de la Plata (Argentina), and Chile, and other recognitions would follow in due course. Recognition had come only after a suitable period of watchful waiting. The United States government had taken an interest from the beginning in the independence movement south of the border. Emissaries of the new governments were received cordially, though unofficially, in Washington, and "agents for seamen and commerce" (for a while, regular consuls) were sent to watch over American interests in the rebellious countries. When the European war ended and Spain undertook by force to recover control in America, the United States adopted a position of neutrality between the parties, thus allowing colonial vessels the privilege of frequenting United States ports and procuring war materials and other supplies. Henry Clay, Speaker of the House of Representatives, called for immediate recognition of the new governments. Exclaiming, "Let us become real and true Americans, and place ourselves at the head of the American System," he attacked the President and Secretary of State, Monroe and Adams, for timidity and subservience to Europe in their postponement of recognition.

Monroe and Adams had good reason for hesitation. Heretofore the recognition by one power of the rebellious subjects of another had been but a prelude to war. The government of France had recognized the independence of the United States only when ready to go to war with England to support it. The British government had accepted the challenge and later had seized upon an unauthorized draft treaty with the United States subscribed to by a Dutch agent as an excuse for making war upon the Netherlands. The United States now had no intention of going to war with Spain in behalf of the revolted colonies, but there was a chance that Spain, following the British precedent, might regard recognition as an act of war and that, if so, she might be aided by the powers of the Quad-

British Prince Regent. The United States was invited to adhere but sent a polite declination. The original signers were the Czar, the Emperor of Austria, and the King of Prussia. Since these three sovereigns were also members of the Quadruple Alliance, it is not surprising that contemporary writers and later historians confused the two alliances. In reality the Holy Alliance was in the clouds, the Quadruple Alliance very much of this world.

ruple Alliance. That was a chance that Henry Clay might be willing to take, but not Adams or Monroe.

Under what conditions could recognition be granted to a state that had established itself by revolution, without giving just offense to the parent state? International law had as yet no clear answer to that question, and the government in Washington had to make its rules as it went. For the recognition of revolutionary governments, Jefferson had stated the thesis, in 1792, during the French Revolution, that "It accords with our principles to acknolege [*sic*] any government to be rightful which is formed by the will of the nation substantially declared." "The only thing essential is the will of the nation," he said on another occasion. This assertion left open the question of how "the will of the nation" was to be ascertained. Henry Clay, in 1818, proclaimed that the essential test for recognition was and had been a more practical one. "We have constantly proceeded on the principle," he announced, "that the government *de facto* [in fact] is that we can alone notice. . . . As soon as stability and order are maintained, no matter by whom, we have always considered and ought to consider the actual as the true government."

Clay came very close to stating what was to become the standard American doctrine of recognition, but Adams added some important qualifications. The government of a state or a colony in rebellion might properly be recognized, he said, "when independence is established as a matter of fact so as to leave the chance of the opposite party to recover their dominion utterly desperate." But he also insisted upon certain standards of behavior in the government of the new state: it must carry out its responsibilities and duties as a member of the international community. Complaining of the lawless acts of privateers carrying letters of marque from the unrecognized Latin American governments, Adams wrote that those governments "cannot claim the rights & prerogatives of independent States, without conforming to the duties by which independent States are bound."

In these discussions, brought on by the Latin American wars of independence, can be found the principles of the permanent recognition policy of the United States. A government that has come to power by revolution (whether in an old or a new state) may properly be recognized when it (1) is effectively exercising the powers of government, (2) shows promise of stability, and (3) shows willingness and ability to carry out its international obligations.

The problem of Monroe and Adams was to ascertain, first, whether these requirements were met by the new Latin American governments, and, second, whether Spain and her European friends would resent an act of recognition to the point of taking hostile action against the United States.

In 1817, when Clay began his campaign for recognition, victory for the revolutionists was still far from certain and the quality of the new governments was open to doubt. Commissioners sent by Monroe to Buenos Aires and elsewhere in South America disagreed among themselves as to whether the situation would justify recognition. Nevertheless, Adams, at Monroe's suggestion, inquired of Great Britain, France, and Russia whether they were disposed to join the United States in recognizing the new governments. When the responses were negative, the Washington statesmen thought it best to postpone action until the new governments could give better evidence of permanence and stability.

By 1822 military victories over Spanish arms in South America had made it obvious that Spain, unaided, could never restore her rule on the mainland. The emancipated colonies were making encouraging progress toward orderly government, and some of them, at least, had put an end to privateering under their authority. It seemed unlikely that recognition would lead to war with Spain or her European backers. The time had come, thought Monroe and Adams, to recognize the new governments to the south without awaiting the concurrence of the powers of Europe. A special message of March 8, 1822, conveyed that opinion to Congress, which responded with an appropriation to cover the expenses of diplomatic missions to such of the American nations as the President might deem proper. By the end of January 1823, accordingly, the United States had entered into formal diplomatic relations with Colombia (comprising not only northern Colombia, but also Ecuador and Venezuela), Mexico, Chile, and the United Provinces of Rio de la Plata. Having officially recognized these states as independent sovereignties, the American government was even less sympathetic than formerly to any plan for the suppression of their independence by force.

Canning and Monroe Warn the European Allies

Such was the situation in the Americas in August 1823, when reports reached George Canning, British Foreign Secretary, that when France had completed her work of intervention in Spain, a new congress of the powers would probably be convoked to deal with the colonial question. Canning had already, in the preceding March, warned France that any attempt on her part to appropriate any of the Spanish colonies would be opposed by Great Britain. He now suggested to Richard Rush, the United States minister in London, that either by signing a convention or by an exchange of notes, the British and American governments signify their disapproval of any attempt by the European powers to restore the rule of Spain to her lost colonies. Great Britain, he said, subscribed to the

following principles, which he believed to be also accepted by the United States:

1. We conceive the recovery of the Colonies by Spain to be hopeless.
2. We conceive the question of the recognition of them, as Independent States, to be one of time and circumstances.
3. We are, however, by no means disposed to throw any impediment in the way of an arrangement between them, and the mother country by amicable negotiations.
4. We aim not at the possession of any portion of them ourselves.
5. We could not see any portion of them transferred to any other Power, with indifference.

If any European power, Canning added, contemplated the forcible subjugation of the former colonies on behalf of Spain or in her name, or the acquisition of any of them for itself, a joint declaration by Great Britain and the United States of the principles indicated "would be at once the most effectual and the least offensive mode of intimating our joint disapprobation of such projects."

Since Great Britain alone, with her unchallenged control of the seas, would have been able to veto any attempt of the continental powers to restore Spanish rule in America, why should Canning have sought the cooperation of the United States? It seems obvious, in the first place, that such cooperation, even though the United States of 1823 was less than second-rate in naval and military power, would have bolstered England's diplomatic position. But scholars have suggested further reasons for Canning's proposal. Acceptance by the United States of Canning's fourth principle would be agreeable to Canning as a disclaimer of any American intent to acquire Cuba. It has been conjectured, furthermore, that Canning hoped, through courting American cooperation in the international field, to secure a continuance of a tariff-free American market for British textiles and ironware—a hope, however, which received a rebuff in protectionist proposals in Monroe's famous message.[5]

Rush had no instructions that would have empowered him to join with Canning in such a statement. He was, nevertheless, greatly attracted by the proposal. Could he have secured from Canning an immediate recognition of the independence of the Spanish American states, he would have been ready to make a statement on behalf of his government that it would "not remain inactive under an attack upon the independence of those states by the Holy [Quadruple] Alliance," leaving it for his government to disavow his action if it saw fit. But Canning, whose policy, though backed by the Prime Minister, Lord Liverpool, was opposed by other cabinet colleagues and by the King, was not ready to risk recognition;[6] nor was Rush willing to accept a mere promise of future recognition, which Canning tentatively offered. Rush, therefore, could do no more than report the negotiations to his government and await instructions.

Adams was at home, in Quincy, Massachusetts, when Rush's account of the momentous conversation reached Washington. Monroe sought the advice of the two living Virginian ex-Presidents, Jefferson and Madison. Should the United States join with Great Britain in the proposed declaration? Both elder statesmen answered affirmatively. Madison even proposed that the "avowed disapprobation" be extended to cover the French intervention in Spain and that the two governments issue also a declaration in behalf of the Greeks, then engaged in their war for independence against Turkey.

John Quincy Adams was yet to be heard from. In November, when Monroe's cabinet discussed Canning's proposal, the Secretary of State frankly opposed joint action with Great Britain. "It would be more candid, as well as more dignified," he argued, "to avow our principles explicitly to Russia and France, than to come in as a cock-boat in the wake of the British man-of-war." Adams' ideas prevailed. Rush was instructed to decline Canning's proposal for a joint declaration, though at the same time assuring the Foreign Secretary that the United States accepted all of his stated principles except the second, which left the question of recognition to "time and circumstances." On this point, said Adams, "we considered that the people of these emancipated Colonies, were, *of right* independent of all other nations, and that it was our duty so to acknowledge them." Adams made no reservation on the fourth point, though he suspected its purpose in relation to Cuba. He added, on behalf of the United States,

that we could not see with indifference, any attempt by one or more powers of Europe to restore those new states to the crown of Spain, or to deprive them, in any manner, whatever of the freedom and independence which they have acquired.

The note did not close the door entirely to the possibility of a joint declaration,[7] should an emergency make it expedient, but the decision upon such a declaration was reserved to the Washington authorities, who would, said Adams, "according to the principles of our Government, and in the forms prescribed by our Constitution, cheerfully join in any act by which we may contribute to support the cause of human freedom, and the Independence of the South American Nations."

It was President Monroe who proposed

[5]George Dangerfield, *The Era of Good Feelings* (New York: Harcourt, Brace & World, Inc., 1952), pp. 291–92, 319.

[6]Bradford Perkins, *Castlereagh and Adams: England and America, 1812–1823* (Berkeley: University of California Press, 1964), pp. 321–23.

[7]This point is well developed in G. W. McGee, "The Monroe Doctrine—A Stopgap Measure," *Mississippi Valley Historical Review,* 38 (1951), 233–50.

that the American position be announced to the whole world through a presidential message instead of being buried in diplomatic correspondence. The notes for his annual message, which he read to his cabinet, included a vigorous statement of the noninterference principle; they also expressed disapproval of the French intervention in Spain and sympathy with the Greek revolt. To these latter expressions Adams objected. "The ground I wish to take," he said, "is that of earnest remonstrance against the interference of European powers by force in South America, but to disclaim all interference on our part in Europe; to make an American cause, and adhere inflexibly to that." The President yielded. The message, while branding European intervention in the New World as "dangerous to our peace and safety" and as "the manifestation of an unfriendly disposition toward the United States," likewise disclaimed on the part of the United States the taking of any part "in the wars of the European powers *in matters relating to themselves.*"

The last phrase is here italicized because it left a door wide open for American participation in the wars of Europe, if and when such wars should invade or seriously menace American rights or American security. When this passage was written, the Treaty of Ghent was less than eight years old. Monroe, who had been Secretary of State and for a short time Secretary of War during the War of 1812, had not forgotten that the wars of the European powers were not always concerned solely with "matters relating to themselves." They could endanger the rights, even the security of the United States.

Effects of the Message in Europe

To James Monroe and the members of his cabinet, who concurred in the content and phraseology of his message to Congress of December 2, 1823, the threat of European intervention in America was real—to all, at least, except Adams, who was convinced that it would not be tried. The British warnings had been reinforced by a communication from the Russian Foreign Office exulting over the successes of the Quadruple Alliance in Europe and declaring it to be the Czar's policy to guarantee "the tranquility of all the states of which the civilized world is composed"—an expression which, the Russian minister informed Adams, comprehended "the supremacy of Spain over the revolted colonies." The warning against intervention was therefore appropriate. For a young and weak nation thus to challenge the four principal powers of continental Europe appeared audacious, but Monroe was not bluffing; he had an "ace-in-the-hole"—the British navy. For while there was no agreement, not even an "understanding," with Great Britain, Canning had revealed enough to Rush to assure Monroe that Great Britain would oppose armed intervention in the Americas.

What neither Monroe nor Adams knew was that Canning had already served an ultimatum on France and received a satisfactory response. Discouraged by Rush's insistence upon conditions that he was unwilling to meet, Canning had approached the Prince de Polignac, the French ambassador in London, and in a series of conferences in October had received from him assurances that France had no intention or desire to appropriate to herself any of the Spanish possessions in America, nor "any design of acting against the Colonies by force of arms." With the substance of these assurances embodied in a memorandum, Canning had lost interest in obtaining cooperation from the United States; he no longer needed it to secure British objectives, and he dropped the matter with an abruptness that shook American confidence in his good faith.

After the secret Canning-Polignac conversations, there was no danger that the Quadruple Alliance powers would intervene by force in Latin America, if, indeed, any such danger had ever existed. Modern scholarship, especially the work of Dexter Perkins, has shown that no one of the four governments involved—French, Russian, Austrian, and Prussian—had any matured plan for the use of force against Spain's former colonies, and that Prince Metternich, most influential of Quadruple Alliance statesmen, was realist enough to know that the restoration of Spain's rule in the New World was impossible.[8] Under these circumstances, it can hardly be supposed that a congress, had one been held, could have agreed upon a policy of force in America. Certainly after the Canning-Polignac conversations in October, such an outcome was unthinkable.

Unknown to Monroe and Adams, therefore, a practically nonexistent danger had been completely dissipated by Canning's warning to Polignac nearly two months before Monroe's message went to Congress. The message, consequently, had little or no practical effect upon the course of events in Europe. Canning was probably exaggerating its effectiveness when he declared that the proposed congress on the "colonial question" "was broken in all its limbs before, but the President's speech [sic] gives it the *coup de grace.*"

From the courts of the continental powers, the message elicited considerable unofficial abuse—it was described as "blustering," "monstrous," "arrogant," "haughty," and "peremptory,"—but no official protests. The United States was still a small power, and its attitude on international questions was of minor significance. Continental reaction to Monroe's message may be summarized as holding that his declaration was impertinent but unimportant.

George Canning, whose proposals to Rush had led to the inclusion of the nonin-

terference principle in Monroe's message, was understandably annoyed at Monroe's independent pronouncement—a pronouncement that rested upon a knowledge of Canning's position but gave him no credit for it. Monroe, he felt, had stolen a march upon him and was courting the favor of the Latin American republics as the principal protector of their independence. To establish British priority in that role, Canning published the Polignac memorandum of October 1823, which showed that the British government had anticipated the United States in warning the continental powers against intervention. Later, after Great Britain had extended recognition to the new governments in December 1824, Canning boasted, "I called the New World into existence to redress the balance of the Old." By such claims, and in more direct ways, he sought to undermine the prestige of the United States with the Latin American governments and to establish England as their first and most powerful friend.

The other basic dogma of Monroe's message, the noncolonization principle, contributed further to Canning's pique at the United States. With vast portions of North America still unoccupied, Great Britain could not assent to the right of the United States to veto all further colonizing enterprises in that area. For this reason, Canning refused to join the United States in tripartite negotiations with Russia over claims on the northwest coast and took an unyielding stand toward the United States on the Oregon boundary question. In the course of time, Great Britain and the United States would come to see eye to eye on the Monroe Doctrine, but the initial effect of Monroe's message upon Anglo-American relations was irritating rather than soothing.

As for Russia, against whose expanded territorial claims the noncolonization principle had been ostensibly directed, she readily consented, in separate treaties with

---

[8]Dexter Perkins, *The Monroe Doctrine, 1823–1826* (Cambridge: Harvard University Press, 1927), chap. 4.

the United States (1824) and Great Britain (1825), to limit her territorial claims in North America to the area north of latitude 54° 40 ′. This she would have done, it seems safe to say, even had she never been confronted with the sweeping assertion put forth by John Quincy Adams.

The Reception of the Message in America

Monroe's message was received with some enthusiasm by the press of the United States. In Congress there was both praise and criticism. A resolution of endorsement, introduced by Henry Clay in the House of Representatives, never came to a vote. The principles of the message remained, therefore, a simple pronouncement of the President of the United States, without legal standing at home or in the international community.

In the Latin American states, supposedly the beneficiaries of the message, liberal and republican elements applauded the American President's declaration, but they soon discovered that the United States was little prepared to back up words with action. Five of the new governments, Argentina, Brazil, Chile, Colombia, and Mexico, applied to the authorities in Washington for either treaties of alliance or promises of assistance against possible European intervention. All received negative replies. Of special interest was John Quincy Adams' reply (August 6, 1824) to the Colombian minister in Washington, since it plainly meant that without the support of Great Britain, the United States could not undertake to defend the Americas against the Quadruple Alliance. Thus Latin American liberals learned what their conservative and monarchist rivals had known from the beginning, that the chief bulwark of their newly won independence was the British navy, not the pronouncement of an American President.

A Diplomatic Miscellany

In the two decades following the issuance of the Monroe Doctrine, there were a number of international problems that were provocative of serious frictions until their solutions were found. Among them were questions of boundaries, suppression of the slave trade and the *Caroline* affair.

The Northeastern Boundary Dispute

Failure of the joint commissions provided for by the Treaty of Ghent to agree on the northeastern boundary and on the line from the Neebish Rapids to the Lake of the Woods and the subsequent rejection of the recommendation of the King of the Netherlands for settlement of the former controversy threw these two problems again into the hands of the diplomats. It will be well here to examine the conflicting conceptions of the boundary between the state of Maine and the British provinces of New Brunswick (detached from Nova Scotia in 1784) and Quebec.

The dispute over this section of the boundary turned upon the meaning of the language of Article II of the treaty of peace with Great Britain of 1783, the relevant portion of which described the boundary as follows:

. . . From the NorthWest Angle of Nova Scotia, viz. That Angle which is formed by a Line drawn due North from the Source of Saint Croix River to the Highlands along the said Highlands which divide those Rivers that empty themselves into the River St. Lawrence, from those which fall into the Atlantic Ocean, to the Northwestern-most Head of

Connecticut River: Thence down along the middle of that River to the forty-fifth Degree of North Latitude; From thence by a Line due West on said Latitude until it strikes the River Iroquois or Cataraquy [St. Lawrence]; . . .

The identity of the St. Croix River having been established and its source located pursuant to the Jay treaty, the Americans proposed to draw a line from that point due north to the watershed between the St. Lawrence basin and the southward-flowing rivers and to follow that watershed to the northwestern source of the Connecticut. That seemed, and still seems, the plain meaning of the treaty. The British, however, demurred. From their point of view, there were practical objections to a line so drawn. Such a line, as the map will show, would cut across the St. John River, leaving its source in Maine and its mouth in New Brunswick. It would also, by pushing the boundaries of Maine far up toward the St. Lawrence, drive a wedge between the provinces of Quebec and New Brunswick and interfere with British plans for a vital military road to run from Fredericton, New Brunswick, to Riviere du Loup on the St. Lawrence.

The British, therefore, insisted that the line should be drawn south of the St. John River, leaving the river and the line of the proposed military road in British possession. They resisted the American interpretation of the treaty, in the first place, by arguing that the rivers flowing south from the highlands picked by the Americans drained not into the Atlantic Ocean, but into the Bay of Fundy. Hence, they said, these could not be the highlands of the treaty. The Americans, on their side, contended that the Bay of Fundy was comprehended under the term Atlantic Ocean. The more persuasive British argument was based upon what they contended must have been the intent of the treaty-makers. These negotiators, they argued, would not knowingly have divided the source of an important river like the St. John from its outlet or have driven a wedge between two of His Majesty's provinces. Finally, they asserted, where the treaty spoke of "Highlands," it must have referred to some conspicuous elevation, not to the almost indistinguishable line that divided the tributaries of the St. Lawrence from the streams flowing southward. Such a conspicuous elevation was conveniently found in Mars Hill south of the St. John and a line of hills running thence westward, always south of that stream. There, said the British, must be the "Highlands" mentioned in the treaty.

The Americans, in addition to having what seems the fairest interpretation of the treaty in support of their case, had also, like the British, material reasons for insisting on their claims. North of Mars Hill and south of the St. John lay the valley of the Aroostook, a tributary of the St. John, a fertile valley constituting Maine's "last agricultural frontier." This area the people of Maine and their backers in Massachusetts (which still held title to lands in Maine) were determined not to give up.[9] When lumbermen from New Brunswick entered the Aroostook Valley and began cutting timber, they were expelled by Maine militia in what was locally dubbed the "Restook War" of 1838–1839. Serious trouble threatened. General Winfield Scott was sent to the Aroostook, where he arranged a *modus vivendi* between Maine and New Brunswick, each party to remain in possession of territory actually occupied without prejudice to its disposition in a final settlement.

The Webster-Ashburton Treaty

A final settlement was manifestly desirable, but until 1842 every attempt to negotiate a settlement or to submit the dispute a second

[9]Thomas LeDuc, "The Maine Frontier and the Northeastern Boundary Controversy," *American Historical Review,* 53 (1947), 30–41.

time to arbitration encountered insuperable obstacles. For the United States, any compromise arrangement was rendered difficult by the contention of Maine and Massachusetts, both politically important, that no abatement of the American claim could be made without Maine's consent. In 1842 there arrived in Washington Alexander Baring, Lord Ashburton, commissioned as special envoy of the British government to seek a settlement of all existing difficulties between Great Britain and the United States. Among the chief of these was the northeastern boundary dispute. Daniel Webster, Secretary of State under President John Tyler, was, like Lord Ashburton, anxious to reach a settlement. Both men were prepared to make concessions.

The British had been willing, since 1831, to accept a compromise line similar to that proposed by the King of the Netherlands—a line that in its most vital portion would follow the west-east course of the St. John River, roughly halfway between Mars Hill on the south and the highlands claimed by the Americans to the north. Such a line would leave the Aroostook Valley to the people of Maine and the site for the military road to the British. For such a line Lord Ashburton was ready to make concessions on other points. He was empowered to permit the Americans of the Aroostook the free navigation of the St. John to its mouth for the exportation of their farm and forest products. He was empowered to yield to the American claims on several other unsettled portions of the boundary. He might accept the American contention that the head of Hall's Stream was the northwesternmost source of the Connecticut River, thereby yielding to the United States some 150 square miles of forest land claimed by Great Britain. He might also accept, in lieu of the true 45th parallel from the Connecticut to the St. Lawrence, the line inaccurately surveyed as such in 1774, which lay about three-fourths of a mile north of the true line. This discrepancy was important chiefly because Fort Montgomery, a newly constructed American military work on Rouse's Point at the outlet of Lake Champlain, was situated just north of the true 45th parallel. Retention of the old line would leave the fort in United States territory. The importance attached to this fort and to the British plan for a military road throws interesting light on the myth of the "unguarded frontier" in this period. Lord Ashburton was also authorized to make concessions to the United States on the boundary from the head of Lake Huron to the Lake of the Woods.

The chief obstacle to an agreement on the lines indicated was the opposition of the people and authorities of Maine to the relinquishment of their claims north of the St. John River. This opposition was quieted, partly by compensating Maine and Massachusetts, $150,000 to each, for the land titles surrendered; partly by skillful newspaper propaganda, some of it apparently paid for out of the secret service fund at Webster's disposal;[10] partly by bringing secretly to the attention of the Maine and Massachusetts authorities certain old maps that appeared to support the British contention in regard to the identity of the "Highlands" of the treaty. Though subsequent discoveries have shown that Webster's maps were without authority and that authentic maps, which were not known to the negotiators, supported the American claim, Webster's strategy was effective, and the New Englanders agreed not to obstruct the compromise settlement.[11]

[10] R. N. Current, "Webster's Propaganda and the Ashburton Treaty," *Mississippi Valley Historical Review,* 34 (1947), 187–200.

[11] For a discussion of the famous episode of the "red line maps," see S. F. Bemis, *John Quincy Adams and the Foundations of American Foreign Policy* (New York: Alfred A. Knopf, Inc., 1949), chap. 23. Professor Bemis is scathing in his criticism of Webster, who, as he says, "wilfully relinquish[ed] millions of acres of good American territory." He implies that Webster was motivated by selfish personal, even pecuniary, considerations in making his "surrender." It may be guessed that the final verdict of history will treat Webster more charitably. Lord Ashburton's British critics charged that it was he who had made the surrenders.

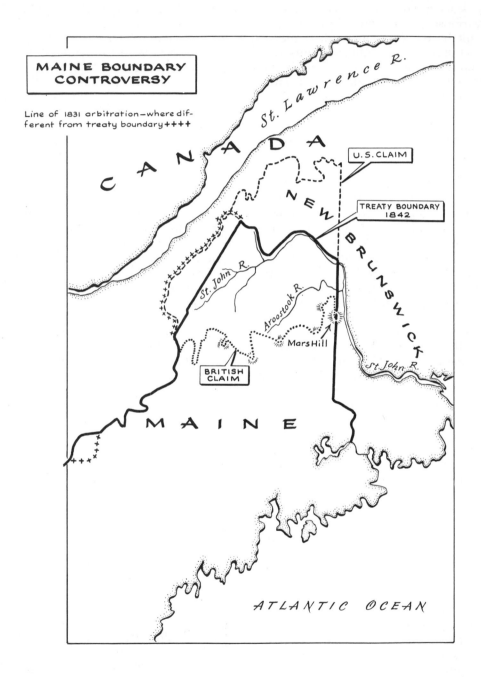

MAINE BOUNDARY CONTROVERSY

Line of 1831 arbitration—where different from treaty boundary ++++

St. Lawrence R.

CANADA

U.S. CLAIM

NEW BRUNSWICK

TREATY BOUNDARY 1842

St. John R.

Aroostook R.

Mars Hill

BRITISH CLAIM

St. John R.

MAINE

ATLANTIC OCEAN

By the Webster-Ashburton treaty, signed August 9, 1842, the United States secured slightly less of the disputed territory in Maine than it would have received by accepting the arbitral recommendation of the King of the Netherlands, as the following figures indicate:

	Arbitral Award 1831	Treaty 1842
To the United States	7,908 sq. mi.	7,015 sq. mi.
To Great Britain	4,119 sq. mi.	5,012 sq. mi.

Granting that on the best interpretation of the treaty of 1783 the United States had a sound claim to the whole of the disputed territory, and granting that Webster could have exacted a better price from Lord Ashburton for what he yielded—the latter certainly could have been persuaded to foot the bill for compensation to Maine and Massachusetts and would probably have consented to grant the navigation of the St. Lawrence River—one may still feel considerable satisfaction at the termination of this long controversy. It is not clear that continued insistence upon all that the United States believed it was entitled to under the treaty would have exacted a peaceful surrender from Great Britain. It will hardly be contended that the five thousand square miles relinquished were worth a war.

The boundary settlements of the treaty, furthermore, cannot be assessed properly without weighing gains in the west against losses in the east. Webster and Ashburton inherited the unsettled boundary from the Neebish Rapids to the Lake of the Woods, a segment of the line that had baffled the Treaty of Ghent commissioners. The chief points in controversy in this area were the ownership of St. George's or Sugar Island

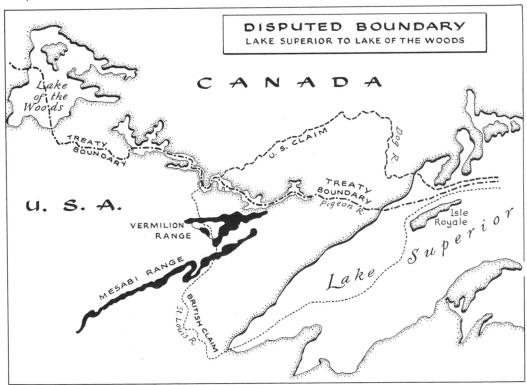

in the St. Mary's River and the location of the line from Lake Superior to the Lake of the Woods. The treaty of 1783 described the boundary as leaving Lake Superior at "Long Lake" and running thence by the water communication to the Lake of the Woods. The commissioners found no "Long Lake" emptying into Lake Superior, but Mitchell's Map of North America of 1755, which they had every reason to suppose had been used by the peace commissioners, showed a Long Lake in the position of what had come to be called Pigeon River, which was not a lake at all. Both commissioners were at first disposed to run the line through Pigeon River, but Anthony Barclay, the British representative, later claimed that St. Louis River at the extreme western end of Lake Superior best answered the description of the treaty. Choice of this line would have added some 6,500 square miles of territory to the British possessions. Thereupon the American agent, Joseph Delafield, made out a case for the Kamanistegua or Dog River, some distance east of the Pigeon, as the proper boundary. He showed that its course included a stretch of water called Long Lake (though some distance from Lake Superior) and that a water route, with portages, led thence to the Lake of the Woods. It was the expectation of Delafield and of Peter B. Porter, the American commissioner, who adopted his claim, that the British would agree to accept Pigeon River as a compromise. The British stood firm for the St. Louis, however, and this portion of the boundary remained undetermined until the Webster-Ashburton negotiations. The diplomats then assigned St. George's Island to the United States and adopted Pigeon River as the "Long Lake" of the earlier treaty.[12]

By relinquishing the British claims between Lake Superior and the Lake of the Woods, Lord Ashburton yielded to the United States some 6,500 square miles of territory, which, though the negotiators were unaware of it, embraced a large proportion of the future iron ore fields of northern Minnesota, including the eastern portion of the famed Mesabi range. In any economic balance, the iron deposits of this section of Minnesota would certainly outweigh the forests surrendered to New Brunswick.[13]

The African Slave Trade and the Right of Search

Webster and Ashburton included in their treaty an article providing for cooperative American and British action to further the suppression of the traffic in African slaves. Both governments had long since forbidden the slave trade to their own citizens or subjects (the United States as of January 1, 1808); and both had followed up the prohibitions by declaring the trade to be piracy, punishable by death. British and American action alone, however, could not give the slave trade the status of piracy under international law; and in the absence of special treaties providing for international action, each nation could enforce the law only against its own nationals.

By Article Ten of the Treaty of Ghent, the British and American governments had promised to "use their best endeavors to accomplish" the "entire abolition" of the slave trade. In 1824 British and American negotiators agreed on a convention that would have permitted reciprocal right of search of vessels suspected of engaging in the forbidden traffic; British cruisers could

[12]Robert McElroy and Thomas Riggs, eds., *The Unfortified Boundary; A Diary of the First Survey of the Canadian Boundary Line from St. Regis to the Lake of the Woods, by Major Joseph Delafield* (New York: Privately printed, 1943), pp. 63–123.

[13]Thomas LeDuc, "The Webster-Ashburton Treaty and the Minnesota Iron Ranges," *Journal of American History,* 51 (December 1964), 476–81.

have searched ships flying the American flag and vice versa. The proposal called up old and bitter memories of British cruisers hovering off American ports and searching American ships for alleged deserters from His Majesty's navy. The Senate, therefore, amended the convention to make it inapplicable to waters off the North American coast. The British government refused to accept this amendment, and the convention was never ratified.[14]

The division in the Senate over the convention of 1824 was not sectional, but within a few years thereafter, the American controversy over slavery grew bitter, while Great Britain, abolishing slavery in her colonies, in 1833, became the international champion and promoter of the antislavery movement. This combination of circumstances aroused the slaveholding South to oppose any arrangement that would concede to British cruisers the right to search American ships for evidence that they were carrying slaves; and northern allies of the South, such men as Lewis Cass of Michigan, took the same view. When, in the late 1830's, British men-of-war off the African coast began stopping vessels flying the American flag, John Forsyth of Georgia was Secretary of State, and Andrew Stevenson of Virginia was minister to Great Britain. Forsyth and Stevenson took violent exception to this new British assertion of the right of search.

Lord Palmerston, British Foreign Secretary, was as vigorous in stating the British case as was Stevenson in setting forth that of the United States. He claimed for Great Britain, he said, not the right of search but merely a "right of visit"—the right to board a ship to ascertain whether she was really of the nationality that her flag indicated. He pointed out that, since England had treaties permitting reciprocal rights of search with numerous states of Europe and Latin America, it was becoming common practice for slave traders of various nationalities to seek protection by flying the United States flag. If British cruisers were debarred from visiting such vessels to discover whether they were bona fide American or were sailing under false colors, said Palmerston, suppression of the slave traffic would be impossible.

Stevenson replied that the "right of visit" was merely the right of search under another name, and that the United States would never consent to having its ships searched by foreign cruisers except for contraband or evidence of other illegal trade in time of war. The controversy grew warm and, added to the disputes over the Maine boundary and others over the *Caroline* and Alexander McLeod, to be described below, produced something of a crisis in Anglo-American relations in 1841.

Chances for a friendly settlement improved when the conciliatory Lord Aberdeen replaced Palmerston in the Foreign Office and the conciliatory Webster succeeded Forsyth as Secretary of State. The questions of the slave trade and the right of search in connection with it were included in the agenda for the Webster-Ashburton conferences. To Lord Aberdeen, Ashburton pointed out that the American objection to the right of search arose largely from its association with the impressment controversy and asked permission to conciliate American opinion by assuring Webster that Great Britain no longer claimed the right to impress sailors from American ships. This proposal was firmly rejected by the Foreign Secretary, but Ashburton nevertheless assured Webster in writing that the practice of impressment had "wholly ceased" and could not be "under present circumstances renewed."[15]

This concession, unauthorized by the

---

[14]This whole subject is well covered in H. G. Soulsby, *The Right of Search and the Slave Trade in Anglo-American Relations, 1814–1862* (Baltimore: The Johns Hopkins Press, 1933).

[15]Soulsby, *The Right of Search*, pp. 84–85.

British government, did not alter the American attitude toward the right of search. Webster and Ashburton sought to terminate the controversy by eliminating the need for reciprocal rights of visit and search. Article Eight of the treaty stipulated that each government should maintain off the African coast an adequate cruising squadron carrying not fewer than eighty guns, "to enforce, separately and respectively, the laws, rights, and obligations, of each of the two countries, for the suppression of the Slave Trade, . . ." The two squadrons would be independent of each other, but it was agreed that the two governments would give such orders to their squadron commanders as would "enable them most effectually to act in concert and cooperation, upon mutual consultation, as exigencies may arise, . . ."

Thus the United States agreed to take measures adequate to enforce, against its own nationals or ships flying the American flag, its laws forbidding the African slave trade. This solution removed the issue from the field of controversy for fifteen years but did not settle it. The United States failed to implement the agreement effectually. It fulfilled its promise to keep eighty guns in African waters by using a few large and slow sailing ships when the situation called for numerous small but speedy craft. It was tardy in assigning steamers to the service. The base of the American squadron, in the Cape Verde Islands, was too far from the slave coast to permit effective operation. The slave trade, therefore, continued to flourish, a large share of it under the United States flag. Until 1857, nevertheless, the British refrained from visiting suspicious vessels flying the Stars and Stripes. In that year they renewed the practice and thereby revived the controversy. Lewis Cass, now Secretary of State,[16] com-

batted vigorously the British reassertion of the "right to visit." This time the British government gave ground, abandoning in 1858 its claim to rights of visit and search in time of peace, except where such rights were specially conceded by treaty.

The final chapter of the story was written in 1862, after the secession from the Union of the slaveholding South. A treaty with Great Britain, then signed and ratified, permitted the cruisers of each power not only to search ships of the other but also, if the search showed reasonable grounds for suspecting participation in the slave trade, to seize the suspect ship and send it for adjudication to one of several mixed British and American courts created for the purpose. The end of slavery in the South removed one important market of the illicit traffic. This event was soon followed by the abolition of slavery in the remaining civilized lands where it still had legal existence: in Brazil, between 1871 and 1888; in Puerto Rico, in 1873; and in Cuba, in 1880. The closing of these last markets removed all incentive to the prohibited commerce.

The Caroline and Alexander McLeod

Another controversy that Webster and Ashburton inherited from their predecessors and succeeded in terminating amicably was the affair of the steamer *Caroline,* an outgrowth of a short-lived Canadian rebellion against British rule in 1837–1838. In this minor civil struggle, the United States, following the precedent that it had set in the Spanish-American wars of inde-

---

[16]In 1841, as United States minister in Paris, Cass had worked against French ratification of a quintuple treaty (Great Britain, France, Austria, Prussia, Russia) declaring the slave trade piracy and allowing limited

reciprocal rights of search. Such a treaty would have gone far to isolate the United States in regard to the slave trade. Whether or not because of Cass' exertions, France withheld ratification. Four years later she abrogated an earlier treaty with Great Britain permitting reciprocal rights of search. France, however, acted more vigorously than the United States in preventing slavetrading by its own nationals.

pendence, declared its neutrality. In a proclamation of January 5, 1838, President Van Buren warned citizens of the United States against committing any act that would "compromise the neutrality of this Government."

Despite official American efforts to prevent the giving of aid to the Canadian insurgents, the American lake steamer *Caroline* was used for the running of arms and recruits from Buffalo to an insurgent encampment on Navy Island in the Niagara River. On the night of December 29, 1837, a party of Canadian militia crossed the river to Schlosser on the American shore (now in Niagara Falls, New York), boarded the *Caroline,* routed her crew, killing at least one American, set her on fire, and towed her out into the river, where she sank.

This flagrant invasion of American territorial waters the British sought to justify on the ground that the rebellion was a criminal conspiracy and hence that the *Caroline* had the character of a pirate craft and might, as such, be destroyed wherever found. This whole argument was denied by the United States, which demanded apology for the attack on the *Caroline* and asserted that the rebellion must be regarded as a war, conferring belligerent status on the participants.

The *Caroline* affair remained unsettled for nearly five years. Meanwhile, in 1840, a Canadian named Alexander McLeod, a deputy sheriff whose efforts to prevent gunrunning had made him enemies on the American side of the line,[17] was arrested in New York and indicted by a state grand jury on charges of having participated in the attack on the *Caroline* and hence of being guilty both of arson and of the "murder" of Amos Durfee, the one American known to have lost his life in the encounter.

Lord Palmerston, for the British government, demanded McLeod's release on the ground that any share he might have had in the affair was performed under orders from the British authorities in Canada and hence that he was not personally responsible for his act. Should New York State hang McLeod for murder, Palmerston threatened, Great Britain would fight to avenge his death.

Webster, who became Secretary of State in the midst of this crisis, accepted the British contention that McLeod could not be held responsible for acts committed under orders. But McLeod was in the hands of the sovereign state of New York, which insisted that the trial must go on. The New York Supreme Court refused to order his release but did direct a change of venue from Lockport, where feeling against McLeod was strong, to Utica, distant from the scene of the "crime." At the trial, McLeod produced an alibi, and state witnesses who were reported to have seen him in the *Caroline* affray failed to appear. McLeod was acquitted, and the crisis passed.[18]

To prevent the recurrence of such collisions between state and national authority, Webster suggested and Congress passed (1842) an act providing that, in the future, cases against persons acting under the authority of a foreign government could be removed from state to federal jurisdiction.

With McLeod safely restored to his family and fireside, Webster and Ashburton could turn calmly to a settlement of the *Caroline* case. The British government had dropped its contention that the *Caroline* was, in effect, a pirate ship and excused the admitted invasion of United States territory

---

[17]Alastair Watt, "The Case of Alexander McLeod," *Canadian Historical Review,* 12 (1931), 145–67, refutes the traditional story that McLeod's arrest followed his drunken boasting of his share in the *Caroline* raid.

[18]Alastair Watt contends that McLeod was not in the *Caroline* party but that his brother, Angus McLeod, was a member of it. William H. Seward, governor of New York, refused to halt the prosecution but assured Webster privately that McLeod had an alibi but that if nevertheless he should be convicted, he would be pardoned.

as an act of necessary self-defense. But although he claimed that "there were grounds of justification as strong as were ever presented in such cases," Lord Ashburton added that "no slight of the authority of the United States was intended" and expressed regret "that some explanation and apology for this occurrence was not immediately made." He hoped that "all feelings of resentment and ill will, resulting from these truly unfortunate events, may be buried in oblivion, and that they may be succeeded by those of harmony and friendship." This quasi-apology atoned for the violation of American sovereignty. Since the *Caroline* had confessedly been engaged in illegal activity, no reparation for her loss was demanded.

ADDITIONAL READINGS

BEMIS, SAMUEL F., The *Latin American Policy of the United States.* New York: Harcourt Brace Jovanovich, Inc., 1943.

CURTI, M. E., *The American Peace Crusade, 1815–1860.* Durham, N.C.: Duke University Press, 1929.

GILL, GEORGE G., "Edward Everett and the Northeastern Boundary Controversy," *New England Quarterly,* 42 (1969), 201–13.

JONES, HOWARD, *To the Webster-Ashburton Treaty.* Chapel Hill, N.C.: University of North Carolina Press, 1977.

LOGAN, J. A., JR., *No Transfer: An American Security Principle.* New Haven: Yale University Press, 1961.

MAY, ERNEST R., *The Making of the Monroe Doctrine.* Cambridge: Harvard University Press, 1975.

MERK, FREDERICK, *Fruits of Propaganda in the Tyler Administration.* Cambridge, Harvard University Press, 1971.

WHITAKER, A. P., *The United States and the Independence of Latin America, 1800–1830.* Baltimore: The Johns Hopkins Press, 1941.

6. Oregon, Texas, and the Diplomacy of Annexation—Part I

The Oregon country was, by the treaty of 1818, open to the use and occupation of both British subjects and American citizens. For many years this arrangement played into the hands of the British, for it was they who were on the ground, with the organization and experience needed to exploit the country. The North West Company, which had purchased Astor's post and trading goods in 1813, monopolized the trade of the Columbia River until the company itself was absorbed in 1821 by its rival, the Hudson's Bay Company. The Hudson's Bay Company tightened still further the monopoly of the Oregon trade, until there were few areas west of the Rockies in which traders from the United States dared compete with the great corporation. With the fur trade effectually closed to Americans, Oregon seemed for the moment to have little else to offer. Not only was it difficult of access, but Lewis and Clark and other early explorers had pictured it as mountainous, barren, and unattractive, and this remained the popular impression for many years.

The United States, nevertheless, maintained an interest in the Oregon country. A few men in Congress, notably Senator Thomas Hart Benton of Missouri, and Representative John Floyd of Virginia, repeatedly called attention to its future importance to the United States, Benton viewing it as part of a route to the commerce of the Orient. In diplomatic negotiations in the 1820s, the United States, while asserting the validity of its claim to the entire area, adhered to its offer of 1818, to accept the 49th parallel as the boundary. The British with equal consistency insisted upon the Columbia River, from its mouth to its intersection with the 49th parallel, as the dividing line. They were willing, however, to concede to the United States a detached fragment of territory, an enclave, on the Olympian peninsula, giving access to harbors on Puget Sound.[1] Since neither government was willing to back down, and since the ten-year period of joint occupation would terminate in 1828, the negotiators agreed simply to extend that arrangement indefinitely, with the proviso that either party might terminate it by giving twelve months' notice. A convention to that effect was signed on August 6, 1827.

Americans Colonize Oregon

Although some efforts had been made to settle the area, it was not until the early 1840s, however, that migration to Oregon

[1]The United States based its claim to Oregon upon (1) the principle of "contiguity," Oregon being regarded as a natural extension of Louisiana; (2) the explorations of Captain Gray and Lewis and Clark, and the settlement of Astoria; (3) the acquisition of Spanish rights under the treaty of 1819. The British denied the validity of (1) and (3). Any exclusive Spanish rights, they contended, had been canceled by the Anglo-Spanish Nootka Sound Convention of 1790. This also disposed of the claim derived from Louisiana, which in 1790 was a Spanish possession. They admitted that American explorations had some weight but asserted that their own explorations gave them claims as good as the American to the Columbia River and better to the north of it.

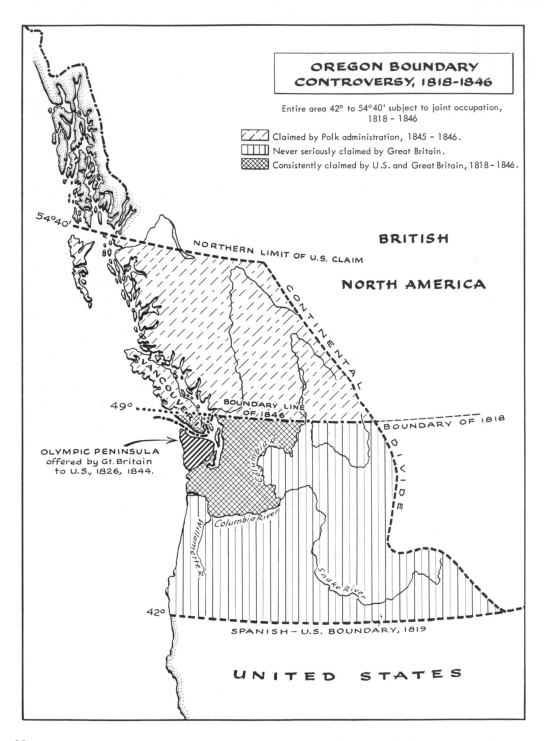

**OREGON BOUNDARY
CONTROVERSY, 1818-1846**

Entire area 42° to 54°40' subject to joint occupation,
1818 – 1846

Claimed by Polk administration, 1845 – 1846.

Never seriously claimed by Great Britain.

Consistently claimed by U.S. and Great Britain, 1818 – 1846.

54°40'

NORTHERN LIMIT OF U.S. CLAIM

BRITISH

NORTH AMERICA

CONTINENTAL

VANCOUVER

49°

BOUNDARY LINE
OF 1846

BOUNDARY OF 1818

OLYMPIC PENINSULA
offered by Gt. Britain
to U.S., 1826, 1844.

DIVIDE

Columbia R.

Columbia River

Willamette R.

Snake River

42°

SPANISH – U.S. BOUNDARY, 1819

UNITED STATES

reached significant proportions. The one hundred emigrants of 1842 swelled to nearly a thousand the following year. A census taken in 1845 showed 2,109 persons in Oregon, and the migration of that year brought nearly three thousand more. These settlers had need of some regular form of government and of some means of securing titles to the lands they occupied.

These purposes could have been accomplished through the establishment of either British or United States control, but since a great majority of the settlers had come from the United States, they hoped to see Oregon become American. Following the dispatch of several petitions to Congress asking that the United States assume control of the area, the settlers in July 1843 established an Oregon Provisional Government. In amending their organic act two years later, they stated in a preamble that its provisions were to apply only "until such time as the United States of America extend their jurisdiction over us." The next move was up to the Congress and the diplomats.

The Oregon Question in Politics

Neither Congress nor the diplomats had been entirely idle. In Congress, Senator Lewis F. Linn of Missouri had assumed the role of protagonist of American rights in Oregon. Beginning in 1838, he introduced a series of resolutions which, though they never became law, furnished a sort of program for advocates of American supremacy in Oregon. They asserted the American right to Oregon as beyond dispute, called for extension of American law over American citizens in Oregon and for military protection of the emigrant road, and proposed a grant of 640 acres of land to every white male inhabitant of Oregon who should cultivate and use the tract for five consecutive years. Explicitly or implicitly

they called upon the President to give the necessary twelve months' notice of the termination of joint occupation.

During the Webster-Ashburton negotiations of 1842, so successful in settling other matters in controversy, informal discussion revealed that Great Britain was still, as in 1827, unwilling to concede to the United States the territory between the Columbia River and the 49th parallel. President Tyler suggested a possible compromise solution. If Great Britain would induce Mexico to recognize the independence of Texas and to cede Upper California to the United States, Tyler would be willing to accept the Columbia River as a northern boundary. Lord Ashburton stated that he had no authority to enter into any such arrangement. Acceptance of the Columbia River line would, in fact, have brought practically all the Oregon settlers under American jurisdiction, concentrated as they were in the Willamette Valley. The idea of surrendering the region north of the Columbia was discouraged, however, by reports from United States naval officers of the formidable bar at the mouth of the Columbia and excellent harbors on Puget Sound. The subject of Oregon, at any rate, never reached the stage of formal negotiation between Webster and Ashburton.

Rumors that Webster had offered to surrender northern Oregon in exchange for California created an uproar in the western states. It is evident that Senator Linn's Oregon proposals had struck a popular note among the people of the upper Mississippi Valley. Western newspapers and "Oregon conventions" in western towns expressed indignation at the suggestion of surrendering Oregon to Great Britain. The climax of this western agitation came in July 1843, when some 120 delegates from six states met in Cincinnati. Declaiming that the right of the United States to the whole of Oregon from 42° to 54° 40′ north latitude was "unquestionable," the delegates asserted it to be "the imperative duty of the General

Government forthwith to extend the laws of the United States over said territory." The meeting directed that its declarations be sent to the President, to members of Congress, and to the governors of all the states.[2]

The United States was now on the eve of a presidential campaign in which the annexation of Texas was certain to figure as a major issue. To strategists of the Democratic party, the party of expansion, it appeared expedient to link the two expansionist issues, Texas and Oregon, so that western votes for Texas might be obtained in return for southern votes for Oregon. After nominating James K. Polk, himself an advocate of taking possession of Oregon, the Democratic National Convention at Baltimore accordingly adopted the following platform declaration:

> *Resolved,* That our title to the whole of the territory of Oregon is clear and unquestionable; that no portion of the same ought to be ceded to England or any other power; and that the re-occupation of Oregon and the re-annexation of Texas at the earliest practicable period are great American measures, which this convention recommends to the cordial support of the Democracy of the Union.

The syllable "re" prefixed to "occupation" and "annexation," was designed to allay charges of aggression by suggesting that the nation was merely about to resume possession of what had once and rightfully been hers.

President Polk Looks John Bull in the Eye

Texas was more of an issue in the campaign than was Oregon. The phrase "Fifty-four forty or fight," traditionally supposed to

have been a campaign slogan, was actually coined after the campaign, not during it.[3] But as there had been no serious Whig opposition to the Democratic pronouncement on Oregon, President Polk was within his rights in interpreting his electoral victory as a popular verdict in favor of a vigorous Oregon policy. Whether the verdict called for assertion of the claim to all of Oregon, even at the risk of war, or merely for a division at the 49th parallel, no one could be sure.

In his inaugural address Polk asserted, quoting the Democratic platform, that the American title to all of Oregon was "clear and unquestionable." But inasmuch as his predecessors had offered to settle for the 49th parallel, he instructed his Secretary of State, James Buchanan, to repeat the offer. When Richard Pakenham, the British minister, declined the proposal without even referring it to London, Polk directed Buchanan to withdraw it, intimating that the United States would stand upon its rights to the whole of Oregon. He was now determined to leave the next move to England and refused to permit Buchanan even to say that the United States would consider any proposal that the British government might care to make.

In his first annual message, December 2, 1845, Polk informed Congress of the course of the negotiations to that time. He was convinced, he said, "that the British pretensions of title could not be maintained to any portion of the Oregon territory upon any principle of public law recognized by nations." He had, nevertheless, made an offer of compromise. That offer, upon its being refused, had been withdrawn, "and our title to the whole Oregon territory asserted, and, as is believed, maintained by irrefragable facts and arguments." He recommended that Congress authorize him to give the required one year's notice of termination of joint occupation, that it ex-

---

[2]M. C. Jacobs, *Winning Oregon: A Study of an Expansionist Movement* (Caldwell, Idaho: Caxton Printers, 1938), pp. 124–39, 169–76.

[3]Edwin A. Miles, "'Fifty-four Forty or Fight'—An American Political Legend," *Mississippi Valley Historical Review,* 44 (September 1957), 291–309.

tend the laws and jurisdiction of the United States over American citizens in Oregon, that it likewise extend to Oregon the laws regulating trade with the Indians, that it provide for a line of fortified posts from the Missouri to the Rockies and for the establishment of an overland mail route to the Columbia.

> At the end of the year's notice [said Polk], . . . we shall have reached a period when the national rights in Oregon must either be abandoned or firmly maintained. That they cannot be abandoned without a sacrifice of both national honor and interest, is too clear to admit of doubt.
>
> Oregon is a part of the North American continent, to which, it is confidently affirmed, the title of the United States is the best now in existence. . . . The British proposition of compromise . . . can never for a moment, be entertained by the United States without an abandonment of their just and clear territorial rights, their own self-respect, and the national honor.

Polk appeared to have closed the door to compromise, and the appearance was heightened some weeks later when Buchanan, under instructions from Polk, declined successively two British offers of arbitration, the first proposing to arbitrate an equitable division of the territory; the second, to arbitrate the whole question of title. To a timorous congressman, who expressed alarm lest Polk's bold stand lead to war with Great Britain, the President replied that "the only way to treat John Bull was to look him straight in the eye; . . . that if Congress faultered [*sic*] or hesitated in their course, John Bull would immediately become arrogant and more grasping in his demands."

John Bull Will Not Be Bluffed

President Polk has usually been given credit for adhering to this firm policy of looking John Bull straight in the eye, maintaining the American right to the 54° 40′ line, until the British government retreated, offering the traditional American solution of division at the 49th parallel. This impression, though doubtless the one that Polk wished to leave, credits him with more firmness and less discretion than he really exercised. Within a few days after his annual message, he permitted Buchanan to inform United States Minister Louis McLane, in London, that the President would feel inclined to submit to the Senate any reasonable proposal that the British government might make. Six weeks later, McLane was told that he might say to Lord Aberdeen, British Foreign Secretary, that although the President "would accept nothing less than the whole territory unless the Senate should otherwise determine," he might submit to the Senate for its advice a British proposal for a division at the 49th parallel.

Meanwhile, McLane was reporting two alarming interviews with Lord Aberdeen. Queried as to the purpose of extensive military preparations under way in England, the Foreign Secretary had expressed the conviction that "the President had determined to discourage any new proposition on the basis of compromise, and to concede nothing of the extreme demand." If this was true, said Aberdeen, he would not oppose measures for the defense of Canada and even for "offensive operations." McLane understood that such measures would include "the immediate equipment of thirty sail of the line, besides steamers and other vessels of war."[4]

McLane's dispatch conveying this information created distinct alarm in Polk's official circle, as well it might. Relations

[4]J. W. Pratt, "James K. Polk and John Bull," *Canadian Historical Review*, 24 (1943), 341–49. That Polk's retreat from his claim to the 54° 40′ boundary was hastened by McLane's report of February 3, 1846, is questioned by Frederick Merk, *The Oregon Question: Essays in Anglo-American Diplomacy and Politics* (Cambridge: Harvard University Press, 1967), pp. 337–47, but is borne out in Charles Sellers, *James K. Polk, Continentalist, 1843–1846* (Princeton: Princeton University Press, 1966), pp. 380–83.

with Mexico had reached a state in which war was practically certain. A war with Mexico and Great Britain at the same time could easily prove disastrous to the United States. Polk had carried his game of bluff too far and was sensible enough to realize it. Though publicly preserving a bold front, he permitted Buchanan to rush off by the next steamer a note to McLane in which the Secretary made a further bid for a compromise settlement. The President, he said, had always been ready "to receive and to treat with the utmost respect" any compromise proposal from the British government. McLane had expressed the opinion that he could secure from Lord Aberdeen an offer of settlement at the 49th parallel with one of several alternative modifications. Such an offer, Buchanan assured McLane, the President would send to the Senate; and he added in a private note that the Senate would certainly approve it.

Moderation Wins in Congress

Thus the President, through Buchanan's note to McLane (February 26, 1846), abandoned the claim to 54° 40′ and secretly reverted to the 49th parallel boundary repeatedly proposed by his predecessors. However, there were still "Fifty-four forty" men in Congress. Early in February, the House of Representatives had passed a bill directing the President to give the year's notice of abrogation of the joint-occupation agreement, but only after prolonged wrangling did the Senate pass the measure. The Oregon debate in both houses was notable for two things: the popularization of the phrase "manifest destiny" and a dispute between spokesmen of the Northwest and the South over the proposed compromise on the boundary question.

The phrase "manifest destiny" had apparently been coined by one John L. O'Sullivan and first used in an editorial on the Texas question printed in the *Democratic*

Review for July and August 1845. It appeared again in the New York *Morning News* (also edited by O'Sullivan) of December 27, 1845, in an editorial setting forth the writer's conception of "the true title" to Oregon. The "true title," according to this argument, was not to be found in rights of discovery, exploration, settlement, and contiguity—strong though the American case was on these grounds—but rather in

the right to our manifest destiny to overspread and to possess the whole of the continent which Providence has given us for the development of the great experiment of liberty and federated self-government entrusted to us. . . . The God of nature and of nations has marked it for our own; and with His blessing we will firmly maintain the incontestable rights He has given, and fearlessly perform the high duties he has imposed.

Within a few days the phrase "manifest destiny" was being quoted in Congress by opponents as well as advocates of terminating joint occupation; and though the opposition quoted it only to ridicule it, expressing mock surprise that so important a principle of international law was not mentioned by Grotius or Vattel and branding it as "the robber's title," the supporters of President Polk's policy were not ashamed now to cite "destiny" as an argument for expelling the British from Oregon.[5]

The sectional controversy arose from the fact that southern leaders like Calhoun, having secured Texas,[6] now favored compromise with Great Britain on Oregon. Northwestern expansionists, for whom Democratic Senators Hannegan of Indiana and Allen of Ohio were leading spokesmen,

[5] J. W. Pratt, "The Origin of 'Manifest Destiny'," *American Historical Review,* 32 (1927), 795–98; "John L. O'Sullivan and Manifest Destiny," *New York History,* 45 (1933), 213–34.

[6] Texas was admitted to the Union December 29, 1845. A fine analysis of the Oregon debate in Congress is Merk, *The Oregon Question,* chap. 13.

asserted that the Democrats had agreed at the Baltimore Convention that the South should get Texas and the Northwest the whole of Oregon, up to 54°40′. They took literally the slogan "Fifty-four forty or fight," though professing to believe that England would not fight if the United States stood firm. Hannegan not only charged the South with "Punic faith" in deserting the West after realizing its own objectives; speaking of rumors that Polk would compromise with Great Britain, he declared that, in that event: "I shall hold him recreant to the principles which he professed, recreant to the trust which he accepted, recreant to the generous confidence which a majority of the people reposed in him."

Southern Democratic senators, on the other hand, joined with Whigs to pave the way for compromise. Whig senators shared the alarm of business and commercial groups at the possibility of a costly war with England. Calhoun's advocacy of compromise received warm praise in New York and New England. Daniel Webster, who set a low value upon Oregon and a high value upon peace with England, was working for compromise both in the Senate and out. The aged Albert Gallatin wrote a seventy-five page argument for postponement of the Oregon crises, including an estimate of "War Expenses" covering over twenty pages. An anonymous pamphlet published in Philadelphia declared that "monied men, for the most part, think very unfavorably of belligerent measures for the acquisition of Oregon" and declared that such men would not deem it prudent to invest money in government bonds "issued for the purpose of asserting a claim to worse than useless territory on the coast of the Pacific."[7]

Under such influences, the curt resolu-

[7]Albert Gallatin, *The Oregon Question* (New York: Bartlett & Welford, 1846); *Oregon. The Cost and the Consequences*, by "a Disciple of the Washington School" (Philadelphia: J. C. Clark's Bookstore, 1846).

tion passed by the House of Representatives was softened in the Senate. As amended and finally passed by both houses (April 23, 1846), it authorized the President to give the year's notice instead of directing him to do so. It made no mention of "clear and unquestionable" rights to all of Oregon but expressed a hope for "a speedy and amicable adjustment" of "the respective claims of the United States and Great Britain." Its adoption by the Senate by a vote of 40 to 14 gave assurance that the Senate would not reject a compromise settlement.

The Controversy Is Settled

Five days after passage of the resolution, Buchanan forwarded the formal notice to McLane for transmission to the British government. In doing so he reiterated the President's willingness to consider any suitable proposal made by Great Britain and his desire to preserve amicable relations.

Lord Aberdeen had awaited final congressional action upon the resolution before submitting the new British offer. Aberdeen, personally, had long been ready to accept the 49th parallel as a boundary. He attached little value to the disputed territory—to the whole of Oregon, in fact. He had, naturally, resented Polk's inaugural declaration that the American title to Oregon was "clear and unquestionable" and had replied, in a speech in the House of Lords, that England also possessed rights in Oregon which were "clear and unquestionable" and which, he added, "by the blessing of God, and with your support, . . . we are fully prepared to maintain." Undoubtedly the British government would have met with force any American attempt to occupy all of Oregon, but Aberdeen, at least, was ready to accept any compromise that could be reconciled with the national honor.

Aberdeen's real problem, in abandoning the British claim to the Columbia boundary

and proposing the line that had been repeatedly offered by the United States and
as often rejected by Great Britain, was to
reconcile British opinion to the retreat. He
must convince the British public that no
vital British interests were being surrendered, and he must guard the cabinet, the
Peel ministry, which had but a slender majority in Parliament, against a Liberal attack
upon their conciliatory policy.

In the first undertaking, Aberdeen was
assisted by events in Oregon itself. In past
negotiations, the chief reason for insisting
upon the Columbia River boundary had
been the interest of the Hudson's Bay
Company in that river and its watershed. In
1845, however, because of the decline of
the fur trade on the Columbia and growing
friction between the company's establishment at Fort Vancouver and the American
settlers south of the river, the company had
moved its headquarters from Fort Vancouver to Vancouver Island, thus virtually
abandoning the river. It was now possible,
therefore, for Lord Aberdeen and his supporters to argue that the Columbia River
boundary was not worth contending for.[8]

At home, Aberdeen and his associates
were able to win over a large section of the
British press to advocacy of compromise,
and leaders of the Liberal party, now in
opposition, prevailed upon the chauvinistic
Viscount Palmerston, their spokesman in
foreign affairs, to abstain from attack upon
the proposed Oregon settlement. The
prospect, furthermore, of an enlarged
trade with the United States, founded upon
the imminent repeal of the Corn Laws in
Great Britain and the low-tariff policy of
the Polk Administration, contributed to the

desire for a friendly settlement of the Oregon question; and the work of the peace
societies on both sides of the Atlantic, which
were active in petitioning both governments and in promoting "friendly addresses" between English and American cities,
should not be overlooked. All in all, by the
spring of 1846, Aberdeen was sure of his
ground in England and could make a compromise proposal with assurance of its receiving British approval.

Aberdeen's offer, in the form of a treaty,
was received in Washington on June 6. It
proposed to draw the boundary line along
the 49th parallel from the Rocky Mountains to the channel separating Vancouver
Island from the mainland and thence
through the channel around the south end
of the island, leaving the entire island to the
British. Other clauses recognized and
safeguarded the lawfully acquired property rights, both north and south of the
Columbia, of the Hudson's Bay Company
and other British corporations and subjects. These provisions were acceptable to
Polk. He objected, however, to a provision
that navigation of the Columbia from the
boundary line to its mouth should be "free
and open to the Hudson's Bay Company,
and to all British subjects trading with the
same." In fact, he had said categorically that
he would not accept such a provision. But
the situation did not admit of delay. War
with Mexico had begun, making a settlement with England imperative. In England, the Peel ministry, with Aberdeen as
Foreign Secretary, retained power by a
precarious hold, and Lord Aberdeen's successor was likely to be less compliant than
he. On the advice of his cabinet, therefore,
Polk resolved to send the treaty project to
the Senate as it stood and to give or withhold his sanction depending upon the Senate's advice. Declaring, with dubious ve-
racity, that the opinions expressed in his
December message remained unchanged,
Polk "passed the buck" to the Senate.

Two days later, on June 12th, the Senate

---

[8]Merk, *The Oregon Question,* chap. 8. In promoting,
through their obstreperous behavior, the company's
abandonment of Fort Vancouver, the pioneers made a
contribution of a sort to American acquisition of the
territory between the Columbia River and the 49th
parallel. Certainly they had not "occupied" the disputed territory, for not more than thirty-one Americans had settled north of the Columbia by 1846.

voted, 38 to 12, to advise acceptance of the British proposal without change. The treaty was formally signed on June 15, and on June 18 the Senate gave its advice and consent for ratification by a vote of 41 to 14. The treaty was proclaimed on August 5, 1846. The long controversy was settled, apparently to the satisfaction of nearly everyone except the little group of "Fifty-four forty" men from the Old Northwest.

Texas

Some twenty years before the westward movement of population reached Oregon, it had begun to flow into Texas. Here there were no formidable physical barriers to migration, and the Spanish government, which had long prohibited the entry of Americans into Texas, modified that policy in 1821. In that year it granted to Connecticut-born Moses Austin, who had lived for a while under Spanish rule in upper Louisiana, permission to settle three hundred Louisiana families in Texas. The new policy was continued by the government of Mexico, which became independent soon thereafter. Moses Austin died before he could carry out his plan, and his son, Stephen F. Austin, assumed charge of the enterprise.

Under contracts with the Mexican authorities, Austin and other empresarios (contractors) received permission to settle specified numbers of families in the central portion of Texas. Mexican federal and state regulations made the acquisition of land easy and at a price far below that of public land in the United States. The population of Texas grew rapidly. Geographical location, soil, climate, the easy evasion of Mexican laws against slavery, all made Texas more attractive to the South than to other sections of the United States. By 1835 the population of Texas approximated thirty thousand, nearly all from the United States

and the great majority from the slave states of the South.

In the meantime, the United States had sounded out the Mexican government as to its willingness to part with Texas. John Quincy Adams, in his negotiations with Spain, had surrendered the claim to Texas with reluctance, and the surrender had been criticized in the Southwest. As President, Adams permitted Joel R. Poinsett, first United States minister to Mexico, to suggest that Mexico celebrate her independence by making a new boundary treaty instead of accepting that made by Spain; but when the Mexican government showed no willingness to give up Texas or any part of it, Poinsett dropped the subject. A treaty signed in 1828, but not ratified until four years later, simply confirmed the boundary agreed upon between the United States and Spain in 1819. Andrew Jackson, when he became President, replaced Pointsett with Anthony Butler. "Vain, ignorant, ill-tempered, and corrupt,"[9] Butler was a disgrace to the diplomatic service. His fruitless efforts to secure Texas by bribing Mexican officials led tardily to his recall in 1835.

Texans Win Their Independence

Alarmed by such attempts as Butler's and awake to the possibility that Texas might be lost through revolution by its American-born inhabitants (as West Florida had been lost by Spain in 1810–1811), the Mexican government tried too late to check the flow of immigrants or to subject them to military control. Such measures produced resentment without achieving their purpose. General Antonio Lopez de Santa Anna, elected President of Mexico in 1833, undertook a more drastic solution of the Texas problem. Abolishing the federal constitu-

[9]G. L. Rives, *The United States and Mexico, 1821–1848,* 2 vols. (New York: Charles Scribner's Sons, 1913), 1: 235–36.

tion, he transformed Mexico into a centralized state, in which the people of Texas stood to lose any vestige of local autonomy. The Texan response was rebellion, a declaration of independence (March 2, 1836), and the crushing defeat and capture of Santa Anna at the battle of San Jacinto (April 21, 1836). The remnant of Santa Anna's invading army retreated beyond the Rio Grande, and Texas had won *de facto* independence. Sam Houston, who had commanded the Texan army at San Jacinto, was rewarded for his victory by election to the presidency of the Republic of Texas.

The United States and the Texan Revolution

The Texans' fight for life against Santa Anna evoked widespread sympathy and material support from the United States. "Texas meetings" were held in cities ranging from New Orleans to Boston. Money and supplies were sent to Texas by sea, and hundreds of volunteers from the United States swelled the ranks of Houston's army. President Jackson, despite sympathy with the Texans and especially with Sam Houston, an old friend and comrade in arms, issued the appropriate orders for the enforcement of the neutrality laws. That these orders were not rigorously enforced was the result of strong pro-Texas feeling in the Southwest, which infected even federal district attorneys and United States army officers. The Mexican minister in Washington lodged protest after protest with the State Department against American activities in support of Texas and finally became so incensed that he withdrew from the capital.

Meanwhile both Congress and the President were weighing the question of recognition. Proposals for such action were heard in Congress as early as April 1836. The news of San Jacinto greatly

strengthened the case for recognition. But aside from caution in recognizing a government that had not yet demonstrated a capacity to maintain itself, there was another obstacle in the rising antislavery sentiment of the North. Abolitionists opposed recognition as a step toward annexation. Once annexed, they feared, Texas might be subdivided into four or five new slave states. Despite such opposition—which found a powerful spokesman in ex-President John Quincy Adams, now a representative from Massachusetts—Congress and the President moved step by step toward recognition. On March 3, 1837, just before relinquishing the presidency, Jackson nominated a chargé d'affaires for Texas, and formal diplomatic relations were established in the following July.

But annexation was another matter. It was formally proposed by the Texan minister in August 1837 and was warmly favored by southern leaders. But Martin Van Buren's administration, already staggering under the burden of nationwide financial panic and economic depression, had no wish to take on a fight with the antislavery forces. The Texan offer of annexation was politely declined. Texas thereupon withdrew the proposal, and from 1838 to 1842 talk of annexation subsided in both countries.

The Texas Question in Party Politics

By 1842 annexation was taking on new attractiveness on both sides of the border. Sam Houston, again elected to the presidency after three years out of office, found his government facing a heavy debt, an empty treasury, and renewed hostilities with Mexico. He saw two possible avenues of escape from these difficulties: annexation by the United States or continued independence under British protection. When he approached Washington on the possibility of annexation, he found the Virginian President, John Tyler, personally sympathetic but unable to act because of the opposition of his Secretary of State, Daniel Webster. But Webster resigned in May 1843, and his successor, Abel P. Upshur, like Tyler a Virginian, shared Tyler's desire to bring Texas into the Union.

The prospect that Texas might turn to Britain for protection, and the growth of British interest and influence in the "Lone Star Republic" had, in fact, aroused serious concern in all sections of the United States. It was the aim of Lord Aberdeen, British Foreign Secretary, to keep Texas independent, a market for British manufacturers, and a source of cotton for British mills. To remove the appeal of annexation by the United States, he sought to induce Mexico to recognize Texan independence. If, at the same time, Texas could be induced to follow Britain's example and abolish slavery, so much the better.

No part of this program was secret, and each part of it created alarm in the United States. To the South it meant danger to slavery as well as competition with the South's principal staple. To the commercial North it meant diversion of Texan trade from the United States into other hands—a diversion that was indeed already a reality. The surest cure for all these dangers was annexation. Annexation would also be profitable to an unknown number of speculators who held certificates of the Texas debt and scrip entitling them to Texas lands.

North as well as South, then, had begun to see advantages in the acquisition of Texas. When Secretary Upshur informed Houston in September 1843 that the administration had changed its policy and would be glad to conclude a treaty of annexation, he felt safe in assuring the Texan that such a treaty would certainly receive the Senate's approval.

Houston consented. Negotiations were interrupted by the death of Upshur but

were resumed under his successor, John C. Calhoun, and on April 12, 1844, an annexation treaty was signed. Texas was to be annexed to the United States as one of its territories, surrendering its public lands to the United States, which in turn would assume the Texan public debt to an amount not exceeding ten million dollars.

Had the treaty been acted upon promptly by the Senate, it would perhaps have received the better than two-thirds majority that had been indicated by a poll in January. The Senate, however, deferred action until after the party nominating conventions in May, and there events took a turn that sealed the treaty's fate. On the eve of the conventions the leading contenders for the nominations, Martin Van Buren, Democrat, and Henry Clay, Whig, published letters in which both opposed the immediate annexation of Texas, though leaving the door open to its future accomplishment. True to expectations, the Whig Convention nominated Clay and thereby committed the party against immediate annexation. The Democrats, on the other hand, unwilling to accept Van Buren's anti-Texas stand, set him aside and nominated the comparatively little known James K. Polk, a thorough-going expansionist. The Democrats also wrote into their platform a plank declaring for "the re-annexation of Texas and the re-occupation of Oregon." By both their candidate and their platform, the Democrats labeled themselves the party of expansion.

The effect of these party maneuvers was seen when the Senate, on June 8, 1844, voted on the Texas treaty. In view of Clay's stand against annexation, Whig senators could hardly support the treaty even if they so desired. The Van Buren Democrats, furthermore, were offended at the defeat of their hero and for the time being were unwilling to vote for a policy that he opposed. Thus party and factional politics had more weight than conviction in determining votes on the treaty. Of twenty-nine

Whig senators, all but one (Henderson of Mississippi) voted No, and they were joined by seven of the twenty-four Democrats, while one Democratic senator did not vote. Thus, instead of the two-thirds vote for ratification predicted by Upshur in January, the vote stood thirty-five to sixteen against it.[10]

Whether defeat of the treaty disposed finally of Texan annexation, as some observers believed, or whether, as President Tyler suggested, there might be other means of accomplishing the same objective was not immediately apparent. At any rate, nothing further could be done about it until the country had spoken in the presidential election. When the nation did speak, however, it was not in a clear-cut manner. In a hotly-contested election, Polk received 170 electoral votes, carrying 15 of the 26 states. The popular vote was much closer—Polk, 1,337,243 vs. Clay, 1,299,068. Whatever the student of history may think of the meaning of the election, President Tyler, the first President who failed to run for a second term, admitted no doubt. As he told Congress in his annual message, it appeared to him that both the people (through the popular vote) and the states (through the electoral vote) had decided. "A controlling majority of the people," he asserted, "and a large majority of the States, have declared in favor of immediate annexation." He recommended, therefore, that Congress should embody the terms of the

late treaty in an act or joint resolution, "to be perfected and made binding on the two countries, when adopted in like manner by the government of Texas."

Invitation by Joint Resolution

The obvious advantage of action by joint resolution instead of treaty was that a resolution could be passed by a majority vote in each house of Congress as compared with the two-thirds vote in the Senate required for a treaty. A joint resolution providing for admission of Texas to the Union as a state was passed by the House of Representatives on January 25, 1845. The change from the territorial status proposed by the treaty to that of statehood was designed to meet a constitutional point. For authority to acquire territory by joint resolution, the annexationists relied upon the constitutional provision that "new States may be admitted by the Congress into this Union."

In the Senate the Whig-dominated Committee on Foreign Relations reported against the resolution on the ground that foreign territory could be acquired only by treaty. While the Senate debated the committee's report, public opinion was expressing itself through the press, petitions to Congress, and resolutions of state legislatures. A preponderance of such sentiment, especially in the South and West, appears to have favored immediate annexation. Even in New England, the legislatures of Maine and New Hampshire passed annexationist resolutions. Goaded by instructions from the Missouri legislature, Senator Thomas H. Benton, who had opposed Tyler's treaty as likely to lead to war with Mexico, introduced a substitute for the House resolution, providing for admission of Texas upon terms to be agreed on by negotiation with Texas instead of terms defined unilaterally by the United States, as in the House measure.

---

[10]Some northern votes for the treaty may also have been lost by publication of a note from Calhoun to the British minister in which he defended the treaty as necessitated by British encouragement of emancipation in Texas. He had added a long argument in defense of slavery and had cited facts and figures purporting to show the ill effects of freedom upon the health, morals, and general well-being of the Negro. This communication naturally antagonized northern opinion by stamping annexation as a proslavery measure. Not intended for publication, it had been leaked to the press by an antislavery senator. C. M. Wiltse, *John C. Calhoun, Sectionalist, 1844–1850* (Indianapolis: The Bobbs-Merrill Company, Inc., 1951), pp. 170–71.

In order to secure Benton's vote and the votes of other wavering senators, the Democratic managers attached Benton's bill to the House resolution as an alternative, giving the President the authority either to invite Texas into the Union on the House terms or to negotiate an agreement as Benton proposed. Upon assurances, as Benton later claimed, that Tyler would leave the choice of alternatives to Polk and that Polk would elect negotiation under Benton's plan, Benton and several other senators who had opposed the House resolution now voted for it in its amended form, and at a night session on February 27, 1845, the amended resolution passed the Senate by a vote of 27 to 25, the majority comprising all Democratic senators and three southern Whigs. The House promptly passed the amended measure, and President Tyler signed it on March 1, 1845.

Tyler and Calhoun resolved to act in the short time remaining before the change in administration, and on March 3, Calhoun sent instructions to A. J. Donelson, the American chargé d'affaires for Texas, who was waiting in New Orleans, to invite Texas to enter the Union under the terms of the House resolution. Thus they discarded Benton's plan, much to the chagrin of that senator, and Polk, after a few days of apparent hesitation, decided to let Donelson proceed under Calhoun's instructions.

Texas Accepts Annexation

Under the terms thus offered, Texas was invited to become a state in the Union, comprising "the territory properly included within, and rightfully belonging to the republic of Texas." All questions of the state's boundaries were to be left to negotiation between the government of the United States and "other governments." Texas was to cede to the United States its public buildings, ports, harbors, fortifications, and other means of defense, but it was to retain its public lands and to remain responsible for its debts; the latter should never become a charge upon the United States. A state constitution, republican in form, must be submitted to Congress on or before January 1, 1846. Additional states, not over four in number, might, with the consent of Texas, be formed out of her territory. In any such states lying north of 36° 30′, the Missouri Compromise line, slavery was to be prohibited; states south of that line might be admitted with or without slavery, as the people thereof should determine.

Congress had acted. It was now for Texas to decide whether to accept annexation on the terms offered. There much depended upon Sam Houston. His term as President ended in December 1844, when he was succeeded by Anson Jones, but his influence outlived his term in office. Houston had given his support to the treaty of annexation, but he had served notice that if Texas were again rejected by the United States, she would *"remain forever separate,"* and that the United States must expect that "she would seek some other friend." Texas had been again rejected, and Houston's attitude remained problematical.

Tyler and Calhoun, while they remained in office, did everything they could to conciliate Houston. In particular they sought to make use of Andrew Jackson's well known influence over the Texan. In August 1844, they had sent to Texas as chargé d'affaires Andrew Jackson Donelson, nephew and close friend of the old hero of the Hermitage. Through letters to both Houston and Donelson, Jackson sought to play upon whatever remained of Houston's loyalty to the United States in order to save him from falling under British influence. "How much more honorable," Jackson wrote, ". . . to be a senator representing a free and enlightened people, than the president of a people, a mere colony of England, and fighting against the United

States that gave them birth, . . .'' While Jackson thus hinted at a senatorship for this friend if Texas were annexed, other correspondents suggested that even the presidency of the United States might be within his reach.

Houston remained coy to such hints of preferment in the United States. In view of the uncertain temper of Congress, both he and Anson Jones would have been negligent of the true interests of Texas had they entirely closed the door upon a career of independence under British protection. At the same time, however, they left open the door to annexation. In his valedictory message to the Texan Congress (December 9, 1844), Houston pictured in glowing terms the future that might lie before an independent Texas, but at the same time spoke sympathetically of a possible union with "the beloved land from which we have sprung—the land of the broad stripes and bright stars"; and a few days later he wrote Jackson that if the United States should now make a proper offer of annexation, he would "not interpose any individual obstacle to its consummation."

Such was the situation in Texas when Congress passed the joint resolution, and Donelson hastened back to Texas from New Orleans with the proposal made by Tyler and confirmed by Polk. Donelson found Houston at first seriously dissatisfied with the terms of the offer and disposed to insist upon negotiating under Benton's plan; but President Anson Jones, although agreeing with Houston that the United States should have offered better terms, assured Donelson that he would submit the proposal of the Congress to the people of Texas and that a special session of Congress for that purpose would be called to meet on June 16.[11] Weeks before that date, Houston

had been won over to support of annexation upon the terms offered.

The British government made a final effort to prevent annexation.[12] In the spring of 1845, Captain Charles Elliot, British chargé d'affaires in Texas, visited the Mexican capital, where he persuaded the Mexican government to agree to a treaty by which Mexico would recognize the independence of Texas in return for a promise by Texas never to annex herself to another power, the question of boundary being left for future adjustment. Elliot returned to Texas with this document shortly before

---

Jones, *Memoranda and Official Correspondence Relating to the Republic of Texas, Its History and Annexation* (New York: Appleton-Century-Crofts, 1859), pp. 44, 58, 80–81. His statements, about both himself and Houston, need to be discounted. See Herbert Gambrell, *Anson Jones, The Last President of Texas* (Garden City: Doubleday & Company, Inc., 1948). Jones also asserted (pp. 46–51) that agents of President Polk tried to instigate him to renew hostilities with Mexico "so that, when Texas was finally brought into the Union, *she might bring a war with her.*" Some revisionist historians have seen in this incident evidence of a scheme by Polk to bring on a war with Mexico that would enable him to seize California (as actually happened a year later). See R. R. Stenberg, "The Failure of Polk's War Intrigue of 1845," *Pacific Historical Review,* 4 (March 1935), 39–69; G. W. Price, *Origins of the War with Mexico: The Polk-Stockton Intrigue* (Austin: University of Texas Press, 1967). There is no doubt that such agents, notably Commodore Robert F. Stockton of the Navy, tried to persuade Jones to permit the commander of the Texas militia to seek a confrontation with Mexican troops on the Rio Grande, but the contention that they were doing Polk's bidding in that respect lacks adequate proof and is contradicted by other known facts of Polk's policy at this time. See Charles Sellers, *James K. Polk, Continentalist, 1843–1846* (Princeton: Princeton University Press, 1966), pp. 222–26.

[12]When the treaty of annexation was published in the spring of 1844, Lord Aberdeen had proposed an ambitious plan to preserve Texan independence. His scheme was what he called a "diplomatic act" by which Great Britain and France should join with Mexico and Texas in guaranteeing the independence of Texas and the boundaries of Mexico. France was interested, but the plan was dropped on the advice of the British and French ministers in Washington. Any such European intervention, they warned, was certain to heighten the expansionist fever in Washington and to insure the election of Polk, the expansionist candidate.

---

[11]Jones, in later years, claimed to have been "the architect" of annexation. He favored annexation, so he said, when Houston opposed it, and he took credit for the various measures that aroused and kept alive annexation sentiment in the United States. Anson

the Texan Congress met in June, and Jones laid before Congress both the proposed treaty with Mexico and the proposal of annexation from the United States. Jones hoped, with the Mexican offer in hand, to be able to bargain for better terms from the United States, but Texan sentiment for annexation had become so overwhelming that the Texan Congress threw away the opportunity. By unanimous vote the Texan Senate rejected the treaty with Mexico, and both houses of Congress voted without dissent for annexation upon the terms offered. On July 4, a special convention confirmed this choice, and the convention's action, together with the state constitution that it had prepared, was ratified by popular vote in October. The final resolution admitting Texas as a state of the Union was passed by the American Congress and signed by President Polk on December 29, 1845.

ADDITIONAL READINGS

ADAMS, E. D., *British Interests and Activities in Texas, 1838–1846.* Baltimore: The Johns Hopkins Press, 1910.

GRAEBNER, NORMAN A., *Empire on the Pacific: A Study in American Continental Expansionism.* New York: The Ronald Press Company, 1955.

MERK, FREDERICK, *The Monroe Doctrine and American Expansionism.* New York: Alfred A. Knopf, Inc., 1966.

PLETCHER, DAVID M., *The Diplomacy of Annexation: Texas, Oregon, and the Mexican War.* Columbia, Mo.: University of Missouri Press, 1973.

7. War and Peace with Mexico and the Diplomacy of Annexation—Part II

The acquisition of Texas and of a clear title to Oregon south of the 49th parallel was quickly followed by the war with Mexico of 1846–1848 and the resulting addition of a still more notable slice of territory to the American domain. By the treaty that put an end to that two-year struggle, the United States secured the Rio Grande boundary, Upper California, and the vast intermediate region known as New Mexico. In three years, 1845–1848, the area of the United States had grown by over 1,200,000 square miles, an increase of more than 66 percent. It was no wonder that expansionist-minded Americans proclaimed their faith in Manifest Destiny, and, as later embodied in the writings of Theodore Roosevelt and others, an heroic view of American expansionism.[1]

Subjects of Contention with Mexico

The complicated factors that gave rise to the war with Mexico may be thus summarized: (1) Mexican resentment over the annexation of Texas by the United States, (2) a dispute as to what in reality constituted the southwestern boundary of Texas, (3) the failure of Mexico to pay certain damage claims of citizens of the United States, (4) President Polk's anxiety to acquire California for the United States. These factors interacted upon one another in a manner adverse to a maintenance of peaceful relations, Mexico's resentment over the annexation of Texas proved an insuperable obstacle to amicable negotiation over claims and boundary, and the glitter of California in the eyes of James K. Polk—for its shining harbors, not its still unknown golden treasure[2]—probably made him less forbearing toward Mexico on other points than he might otherwise have been.

From the time in Tyler's administration when the annexation of Texas was first seriously contemplated, Mexico had repeatedly served notice that it would regard such action on the part of the United States as a *casus belli*. Such warnings had been delivered in the summer of 1843 and the spring of 1844. Calhoun, after signing his abortive treaty of annexation in April 1844, had sent a special messenger to Mexico in a fruitless effort to mollify the Mexican government, which refused to negotiate on the

---

[1] The latest, most extensive treatment of this subject is found in David M. Pletcher, *The Diplomacy of Annexation: Texas, Oregon, and the Mexican War* (Columbia, Mo.: University of Missouri Press, 1973).

[2] N. A. Graebner, *Empire on the Pacific: A Study in American Continental Expansion* (New York: The Ronald Press Company, 1955), emphasizes commercial interest in Pacific harbors as a major factor in the expansionism of the 1840's.

subject but as yet maintained diplomatic relations with Washington. When, however, in March 1845, the joint resolution of annexation was passed by Congress and signed by President Tyler, the Mexican minister in Washington asked for his passport and shortly thereafter took his departure from the United States. As the Mexican government at the same time terminated relations with the United States minister, all formal diplomatic intercourse ceased. Mexico, however, fresh from one revolution and with another on the horizon,[3] was in no condition to inaugurate a war with the United States. It seems probable that Mexico would eventually have acquiesced in the accomplished fact of annexation had that been the sole subject of contention.

The dispute over annexation, however, was further embittered by a controversy over just what had been annexed. The United States, convinced of the propriety of its annexing Texas, had adopted the Texan claim that its boundary was the Rio Grande. Mexico, indignant that annexation had occurred at all, further insisted that Texas had never extended west or south of the River Nueces. The boundary question was of a kind that should have been susceptible of friendly adjustment had both sides been willing to await an examination and negotiation. An impartial examination would probably have sustained the Mexican contention. Texas, under Spanish and Mexican rule, it seems well established, had never extended beyond the Nueces. The

Texan claim to the Rio Grande boundary rested upon an early act of the Texan Congress, which could have no force against Mexico, and upon the fact that Santa Anna's armies, after San Jacinto, had retired beyond the Rio Grande. Thereafter, the land between the rivers had not been effectively occupied or controlled by either party to the dispute. The Texans had a settlement at Corpus Christi, south of the Nueces at its mouth; the Mexicans had a few scattered ranches and villages just north of the Rio Grande. Otherwise the strip was virtually no man's land. Texas had thus done little or nothing through *de facto* occupation to counter Mexico's historic claim. The claim of the United States was as strong as that of Texas, and no stronger. The joint resolution of annexation had merely provided that the boundaries of Texas should be subject to the adjustment between the United States and other powers. American diplomats, indeed, now revived the claim that the Rio Grande had been the ancient boundary of Louisiana, but since the United States had definitely given up that claim by the treaty of 1819, it is difficult to see what bearing it had upon the question of the limits of Texas.

It seems regrettable, in retrospect, that the United States and Mexico did not agree to abstain from any attempt to occupy the disputed area until a settlement could be reached. On the Mexican side, however, such an agreement would have meant acquiescence in the annexation of Texas proper, and for this, Mexico was not ready. President Polk, on the other hand, was determined to uphold the Texan claim to the Rio Grande boundary. He was willing to recognize merit in the Mexican contention to the extent of cancelling several millions of dollars of damage claims against Mexico in return for its surrender but was not willing, in the meantime, to forgo occupation of the disputed territory.

In July 1845, as soon as the Texan legislature and convention had voted for annex-

---

[3]Santa Anna, after his defeat and capture at San Jacinto had returned to Mexico in 1837. In the following year he had lost a leg but won additional military distinction in defending Vera Cruz against a French attack. From 1841 until November 1844, he was again President of Mexico but was then overthrown and banished. Herrera was then President for a brief period. In December 1845, he was overthrown by General Paredes, the same military chieftain who had engineered the revolution against Santa Anna thirteen months before.

ation, Brigadier General Zachary Taylor, with some 3,900 United States troops, was ordered from the Sabine into Texas to defend it against an anticipated Mexican invasion. He was instructed to take up a position south of the Nueces and as near the Rio Grande "as prudence will dictate," but not to disturb any posts occupied by Mexican troops or Mexican settlements not under Texan jurisdiction. The obvious intent of these instructions was, while asserting title to the disputed territory, to avoid the initiative in any clash with Mexican forces. Exercising the discretion allowed him, Taylor in August stationed his army at Corpus Christi at the mouth of the Nueces, at a prudent distance from the Rio Grande. There he remained until March 1846.

A third subject of dispute with Mexico was the latter's failure to settle claims of American citizens to the amount of some millions of dollars. These claims had originated in supplies purchased on credit by the Mexican government and never paid for and in damages to persons and property of United States citizens suffered during revolutionary disorders in Mexico. A treaty of 1839 had set up a mixed claims commission that had considered claims of over eight million dollars and made awards of slightly over two millions. Additional claims of over three millions had been submitted too late for adjudication by the commission. The two millions adjudicated, Mexico had agreed to pay in twenty installments over a five-year period; she had paid three installments, together with arrears of interest to April 30, 1843, and then had suspended payments. Since the Mexican treasury was chronically empty, there was little hope that payments in money would be resumed at any early date, if ever. But an alternative mode of settlement was possible. Following the precedents of the Louisiana and Florida transactions, Polk was willing to accept a boundary settlement in lieu of money. Specifically, if Mexico would recognize the annexation of Texas

with the Rio Grande boundary, Polk would release Mexico from all monetary claims of American citizens, which would then be settled out of the treasury of the United States. But Polk wished to carry the settlement still further. If Mexico would yield additional territory, dearly coveted by Polk, the President stood ready to fill the bare Mexican treasury with good American dollars.

Polk's California Policy

In a conversation with George Bancroft, his Secretary of the Navy, soon after taking office, Polk remarked that two of the "great measures" of his administration would be "the settlement of the Oregon boundary question" and "the acquisition of California."[4] His success in settling the Oregon question has been described. In the acquisition of California he was likewise successful, but not without bloodshed.

California, the youngest of Spain's colonial enterprises in America, had received its first Spanish settlers at the time of the American Revolution. The area of effective Spanish, and later Mexican, control never extended farther north than the shores of San Francisco Bay or farther inland than the coastal area. The great inland valleys of the Sacramento and San Joaquin Rivers

[4]James Schouler, *History of the United States of America under the Constitution,* revised edition, 7 vols. (New York: Dodd, Mead & Co., 1894–1913), 4:498. The paging differs slightly in different printings of this work. The source of the quotation is a letter from Bancroft to Schouler of February 1887. Schouler says the conversation between Polk and Bancroft is "still preserved." This may mean that Bancroft had preserved a contemporary memorandum of the conversation. If he relied upon his memory only, after forty-two years, we should of course question the accuracy of his statement. Polk mentioned "four great measures," of which the other two were "a reduction of the tariff" and "the independent treasury." Since all four were realized, Polk deserves to rank as one of our most successful presidents—if success is to be measured by having a definite program and carrying it out.

remained practically untouched until the coming of the Americans. Aside from the presidios and Franciscan missions, Spanish activities consisted principally of sheep and cattle ranching. The agricultural possibilities and mineral wealth of California were unexploited and almost undreamed of, and as late as 1846, the entire population of Spanish descent probably did not exceed seven thousand persons.

The first visitors to California from the United States came by sea, but in the 1820's, American fur traders were beginning to make their way overland, and soon there was a sparse population of drifting "mountain men" living among the Indians in the interior. The first party of bona fide homeseekers crossed the mountains in 1841, and thereafter there was a steady trickle of immigrants, who followed the Oregon Trail to Fort Hall in modern Idaho, and then turned southwest to cross the Great Basin and the Sierras.

Two reports of official explorations, both published in 1845, contributed to the growing interest in California. Lieutenant Charles Wilkes, commander of a naval exploring expedition, spent several months in Oregon and California in 1841. In his report, published four years later, he praised San Francisco harbor as "one of the finest, if not the very best harbour in the world." He found the country potentially rich but ill-governed under Mexico. He predicted that it would become independent and, probably joined with Oregon, would "perhaps form a state that is destined to control the destinies of the Pacific." John C. Frémont, a lieutenant in the Topographical Corps of the Army, after surveying the Oregon Trail, crossed the Sierras into California in the winter of 1843–1844 and returned to the United States by a southern route. His report painted an attractive picture of the California valleys.

Most important of the Americans living in California was Thomas O. Larkin of Monterey. Larkin, a New Englander, had come by sea in 1832 and had built up a prosperous trade. About 1840 he began writing articles about California for Boston and New York newspapers that became the foremost sources of information for readers in the eastern United States. In 1843 Larkin was appointed first United States consul in Monterey.

By 1846, according to the estimates of Consul Larkin, there were some nine hundred Americans in California, as well as three hundred non-Spanish whites of other nationalities, and the American contingent was rapidly growing; the newcomers of 1845 alone had numbered between four and five hundred. This infusion of American blood into a Mexican province inevitably called to mind the histories of West Florida and Texas. Larkin's eastern correspondents began asking him whether there were not "enough wild Yankees in California to take the management of affairs in their own hands" and predicting that the American population would soon be "sufficiently numerous to play the Texas game."

The danger of another "Texas game" in California was quite apparent to the government in Mexico, but all orders from Mexico City for halting American immigration or expelling the Americans already there were disregarded by the local officials, who had neither the will nor the power to enforce them. In fact, the hold of Mexico upon California grew steadily weaker, and it was clear to visitors as well as to residents in the country that the sands of Mexican rule were running out. Lieutenant Wilkes foretold an independent California, perhaps joined with Oregon. With greater realism, Sir George Simpson of the Hudson's Bay Company, who visited California in 1842, warned his countrymen that only prior occupation by Great Britain could save it from falling into the hands of the United States. The hour was approaching when vigorous action by the United States might bring about a notable extension of American territory.

Presidents Jackson and Tyler had both displayed an interest in the possibility of acquiring California, and Tyler had received from Lord Ashburton an assurance that Great Britain would not object to such an accession to American territory. Despite such assurances, there was a growing suspicion in the United States not only that Great Britain would oppose the acquisition of California by this country, but that she sought it for herself. Rumors emanating from Mexico City had it that Mexico had mortgaged or would mortgage California to Great Britain as security for the large Mexican debt held by British subjects. No such plan really existed, but British subjects in Mexico and California persistently reminded the British government of the value of California, the danger of its falling to the United States, and the comparative ease with which Great Britain might take possession of it. Such suggestions were discouraged by Lord Aberdeen, who clearly had no desire for California. By the close of 1844, however, when he faced defeat in his efforts to save Texas from the United States, he had become distinctly averse to the thought of California's suffering a similar fate. He therefore directed that Californians who contemplated throwing off Mexican rule should be warned that Great Britain would be displeased by their accepting a protectorate from any foreign power; but neither British naval officers nor other British officials on the West Coast received orders to oppose actively the occupation of California by the United States. The British government was certainly not prepared to oppose American policy in California at the risk of war.

President Polk was not informed of the exact nature of British policy in California. He was well aware of Lord Aberdeen's attempt to thwart American policy in Texas, and the persistent rumors of British designs upon California must have seemed to him entirely credible. His anxiety for an early acquisition of that territory, there-fore, was founded largely upon a genuine fear that if the United States failed to acquire it, Great Britain would do so.

Aside from war and conquest, Polk saw two possible methods of acquiring California. It might be purchased, if Mexico would listen to reason, and Polk was determined to try this if he received the slightest encouragement from Mexico City. But if Mexico refused to negotiate, the Californians might be induced to join the United States of their own free will. Polk's reliance here was not upon the recent immigrants from the United States, who might have evinced a willingness to "play the Texas game"; it was rather upon the bona fide Californians of Spanish descent. He was well informed, through Larkin and others, of the shaky hold of the distant Mexican government upon California, of the impatience of many of the native Californians with the ineptitude and inefficiency of Mexican rule. Was it unreasonable to suppose that these people might be persuaded to sever their ties with Mexico and to form with the United States a close connection that would eventually lead to statehood? At least it was worth the effort, if purchase failed. Indeed, both methods might be tried at once.

Thomas O. Larkin's informing reports had been so satisfactory that it was now resolved to make him the confidential agent of the government and to entrust to him the execution of one of the two branches of Polk's California policy. In instructions written by Secretary of State Buchanan and dated October 17, 1845, Larkin received his new appointment and was informed of his new duties. He was to seek to counteract foreign influence in California. He was to supply his government with full information in regard to conditions in the territory, the identity of its leading citizens and officials, its trade, and the amount and character of immigration from the United States. More significantly, however, Larkin was directed to do whatever he could to win the friendship of the Californians and to assure them that if California should decalre her independence of Mexico, "we shall render her all the kind offices in our power as a sister republic." The United States, they were to be told, did not desire to extend its boundaries "unless by the free and spontaneous wish of all the independent people of adjoining territories." But, the instructions continued:

> Whilst the President will make no effort and use no influence to induce California to become one of the free and independent States of this Union, yet if the people should desire to unite their destiny with ours, they would be received as brethren, whenever this can be done without affording Mexico just cause of complaint.

But although expansion by compulsion was not its policy, the United States could not view with indifference the prospect of California passing under the control of Great Britain or any other European power. In the absence of any attempt at such a transfer, the true policy for the Californians should be to let events take their course—a course which, the writer evidently felt, would lead eventually to a voluntary union of California with the United States. These instructions, which could easily be interpreted as an invitation to the Californians to revolt from Mexico and join the United States, were entrusted to Lieutenant Archibald H. Gillespie of the Marine Corps and reached Larkin on April 17, 1846.

Polk Reasserts the Monroe Doctrine

While awaiting an expression from the Californians of their desire for union with the United States, Polk made use of his annual message (December 2, 1845) to notify Europe in general and Great Britain in particular that California was not open to European colonization and that a voluntary union of California and the United States would be the business of no one but the people directly concerned. In making the first point, he cited President Monroe's message of exactly twenty-two years earlier, thus becoming the first President since Monroe to refer to the Monroe Doctrine as a statement of official American policy. After quoting Monroe's noncolonization dictum, Polk continued:

> This principle will apply with greatly increased force should any European power attempt to establish any new colony in North America. In the existing circumstances of the world the present is deemed a proper occasion to reiterate and reaffirm the principle avowed by Mr. Monroe and to state my cordial concurrence in its wisdom and sound policy. . . . it should be distinctly announced to the world as our settled policy that no future European colony or dominion shall with our consent be planted or established on any part of the North American continent. . . .[5]

Having thus warned England to keep hands off California, Polk laid down another principle which has sometimes been called the "Polk corollary" to the Monroe Doctrine.

> We must ever maintain the principle [he wrote] that the people of this continent alone have the right to decide their own destiny. Should any portion of them, constituting an independent state, propose to unite themselves with our Confederacy, this will be a question for them and us to determine without any foreign interposition.

This declaration was a rebuke to the British government for its recent efforts to prevent

[5]It is to be noted that Polk referred repeatedly to *North* America, thus seeming, whether intentionally or not, to restrict the application of the noncolonization principle to that part of the western hemisphere. For comment, see Dexter Perkins: *The Monroe Doctrine, 1826–1867* (Baltimore: The Johns Hopkins Press, 1933), chap. 2.

the annexation of Texas. It was a rebuke to the French government for a recent speech in which Guizot, the Premier, had declared that there ought to be a "balance of power" in the Americas, in other words, a Latin counterweight to the United States. Most of all, perhaps, it was a warning that the United States would brook no European interference with its plan for the peaceful annexation of California. The reader, remembering that it was in this same message that President Polk asserted against Great Britain the American claim to all of Oregon, will hardly deny that this is one of the most nationally self-assertive documents in American history.

John Slidell's Mission

Thus Polk sought to pave the way for voluntary union of California with the United States and to forestall foreign objection to such a union. At the same time, he was attempting to bring about a restoration of diplomatic relations with Mexico and at one stroke not only to purchase California but to effect a peaceful settlement of all questions in dispute with that country. Discreet inquiries as to whether the Mexican government would receive a minister and thus resume official intercourse were apparently well received in Mexico. When Polk sought more than verbal assurances, Consul Black obtained from Peña y Peña, Mexican Foreign Minister, a statement in writing (October 15, 1845) that President Herrera was "disposed to receive the commissioner [comisionado] of the United States, who may come to this capital with full powers from his government to settle the present dispute in a peaceable, reasonable, and honorable manner."

Thinking this invitation adequate, Polk at once despatched John Slidell of Louisiana to Mexico bearing a commission as envoy extraordinary and minister

plenipotentiary of the United States. Polk and his cabinet had previously agreed to propose a boundary line following the Rio Grande from its mouth to El Paso in latitude 32° north or thereabouts, and thence directly westward to the Pacific—thus giving to the United States New Mexico and Upper California as well as the Rio Grande boundary. Polk believed such a line might be obtained by a payment of fifteen or twenty million dollars, but he was willing to pay as much as forty millions for it, if necessary.

Buchanan's instructions to Slidell (November 10, 1845) proposed a boundary settlement such as that described but showed a willingness to accept less as a minimum. Slidell was given four alternative propositions. If Mexico would accept the Rio Grande boundary and cede to the United States New Mexico and enough of California to include both Monterey and San Francisco, the United States would assume the American claims against Mexico and pay in addition twenty-five million dollars. If Mexico insisted upon holding Monterey but would accept these terms in other respects, the United States would assume the claims and pay twenty millions. For the Rio Grande boundary and New Mexico without California, the United States would assume the claims and pay five millions; for the Rio Grande boundary alone, it would assume the claims. This last proposal was practically an ultimatum. Slidell should make no settlement that did not secure the Rio Grande boundary in return for the assumption of the claims. But it is to be noted that Polk was willing to come to terms with Mexico without securing California or New Mexico— except that part of the latter east of the upper Rio Grande.[6] If California

---

[6] Under the minimum proposal, the line would follow the Rio Grande from mouth to source, thus depriving Mexico of the eastern portion of New Mexico, including Santa Fe and Taos, and thence run due north to the 42nd parallel.

could not be purchased, there was always the other alternative.

When Slidell arrived in Mexico, the government of President Herrera was facing imminent overthrow and dared not antagonize public opinion by an appearance of concessions to the United States. By way of excuse, Peña y Peña complained that instead of a *comisionado*—a commissioner authorized merely to settle the Texas question as a preliminary to the restoration of friendly relations—the United States had sent an envoy extraordinary and minister plenipotentiary, implying a full restoration of diplomatic relations. In that capacity, said the Foreign Minister, Slidell could not be received. While Slidell waited, Herrera's goverment fell, and on January 2, 1846, General Paredes entered Mexico City and assumed the presidential authority. Slidell withdrew to Jalapa to await the decision of the new government. But Paredes, who had used Herrera's alleged friendliness to the United States as a weapon with which to overthrow him, was in no position to be conciliatory himself. On March 12, his Foreign Minister informed Slidell that he would not be received. "Be assured," wrote Slidell to Buchanan as he prepared to come home, "that nothing is to be done with these people, until they shall have been chastised." Polk was already of much the same opinion.

Polk Ponders War

Polk's attitude toward Mexico from first to last combined simultaneous gestures with the sword and the olive branch. Always willing to make what he considered a liberal settlement with Mexico, he was determined to have as a minimum the Rio Grande boundary as compensation for the American claims. He was, it seems safe to assume, sincerely hopeful that Slidell's mission would result in such a settlement, but if

Mexico declined to accept that proffered olive branch, the sword was ready. A little saber rattling, he believed, might facilitate negotiations. Thus, on January 13, 1846, upon learning of Herrera's refusal to negotiate, he ordered General Taylor to advance from Corpus Christi and take up a position on the Rio Grande.

A month later (February 13), Polk was visited by one Colonel A. J. Atocha, a friend of Santa Anna who was then in exile at Havana. Presumably speaking for the exiled dictator, Atocha assured Polk that if Santa Anna were again in power, as he soon expected to be, he would gladly, for a sufficient consideration, make such a territorial settlement as Polk desired. Such a settlement might even be made, he hinted, with the existing government, but to reconcile Mexican public opinion to a cession of territory, the United States would have to take stronger measures. The army should advance to the Rio Grande (as it already had orders to do), and Slidell, if he were not received, should go on board a United States man-of-war at Vera Cruz and deliver an ultimatum supported by the guns of the fleet.

Polk was favorably impressed by Atocha's suggestions. Having already ordered General Taylor to the Rio Grande, he now proposed to his cabinet that Congress be requested to authorize the President, first, to present Mexico with an ultimatum, and second, if Mexico still rejected his terms, "to take redress into our own hands by aggressive measures." This was at a time, however, when the Oregon controversy was approaching a crisis, and Polk accepted the advice of Secretary of State Buchanan, who preferred not to precipitate war with Mexico till he was sure of peace with England. For the time being, the suggestion of an ultimatum was dropped, and Slidell was told not to hurry home even if Paredes refused to receive him, since his return, before settlement of the Oregon dispute, "would produce considerable alarm in the public mind and might possibly exercise an injurious influence on our relations with Great Britain."

Early in April Slidell's failure was known in Washington. Polk, determined to take drastic measures against Mexico, delayed action until Slidell could report to him in person. Slidell reached Washington May 8, still of the opinion that only "chastisement" could bring Mexico to terms. Saturday, May 9, Polk informed his cabinet of his intention to send to Congress the following Tuesday a message recommending a declaration of war against Mexico. All concurred except George Bancroft, Secretary of the Navy, who, as recorded by the President, "dissented but said if any act of hostility should be committed by the Mexican forces he was then in favour of immediate war." On that very evening came tidings that such an "act of hostility" had occurred.

The Clash of Arms

General Zachary Taylor, under his orders of January 13, had set out with his army early in March from Corpus Christi for the Rio Grande. On the twenty-eighth he had reached the river without meeting armed resistance and had occupied and fortified the east bank some miles from its mouth at the present site of Brownsville, Texas, opposite the Mexican town of Matamoros. Taylor's advance to the farther edge of the disputed territory brought to Matamoros the Mexican General Ampudia, who on April 12 warned Taylor, upon pain of hostilities, to withdraw his army beyond the Nueces—thus, it would seem, giving a sort of tacit assent to the annexation of Texas and narrowing the quarrel to the controversial area between the Nueces and the Rio Grande. In reply, Taylor cited his orders from the Secretary of War as authority for his movements. Furthermore, in retaliation for the Mexican refusal to permit him to use the river as a supply line, he instituted a blockade at its mouth, thereby denying its use to the Mexicans at Matamoros. This measure Taylor characterized as "a simply defensive precaution." It was, in reality, an act of war.

Upon receipt of the news of Taylor's blockade, President Paredes, April 23, proclaimed the existence of a "defensive war" against the United States. Next day (unaware as yet of Paredes' proclamation) a Mexican force crossed the river above Taylor's position. On the twenty-fifth, a party of Mexican cavalry attacked a company of sixty-three American dragoons commanded by a Captain Thorton, killed or wounded sixteen, and captured the remainder. So began the war with Mexico.

This was the news that reached President Polk on Saturday evening, May 9, 1846. Another cabinet meeting and a busy Sabbath produced a "war message" that went to Congress on Monday. The bulk of the message was—as Polk had planned it prior to the coming of the news from the Rio Grande—a summary of Mexican offenses against the United States, with emphasis upon her "breach of faith" in refusing to receive Slidell after having agreed to do so. But the latest act in the drama enabled Polk to add a paragraph well calculated to fire the patriot heart.

> The cup of forbearance [he wrote] had been exhausted even before the recent information from the frontier of the Del Norte. But now, after reiterated menaces, Mexico has passed the boundary of the United States, has invaded our territory and shed American blood upon American soil. She has proclaimed that hostilities have commenced, and that the two nations are now at war.

Had Polk sent his contemplated message to Congress before the clash of arms on the Rio Grande was known, or had there been no such clash, there would almost certainly have been a long and bitter fight over the proposed declaration of war. But the shedding of American blood on "American soil," even though the soil in question was claimed with at least equal right by Mexico, supplied the necessary emotional element to give Polk the war he desired. Within two days Congress, by a vote of 173 to 14 in the House and 42 to 2 in the Senate, had declared that a state of war existed "by the act of the Republic of Mexico," had authorized the President to call out fifty thousand volunteers, and had appropriated ten million dollars for military and naval expenditures.[7]

Thus to the American public, unacquainted with the deliberations in Polk's cabinet, the ostensible cause of the war with Mexico was the Mexican attack upon Captain Thornton's dragoons. Thanks to James K. Polk's meticulous recording of his daily activities in his diary, it is now clear that he and his advisers, with a single dissenting vote, had chosen war before they knew of the attack—a war to punish the weak Mexican government for its refusal to receive Slidell and negotiate a settlement of the American claims and the disputed boundary. Back of these reasons lay Polk's determination to possess California—peaceably if he could, forcibly if he must.

Initiating the Peace

Immediately after the declaration of war, steps were taken toward making peace

[7]The entire opposition vote was cast by northern Whigs: in the Senate, one vote from Massachusetts and one from Delaware; in the House, five votes each from Massachusetts and Ohio and one each from Maine, Rhode Island, New York, and Pennsylvania. Present but not voting in the Senate, however, in addition to a Whig Senator from Maine, were Berrien, a Whig from Georgia, and Calhoun of South Carolina, the sole Democrat to withhold a vote for war. There is an excellent analysis of the debate on the war resolutions in Charles Sellers, *James K. Polk, Continentalist, 1843–1846* (Princeton: University Press, 1966), pp. 416–21.

through Santa Anna, and it was no doubt in the expectation that these efforts would succeed that members of Congress had been promised a short and easy war. The commander of the American naval squadron off Vera Cruz was instructed to let Santa Anna enter Mexico should he attempt to do so. A few weeks later Polk sent a personal representative, Commander Alexander Slidell Mackenzie of the Navy, to interview Santa Anna in Havana. To Mackenzie, Santa Anna expressed a desire to return to Mexico and "govern in the interest of the masses, instead of parties, and classes."

In expectation of Santa Anna's return to power, Secretary of State Buchanan on July 27 addressed a note to the Mexican Foreign Minister proposing negotiations for "a peace just and honorable for both parties." Before this note reached Mexico City, Santa Anna had actually returned to Mexico and assumed command of the "Liberating Army." While ostensibly keeping aloof from politics, he became in reality the directing force in the Mexican government. To Santa Anna's decision, therefore, is to be attributed the Foreign Minister's reply to Buchanan, postponing consideration of the peace offer until a new Mexican congress should meet in December. Justifiably angry at Santa Anna's double dealing, Buchanan rejoined that no choice remained for the United States "but to prosecute the war with vigor" until Mexico herself should exhibit a desire for peace.

Defining the Objects of the War

Long before this fading of the hope of an early peace, the objects of the war had come under discussion in Polk's cabinet. The first such discussion was precipitated by a proposal from Buchanan that a circular note be sent to the diplomatic corps disclaiming any intention of dismembering Mexico or acquiring New Mexico or California. Unless some such declaration were made, Buchanan feared intervention by foreign powers, especially England, with whom the Oregon settlement was not yet complete. Buchanan's fears were not shared by other members of the cabinet or by the President. Polk remarked that acquisition of territory was not the aim of the war, but that being in it, the United States must not fail to take California as its sole means of indemnification. He would "meet war with either England or France or all the Powers of Christendom" rather than make such a pledge as Buchanan proposed. A further discussion some weeks later resulted in a general agreement that as a minimum the United States must secure the Rio Grande line, New Mexico, and Upper California—the maximum for which John Slidell had been directed to ask.

In order to make good these plans, it was proposed that General Taylor, already on the Rio Grande, should advance "toward the heart of the enemy's country" to bring Santa Anna to terms, while another expedition, setting out from Fort Leavenworth, should proceed to Santa Fe and thence to California, should occupy both California and New Mexico, and establish temporary governments therein.

The War in Northern Mexico

Taylor's army, already on the Rio Grande, was naturally the first in motion. During May, Taylor drove the Mexican forces beyond the Rio Grande, crossed the river himself, and occupied Matamoros against but slight opposition. By the capture of Monterey in September, enemy resistance in northeastern Mexico was effectually broken, and Taylor was enabled to push on and take possession of Saltillo and Victoria. Thus before the close of 1846 the capitals of three Mexican states, Nueve Leon,

Coahuila, and Tamaulipas, were in American hands. Another American column, commanded by Colonel A. W. Doniphan, separating at Santa Fe from Brigadier General Stephen W. Kearny's California expedition, descended the Rio Grande to El Paso, pushed from there into the interior, and in March 1847 occupied Chihuahua.

The Occupation of California

Long before Doniphan reached Chihuahua, California had passed securely into American hands, but not through the peaceful agreement with the Spanish Californians for which Polk had hoped. Consul Larkin at Monterey received in April 1846 the secret instructions of the preceding October. He began conversations, as directed, with some of the leading Californians, but his efforts to win their loyalty were interrupted by the strange behavior of Captain John C. Frémont. This young Army officer, already a noted explorer, had set out for California in the spring of 1845 with a party of sixty-two soldiers. His ostensible purpose was to determine the most feasible route from Missouri to California. When Frémont undertook to winter in California, the presence of so many armed Americans alarmed the Mexican commandant at Monterey, who ordered the Americans to leave the province. This Frémont did after considerable bluster, leading his men up the Sacramento Valley and north into Oregon. Here, in May 1846, he was overtaken by Lieutenant Gillespie, who had brought instructions to Larkin and letters to Frémont. What the letters contained, or what verbal messages Gillespie may have brought, is not known. Obviously, they could not have conveyed tidings of war with Mexico, as Frémont later asserted. At any rate, Frémont returned to California and to the vicinity of San Francisco Bay, where he lent assistance to a group of American frontiersmen in an unprovoked rebellion against the Mexican authorities—the so-called Bear Flag revolt. This action brought him into direct conflict with the Spanish Californians whom Polk wished to conciliate, and worked at cross-purposes with Larkin's efforts to win their confidence.

Having begun a private war of his own, out of harmony with the policy of his government. Frémont was rescued from serious embarrassment by receipt, early in July, of unofficial information that the United States and Mexico were at war. Frémont could now cooperate with Commodore John D. Sloat, and later with Captain Robert F. Stockton, both of the Navy, for the occupation of all California, but his erratic behavior had lessened the chances of effecting that occupation with the good will of the Californians.

Before the end of July, the United States flag was flying over all the settlements north of Monterey. Stockton and Frémont, accompanied by Larkin, then took their commands by sea to southern California, where in August they took possession of San Diego, San Pedro, and Los Angeles, meeting no armed resistance from the Mexicans.

There now arrived from Washington the first official news of the declaration of war, and Stockton proclaimed the annexation of California by the United States.

So far, with the exception of the Bear Flag episode, the conquest had proceeded smoothly enough; but in September latent Mexican resentment flared into open revolt in Los Angeles, the small American garrison retreated to the coast, and for nearly four months the Americans were unable to re-establish their authority in the south. Not until after Brigadier General Stephen W. Kearny arrived in December with a hundred cavalrymen—he had sent the rest back to Santa Fe upon learning of Stockton's "conquest"—was it possible to repossess Los Angeles and reassert the authority of the United States. On January 10, 1847, the combined forces of Kearny and Stockton entered the city, and the conquest of California was complete.

A Blow at the Heart of Mexico

At every point American arms had triumphed, and all the territory that the administration desired to wrest from Mexico had been occupied. There remained the problem of terminating the war through a treaty by which Mexico would confirm such cessions as the United States wished to exact. Santa Anna, however, as yet showed no inclination to discuss peace terms. What, then, was to be done? One possible course, recommended by General Taylor, was simply to hold what had been taken and wait for Mexico to propose a settlement. This procedure at first appealed to Polk and most of his cabinet but, largely at the insistence of Senator Benton, was set aside for a more aggressive policy and Polk resolved that an expedition should be despatched to seize Vera Cruz and thence, if circumstances seemed propitious, to advance against Mexico City. Since the existing military force was inadequate for such a campaign, ten regiments were to be added to the Regular Army, and these were to be supplemented by nine regiments of volunteers to serve for the duration of the war. In selecting a commander for the expedition, Polk, the politician, was embarrassed by the fact that Major General Winfield Scott, the highest ranking as well as the most capable general officer in the service, was a Whig in politics. After searching in vain for a competent Democratic general, Polk did the sensible thing by giving the command to Scott.

Scott's army of some 10,000 men consisted partly of new regiments from the United States, partly of units detached from Taylor's command. The army was put ashore south of Vera Cruz early in March, 1847, and on March 29 received the surrender of the city. Not until Scott undertook to scale the mountain barrier back of Vera Cruz did he encounter the main Mexican force under General Santa Anna. The Mexican leader had seen an opportunity to overwhelm General Taylor's depleted army in the north, only to be himself soundly beaten in the hard-fought battle of Buena Vista (February 23–24, 1847). He was now routed again by Scott at the pass of Cerro Gordo, after Captain Robert E. Lee discovered a path through ravines and jungle to the Mexican rear. Scott pushed on to Puebla, Mexico's second city, which surrendered without opposition on May 15. The road to Mexico City lay open, but at Puebla, Scott found it necessary to await replacements for nearly four thousand of his one-year volunteers. Their terms of enlistment were near expiration and only a handful proved willing to re-enlist.

The Mission of Nicholas P. Trist

While Scott and his army rested at Puebla, a new attempt was made to bring the slippery Santa Anna to terms without further bloodshed. In violation of his promises, made through Colonel Atocha and Commander Mackenzie, Santa Anna had hitherto refused to negotiate, demanding withdrawal of all American troops from Mexico as a condition precedent. News of the American victories at Buena Vista and Vera Cruz seemed to the administration in Washington to offer new opportunities for negotiation. On the chance that Santa Anna might now be ready to discuss peace, Polk resolved to send a commissioner to Scott's headquarters, empowered to negotiate a treaty whenever the Mexicans showed a willingness to talk.

The agent selected for this responsibility was Nicholas P. Trist, chief clerk of the State Department, who had formerly served as consul in Havana, who knew the Spanish language and was supposed to have some understanding of the Spanish character. Trist's instructions, drafted by Buchanan and signed April 15, 1847, directed him to insist upon the Rio Grande boundary and the cession of New Mexico and Upper California as a minimum. In compensation for such a boundary, the United States would assume the claims against Mexico and would pay, in addition, as much as $20,000,000, though Trist was to offer only $15,000,000 and was not to exceed the latter figure unless necessary to prevent a rupture of the negotiations. He was authorized, however, to pay an additional $5,000,000 for Lower California and a similar sum for the right of transit across the Isthmus of Tehuantepec—an outside figure of $30,000,000 for the maximum cessions suggested.

Trist arrived at Vera Cruz on May 6 and at once opened communications with Scott, to whom the visit of the commissioner was a complete surprise. Unfortunately General Scott, who already had reason to feel that he was not trusted by the President, received the not incorrect impression that Trist, a civilian and a mere departmental clerk, had come to Mexico with authority superior to his own. The general took offense and not only refused to transmit Trist's communications to the Mexican government but also sent Trist a lecture upon the latter's effrontery. Trist replied in kind, and the two men were presently engaged in an epistolary duel that did no credit to either. After some weeks of these unfortunate exchanges, the antagonists became reconciled, partly at least through the general's graciousness in sending a jar of guava jelly to his ailing opponent, and thenceforward the two worked in friendship and in perfect harmony.[8]

[8]The best defense of Trist is still an article by L. M. Sears, "Nicholas P. Trist, a Diplomat with Ideals," *Mississippi Valley Historical Review*, 11 (1924), 85–98.

Before the reconciliation with Scott, which occurred at the beginning of July, Trist had made contact with Santa Anna through the good offices of Charles Bankhead, the British minister in Mexico City. Through this channel came an intimation that the use of money would facilitate the opening of negotiations; specifically, that Santa Anna would consent to treat for peace if he could have $10,000 at once and a promise of $1,000,000 upon ratification of a treaty by Mexico. Trist informed Scott of this proposal and the latter, after conferring with his officers, made the initial payment of $10,000 from his secret service fund. Once more Santa Anna doublecrossed the Americans. After receiving the money, he pleaded the unwillingness of Congress as a bar to negotiations. Scott then had no alternative but to advance upon the Mexican capital.

On August 7, Scott broke camp at Puebla and, with less than eleven thousand able-bodied troops, began the march to Mexico City. In command at the capital was Santa Anna with an army several times the number of Scott's. But Santa Anna's force was poorly led, poorly disciplined, and poorly equipped; and to make matters worse, bitter feuds raged between Santa Anna and his generals and between Santa Anna, who had again assumed the presidential title, and rival politicians. The country was hopelessly divided in the face of the invader. Furthermore, Scott's fair and generous dealing with the Mexican people along the route of his invasion had won their friendship and removed the menace of a hostile population to his long line of communications.[9] The American advance encountered no resistance until it had penetrated the mountain rim of the Valley of Mexico and reached the immediate approaches to the city. Here Scott cleverly avoided the strong defenses guarding the more direct and obvious route and by a

turning movement to the south and two brilliant victories at Contreras and Churubusco (August 20, 1847) found himself at the southern gates of the Mexican capital.

Now, at last, Santa Anna sent to Scott through the British legation a proposal for a suspension of hostilities, and on August 23, commissioners from the two camps agreed upon an armistice to last until the end of peace negotiations or until forty-eight hours after either party should have given notice of its termination. It soon appeared that Santa Anna was but stalling for time. Upon his refusal to accept the terms offered by Trist, the negotiations were declared at an end, and with them the armistice. Hostilities were resumed, and on September 13 the Americans stormed the fortress of Chapultepec and on the following day occupied Mexico City. Santa Anna, with the remainder of his army, withdrew from the city and two days later resigned the presidency. A new government, headed provisionally by Peña y Peña, was set up at Querétaro, and early in October, Santa Anna was deprived of his military command.

Manifest Destiny

News of the breakdown of Trist's negotiations and the termination of the armistice reached Washington early in October. It was at once decided to recall Trist, to instruct Scott to occupy Mexico City and additional territory as rapidly as reinforcements made it practicable, and to await peace proposals from Mexico. Orders to this effect were sent to Trist and Scott on October 6.

Exasperated at Mexico's refusal to accept what they deemed generous terms of peace, Polk and his cabinet now talked of exacting from the defeated enemy much more than had at first been contemplated. They were agreed that the war should be

---

[9]R. H. Gabriel, "American Experience with Military Government," *American Historical Review,* 49 (1944), 630–43, especially 630–37.

prosecuted with increased energy, that the costs of occupation should be levied upon the Mexican people, that New Mexico and California should be regarded forthwith as permanent possessions of the United States and provided with territorial governments, and that, if necessary, the army in Mexico should assist in setting up and protecting temporarily a republican government willing and able to conclude an honorable peace.

There remained the question of what should be done if it proved impossible to make a satisfactory treaty even with a government set up under the protection of the United States. Two members of the cabinet, Buchanan and Secretary of the Treasury Robert J. Walker, were not averse to the possibility of conquering and absorbing all of Mexico, and both wished the President to intimate as much in his annual message, Buchanan suggesting a statement that "we must fulfill that destiny which Providence may have in store for both countries." Polk preferred to say that we should "take the measure of our indemnity into our own hands," and this was the wording of the message; but Walker and Buchanan were expressing the thought of a vocal group of politicans and journalists.

"Continental Democrats," as they were sometimes called, were urging the annexation of all of Mexico, or at least much more of it than had been contemplated at the beginning of the war. The long-prevalent view of this movement, like that of the war itself, ascribed the annexationist sentiment to southern cupidity for more slave territory and slave states. James Russell Lowell, in his antiwar and antisouthern *Biglow Papers*, announced:

> They just want this Californy
> So's to lug new slave-states in,

and derisively instructed the recruiting squad:

> Wal, go' long to help 'em stealin'
> Bigger pens to cram with slaves!

In reality, as even a casual examination of the evidence shows, there was nothing peculiarly southern about either the promotion of the war or the propaganda for larger annexations of Mexican territory. On the other hand, southern Whigs almost unanimously, and Calhoun and many southern Democrats, condemned the war and deplored the prospect of acquisitions of new territory. If they coveted more land for the slave economy, they saw little prospect of finding it in Mexico, where slavery had long since been abolished by Mexican law and where soil and climate were not propitious for the extension of the system. Even if physical conditions had been more favorable, the passage several times by the House of Representatives of the Wilmot Proviso, prohibiting slavery or involuntary servitude in any territory to be acquired from Mexico, had warned southerners that any attempt to extend slavery into new territory would meet with determined opposition from the North. So evident, in fact, did it become that any territory to be acquired from Mexico would be "free soil," that a few abolitionists abandoned their opposition to the war and to the absorption of territory and were ready to welcome new states from Mexico into the Union.[10]

The "all-Mexico" movement, however, was mainly neither proslavery nor antislavery. Sectionally, its greatest strength, or at least its most vocal support, was in New York and in the western states, from Ohio to Texas. Almost without exception its adherents were Democrats, and the arguments used in its behalf were those of Manifest Destiny. The *Democratic Review*, original propagator of that phrase, declared in October 1847: "This occupation of territory by the people, is the great movement of the age, and until every acre of the North American continent is occupied by citizens

[10] An excellent analysis of the rise and decline of the movement for "all Mexico" is Frederick Merk, *Manifest Destiny and Mission in American History: A Reinterpretation* (New York: Alfred A. Knopf, Inc., 1963), chaps. 5–8.

of the United States, the foundations of the future empire will not have been laid." Similar ideas were expressed by the New York *Herald* and *Sun*. The New Orleans *Picayune* predicted that "the better order of Mexicans" would claim the protection of a power whose martial law they had found superior to the sort of native government they had experienced. "Nor is it," this journal added, "prophetic of the long dominion of a hybrid people, to have their flowers scented by any of Saxon origin." The incapacity for self-government of the Indian race, forming a large part of the Mexican population, was dwelt upon by the *Democratic Review* and the New York *Evening Post,* the latter remarking: "The aborigines of this country have not attempted and cannot attempt, to exist *independently* alongside of us. . . . The Mexicans are *aboriginal Indians,* and they must share the destiny of their race."

These are but a few samples of the type of expression that was becoming common in Congress and the press. *Niles' Register* printed a column of " 'Manifest Destiny' Doctrines," and Calhoun, battling in the Senate against the proposed incorporation of Mexico with its hybrid race, declared: "I should be very glad indeed to think . . . that there is no person in the country who thinks of the extinction of the nationality of Mexico. Why, you can hardly read a newspaper without finding it filled with speculation upon the subject."

It was evident, then, that if the war should continue and American armies should occupy more and more of Mexico, there would be a numerous faction in the United States that would oppose surrendering any of the occupied territory. President Polk had not, as yet, aligned himself with this faction. Perhaps he would never have done so; yet the passage in his December message in which he said that if Mexico rejected peace offers, we "must continue to occupy her country with our troops, taking the full measure of indemnity into our own hands," was sufficiently

elastic to cover all eventualities. This was the state of affairs in the United States when, quite unexpectedly, there arrived in Washington a messenger bearing a peace treaty which Trist, despite his recall as commissioner, had negotiated with the provisional government of Mexico.

Mr. Trist Makes a Treaty

Not until November 16 did Trist receive Buchanan's letter of October 6 recalling him to Washington. In the same mail came a later note reiterating the order to return and rebuking him for alleged disregard of his instructions. In the meantime Trist had opened communications with the new Mexican government at Querétaro and had been informed that the government was anxious for peace and was about to appoint commissioners to treat with him. Trist's first act upon receiving his recall was to send to Querétaro an informal notice of the situation and to invite the Mexican government to give him peace proposals to take to Washington. The Mexican authorities, however, urged Trist to remain and negotiate despite his recall, and similar advice was given by General Scott and by Edward Thornton of the British legation, who played a useful role in bringing the parties together. For several weeks Trist hesitated, but on December 3 he informed the Mexican commissioners that he would withdraw his notice of recall and would proceed to negotiate if assured that Mexico would accept the minimum territorial demands of the United States.

The reasons for this unprecedented act of insubordination on Trist's part are clear to his credit. He knew, much better than Polk or Buchanan, the political situation in Mexico and the nature of the people with whom he had to deal. He knew that neither the existing Mexican government nor any other could ever send a commission to Washington to sue for peace without committing political suicide. He knew also that the faction at that moment in power, the *Moderado* or Moderate party, was the only group in Mexico with which there was any hope of making a reasonable treaty. Experience had shown that Santa Anna and his following could never be dealt with. Certain other factions, such as the *Puros* (idealistic republicans) and the more substantial business elements, were attracted by the possible advantages of prolonged or permanent American rule. Knowing something too of the programs of the "all-Mexico" movement in the United States, and suspecting that Polk was in sympathy with it, Trist was convinced that the choice lay between a peace made at once with the Moderates on the basis of his original instructions and a protracted military occupation of Mexico, complicated by guerrilla warfare and possibly ending in annexation of the whole country. The latter course he believed, as did Calhoun and many others, would be a major calamity for the United States; and he therefore resolved to disregard his recall and attempt to make a treaty, though he must have realized that a treaty made under these circumstances might be rejected in Washington and that in any case he was terminating his own official career.

Despite good will on both sides, the negotiations moved slowly, and it was not until February 2, 1848, that the treaty was signed at Guadalupe Hidalgo, a suburb of Mexico City.

The treaty embodied the minimum territorial demands and the minimum monetary compensation proposed in Trist's instructions of April 15, 1847. The boundary line was to follow the middle of the Rio Grande from its mouth to the point where it crossed the southern boundary of New Mexico; was to follow that boundary to the southwest corner of New Mexico and proceed thence due north till it reached the nearest branch of the Gila River, which it was to follow to its junction with the Colorado; and was to cross from the Colorado

to the Pacific by way of the existing boundary line between Upper and Lower California. Thus the United States would secure the Rio Grande boundary and retain New Mexico and Upper California, both of which it had already occupied. The boundary rivers were to be open to the navigation of both parties, and the Colorado below the boundary line, as well as the Gulf of California, open to ships of the United States. The United States was to release Mexico from responsibility for all existing claims and to settle such claims itself to an amount not exceeding $3,250,000 and was to pay to Mexico $15,000,000.

The arrival of the treaty placed Polk in a serious dilemma. He was indignant at Trist, not only for his disregard of his letter of recall, but also because of the tone of his recent communications, which had been outspokenly critical of the President and had contained insinuations that Polk was really planning to extinguish Mexican nationality. Polk had come to regard Trist as "a very base man" and could not without pain accept his handiwork. On the other hand, Trist's treaty conformed to his official instructions and to Polk's public profession of his war aims, and if he rejected it merely because of the irregularity in its negotiation and chose to carry on the war, the President knew that he would be fiercely criticized and would meet with intensified opposition in Congress, where the Whigs, since the elections of 1846, held a majority of the House of Representatives.

In view of all the facts, it seemed best to Polk not to reject the treaty. With suggestions for certain minor changes, but with a cautious statement of approval, he sent it to the Senate on February 22, 1848.

In the Senate the treaty was opposed by a strange alliance made up of those who wanted less territory than it secured, and those who wanted more. The former were Whigs; the latter, expansionist Democrats. Daniel Webster, despite his well-known concern for Pacific commerce, declared

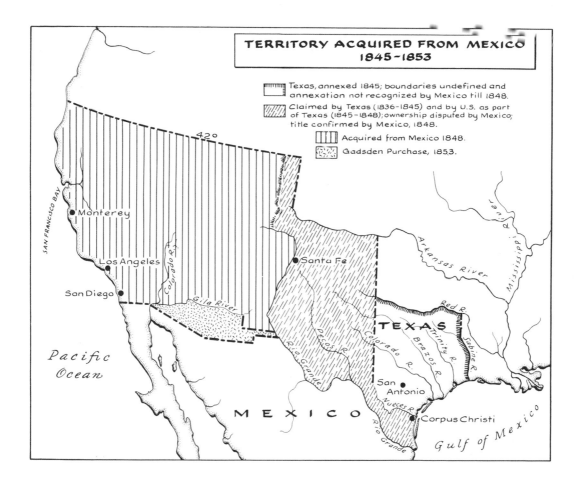

TERRITORY ACQUIRED FROM MEXICO
1845-1853

Texas, annexed 1845; boundaries undefined and annexation not recognized by Mexico till 1848.

Claimed by Texas (1836-1845) and by U.S. as part of Texas (1845-1848); ownership disputed by Mexico; title confirmed by Mexico, 1848.

Acquired from Mexico 1848.

Gadsden Purchase, 1853.

that New Mexico and California together were "not worth a dollar." He and fourteen other Whig senators joined in voting for an amendment that would have handed back to Mexico all territory west of the Rio Grande. On the other side, eleven Democrats, one from New York and ten from the West and South, supported an amendment that would have added to the Mexican cession all or large parts of the states of Chihuahua, Coahuila, Nuevo Leon, and Tamaulipas. Had the two groups of malcontents held together in opposition to the treaty, they would easily have defeated it. In the final vote, however, neither group held its lines intact, and the treaty was approved, March 10, by a majority of 38 to 14. Twenty-six Democrats and twelve Whigs made up the majority while each party contributed seven votes to the minority.

The Senate had amended the treaty in a number of minor particulars, and it was therefore necessary to send commissioners to Mexico to explain the changes and secure the concurrence of the Mexican Congress. On May 19, 1848, that body approved the amended treaty, and on the thirtieth, ratifications were exchanged at Querétaro. The war was over, and by July 30 the last soldiers of the invading army had embarked from Vera Cruz for home.

In his message to Congress on July 6,

1848, announcing the completion of the treaty, Polk expressed satisfaction that the annexed territories, which in Mexican possession had lain undeveloped and almost useless, would now be "productive of vast benefits to the United States, to the commercial world, and the general interests of mankind." Well might Polk feel gratification at the achievements of his three and a quarter years in the Presidency. A firm believer in the desirability of territorial expansion, he had completed the annexation of Texas, had acquired full title to the more valuable portion of Oregon, and by a short war, glorious to American arms and rela- tively inexpensive in lives and money, had secured the Rio Grande boundary, New Mexico, and the still unrealized wealth of California. Within less than two years the United States had become a Pacific power with a coastline stretching from San Diego to Puget Sound. Polk had taken serious chances, risking both a war with England and a prolonged and costly occupation of Mexico. If he owed his successes as much to good luck as to good management, the suc- cesses were nevertheless impressive, and it was but natural that he should claim for himself the chief credit.

ADDITIONAL READINGS

BAUER, KARL JACK, *The Mexican War, 1846–48*. New York: The Macmillan Company, 1974.

MORISON, SAMUEL ELIOT, FREDERICK MERK, and FRANK FREIDEL, *Dissent in Three American Wars*. Cambridge: Harvard University Press, 1970.

SCHROEDER, JOHN H., *Mr. Polk's War*. Madison, Wisconsin: University of Wisconsin Press, 1973.

SMITH, JUSTIN H., *The War with Mexico*. 2 vols. New York: The Macmillan Company, 1919.

8. Open Doors, Frustration, and Other Aspects of Pre-Civil War Diplomacy

Agents of Commerce in the Far East

Long before the first American explorer reached the Pacific overland, ships from New York and New England were making the United States flag a familiar sight from the shores of California and Oregon to those of China and Southeast Asia. The search for new markets, so keenly pressed after the Revolution, led American merchants into distant seas where as colonials they had never ventured. As British subjects, they had been excluded from the trade of the Far East by the monopoly conferred upon the British East India Company. Now, as citizens of an independent state, Americans had no longer to respect that monopoly. The British themselves, by the Jay Treaty, admitted American ships to the trade with the British East Indies. In other Far Eastern lands they needed only to secure the permission of the governments concerned. It was not long before Yankee skippers were trading with Oman, on the Indian Ocean, with Batavia in the Dutch East Indies, with Manila in the Spanish Philippines, with the kingdom of Siam, with Botany Bay in Australia, but above all, with the Chinese port of Canton.

The "Middle Kingdom" and Its Neighbors

The Chinese Empire of 180 years ago looked upon itself as the possessor of the world's only true civilization. It was the "Middle Kingdom," and those members of the human race outside its sacred circle were "barbarians" or "foreign devils," with whom the Chinese desired no intercourse. But as a favor, the foreigners were allowed very restricted privileges of trade. Foreign ships were admitted to the single port of Canton in south China, and at the same port foreign merchants were allowed to live in "factories" outside the city walls. Here they were shut off from all contact with the local population except the "co-hong" merchants, the small group of Chinese who had a monopoly of the foreign trade. China had no regular diplomatic relations with the outside world, no ambassadors or ministers abroad, no embassies, legations, or even recognized consulates in China. Foreign ambassadors were received at Peking only as tribute-bearers from governments of inferior states. The Emperor of the Middle Kingdom recognized no equals.

China's neighbors, Japan and Korea, were even more isolated from the outside world than was China. Korea acknowledged the overlordship of China, and her foreign trade was almost exclusively with that country. The Japanese had once been an active seafaring people; their ports had been open to foreign traders and even to Christian missionaries, who had made many native converts. But early in the seventeenth century, under Shoguns of the Tokugawa clan, Japan had closed her doors to the world, forbidden Japanese to go abroad, expelled the missionaries, and outlawed native Christianity. As one slight exception to this policy of exclusion, the Dutch were permitted to keep a trading post on Deshima Island in the harbor of Nagasaki, to which they might bring one ship a year. Some trade with China was also allowed through Nagasaki, but otherwise the policy of Japan was to shield its people from all outside contacts and influences.

American Far Eastern Policy

Between the winning of American independence and the close of the nineteenth century, profound changes occurred in these nations of the Far East and in their relations with the Occident—changes to which the United States made important contributions. In China, the growth of trade led to the opening of regular diplomatic relations. In Japan (and in a much less significant way in Korea) the opening of diplomatic relations paved the way for the beginning of trade. In opening commercial and diplomatic relations with the Far East, the United States sometimes followed, sometimes preceded, the European powers. In its Chinese policy it at first followed England; in its Japanese policy, it led, and Europe followed.

But American policy in the Far East developed in a somewhat different direction from the policy of Europe. American aims in this area were purely commercial; as yet the United States had no colonial ambitions. For its commerce it desired nothing better than most-favored-nation treatment, equality, or the "open door" as it came later to be called. When trade had once been opened, threats to the open door came not from China and Japan but from the colonizing powers of Europe, which were on the lookout for colonies, spheres of interest, and special favors in the Far East. A weak China or a weak Japan would be more likely to yield to such demands than a strong China or Japan. It was to the interest of the United States, therefore, to maintain or to build up the strength of both China and Japan. It was China's fate to be almost torn apart by internal strains and the encroachments of foreign powers. It was American policy to help China resist those disruptive forces—to maintain China's independence and "territorial integrity." Japan, on the other hand, after opening her door to western influences, began an amazing program of speedy westernization and modernization, building a strongly centralized government in place of a loose feudal organization. This course she followed in order to save herself from the helplessness against the West that she saw in China. In this policy of self-strengthening, which Europe at times sought to obstruct, Japan had the sympathy and moral support of the United States.

These American policies are usually associated with the period just before and after 1900, but they had their beginnings much earlier. Their chief objectives were:

1. To secure and maintain an open door for American trade.
2. To keep China and Japan unified and strong as the surest means of keeping the door open.

Negatively, the United States had no wish for territorial acquisitions in the Far East; and it abstained from the use of force in pursuing its objectives. Other nations, the British and French, might use force. Whatever rights they gained, the United States gained too, through the operation of the most-favored-nation clauses in its first treaties with China and Japan. Thus its gains were made without bloodshed and without incurring the enmity of Chinese and Japanese. The development of these American policies will now be examined in some detail.

The "Old China Trade"

The first American ship to visit Canton was the *Empress of China,* which left New York in February 1784 and returned in May 1785. Her example was quickly followed by ships from New York, Boston, and other Atlantic ports, and before 1800 dozens of American vessels were engaged in the China trade. In the beginning these traders went primarily to bring back Chinese products—tea, spices, silk and cotton fabrics, chinaware—for which there was a market in the United States, and were hard put to it to find American commodities that could be disposed of in self-sufficing China. One such article was ginseng, a root found plentifully in the eastern United States, and esteemed in China for its supposed medicinal properties. Furs, from the sea otter of the northwest coast or the fur seals of the South Pacific, brought good prices in Canton. The value of such articles, however, was inadequate to pay for the return cargoes, and the balance was made up in Spanish silver dollars or in opium, for which China provided a growing but illicit market.

Beginning in the middle 1820's the United States exported to China growing amounts of coarse cotton cloth, and although imports from China remained far in excess of exports to it, Americans came to look upon China more and more as a future market for American manufactured goods.

"After 1840," writes Tyler Dennett, "American policy in Asia was always directed with an eye to the future—to the day when Americans would supply the seemingly limitless markets of the East."[1]

The First Treaties with China

The first effective blow against the Chinese policy of exclusion was struck by the British in the Opium War of 1839–1842. The Chinese authorities had long connived in the smuggling of opium. Most of this came from British India, where the tax on its production was the principal source of government revenue. Without warning, a new imperial official in 1839 suddenly cracked down on the practice, compelling British merchants to hand over 20,000 chests of opium valued at more than £2,000,000. This and other punitive measures against the British led to open hostilities, in which Chinese armies, fleets, and fortifications proved ineffectual against European armaments. The Chinese government was forced to capitulate. By the Treaty of Nanking, August 29, 1842, China ceded to Great Britain the island of Hong Kong, opened four new ports for trade, and agreed to pay an indemnity of $21,000,000 for the confiscated opium, the cost of the war, and debts owing to British merchants. The co-hong system was abolished; British traders might do business with any Chinese in the open ports. Aside from a boundary treaty with Russia in 1689, the Nanking treaty was the first made by China with any European power. It was the first step in a general opening up of China to western diplomacy, trade, and culture.

The United States was quick to follow the British lead. Caleb Cushing, a Whig politician from Massachusetts, was sent to China

[1]Tyler Dennett, *Americans in Eastern Asia* (New York: The Macmillan Company, 1922), p. 74.

CHINA COAST AND JAPAN

by President Tyler to make sure that American ships and trade should enjoy privileges at least equal to those granted to the British. Both Cushing and Secretary of State Daniel Webster, who wrote his instructions, represented that section of the country most interested in the China trade.

On July 3, 1844, Cushing and a Chinese commissioner signed the Treaty of Wanghia (the name of a Chinese village near Canton). The treaty opened to American ships and trade the five ports of Canton, Amoy, Foochow, Ningpo, and Shanghai and authorized the stationing of United

States consular officers at these ports. It permitted American citizens to reside in the open ports with their families, to acquire sites for houses, places of business, hospitals, churches, and cemeteries, to purchase books, and to employ scholars to teach the Chinese language. It also gave to Americans residing in China the right of extraterritoriality; that is, the right, when accused of crime or involved in civil cases, to be tried before an American official (normally the consul) and according to American law. It fixed at a low level the tariff to be paid by Americans on imports and exports and stipulated that the rates should not be changed without American consent. Finally, it contained a most-favored-nation article, assuring to the United States any additional rights or privileges that might be gained by any other power.

A few words of comment on some of these provisions are in order. The clauses permitting the building of churches, purchase of books, and employment of Chinese scholars were inserted at the insistence of American missionaries who served Cushing as interpreters. The most notable of these was Dr. Peter Parker, a medical missionary who since 1834 had conducted a hospital at Canton.

The principle of extraterritoriality was supported by the arguments (1) that Chinese courts were unreliable, (2) that Chinise law, both civil and criminal, was so different from western law that the results of its application were often palpably unjust by western standards. The giving of criminal jurisdiction to American consuls was, however, attended with serious abuses. Consuls were rarely well trained for such duties or adequately paid, and there were no American jails for the confinement of convicted criminals.

For the fixing of tariff rates by treaty, instituted by the British in the Treaty of Nanking, it is difficult to find a valid excuse. Such a practice was wholly one-sided and subjected China to a surrender of sovereignty to which no western power would itself have submitted. It restricted the Chinese government's use of an important source of revenue and prevented the imposition of a duty on imports sufficient for the encouragement of domestic industry. There was much more justification for placing the collection of customs under the administration of foreigners, since native officialdom was both inefficient and corrupt. The Imperial Maritime Customs, staffed by foreigners of many nationalities but headed by Englishmen, originated in the 1850's during the disorders of the Taiping Rebellion and continued to administer the customs until the eve of World War II. It won an enviable reputation for honesty and efficiency.

Because of the inclusion of extraterritoriality and tariff limitation in the Chinese treaties with Great Britain and the United States and in later treaties with the other European powers, these documents came to be referred to as the "unequal treaties" and became a standing grievance of China against the West; but not until the western powers needed China as an ally in World War II were the last of these unequal provisions abrogated.

The United States
Takes an Interest in Japan

In the opening of China it was Great Britain that played the leading role. In the opening of Japan the United States played the lead. Prior to 1853, British, Russians, and Americans had tried in vain to open diplomatic and trade relations with the island empire. American ships, government and private, which visited Japanese ports were received with varying degrees of courtesy but were always required to depart without doing business. Sailors from American whaling ships who, by mischance or design—as in the case of a group of deserters from the *Lagoda*—found themselves marooned on Japanese shores, were placed in confinement and transported to Deshima, whence they were repatriated via Dutch ships or, in one case, an American naval vessel. Those who complained of cruel treatment seem to have brought it upon themselves by unruly behavior,[2] but their complaints nevertheless helped to shape American policy.

In the meantime, the United States was rapidly becoming a Pacific power. The settling of the Oregon question in 1846 and the acquisition of California from Mexico in 1848 gave it a frontage of over 1,200 miles on the Pacific Ocean with magnificent harbors in San Francisco Bay and Puget Sound. Forward-looking Americans saw the dawn of a great commercial era on the Pacific. Japan's harbors lay close to the Chinese coast. Japan, furthermore, was reputed to have valuable deposits of coal, and coal was becoming a necessity of ocean commerce as the steamship nosed its way into the sea lanes. To open Japanese ports to trade, to gain access to Japanese coal, to insure humane treatment for American sailors shipwrecked on Japanese shores— these became objectives of American foreign policy in the 1850s. The efficient agents in attaining them were Matthew Calbraith Perry, the naval officer, and Townsend Harris, the diplomat.

Commodore Perry's original instructions, like those to Caleb Cushing, were written by Daniel Webster, serving now as Secretary of State under President Millard Fillmore (1850–1853), but Perry was permitted to rewrite the instructions to suit himself. He was, if possible, to deliver a letter from the President (Franklin Pierce

[2]Shunzo Sakamaki, *Japan and the United States, 1790–1853 (The Transactions of the Asiatic Society of Japan,* second series, Vol. 18, Tokyo, 1939). This study corrects the common impression that inhumane treatment of shipwrecked American sailors was standard Japanese practice. This myth is perpetuated in S. E. Morison, *"Old Bruin": Commodore Matthew C. Perry, 1794–1858* (Boston: Little, Brown and Company, 1966), p. 266.

replaced Fillmore in 1853), to the Emperor. He was to seek permission for American vessels to enter one or more of the ports of Japan for the purpose of selling their cargoes and obtaining supplies, including coal; permission to establish a coal depot on one of the islands was to be obtained if possible. But the objective most emphasized was assurance of protection of American seamen and property wrecked on the islands or driven into their ports by storm. Unless this was promised, the commodore was to warn the Japanese that any future acts of cruelty would "be severely chastised."

Perry paid two visits to Yedo (later Tokyo) Bay in July 1853 and February 1854. The Japanese were impressed by the haughty and determined demeanor assumed by the commodore and by his formidable naval squadron. They were also aware of Oriental weakness vis-à-vis western naval armament, as shown in the recent Opium War, and they knew that both Britain and Russia were planning demonstrations for ends that might be more drastic than those sought by the United States. They considered it expedient, therefore, to give the American commodore most of what he asked for. Moderate concessions to the United States might shield them from immoderate demands of other powers. These factors help to account for Perry's success.

On his first visit Perry was able to deliver the President's letter to a representative not of the Emperor but of the Shogun, at this time the effective head of the Japanese government. When he returned seven months later, he found the Shogun's government ready to sign a treaty, and this ceremony took place at the village of Yokohama on March 31, 1954.

By Perry's treaty, the United States merely got a toe, so to speak, inside the Japanese door; the door was not really opened. American ships, it was agreed, might enter two Japanese ports to procure supplies. The ports were isolated and unimportant—Shimoda, southwest from

Yedo Bay, and Hakodate, in the northern island of Hokkaido—and all business must be transacted through Japanese officials; no trade with private individuals would be permitted. There was no mention of a coal depot, though coal was listed among the supplies that might be purchased. A United States consul would be permitted to reside at Shimoda. Japan agreed to give proper treatment to shipwrecked American sailors, and a most-favored-nation clause assured to the United States any rights that might subsequently be granted to any other power.

The United States Defines Its Policy in the Far East

As the treaties of Nanking and Wanghia had served as the models for other treaties with China, so Perry's treaty was accepted as the pattern for Japan. Within a few months after its signature, Japan had signed very similar treaties with Great Britain, Russia, and the Netherlands. Both China and Japan had made their first treaties under duress—China as a result of defeat in war, Japan under threat of unpleasant consequences if she refused. Neither nation intended to go further than it was compelled to go in carrying out the spirit or even the letter of its new obligations. The western powers, on the other hand, including the United States, were determined not only to enjoy the rights they had secured by the treaties but to gain additional rights as soon as possible. What methods were to be used in enforcing and enlarging treaty rights in China and Japan? Should reliance be placed upon force or persuasion?

Both Perry and Dr. Peter Parker, the medical missionary, who became United States commissioner to China in 1855, advocated an aggressive policy. As Britain had obtained a base at Hong Kong, they urged that the United States secure territorial bases in Far Eastern waters from which it

might defend and promote its interests. Perry occupied the Bonin Islands, arranged for a supply depot on Okinawa in the Ryukyus, and suggested a protectorate over Formosa. Parker also had schemes for making Formosa a protectorate.

But as advocates of American territorial expansion in the Far East, both Perry and Parker were a half-century ahead of their time. The government in Washington turned a deaf ear to their proposals. Parker's successor as commissioner, appointed by President Buchanan in 1857, was told that the only interests of the United States in China were in "lawful commerce" and "the protection of the lives and property of its citizens." The United States had no motive "for territorial aggrandizement or the acquisition of political power in that distant region." Parker's suggestions for seizure of Formosa were ignored. Nothing was done to follow up Perry's occupation of the Bonins, and when Japan in 1861 reasserted an old claim to those islands, the American government made no objection.

The Tientsin Treaties

The United States in the 1850s had no wish for territorial conquest in the Far East, nor would it, like France and Great Britain, use armed force to advance its interests there.[3]

[3]American naval commanders in the Far East in a few instances used force on their own responsibility. In November 1856, while the Chinese were engaged in hostilities with the British at Canton, Chinese forts below the city fired on an American naval launch. Failing to receive a satisfactory explanation from the Chinese viceroy, U.S. Flag Officer James Armstrong silenced the forts by a naval bombardment and sent ashore a landing party which effectually demolished them. J. W. Pratt, ed., "Our First 'War' in China: The Diary of William Henry Powell, 1856," *American Historical Review*, 53 (1948), 776–86. In June 1859, U.S. Commodore Josiah Tattnall was present as an observer while British ships engaged the Chinese forts on the Pei-ho River below Tientsin. In the midst of the battle he went on board the British flagship to pay his respects to the wounded British admiral and with the celebrated remark, "Blood is thicker than water!" ordered the crew of his barge to assist the British seamen in serving the guns.

It placed reliance upon the good faith of the Chinese and Japanese governments, upon the persuasiveness of its diplomats, and, in China especially, upon the operation of the most-favored-nation article in its treaty with that country.

In 1857 the French and British went to war with China in order to enforce respect for their rights under the earlier treaties and to gain further privileges. The United States and Russia remained neutral but sent their diplomatic representatives to cooperate with those of the allies in the negotiation of new treaties with China. Treaties with all four powers were signed at Tientsin in 1858. Through its own treaty or as a consequence of the treaties of the other powers, the United States gained for its citizens access to eleven additional ports on the coast and on the Yangtse River, the right to navigate the Yangtse as far as Hankow and to travel in the interior, and toleration for the Christian religion. Like the other governments concerned, the United States at last secured the right of diplomatic representation at Peking and the abandonment of the Chinese Emperor's pretensions to a status above that of other monarchs. Further fighting and the occupation of Peking by British and French forces proved necessary before the Emperor could be induced to ratify the treaties, but this final step was accomplished in 1860.

The chief gainer from the hostilities of 1857–1860 was neutral Russia. By the Treaty of Aigun (1858) China ceded to Russia the northern watershed of the Amur River. In the negotiations over ratification of the Tientsin treaties the Russian representative, General Ignatiev, acted as mediator between China and the allies and was rewarded by the further surrender of the area lying between the Amur and the Ussuri Rivers and the Sea of Japan. Thus the Czar's government came into possession of the Maritime Province and forthwith established the port of Vladivostok at its southern extremity.

The United States Opposes Partition of China

By its own Treaty of Tientsin and the inclusion in it of a new most-favored-nation article, the United States was maintaining the principle of equality of treatment, or the open door. In the 1850's and 1860's also it was taking a stand against the disruption of the Chinese Empire, or in behalf of the preservation of China's territorial integrity. When the great Taiping Rebellion (1851–1865) in southern China threatened to split the empire asunder, the American commissioner at Canton, Humphrey Marshall, gave his sympathy to the imperial government in its struggle to hold China together. He suspected Great Britain and Russia of plans to take advantage of the rebellion by partitioning the country between them. Anson Burlingame, United States minister to China from 1861 to 1867, found the representatives of Great Britain, France, and Russia ostensibly willing to drop any claims for special privileges in China and any demands for further cessions of Chinese territory. His agreement with them, he reported to the Secretary of State, "is a guarantee of the territorial integrity of the Chinese Empire."

Townsend Harris and Japan

In China the United States had been content to leave leadership to the more aggressive British and French and to profit from their exploits. In Japan, on the other hand, it continued for some time to hold the leading position that it had assumed under Perry. The first American consul at Shimoda, appointed in accordance with the provisions of Perry's treaty, was Townsend Harris, a New York businessman who had had some years of experience in the Far East. It was his task to push open the door that Perry had merely unlocked.

When Harris was deposited by an American warship at Shimoda in August 1856, he met with anything but a hospitable reception. In spite of the treaty, the Japanese had no wish to permit a foreign official to reside at Shimoda, and for months they made his stay as uncomfortable and as dreary as possible in the hope that he could be persuaded to leave. But Harris was a man of persistence, patience, and tact. Before many months he had won the respect if not the friendship of the officials. Within a year he had persuaded them to sign a convention (June 17, 1857) materially enlarging American privileges in Japan; and in the following year he was permitted to travel in state to Yedo, seat of the Shogun's government, where he secured (July 29, 1858) the first full-fledged commercial treaty that Japan signed with any western power. In obtaining Japan's signature to this treaty, Harris was aided by contemporary events in China, where the British and French had soundly beaten the Chinese forces and compelled China to sign the treaties of Tientsin. Harris argued with effect that by accepting a reasonable treaty with the United States, Japan could divert the other powers from making excessive demands. The American treaty did, in reality, become the model for those soon after made with the Netherlands, Russia, Great Britain, and France.

The convention of 1857 and the treaty of 1858 together opened four new ports to American ships, authorized the appointment of consuls for all the open ports, permitted trade with private parties in those ports, and gave to Americans the right to reside in the open ports, there to hold property, build churches, and practice their religion. After January 1, 1862, American citizens might also reside in Yedo, the Shogun's capital. The treaty permitted each government to appoint a diplomatic representative to reside at the capital of the other. Like the Chinese treaties, it gave extraterritorial status to Americans living in the Oriental country and fixed upper limits for duties on imports and exports. Perry had not included extraterritoriality in his treaty with Japan, and Harris did not approve the principle; but since the British, Dutch, and Russians had all inserted extraterritorial provisions in their treaties, Harris could not well forgo securing the same privilege for the United States. Thus Japan, like China, became a victim of "unequal treaties." The United States, however, was to be the leading advocate of a restoration to Japan of tariff autonomy and full jurisdiction over foreigners in her territory. Japan was relieved of the handicap of extraterritoriality before the end of the century and achieved tariff autonomy soon thereafter.

The End of Japanese Isolation

The treaties of 1858 were followed by a period of internal discord and strife in Japan. The Shogun's government had negotiated the treaties in the conviction that Japan must either make concessions to the western powers or, like China, suffer defeat and humiliation at their hands. The isolationist elements in society and those who were simply jealous of the Shogun, gathered around the Emperor, and for several years the imperial court at Kyoto was the center of opposition to the admission of the foreigners. An imperial decree ordered all foreigners out of the empire by June 25, 1863, and while no real effort was made to enforce this edict, foreigners were attacked and even murdered from time to time by irresponsible adherents of the isolationist party. In this difficult period the United States cooperated closely with the other powers in Japan, as it was doing in China under Minister Burlingame. United States naval forces joined in a punitive expedition against rebellious clans in southwestern Japan, and the American minister was present (though on a British warship) at a joint naval demonstration at Osaka in 1865, which finally persuaded the Emperor to give his approval to the treaties signed seven years before. The period ended with the overthrow of the Shogunate and the "restoration" of the Emperor to the actual possession of sovereign power. After this "Meiji Restoration" of 1868, the imperial court, its seat removed to Yedo, now rechristened Tokyo, was quickly converted to a belief in the necessity of throwing the door open to western ideas and western technology. Then began the marvelous transformation that was to bring Japan within a generation to a position among the leading world powers.

A Decade of Frustration

If the 1840's are labeled the decade of the Manifest Destiny Triumphant, the succeeding ten years may well be called the era of Manifest Destiny Frustrated. The faith in American democracy that had made acquisitions of new territory seem merely "extending the area of freedom" still persisted. So strong indeed was the democratic faith that not a few Americans were tempted to intervene in behalf of struggling democracy in Europe, in disregard of the warnings of earlier statesmen.

Such impulses were seen in the tumultuous enthusiasm that greeted the exiled Hungarian patriot, Louis Kossuth, when he visited the United States in 1851. In Washington, Kossuth was lavishly entertained at a banquet sponsored by members of Congress from both parties. He was cordially recieved by President Fillmore but was clearly told by both the President and Secretary of State Webster that the United States would not depart from its policy of noninterference in the affairs of Europe. Kossuth was assured that Hungary's struggle for independence had American sympathy but could expect no American aid. Members of a group in the Democratic party calling themselves "Young America" were ready to go to almost any length in support of liberal or revolutionary movements in Europe, but their attempts were brought to nought by more conservative elements in the party.

Faith in democracy, together with strategic and economic considerations, produced a profusion of new projects of territorial expansion, looking to the north, west, and south. But so deeply, in this decade, was the nation divided over the slavery question, that any proposal of expansion put forward by the pro-southern administration of either Franklin Pierce or James Buchanan was sure to be viewed with suspicion by the antislavery forces of the North. For this and for other reasons, few of the proposals for expansion were carried out. The only achievements of the decade in this respect were the narrow strip of territory purchased from Mexico by James Gadsden, certain rights of interoceanic transit across the Isthmuses of Panama and Tehuantepec, and a few scattered and isolated "guano islands" in the Pacific and elsewhere.

Canada—Annexation or Reciprocity?

There seemed a possibility in the early 1850's that Canada, an objective of American arms and diplomacy in the Revolution and again in the War of 1812, might join the United States of its own accord. Dissatisfaction with a change in British commercial policy—repeal of the Corn Laws and the resulting loss of Canada's preferred status in British markets—combined with political discontents to produce a movement for peaceful separation from the British Empire and annexation to the United States. As was to be expected, the British government opposed any such solution for Canada's difficulties, and it undertook to meet these problems by liberalizing trade between Canada and her sister provinces[4] on the one hand and the United States on the other. This was accomplished by a reciprocity treaty, signed June 5, 1854, by Secretary of State William L. Marcy and the Earl of Elgin and Kincardine, governor general of Britain's North American Provinces. The treaty provided free entry from Canada and the Maritime Provinces to the United States, and vice versa, of a long list of raw and semi-finished commodities, the products of farm, forest, mines, and the sea. It admitted American fishermen to the inshore fisheries of the British provinces from which they were excluded under the treaty of 1818 and gave similar privileges to Canadian fishermen on the eastern coast of the United States north of the 36th parallel of latitude. It also opened the St. Lawrence River and its canals to navigation by citizens of the United States and in return admitted British subjects to the navigation of Lake Michigan.

The Marcy-Elgin Treaty was to remain in force for ten years, after which either party might terminate it by giving a year's notice. It proved beneficial to both countries but was terminated by the United States in 1865. The principal reasons for this action were irritation at the allegedly pro-southern attitude of Canada during the Civil War, a belief that Canada profited more from the treaty than did the United States, and the protectionist philosophy of the then dominant Republican party.

[4]Canada in 1849 comprised Quebec and Ontario (formerly Lower and Upper Canada), which had been united by the British Act of Union of 1840. Separate provinces or colonies were New Brunswick, Nova Scotia, Prince Edward Island, and Newfoundland. The Dominion of Canada, created by the North America Act of 1867, included at first Quebec, Ontario, New Brunswick and Nova Scotia. Manitoba became a province of the Dominion in 1870; British Columbia, in 1871; Prince Edward Island, in 1873; Alberta and Saskatchewan, in 1905; Newfoundland, in 1950.

The Pacific

The settlement of the Oregon boundary controversy and the acquisition of California made the United States a Pacific power. The opening of official relations with China and Japan in 1844 and 1854 respectively held out the prospect of a greatly increased commerce on the Pacific. Commodore Perry and Dr. Peter Parker, it will be recalled, urged the United States to follow the British example set at Hong Kong and acquire outposts of its own in the western Pacific, but the government in Washington repudiated such proposals.

The Hawaiian Islands were a different matter. Geographically an outpost of North America, they had come increasingly under United States influence. New England trading ships had begun frequenting them in the 1790s. New England whalers appeared some years later. New England missionaries, sent out in 1820 by the American Board of Commissioners for Foreign Missions, gained the ears of the royal family and within a few years had converted the entire Polynesian population to at least a nominal acceptance of Christianity. With Christianity in its American Calvinist form, the missionaries brought American ideas of education and of government. They set up printing presses, reduced the native language to writing, and provided a written constitution for the formerly despotic monarchy.

Culturally, Hawaii was becoming a colony of the United States. That it should not become politically a colony of any other power came to be a tenet of American foreign policy, first announced in 1842 by President Tyler and Secretary of State Webster. This was as far as they cared to go. Nine years later, in restating the principle, as in the earlier instance, against threatened interference by France, Webster declined an offer of a protectorate and disclaimed any thought of annexing the islands.

Franklin Pierce, Democratic President (1853–1857), was ready to adopt a more aggressive Hawaiian policy than his Whig predecessors. A treaty of annexation was actually negotiated in Honolulu in 1854, but the death of the reigning monarch produced a change in Hawaiian policy, and the treaty was never signed.

The only Pacific islands that came under American sovereignty in the 1850s were acquired as a result of the "Guano Law" of 1856. The law was the consequence of the discovery by American ship captains of deposits of guano, a valuable fertilizer, on certain uninhabited islands in the Pacific. It provided that such islands, if taken possession of and occupied by citizens of the United States, might "at the discretion of the President, be considered as appertaining to the United States." The first "appurtenances" acquired under this law were Baker and Jarvis Islands. Dozens of others were added in due course, most of them in the Pacific, a few in the Atlantic and Caribbean. Of no value then, save for the guano deposits, some of them were to assume unexpected importance in the air age.

One other possible Pacific acquisition, Russian America (or Alaska), received some attention at this time. Russia was not averse to selling, and President James Buchanan (1857–1861) let it be known that he stood ready to pay $5,000,000 for it. The project was dropped when the Russian minister in Washington informed his government that under existing relations between President and Congress, no treaty sponsored by Buchanan was likely to get Senate approval.

Approaches to the Pacific: Railroad Schemes

Men who predicted a great future for the United States in the Pacific looked forward to speedier means of getting there than the prairie schooner plodding along the Oregon trail or the sailing ship beating laboriously around the Horn. There would be railroads across the continent or a canal through the isthmus; probably both. Asa Whitney, a New York merchant who had made a fortune in the China trade, labored vainly for years to persuade Congress to finance the building of a railroad from Lake Michigan to the mouth of the Columbia River. It proved easier to interest Democrats in Washington in a railroad by a southern route. The acquisition of such a route was warmly sponsored by Jefferson Davis, Secretary of War in Pierce's cabinet, and became an important object of James Gadsden's mission to Mexico in 1853.

The Gadsden Purchase

Gadsden was directed by William L. Marcy, Secretary of State, to secure a southward readjustment of the boundary with Mexico, between the Rio Grande and the Colorado, sufficient to permit the construction of a railroad within the limits of the United States. For this he could offer a maximum of $15,000,000. If Mexico would cede additional territory, Gadsden might offer more money, up to a top figure of $50,000,000 for a wide strip of northern Mexico, embracing portions of five states, and the peninsula of Lower California. In all, five alternative boundaries were suggested. Gadsden was also to secure the release of the United States from certain responsibilities of border policing that it had accepted in the Treaty of Guadalupe Hidalgo.

Events now began to take on a familiar pattern. The notorious Santa Anna was again in power in Mexico City and, as usual, was in need of money. Whether there was a duplicate of Colonel Atocha to carry hints to Gadsden the records do not reveal, but soon the minister was suggesting to Washington that an offer of a liberal down payment backed by threats of force might be expected to win valuable concessions. Accordingly, Gadsden was authorized to promise a large installment in cash for any one of the proposed cessions, and United States troops were moved ominously toward the Rio Grande.

Santa Anna this time proved compliant, but only to the extent of the minimum cession proposed by Gadsden. A treaty was signed on December 30, 1853. In the Senate it underwent considerable modification. As it emerged with Senate approval on April 25, 1854, it contained, in addition to the cession of territory between the Rio Grande and the Colorado, a guarantee to the government and the citizens of the United States of the use of any means of transit across the Isthmus of Tehuantepec, including the right of the government to protect the transit "when it may feel sanctioned and warranted by the public or international law." These rights, though never used, were not formally surrendered until 1937. The amended treaty also cancelled Article XI of the Treaty of Guadalupe Hidalgo, which had made the United States responsible for depredations that might be committed in Mexico by Indians from north of the border. The Senate reduced the monetary compensation from $20,000,000, of which $5,000,000 was to be paid to claimants in the United States, to $10,000,000, all to go to Mexico. All amendments were accepted by Santa Anna, and ratifications were exchanged in Washington June 30, 1854. Thus was acquired the route for a railroad subsequently utilized by the Southern Pacific.

Later attempts to secure rights-of-way on other possible railroad routes through Mexican territory were associated with chaotic political conditions in Mexico and the resulting danger of intervention from Europe. After Santa Anna's final elimination from Mexican politics in 1855, presidents followed one another in rapid succession, and soon there were rival governments at Mexico City and Vera Cruz. Americans and other foreigners lost lives and property in the disorders, and neither government would assume the obligation to settle damage claims. The situation was a standing invitation to foreign intervention, and President Buchanan feared that if the United States did not intervene, some European power or powers would do so, as eventually they did. He asked authority, therefore, to intervene by force in behalf of the "constitutional" government of Benito Juarez at Vera Cruz, to help in restoring order, and to establish, temporarily, a protectorate over certain of the northern states of Mexico. "As a good neighbor," he asked Congress, "shall we not extend to her a helping hand to save her?"

Northern men in Congress, suspecting that Buchanan's "good neighbor policy" cloaked designs for the extension of slave territory, saw to it that Congress refused or ignored all his requests. When his miniser, R. M. McLane, signed a treaty with the Juarez government granting to the United States for $4,000,000 rights-of-way on two railroad routes—from the lower Rio Grande to Mazatlán and from Nogales to Guaymas—and the right to intervene for the protection of its citizens in Mexico, the Senate rejected it (May 31, 1860) by a vote of eighteen ayes to twenty-seven noes. Thus the way was left open for the Anglo-French-Spanish intervention of 1862 and the reign of Maximilian.

The Search for a Canal Route: The Clayton-Bulwer Treaty

Keener than the interest in a transcontinental railroad route was that in the possibility of an interoceanic canal. Two sites for such a canal presented obvious advantages: Panama, where the inter-American isthmus was narrowest, and Nicaragua, where a natural water communication by

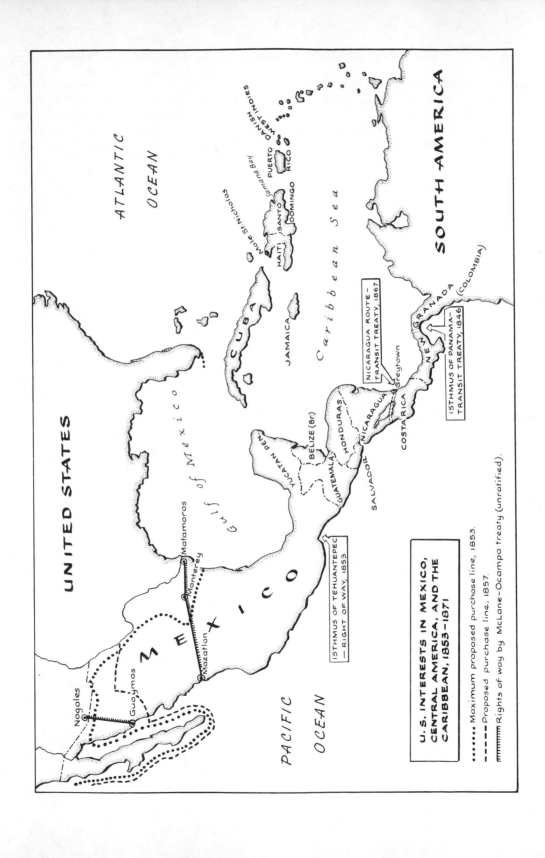

U.S. INTERESTS IN MEXICO, CENTRAL AMERICA, AND THE CARIBBEAN, 1853–1871

.... Maximum proposed purchase line, 1853.

– – – – Proposed purchase line, 1857.

ıııııııı Rights of way by McLane-Ocampo treaty (unratified).

UNITED STATES

ATLANTIC OCEAN

MEXICO

Gulf of Mexico

PACIFIC OCEAN

Nogales
Guaymas
Mazatlan
Monterey
Matamoros

ISTHMUS OF TEHUANTEPEC – RIGHT OF WAY, 1853

Caribbean Sea

CUBA

JAMAICA

HAITI
Mole St. Nicholas
Samana Bay
SANTO DOMINGO
PUERTO RICO
DANISH WEST INDIES

YUCATAN PEN.

BELIZE (Br.)
GUATEMALA
HONDURAS
SALVADOR
NICARAGUA
COSTA RICA
Greytown

NICARAGUA ROUTE – TRANSIT TREATY, 1867

NEW GRANADA (COLOMBIA)

ISTHMUS OF PANAMA – TRANSIT TREATY, 1846

SOUTH AMERICA

lake and river traversed all but a dozen miles of the distance between Pacific and Caribbean.

At Panama the United States had already, through no initiative of its own, acquired both rights and responsibilities. In 1846 Benjamin Bidlack, United States minister to New Granada (later known as Colombia), which embraced the isthmus, had been suddenly confronted with a surprising offer from the New Granadan government. If the United States would guarantee the neutrality of the isthmus and the sovereignty of New Granada therein, the government of New Granada would in return guarantee to the citizens of the United States the use of any means of transit that might be constructed across the isthmus upon the same terms as those enjoyed by the citizens of New Granada. Bidlack, though without instructions for such a contingency, signed the proposed treaty. Polk, after some hesitation because of the novel character of the plan, sent the treaty to the Senate, which eventually approved it.

Over control of the Nicaragua route an intense rivalry developed between local representatives of the United States and Great Britain. Fortunately, the governments in Washington and London were less ambitious and combative than the agents on the spot. A compromise settlement was achieved in a treaty signed by Secretary of State John M. Clayton and the British minister, Sir Henry Bulwer, April 19, 1850. Each party agreed never to obtain or maintain any exclusive control over the proposed Nicaraguan canal, never to erect fortifications in its vicinity, and never to colonize, or exercise dominion over, any part of Central America. Both agreed to lend support and encouragement to any company that should undertake the construction of a canal, to guarantee neutrality of the canal when built, and to invite other friendly states to become parties to the treaty.

There were ambiguities in the Clayton-Bulwer Treaty, which resulted in misunderstanding and bickerings through much of the following decade. These concerned principally the question of whether the treaty required Great Britain to surrender certain holdings in the area, such as her protectorate over the Mosquito Indians of Nicaragua, or merely to refrain from acquiring new ones. In the diplomatic debates over these issues, the United States relied not only upon its interpretation of the treaty, but also upon President Monroe's message of December 2, 1823, which now for the first time came to be referred to as the Monroe Doctrine. Great Britain adhered to her own interpretation of the treaty and would admit no validity in the Monroe Doctrine. In practice, however, she eventually gave in, surrendering the footholds to which the United States had objected. In these British retreats, which were in keeping with the current loss of interest in colonial possessions in general, one may perhaps see the first real victory of the Monroe Doctrine.

There was to be no isthmian canal for half a century, but both the Panama and Nicaragua routes were soon accommodating numerous travelers to and from the west coast of the United States. In Nicaragua, beginning in 1850, Cornelius Vanderbilt's Accessory Transit Company carried passengers by small steamer and coach between the Caribbean and the Pacific termini, to which steamers operated from New York and San Francisco. At Panama, by 1855, a railroad had replaced mule-back and other primitive modes of transportation across the isthmus.

Occasional disorders on both transit routes led to proposals for some sort of supervision by the United States. Riots in Panama disrupted transportation by that route. In Nicaragua, the incursion of the filibuster William Walker, the "grey-eyed man of destiny," kept things in turmoil for a year or two. To such interruptions of transportation over the isthmian routes President James Buchanan invited the attention of Congress in his first annual message in 1857 and in several subsequent messages. He proposed that Congress authorize the President to use the armed forces of the United States to keep the routes open.

One supporter of Buchanan's proposals was Sam Houston, now a senator from Texas. Houston questioned whether the United States had a right, under the Monroe Doctrine, to exclude European powers from intervention in the Americas "and yet do nothing ourselves by which these nations may be made useful to the community of nations, and advantageous to the cause of commerce, social organization and good government." Houston's position was close to that preached and practiced by Theodore Roosevelt half a century later. But Congress, where antislavery men suspected another scheme for extending slave territory, took no action. Buchanan was left to do what he could through normal diplomatic approaches to Nicaragua and New Granada.

Approaches to the Isthmus:
The Cuban Question

The eastern approaches to the isthmus lie through the Caribbean, and the Caribbean is rimmed on the northwest and north by the peninsula of Yucatán and by Cuba, Hispaniola, and other islands to the eastward. Peninsula and islands command the sea lanes into the Caribbean, and Cuba, in addition, shares with Florida control of the eastern gateway of the Gulf of Mexico. In an era when the isthmian routes had become of such vital concern to the United States, it was inevitable that a similar concern should be felt for the territories dominating the entrances to the Caribbean. It is not surprising, therefore, that the expansionists of the period following the Mexican War sponsored projects for securing footholds for the United States in Yucatán, Hispaniola, and Cuba.

In Yucatán, which at the time considered itself independent of Mexico, the white inhabitants were endangered by a formidable Indian revolt. Through an agent in Washington, in April 1848, they offered the United States "dominion and sovereignty" over the peninsula in return for military aid against the Indians. Notification that similar offers had been made to Spain and Great Britain led President Polk to send the correspondence to Congress. There a debate on the desirability of forestalling Britain by taking possession of Yucatán was terminated by news that whites and Indians in the peninsula had patched up their differences.

Six years later, the expansionist administration of Franklin Pierce made an attempt to secure by cession or lease a site for a naval base at Samaná Bay in the Dominican Republic on the island of Hispaniola. The American agent, William L. Cazneau, seemed on the point of success when intervention by the British and French consuls dissuaded the Dominican government from executing the cession.

Far more important in American eyes than Yucatán or Samaná Bay was the island of Cuba. Thomas Jefferson and John Quincy Adams had viewed Cuba as inescapably linked by fate with the United States, and Adams and Henry Clay had warned Spain that the United States could never consent to its transfer to another European power. The new importance of Cuba in relation to the isthmian routes, renewed hints of British and French interest in the island and of projects for the emancipation of Cuban slaves, sympathy for an oppressed colonial people who made sporadic attempts to throw off Spanish rule—all linked themselves with the prevalent expansionist fever in the United States to promote a succession of schemes for the "liberation" of Cuba and its eventual annexation.

An informal offer from President Polk to purchase the island for $100,000,000 was emphatically rebuffed by the Spanish government. The Whig administrations of Taylor and Fillmore (1849–1853) showed no interest in the acquisition of Cuba and did what they could to prevent the filibustering adventures of the exiled Cuban patriot, Narciso Lopez. Lopez, whose ostensible object was an independent Cuba, nevertheless had the support of such American expansionists as John L. O'Sullivan of New York and Governor John A. Quitman of Mississippi. Twice he succeeded in slipping out of New Orleans and landing several hundred men on Cuban shores. Both attempts failed, and the second, in August 1851, ended in the capture and execution of Lopez and many of his followers.

Spain had appealed for British and French aid in resisting the filibusters. In the spring of 1852 the British and French ministers in Washington invited the United States to adhere to a tripartite convention by which the three governments would disclaim for all time any intention of acquiring the island of Cuba and would promise to discourage any such design on the part of other powers or individuals. This proposal was rejected by the Fillmore administration. Edward Everett, who had become Secretary of State upon Webster's death, informed the two ministers that although the United States did not seek the acquisition of Cuba, he considered its status "mainly an American question." The proposed agreement, he continued, was unequal, since the fate of Cuba was of much more vital importance to the United States than it could be to France or Great Britain. While Spain stood still, furthermore, the United States was an expanding power whose growth could not be arrested by any such paper agreement as that proposed. Such reasoning by the Whig Secretary of State was a close approximation to the Democratic dogma of Manifest Destiny.

The Pierce Administration and Cuba

Before Everett's note was written, the November elections had resulted in the defeat of the Whigs and the choice of the Democrat, Franklin Pierce, for the presidency. The new administration was avowedly expansionist. Pierce's inaugural declaration that his policy would "not be controlled by any timid forebodings of evil from expansion" probably alluded to a warning from outgoing President Fillmore that "serious peril" might result from the acquisition of Cuba. Pierce believed, on the contrary, that the acquisition of certain possessions—not named but certainly including Cuba—was "eminently important for our protection."

Spain's aversion to the idea of parting with Cuba was well known. Pierce and his Secretary of State, William L. Marcy, would perhaps have been willing to resort to other methods than negotiation had they been sure of support within their party. The *Black Warrior* incident seemed for a while to offer an opportunity. On February 28, 1854, Spanish authorities in Havana confiscated the cargo of the American steamer of that name for a purely technical violation of the customs regulations. This action drew from Washington a strong remonstrance and a demand for redress, refusal of which might conceivably be used as an excuse for war and the seizure of Cuba. At the same time, John A. Quitman, the former Mississippi governor who had supported Lopez, was organizing a filibustering plan of his own to save "white civilization" in Cuba and to bring the island into the Union as a slave state. Pending in the Senate was a proposal to suspend the neutrality laws, thus removing a barrier to Quitman's plan. England and France, now involved in the Crimean War, would hardly be in a position to interfere.

This seemingly fair prospect was dissipated by a rift within the Democratic party.

Pierce's sponsorship of Senator Stephen A. Douglas' Kansas-Nebraska bill, opening Kansas and Nebraska territories to slavery, had incurred the displeasure of important sections of the northern Democracy. Virtual sponsorship of filibustering attacks on Cuba, demanded by proslavery southerners, might completely disrupt the party. In an attempt at compromise, Pierce repudiated the filibustering scheme and relaxed pressure on Spain for settlement of the *Black Warrior* claims but promised more energetic measures for the acquisition of Cuba by diplomacy.

The American minister to Spain was Pierre Soulé, French-born radical and expansionist from Louisiana. He had been authorized by Marcy to attempt to purchase Cuba for as much as $130,000,000 and if purchase proved impossible, to seek other means "to detach that island from the Spanish dominion and from all dependence on any European power." Soulé's efforts had availed nothing. Marcy now proposed that Soulé, James Buchanan, minister to Great Britain, and John Y. Mason, minister to France, meet, consult together, "compare opinions as to what may be advisable, and . . . adopt measures for perfect concert of action in aid of [Soulé's] negotiations at Madrid." They were directed to report the result of their deliberations to Marcy by confidential messenger.

Out of the meetings of the three envoys at Ostend and Aix-la-Chappelle came their report, dated October 15, 1854, which was to become notorious as the "Ostend Manifesto." The term is a misnomer. The document was a confidential report to the Secretary of State and was published only at the insistence of the administration's enemies in the House of Representatives. It failed to give what Marcy presumably had desired—an objective appraisal of the attitudes of the principal European governments toward the Cuban question. It consisted principally of advice to the govern-

ment of the United States as to why it needed Cuba and of advice to Spain on the advantages which that country could derive from selling the island. The sensational portion of the "manifesto" was a declaration that if Spain refused to sell Cuba and if conditions in Cuba should seriously endanger "our internal peace and the existence of our cherished Union," the United States would be justified in seizing the island upon the principle of self-defense.

The "Ostend Manifesto" failed completely in its purpose. Marcy repudiated the proposal for seizure, "the robber doctrine" he called it, whereupon Soulé resigned as minister. In December the Spanish Foreign Minister stated to an applauding Cortes: "To part with Cuba would be to part with the national honor." In the United States, the November elections went against the administration. Whatever chance Franklin Pierce may have had to acquire Cuba had been destroyed by the adverse northern reaction to the Kansas-Nebraska Act.

Pierce's successor, James Buchanan, fared no better than Pierce with respect to Cuba. The co-author of the Ostend Manifesto repeatedly called upon Congress for funds to facilitate negotiations with Spain for the acquisition of the island, but in the face of growing opposition, his efforts were fruitless.

Could Buchanan have had his way, he would have purchased Cuba, stationed United States troops in Nicaragua and on the Isthmus of Panama, and used the army in Mexico to establish an orderly and solvent government. In proposing these policies, it seems safe to say, Buchanan was seeking to promote national rather than sectional interests—to guard the isthmian transit and the approaches to it and to forestall European intervention by removing the justification for it. He ultimately failed because of the identification of his plans with the interests of slavery.

ADDITIONAL READINGS

CURTI, M. E., "Young America," *American Historical Review,* 32 (1926), 34–55.

FAIRBANK, J. K., " 'American China Policy' to 1898: A Misconception," *Pacific Historical Review,* 39 (1970), 409–20.

————, *Trade and Diplomacy on the China Coast: The Treaty Ports, 1842–1854.* 2 vols. Cambridge: Harvard University Press, 1953.

IRIYE, AKIRA, *Across the Pacific: An Inner History of American Far Eastern Relations.* New York: Harcourt Brace Jovanovich, Inc. 1967.

OFFICER, L. H. and L. B. SMITH, "The Canadian-American Reciprocity Treaty of 1855 to 1866" *Journal of Economic History,* 28 (1968), 598–623.

PINEAU, ROGER, ed., *The Japan Expedition, 1852–1854: The Personal Journey of Commodore Matthew C. Perry.* New York: Random House, Inc., 1969.

RAUCH, BASIL, *American Interest in Cuba, 1848–1855.* New York: Columbia University Press, 1955.

STATLER, OLIVER, *Shimoda Story.* New York: Random House, Inc., 1969.

9. The Diplomacy of the Civil War

The attack on Fort Sumter by the forces of the Southern Confederacy, April 12, 1861, opened the four-year struggle usually referred to as the American Civil War. Seven states of the lower South had seceded as a consequence of the election of Lincoln and at Montgomery, Alabama, had organized the Confederate States of America. Four additional states, Virginia, North Carolina, Tennessee, and Arkansas, joined them after the firing on Fort Sumter and Lincoln's call upon the states for troops to assist in suppressing the insurrection. The Atlantic and Gulf coasts from Chesapeake Bay to the Rio Grande lay within the Confederacy. This fact made it certain that the war would be fought by sea as well as by land and would involve many of the same troublesome questions between belligerents and neutrals that had been raised in the Napoleonic Wars.

The United States now found itself in an unaccustomed role—that of a belligerent in a war in which the great powers of Europe were neutral. It may be said, in general, that although the United States repudiated none of the principles for which it had previously contended, it adopted a new emphasis in their interpretation. It now insisted upon the *rights* of belligerents rather than their obligations, upon the *obligations* of neutrals rather than their rights. The consequence was an enlargement of belligerent rights and a more precise and exacting definition of neutral duties.

But the most momentous question that confronted the United States after the outbreak of hostilities was whether Europe, especially England and France, would remain neutral. It was the hope of Confederate leaders in 1861 that intervention by one or more of the European powers would insure the independence of the South, much as the intervention of France in 1778 had insured the independence of the United States. By the same token, avoidance of European intervention was vital to the triumph of the North.[1]

The Downfall of King Cotton

The first step toward intervention in behalf of the South would be formal recognition of the Confederacy as an independent state, and for this, Confederate agents in England and France, worked unceasingly throughout the conflict. Napoleon III, the French Emperor, was frankly pro-southern in sympathy. He was ready to recognize the Confederacy and to intervene at any time when the British government would cooperate. Without British support he dared not risk such action. All depended, therefore, upon the British attitude, and this in turn was determined by a number of factors.

The South had relied heavily upon the

[1] William H. Seward, Lincoln's Secretary of State, suggested to Lincoln (April 1, 1861) that provoking a foreign crisis, even war with Spain and France, might restore the Union. His suggestion was tactfully set aside by the President. Seward soon recovered from this "foreign war panacea" illusion and thereafter conducted the delicate diplomacy of wartime with exemplary discretion.

power of "King Cotton" to compel European intervention. This reliance proved illusory. Confidence that Europe, especially England, was so dependent upon the South's cotton that it must intervene to gain access to the white staple had failed to take account of the large surpluses of cotton and cotton goods in European warehouses in 1861. To the owners of these stocks, the cutting off of further supplies was a boon. By the time the surpluses were exhausted, substitutes were available. Neither the owners nor the employees of British cotton mills agitated for intervention.[2] Economic considerations, in fact, were more conducive to nonintervention than to intervention by Britain in the American war. Continuance of the war was profitable to British interests, not only in the enhanced prices of textiles, but also in the sale of war supplies to both sides and in the opportunity for destruction by Confederate cruisers of northern shipping, the chief competitor of England's merchant marine.[3] Intervention, furthermore, involving a break with the North, would entail serious risks for Great Britain. In Canada and the British merchant marine, the North held hostages for Britain's good behavior.

Apart from such material factors, British sympathies divided largely along class and ideological lines. The aristocracy, at that time still to a large degree the governing class, had much in common with the planter class of the South and were inclined to welcome the breakup of the Union as an object lesson in the failure of democracy. British liberals, like John Bright, likewise looked upon the war as a test of democracy and for that reason hoped for a northern victory and the preservation of the Union. British labor also favored the North, and though still unenfranchised, made its influence felt through numerous mass meetings and other forms of demonstration. Lincoln's emancipation policy, although deplored by the upper classes as a last desperate gamble and an invitation to a servile war, strengthened the support of the North on the part of liberal and labor groups.[4]

Viscount Palmerston and Earl Russell, Prime Minister and Foreign Secretary, respectively, shared the sympathies of the British upper classes, but in so far as their official policy could be called pro-southern, it was the result of a widely held conviction that southern victory was inevitable and that hence the prolongation of the war meant useless bloodshed and destruction of property. In this conviction and under Russell's leadership, the cabinet was on the verge of intervention in October of 1862.

News of the southern repulse at Antietam, arriving at an opportune moment, made southern victory less certain and strengthened the opponents of intervention. The cabinet drew back. In November the government rejected French proposals for joint intervention. Never again did Palmerston and Russell approach so close to recognition of the Confederacy.

The War and Belligerent Rights

Although the Confederacy never secured the coveted recognition of its independence, the British government was prompt in granting it belligerent rights. Such a course was not only in accord with Ameri-

---

[2]F. L. Owsley, *King Cotton Diplomacy: Foreign Relations of the Confederate States of America* (Chicago: University of Chicago Press, 1931), chap. 2; E. D. Adams, *Great Britain and the American Civil War*, 2 vols. (New York: Longmans, Green & Company, Inc., 1925), 2, chap. 10. The theory that accounts for British nonintervention by a supposed British dependence upon northern wheat is not tenable. Wheat was obtainable elsewhere. It came from the United States in large quantities chiefly because sale of war supplies to the North created a favorable exchange rate.

[3]Owsley, *King Cotton Diplomacy*, chap. 19.

[4]Adams, *Britain and Civil War*, 2, chap. 12; J. G. Randall, *Lincoln the President*, 3 vols. (New York: Dodd, Mead & Co., 1945–1953), 2: 176–80; 3, chaps. 13, 14. Public reaction in favor of emancipation and hence in favor of the North was apparently much more general in France and Spain than in England.

can practice, as seen in connection with the Canadian rebellion of 1837, it was rendered unavoidable by the magnitude of the military preparations in America and by the Federal government's institution of a naval blockade of southern ports—clearly an act of one belligerent against another. British recognition of Confederate belligerency, accomplished through the issuance of a neutrality proclamation on May 13, 1861, was promptly imitated by the other principal European governments. In practice it meant chiefly that Confederate naval vessels or privateers would be treated as legitimate ships of war, not as pirates. Though Lincoln and William H. Seward, his Secretary of State, resented the British proclamation as unfriendly, or at least as premature, nevertheless they found it necessary themselves to treat the Confederacy as a belligerent, not as a domestic insurrectionary movement, as Seward at first hoped.

The war, therefore, raised many of the old questions concerning the rights and duties of belligerents and neutrals.

To a considerable extent, these questions had been answered, for Europe at any rate, by the Declaration of Paris, adopted April 16, 1856, at the close of the Crimean War. The powers concerned (Austria, France, Great Britain, Prussia, Russia, Sardinia, and Turkey), had joined in declaring the following principles:

1. Privateering is, and remains, abolished;
2. The neutral flag covers enemy's goods, with the exception of contraband of war;
3. Neutral goods, with the exception of contraband of war, are not liable to capture under the enemy's flag;
4. Blockades, in order to be binding, must be effective; that is to say, maintained by a force sufficient really to prevent access to the coast of the enemy.

To this declaration the United States was invited to adhere. The second, third, and fourth articles stated principles for which the United States had long contended and which it rejoiced to see thus formally accepted by the great powers. But for the abolition of privateering it was not then ready. The United States had a large merchant marine but a navy far inferior to the navies of several European states. If it were unable, in a war with a European power such as England, to supplement its inadequate navy with privateers, it would be at a serious disadvantage. Its own merchant marine might be destroyed or driven from the seas by the British navy, while the American navy could inflict only trifling losses on British commerce. Only on one condition would the United States consent to end privateering—if the other powers would agree to the immunity of all noncontraband belligerent property at sea. Secretary of State Marcy offered American adherence to the declaration if it were amended to include this principle. There the negotiations had ended.

In the war now begun, privateering might well work to the advantage of the Confederacy and to the detriment of the United States. Lincoln and Seward, consequently, had reason to regret that their predecessors had not subscribed to the Declaration of Paris, which might now have been invoked to outlaw privateering under the Confederate flag. Seward, in fact, proposed to Great Britain and other signatories that they accept the adherence of the United States to the declaration without the amendment upon which it had formerly insisted. Earl Russell in reply offered to accept the adherence of the United States, but only with the understanding that such acceptance should not "have any bearing . . . on the internal differences now prevailing in the United States." The qualification meant, of course, that Great Britain would not regard the ban upon privateering as applicable in the current conflict. Seward declined the offer thus qualified but made it plain to the British Foreign

Office that the United States proposed to adhere to the second, third, and fourth articles of the declaration.[5]

In reality, all four principles of the Declaration of Paris came to be observed during the war. The Confederacy, after a few experiments with privateering, abandoned the practice as unprofitable. As for the North, although Congress in 1863 authorized President Lincoln to issue letters of marque, the President never made use of that authority.

Blockading the Confederacy

Observance of the fourth principle of the Declaration of Paris—that "blockades," in order to be binding, must be effective"—presented serious problems to the government in Washington. In a proclamation of April 19, 1861, Lincoln announced the intention of the government to institute a blockade of the ports of the seceded states. These ports, after Virginia and North Carolina joined the Confederacy, were scattered along 3,000 miles of coastline stretching from Chesapeake Bay to the Rio Grande. The Navy which would bear responsibility for closing some 185 ports or openings in this extensive coastline comprised initially about one hundred vessels, of which two-thirds were antiquated sailing vessels, while a number of the better steamers were in navy yards awaiting repairs. These were supplemented as rapidly as possible by the purchase of vessels of the most diverse types—steamers, tugs, ferryboats, even sailing vessels—since any craft that could carry a few guns and remain at sea could be utilized for blockade purposes. Over four hundred vessels were thus acquired during the war.[6]

Whether the blockade thus instituted was technically effective was at the time, and has been since, a matter of controversy.[7] There were a great many successful violations; just how many is not known. On the other hand, over 1,500 ships were captured or destroyed in attempted violations, and before the end of the war, the principal Confederate ports were in Union hands. The British government, at any rate, accepted the blockade as effective and hence as binding under international law. Legality did not require, as Earl Russell wrote, that a blockade make access to a port impossible; it was sufficient if it created "an evident danger of entering or leaving it." There is good reason to suppose that the British government was not displeased at seeing the United States hitherto the champion of neutral rights, now extending the rights of belligerents and setting precedents that might be useful to England in the future—as indeed they were.[8]

One of the precedents that was to prove of great value to Great Britain in years to come was the American application to blockade of that British invention, the doctrine of continuous voyage. This doctrine, it will be recalled, had first been announced by British courts in the case of the *Essex* (1805) in connection with the rule of 1756.

[5]Department of State, *Policy of the United States toward Maritime Commerce in War*, prepared by Carlton Savage, 2 vols. (Washington, D.C.: Government Printing Office, 1934–1936), 1: 416–19, 432–35. Before answering Seward, the Foreign Office had sounded the Confederate government unofficially through the British consul at Charleston and had been informed that it would accept all articles of the Declaration of Paris except the first, which abolished privateering; Adams, *Britain and Civil War*, 1, chap. 5.

[6]C. S. Alden and Allan Westcott, *The United States Navy: A History* (New York: :J. B. Lippincott Co. 1943), p. 144.

[7]Department of State, *Policy toward Maritime Commerce*, 1: 442. The leading modern critic of the blockade is Professor Owsley, who concludes, largely on the basis of estimates, that for the first two years of its duration the blockade of the South "made the old-fashioned English blockade look like a stone wall in comparison." Owsley, *King Cotton Diplomacy*, chap. 8.

[8]J. P. Baxter, III, "The British Government and Neutral Rights, 1861–1865," *American Historical Review*, 34 (1928), 9–29.

American courts adopted it in the enforcement of the Civil War blockade.

The actual running of the blockade was most successfully carried out by specially adapted steamers that brought cargoes from Bermuda, Nassau, or Havana into the ports of the Confederacy. Such steamers were hard to intercept, hard even to see. It was much easier to catch ships of more conventional type that brought the goods from Europe to the intermediate neutral ports. But could a voyage from Liverpool to Nassau be interfered with on the ground that the ultimate destination of the cargo was a blockaded port? The United States Supreme Court answered affirmatively. If the ship's papers or the character of the cargo showed conclusively that its real destination was a blockaded port, that the neutral destination was a subterfuge, then the voyage was *continuous* (even though in different ships) from origin to ultimate destination, and the cargo, whether contraband or not, was liable to confiscation for breach of blockade. If the owners of the ship were aware of the ultimate destination of the cargo, the ship was also subject to confiscation.

Such was the opinion of the Supreme Court in the cases of the *Bermuda* and the *Springbok,* where the ultimate destination of the cargo was a blockaded port of the Confederacy. In the case of the *Peterhoff,* intercepted en route to Matamoros, Mexico, with a cargo destined for the Confederacy but not through a port actually blockaded, the court held that no breach of blockade was involved and that only the contraband goods in the cargo were seizable.[9]

It is significant that although continental jurists—French, German, and Dutch— vigorously attacked the doctrine of continuous voyage as applied by the Supreme

[9]*Bermuda,* 3 Wall. 514 (1865); *Springbok,* 5 Wall. 1 (1866); *Peterhoff,* 5 Wall. 28 (1866). J. W. Pratt, "The British Blockade and American Precedent," *U.S. Naval Institute Proceedings,* 46 (1920), 1789–1802.

Court in these cases, the British government said not a word in protest, although the property condemned was the property of British subjects. Apparently the British were content to see the United States adopt, adapt, and improve upon, a theory very useful to a belligerent controlling the sea lanes.

A Crisis with Great Britain: The Trent Affair

There were limits, however, to Britain's acquiescence in the stretching of the law and precedent by the United States. An instance in which the British government firmly called a halt was the *Trent* affair in the first year of the war.

In November 1861, Captain Charles Wilkes, in the United States cruiser *San Jacinto,* took from the British mail steamer *Trent* the Confederate agents James M. Mason and John Slidell and their secretaries. Mason and Slidell, en route to represent the Confederacy in England and France respectively, had slipped through the blockade to Havana and there had taken passage on the *Trent* to St. Thomas, Danish West Indies, on their way to Europe. Wilkes, who had learned of their presence on the *Trent,* halted the ship and removed the four men over their protests and those of the British commander of the *Trent.* A week later (November 15) he landed them at Fortress Monroe, Virginia.

The news of Wilkes' bold action, which was taken wholly on his own responsibility, created great excitement in both the United States and England—in the former, exultation over the seizure of two important and dangerous Confederate personages with a slap at John Bull in the process; in the latter, resentment at an indignity to the British flag and insistence that the envoys be released and apologies made. In the United States, Wilkes was praised almost unanimously by the press and congratulated by the Secretary of the Navy. The House of Representatives passed a resolution thanking him for his "brave, adroit, and patriotic conduct." In England, Earl Russell penned instructions to Lord Lyons, British minister in Washington, directing him to demand the release of the envoys and an apology, and if these demands were not granted within seven days from their presentation, to close the legation and leave Washington. Few persons in England expected the United States to yield. Seward was suspected of a desire to provoke a war with Great Britain, and it was widely assumed that Wilkes had acted under his instructions. Since war seemed likely, British troops were ordered to Canada and the Navy was put in readiness for action.

Yet neither the British public nor the British government wished war. War with the United States would again endanger Canada, bring disaster to the British merchant marine, and align Great Britain, leader in the crusade to end slavery, on the side of the slaveholding South. The instructions to Lyons had been softened, largely at the instance of Albert, the Prince Consort: the minister was not to "menace" the United States or to inform Seward of the seven-day time limit. Later he was told that an explanation would be accepted instead of an apology.

Seward was in a difficult dilemma. He knew that Wilkes' action had been irregular, that in defending him the United States would have a poor case, that European opinion solidly supported England, and that to refuse the release of Mason and Slidell would mean war with England and the almost certain victory of the Confederacy. Seward, who had long since discarded his "foreign war panacea," wanted none of this. On the other hand, to surrender the Confederate agents would be flouting public opinion in the United States and might be politically disastrous to the administration.

Seward escaped from the trap with great skill. Having won Lincoln and the cabinet to his way of thinking in two long meetings, December 25 and 26, 1861, he promised the British minister that Mason and Slidell would be released but gave the promise in a paper, at once made public, in which he made it appear that in releasing them, he was vindicating a principle which the United States had long cherished and England had flouted. Reviewing Wilkes' conduct, he argued that the officer had been within his rights and had followed correct procedures in stopping and searching the *Trent* and that Mason and Slidell were properly liable for capture since—and here Seward advanced a novel doctrine—"persons, as well as property, may become contraband."[10] Wilkes' only error had been in removing the envoys on his own responsibility instead of bringing the *Trent* before a prize court where their status could be determined by proper judicial authority. But in committing this one error, Wilkes had been guilty, said Seward, of the very practice of which the United States had complained so bitterly when it was followed by Great Britain—the arbitray action of naval officers in assuming the right to remove persons from neutral ships. What was this but impressment? Seward continued:

> If I decide this case in favor of my own government, I must disavow its most cherished principles, and reverse and forever abandon its essential policy. The country cannot afford the sacrifice. If I maintain those principles, and adhere to that policy, I must surrender the case itself. . . . We are

[10] In instructions of the Secretary of the Treasury, May 23, 1862, only "military persons in the service of the enemy" were listed as contraband. This list was adopted by the Secretary of State in instructions to consular representatives, May 30, 1862. Mason and Slidell were of course not "military persons." A further difficulty about considering them as "contraband" was the fact that they were in transit between two neutral ports and that even their "ultimate destination" was not enemy territory.

asked to do to the British nation just what we have always insisted all nations ought to do to us.

By the proposed adjustment of the present case, therefore, Seward declared, a question which had alienated the two countries for more than half a century would be "finally and rightly settled between them."

Seward could not resist the opportunity to take a dig at the two southern envoys, whose "comparative unimportance," he remarked, together with the "waning proportions of the existing insurrection," made it unnecessary for him to detain them on grounds of national security. Their self-esteem received a further blow when, upon reaching Europe, they not only met with a cool reception and no encouragement as to recognition, but were informed editorially by the London *Times* that "We should have done just as much to rescue two of their own Negroes."

Seward's surrender on these terms was well received in the United States and gladly accepted in England, though Earl Russell made it plain that he did not accept all of Seward's reasoning. Only southern agents and their sympathizers were disappointed. They found, in fact, that the crisis and its settlement had reacted against them and in favor of the North. Minister Adams reported to Seward that the *Trent* affair, "with just the issue that it had, was rather opportune than otherwise"; and Henry Hotze, the Confederate agent, complained that "the *Trent* affair has done us incalculable injury" and that Earl Russell was now "an avowed enemy of our nationality."[11]

The War and Neutral Obligations: The Confederate Cruisers

Except for the *Trent* affair and the close approach to British recognition of the Confederacy in the fall of 1862, the only mis-

[11]Adams, *Britain and Civil War,* 1: 243.

understanding with England that reached crisis level concerned the building of ships for the Confederate Navy in British shipyards and subsequent hospitality to such ships in British Empire ports. These activities were made possible, as Americans saw it, by the inadequacy of the British neutrality laws and their lax enforcement.

The British statute on neutral conduct, the Foreign Enlistment Act of 1819, forbade the equipping, furnishing, fitting out, or arming within British jurisdiction of vessels for the purpose of attacking the commerce of friendly powers, or the augmentation of "the warlike force" of such vessels, but did not prohibit the building of such vessels. Taking advantage of this loophole in the law, Captain James D. Bulloch, the Confederate agent charged with such business, arranged with English shipbuilding firms for the construction of the ships, originally known as the *Oreto* and "No. 290," which became famous as the Confederate cruisers *Florida* and *Alabama*. In each case the ship was built but not "equipped, fitted out, or armed" in a British shipyard. Each put to sea without equipment and in a remote and unpoliced sanctuary—the *Florida* in the Bahamas, the *Alabama* in the Azores—met another steamer bringing her armament, officers, and crew. Each was then duly commissioned as a ship of the Confederate Navy and began her career as a commerce destroyer. The *Florida* made over forty prizes before she was herself captured by the U.S.S. *Wachusett*—by a violation of neutrality—in the port of Bahia, Brazil. The *Alabama* destroyed fifty-seven prizes and released many more on bond before she was sunk in a duel with the U.S.S. *Kearsarge* off the port of Cherbourg, France. Next after these two in destructiveness and notoriety was the *Shenandoah*, purchased for the Confederacy from her English owners and armed and manned at sea. Beginning her career late and cruising in the Pacific, she destroyed a large part of the New England whaling fleet at a time when, unknown to her officers or their victims, the Confederacy had ceased to exist.

In the cases of the *Florida* and *Alabama,* Charles Francis Adams, the United States minister to the Court of St. James, had laid before the British government evidence that the ships were being prepared for the service of the Confederacy. The evidence against the *Alabama* was so strong that at the last moment Earl Russell ordered her held. The order came too late. The *Alabama* had steamed out of the Mersey River on a "trial trip" from which she never returned. The United States held Great Britain guilty of breaches of neutrality in permitting her escape and in the construction of the *Florida.*

The United States held also that Great Britain had violated the principles of neutrality in permitting Confederate cruisers to augment their strength in ports of the British Empire. The *Shenandoah,* for example, had put in at Melbourne, Australia, where, in spite of protests from the United States consul, she was allowed to make repairs, take on a supply of coal, and recruit additions to her crew. In addition to the actual destruction wrought by the *Alabama, Florida, Shenandoah,* and less celebrated raiders, their depredations had caused a skyrocketing of insurance rates, kept ships idle in port, and driven many northern shipowners to sell their vessels or transfer them to foreign registry. For all these losses, British negligence or partiality was held responsible.

The *Alabama* began her career in August 1862. Even before her escape, Captain Bulloch signed a contract with her builders, Laird Brothers, of Birkenhead, for the construction of two armored steamers, each to be equipped with four rifled guns mounted in turrets, and armed with a ram at the bow—ships more powerful than any in the United States Navy. It was reported that the "Laird rams," as the vessels were called, were being built for France or for the viceroy of Egypt, but their real destination was common knowledge and their possession by the Confederacy would imperil the blockade and might well decide the out-come of the war. Adams bombarded Earl Russell with evidence of the true character and destination of the rams, most of it gathered by Thomas H. Dudley, the efficient United States consul at Liverpool. Adams' protests reached a climax with the warning, September 5, 1863, that should the rams be allowed to depart, "It would be superfluous in me to point out to your lordship that this is war."

Before receiving Adams' threat, Russell had ordered the rams detained; eventually they were purchased by the British government. There was, in reality, no danger that the rams would be allowed to escape. Russell was merely awaiting the most opportune time to halt them. Months earlier the British government had decided that it would not risk serious trouble with the United States by permitting repetitions of the *Alabama* episode. In April it had proceeded against the *Alexandra,* whose case resembled the *Alabama's,* and in September it detained the Laird rams. There were no more such incidents.

The suppression of Confederate transactions in English shipyards, together with England's continued refusal to recognize the Confederacy, made it clear to the Confederate government and its agents in Europe that British policy was actually beneficial to the North rather than the South. Mason withdrew from England under instructions in 1863, and in the same year British consuls in the South were expelled by the government at Richmond. Nonexistent diplomatic relations could not be broken, but these Confederate gestures were an equivalent manifestation of displeasure.

The Alabama Claims and the Geneva Arbitration

The British government's action against the *Alexandra* and the rams, although gratifying, did not atone for its earlier laxness, which had permitted the escape of the

Alabama and *Florida* and had facilitated the destructive careers of those cruisers and the *Shenandoah*. The war's end, therefore, left the United States with a sense of grievance and a determination to insist upon compensation for damages resulting from Great Britain's too casual observance of neutral obligations.

An American proposal that the question of Great Britain's responsibility for the depredations of the Confederate cruisers be submitted to arbitration was at first rejected by the British government. By 1869, however, that government had concluded that the precedents set by the *Alabama* and her sisters might be injurious to British interests. In the event of an Anglo-Russian war, which seemed not unlikely, American shipyards might build cruisers for the Czar's navy, with disastrous consequences to the British merchant marine.[12]

Fear of such developments was at least one of the influences that led a new British ministry to agree, in 1869, to the Johnson-Clarendon convention, which provided for submission to arbitration of all claims on either side that had arisen since 1853, the year of the last general settlement. The "*Alabama* claims," as they were now called, were mentioned, but without special emphasis. There was no expression of regret or apology for British delinquencies, and the neutral member of the proposed court of arbitration was under certain circumstances to be chosen by lot, leaving much to chance.

All of these defects in the treaty, from the American point of view, help to explain its rejection by an unfriendly Senate with only a single vote in its favor. Charles Sumner, chairman of the Foreign Relations Committee, in a celebrated speech, put forward additional reasons. The proposed arbitration, he complained, took account of but a small fraction of England's debt to the

United States. England should pay, he argued, not only the value of the ships and cargoes destroyed by the English-built cruisers, estimated at $15,000,000; she should pay also for the losses resulting from increased insurance rates and commerce driven from the sea or to the coverage of neutral flags. These items he put at $110,000,000. But that was not all. Only British encouragement, Sumner argued, had kept the Confederacy fighting after the battle of Gettysburg in July 1863. Britain ought, therefore, to pay half the cost of the war to the North, or two billion dollars. The total bill of $2,125,000,000, Sumner let it be known, could be paid only by ceding Canada and Britain's other American possessions to the United States.

Sumner's speech and the Senate's apparent endorsement of it in the 54 to 1 vote against the Johnson-Clarendon convention placed an obstacle in the path of any settlement of the *Alabama* claims. No British government could agree to the "indirect claims," as Sumner's second and third categories were called. British spokesmen in Washington also pointed out that Canada could not be ceded contrary to its own wishes, and few Canadians wished for annexation by the United States.

Hamilton Fish, Secretary of State under President Grant, was anxious for a friendly settlement with Great Britain. He did not take Sumner's indirect claims seriously but did believe that they should be put forward, if only to be set aside by an authoritative arbitral body. With the concurrence of Grant (who had at first been disposed to back Sumner's position), he brought this matter and others before a joint high commission (five Americans, four British, and one Canadian), which met at Washington in the spring of 1871. The resulting Treaty of Washington, signed May 8, 1871, provided, among other things, for the arbitration of the *Alabama* claims.[13]

---

[12]This danger was emphasized when the House of Representatives in July 1866 voted to repeal those clauses of the neutrality laws which forbade the sale of ships to belligerents.

[13]In addition to providing for arbitration of the *Alabama* claims, the Treaty of Washington provided

The treaty featured an unqualified expression of

the regret felt by Her Majesty's Government for the escape, under whatever circumstances, of the Alabama and other vessels from British ports, and for the depredations committed by those vessels.

Although not exactly an apology or an admission of wrongdoing, this statement went far enough to satisfy most Americans. The treaty then provided for a tribunal of arbitration of five persons, one each to be named by the President of the United States, the Queen of Great Britain, the President of the Swiss Confederation, the King of Italy, and the Emperor of Brazil. To this body were to be submitted all claims growing out of the acts committed by the *Alabama* and other vessels, "generically known as the 'Alabama Claims.'" In reaching decisions the arbitrators were to be governed by three rules, in addition to such principles of international law as they might consider applicable. The three rules were crucial.

Of special importance was the first. It filled the principal gap in the foreign enlistment act by making it the duty of a neutral government to use due diligence to prevent the departure from its jurisdiction of any vessel intended to carry on war against a friendly power, "such vessels having been specially adapted, in whole or in part, within such jurisdiction, to warlike use." Since there could be little doubt that the

Alabama and *Florida* had been so adapted within British jurisdiction, acceptance of these rules by the British government came close to being a surrender of its case.

But when all seemed set for a happy ending to the controversy, a new crisis arose. When the court of arbitration convened in Geneva in December 1871, the case presented by the United States included the indirect claims, much as they had been drawn up by Charles Sumner. This course was adopted not with any expectation that the judges would accept them, but to satisfy the Senate and public opinion in the United States and, as Secretary Fish viewed the matter, to have the claims judicially disposed of, once and for all. The British, however, were under the impression that the United States had tacitly abandoned the indirect claims. They charged bad faith and refused to consent to any consideration of these claims by the court. It appeared that the court might have to adjourn with nothing accomplished, but a way was finally found around the obstacle. The court, in the absence of the British member, delivered an extrajudicial statement to the effect that the indirect claims were inadmissible. The opinion was promptly accepted by both British and American governments, and the tribunal proceeded to a consideration of the direct claims.

The decision of the tribunal was made public on September 14, 1872. On British responsibility for the depredations of the *Alabama,* the judges were unanimous. That the British government was also responsible for the careers of the *Florida* and the *Shenandoah* the court held by votes of four to one and three to two respectively, the British member in each case voting in the negative. Claims based upon the careers of other cruisers were unanimously rejected. For the destruction wrought by the *Alabama, Florida,* and *Shenandoah,* the court awarded damages of $15,500,000 to the United States. Sir Alexander Cockburn, the British member of the tribunal, declined to sign the award and in other ways showed

---

the following modes of settlement for other controversies: A mixed commission on British claims for property seized during the Civil War awarded $1,929,819 to British subjects. A mixed commission on the value of inshore fisheries (reciprocally agreed to for 12 years by the treaty) awarded to Great Britain (over U.S. protest) $5,500,000 for the estimated difference between the value of the privilege to Americans and that to British subjects. A dispute over the ownership of the San Juan Islands, lying in the straits between Vancouver Island and Washington Territory, was submitted for arbitration to the German Emperor, who in 1872 decided in favor of the American claim.

himself a poor loser, but the British government promptly paid the bill. A troublesome controversy was settled, Anglo-American relations were restored to a cordial footing, and the obligations of neutrals were established with new precision.

ADDITIONAL READINGS

BERNATH, STUART L., *Squall Across the Atlantic: American Civil War Prize Cases and Diplomacy.* Berkeley, Calif.: University of California Press, 1970.

COOK, ADRIAN, *The Alabama Claims.* Ithaca, New York: Cornell University Press, 1975.

CROOK, D. P., *The North, The South, and the Powers, 1861–1865.* New York: John Wiley & Sons, 1974. In abridged form, *Diplomacy during the American Civil War.* New York: John Wiley & Sons, 1975.

KUSHNER, HOWARD L., "The Russian Fleet and the American Civil War: Another View," *Historian,* 35 (1972), 633–49.

10. From the Civil War to the Spanish American War

The secession of the southern states and the ensuing Civil War had put an end, for the time being, to plans for national expansion. The years immediately following the war, however, were almost as prolific in expansionist projects as the 1850s had been, though with different sponsorship and different motives. The Democratic party, formerly the party of Manifest Destiny, went into a long political eclipse. A few prominent individuals in the dominant Republican party—notably Secretary of State William H. Seward—became devotees of that doctrine but did not succeed in converting many of their colleagues. Several of the motives for expansion operative in the 1850's had disappeared in whole or in part. Slavery in the United States was ended. The need for an isthmian route to the Pacific became less urgent with the construction of the first transcontinental railroad—the Union Pacific—Central Pacific line—authorized in 1862 and completed in 1869. The menace of European intervention in the Caribbean region was removed; for Spain, which had reannexed her former colony of Santo Domingo in 1861, withdrew four years later, and France in 1867 abandoned her support of Maximilian's empire in Mexico.

On the other hand, the experiences of the United States Navy during the Civil War had called attention to the need for insular naval bases in both the Caribbean and the Pacific. Seward, Secretary of State (1861–1869), sought to meet this need, as did President Grant after 1869. Seward in 1867 negotiated a treaty with Denmark for the purchase of the islands of St. Thomas and St. John in the Virgin Islands group, attractive to Seward and the Navy because of the fine harbor of Charlotte Amalie in St. Thomas. The price, $7,500,000, seemed excessive to many members of the American Congress; the more so since just at that time the islands were devastated by a series of natural disasters—an earthquake, a tidal wave, and a tropical hurricane. The House of Representatives warned that it would not feel bound to appropriate the money, and in the Senate, the treaty was never brought to a vote.

Seward then turned to dicker with the current dictator of the Dominican Republic, or Santo Domingo, for purchase or lease of Samaná Bay, a capacious harbor at the northeastern corner of the island. Buenaventura Báez, the dictator-president, was ready for a deal, as was President Andrew Johnson, but Congress showed itself averse to this proposal also, and soon thereafter Seward went out of office with the Johnson Administration.

President Ulysses S. Grant (1869–1877) took up the Santo Domingo project where Seward had left it. Influenced by a pair of American speculators with axes to grind, and against the advice of his able Secretary of State, Hamilton Fish, he sponsored the negotiation of a treaty for the annexation of Santo Domingo by the United States and tried to force it through the Senate. The Senate was inhospitable. It resented Grant's highhanded methods and an odor of corruption that sullied the entire transaction, and certain senators warned against the dangers inherent in an effort to extend American institutions into a climate, physical and human, where they could not flourish. Such a procedure, said one senator, would be to "embark the Government of the United States upon the vast and trackless sea of imperialism." The Senate rejected Grant's treaty by a vote of 28 to 28.

The Purchase of Alaska

But though Seward and Grant both met failure in their quest for Caribbean bases, Seward was more successful in another of his ambitions—his desire to make the United States a great Pacific power. By a treaty signed March 30, 1867, he acquired Russian America, thenceforth to be known as Alaska, an Indian name meaning "great land." Alaska had virtually become a white elephant to the Czar's government, which for some years had been willing to dispose of it at a suitable price. This was intimated to Seward by the Russian minister, Baron Stoeckl, when he returned from a visit to St. Petersburg in the spring of 1867. Seward made an offer, and the two diplomats quickly agreed on a price of $7,200,000.

The treaty was promptly approved by the Senate, where it had the vigorous support of Charles Sumner, chairman of the Committee on Foreign Relations. Sumner made much of the importance of cultivating and perpetuating friendship with Russia, the only major power that had shown sympathy for the North in the recent war. He also argued that the acquisition of Alaska was one more step in ousting the European monarchies from America. He and other legislators intimated that it was Britain's turn to go next—an idea that fitted in with several contemporary popular schemes for the annexation of Canada.

One member of the House of Representatives predicted that the British Empire would be shorn of its American possessions by Russia and that the day would come when "the two great Powers on earth will be Russia and the United States."

By the purchase of Alaska the United States made its final acquisition of continental territory. It was a significant addition. Alaska contained mineral, forest, and animal resources that were to prove a mine of wealth. Although it was not, as many of its advocates predicted, a prelude to the absorption of Canada, it brought the United States, at Bering Strait, into sight of Asiatic shores, and in the Aleutian Islands to the south, carried the American flag into the western Pacific, in the longitude of the Marshall Islands and New Zealand. In that respect the purchase of Alaska was prophetic, as presumably Seward intended, of the destiny of the United States as a Pacific power.

In another respect the Alaska purchase was a turning point in the history of American expansion. In all earlier acqusitions of territory by treaty—Louisiana, Florida, the Mexican cession, the Gadsden purchase—the treaties of cession had stipulated, not only that the inhabitants of the ceded territory should enjoy the rights and privileges of United States citizenship, but also that they should be, in the language of the Louisiana treaty, "incorporated in the Union of the United States." The Alaska treaty provided that such civilized inhabitants as chose to remain in the territory should "be admitted to the enjoyment of all the rights, advantages and immunities of citizens of the United States"; but it made no promise of incorporation. Thus Alaska became the first bit of American soil not legally destined for statehood. Promising citizenship but not incorporation, the Alaska treaty was a transitional episode between the earlier treaties, which promised both, and the treaty of 1898 with Spain, which promised neither. It was the first step on the road to "imperialism."[1]

Midway Island—and the End of an Era

Alaska and Midway Island were the only new possessions actually acquired in the immediate postwar period. Midway Island, about a thousand miles northwest of the Hawaiian group, was occupied by the Navy in the summer of 1867, at the suggestion of the China Mail Steamship Company. Under orders from the Navy Department, Captain William Reynolds, of the U.S.S. *Lackawanna,* took possession of the island in the name of the United States on August 28, 1867. Formerly known as Brooks Island from the name of its discoverer, it was re-christened in recognition of its situation approximately halfway from San Francisco to Yokohama. An attempt to dredge the entrace to the harbor was abandoned as too costly. In 1903 Midway became a station on the first transPacific cable. Otherwise it had no importance till the advent of transPacific air transportation some thirty years later.

The failure of Grant's attempt to annex Santo Domingo marked the end of the postwar revival of Manifest Destiny. The American public and the American Congress were, for the time being, simply not interested in schemes for the acquisition of insular possessions. But commercial expansion was another matter. The years after 1850 were the years of the industrial revolution in the United States. With the Civil War ended, American factories (like American farms) were soon turning out more products than the home market could absorb. The need for expanding foreign markets, therefore, impressed every administration from Grant's to McKinley's and became a constant, though generally undramatic, factor in the foreign policy of those decades. It played a part in President Cleveland's somewhat strained application of the Monroe Doctrine against Great Britain in Venezuela. Quite distinct in itself from the desire for further territorial acquisitions, it nevertheless on occasion provided a motive for such acquisitions, as at the time of the Spanish American War in 1898. In the meantime, during Grant's years and later, it helped to account for a continuing American interest in the isthmian region, Hawaii, and the remote Samoan Islands.

The Isthmian Canal Question

The building of the transcontinental railroads diminished but did not eliminate the importance of the isthmian transit routes. Seward negotiated with Nicaragua a treaty which, like that of 1846 with New Granada (Colombia after 1863), insured to citizens of the United States equal rights with citizens of the sovereign state in the use of such transit facilities as might be constructed. President Grant was the first American statesman to proclaim publicly, in disregard of the Clayton-Bulwer Treaty with Great Britain, that any canal should be under the exclusive control of the United States. Grant in 1869 appointed an Interoceanic Canal Commission, which directed surveys of several proposed canal routes and in 1876 reported unanimously in favor of the route through Nicaragua.

While the United States deliberated, however, Europeans began to make the dirt fly. In 1881 a French corporation headed by Ferdinand de Lesseps, builder of the

---

[1]Although the Alaska treaty said nothing of incorporation, the Supreme Court later held that the treaty together with subsequent legislation extending the customs and other laws to Alaska had the effect of making Alaska an incorporated territory. *Rassmussen v. U.S.,* 197 U.S. 516 (1905). Alaska became a state in 1959.

Suez Canal, operating under a concession from the government of Colombia, began the digging of a canal through the Isthmus of Panama. The prospect of a canal at Panama under European auspices was not relished in the United States. It was denounced as being in violation of the Monroe Doctrine. It brought from President Rutherford B. Hayes (1877–1881) a declaration that "The policy of this country is a canal under American control." An isthmian canal, he continued, would be "virtually a part of the coast line of the United States," and it was "the right and duty of the United States to assert and maintain such supervision and authority over any interoceanic canal . . . as will protect our national interests." Hayes had voiced what was to become accepted American opinion—that sound national policy called for a canal controlled exclusively by the United States.

No attempt was made, however, to interfere with the operations of the French company. Instead, Congress chartered an American corporation, the Maritime Canal Company of Nicaragua, to exploit the rival Nicaraguan route, while Secretaries of State Blaine and Frelinghuysen strove in vain to induce Great Britain to abrogate or amend the Clayton-Bulwer Treaty and thus open the way for a canal nationally owned or controlled. Secretary Frederick T. Frelinghuysen, contending that the Clayton-Bulwer Treaty was no longer binding, negotiated in 1884 a treaty with Nicaragua, which gave the United States exclusive rights to the Nicaraguan route in return for a permanent alliance and a guarantee of Nicaragua's territorial integrity. This treaty was pending in the Senate when a change of administration in 1885 brought Grover Cleveland to the White House for his first term (1885–1889) and Thomas F. Bayard to the State Department. Upon Bayard's advice, Cleveland withdrew the treaty from the Senate. Its

approval would certainly have brought on a controversy with Great Britain.

By the early 1890's the French company had gone bankrupt with only a minor portion of its work completed, and the Maritime Canal Company had failed to raise funds for its enterprise. It was evident that the United States government alone possessed the resources and the ability to do the work. The barrier to such a course was the Clayton-Bulwer Treaty, to which Great Britain as yet firmly adhered.

International Rivalry in Samoa

President Grant's susceptibility to the pressures of businessmen and speculators, noted in connection with Santo Domingo, was also responsible for his interest in the Samoan Islands. In this case it was the head of a steamship company running steamers between San Francisco and Australia and New Zealand who drew the President's attention to the fine qualities of Pago Pago harbor in the Samoan isle of Tutuila. An American naval officer negotiated with the native chief of Tutuila a treaty giving the United States exclusive rights in Pago Pago harbor in return for assumption by the United States of a protectorate over the native government. Submitted to the Senate with Grant's qualified endorsement, the Samoan treaty was never brought to a vote.

In 1878 a native Samoan delegation visited Washington, seeking annexation or a protectorate. They were informed that this was impossible but were given instead a treaty by which the United States agreed merely to use its "good offices" for the adjustment of differences that might arise between Samoa and any other government "in amity with the United States." In return the United States received the right to establish a coaling station in Pago Pago harbor. In the meantime, the Samoan

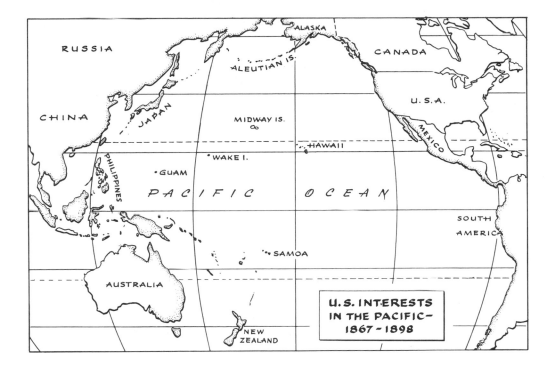

U.S. INTERESTS
IN THE PACIFIC—
1867-1898

economy had fallen under German domination, while the proximity of Samoa to Australia and New Zealand had led the British government to take a lively interest in the fate of the islands. The resulting three-power rivalry reached an intensity quite out of proportion to the weight of the issues involved. In the United States there was even reckless talk of war with Germany.[2] A three-power conference in Washington in 1887 failed to settle the controversy, but a second conference in Berlin two years later agreed on a compromise. The Treaty of Berlin, signed June 14, 1889, paid lip service to Samoan "independence" but in reality set up a three-power protectorate or condominium. Though the Samoan

[2]On one occasion, in March 1889, American and German naval vessels were apparently on the verge of exchanging shots when a timely hurricane wrecked both squadrons on the reefs and beaches of Apia harbor.

natives were given the right to choose their own "king," real power thereafter resided in officials chosen by the three governments. The arrangement, though a clumsy one, was a victory for American policy. It prevented German political domination and preserved American rights in Pago Pago. Though it did not work without friction and left a residue of ill will against Germany, it did prevent serious international controversy during the ten years of its operation.

Toward Hawaiian Annexation

Unlike Samoa, Hawaii was a natural outpost of North America, and the interest of the United States in its destiny was almost as old as American independence. The attempt to annex Hawaii made by the Pierce administration in 1854 was not renewed in the immediate postwar years. Seward, however, in negotiation over a proposed treaty of commercial reciprocity in 1867, informed the American minister in Honolulu that

> a lawful and peaceful annexation of the islands to the United States, with the consent of the people . . . is deemed desirable by this Government; and that if the policy of annexation should really conflict with the policy of reciprocity, annexation is in every case to be preferred.

Apparently some senators agreed with Seward in their preference for annexation rather than reciprocity, for some of the Senate votes that defeated the reciprocity treaty in 1867 were attributed to a fear that such an agreement might stand in the way of annexation.

In 1875, however, another attempt at reciprocity succeeded. A warning that Hawaiian sugar planters, if they failed to obtain a free market in the United States, might divert both their trade and their political attachments to the British Empire, proved efficacious in securing American consent to the treaty. Its value to the United States was political and strategic, not economic. Exports from the United States to Hawaii expanded substantially under the stimulus of the free market, but the total value of such exports during the period of reciprocity was only some $82,000,000, while the loss of revenue to the United States treasury from the free admission of sugar and other Hawaiian products amounted to $91,000,000. Obviously, the arrangement was not good business, considered in terms of dollars and cents. Its advantage to the United States lay in the fact that by holding Hawaii in the American economic sphere, it also held the little kingdom in the American political sphere. The treaty pledged the Hawaiian government not to alienate any port or territory in the islands to any other power and not to grant to any other power the commercial privileges that the treaty conferred upon the United States.

The reciprocity treaty of 1875 was terminable by either party after seven years. A renewal treaty was negotiated in 1884, but the United States Senate, before approving it in 1887, attached an amendment by which the United States was to enjoy the exclusive right to the use of Pearl Harbor in the island of Oahu as a coaling and repair station for its naval vessels. The reciprocity arrangement was thus extended to 1894 at least, and the United States was free during the same period to develop and use Pearl Harbor—a privilege of which it made no use.

The free American market provided by the reciprocity treaty gave a great stimulus to Hawaiian sugar production, which multiplied tenfold in the next twenty years. It also made Hawaiian prosperity so dependent upon the American market that a change in American tariff policy in 1890, admitting other foreign sugar on equal terms with Hawaiian and giving a bounty to American domestic producers, brought about an economic crisis, and contributed to a political crisis, in the Hawaiian kingdom.

The imperfect integration of two cultures in Hawaii had resulted in the existence side by side of a modern system of economy and a monarchical government that retained not a few primitive features. The dissolute and corrupt behavior of the last-but-one of the native monarchs, King Kalakaua, 1874–1891, invited revolution. In a bloodless coup in 1887, leaders of the white business community forced on Kalakaua a new constitution that effectually clipped his wings, making his ministers (without whose consent he could perform no official act) responsible to the legislature and so restricting the suffrage as to make the legislature appear securely under the control of the propertied classes.

Kalakaua was succeeded in 1891 by his

sister, Liliuokalani. Educated in the local mission schools, active in local philanthropies, a composer of musical lyrics of some merit, "Queen Lil" was not endowed with political sagacity. She made no secret of her ambition to recover for herself and her native subjects the prerogatives and rights that her brother had signed away. In laying such plans, she underestimated the ability and determination of the white elite who had compelled Kalakaua to accept the reforms of 1887. Filled with apprehension at the course the Queen might follow and suffering from the economic depression induced by the change in American tariff policy, many white businessmen and lawyers in the islands came to look upon annexation by the United States as a guarantee of both stable government and economic prosperity. They therefore planned to persuade or compel Liliuokalani to abdicate and then to offer the islands to the United States. One of their leaders, Lorrin A. Thurston, visited Washington in the spring of 1892 and received secret encouragement from members of the cabinet of President Benjamin Harrison (1889–1893) and from leaders in Congress.

Not until January 1893 did the revolutionists find a suitable occasion to carry out their plan. Their cue came in an announcement from the Queen that she proposed to proclaim a new constitution, an act that itself would have been unconstitutional and revolutionary. The annexationists immediately formed a committee of safety, set up a provisional government, and demanded the Queen's abdication. Their course had the sympathetic support of United States Minister John L. Stevens, who landed troops from the cruiser *Boston* and so disposed them as to give the impression that they would, if necessary, defend the provisional government, to which Stevens also granted precipitate *de facto* recognition. In this situation there was no course for the Queen but to yield her authority, as she said, "to the

superior force of the United States of America," until such time as the United States government should "undo the action of its representative" and reinstate her "as the constitutional sovereign of the Hawaiian Islands."

The provisional government at once dispatched a commission to Washington to negotiate a treaty of annexation. In the negotiation they met with no serious difficulty, and on February 15, President Harrison sent to the Senate a treaty providing for the annexation of the Hawaiian Islands as "an integral part of the territory of the United States" and for the payment to the deposed Queen of a life annuity of $20,000. The treaty might well have received Senate approval had not the President-elect, Grover Cleveland, about to take office for his second term (1893–1897), let it be known that he preferred to have it left for him to deal with after the fourth of March. One of Cleveland's first acts as President was to withdraw the Hawaiian treaty from the Senate "for the purpose of reexamination." A few days later he appointed a former Democratic congressman, James H. Blount of Georgia, a special commissioner to the Hawaiian Islands to investigate the character of the annexation movement and especially to report to the President whether Minister Stevens had played an improper part in the revolution and whether annexation was desired by any large proportion of the natives or only by the ruling clique of whites.

Blount's investigation convinced both him and President Cleveland, first, that the revolution would not have been attempted and could not have been carried out without the encouragement and support of Minister Stevens; second, that the great majority of the native people were supporters of the Queen and opposed to annexation. Cleveland, therefore, not only declined to return the annexation treaty to the Senate, but concluded, somewhat quixotically, that he was under a moral obligation to undo "the great wrong done to a feeble but independent State" by restoring the Queen to her throne. But when Cleveland's minister, Albert S. Willis, sent to Honolulu for this purpose, had secured from Liliuokalani a reluctant promise of amnesty for the revolutionists, he received from the provisional government an unqualified refusal of his demand that they step down and make way for restoration of the ex-Queen. Only the superior armed force of the United States, said Hawaiian President Sanford B. Dole, could compel the provisional government (which the United States had formally recognized) to give up its authority.

Unprepared to make war on the provisional government, to right one wrong by committing another, Cleveland referred the whole matter to Congress, which resolved that nothing be done. In Hawaii a constitutional convention, held in 1894, provided the body politic with a regular republican constitution that perpetuated the power of the white minority who had overthrown the Queen. The new instrument worked smoothly; a small royalist uprising in 1895 was easily suppressed; a new United States tariff in 1894 restored Hawaiian sugar to its favored position in the American market. The Hawaiian republic enjoyed several years of peace and prosperity, but its leaders never lost sight of their chief desire, annexation by the United States. They could only wait patiently until a turn in the political wheel should bring into power in Washington an administration willing to reverse the policy of Grover Cleveland.

The Monroe Doctrine and Pan Americanism

In the years in which the United States was uncertainly feeling its way toward a policy of overseas expansion, it was asserting the Monroe Doctrine with new emphasis and new assurance and winning for Monroe's pronouncement the explicit or the tacit assent of Europe's principal Atlantic powers. And while thus taking a more active role than formerly as a guardian of the Western Hemisphere, it was, by launching the Pan American movement, beginning to assume in that hemisphere the place of leadership that Henry Clay had urged in the early years of the century. William H. Seward, Secretary of State under Presidents Abraham Lincoln and Andrew Johnson, was eventually to win a signal victory for the Monroe Doctrine, but his first attempt to apply it earned him only a rebuff. Almost at once upon assuming office, Seward learned that Spain was about to reannex her former colony of Santo Domingo (now the Dominican Republic). The news led Seward to suggest to Lincoln that a war with Spain, and also with France, which was rumored to be involved in the transaction, might regain the loyalty of patriotic Southerners. Lincoln put aside the Secretary's rash proposal, but did not prevent him from sending several strongly worded notes of protest to the Spanish government. In one of these Seward characterized Spain's action as "manifesting an unfriendly disposition toward the United States," and threatened forcible resistance. In another he expressly cited Monroe's message of 1823 as the basis for the American objection to Spain's reannexation of her former colony.

The Spanish Foreign Minister rejected Seward's protests. He acknowledged no legal force in the Monroe Doctrine and pointed out that Spain had agreed to reannex Santo Domingo at the behest of the representatives of the people of the island. By this time the United States was deeply involved in the Civil War. Unable to back his protests with force, Seward wisely dropped the subject. Spain withdrew from Santo Domingo in 1865, not as a result of protests from the United States, but because of armed resistance to her rule by the island population.[3]

Napoleon III and Mexico

A far more serious challenge to the Monroe Doctrine than the short-lived Spanish regime in the Dominican Republic was the contemporary French intervention in Mexico and the establishment there of an empire under a European prince. The mastermind in this scheme to re-establish monarchy in the New World was the French Emperor Napoleon III, but he acted upon what he believed to be ample invitation from Mexico itself.

The monarchical ideal had never wholly disappeared in Mexico; in fact, there had always been a party there that saw in the establishment of a monarchy under a scion of some European royal house a solution for Mexico's internal disorders and a protection against further encroachments by the United States. Alarmed by the loss of Texas, California, New Mexico, and the Gadsden strip, and by the further acquisitive tendencies shown by the American government in the 1850's, monarchist elements in Mexico had repeatedly indicated their willingness to accept a European nominee for the Mexican throne. Many Europeans, too, wished to see a barrier erected which would halt the advance of the United States and preserve a balance of power in America. Europeans in Mexico, furthermore, had lost lives and property in the chronic state of disorder and civil war that beset the country. When, on top of all this, the government of President Juarez in

1861 was forced to suspend payments on its foreign obligations, even Great Britain was ready for a limited intervention in Mexican affairs.

Meeting in London in October 1861, representatives of France, Spain, and Great Britain signed a convention by which the three governments agreed to send a joint military expedition to Mexico. They declared its purpose to be the "more efficacious protection of persons and property of their subjects." They disclaimed any designs upon the territory or the independence of Mexico and any intention of interfering with the right of the Mexicans to decide for themselves upon the form of their government. At the insistence of Great Britain, they invited the United States to participate.

This invitation to the United States Seward declined in a tactful note of December 4, 1861, on the grounds, first, of the American preference for abstaining from alliances with foreign nations, and second, of the friendship felt by the United States for Mexico as a neighboring republic. The President, said Seward, did not question the right of the three powers to make war upon Mexico for the redress of grievances, and he accepted their assurances that they aimed at no acquisition of territory and at no impairment of the Mexican people's right of self-government. Meanwhile, Seward was attempting to arrange a loan (with ample security) to the Mexican government, which might enable it to forestall intervention by meeting its foreign obligations, but this proposal found favor neither with the European governments nor with the United States Senate.

The allied forces landed in Mexico in December 1861 and January 1862. The British and Spanish soon withdrew, finding that France had plans which they were unwilling to support. The French Emperor, in fact, had in mind nothing less than the creation in Mexico of a monarchy, closely associated with France, which should keep

---

[3] In contrast with her attitude in the Santo Domingo affair, Spain in 1864 assured the United States of her intention to return to Peru certain Pacific islands seized in a current controversy. The Monroe Doctrine "would not be called in question," said the Spanish Foreign Office. Perkins, *History of the Monroe Doctrine*, pp. 138–47, covers these episodes.

alive the monarchical idea in the New World and serve as a barrier to the further southward expansion of the United States. Thus he would ensure that "balance of power" in America of which Guizot had spoken sixteen years earlier. France, he thought, would benefit commercially, and he himself might recover the good will of French Catholics, which he had lost by espousing the cause of Italian unification at the expense of the temporal power of the Pope.

Napoleon's candidate for the Mexican throne was the Archduke Maximilian, brother of Emperor Francis Joseph of Austria, a young man of fine character and wholesome ambitions. To him the throne was offered by a handpicked Assembly of Notables, convoked by the French commander after French troops had occupied Mexico City. To satisfy Maximilian's democratic scruples, a "plebiscite" was held, though only the small fraction of Mexico under French control participated, and upon being informed of the favorable result of this dubious popular vote, Maximilian accepted. The new Emperor arrived in his capital in June 1864, only to find that his throne was supported by French bayonets. President Juarez, though driven from the capital, kept up a guerrilla war against the French occupation, and the authority of Maximilian was never secure far beyond the environs of Mexico City. The promised popular support was nonexistent.

Had an empire been erected in Mexico by purely Mexican forces, there is no reason to suppose that the United States would have interfered with it. The American goverment had made no objection to the long continuance of an imperial regime in Brazil (1822 to 1889). It was not monarchy in America in itself to which Monroe had objected, but monarchy imposed upon an American state by European powers. This, Napoleon III's adventure in Mexico certainly was, for though Napoleon may have been led to believe that monarchy would be popular in Mexico, a few months of experiment showed that the Mexican people desired none of it. Maximilian's empire was a thinly veiled French protectorate and, as such, was a manifest violation of the Monroe Doctrine.

The French intervention in Mexico, consequently, was distasteful to government and public in the United States from the time when its purposes first became apparent. The United States, however, involved in a desperate civil conflict, was in no position to offer resistance to the French. From his experience with Spain in the affair of the Dominican Republic Seward had learned the futility of making threats that he could not back with force. From the same experience he had learned that European governments were unimpressed by citations of the Monroe Doctrine. With these lessons in mind, Seward acted with caution and prudence. Although warning that a monarchical regime, especially one headed by a non-Mexican, would be unpopular in the United States, he made no threats that his government would interfere. He refused to receive a representative of Maximilian and continued to recognize Juarez as head of the legitimate Mexican government; but as long as the Civil War lasted in the United States, he did not entirely close the door upon a future recognition of Maximilian. In his correspondence with the French government he made no reference to President Monroe or to the Monroe Doctrine by name; but the principles of that doctrine were, in the words of Dexter Perkins, "implicit in all the more important of his dispatches; . . . they were on the lips of most American public men, and in the columns of many of the newspapers; and . . . they exercised a powerful influence upon the course of events at home and abroad."[4]

As the prospects for Union victory over the Confederacy improved, vocal opinion

[4]Dexter Perkins, *The Monroe Doctrine, 1826–1867* (Baltimore: The Johns Hopkins Press, 1933), p. 420.

in the North and in Washington became bolder in its assertion of the principles of Monroe against the French experiment in Mexico. Both factions of the Republican party, regular and radical, denounced the intervention in their campaign platforms in 1864, and the House of Representatives passed unanimously a resolution referring to "the deplorable events now transpiring in the Republic of Mexico" and declaring that

> it does not accord with the policy of the United States to acknowledge any monarchical government erected on the ruins of any republican government in America under the auspices of any European power.

That the fate of Maximilian's empire might hang upon the outcome of the Civil War in the United States was well enough recognized both in Paris and in Mexico City, and both imperial courts watched the progress of the war with deep concern. Maximilian made repeated efforts to secure a hearing in Washington, where he hoped his efforts to give Mexico a stable and a liberal government would be appreciated. The death of Lincoln was little less of a blow to him than the surrender of Lee, for he had hoped for an understanding with the patient and forbearing man in the White House. Upon learning of these two momentous events, Maximilian dispatched a special envoy to the courts of Napoleon III and of his own father-in-law, Leopold I of Belgium, in the hope of securing a joint guarantee from the principal European powers against interference by the United States. This attempt to call into being a later version of the Quadruple Alliance failed completely. Even Napoleon III was heartily sick of an adventure which had proved costly and unpopular in France and which was not meeting with the anticipated success.

The collapse of the Confederacy left the United States reunited and powerful, with a formidable army and navy. Military leaders, Grant, Sheridan, and Schofield, would have relished the assignment of expelling Maximilian and his French backers from Mexico by force. Seward, confident that the same object could be accomplished peacefully, held the dogs of war in leash but raised the tone of his diplomacy. In November 1865 he informed Napoleon, through the United States minister in Paris, that the French intervention was "disallowable and impracticable" and that recognition by the United States of Maximilian's regime was out of the question. Dispatches from Paris in the weeks that followed made it plain that France was preparing to retreat. By February 1866, Seward was convinced that he could present something approaching an ultimatum without risk of its being rejected. On February 12, accordingly, through the French minister in Washington, he requested the French Emperor to provide "definitive information of the time when French military operations may be expected to cease in Mexico." In the same note, to make the French retreat easier, Seward assured the Emperor that the United States would, after the French withdrawal, adhere to its usual policy of noninterference in the affairs of its neighbors: if Maximilian could sustain himself without French arms, the United States would not aid his foes. Seward made no reference to the Monroe Doctrine, but Monroe would have recognized his apprehensions in the following passage from the note:

> . . . the presence of European armies in Mexico, maintaining a European prince with imperial attributes, without her consent and against her will, is deemed a source of apprehension and danger, not alone to the United States, but also to all the independent and sovereign republican States founded on the American continent and its adjacent islands.

The result of the note was what Seward had expected. Early in April the govern-

ment of Napoleon promised the withdrawal of French troops in three installments, in November 1866, March and
November 1867. In reality, the last French
soldiers embarked from Vera Cruz in the
spring of 1867. Maximilian, rejecting the
pleas of his wife and friends to seek safety in
Europe, was captured and shot by the
forces of Juarez. The persistent opposition
to Maximilian in Mexico, the costliness of
the adventure and its unpopularity in
France, possibly the disturbed international situation in Europe—all or most of
these factors had contributed to Napoleon's
decision. But certainly decisive in timing, if
not in the final result, had been the hostility
of the United States. The Monroe Doctrine
had won an impressive, indeed a tragic,
success.

The application of the Monroe Doctrine,
even though unnamed, in the Mexican
crisis had won for it respect in Europe, in
practice, if not in theory. That respect was
due, rather obviously, to the great increase
in the material and military power of the
United States and the conviction that the
United States would use that power, if
necessary, to prevent political interference
by Europe in the Americas. The Mexican
episode had also had a profound effect
upon the status of the Monroe Doctrine at
home, converting it from a party dogma to
a national principle. It was, significantly, a
Republican Secretary of State, supported
enthusiastically by a Republican Congress,
who had invoked against Napoleon III the
principles originally set forth by a Democratic President. Henceforth the nation
was close to unanimity in its support of the
doctrine.

The Beginning
of the Pan American Movement

The Monroe Doctrine, in its origin and
throughout the first century of its history,
was a purely unilateral policy of the United
States. The United States warned Europe
against undertaking new colonization in
the Americas and against attempting to
shape or control the governments of the
independent American states. This it did in
the interest of its own security. It gave no
promises of protection to other American
states (with the exception of such isolated
cases as the Bidlack treaty with New
Granada). It assumed no obligation to
them and asked no cooperation from them.
The Monroe Doctrine was a policy of the
United States, not a policy of the American
republics.

The idea of cooperation of all the
American republics for common ends and
in support of common principles—an idea
entirely absent from the Monroe Doctrine—is the heart of Pan Americanism. Henry Clay had envisaged an
"American System" of republics, led by
the United States. The Panama Congress of
1826 had been called with some such idea
in mind. Though its promoter, Simon
Bolivar, would have limited the projected
organization to the states of Spanish and
Portuguese origin, the United States was
eventually invited to send delegates. Its
representatives, though appointed, failed
to reach Panama. During the next fifty
years, no progress was made toward the
Pan American ideal. Such congresses as
were held by the Latin American states
were sparsely attended and barren of
achievement. Not until 1881 did the United
States attempt to lead its sister republics
into a cooperative system.

James G. Blaine, Secretary of State in
1881 and from 1889 to 1892, was the chief
agent in reviving the Pan American idea
first voiced by Henry Clay. With the approval of President Chester A. Arthur,
Blaine issued, November 29, 1881, an invitation to the other eighteen American states
to send delegates to Washington in the following year "for the purpose of considering
and discussing the methods of preventing
war between the nations of America."

Blaine's purpose, stated in his own words, was:

> First, to bring about peace and prevent future wars in North and South America; second, to cultivate such friendly, commercial relations with all American countries as would lead to a large increase in the export trade of the United States, by supplying fabrics in which we are abundantly able to compete with the manufacturing nations of Europe.

The maintenance of peace, as Blaine viewed the matter was essential to a healthy growth of trade.

Unfortunately for Blaine's plans, President Arthur, who had inherited Blaine as a member of the cabinet of the assassinated President Garfield, desired a Secretary of State politically more congenial to himself. Consequently, within three weeks of the issuance of the invitations to the conference, Blaine was replaced by Frederick T. Frelinghuysen. The new Secretary disapproved of Blaine's conference plans and, with the President's consent, withdrew the invitations. His official excuse for so doing was fear that friendly European states might regard the calling of an exclusively American conference as an affront to them.

The idea did not die, however. Congress, in 1888, requested the President to call a conference of American states for the purpose of promoting trade and preserving peace among the free nations of the hemisphere. For the promotion of trade, the resolution proposed the creation of an American customs union, the improvement of transportation and communications, and the adoption of uniform customs regulations, a common system of weights and measures, and a common silver coin. For the preservation of peace, it proposed an agreement to submit to arbitration all disputes that could not be settled by ordinary diplomacy. Thomas F. Bayard, Secretary under President Cleveland, sent out the invitations in July 1888. Before the con-

ference met in October 1889, another turn of the political wheel had brought the Republican Benjamin Harrison to the White House and returned Blaine to the State Department. It was Blaine, therefore, who welcomed the American delegates to Washington and was chosen by them to preside over the conference. Thus Blaine, the initiator of the conference in 1881, became its presiding officer when it finally met eight years later.

Invitations had been sent to Mexico, to all the republics of Central and South America, and to Haiti and the Dominican Republic in the Caribbean—eighteen in all. All but the Dominican Republic accepted and sent delegates. Including the United States, therefore, eighteen governments were represented. The delegates, numbering thirty-seven, were organized in fifteen committees to study the proposals made to the conference and to recommend action upon them.

The results were disappointing. The proposal for a customs union was rejected; instead, the conference recommended separate reciprocity treaties. The proposal of a common silver coin (evidently a measure designed to check the falling price of silver) was reported adversely. No progess was made toward uniformity in weights and measures or in customs regulations. A railroad connecting North and South America was recommended, but nothing was done to make it a reality. A general arbitration treaty providing for settlement by arbitration of all questions except such as might compromise the independence of one party, was agreed upon (with the Chilean and Mexican delegations dissenting) but was never ratified. A resolution declaring against recognition of any future acquisition of territory by conquest suffered a similar fate.

The one tangible achievement of the conference was the setting up in Washington of the Bureau of American Republics, later renamed the Pan American Union, essentially an agency for the exchange of information, economic, scientific, and cultural. More significant, however, was the precedent set by the conference of 1889–1890 for the holding of inter-American meetings to discuss problems of common interest. It was the first of a long series of inter-American conferences, which gained in importance with the passage of time. The early conferences avoided all political commitments. Those held in the 1930s and later, on the other hand, were successful in smoothing disagreements, particularly between the United States and its southern neighbors, and in unifying the American republics in resistance to totalitarian aggression from without. In this way, the Pan American movement, in its later phases, virtually adopted and "continentalized" the Monroe Doctrine.[5]

Great Britain and Venezuela

Aggressive assertion of the Monroe Doctrine as a unilateral policy of the United States, interpreted and maintained by the United States alone, reached a climax in 1895 in a diplomatic note penned by Secretary of State Richard Olney and a special message addressed to Congress by President Grover Cleveland.

This episode was the outgrowth of a boundary controversy between the republic of Venezuela and the adjoining colony of British Guiana. Venezuela had won its in-

dependence from Spain in the years after 1810 and had been recognized by the United States in 1822, being then a portion of Colombia. The neighboring western portion of Guiana had been ceded to Great Britain by the Netherlands in 1814. Spain and the Netherlands had never agreed upon a mutual boundary line. In 1840 the British explorer, Sir Robert Schomburgk, drew a line that the British accepted but the Venezuelans rejected. As time passed and gold deposits were discovered in the interior, the drawing of a boundary increased in importance, and both parties inflated their claims. Venezuela, the weaker party, repeatedly proposed arbitration. Great Britain offered to arbitrate her claims west of the Schomburgk line but not east of it, where British settlers had for years occupied areas now claimed by Venezuela. Venezuela insisted upon arbitration without such limitations and made appeal after appeal to the United States for support. Diplomatic relations were broken off, restored, and again severed. The United States recommended arbitration to Great Britain from time to time, but not until 1895 did its recommendations actually assume the nature of an ultimatum.

The new urgency that marked the diplomacy of 1895 must be attributed in part to the economic depression that followed the panic of 1893 in the United States. Every economic depression led to revived emphasis on the need for expanding foreign markets. This one, with its railroad strikes and armies of the unemployed marching on Washington, seemed to pose a particular threat to the nation's social fabric. Foreign markets seemed essential to the preservation of social stability, and American businessmen were eyeing with jealous interest the competition of Europe in the markets of South America. As a British publication remarked in the fall of 1895, there was "an unwritten Monroeism working like yeast in the commercial world of

---

[5]There is a good concise account of the Washington Conference of 1889–1890 in J. B. Lockey's sketch of James G. Blaine, in Samuel F. Bemis, ed., *The American Secretaries of State and Their Diplomacy*, 10 vols. (New York: Alfred A. Knopf, Inc., 1927–1929), 8: 164–81. See also T. F. McGann, *Argentina, the United States, and the Inter-American System, 1880–1914* (Cambridge: Harvard University Press, 1957), chaps. 10–11.

America."[6] There is little doubt that Cleveland and Olney were thinking in terms of this "unwritten [economic] Monroeism," though it must be read between the lines of the official documents.

Skillful propaganda also played a role in bringing on the confrontation. In the previous year, William L. Scruggs, an American and a paid agent of the Venezuelan government, had published a pamphlet entitled *British Aggressions in Venezuela, or the Monroe Doctrine on Trial,* in which he unblushingly set forth the Venezuelan side of the case. To aid in arousing American concern, he advanced the theory that the upper waters of the Orinoco River interlocked with those of the Amazon and the La Plata; hence, if the British held, as they claimed, the southern shore of the Orinoco at its mouth, they would hold "the key to more than a quarter of the whole continent."[7] Scruggs not only secured wide circulation for his pamphlet, he lobbied directly with members of the House, the Senate, the Cleveland administration, and with the President himself. He deserved at least some of the credit when both houses of Congress early in 1895 passed unanimously a joint resolution calling upon the President to recommend "most urgently" to Great Britain and Venezuela that they settle their dispute by arbitration.

Walter Q. Gresham, Cleveland's Secretary of State (1893–1895), began the preparation of a note to Great Britain. Upon his death in May 1895, the task was taken over by his successor, the vigorous Boston lawyer Richard Olney. Olney resolved to rest his case against Great Britain on the Monroe Doctrine as he interpreted it. The "noninterference" principle of the doctrine, he contended, would be violated if Great Britain should take by force any territory claimed by Venezuela without submitting the question of its ownership to impartial adjudication. Such a policy, he argued, "in effect deprives Venezuela of her free agency and puts her under virtual duress."

In an effort to show that the United States had a legitimate interest in such a controversy, Olney resorted to the argument that if Britain succeeded in appropriating Venezuelan territory, other European powers would follow her example; the powers of Europe would be "permanently encamped on American soil," and the United States would be deprived of the happy situation under which it "is practically sovereign on this continent, and its fiat is law upon the subjects to which it confines its interposition."

Olney closed his note by requesting a reply in time for the President to submit it to the session of Congress that would open early in December. The entire note savored of an ultimatum.

Lord Salisbury, British Foreign Secretary, took the American demand less seriously than it deserved. He took his time in replying; his answer—which the United States ambassador forwarded by mail instead of cable—did not reach Washington until after the opening of Congress. At the expenditure of considerable verbiage, it made two simple points: (1) the Monroe Doctrine was in no way binding upon Great Britain, which recognized no special rights of the United States in the Western Hemisphere; (2) even if the Monroe Doctrine were recognized as valid international law, it would have no bearing upon a mere

[6]*British Trade Journal,* quoted in Walter LaFeber, *The New Empire: An Interpretation of American Expansion, 1860–1898* (Ithaca, N.Y.: Cornell University Press, 1963), p. 195. Cleveland's Secretary of State Walter Q. Gresham had already taken vigorous action to sustain a government in Brazil friendly to American business interests and to end the last British pretensions to a protectorate over the Mosquito Indians of Nicaragua. Ibid., pp. 210–29.

[7]John A. S. Grenville and G. B. Young, *Politics, Strategy, and American Diplomacy: Studies in Foreign Policy, 1873–1917* (New Haven: Yale University Press, 1966), chap. 5.

boundary dispute between an American state and a British possession. The British government's position remained unchanged: it would arbitrate claims beyond the Schomburgk line, but not within it.

It is hard to refute the British logic, but the controversy had passed, in the United States, from the area of logic into that of emotion—and of politics. Public opinion, resentful of British procrastination and stubbornness in the Venezuelan affair, had found another grievance in the British occupation, in the spring of 1895, of the Nicaraguan port of Corinto as a means of enforcing payment of claims by Nicaragua. Some Democrats as well as most Republicans were denouncing Cleveland's foreign policy as weak, both in his failure to prevent the Corinto incident and in his shelving of the treaty for the annexation of Hawaii. Cleveland and Olney were being urged to bolster their own position and that of the Democratic party by making a strong stand in support of Venezuela.[8] Cleveland, a stubborn man in his own right, was in no mood to accept Salisbury's rebuff complacently.

In a special message to Congress, December 17, 1895, the President submitted the correspondence with the British government and with it, his recommendations. Since Great Britain had declined to submit her claims to arbitration, he proposed that Congress authorize him to appoint a commission to determine where the boundary ought to be, and that when the commission had reported, the United States assume responsibility for enforcing its decision. The President was aware, he said, of all the consequences that might follow his recommendation. It was, he observed, "a grievous thing to contemplate the two great English-speaking peoples . . . as being otherwise than friendly competitors in the onward march of civilization," but even war, he implied, would be preferable to "a supine submission to wrong and injustice and the consequent loss of national self respect and honor."

Thus Cleveland, like his predecessor, President James K. Polk, looked John Bull "straight in the eye." At home the message received enthusiastic support, and though many bankers and some businessmen, clergymen, and academic people deplored the risk of war over what seemed a trivial matter, Congress promptly gave the President the authority he had asked and provided for the expenses of the proposed commission.

Actually, despite the bold language, there was little risk of war. The message, composed by Olney, "was a most skillful piece of work: it satisfied even the wildest jingoes without, in fact, involving the United States in any real danger of conflict."[9] The work of the proposed boundary commission would take time: not until it was completed would there be a showdown, and in the interval pacific counsels were likely to prevail.

In fact, they prevailed without awaiting the report of the commission. If American opinion was chauvinistic, prevailing British opinion was quite the reverse. Newspapers and public men, including the Prince of Wales, hastened to express themselves in terms of friendship for the United States. The German Kaiser diverted British irritation from Washington to Berlin by a telegram congratulating President Paul Kruger of the Transvaal on the repulse of a filibustering expedition by Englishmen— the Jameson raid. Lord Salisbury wanted no war over the Venezuela boundary. He had underrated American determination and was ready for a retreat if a formula

[8]N. M. Blake, "Background of Cleveland's Venezuelan Policy," *American Historical Review,* 47 (1942), 259–77.

[9]Grenville and Young, *Politics, Strategy, and American Diplomacy,* p. 167; cf. Bradford Perkins, *The Great Rapprochement: England and the United States, 1895–1914* (New York: Atheneum, 1968), p. 17.

could be found that would accept arbitration and yet save British face. Such a formula was advised in a rule that "adverse holding or prescription during a period of fifty years shall make a good title." Thus Great Britain was protected against loss of territory long settled or held by British subjects. A court of arbitration, provided for by treaty between Great Britain and Venezuela and composed of two justices of the United States Supreme Court, two Englishmen, and a Russian jurist selected by the four, rendered its decision in October 1899. The line agreed upon differed from the Schomburgk line chiefly in assigning to Venezuela possession of the south bank of the Orinoco River at its mouth and another bit of territory in the interior.[10]

The Monroe Doctrine had scored a second notable victory, for Lord Salisbury, although denying it in theory, had conformed to it in practice, even in the extreme and questionable interpretation given it by Richard Olney. Judged pragmatically, Cleveland and Olney had been right. Whether they were justified in running the risk of war with England, minimal though it was, over a boundary dispute that in itself was of minor importance, was and remains debatable. It was their contention that by bringing the dispute to a head when they did, they foreclosed a greater risk of war that would have arisen later if Britain and Venezuela had drifted into hostilities.

Strangely enough, a controversy that for a few days had the United States and Great Britain seemingly on the verge of war marked a definite turning point for the better in Anglo-American relations. A general arbitration treaty between the two, the Olney-Pauncefote Treaty negotiated in

[10]The negotiations were cooled by a temporary shift from official to unofficial channels with the editor of the *Times* of London speaking for Salisbury and his American correspondent for Olney. See J. T. Mathews, "Informal Diplomacy in the Venezuela Crisis of 1896," *Mississippi Valley Historical Review*, 50 (September 1963), 195–212.

1897, fell short of Senate approval by only three votes. When the United States went to war with Spain over the Cuban question in 1898, it was warmly supported by British opinion. Within the next dozen years, all Anglo-American misunderstandings of any significance were amicably adjusted, and the way was made easier for Anglo-American cooperation in World War I.

Olney's aggressive assertion of the Monroe Doctrine was less resented in England, at which it was aimed, than on the continent of Europe. In France, Germany, Austria-Hungary, Italy, Spain, Holland, and Russia, official and newspaper opinion showed hostility to this new assumption by the United States of a predominant position in the Western Hemisphere. Nor was Latin America universally appreciative of Uncle Sam's taking upon himself the role of a protector whose "fiat is law" upon the continent. Venezuela, Colombia, Brazil (which had a boundary dispute with French Guiana), Peru, and the states of Central America showed varying degrees of enthusiasm or approval for the Cleveland-Olney policy. In Mexico, Argentina, and Chile, on the other hand, there was suspicion and hostility, and a thinly attended congress of American states, meeting in Mexico City in 1896, clearly betrayed distrust of the growing power and pretensions of the "Colossus of the North." To have a powerful protector was all very well, but it was clear that some of Uncle Sam's neighbors were growing fearful that the protector might lay claim to certain rights of overlordship.

The Venezuela boundary controversy, although the most serious threat, was not the sole threat to Anglo-American amity in the last quarter of the nineteenth century. An ancient dispute over inshore fishing rights along the coasts of British North America flared up with new heat in the 1880s. At about the same time, a fresh misunderstanding arose over the American claim of an exclusive right to regulate the taking of fur seals in the waters of Bering Sea. Both controversies were eventually settled by arbitration; the fur seal dispute in 1893, the northeast fisheries question not until 1910. While the United States was defending its economic interests in these matters in protracted arguments with the British government, it was feeling new concern about a future market for its growing surplus of industrial products and was ready to take alarm when an apparently promising market in China seemed about to be preempted and monopolized by the other powers.

Chinese Immigration Presents a Problem

American interest in the Far East in the thirty years after the Civil War was kept alive by a slow growth of trade and a continuing support by American churches of missionary activity in that area. Relations with Japan after the Meiji Restoration of 1868 were uneventful and generally cordial. There were few causes of friction between the two governments, and the United States sympathized with and encouraged Japan's attempts to throw off the shackles of the unequal treaties.

American relations with China in the same period suffered some deterioration. Anson Burlingame, after serving successfully for six years as United States minister to China, resigned in 1867 to become a member of a three-man commission to represent China in negotiations with the United States and the governments of Europe. His two colleagues were Chinese. In Washington, Burlingame signed with Secretary Seward (July 28, 1868) a treaty assuring most-favored-nation treatment to Chinese visiting or residing in the United States (and reciprocally to Americans in China). It withheld from such Chinese, however, the privilege of naturalization, which by an act of Congress of 1870 was

limited to immigrants of European or African origin.

At the time when this treaty was made and approved, cheap labor was in much demand on the Pacific coast, and no objection was raised to the importation of Chinese of the working class. The completion of the Central Pacific railroad in 1869 threw thousands of laborers out of work and depressed wages. Soon thereafter came the panic of 1873, followed by a long economic depression. It was not surprising that white workers on the Pacific coast and their spokesmen in politics raised a storm against the Chinese, whose customary standard of living was so low that they were glad to work for a fraction of the wage considered adequate by native Americans or Europeans. From California came reports of anti-Chinese riots and insistent demands for prohibition or limitation of Chinese immigration.

When Congress in 1879 passed a limitation bill, however, President Hayes vetoed it as a violation of the Burlingame treaty. An American commission sent to China the next year (1880) returned with a new treaty by which China consented that the United States might "regulate, limit, or suspend, but not absolutely prohibit" immigration of Chinese laborers. Accordingly, an act of 1882 suspended for ten years the immigration of Chinese laborers, and in 1892 the suspension was renewed for an additional ten years. This suspension was later extended to 1904, with Chinese consent, and in 1904, without such consent, the exclusion of working-class Chinese was made permanent.

Such racial discrimination whether justified or not, produced resentment in China. On the other hand, a grudging acceptance by the Chinese of American missionaries and the occasional mistreatment of such persons made for anti-Chinese feeling in the United States. Hence as China and Japan drifted toward war over their conflicting interests in Korea, American sentiment tended to favor Japan rather than China.

Japan and China Fight over Korea

Korea, the "hermit kingdom," had long paid tribute to China, and, until 1832, to Japan also. Such submission, however, was ceremonial rather than political. In 1876 Japan, imitating the technique that Perry had used against the Shogun, made a naval demonstration in Korean waters and secured a treaty by which Korea declared itself to be a sovereign and independent state, thus repudiating any allegiance to China and opening the way for Japanese penetration.

The Chinese government had from time to time denied any responsibility for what befell foreigners in Korea, thus shielding itself from demands for satisfaction for the murder of missionaries or for other wrongs. But when the Chinese saw Japanese footprints leading to the Korean door, they began to assert their claims to suzerainty. Thus when Commodore R. W. Shufeldt of the United States Navy was sent to the Far East with authority to make a treaty with Korea, he found Li Hung-chang, the Chinese viceroy at Tientsin, anxious to demonstrate that the proper approach to Korea was through China.[11] Commodore Shufeldt accepted the proffered good offices. A treaty was negotiated at Tientsin between Li and Shufeldt and signed in Korea on May 22, 1882. The treaty opened Korea to American trade, permitted residence of Americans in the open ports, fixed import and export duties, and provided temporary rights of extraterritoriality.

There now followed a period of intrigue for hegemony in Korea between China and Japan, with Russia, now a neighbor of Korea on the north, also taking a hand. The Russians withdrew for the time being, and after some years of see-saw between China and Japan, marred by assassinations, kidnappings, and deportations, an antiforeign uprising brought both Chinese and Japanese troops into the peninsula. Attempts of the western powers to persuade both to withdraw were unavailing, and on August 1, 1894, Japan declared war upon China. Characteristically, she had struck her first naval blow a week before. The United States was officially neutral and maintained friendly relations with both powers, but its attitude was on the whole more favorable to Japan than to China. It refused to join the other powers in making a one-sided protest to Tokyo against the opening of hostilities by Japan. It gave Japan a friendly warning that if she forced too drastic surrender terms upon China, she might bring on intervention by the European powers—a warning that Japan failed to heed. To both belligerents the United States was useful in helping to initiate peace negotiations, the first steps to which were taken through the American legations in Tokyo and Peking.

Japan surprised the world by winning an easy victory on both land and sea over her gigantic but clumsy foe. In the Treaty of Shimonoseki (April 17, 1895), she exacted hard terms from China—recognition of the independence of Korea (meaning, really, a free hand for Japan in that country), the cession of Formosa and the Pescadores Islands and of the Liaotung peninsula on the mainland of southern Manchuria, the grant of new commerical privileges, and

[11] This was not the first attempt of the United States to open relations with Korea. Secretary Seward was willing in 1868 to join with France in sending a naval expedition to avenge wrongs to missionaries and to effect a forcible opening, but the French government let the matter drop. In 1871 Mr. F. F. Low, the American minister to China, with a naval force, visited the Han River below Seoul, the capital. The squadron was fired upon by the shore batteries. In return it inflicted several hundred casualties on the Korean defenders but failed to open communications with the government.

payment of a large war indemnity. Now, however, came the outside intervention of which the United States had warned Japan. The ink on the treaty was hardly dry when Russia, backed by France and Germany, notified the Tokyo Foreign Office that the three powers, "in the interest of the peace of the Far East," could not consent to Japanese acquisition of territory on the mainland. Japan was forced to return to China the Liaotung peninsula, receiving instead an increased war indemnity. The part played by Russia in this diplomatic maneuver marked her as Japan's next rival.

The Open Door Is Threatened

Over the outcome of the Sino-Japnese war the United States showed no great concern, but it was deeply concerned over the events that quickly followed. The three powers that had vetoed Japan's acquisition of the Liaotung peninsula soon showed that their motive was not the preservation of China's territorial integrity but merely the prevention of its violation by Japan. They had no qualms about taking slices of Chinese territory for themselves.

Early in November 1897 two German missionaries were murdered by Chinese in Shantung province. Within two weeks of the event, a German naval and military force expelled the Chinese garrison at Tsing-tau on Kiaochow Bay on the southern side of the Shantung peninsula and took possession of the port. The German government demanded from China an indemnity for the murders, punishment for the provincial governor, consent to the establishment of a German coaling and naval station in Kiaochow Bay, and exclusive mining and railroad rights in the Shantung province. The Chinese government, having no means of resistance and no allies, bowed to the German demands and on

March 6, 1898, signed a convention granting them in full.

The German action was the signal for similar demands by other powers. Russian naval vessels appeared at Port Arthur on the Liaotung peninsula, and Russia exacted from China a twenty-five year lease of Port Arthur as a naval base, of the neighboring commerical port of Dairen, and of additional portions of the peninsula. With these virtual cessions of territory Russia secured exclusive railway and other economic rights in Manchuria, with privileges of policing and administration that left little more than a shadow of Chinese authority in that area.

France had already (between 1862 and 1885) annexed Cochin China and established a protectorate over the remainder of the Indo-Chinese peninsula, at the expense of Chinese claims to suzerainty. Not to be outdone by Germany and Russia, she now demanded and got a lease of Kwangchow Bay on the south China coast and special mining and railroad rights for French citizens in China's three southern provinces, adjoining the French protectorate.

Great Britain's interests, like those of the United States, would have been best served by preserving China's territorial integrity against such encroachments as those of Germany, Russia, and France, but after trying in vain to dissuade those powers from the game of grab that they were playing, she joined in it herself. For the port of Weihaiwei, facing Port Arthur across the strait of Pechili, she obtained a lease for as long as Russia should hold Port Arthur. She also secured an enlargement of her leased territory of Kowloon on the mainland adjoining Hong Kong and recognition of her peculiar economic interests in the Yangtse Valley.

The "break-up of China" had apparently begun. The Chinese government was unable to resist the aggressions of great powers armed with modern weapons. If the process now begun should continue, China would soon be carved up into colonies and spheres of influence of the competing states of Europe. For American interests in China, the future looked dark. American policy since 1844 had been to insist on equality of opportunity—the open door—for American trade with China; and as a means of keeping the door open, it had fostered the preservation of China's territorial integrity. Now China was faced with being torn apart piece by piece, and who could hope that the powers that appropriated the pieces would not favor their own nationals and discriminate against outsiders like the Americans?

The Chinese Market and the American Surplus

The prospect of being excluded from the Chinese trade was particularly alarming to American business interests in the 1890's, for China had come to hold a prominent place in their vision of future markets for American products. American industry was turning out an increasing surplus of manufactured goods. The agricultural South and West were afflicted with falling prices for their cotton, tobacco, and foodstuffs—the result, in part at least, of inadequate markets. Realizing that if the United States would sell its surpluses abroad, it must accept the complementary surpluses of foreign lands, James G. Blaine and other leaders advocated the reciprocal lowering of tariff barriers. The failure of Blaine's plan for an American customs union was mentioned earlier. Blaine did succeed in securing an amendment to the McKinley tariff of 1890 which empowered the President to impose specified rates of duty upon certain commodities (otherwise duty-free) when imported from any country which should impose upon products of the United States duties which he deemed "reciprocally unequal and unreasonable."

Armed with this bargaining weapon,

Secretary Blaine succeeded in negotiating executive agreements with ten countries by which they reduced or abolished import duties on various American agricultural and manufactured products.[12] The ten were Brazil, the Dominican Republic, Guatemala, Honduras, Nicaragua, Salvador, Spain (for Cuba and Puerto Rico), Great Britain (for her West Indies islands and British Guiana), Germany and Austria-Hungary (the last two as producers of beet sugar). There was also "an informal commerical arrangement with France," by which the French government agreed to apply minimum tariff rates to a small number of American products.[13]

By the Wilson-Gorman tariff of 1894, Congress abruptly terminated these agreements, arousing the resentment of the American and European nations that had participated in them. When the Dingley tariff of 1897 raised American duties to new high levels, European antagonism became more general. The products of American low-cost manufacture were penetrating European markets, competing successfully with European industry in its home area, while Europe on economic grounds found a mouthpiece in the Austria-Hungarian Foreign Minister, Count Goluchowski. In an address in the late autumn of 1897, he complained of the "destructive competition with transoceanic countries" and warned that the peoples of Europe "must fight shoulder to shoulder against the common danger" and "must close their ranks in order successfully to defend their existence"[14]

Anticipating such resentment abroad,

---

[12]The actual negotiation of these agreements was placed in the hands of John W. Foster. See D. S. Muzzey, *James G. Blaine, A Political Idol of Other Days* (New York: Dodd, Mead & Co., 1934), pp. 437–58, for a good account of this episode.

[13]U.S. Tariff Commission, *Reciprocity and Commercial Treaties* (Washington, D.C.: Government Printing Office, 1919), pp. 153–55.

[14]*Literary Digest,* 15 (December 11, 1897), 964.

and realizing that in the long run any nation must import in order to export, advocates of reciprocity had succeeded in incorporating certain mild reciprocity provisions in the Dingley tariff act of 1897. One of these, the so-called "argol provision," empowered the President to lower the American rates on argols, brandies, wines, paintings, and statuary imported from countries that would agree to make equivalent reductions in favor of products of the United States.[15] A second provision directed the President to impose specified duties on coffee, tea, tonka beans, and vanilla beans—articles otherwise on the free list—when imported from any country whose duties or other exactions upon products of the United States the President should deem to be "reciprocally unequal and unreasonable." A third provision empowered the President to negotiate reciprocal trade treaties with other governments but with the "joker" that such treaties must not only be approved by the Senate in the usual way but must also secure approval of the House of Representatives.

The result of these cautious gestures toward reciprocity in a tariff act that erected new high barriers against international trade may be quickly stated. Under the treaty provision, treaties with seven countries were negotiated but never ratified. Threat of imposition of a duty on coffee

under the penalty provision made possible negotiation with Brazil of an agreement establishing favorable rates for American flour, condensed milk, watches and clocks, rubber articles, and other items. The "argol provision" of the act proved to have some bargaining value. Agreements made under this provision secured reductions of tariff rates on American imports into Great Britain, France, Germany, the Netherlands, Italy, Spain, Portugal, and Bulgaria. Most of the reductions in duty thus secured were small, however, and had little effect upon the course of American trade. The agreements were terminated by the next tariff act, adopted in 1909, but most of the reductions made in favor of the United States were permitted to continue.

The "argol agreements" and the prospect (though unfulfilled) of reciprocity treaties to be made under the provisions of the act of 1897 alleviated somewhat the danger of European discrimination against American industry—the threat that Count Goluchowski had voiced so dramatically. The threat itself, however, had the effect of turning American eyes afresh to the Far East, especially to China. China had been to some extent a market for American goods for a century. If Europe should close her markets to American exports, there was still China, where the stirrings of a modernization movement seemed to promise "four hundred million customers" for the products of the West. It was for these reasons that threats to the open door in China were so alarming to some Americans in 1898.

---

[15]*Argol* is defined by Webster as "a grayish or reddish crust or sediment in wine casks; crude tartar."

ADDITIONAL READINGS

BEISNER, ROBERT L., *From the Old Diplomacy to the New, 1865–1900*. New York: Thomas Y. Crowell Co., 1975.

EGGERT, GERALD G., *Richard Olney: Evolution of a Statesman*. University Park, Pa.: Pennsylvania State University Press, 1974.

KENNEDY, PAUL M., *The Samoan Tangle: A Study in Anglo-German-American-Relations, 1897–1900*. St. Lucia, Queensland: University of Queensland Press, 1974.

LAFEBER, WALTER, *The New Empire: An Interpretation of American Expansionism, 1860–1898*. Ithaca, N.Y.: Cornell University Press, 1964.

PLESUR, MILTON, *America's Outward Thrust: Approaches to Foreign Affairs, 1865–1900*. DeKalb, Ill.: Northern Illinois University Press, 1971.

11. The Coming of War with Spain

By the 1890s the United States was, as the naval historian Mahan expressed it, "looking outward." Expansion was again popular; a new phase of Manifest Destiny had begun. The Republicans revived that phrase in 1892 and four years later wrote into their platform an ambitious expansionist program. They called for a foreign policy "firm, vigorous, and dignified," for "a naval power commensurate with [the nation's] position and responsibility," for control of the Hawaiian Islands, for a Nicaraguan canal "built, owned and operated by the United States," and for "a proper and much-needed naval station in the West Indies." The Republican victory in 1896 was followed by the War with Spain, the acquisition of a colonial empire in the Caribbean and the Pacific, and the assumption of leadership among the powers in the defense of the open door in China and of China's territorial integrity. The party that had launched this program won easily at the polls in 1900. The "public mind" evidently approved an aggressive foreign policy.

The New Manifest Destiny

The reasons for this change in popular psychology are not susceptible of precise definition or measurement. It is possible, however, to point to certain intellectual currents and material facts that help to account for the change.

One such intellectual current was the Darwinian theory of evolution, popularized in the United States by historian John Fiske and others. Darwin taught that in the biological world, higher life-forms evolved through natural selection—the "survival of the fittest" in the "struggle for existence." This hypothesis was easily adapted to sociological theorizing, even in the international sphere. If a ruthless struggle for existence among biological species resulted in the survival of the "fittest, or biologically "best," a similar struggle among races or nations might be expected to produce similar results. Thus ruthless international competition could be justified in the name of "progress." With a frank racism, popular writers like Fiske and the Congregational clergyman Josiah Strong foretold the day when Anglo-Saxons, especially the American branch of the family, through their energy and the virtues of their institutions, should dominate the world. "And can anyone doubt," asked Strong, "that the result of this competition of races will be the 'survival of the fittest'?"

Another frankly racist approach was represented by a leading political scientist of the day, Professor John W. Burgess of Columbia University; but Burgess, after two years of advanced study in German universities, included Germans with Anglo-Saxons as constituting the world's elite in the arts of government. The Teutonic nations, which had perfected, in the national state, the best form of government yet devised on earth, were, he wrote, "called to carry the political civilization of the modern world into those parts of the world inhabited by unpolitical and barbaric races; i.e., they must have a colonial policy."[1]

This language would seem to mean that the expansion of the United States into backward and misgoverned areas, which Fiske and Strong had seen as destiny, in Burgess' teaching took on the character of an obligation to civilization. It was apparently so understood by one of his students in Columbia Law School, young Theodore Roosevelt. Ironically, when as a result of the war with Spain, the United States set out to "have a colonial policy," Burgess bitterly dissented and even censured Roosevelt, his own pupil, for his part in promoting that policy.

These men had wide circles of readers, and their expansionist language must have helped to shape the national mood, whether it was basic to their own thinking or only peripheral.

A fourth writer, about whose influence on public opinion and public men there can be no doubt, was Captain (later Rear Admiral) Alfred Thayer Mahan. In the year of Burgess' treatise (1890), Mahan published his own masterpiece, *The Influence of Sea Power upon History, 1660—1783*. The simple thesis of this work was that a wise cultivation of sea power had raised England in a century and a quarter from a second-rate power to the world's most powerful state, and from this he theorized that without sea power no nation could attain a position of first importance in the world. Being a patriotic American, he was naturally anxious to see his own nation profit by the British example. Not only in his original book, but in essays published in various magazines

throughout the 1890s,[2] he urged his fellow countrymen to build up their sea power in order that the United States might be enduringly prosperous and influential. Widely read and respected at home and abroad, friend and confidant of Theodore Roosevelt and Senator Henry Cabot Lodge, Mahan exerted a potent influence upon the current of affairs.

What was the nature of the "sea power" whose possession Mahan thought indispensable to national greatness? He defined it broadly as "all that tends to make a people great upon the sea or by the sea." Thus it included commerce, merchant marine, navy, naval bases at strategic points, and overseas colonies. All of these England had. The United States had a growing commerce—most of it carried in ships under other flags; it had, when Mahan first wrote, only the rudimentary beginnings of a modern navy. It possessed no colonies or outlying naval bases. Without these, the ships of war of the United States would

> be like land birds, unable to fly far from their own shores. To provide resting-places for them, where they can coal and repair, would be one of the first duties of a government proposing to itself the development of the power of the nation at sea.[3]

Specifically, in addition to the building up of its navy, Mahan urged the United States to acquire bases in the Caribbean and the Pacific. Without American control of the Caribbean and the isthmian region, the piercing of the isthmus by a canal would be "nothing but a disaster to the United States." Bases in the Caribbean, then in the hands of other powers, the United States must not obtain "by means other than

[1] J. W. Burgess, *Political Science and Comparative Constitutional Law*, 2 vols. (Boston: Ginn and Company, 1890), 1:30–39.

[2] Collected in the volume, A. T. Mahan, *The Interest of America in Sea Power, Present and Future* (Boston: Little, Brown and Company, 1897).

[3] A. T. Mahan, *The Influence of Sea Power upon History, 1660–1783* (Boston: Little, Brown and Company, 1890), p. 83.

righteous; but," he declared with an obvious fling at the rejection of Seward's and Grant's annexation projects,

> a distinct advance will have been made when public opinion is convinced that we need them, and should not exert our utmost ingenuity to dodge them when flung at our head.[4]

Like Seward, Mahan foresaw a great commercial future in the Pacific. But he went further than Seward in his prophecy that that ocean would be the theater of a gigantic struggle between Western and Oriental civilizations—a struggle in which the United States would be in a front-line position. Hence the possession of outposts in the Pacific was of crucial importance. The issue of such a contest might well be determined by "a firm hold of the Sandwich [Hawaiian] Islands by a great, civilized, maritime power," and the United States was "naturally indicated as the proper guardian for this most important position."

Mahan's philosophy was basically economic. At the root of sea power was trade, the source of national wealth and power. Without trade, a nation might still need a navy for coast defense, but other elements of sea power—colonies, bases, merchant marine—would lose their significance. Thus Mahan was quite in accord with the current urge for trade expansion, for wider foreign markets.

The intensified quest for wider markets was, as noted, one consequence of the economic depression of the 1890s. Another consequence, at least in the opinion of one historian, was a psychic crisis in the American collective mind. The depression, together with the revelation in 1893, in Frederick Jackson Turner's famous essay, "The Significance of the Frontier in American

History," that the American frontier had ceased to be, led to widespread frustration. This feeling was expressed, in the words of Richard Hofstadter, in "an intensification of protest and humanitarian reform" on one hand and, on the other, in a mood "of national self-assertion, aggression, expansion." The war with Spain was to fit this mood exactly, serving "as an outlet for expressing aggressive impulses while presenting itself, quite truthfully, as an idealistic and humanitarian crusade."[5]

The intellectual atmosphere and the psychological mood suggested by these samplings help to explain why American public opinion was more receptive to proposals of overseas expansion in the 1890s than it had been in Seward's day. There was also the contagion of European neo-imperialism. From the 1870s onward, the great powers of Europe were engaged in a new race for colonial possessions, in Asia, in Africa, and among the islands of the Pacific—a race brought home to the United States by the triangular quarrel over Samoa. If there was, indeed, any virtue in colonies, the United States would need to act quickly in order to get its share. "The great nations," wrote Henry Cabot Lodge in 1895, "are rapidly absorbing for their future expansion and their present defense all the waste places of the earth. It is a movement which makes for civilization and the advancement of the race. As one of the great nations of the world, the United

---

[4]Mahan, *The Interest of America in Sea Power*, pp. 102–3.

[5]Richard Hofstadter, "Manifest Destiny and the Philippines," in Daniel Aaron, ed., *America in Crisis: Fourteen Crucial Episodes in American History* (New York: Alfred A. Knopf, Inc., 1952), pp. 173–200. Turner's essay is reprinted in F. J. Turner, *The Frontier in American History* (New York: Henry Holt and Company, 1920), pp. 1–38. Another writer credited with influencing expansionist policy was Brooks Adams, who believed that control of Asia might postpone for America the decline into "barbarism" that was the common fate of empires. See Walter LaFeber, *The New Empire: An Interpretation of American Expansion, 1860–1898* (Ithaca, N.Y.: Cornell University Press, 1963), pp. 80–85.

States must not fall out of the line of march."[6]

The fact should, however, be emphasized that the influences responsible for the new expansionism were as yet chiefly intellectual and emotional, not economic. Despite the growing importance of foreign markets for the surplus of America's industrial production, most businessmen were still unconvinced of the need for colonies. Colonies, in the eyes of the average businessman, were not only difficult and expensive to administer; they meant foreign complications, perhaps war. Rather then engage in risky colonial ventures, he preferred to rely on the high quality and low prices of American products, backed by such assistance as the government could give through favorable treaties and the like, to insure their entry into the world's markets. Not until the spring and summer of 1898 did changes in the international picture persuade the American businessman that colonial possessions might be economically advantageous; and even then, the possessions that caught his eye—the Philippines, primarily—were valued less for themselves than for their supposed utility in affording entry to the markets of China.

Expansion Becomes Republican Policy

The administration of Benjamin Harrison (1889–1893) was the first to show substantial evidence that it had been influenced by the ideas and tendencies just described. Harrison's Secretary of the Navy, Benjamin F. Tracy, had either read the manuscript of Mahan's *Influence of Sea Power upon History* or been otherwise indoctrinated with that author's sea power philosophy. He was the first Navy Secretary since the Civil War to

[6]H. C. Lodge, "Our Blundering Foreign Policy," *The Forum*, 19 (1895), 8–17.

propose the building of an up-to-date fighting fleet. His *Annual Report* of 1889 called for a fleet of twenty battleships, twelve for the Atlantic and eight for the Pacific, equal to the best in armor, armament, and speed. Congress in the next year authorized the building of three first-class battleships, the *Indiana, Massachusetts,* and *Oregon,* which, with the *Iowa,* were to form the backbone of the fleet in the war with Spain in 1898.[7]

Harrison's first Secretary of State, James G. Blaine, emulated Seward and Grant in attempts to secure naval bases in Santo Domingo and Haiti. He failed because of political complications in the two island republics. Harrison himself urged Congress repeatedly but unavailingly to assist in the building of a Nicaragua canal by guaranteeing the bond issues of the Maritime Canal Company and acquiring in return, for the United States, ownership of all or a majority of the company's stock. Harrison, Tracy, and John W. Foster, Blaine's successor in the State Department, were all sympathetic to the proposal for annexation of Hawaii. They would probably have succeeded in accomplishing it by treaty if the opportunity had occurred before the Democratic victory of November 1892.

The second Cleveland administration (1893–1897), therefore, while alert to the need of foreign markets, was, in terms of territorial expansion, an interlude between two Republican regimes, of which the first attempted, and the second carried out, an aggressively expansionist foreign policy. It is true that in the 1896 presidential race the

[7]See Harold and Margaret Sprout, *The Rise of American Naval Power, 1776–1918* (Princeton: Princeton University Press, 1939), chaps. 12, 13; G. T. Davis, *A Navy Second to None* (New York: Harcourt Brace & World, Inc., 1940), chaps. 3–6. The new navy had begun with the authorization in 1883 of three steel cruisers and a dispatch boat (the "White Squadron"). From 1883 to 1889 Congress had authorized some thirty additional vessels, including the second-class battleships *Maine* and *Texas*.

battles over "free silver" and the tariff absorbed popular attention almost to the exclusion of foreign policy issues. It is also true that William McKinley, the successful Republican candidate, had devoted his political career to such domestic problems as tariff and currency and was innocent, when he entered office, of any aggressive intentions in the international sphere. Taking office in the midst of the depression, he hoped, like his friend and political sponsor, Mark Hanna, that his administration could be signalized by a "policy of domestic economic amelioration." Foreign complications were the last thing that he desired. To the anti-expansionist Carl Schurz he gave verbal assurance that under his administration there would be "no jingo nonsense," no scheming for the annexation of Hawaii. The aging John Sherman, his first Secretary of State, was of like mind—"opposed to all acquisitions of territory not on the mainland."

But McKinley was soon to yield to the expansionist forces within the Republican party, and before he had been in the White House eighteen months, the United States had annexed Hawaii and was involved in a war from which it emerged with a colonial empire in the Pacific and the Caribbean.

Hawaiian Annexation Revived

McKinley's first surrender to the expansionists was on the Hawaiian question. Forgetful, apparently, of his promise to Carl Schurz, the President gave his consent to the negotiation of a new treaty of annexation, and such a treaty, providing for the annexation of Hawaii as a territory, was signed on June 16, 1897, and sent to the Senate on the same day. The Senate took no action, however, prior to the adjournment of the special session of Congress.

Former opponents of annexation, Democrats and domestic sugar men, rallied to oppose the new treaty. An unexpected protest from Japan, which had a special interest in Hawaii because of the large number of Japanese that had recently settled in the islands, brought a vigorous response from Washington. Theodore Roosevelt declared to Mahan: "If I had my way we would annex those islands tomorrow . . . I would . . . hoist our flag over the island leaving all details for after action." While the State Department assured the Japanese minister that annexation would not jeopardize vested Japanese rights, secret instructions were sent to the commanding officer of the United States naval forces in Honolulu to raise the United States flag and declare a provisional protectorate over the islands at the first indication of a resort to force on the part of the Japanese, and preparations were made to dispatch the new battleship *Oregon* to Hawaii in case of need. Such precautions proved unnecessary. The Japanese government professed itself satisfied with the assurances given by the State Department, and in December 1897, its protest was withdrawn.

The "yellow peril" in Hawaii, although it stimulated the friends of annexation in the United States, failed to convert its opponents. By March 1898, it was evident that the treaty could never command a two-thirds majority in the Senate. The alternative of a joint resolution had already been considered, and on March 16 such a resolution was introduced in the Senate, only to languish there until the War with Spain and the victory at Manila Bay provided a new argument for the need of Pacific naval bases.

Civil War in Cuba

The War with Spain was itself not the product of an expansionist urge in the United States, but of a distressing situation in Cuba that became intolerable to American sentiment. Spain's misgovernment of its Cuban colony had been notorious for many decades, and Cubans had periodically risen in armed revolt to demand independence or at least autonomy. Reforms promised by the Spanish government at the close of the Ten Years' War (1868–1878) had ended slavery in Cuba but otherwise had brought little relief to the Cuban people. The cost of the war had been saddled upon the island population. Ninety percent of the revenues collected in Cuba went either into service on the debt or into the pockets of Spanish officialdom and military in the island. Cuba continued under the autocratic rule of a Spanish captain general, while a benighted commercial policy hampered Cuba's trade with its neighbors, such as the United States, and even laid heavy taxes on exports to Spain itself.

An already bad situation was made worse by the worldwide economic depression that began in 1893 and by the United States tariff law of 1894, which reimposed a duty upon raw sugar from abroad. Economic distress now combined with political discontent to produce, in February 1895, an armed revolt against Spanish rule. A so-called republican government was set up in eastern Cuba, where large sections fell under insurgent control, and a Cuban *junta* in New York dispensed propaganda and tried desperately to secure money and arms from sympathetic Americans.

In Cuba the war was waged with ruthless ferocity on both sides. The insurgents made it their policy to destroy cane fields, sugar mills, and other property in the hope of thus rendering the island valueless to Spain. In February 1896, the newly appointed captain general, Valeriano Weyler, inaugurated a "reconcentration" policy, ordering the entire population of large districts of central and western Cuba into the cities and towns, which were surrounded with *trochas* or trenches, fortified with barbed wire and guarded by blockhouses at

frequent intervals. Cubans who disobeyed the order were regarded as insurgents and were shot on sight. For the many thousands of women, children, and old men herded in the concentration camps, there was no provision of adequate shelter, food, or sanitation. Famine and disease were rife, and by the spring of 1898 it was estimated that at least 200,000 of the *reconcentrados* had died out of a total population of only 1,600,000.

The Cuban war affected intimately American economic interests and humanitarian sentiment. American capital to the amount of forty to fifty million dollars was invested in Cuba—in sugar and tobacco plantations, sugar mills, manganese and iron mines, and other properties. Trade between Cuba and the United States, in good years, amounted to as much as $100,-000,000. The effect of the war upon many of these enterprises was disastrous. The sugar crop dropped from 1,050,000 tons in 1894 to 200,000 in 1896; tobacco, from 450,000 to 50,000 bales. Exports fell from $60,000,000 in 1895 to $15,000,000 in 1896. American businessmen who made their living from investments in Cuba or trade with Cuba had an obvious reason for desiring a termination of the war. Much more important, probably, was the reaction of humanitarian and religious sentiment in the United States to the barbarities attendant upon the Cuban conflict, especially to the suffering and death inflicted upon innocent noncombatants in the concentration camps.

Of these barbarities the American public was supplied with vivid and frequently exaggerated accounts by the "yellow press," led by William R. Hearst's New York *Journal* and Joseph Pulitzer's New York *World*. These and other papers sent talented reporters and artists to Cuba, and their descriptions of conditions in the island were widely published through the news services of the metropolitan papers that employed them. Spanish atrocities were played up to the virtual exclusion of insurgent ruthlessness, and a wave of sympathy for the *recon-centrados* swept the United States. Americans contributed with customary generosity for the relief of suffering, but as the war dragged on without prospect of victory for either side, there was a rising demand that the United States intervene to end the struggle and to secure independence for Cuba.

The demand for intervention, which would almost inevitably involve war with Spain, arose plainly from humanitarian rather than from economic considerations. While much of the Protestant religious press and numerous daily newspapers, both Democratic and Republicans, clamored for intervention in behalf of the Cubans, mouthpieces of business—trade journals and resolutions of boards of trade and chambers of commerce—with few exceptions advocated a hands-off policy.[8] American business in general, which by the fall of 1897 was rapidly recovering from a prolonged economic depression, was fearful that a war with Spain would interrupt its upward march to prosperity. Fear of the losses that the Spanish navy might inflict upon American commerce was joined with fear that war expenditures might produce inflation. Practically the only business interests that agitated for intervention were seaboard firms that normally engaged in trade with Cuba, and such firms advocated neither Cuban independence nor armed intervention. They voiced a simple desire for the restoration of peace in order that trade might flourish. Nor is there any evidence that Americans with investments in Cuba worked for or desired intervention by the United States. There is proof, on the contrary, that a number of such persons or companies warned the State Department that they would suffer more heavily from a

war between Spain and the United States than from the existing civil war.

Intervention on humanitarian grounds ought to be divorced from any motive of profit for the intervening power, and it is notable in this case that the advocates of intervention usually said nothing of annexing Cuba or, if they mentioned that possibility at all, did so only to disclaim it. Senator Lodge, who in 1895 had spoken of Cuba as a "necessity" to the United States, indicated a year later that he would be satisfied if it were "in friendly hands, in the hands of its own people." Other senators, speaking for intervention, either declared themselves opposed to annexation or professed a willingness to wait until the hand of destiny and the desire of the Cuban people should bring about union in some indefinite future. Most of the prominent newspapers also disclaimed all selfish designs on Cuba. Although the New York *Tribune* preferred to leave the question open, the *Journal, World, Sun, Herald, Times,* and *Journal of Commerce,* of the same city, denounced any suggestion of annexation. "No annexation talk so far as Cuba is concerned!" declared the *Sun.* ". . . For human lives and the liberty of human beings, for Cuba Libre; not for an extension of United States territory!" And the *World* concurred: "We are not going to filibuster under the guise of honor or philanthropy." As far as the American public was concerned, intervention, if it came, should be intervention for *Cuba libre*—for a Cuba free and independent, not a Cuba transformed from a colony of Spain to a colony of the United States.

The United States Intervenes

The situation in Cuba that made such a strong appeal to the humanitarian sentiment of the American public was also one of which the United States government

---

[8]The attitude of business and the churches toward intervention in Cuba is elaborated, together with the other themes in this chapter, in J. W. Pratt, *Expansionists of 1898* (Baltimore: The Johns Hopkins Press, 1936).

could not avoid taking official cognizance.[9] American citizens, usually naturalized Cubans, were frequently arrested by the Spanish authorities, and official interposition was necessary to secure their release, which was effected in every instance. It was also necessary to patrol the coasts of the United States, at considerable expense to prevent or break up attempts at "gun-running" by Cuban sympathizers. In the spring of 1896 both houses of Congress passed a concurrent resolution declaring that belligerent rights should be accorded the insurgents, but this declaration, being merely a statement of opinion on the part of Congress, was ignored by President Cleveland and Secretary of State Richard Olney.

Both Cleveland and President William McKinley, who succeeded him on March 4, 1897, desired to avoid intervention. Both, however, tendered their good offices to Spain for a settlement of the difficulty. Cleveland, furthermore, intimated in his last message to Congress, that the United States could not indefinitely stand aside and watch the cruel struggle continue, and McKinley made this position still clearer in instructions to the new minister to Spain in July 1897. Prospects for a settlement brightened in September when the assassination of the Spanish Prime Minister, Cánovas, brought in the Liberal Sagasta ministry, which was pledged to a more generous and humane colonial policy. The new ministry recalled General Weyler, gave assurance that the reconcentration policy would be abandoned, and promised a limited degree of autonomy to the Cuban people through the election of their own legislature or *cortes*.

President McKinley welcomed the re-

form program in his annual message of December 6, 1897, and bespoke for Spain an opportunity to carry it out, but warned again that if the new policy failed to pacify the island, "our obligations to ourselves, to civilization and humanity" might require intervention.

The grant of limited autonomy to Cuba was, as it turned out, doomed to failure. It was not acceptable to the insurgent leaders, who now declared they would accept nothing short of complete independence, nor was it acceptable to the many peninsular Spaniards in Cuba, who resented the prospect of being ruled by a native Cuban legislature. Any chance for success that it may have had was frustrated by a series of unfortunate incidents that suddenly inflamed relations between Spain and the United States.

On February 9, 1898, the New York *Journal* printed, with a photographic facsimile, a private letter from Dupuy de Lôme, Spanish minister in Washington. The letter, which had been stolen from the minister's correspondent by an insurgent sympathizer in Havana, described President McKinley in unflattering terms as "weak and a popularity-hunter." The letter also raised doubts about Spain's good faith in carrying out the reform program and in current trade negotiations with the United States. De Lôme's immediate resignation and an apology from the Spanish government ended the episode but left an increment of ill will and distrust.

Six days later the United States battleship *Maine* was destroyed by an explosion at her anchorage in the harbor of Havana, whither she had been sent on a "courtesy call" following some rioting in that city early in January. Some 266 American seamen lost their lives. The cause of the catastrophe was never determined. The *Maine's* forward magazines had exploded, but a board of American naval officers, examining the wreck with divers, found unmistakable evidence that the initial explosion had been

[9]For elaboration of the diplomacy leading to the War with Spain, see J. W. Pratt, "The Coming War with Spain," in P. E. Coletta, ed., *Threshold to American Internationalism: Essays on the Foreign Policies of William McKinley* (New York: Exposition Press, 1970), pp. 35–76.

that of a submarine mine, which had in turn set off the magazines.[10]

The report of the navy board was not made public until March 28, when the President sent it to Congress, but in the meantime many of the American people, guided by the sensational newspapers, had adjudged Spain guilty of the act of destruction. "The readers of *The Journal,*" boasted that New York paper in March, "knew immediately after the destruction of the *Maine* that she had been blown up by a Spanish mine."[11] "Remember the Maine!" became the popular watchword.

While Congress, for the most part, refrained from recrimination over the *Maine* tragedy until after the naval experts had reported, there was, after the middle of March, an intensified denunication in the Senate of Spanish atrocities in Cuba. On March 17, Senator Redfield Proctor of Vermont described to the Senate what he had seen and heard during a recent unofficial visit to Cuba, in the course of which he had toured the four central and western provinces. Outside of Havana, where conditions seemed almost normal, the situation, he said, "is not peace nor is it war. It is desolation and distress, misery and starvation." Of about 400,000 persons who had been driven into the concentration camps, "one-half have died and one-quarter of the living are so diseased that they can not be saved." Outisde the camps there was only desolation—no crops, no domestic animals; everything of value was destroyed. He described Captain General Blanco, Weyler's successor, as an "amiable gentleman" with good intentions but without capacity to relieve the situation or put down the rebellion. Proctor made no recommendation beyond remarking that he was opposed to

annexation. He merely reported his observations, in calm and unimpassioned language.

Senator Proctor's speech convinced many who had been skeptical of the revelations of the yellow press. Even the business interests that had hitherto opposed intervention now began to concede that something must be done and that business could stand the shock of war without disaster. The *Wall Street Journal* reported on March 19 that the speech had "converted a great many people in Wall Street." Senator Proctor's statements, "as many of them expressed it . . . made the blood boil."[12]

By this time the President was under heavy pressure from the public, the press, and from virtually all Democrats and many Republicans, in House and Senate, to take vigorous action against Spain. Some historians have pictured him as yielding to such pressure against his better judgment and his devotion to peace. A more likely analysis depicts him as simply following up the policy stated in his July instructions and repeated in his annual message—that is, unless Spain could, within a reasonable time, bring peace to Cuba, the United States would intervene. Spain thus far had not only failed to pacify Cuba; she was now held

---

[10]A second investigation made by the Navy thirteen years later, when the hull was raised, reached the same conclusion. A Spanish board of investigation, meeting just after the disaster, concluded that the only explosion had been an internal one.

[11]*Literary Digest,* 16 (1898), 367.

[12]LaFerber, *The New Empire,* p. 403, conjectures that of the forces pushing McKinley toward war in late March and early April 1898, "perhaps the most important was the transformation of the opinion of many spokesmen of the business community who had formerly opposed war." This idea runs through pp. 379–406. His thesis is repeatedly qualified by "perhaps," as in the sentence quoted. The period that he emphasizes in this chapter is one in which war had become almost inevitable, and businessmen were telling themselves that war might not hurt so much after all and would perhaps be preferable to continued uncertainty. He apparently assumes, furthermore, that businessmen always reached their decisions for business reasons, overlooking the fact that they were not immune to humanitarian sympathy. One need not doubt that the last-minute conversion of many businessmen made it easier for McKinley to follow the course dictated by the logic of his earlier consistent statements, but that is quite different from implying that his decision for war was economically motivated.

responsible for the loss of the *Maine* and the death of 266 American sailors. McKinley's patience was well-nigh exhausted, but he would give the Spanish government one more chance. On March 27, he sent to Madrid his final proposal for a peaceful settlement of the Cuban question. Let Spain, he said, abandon at once the reconcentration policy, grant an armistice until October 1, and enter, through McKinley, into peace negotiations with the insurgents. A telegram on March 28 added that the President regarded Cuban independence as the only satisfactory outcome of the proposed peace negotiations.

In Madrid, the Sagasta ministry was caught on the horns of a dilemma. If it refused McKinley's demands, a disastrous war with the United States appeared certain. If it conceded those demands in full, popular indignation in Spain might overthrow the ministry and even the reigning dynasty. The only hope of salvation lay in securing support from the European powers against intervention by the United States. Such support the Spanish government had already sought from all the major courts and cabinets of Europe, and in every capital except London, it had received expressions of willingness to participate in a joint demonstration against the United States—if someone else would take the lead. The crowned heads of continental Europe, and the government of the French Republic as well, all desired the preservation of the shaky Spanish Empire and dynasty; none was willing to assume leadership in such a crusade. In England, Queen Victoria was sympathetic to the Spanish Queen Regent, as was her Foreign Secretary, Lord Salisbury; but British public opinion was overwhelmingly pro-United States, and neither Salisbury nor any other member of the ministry dreamed of opposing American policy in Cuba. The only result of the Spanish supplications, aside from a hazy suggestion for mediation by the Pope, was a visit to President McKinley

by the ambassadors of six powers on April 6, in which they begged him, in the interest of humanity, to refrain from armed intervention in Cuba. McKinley replied politely that intervention, if it came, would be in the interest of humanity.[13]

Without hope of substantial support from Europe, the Spanish government went as far as it dared toward meeting McKinley's proposals. In its reply (cabled to Washington on March 31) it announced that reconcentration was being abandoned and that an armistice would be granted upon application by the insurgents. Instead of accepting McKinley's proposal of mediation, the note stated that the Cuban parliament, provided for by the autonomy arrangement, was to meet in May and should be the instrument of pacification—an evident rejection of the demand for independence. Spain was willing to submit to arbitration the question of responsibility for the destruction of the *Maine*.

A few days later, April 9, the Spanish government declared an armistice on its own initiative, and on the following day Minister Stewart L. Woodford cabled from Madrid that he believed a solution satisfactory to all parties was obtainable.

Paying slight heed to these last-minute concessions and assurances, which still fell short of his demands, McKinley sent to a warlike Congress on April 11 a message in which he described the outcome of the recent negotiations as unsatisfactory and declared that:

> In the name of humanity, in the name of civilization, in behalf of endangered American interests which give us the right and the duty to speak and to act, the war in Cuba must stop.

He asked authority to use the military and naval forces of the United States "to secure a full and final termination of hostilities

[13]Orestes Ferrara, *The Last Spanish War: Revelations in "Diplomacy"* (New York: Paisley Press, 1937).

between the Government of Spain and the people of Cuba."

Congress, which had been champing at the bit for weeks, seized upon the President's message with eagerness but debated for a week whether the resolutions that it was about to pass should constitute merely a recognition of the independence of the Cuban people or should include also recognition of the existing, but insubstantial, republican government of Cuba. The administration, opposing recognition of the existing regime, which it did not believe could meet Cuba's needs, finally prevailed. Between one and three on the morning of April 20 (though officially on April 19), Congress adopted the resolutions, the final vote being 42 to 35 in the Senate, 311 to 6 in the House.[14]

The resolutions as adopted, and approved by the President on April 20, declared that "the people of Cuba are, and of right ought to be, free and independent," demanded that Spain "at once relinquish its authority and government in the Island of Cuba and withdraw its land and naval forces from Cuba and Cuban waters," and empowered the President to use the armed forces of the United States to enforce this demand. Without a record vote or any expression of dissent, the Senate had adopted, and the House had accepted, a fourth resolution prepared by Senator Henry M. Teller of Colorado, declaring:

> That the United States hereby disclaims any disposition or intention to exercise sovereignty, jurisdiction, or control over said Island except for the pacification thereof, and asserts its determination, when that is accomplished, to leave the government and control of the Island to its people.

[14]The large minority vote in the Senate is not to be construed as opposition to intervention but as dislike of the form of the resolutions. The Senate had originally passed, by a vote of 67 to 21, its own resolutions including recognition of the republican government in Cuba.

The Colorado senator had remarked that he wished to make it impossible for any European government to say, "when we go out to make battle for the liberty and freedom of Cuban patriots, that we are doing it for the purpose of aggrandizement for ourselves or the increasing of our territorial holdings." He wished this point made clear in regard to Cuba, "whatever," he added, "we may do as to some other islands."

Thus with a specific renunciation of annexationist designs in Cuba but with freedom of action with respect to Spain's other colonies—Puerto Rico, the Philippines, the Carolines and Marianas—the United States entered the conflict with Spain. Upon being informed of the approval of the Cuban resolutions, the Spanish government at once severed diplomatic relations and on April 24 declared war. Congress responded with a declaration of war the next day, making it retroactive to April 21. On the twenty-second the President had instituted a blockade of portions of the coast of Cuba.

The war, begun for motives that were primarily humanitarian and sentimental, was to have momentous consequences for both Spain and the United States. For Spain, it meant the loss of the last remnants of her once great colonial empire. To the United States, it brought the sudden assumption of unprecedented imperial responsibilities and elevation to the status of a "world power." And all this was accomplished in one of the shortest and least costly wars in history.

The Collapse of Spanish Power

The military and naval details of the war, which was to have momentous consequences for both Spain and the United States, require only brief mention. The conflict was pathetically one-sided from the beginning. The Spanish navy, which on paper appeared something like the equivalent of the American fleet, had really nothing to match the four new United States battleships, the *Massachusetts, Indiana, Iowa,* and *Oregon,* the last of which had joined the Atlantic Fleet after a two-months' voyage around the Horn from San Francisco. Spanish ships and crews, moreover, were in a wretched state of inefficiency, and the officers were imbued with a defeatist spirit, while the United States Navy, thanks to the energetic efforts of Assistant Secretary Theodore Roosevelt, was well prepared and spoiling for a fight. The Spanish army in Cuba outnumbered the American expeditionary forces but was ill-equipped for war, and though Spanish soldiers fought bravely and stubbornly, the severance of their supply line from Spain made their case hopeless.

Though Cuba had furnished the sole cause of the war, the first important blow fell in the Far East. Months before the outbreak of war, the President had been briefed by Senator Orville H. Platt of Connecticut and by Assistant Secretary of the Navy Theodore Roosevelt on the importance of Manila as a commercial port, and Roosevelt had submitted a memorandum suggesting that in the event of war with Spain, the Asiatic squadron "should blockade, and if possible take Manila."[15] Even earlier, in June 1896, a naval officer, Lieutenant William W. Kimball, had prepared a contingency plan for such an operation.[16] Contrary to long tradition, therefore, Roosevelt was not acting on a sudden inspiration on February 25, 1898, when he cabled Commodore George Dewey, in Hong Kong, to "begin offensive operations in the Philippines" as soon as he should be informed of a declaration of war. And although other drastic orders issued by the

impatient Roosevelt on that day when Secretary Long had left him as acting Secretary were countermanded by his superiors, the orders to Dewey were allowed to stand. It may be assumed, therefore, that they represented administration policy.

Dewey, whom Roosevelt had personally picked for the command and had provided with the necessary ships and ammunition, received the news of war at Hong Kong. After putting his ships into war trim at neighboring Mirs Bay on the Chinese coast, he steamed south to the Philippines and in the early morning of May 1 led his squadron of light cruisers past the forts and through the rumored mine fields that guarded the entrance to Manila Bay. At dawn he spied the Spanish ships, equal in number to his own but hopelessly antiquated, anchored in line off the naval station of Cavite. Circling repeatedly past the enemy squadron, the American cruisers fired so effectively that before noon the entire Spanish naval force lay sunk or burning, at the cost, to the American squadron, of eight men slightly wounded. Dewey occupied Cavite and held control of Manila Bay, while the War Department prepared to send an army to take possession of the city of Manila, the Philippine capital. By the end of July, some eleven thousand United States troops under General Wesley Merritt had arrived in the Philippines, and on August 13 they entered Manila against little more than token resistance by the Spanish. As an incident of their expedition to the Orient, the American forces had occupied the island of Guam in the Spanish Marianas. Unconnected with the outside world by cable, the Spanish officials in Guam knew nothing of the war until the cruiser *Charleston* entered Apra harbor and tossed a few shells into a deserted fort. Unable to return the fire, which they had at first mistaken for a salute, they surrendered without resistance.

Meanwhile, the main Spanish fleet, four armored cruisers and three destroyers,

[15]T. J. McCormick, *China Market: America's Quest for Informal Empire, 1893–1901* (Chicago: Quadrangle Books, 1967), pp. 107–8.

[16]J. A. S. Grenville and G. B. Young, *Politics, Strategy, and American Diplomacy* (New Haven: Yale University Press, 1966), pp. 269–78.

commanded by Admiral Cervera, had left the Azores for Cuban waters. Dodging American patrols, it slipped into Santiago harbor on the south coast of Cuba. Capture or destruction of this fleet now became the prime objective of the war in this theater, since without a fleet Spain could not possibly defend Cuba for any extended period. The Atlantic Fleet, under Commodores William T. Sampson and Winfield Scott Schley, closed in around the narrow entrance to Santiago Bay, while an army of sixteen thousand regulars and volunteers, commanded by Major General W. R. Shafter, landed on the Cuban coast a few miles east of Santiago and fought its way toward that city. On July 1, in the hard-fought engagements of El Caney and San Juan Hill, the Americans pierced the outer defenses of Santiago and reached high ground, whence they could look down on the city and harbor. Cervera was caught between the Army and Navy of the United States. On the morning of July 3, under orders from the captain general in Havana, he led his squadron out of the harbor in a dash for a safer haven farther west. In a running fight westward along the coast, all his ships were sunk or run ashore in a burning condition. American losses were one man killed and one wounded. On July 16 the city of Santiago was surrendered to the Americans.

The war was now virtually over, and on July 18 the Spanish government requested the good offices of France in arranging for a termination of hostilities. Before the fighting ended, however, another American expeditionary force, commanded by General Nelson A. Miles, landed in Puerto Rico and proceeded, against feeble Spanish resistance, to take possession of that island.

McKinley and the Philippines

With the Spanish application for peace terms before them, President McKinley and his advisers had some difficult decisions to make. The independence of Cuba was a foregone conclusion; it must obviously be detached from Spain, and the Teller Amendment to the resolutions of intervention eliminated the possibility of annexation. But what of Spain's other islands— Puerto Rico, Guam, and above all the Philippines, an extensive and populous area where Spanish misrule had brought about native rebellion only less formidable than that in Cuba? The Teller Amendment said nothing of these, and its author had expressly excluded "some other islands" from his ban on the annexation of Cuba.

McKinley had, after all, approved the plan to attack the Philippines. On the day after Dewey's victory, and before its completeness was known in Washington, the President decided to send an army to occupy Manila, and on May 11 he approved a State Department proposal to insist on cession by Spain of a "coaling station" in the Philippines, presumably Manila. The intention at this stage was to allow Spain to retain the remainder of the archipelago. That plan was abandoned in the course of the summer. The point to be emphasized here is that McKinley was well aware of the significance of the Philippines in the commercial strategy of the Far East and was determined to profit from Dewey's victory by acquiring a base within five hundred miles of the coast of China. Decisions to push the annexation of Hawaii and to occupy Guam as a stepping stone between Hawaii and the Philippines were part of the same pattern.

McKinley, then, seems to have needed little prodding from the group of Republicans in Washington who had been urging expansion ever since Hawaii had invited annexation five years ealier. Prominent in this group were Roosevelt, Senator Henry Cabot Lodge, and Captain Mahan, who had been recalled from inactive duty to help guide the strategy of the war as a member of the Naval War Board. Roosevelt had resigned his office as Assistant Secretary of the Navy to go to Cuba as lieutenant colonel of the "Rough Riders" regiment, but he kept in touch by letter with his friend Lodge. Before going to Cuba, he seems to have felt some temporary qualms about taking the Philippines[17] but he was soon writing Lodge of the importance of securing possession of those islands as well as Puerto Rico. Lodge had written to another friend, three days after Dewey's victory: "We hold the other side of the Pacific, and the value to this country is almost beyond recognition." On no account, he added, must we "let the islands go . . . they must be ours under the treaty of peace." Now he was able to assure Roosevelt: "Unless I am utterly and profoundly mistaken the Administration is now fully committed to the large policy that we both desire."[18]

A number of influential senators also favored the "large policy," as did the powerful New York *Tribune* and large sections of the press that spoke for business and religion.

American businessmen, who had generally opposed intervention in Cuba and had seen no need for colonies, underwent a sudden conversion on the latter point in the spring of 1898. It was at this time that American business was taking alarm at the aggressions of the powers in China, described in an earlier chapter. In February and March, chambers of commerce and boards of trade in cities on both the east and west coasts of the United States were urging the State Department to take energetic measures for the protection of American interests. An American Asiatic Association

was formed in New York to agitate for the preservation of American rights and interests in the Orient. The New York *Journal of Commerce,* which had hitherto scoffed at colonies, isthmian canal schemes, and big-navy programs, now declared itself in favor of an isthmian canal, the annexation of Hawaii, and an increased navy—all for the purpose of strengthening the United States in the Pacific and safeguarding its rights in China.

Dewey's victory at Manila found the Chinese situation unimproved but seemed to many to offer an effective remedy. With a naval base in the Philippines, way-stations in Hawaii and perhaps in Guam, with a growing navy and the prospect of an isthmian canal through which the fleet could slip easily into the Pacific, might not the United States become at last a great Pacific power, quite capable of defending its interests in the Orient against aggressions from Europe? Many trade journals in all parts of the country agreed with the New York *Journal of Commerce,* which declared that to give up those islands now "would be an act of inconceivable folly in the face of our imperative future necessities for a basis of naval and military force on the Western shores of the Pacific."

Converted to a belief in colonialism by the special situation in the Far East, American businessmen found it easy to apply the same philosophy to the Caribbean. The erstwhile anti-imperialist *Journal of Commerce* insisted that Puerto Rico be retained and suggested that it might be necessary to keep control over Cuba in spite of the Teller Amendment. The former Spanish islands might furnish not only outlets for trade but also profitable fields for investment. It seemed that the war for humanity might be made to pay dividends in hard cash.

But the war might also pay dividends in the salvation of human souls. Of this the larger Protestant churches were as firmly convinced as were businessmen of its mate-

[17]R. H. Miller, ed., *American Imperialism in 1898: The Quest for National Fulfillment* (New York: John Wiley and Sons, Inc., 1970), p. 10.

[18]Except as otherwise indicated, the account of the settlement with Spain is based chiefly on *Expanionists of 1898,* pp. 259–78, 289–316, and chap. 9. For a recent detailed account of the negotiations, see P. E. Coletta, "The Peace Negotiations and the Treaty of Paris," in Coletta, *Threshold to American Internationalism,* chap. 4.

rial advantages.[19] Religious groups that had favored the war as a humanitarian crusade regarded the quick and easy victory as a sure sign of divine approval and as a divine command to continue the good work in islands freed from Spanish tyranny. Although there were some dissenting voices, in general Methodists, Baptists, Presbyterians, Congregationalists, and Episcopalians, together with several of the minor sects, united in urging that the United States accept the civilizing and Christianizing mission that Providence had placed before it; and just as businessmen prepared to take advantage of the opportunities for trade and investment in the former possessions of Spain, so the churches began laying plans for new missionary enterprise. If the new career upon which the United States was about to enter was to be tinged with economic imperialism, it was also to be, as one religious writer remarked, "the imperialism of righteousness."

Businessmen were interested in the Philippines principally because of their proximity to China and would presumably have been satisfied with the retention of a secure naval base in the islands. To that, McKinley had been committed since the first week of the war. But the churches wanted something more—an opportunity to practice their benevolence among the seven million people of the Philippines. Their zeal may have helped to shape the President's decision to demand cession of

[19]Quakers and Unitarians, who had opposed the war, were skeptical of any benefit accruing from "imperialism." The Catholic Church was excusably dubious about Protestant enthusiasm for missionary work in islands that had for centuries been Catholic under Spanish rule. "The unfortunate people of Manila," said *Ave Maria*, "will remember Dewey's bombardment as a restful holiday compared with the times that will come if the preachers ever invade the Philippines, bringing divorce and sundry other things with them." Other Catholic publications, however, and several members of the Catholic clergy joined with Protestants in welcoming the opportunity for civilizing work in the islands. They expressed little fear of the results of Protestant competition.

the entire archipelago. On one occasion, at any rate, he attributed his decision to religious influence. Months after the decision had been reached, he told a Methodist delegation at the White House that in answer to his earnest prayers for guidance the revelation had one night come to him that "there was nothing left for us to do but to take them all, and to educate the Filipinos, and uplift and civilize and Christianize them, and by God's grace do the very best we could by them as our fellow-men for whom Christ also died."

Spain Surrenders Her Colonial Empire

The decision to demand from Spain the cession of all the Philippines was not reached, however, until after months of uncertainty. The reply to the Spanish request for peace terms offered an immediate cessation of hostilities on condition that Spain relinquish all authority over Cuba, cede to the United States Puerto Rico and an island in the Ladrones (Marianas), and consent to American occupation of the city and harbor of Manila pending the conclusion of a definitive peace treaty that should determine the future of the Philippines. On this basis an armistice protocol was signed on August 12. American and Spanish peace commissioners were to meet in Paris not later than October 1. Thus several months would be allowed for discussion and the testing of public opinion before the final decision on the Philippines would need to be made.

As peace commissioners to represent the United States, the President selected William R. Day, who resigned as Secretary of State to become chairman of the commission, Senators Davis and Frye, Republicans, and George Gray, Democrat, and editor Whitelaw Reid of the New York *Tribune*. A majority of the commission—Davis, Frye, and Reid—were expansionists; all three favored retention of the entire Philippine ar-

chipelago. Gray, formerly a strong supporter of Cleveland's Hawaiian policy, was
still an "anti," while Day occupied a middle
ground.

Instructions to the peace commissioners
were dated September 16. By this time the
desires of American business and religion
had had ample opportunity to be heard,
and McKinley had also received from
abroad significant hints that the United
States would do well to retain the Philippines. John Hay, formerly ambassador to
Great Britain, who now succeeded Day as
Secretary of State, had previously sent
word that England would be glad to see the
United States keep the islands. Japan expressed a similar preference, though adding that Japan herself would be willing to
join with the United States and a third
power in a joint administration. These
friendly gestures were presumably designed to forestall the possibility that the
Philippines might fall into the possession of
a Germany still hungry for Pacific islands.
The American ambassador in Berlin, Andrew D. White, had dropped an unauthorized hint, after Dewey's victory, that
the United States did not wish the islands,
and the Germans had sent a naval squadron
to Manila, where its commander, Admiral
von Diederichs, made things difficult for
Dewey by his disregard of the latter's rules
of blockade. Should the United States decide to abandon the Philippines, the Germans were on hand to promote their own
interests.[20]

By the instructions of September 16, the
American commissioners were told that the
United States could not accept less than full
sovereignty over the principal island of Lu-
zon. In Paris the commissioners were advised by Americans who had been in the

Philippines that division of the islands was
undesirable. The archipelago formed an
economic unit with Manila as its commercial center. Davis, Frye, and Reid, accordingly, cabled to the President a strongly
worded argument for the retention of the
entire group. McKinley, who had just
sounded public opinion during a tour of
the Midwest, had apparently reached a
similar conclusion. On October 26 Secretary Hay cabled the commissioners that the
United States must retain all the Philippines. Small heed was paid to the group of
Filipino natives, led by Emilio Aguinaldo,
who demanded independence and had set
up a government of their own near Manila.
It was generally agreed, by whites who
knew the Philippines, that the natives were
not prepared for self-government. Independence under these conditions might
breed anarchy, and anarchy would invite
foreign—quite possibly German—intervention.

Spain, reluctant to surrender the last
remnants of her once great colonial empire, held out as long as possible for retention of all or part of the Philippines but in
the end could do nothing but accept the
American terms. The blow was softened
somewhat by an agreement to pay her
$20,000,000 for public works and im-
provements in the islands.[21]

By the treaty of peace signed in Paris on

---

[20]The old notion that either von Diederichs or his
government wished to provoke hostilities with the
United States or to seize the Philippines by force has
been discredited. See T. A. Bailey, "Dewey and the
Germans at Manila Bay," *American Historical Review*, 45
(1935), 59–81; L. B. Shippee, "Germany and the
Spanish-American War," ibid., 33 (1925), 754–77.

[21] The American commissioners were unsuccessful
in an attempt to purchase the island of Kusaie in the
Carolines, which was of considerable interest to
American missionaries and was also desired as a cable
station by capitalists planning to lay a cable from
Hawaii to Manila. The German government, disappointed in the Philippines, had exacted from Spain a
secret promise not to cede the Carolines to the United
States. They were subsequently sold to Germany, and
with them went also the Pelew Islands and the
Marianas with the exception of Guam. Pratt, *Expansionists of 1898*, pp. 302–4, 340–44. Aside from the
disposition of the Philippines and Carolines, the only
serious disagreement between the American and
Spanish commissioners at Paris was over the Cuban
debt. Spain wished this assumed by either the Cubans
or the United States. The United States insisted successfully that responsibility for it be retained by Spain.

December 10, 1898, Spain relinquished "all claim of sovereignty over and title to Cuba," ceded to the United States the Philippine Islands, Guam in the Marianas or Ladrones, Puerto Rico, "and other islands now under Spanish sovereignty in the West Indies."[22] The inhabitants of the ceded territories were promised "the free exercise of their religion," but it was stipulated that their "civil rights and political status" should "be determined by the Congress." For the first time, in a treaty acquiring territory for the United States, there was no promise of citizenship. As in the case of Alaska, there was no promise, actual or implied, of statehood. The United States thereby acquired not "territories" but possessions or "dependencies" and became, in that sense, a "colonial" power.

The Senate Debates Imperialism

The treaty, however, still had to run the gauntlet of the Senate, and there it encountered determined opposition. Few senators appear to have objected seriously to the annexation of tiny Guam or of Puerto Rico, which was nearby and peopled chiefly by the white race, though of alien tongue. But annexation of the Philippines was a much greater break with American tradition. Their distance, six thousand miles from San Francisco, their population of seven million Malays, including a minority of pagans and Moslems, the existence of a vigorous independence movement whose leaders were as hostile to American as to Spanish sovereignty—all these factors made their acquisition seem to many, in and out of the Senate, a dangerous

---

[22]The "other islands" of Spain in the West Indies were Culebra, and tiny islands off the east end of Puerto Rico and the Isle of Pines south of the west end of Cuba. Long in dispute between Cuba and the United States, the Isle of Pines was finally made over to Cuba in 1925.

venture in imperialism and a violation of time-honored American principles. An Anti-Imperialist League was organized to combat annexation, while in the Senate many Democrats and a few Republicans made clear their purpose to vote against ratification of the treaty.

Debate on the treaty was in executive session, but beginning weeks before the treaty was sent to the Senate (January 4, 1899), senators found opportunity for public expression of their views in debating a number of resolutions dealing with the acquisition of colonial territory. The most important of these, introduced by Senator Vest of Missouri, declared:

> That under the Constitution of the United States no power is given to the Federal Government to acquire territory to be held and governed permanently as colonies.

Democratic senators, ably supported by Republican George F. Hoar of Massachusetts, argued that under the Constitution there was no place for a colonial system like that of the European powers—a system based "upon the fundamental idea that the people of immense areas of territory can be held as subjects, never to become citizens." It was against that very system that Americans had rebelled in 1776. If the Philippine Islands were taken under American sovereignty, therefore, their inhabitants must become citizens with all the rights of citizens. They could not be governed as subjects, nor could they and their products be excluded from the United States by restrictions on immigration and importation. American agriculture and American labor would thus be subjected to unchecked competition from the Filipinos. It was foolish to suppose, furthermore, that American free institutions would operate successfully among a people so widely different in race, language, religion, and customs from the people of the United States. Both those who opposed and those who favored annexation regarded colored races and any bred in the tropics as unqualified to participate in democratic self-government.[23]

But even if it were granted that the United States might constitutionally annex the Philippines and govern them as a colony, was it expedient to do so? No, answered opponents of the treaty. Departure from the spirit of our republican institutions in the government of colonies would spell the destruction of those institutions at home. Possession of the Philippines, moreover, would embroil the United States in the international politics of the Far East and endanger the Monroe Doctrine. How could we forbid Europe to interfere in the Western Hemisphere when we were interfering in the Eastern? "The Monroe Doctrine is gone!" lamented Senator Hoar. Opposition senators also minimized the trade advantages to be expected from annexation and ridiculed the religious argument. "In order to Christianize these savage people," said one senator, "we must put the yoke of despotism upon their necks; . . . Christianity can not be advanced by force."

All of these arguments were answered by the supporters of the treaty. Of special interest is the constitutional argument advanced by Senator Orville H. Platt of Connecticut, since it anticipated subsequent decisions of the Supreme Court.[24] The right to acquire and the right to govern territory, said Platt, were sovereign rights, which the United States enjoyed in common with other sovereign nations, and the right to govern implied the right to establish whatever form of government was suitable to the condition of the territory and the character of its inhabitants—be they savages, barbarians, or civilized folk. Platt de-

nied that there would be any obligation to admit the Philippines as a state or to confer citizenship upon the Filipinos. He denied that either the people or the products of the islands could be admitted to the United States without the consent of Congress.

Senator Platt affirmed, in brief, precisely what his opponents denied—that the United States had all the powers necessary to establish and maintain a full-fledged colonial system.

The debate continued from early December until February 6, 1899, the date set for a vote on the treaty. Since Democratic votes were essential for ratification, it was important that Senator Gray of Delaware, a leading Democrat, who had been a member of the peace commission, and though at first opposed to taking the Philippines, now defended the treaty in the Senate. William Jennings Bryan, titular head of the Democratic party, came to Washington to urge Democratic support of the treaty, arguing that peace should be made as soon as possible and that the question of freeing the Philippines could be disposed of later. It is possible that he won two votes that might otherwise have been cast against the treaty.[25] On February 6, 1899, the Senate approved the treaty by a vote of 57 to 27—a single vote above the necessary two-thirds majority. Fifteen Democratic, Populist, or Independent senators voted with the Republican majority, while two Republicans, Hoar of Massachusetts and Hale of Maine, voted in the negative.

Meanwhile, on February 4, two days before the Senate approved the treaty, hostilities had broken out between American troops at Manila and Filipino insurgents led by Aguinaldo, who were ready to fight for their independence against Americans as they had fought against Spaniards. In annexing an empire the United States had

[23]Christopher Lasch, "The Anti-Imperialists, the Philippines, and the Inequality of Man," *Journal of Southern History*, 24 (August 1958), 319–31.

[24]*Downes* v. *Bidwell*, 182 U.S. 244 (1901); see also J. W. Pratt, *America's Colonial Experiment* (Englewood Cliffs, N.J.: Prentice-Hall, Inc., 1950), pp. 157–64.

[25]P. E. Coletta, *William Jennings Bryan*, 3 vols. (Lincoln: University of Nebraska Press, 1964–1970), 1: 233–36.

also annexed a war, which was to prove much longer and more troublesome than that with Spain. Not until July 1902 was armed resistance in the Philippines effectually subdued.

Hawaii, Wake, and Tutuila

The War with Spain, which gave the United States Puerto Rico, the Philippines, and Guam, also furnished the impetus necessary to effect the long-delayed annexation of Hawaii, and it was followed within a year by the partition of the Samoan group, in which the United States received the island of Tutuila, where since 1878 it had possessed rights for a coaling station in Pago Pago harbor.

In March 1898, as previously noted, the advocates of Hawaiian annexation abandoned hope of accomplishing their object by treaty and brought into the Senate a joint resolution of annexation. The resolution, however, made no headway until June.[26] Dewey's victory at Manila turned American eyes to the Pacific as never before. If the American flag was to remain in the Philippines—if the United States, from the Philippines as a base, was to defend its rights in China—Hawaii, it was argued, was essential as a naval base and coaling station en route to the Far East.[27] The Hawaiian government, on advice from its minister in Washington, instead of proclaiming its neutrality in the war, placed all the facilities of Honolulu harbor at the disposal of the United States and even offered to make an

alliance. The alliance offer was not accepted, but the friendly attitude of Hawaii and the fact that by aiding the United States it was subjecting itself to possible Spanish reprisals enabled the annexationists to argue that Hawaii should be brought under the American flag as a reward for friendly aid and for its own protection. Thus the war situation greatly strengthened the case for annexation. Much was also said of the "yellow peril" in Hawaii—the rapid growth of its Japanese population and the danger that Hawaii might be absorbed in Japan's waxing empire.

These arguments proved adequate, in the end, to secure a victory for the annexationists. A new joint resolution was introduced in the House of Representatives on May 4, three days after Manila Bay, and passed the House by a large majority on June 15. Senate opponents brought out all the timeworn arguments. They could delay but could not defeat the measure, which passed the Senate on July 6, 1898, by a vote of 42 to 21, and received the President's signature on the seventh. On the following August 12—the date of the signature of the armistice protocol with Spain—Hawaii passed formally under the jurisdiction of the United States as a part of its territory.

The Hawaiian Islands, their outpost at Midway, acquired by the United States in 1867, and Guam provided stepping stones to the Philippines and the Far East in general. The wide gap between Midway and Guam was soon filled in by the annexation of Wake Island, 2,130 miles west of Honolulu and 1,034 miles from Midway. The naval explorer, Commander Charles Wilkes, had asserted title to Wake for the United States in 1841, but for nearly sixty years no effort had been made to enforce the claim. On January 17, 1899, Commander E. D. Taussig, commanding the gunboat *Bennington,* landed at Wake and took formal possession in the name of the United States.

The year of the Spanish-American War

---

[26]For details of the passage of the joint resolution annexing Hawaii, see Pratt, *Expansionists of 1898,* pp. 317–26.

[27]Opponents of annexing Hawaii argued that the United States already had, at Kiska in the Aleutians, a fine harbor much nearer the great-circle route to the Orient than was Hawaii. The claim was correct as far as it went, but it took no account of climatic and supply difficulties in the Aleutians.

witnessed a new outbreak of native trouble and international friction in Samoa, which was solved the following year by a partition of the islands, the United States receiving Tutuila, while Upolu and Savaii passed to Germany. Britain relinquished all claims to Samoa, receiving as compensation the surrender of German rights in the Tonga and part of the Solomon Islands and territorial concessions in Africa. A treaty of partition was signed in Washington on December 2, 1899. From the treaty the United States obtained no title to Tutuila (subsequently, with the small neighboring islands, known as American Samoa), but merely a renunciation in its favor of German and British claims. All three powers had hitherto maintained the fiction of Samoan sovereignty and independence. The native chiefs of Tutuila, however, formally ceded their island to the United States in 1900, and those of the nearby Manu'a group followed suit in 1904. These cessions were accepted by President Theodore Roosevelt without submission to the Senate or to Congress. The American title seems not to have been questioned, but to remove all doubt, Congress, by a joint resolution of February 20, 1929, accepted, ratified, and confirmed the cessions of 1900 and 1904.

The People's Verdict

The expansionist policies growing out of the War with Spain had, in general, been sponsored by Republicans and opposed by Democrats, though with many exceptions in both parties. Under the circumstances it was perhaps inevitable that "imperialism" should become an issue in the presidential campaign of 1900 and that the Democrats should attack their opponents for holding the Philippines by armed force against the will and despite the resistance of the most vocal native faction. Accordingly, while the Republican platform of that year sought to justify the establishment of American sovereignty in the Philippines as a necessary consequence of the breakdown of Spanish rule and promised to confer upon the Filipinos "the largest measure of self-government consistent with their welfare and our duties," the Democrats officially denounced "the Philippine policy of the present Administration" and "the greedy commercialism" which had dictated it. "We are unalterably opposed," said the Democratic platform, "to the seizing or purchasing of distant islands to be governed outside the Constitution and whose people can never become citizens."

. . . we favor [the platform continued] an immediate declaration of the Nation's purpose to give the Filipinos, first, a stable form of government; second, independence; and third, protection from outside interference such as has been given for nearly a century to the republics of Central and South America . . .

the last reference obviously being to the Monroe Doctrine. "Imperialism," said the Democrats, "is the paramount issue" in the campaign.

Mr. Bryan, the Democratic candidate, fully endorsed—probably had dictated—the party's platform declarations with regard to the Philippines. The attack upon imperialism, however, was not confined to the Democrats. Many prominent men of both parties joined hands in the Anti-Imperialist League, which conducted a vigorous campaign of propaganda based upon the principle of "government by the consent of the governed."[28] Opposed, from the beginning, to annexation of the Philippines, the League joined the Democratic party in denouncing the war of subjugation against the Filipino insurgents and in de-

[28]F. H. Harrington, "The Anti-Imperialist Movement in the United States, 1898–1900," *Mississippi Valley Historical Review*, 22 (1935), 211–30; R. L. Beisner, *Twelve against Empire: The Anti-Imperialists, 1898–1900* (New York: McGraw-Hill Book Company, 1968).

manding that they be given independence. After some discussion of the formation of a third party, the League's leaders resolved instead to support Bryan for the Presidency.

Thus, on the surface, the political issue for 1900 seemed clear-cut, but as usual in presidential campaigns, the "paramount issue" did not stand alone.[29] Bryan had insisted upon incorporating, as in 1896, a "free-silver" plank in the Democratic platform. "Bryan would rather be wrong than President," quipped Thomas B. Reed, Republican Speaker of the House. Many Republican anti-imperialists, like Senators Hoar and Hale, discovered that they preferred McKinley, with the gold standard and a little imperialism, to Bryan and free silver. Bryan himself, as the campaign progressed, found that his diatribes against imperialism excited little popular enthusiasm and shifted his emphasis to an attack on the trusts, the plutocracy, and special privilege. But even if attention had been concentrated on the single issue, there was no black and white difference between the Democratic and Republican positions on the Philippines. Republicans promised "self-government" and had never expressed a determination to hold the Philippines as a permanent possession. The Democrats made no proposal to surrender

[29]T. A. Bailey, "Was the Presidential Election of 1908 a Mandate on Imperialism?" *Mississippi Valley Historical Review*, 24 (1937), 43–52.

to Aguinaldo and his insurgents. They promised to "give" the Filipinos "a stable form of government" and independence, but under "protection from outside interference"—a "protectorate" of undefined duration. Who could say whether Filipino liberties would be safer under Republican or Democratic auspices, or under which the United States would run less risk of being involved in Far Eastern politics?

Thus when American voters went to the polls in November 1900, to cast their ballots for McKinley or Bryan, it is none too clear what their votes meant with respect to policy in the Philippines or colonial expansion in general. Certainly those who wished to vote for McKinley and the gold standard, or for McKinley and a continuation of the prosperity that had come in with his administration, could persuade themselves that they were voting for litte more "imperialism" than was implicit in the Democratic proposals. But there must have been very many, influenced by the propaganda of business and the churches, who were anxious to vote for a profitable imperialism that was at the same time an "imperialism of righteousness."

At any rate, when McKinley and Roosevelt won the election by a handy popular plurality of nearly 900,000 votes, the Republicans could be pardoned for assuming that the nation had accepted and approved their "large policy" of territorial expansion.

ADDITIONAL READINGS

HOFSTADTER, RICHARD, *Darwinism in American Thought, 1860–1915*. Philadelphia: University of Pennsylvania Press, 1944.

LEUCHTENBURG, WILLIAM E., "Progressivism, Imperialism: The Progressive Movement and American Foreign Policy, 1898–1916," *Mississippi Valley Historical Review*, 39 (1952), 483–504.

MAY, ERNEST R., *Imperial Democracy: The Emergence of America as a Great Power.* New York: Harcourt Brace Jovanovich, Inc., 1961.

MORGAN, H. WAYNE, *America's Road to Empire: The War with Spain and Overseas Expansionism.* New York: John Wiley & Sons, Inc., 1965.

———, *William McKinley and His America.* Syracuse, N.Y.: Syracuse University Press, 1963.

SIRACUSA, JOSEPH M., "Progressivism, Imperialism, and the Leuchtenburg Thesis, 1952–1974: an Historiographical Appraisal," *Australian Journal of Politics and History,* 20 (1974), 312–25.

SPECTOR, RONALD, *Admiral of the New Empire: The Life and Career of George Dewey.* Baton Rouge, La.: Louisana State University Press, 1974.

12. The Problems
of a World Power

The Spanish-American War, it has been often said, raised the United States to the status of a "world power." After 1898, certainly, the weight and influence of the United States were felt throughout the world as never before. Three phrases sum up the new role of the United States in international politics: (1) dominance in the Caribbean, (2) leadership in the Far East, (3) participation (in a modest way until 1917) in the affairs of Europe. The nation that had suddenly acquired Puerto Rico, Hawaii, and the Philippines had ceased to be land-bound and isolationist. These acquisitions did not cause Uncle Sam's assumption of new world responsibilities; rather, they were a result and a symbol of a new attitude toward the world. Had the United States not been ready to play a part as a world power, it would hardly have insisted upon keeping the Philippines.

The policies that the United States followed during the war and after it were precisely the policies that Admiral Mahan had been preaching throughout the 1890s. Build up the Navy, he had urged; own and control fully whatever isthmian canal is dug; make sure of bases on the Caribbean approaches to the canal; secure Hawaii as an outpost of the Pacific coast. Part of this program was achieved by the events of the war and the resulting Treaty of Paris. The remainder of it was rapidly accomplished thereafter, particularly under the direction of Mahan's disciple, Theodore Roosevelt, who entered the White House in September 1901, after McKinley's assassination.

Roosevelt found a Navy that already comprised some seventeen battleships, built and building. Under his leadership it grew steadily. The United States, which in 1890 had been negligible as a naval power, stood in fifth place in naval strength in 1904, in second place in 1907. After 1912 the German fleet took a small lead, but when war began in 1914, the United States was easily one of the three foremost powers in battleship strength.[1] Outlying naval bases had been developed at Guantanamo Bay in Cuba and at Pearl Harbor in the Hawaiian island of Oahu. In the meantime the United States had built its own isthmian canal at Panama and, as a means of safeguarding that vital defense link against European interference, had ringed the Caribbean Sea with protectorates whose governments were friendly and dependable.

The attainment of American supremacy in the Western Hemisphere was facilitated by British accommodation. British retreat in the Venezuela controversy and British friendliness during the Spanish-American War were early steps in what has been called "the great rapprochement," a process that removed all serious causes of Anglo-American friction before the outbreak of war in Europe in 1914. Alarmed by the threat of rising German commercial and naval rivalry, Britain closed or deactivated her naval bases at Halifax and on Puget Sound, concentrated her naval power in

[1] G. T. Davis, *A Navy Second to None* (New York: Harcourt, Brace & World, Inc., 1940), chaps. 8, 9.

European waters, and conceded naval supremacy on both American coasts and in the Caribbean to the United States. In the same spirit she yielded to American desires with reference to isthmian canal policy and the boundary of Alaska, approved the institution of American protectorates in the Caribbean, settled by arbitration a long-standing dispute over fishing rights, and accepted an American policy for Mexico with which her statesmen strongly disagreed. The traditional enemy had thus become a cooperative friend.[2]

Acquiring the Panama Canal Zone[3]

The focal point of American interest in the Caribbean region was at the site, whether in Nicaragua or Panama, of the future isthmian canal. Here was the key to the naval strategy and national security of the future—a boon to the United States if firmly held in American hands, a menace if controlled by potential enemies. The initial failure of French efforts at Panama, the attempt by American private capital to construct a canal through Nicaragua, and the growing belief in the United States that only a canal under American control was admissible have already been recounted. The events of the war with Spain—the voyage of the *Oregon*, the acquisition of new possessions and new interests in the Pacific—had hardened this belief into a national conviction that was well voiced by President McKinley when he remarked in his annual message of December 5, 1898, that "the construction of such a maritime highway is now more than ever indispens-

able" and that "our national policy now more imperatively than ever calls for its control by this Government."

For the successful pursuit of such a "national policy" the situation in 1898 seemed more favorable than ever before. Both the Panama and Nicaragua routes were available. At Panama, the new Panama Canal Company, successor to the original French company, had come to the end of its resources and was willing to dispose of its rights if the consent of Colombia could be obtained. In Nicaragua, the Maritime Canal Company had forfeited its concession because of failure to fulfill its contract. The governments of Nicaragua and Costa Rica were willing to dicker with the United States for the rights necessary for the construction of a·canal by that route. Finally, Great Britain, which since 1850 had clung to the Clayton-Bulwer Treaty, barring national control of an isthmian canal, was at last in a mood to withdraw or modify that prohibition.

The obstruction of the Clayton-Bulwer Treaty was removed by a new treaty signed by Secretary of State John Hay and Lord Pauncefote, the British ambassador, on November 18, 1901.[4] The new treaty expressly abrogated the Clayton-Bulwer Treaty, thus freeing the United States to construct, manage, and police its own canal. The only obligation assumed by the United States was a guarantee that the canal should be open to the vessels of commerce and war of all nations "on terms of entire equality." The treaty was approved by the Senate on December 4, 1901.

The choice of a route was the next hurdle to be overcome. Nicaragua had for years been the favorite location, and it was powerfully supported in Congress by Senator John T. Morgan of Alabama. But

[2]Bradford Perkins, *The Great Rapprochement: England and the United States, 1895–1914* (New York: Atheneum, 1968), pp. 157–59, 185, 230, *et passim*.

[3]The account of the acquisition of the Panama Canal Zone and the institution of the Caribbean protectorates is condensed from J. W. Pratt, *America's Colonial Experiment* (Englewood Cliffs, N.J.: Prentice-Hall, Inc., 1950), chaps. 3 and 4. Source citations will be found in that work.

[4]This was the second of two canal treaties signed by Hay and Lord Pauncefote. The first had been amended by the Senate in ways that the British government refused to accept, but the second treaty actually embodied the substance of the Senate's amendments.

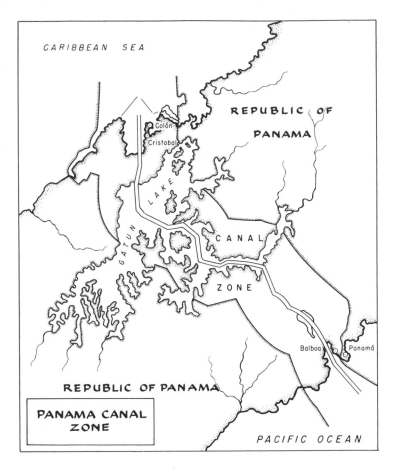

CARIBBEAN SEA

REPUBLIC OF PANAMA

Colón
Cristobal

GATUN LAKE

CANAL

ZONE

Balboa   Panamá

REPUBLIC OF PANAMA

PANAMA CANAL
ZONE

PACIFIC OCEAN

Panama now had persuasive advocates, notably William Nelson Cromwell, of the New York law firm of Sullivan and Cromwell, and the Frenchman, Philippe Bunau-Varilla. Both represented the interests of the New Panama Canal Company, whose only hope of saving something from the wreck of its enterprise lay in sale to the United States. They were fortunate in enlisting in their cause the influential Senator Mark Hanna of Ohio.

The battle of the routes makes a long story, of which only a few high spots will be related here. A commission of engineers reported first in favor of Nicaragua, then switched to Panama when the Company lowered its price for its rights from $109,000,000 to $40,000,000, the figure which the commission had suggested as reasonable. The House of Representatives passed a bill for a Nicaraguan canal. The Senate, after a long debate, amended it to favor Panama. The report of the commission and the persuasive argument of Mark Hanna largely accounted for the change, but they were aided by convulsions of nature. A major volcanic eruption in the island of Martinique and reports of a minor one and an earthquake in Nicaragua itself pointed to danger to a canal in that volcanic country. Panama seemed exempt from such phenomena.[5] The Isthmian Canal

[5] Bunau-Varilla took advantage of the Martinique disaster by placing on the desk of every Senator a Nicaraguan postage stamp featuring a smoking volcano in the middle of Lake Nicaragua. Though there

Act, making the Panama route the first choice, was signed by President Theodore Roosevelt on June 28, 1902.

The next act in the drama is one of the most controversial episodes in the history of American foreign policy. The United States needed the consent of Colombia to the transfer of rights from the New Panama Canal Company to the United States and its consent also to the exercise by the United States in the proposed Canal Zone of the authority necessary to operate and protect the canal. The consent was given in a treaty signed by Secretary of State John Hay and Colombian chargé d'affaires Dr. Tomás Herrán, January 22, 1903. The Colombian Senate, however, unanimously rejected the treaty, holding that the price ($10,000,000) was too low and the impairment of Colombian sovereignty too sweeping.[6] Thereupon the Department of Panama revolted, was promptly recognized as independent, and shielded from Colombian vengeance by the United States. A few days later, November 18, 1903, its representative in Washington signed a treaty giving the United States even more privileges than it would have received under the treaty with Colombia. The United States received in perpetuity the use of a zone across the isthmus, ten miles in width (five miles on each side of the canal), in which it might exercise all the rights and authority that it would possess if actually sovereign. It might take steps to ensure sanitation and to maintain public order in the cities of Colon and Panama, and it might fortify and defend

the canal. The United States, in turn, would pay to Panama $10,000,000 at once and $250,000 annually beginning after nine years—the same compensation earlier offered Colombia. In addition, the United States guaranteed and promised to maintain "the independence of the Republic of Panama."

The treaty, it is interesting to observe, was signed for Panama by Philippe Bunau-Varilla. The Frenchman had promoted and helped to finance the revolution and in return had been named the first minister of Panama to the United States.

The circumstances of the Panama revolution—the appearance of the American collusion, the veto by the United States of Colombian attempts to suppress the uprising, the unusual haste with which recognition was extended and an advantageous treaty made—created bitter resentment in Colombia and divided opinion in the United States. Mr. Roosevelt, supported by his Secretaries of State and War (Hay and Elihu Root), energetically defended his handling of the Panama crisis. "By far the most important action I took in foreign affairs," he said of it in his *Autobiography*. "I took the canal zone and let Congress debate," he boasted in a public address in 1911. Recent scholars have not shared Roosevelt's confident assurance that he followed the only right procedure but are inclined to think his action unnecessarily precipitate and unjustified by treaty or precedent.

Colombia, understandably, believed that she had suffered a grievous wrong at the hands of the United States. For nearly twenty years all attempts to appease her failed. The United States consistently refused to submit the propriety of its conduct to arbitration. Finally, in 1921, the United States paid Colombia $25,000,000, the amount that the Colombian Senate presumably would have settled for in 1903. The payment, though accompanied by no apology, was a tacit admission of wrongdoing on the part of the United States. It

---

was no love lost between Bunau-Varilla and Cromwell, and though each later spoke disparagingly of the other, the two appear to have worked cooperatively during the "battle of the routes" in 1902. See C. D. Ameringer, "The Panama Canal Lobby of Philippe Bunau-Varilla and William Nelson Cromwell," *American Historical Review*, 68 (January 1963), 346–63; but cf. A. H. Dean, *William Nelson Cromwell, 1854–1948* (New York: Privately printed, 1957), pp. 140, 147.

[6]D. C. Miner in *The Fight for the Panama Route* (New York: Columbia University Press, 1940), is an adequate account in English of conditions in Colombia at the time of the canal negotiations.

was reported that senatorial approval of the treaty was made easier by pressure from American capitalists who were to be rewarded with oil concessions in Colombia for bringing about a satisfactory settlement of the old quarrel over Panama.[7]

Transfer of the French property on the Isthmus to the United States took place on May 4, 1904. Construction of the canal, though attended with some bungling at the outset, went forward rapidly, and on August 15, 1914, the Panama Canal was opened to the traffic of the world.

Protectorates in the Caribbean

Control of the Caribbean did not rest solely upon outright annexations of territory, as in Puerto Rico, acquired from Spain in 1898, and the Virgin Islands, purchased from Denmark in 1916,[8] or upon perpetual leases, almost the equivalent of annexation, as in the Panama Canal Zone. Between 1901 and 1917 the United States instituted a system of "protectorates," by which it gained sufficient control of a number of small republics rimming the Caribbean to bind them securely into an American

[7]J. F. Rippy, *The Capitalists and Colombia* (New York: Vanguard Press, Inc. 1931), pp. 103–21.

[8]The United States had several times negotiated for the purchase of the Danish West Indies, the islands of St. Thomas, St. John, and St. Croix. Seward's treaty of 1867 had died in the Senate. John Hay had signed a second treaty in 1902, only to see it defeated in the Danish Parliament. Fear that Germany might absorb Denmark and claim the islands led Secretary of State Lansing in 1916 to make a generous offer, coupled with a warning that the United States might find it necessary to seize them to prevent their falling into German hands. By a treaty signed on August 4, 1916, the United States purchased the three islands for $25,000,000. After the transfer of sovereignty, March 31, 1917, they were known as the Virgin Islands of the United States. The entire story of the efforts of the United States to acquire the islands is told in C. C. Tansill, *The Purchase of the Danish West Indies* (Baltimore: The Johns Hopkins Press, 1932).

"sphere of influence." The term "protectorate," however, like the word "colony," had no place in the American official vocabulary.

The principal recipients of American "protection" were Cuba, Panama, the Dominican Republic, Nicaragua, and Haiti. The special relations of the United States to these republics were embodied in treaties, no two of which were exactly alike. To only one such state—the Republic of Panama—did the United States actually promise "protection," in the declaration that "the United States guarantees and will maintain the independence of the Republic of Panama." Other treaties, such as those with Cuba and Haiti, contained engagements on the part of the "protected" states not to impair their independence or cede any of their territory to a third party; and the same two treaties permitted intervention by the United States for the maintenance of independence or of orderly government. Since careless public finance was likely to lead to foreign intervention and possible loss of independence, a number of the treaties—those with Cuba, Haiti, and the Dominican Republic—contained restrictions upon, or gave the United States supervision over, financial policy. By the treaties with Cuba and Nicaragua, the United States gained the privilege of using naval bases within the territorial limits of the "protected" states, and by that with Nicaragua, it obtained exclusive canal rights through Nicaraguan territory.

In all the countries of this Caribbean semicircle of protectorates American investments existed. These no doubt benefited from the increased stability and financial responsibility induced by governmental policy. In the Dominican Republic, Haiti, and Nicaragua that policy resulted in a transfer of the ownership of government obligations from European to American bankers. Yet in none of the five republics save Cuba was American financial interests large or important, and the charge that the Caribbean policy of the United States was primarily one of "financial imperialism" is not sustained by the facts. The dominant motive was clearly political and strategic rather than economic. The acquisition of the Canal Zone and the building of the Panama Canal made the isthmian area a vital spot in the American defense system. It became, then, a matter of the utmost importance that the United States itself should control the bases requisite for the defense of the canal and that no rival great power should obtain a foothold in the vicinity of the canal or on the approaches to it. Hence the United States secured base rights in Cuba and Nicaragua, and hence exacted nonalienation agreements from Cuba and Haiti and controlled the public finance of these and other Caribbean republics. The establishment of protectorates thus became a species of "preventive intervention," which Theodore Roosevelt, in his celebrated "corollary" message of December 1904, sought to justify as merely an application of the Monroe Doctrine. Still another motive, which influenced different administrations in the United States to varying degrees, was a genuine desire to substitute orderly democratic processes for the chronic addiction to armed revolution that afflicted most of the Caribbean and Central American states.

Panama, whose special relations with the United States have just been described, was the second Caribbean republic to become a protectorate of the United States. Cuba had preceded it, and it was followed by the Dominican Republic, Nicaragua, and Haiti.

Cuba and the Platt Amendment

The end of the war with Spain had left Cuba occupied by the armed forces of the United States but with its future status not clearly defined. Spain had relinquished sovereignty over the island, and the United States had renounced any thought of an-

nexing it. But that renunciation did not absolve the United States, in its own eyes, from responsibility for Cuba's future. President McKinley remarked in his annual message of December 5, 1899, that the United States had assumed "a grave responsibility for the future good government of Cuba." The island, he continued, "must needs be bound to us by ties of singular intimacy and strength if its enduring welfare is to be assured."

What those ties were to be was defined by Elihu Root, McKinley's Secretary of War. General Leonard Wood, who had achieved many useful reforms as military governor of Cuba, convoked a Constitutional Convention, which sat in Havana from November 1900 to February 1901. It completed a constitution for independent Cuba but failed to carry out a directive of the governor to provide for the relations to exist between the Cuban government and the government of the United States. Secretary Root, outlined his concept of what those relations should be in a set of proposals which were introduced in the Senate by Senator Orville H. Platt of Connecticut and were known henceforth as the Platt Amendment. Actually an amendment to the Army Appropriation Bill of March 2, 1901, the amendment authorized the President to terminate the military occupation of Cuba as soon as a Cuban government should have been established under a constitution which provided, among other things, that Cuba should never permit any "foreign power" to gain foothold in its territory, or contract any debt beyond the capacity of its ordinary revenues to pay; that Cuba should consent that the United States might intervene in its affairs for the preservation of Cuba's independence or "the maintenance of a government adequate for the protection of life, property, and individual liberty"; and that Cuba should lease or sell to the United States lands necessary for coaling or naval stations at points to be agreed upon.

The Cuban Convention at first rejected the terms of the Platt Amendment but later accepted them after receiving assurances from Secretary Root that the United States would exercise the right of intervention only in the event of foreign threat or serious domestic disturbance, not in a spirit of "intermeddling or interference with the affairs of the Cuban government."

The new Cuban government was inaugurated on May 20, 1902. The Platt Amendment took its place as an Annex to the Cuban Constitution and was embodied in the permanent treaty of 1903 between Cuba and the United States. It remained in force until 1934, when all of the treaty except the naval base article was abrogated. Under that article the United States enjoyed the use of Guantanamo Bay, on the south coast near Santiago, as a naval station. Under Article 3 the United States exercised the right of intervention from time to time, notably in 1906–1909, following a breakdown of the Cuban government, but so frequently in subsequent years as to violate, in the opinion of many, Root's promise that the article would not result in "intermeddling or interference."[9] Such intervention ceased after 1934, with the treaty basis for it. In the meantime the United States had not only its naval base at Guantanamo, which it kept after 1934, but also the assurance that no rival power would secure a foothold in Cuba.

The Roosevelt Corollary
of the Monroe Doctrine

Secretary Root had spoken of the Platt Amendment as supplying a basis in international law for intervention by the United States under the Monroe Doctrine to pro-

[9]T. P. Wright, Jr., "United States Electoral Intervention in Cuba," *Inter-American Economic Affairs*, 13 (Winter 1959), 50–71.

tect the independence of Cuba. But with how much justice or logic could the United States enforce the Monroe Doctrine against European intervention in turbulent American republics if it took no responsibility for the behavior of such republics or for the fulfillment of their obligations to Europe? The Platt Amendment, by restricting the debt-contracting power of Cuba and by permitting the United States to intervene for the preservation of orderly government, had hinted that the Monroe Doctrine involved certain policing responsibilities for the United States. That idea, though previously suggested from time to time, was now for the first time written into law. Need for such a principle was emphasized by events in Venezuela in 1902–1903.

In 1901, when the German and British governments were contemplating the use of force to collect debts from the Venezuelan dictator, Cipriano Castro, Roosevelt (as yet only Vice President) wrote to a German friend: "If any South American country misbehaves toward any European country, let the European country spank it"; and in his first annual message as President, a few months later, he declared that the Monroe Doctrine gave no guarantee to any American state against punishment for misconduct, provided that punishment did not take the form of acquisition of territory. When, however, in the winter of 1902–1903, Germans and British actually undertook to bring Castro to terms by a "pacific blockade," anti-German sentiment flared up in the United States, and Roosevelt became alarmed over the possibility that such a situation might produce a serious quarrel between the United States and some European power. The Venezuelan crisis was settled when Castro agreed to submit the question of his debts to arbitration, but no one knew when Venezuela or one of its neighbors might present a new invitation to coercion. It seemed to Roosevelt desirable to find a formula by which all excuse for European intervention in the New World might be removed.[10]

The formula was announced by Roosevelt in 1904, first in May in a letter to Secretary Root, later, in almost identical language, in his annual message of December 6, 1904. As stated in the annual message it read as follows:

> Any country whose people conduct themselves well can count upon our hearty friendship. If a nation shows that it knows how to act with reasonable efficiency and decency in social and political matters, if it keeps order and pays its obligations, it need fear no interference from the United States. Chronic wrongdoing, or an impotence which results in a general loosening of the ties of civilized society, may in America, as elsewhere, ultimately require intervention of some civilized nation, and in the Western Hemisphere, the adherence of the United States to the Monroe Doctrine may force the United States, however reluctantly, in flagrant cases of such wrongdoing or impotence, to the exercise of an international police power.

The Dominican Receivership

This "Roosevelt Corollary of the Monroe Doctrine"—so called because it was assumed to follow as a necessary consequence of the Monroe Doctrine—was to serve, whether expressly mentioned or not, as the theoretical basis for the subsequent

[10]Roosevelt's handling of the Venezuela crisis of 1902–1903 is still a subject of disagreement among historians. One recognized authority, Dexter Perkins, in *The Monroe Doctrine, 1867–1907* (Baltimore: The Johns Hopkins Press, 1937), chap. 5 and pp. 407–11, discounts completely Roosevelt's dramatic story of how he brought the Kaiser to accept arbitration. On the other hand, Howard K. Beale, in *Theodore Roosevelt and the Rise of America to World Power* (Baltimore: The Johns Hopkins Press, 1956), pp. 395–431, and J. W. Pratt in *Challenge and Rejection* (New York: The Macmillan Company, 1967), pp. 22–28, express the belief that the story had some factual basis. Many others have argued that question, pro and con.

establishment of protectorates in the Caribbean—in the Dominican Republic, Nicaragua and Haiti. Uncle Sam now assumed the role of international policeman—kindly to the law-abiding, but apt to lay a stern hand upon little nations that fell into disorder or defaulted on their obligations, since disorder or default, if allowed to continue, might invite intervention from outside the hemisphere. The first application of the new doctrine was in the Dominican Republic. In fact, it was a threatening situation in the Dominican Republic that had led to Roosevelt's pronouncement.

The government of the Dominican Republic, or Santo Domingo, since that state won its independence from Haiti in 1844, had been a dictatorship generously tempered by revolution. Revolutions are costly, and by 1904 the Dominican debt had grown to a figure—some $32,000,000—which the national revenues, as administered by native collectors of taxes and customs, were incapable of servicing. The foreign debt was widely distributed. Portions of it were held in France, Belgium, Italy, and Germany. The largest single creditor, representing both American and British capital, was the San Domingo Improvement Company of New York. From time to time the Dominican government had pledged the customs duties at various ports as security for its debts, and the pledges sometimes conflicted. Intervention by the United States in behalf of the Improvement Company resulted, in 1903 and 1904, in that company's being placed in charge of the collection of customs at Puerto Plata and Monte Cristi on the north coast, bringing protests from the European creditors, who claimed that those same revenues had previously been pledged to them. An international scramble for control of the Dominican custom-houses threatened, with the possible development of a situation resembling that in Venezuela which had alarmed Roosevelt a scant two years earlier.

It was under these circumstances that

Roosevelt formulated his famous "Corol-lary," which was without doubt intended as a forecast of coming events. With the en-couragement of Thomas C. Dawson, United States minister to the Dominican Republic, President Morales invited the United States to take charge of the nation's custom-houses and administer the collec-tion of import duties for the purpose of satisfying the creditors of the Republic and providing its government with revenue. An executive agreement to this effect was signed on January 20, 1905, but this at-tempt of Roosevelt to bypass the Senate excited so much criticism that Minister Dawson was instructed to put the agree-ment into the form of a treaty, subject to ratification in the constitutional manner. The treaty was duly signed and its approval urged upon the Senate by President Roosevelt with reasoning based, like his Corollary message, upon the Monroe Doc-trine.

Democratic opposition prevented action upon the treaty, but the President, with characteristic determination, put the es-sence of the arrangment into effect by a new executive agreement, referred to as a *modus vivendi*, signed April 1, 1905. The Dominican government agreed to appoint as receiver of customs a citizen of the United States who should have been nomi-nated by the American President. As in the proposed treaty, 45 percent of the receipts were to be turned over to the Dominican government; the remainder, less costs of collection, was to be deposited in a New York bank, to be apportioned among the creditors of the republic if the Senate ap-proved the treaty, or returned to the Dominican government if the treaty was finally rejected.

The *modus vivendi* remained operative for over two years. During that period the creditors of the Dominican government agreed to a downward adjustment of the debt from over $30,000,000 to $17,000,-000. A new $20,000,000 bond issue was floated in the United States, and the pro-ceeds were applied to the paying off of the adjusted debt and to the execution of need-ful public works in the island. In February 1907, a new treaty was signed, which the Senate promptly approved through the switch of a few Democratic votes to its sup-port. The treaty, proclaimed July 25, 1907, perpetuated the arrangement under the *modus vivendi*, with minor modifications. A general receiver of Dominican customs, named by the President of the United States, was to have full control of the collec-tion of customs duties until the $20,000,000 bond issue should have been liquidated.

The Dominican receivership, under the *modus vivendi* and the subsequent treaty, produced gratifying results. For some four years after the conclusion of the treaty the Republic experienced the unaccustomed blessings of financial solvency and political stability. Then began a new series of rev-olutionary disturbances that led to a more drastic form of intervention by the United States.

"Dollar Diplomacy" in Nicaragua

The next Caribbean country to receive the "protection" of the United States was Nicaragua. Intervention in Nicaragua, in-itiated under William H. Taft as President (1909–1913) and Philander C. Knox as Sec-retary of State, was a prominent example of the "dollar diplomacy" usually associated with that administration. Dollar diplomacy had a dual character. On one side, it was the use of diplomacy to advance and protect American business abroad; on the other side, it was the use of dollars abroad to pro-mote the needs of American diplomacy. In the first sense it was practiced by many an administration before Taft and since. The employment of American dollars to ad-vance the political and strategic aims of di-plomacy was a less familiar technique.

There was a hint of it in the Platt Amendment. It was plainly seen in the refunding of the debt and the instituting of the receivership in the Dominican Republic under Theodore Roosevelt. Invoking, as Roosevelt had done, the Monroe Doctrine as their justification, Taft and Knox made a similar arrangement with Nicaragua and sought unsuccessfully to do the same with Honduras and Guatemala.

The setting up of the Nicaraguan customs receivership came at the conclusion of some years of turmoil in Central America, largely the work of the Nicaraguan dictator, José Santos Zelaya. Having lent support to the ousting of Zelaya, Taft and Knox were anxious to bring peace and order to Central America by applying there the same remedy that had been applied with some success for the Dominican Republic. They found a cooperative leader in Nicaragua in the person of Adolfo Días, who had eventually succeeded Zelaya as President. A businessman who despised militarism and craved order and good government, Días was willing to compromise his country's independence by granting to the United States broad powers of intervention. When he was faced with insurrection, the United States, at his request, landed over two thousand marines in Nicaragua, suppressed the rebellion, deported its leaders, and left at Managua, the capital, a "legation guard" of marines that for the next thirteen years (1912–1925) "stabilized" the Nicaraguan government under Días and his successors.

Secretary Knox's attempt, with the aid of Días, to set up a customs receivership in Nicaragua by treaty was blocked in the Senate, but a receivership was established nevertheless by agreement between Nicaragua, certain American banks, and the State Department. A mixed claims commission reduced claims against Nicaragua from $13,750,000 to a mere $1,750,000. Another mixed commission was given limited control over Nicaragua's spending policy. The policy of Taft and Knox was continued by their successors, President Woodrow Wilson and his first Secretary of State, William Jennings Bryan. To meet Nicaragua's urgent need for funds, and at the same time to provide for the future canal needs of the United States, a treaty signed August 5, 1914, and approved nearly two years later, the Bryan-Chamorro Treaty, provided for a payment of $3 million to Nicaragua in return for the grant of certain concessions to the United States. These included the perpetual and exclusive right to construct a canal through Nicaragua and the right for ninety-nine years to establish naval bases at either end of the route, in the Corn Islands in the Caribbean and on the Gulf of Fonseca on the Pacific.

Two of Nicaragua's neighbors, Costa Rica and El Salvador, contested Nicaragua's right to grant these concessions, which they claimed infringed on their sovereignty. The governments submitted their case to the Central American Court of Justice, where they won a verdict against Nicaragua. Neither Nicaragua nor the United States accepted the decision. The Court, created in 1907 with the blessing of the United States, went out of business in 1918 as a consequence of this defiance of its authority.

Thus by 1916 the United States had secured from Nicaragua at trifling cost a perpetual monopoly of the canal route through that country and the privilege of setting up naval bases, if they should be needed, at each end of the route. It had also succeeded, not by treaty but by informal agreement with Nicaragua and the bankers, in reducing and simplifying the Nicaraguan debt and in setting up a customs receivership which would see to it that a suitable portion of the national revenue was applied on the debt. Application of the Roosevelt Corollary, implemented by dollar diplomacy and the landing of a few marines, had made Nicaragua secure against any violation of the Monroe Doctrine.

Wilsonian Intervention

That the treaty which consummated the success of dollar diplomacy in Nicaragua bore the name of William Jennings Bryan was ironic, for Bryan, out of office, had been a severe critic of dollar diplomacy. Other inconsistencies were to follow. The anti-imperialist Wilson administration (1913–1921), with first Bryan and later Robert Lansing as Secretary of State, although promoting independence for the Philippines and self-government for Puerto Rico, was to impose upon Haiti a protectorate treaty of unprecedented severity, and to set up a regime of pure force in the Dominican Republic.

There is perhaps less of contradiction than at first appears between the new administration's policy in the Philippines and Puerto Rico and its policy toward the independent republics of the Caribbean. The Philippines and Puerto Rico, under American tutelage, had been learning the lessons of democracy and conducting orderly elections in which ballots, not bullets, determined the outcome. Perhaps a few years of American tutelage would suffice to complete the political education of the natives of Haiti and the Dominican Republic, who hitherto had found the bullet a more congenial instrument than the ballot. At the very beginning of his administration, Wilson made it clear that he would frown upon revolutions in the neighboring republics. "I am going to teach the South American republics to elect good men!" he remarked with optimism to a British visitor.

Such remarks foreshadowed a new turn in American interventionist policy, in which the promotion of democracy would take its place as an objective beside the preservation of the Monroe Doctrine and the protection of the economic and strategic interests of the United States. Unfortunately, although the new measures were effective in restoring order and preventing revolutions by force, they did little or nothing toward providing a substitute for revolutions in the form of free and fair elections. Whether because of the absorption of effort in World War I or for other reasons, the Washington schoolmaster quite neglected to "teach the . . . republics to elect good men," or to elect any men at all by democratic methods.

Haiti—the Fifth Protectorate

The Negro republic of Haiti, unlike the Dominican Republic, had maintained its independence continuously since the time of Toussaint L'Ouverture. It had also been more successful than its neighbors in meeting the interest payments on its rather large foreign debt; but in the prevalence of corrupt tyranny complicated by frequent revolution, it surpassed its rival on the island. In the early twentieth century, corruption grew more flagrant and revolution more frequent, and bankruptcy, default, and the menace of European intervention loomed on the horizon.

Under these circumstances the United States began urging upon Haitian Presidents measures designed to bring some order out of the chaos into which the country had fallen and to guard against European intervention. Mr. Bryan asked for the United States the right to appoint a customs receiver, as in Santo Domingo, and a financial adviser. He asked the right to supervise Haitian elections, and he asked a nonalienation pledge as to Môle St. Nicolas, a potential naval base at the northwest corner of the island. Negotiations along these lines proceeded, but so kaleidoscopic were the changes in Haitian administrations that no results had been achieved by July 1915, when President Guillaume Sam, following the coldblooded massacre of 170 political prisoners in the government jail, was pulled by an angry mob from his sanctuary in the French legation, thrown into the street, and there assassinated. On the same afternoon (July 28), the U.S.S. *Washington,* flagship of Rear Admiral Caperton, dropped anchor in Port au Prince harbor, and before nightfall the marines had occupied the town.

Exasperated at the long reign of anarchy in Haiti and at the failure of treaty negotiations, Washington was resolved to use the new crisis to enforce its demands upon the Haitian government. By taking control of the custom-houses and impounding the revenue, and by the threat of continued military government if its wishes were not obeyed, the United States was able to dictate the choice of a President as successor to Guillaume Sam and to prevail upon him and the National Assembly to accept a treaty embodying all the American demands.

The Treaty of 1915 with Haiti went further in establishing American control and supervision than the Platt Amendment treaty with Cuba or the Dominican treaty of 1907, or than both combined. It provided that the following officials should be appointed by the President of Haiti upon nomination by the President of the United States: a general receiver of customs, a financial adviser, an engineer, or engineers to supervise measures of sanitation and public works, and officers of the newly organized native constabulary. All Haitian governmental debts were to be classified, arranged, and serviced from funds collected by the general receiver; Haiti was not to increase its debt without the consent of the United States. Haiti agreed to do nothing to alienate any of its territory or impair its independence. Finally, as in the case of Cuba, the United States might take any necessary measures to preserve Haitian independence or to maintain "a government adequate for the protection of life, prop-

erty, and individual liberty." The treaty was to remain in force for ten years, but a clause permitting its extension for another ten-year period upon either party's showing sufficient cause was invoked by the United States in 1917, thus prolonging to 1936 the prospective life of the treaty.

Aside from the immediate restoration of order and the elimination of all excuse for European intervention, it was presumably hoped that the tying up of the revenues and the organization of an efficient constabulary would remove at once the chief motive for revolution and the chance of its succeeding. Unfortunately neither at this time nor in the new constitution, drafted with American aid in 1918, were any steps taken to complement these reforms with the introduction of democratic political processes. The result was a reasonably efficient dictatorship dominated by the United States treaty officials with the support of the Navy and Marine Corps.

The Navy Governs
the Dominican Republic

Interest in the Caribbean area now shifted eastward to the Dominican Republic. Here, until 1911, the customs receivership of 1905 and 1907 had worked admirably. Under the Presidency of Ramón Cáceres (1906–1911) stable government and orderly finance had been the rule; constitutional reforms had been adopted, and surplus revenues had been applied to port improvements, highway and railroad construction, and education. Such a novel employment of the powers and resources of government was displeasing to many Dominican politicans, and on November 19, 1911, Cáceres fell victim to an assassin's bullet. At once the Republic reverted to its seemingly normal condition of factional turmoil and civil war, and the necessities incident to the conducting and suppressing of revolutions resulted in the contraction of a large floating debt, contrary to the spirit, if not the letter, of the 1907 treaty with the United States.

Thus the Wilson administration found in the Dominican Republic a situation as difficult as that in Haiti. Under a plan drafted by Wilson himself and accepted by the Dominican leaders, the United States supervised the 1914 elections. From the new President, Jiménez, the United States now demanded a treaty providing for the appointment of a financial adviser with control over disbursements, for the extension of the authority of the general receiver to cover internal revenue as well as customs, and for the organization of a constabulary. These demands were rejected as violative of Dominican sovereignty, and in the spring of 1916 the situation went from bad to worse when the Dominican Secretary of War, Desiderio Arias, launched a new revolution and seized Santo Domingo, the capital. On May 15 United States Marines were landed in Santo Domingo, and their occupation was gradually extended to other ports and the interior of the island. Jiménez resigned the presidency. His successor, chosen by the legislature, also refused to accept the proposed treaty. President Wilson thereupon directed that the Dominican Republic be placed under military government.

Accordingly, on November 29, 1916, Captain H. S. Knapp, the naval officer commanding at the capital, proclaimed the establishment of a military government by the forces of the United States in Santo Domingo. Cabinet posts were taken over by Marine Corps officers, the legislature was suspended, and for the next six years the government of the Dominican Republic was administered by the United States Navy Department. The situation differed from that in Haiti in that the Haitian government by consenting to the protectorate treaty demanded by the United States, had pre-served some vestiges of its independence, whereas the Dominican government by refusing less drastic demands, had seen all its functions taken over by officers of a foreign power. Had Haiti similarly refused, there is little doubt that it likewise would have been subjected to alien military rule. In both republics, though in slightly different ways, the Wilson Administration had carried to its logical conclusion the "international police power" doctrine of Theodore Roosevelt.

Wilson and Mexico

The problems presented by the little states of the Caribbean were solved, after a fashion, by bringing their governments under varying degrees of control by the United States. No such simple solution sufficed for the most serious crisis in Latin American affairs that confronted Wilson during his early years in the White House. In Mexico the dictator-President, Porfirio Díaz, who had governed the country since 1877, had been overthrown in 1911. Leader of the revolution against Díaz, and his successor for a brief period of sixteen months, was Francisco I. Madero, a man of good will, who attempted to give Mexico a democratic government and to reform the Mexican economy in the interest of small farmers and landless workers, both rural and urban. Powerful interests, foreign as well as Mexican, opposed his program. Madero lacked the political adroitness that might have brought lasting success. In February 1913, his foes engineered a revolt of elements in the army at Mexico City. General Victoriano Huerta, to whom the President had entrusted the defense of the government, betrayed him, ordered his arrest, and, after compelling him to resign, had him shot. The official excuse asserted that the shooting occurred during an attempt by

Madero's followers to rescue him, but the evidence pointed to a coldblooded assassination.

Huerta then arranged for his own elevation to the Mexican presidency. Foreign interests, including the American ambassador, Henry Lane Wilson, welcomed the accession of Huerta. They had had little patience with Madero's attempted reforms and looked upon Huerta as a strong man, another Díaz, who would keep the Mexican peon in his place and continue Díaz' considerate treatment of foreign capital.[11] Huerta's government, though facing armed opposition from former followers of Madero, was recognized by Great Britain, by other European powers, and by Japan.

President Taft, in the few days that remained of his administration, took no step toward recognition of the Huerta government. The omission was the result, not of any qualms about the means of Huerta's rise to power, but rather of the State Department's hope of securing settlement of certain disputes as the price of recognition. Wilson and Bryan viewed the question differently. Shocked by the assassination of Madero, Wilson looked upon the Huerta regime as "a government of butchers," unworthy of recognition.[12] On March 11, 1913, he announced in a press release that friendship and cooperation with the "sister republics" of Latin America would be possible

> only when supported at every turn by the orderly processes of just government based upon law, not upon arbitrary or irregular

force. . . . We can have no sympathy with those who seek to seize the power of government to advance their own personal interests or ambition.

Although called forth by rumors of revolutionary plots in Nicaragua, this statement was obviously applicable also to Mexico. It hinted at what was to become an established feature of Wilson's foreign policy vis-à-vis Latin America: a refusal to recognize governments that had attained power only by force and violence. Thus he deviated from the practice, followed quite consistently since Jefferson's day, of recognizing, regardless of origin, any government that was firmly seated and capable of performing its duties, internally and externally.

Refusing to be guided by the advice of Ambassador Henry Lane Wilson, the President sent his own investigators to Mexico to inform him of the character of Huerta's regime. Their unfavorable reports confirmed the conclusions he had reached through reading and reflection about Mexico. He had come, he said, to feel a "passion . . . for the submerged eighty-five percent of the people of that Republic who are now struggling toward liberty."[13] Huerta, he believed, besides owing his position to brute force, would not serve the interests of "the submerged eighty-five percent." He let it be known that he would recognize Huerta only if the latter would agree to hold a fair election in which he himself should not be a candidate. When Huerta not only refused these promises but also, on the eve of the election, arrested 110 opposition members of the Mexican Congress, Wilson made up his mind that the dictator must go.

In determining to oust Huerta from the

[11]For a competent account of the Madero regime and Huerta's *coup d'état* see C. C. Cumberland, *Mexican Revolution: Genesis under Madero* (Austin: University of Texas Press, 1952).

[12]A. S. Link, *Woodrow Wilson and the Progressive Era, 1910–1917* (New York: Harper & Row, Publishers, 1954), p. 109. Chapter 5 of this work gives an excellent analysis of Wilson's Mexican policy. See also H. F. Cline, *The United States and Mexico* (Cambridge: Harvard University Press, 1953), chaps. 7–9.

[13]R. S. Baker, *Woodrow Wilson, Life and Letters,* 8 vols. (Garden City, N.Y.: Doubleday & Company, Inc., 1927–1939), 4: 245.

U.S. POSSESSIONS AND PROTECTORATES IN THE CARIBBEAN

GULF OF MEXICO

ATLANTIC OCEAN

FLORIDA

Key West

BAHAMA ISLANDS

NASSAU

ISLE OF PINES

C U B A

Guantánamo

JAMAICA

HAITI

DOMINICAN REPUBLIC

PUERTO RICO

VIRGIN ISLANDS

LEEWARD ISLANDS

WINDWARD ISLANDS

C A R I B B E A N   S E A

MEXICO

BRITISH HONDURAS

GUATEMALA

HONDURAS

SALVADOR

FONSECA BAY

NICARAGUA

CORN IS.

COSTA RICA

PANAMA

Colón

Panamá

COLOMBIA

VENEZUELA

PACIFIC OCEAN

U.S. Possessions or equivalent.

U.S. Protectorates, c. 1917.

Mexican presidency, Wilson was clearly intervening in the domestic politics of Mexico. This act of intervention he justified on the ground that it was in the interest of the Mexican people and that, as he later told a group of Mexican editors:

> . . . our sincere desire was nothing else than to assist you to get rid of a man who was making the settlement of your affairs for the time being impossible.[14]

Not until July 1914 did Wilson's campaign against Huerta achieve its result in the latter's resignation and flight to Europe. In attaining his end Wilson had withheld recognition; had lifted a previously instituted arms embargo, thus enabling Huerta's opponents to secure arms in the United States; had persuaded the British government to remove from Mexico a minister, Sir Lionel Carden, antagonistic to American policy; and finally had occupied the city and port of Veracruz (April 21, 1914). The occupation of Veracruz, accomplished only after considerable fighting, was ostensibly designed to secure an apology for a minor indignity to the United States flag; in reality it was a means of ousting Huerta by depriving him of the revenues from an important port and cutting him off from European sources of arms and ammunition. It was, of course, an act of war; but Wilson insisted that he was not making war upon Mexico, only upon Huerta and his supporters.

When Huerta resigned, July 14, 1914, he left as his leading opponent and probable successor Venustiano Carranza, a former follower of Madero and governor of Coahuila, who had taken up arms against Huerta after Madero's death. Carranza and his forces, Constitutionalists as they called themselves, occupied Mexico City on August 20, 1914, but peace did not come to Mexico nor harmony to Mexican relations with the United States. Carranza's rule was

[14]Baker, *Woodrow Wilson*, 8: 195.

contested by Emiliano Zapata in the south and by Francisco Villa, a former Carranza lieutenant, in the north. Civil war continued, and with it loss of lives and property of foreigners. Carranza, though he had risen to power as a result of Wilson's policy, was so unreceptive to suggestions from Washington that Wilson and Bryan for a while looked with favor upon Villa, the illiterate ex-bandit, as a probable successor to Carranza. This idea had to be abandoned when Carranza's forces, led by General Álvaro Obregón, soundly defeated Villa and drove him back into northern Mexico. Lansing, now Secretary of State, sought aid from other American republics. In the previous year (1914), in its dispute with Huerta, the United States had accepted an offer of mediation from Argentina, Brazil, and Chile. Lansing now called into conference the representatives of these "ABC" powers, together with those of Uruguay, Bolivia, and Guatemala. The conference recommended recognition of Carranza as head of a *de facto* government of Mexico, and the United States took this step in October 1915.

Carranza's enemies continued their resistance. It became the object of Villa to embroil Carranza with the United States. To this end his guerrilla forces, in January 1916, held up a train carrying seventeen American mining engineers and shot all but one. On the following March 9, Villa's cavalry dashed across the international border and shot up the peaceful town of Columbus, New Mexico. A punitive expedition under Brigadier General John J. Pershing followed Villa into Mexico but failed to catch him. Although Carranza had given grudging consent to the pursuit of Villa, he resented the presence of United States troops in Mexico, and on June 21, 1916, in a clash with Mexican government forces at Carrizal, twelve United States soldiers were killed and twenty-three captured. Thereupon Wilson ordered the National Guard to the border, and the two nations were very close to war. The United States declined another Latin American offer of mediation but accepted a suggestion from Carranza (who wanted war no more than did Wilson) for the setting up of a joint commission to study the entire situation. The commission sat from September 1916 to January 1917. It found no solution acceptable to both governments, but the United States members finally advised withdrawal of troops from Mexico and the granting of full diplomatic recognition to the Carranza government.

In accordance with this advice, General Pershing and the last of his troops left Mexican soil on February 5, 1917, and on March 3, Mr. Henry P. Fletcher presented his credentials as ambassador of the United States. Within a few weeks thereafter the United States entered the war against Germany. Throughout the period of that conflict, relations with Mexico continued to be marked by bickering—now over border disturbances, now over threatened expropriations of American property under the new Mexican constitution—but there was no further danger that the United States might have to fight a war in its back yard as well as upon and across the Atlantic.

Woodrow Wilson's Mexican policy had been marred by errors, inconsistencies, and vacillations. These had resulted, in large part, from his own misjudging of the Mexican character and his lack of well qualified advisers. But when all is said, his policy had had three merits that outweighed its faults. First, he had avoided war with Mexico when to drift into war would have been easy and even popular. Second, he had shown a willingness to consult the other American republics in shaping his course toward Mexico. Third, he had contributed to the success of a regime committed to the social progress of the Mexican people rather than to the exploitation of Mexican riches by foreign capital.[15]

[15]The revolution of Madero and Carranza was strongly anticlerical, that is, opposed to the power of

A Policy of Contradictions

Viewed as a whole, Woodrow Wilson's policy toward Latin America presented curious contradictions, which are confusing to the historian and must have been still more confusing to Wilson's Latin American contemporaries. Wilson was aware, when he took office, of a growing air of suspicion toward the United States on the part of its southern neighbors. Theodore Roosevelt's support of revolution in Panama; the Roosevelt Corollary; the interventions in Cuba, the Dominican Republic, and Nicaragua; the frank invoking of dollar diplomacy by Taft and Knox—all had contributed to distrust of "Yankee imperialism." Apprehensive of further interventions by the United States or "imperalist" powers of Europe, the Latin Americans had evolved formulas for the protection of borrowing countries against the exactions of their creditors. The "Calvo Doctrine," first announced by an Argentine jurist of the last century, attempted to bind the foreigner who invested in an American country not to go beyond the courts of the latter in seeking protection for his investment; to bind him, in other words, not to seek the intervention of his home government in support of his interests. Another Argentinian, Foreign Minister Luis M. Drago, later set forth the doctrine that bears his name. Suggested by the Anglo-German blockade of Venezuela in 1902–1903, it declared inadmissible armed intervention to enforce payment of the public debt of an American nation. A convention adopted at the Second Hague Conference in 1907 accepted the Drago Doctrine with the qualification that intervention was

the Roman Catholic Church in Mexico; it was sometimes marked by acts of violence against church property, priests, and nuns. By giving aid and comfort to such a regime Wilson incurred the enmity of much of the Catholic hierarchy in the United States. Link, *Wilson and the Progressive Era*, p. 135.

permissible if the debtor government refused arbitration or, having accepted arbitration, refused to carry out the award. This qualified acceptance of the principle failed to satisfy the Latin Americans. No South American country ratified the convention; distrust and suspicion lived on.

It was Wilson's desire to reassure the Latin Americans by convincing them that the United States had no aggressive purposes. In his public statement of March 11, 1913 (quoted above in connection with Mexico), he declared:

> One of the chief objects of my administration will be to cultivate the friendship and deserve the confidence of our sister republics of Central and South America. . . .

Later in the year, addressing a Southern Commercial Congress at Mobile (October 27, 1913), he denounced the "hard bargains" that had been driven with the Latin American states by foreign moneylenders and added: "I rejoice in nothing so much as in the prospect that they will now be emancipated from these conditions, and we ought to be the first to take part in assisting that emancipation." Later in the same address he declared: "I want to take this occasion to say that the United States will never again seek one additional foot of territory by conquest."

Such words as these must have sounded hopeful to Latin American ears; yet before many months had passed, the Wilson administration twice sent armed forces into Mexico; acquired from Nicaragua exclusive rights to the canal route and to naval base sites on both coasts; flouted a decision of the Central American Court of Justice; landed marines in Haiti and forced both a treaty and a constitution upon that ill-governed little state; and handed to the Navy the task of governing the Dominican Republic. These actions, though almost certainly intended in the interest of the people concerned, were hard to reconcile with the anti-imperialist professions of both

Wilson and his first Secretary of State, William Jennings Bryan.[16]

But against these interventionist actions, again, must be weighed other acts indicative of a very different attitude. Wilson sponsored the negotiation of a treaty (not then ratified) with Colombia, bestowing an apology and substantial compensation for the loss of Panama. Far from adopting a go-it-alone policy toward Mexico, he called other American republics into consultation and was largely guided by their advice. And he refrained, though sorely tempted, from making actual war upon Mexico. Finally, he proposed for adoption, first by the United States and the "ABC" powers, eventually by all the American republics, a Pan American treaty mutually guaranteeing the territorial integrity and political independence under republican forms of government of all the signatories. A precursor of the famous Article X of the League of Nations Covenant, the proposed guarantee was also an anticipation of the "continentalizing" of the Monroe Doctrine, later accomplished by Franklin D. Roosevelt.

The United States and the Far East, 1898–1914

On the eve of the Spanish-American War, it will be recalled, Germany, Russia, France, and Great Britain had seized harbors suita-

[16]Bryan, a severe critic of Taft's dollar diplomacy, would, had Wilson permitted, have carried dollar diplomacy a step further than Taft had done. Once Secretary of State, he became as sensitive as his predecessors to any threat to the security of the Canal Zone. To keep dangerous rivals at a distance, he proposed a new corollary to the Monroe Doctrine by which the United States government should itself become banker to the republics of the Caribbean, supplying on easy terms the funds needed to liquidate their European debts and to promote essential economic development and social services. Wilson never accepted this proposal. Selig Adler, "Bryan and Wilsonian Caribbean Penetration," *Hispanic American Historical Review*, 20 (1940), 198–226; P. E. Coletta, "Bryan, Anti-Imperialism, and Missionary Diplomacy," *Nebraska History*, 44 (September 1963), 167–87.

ble for naval bases on the coast of China and had exacted from the Chinese government long-time leases of these harbors and grants of economic concessions in the neighboring areas, which thereby became "spheres of interest" of the powers named. The United States had a small but at this time a rapidly growing trade with China. It was looking to China as a market for the surplus products of its industry, which European statesmen were threatening to exclude from their own shores. Since signing its first treaty with China in 1844, the United States had been assured of most-favored-nation treatment, or the "open door," in its trade with that country. That open door now appeared to be threatened by the creation of spheres of interest in the hands of governments which might be expected to discriminate in favor of the trade and other interests of their own nationals. It was largely the belief that a foothold in the Philippines would enable the United States better to defend its interests in China that had led to the decision to keep the islands.

John Hay
and the Open Door in China

Of all the powers concerned, Great Britain had interests most akin to those of the United States. An invitation from Great Britain to join with her in defending the open door in China was rejected by Secretary of State John Sherman in March 1898. But Sherman soon gave place to Willian R. Day and he in turn (August 1898) to John Hay, who came home from the London embassy to take the job. Admittedly an Anglophile, Hay would have welcomed close cooperation with Great Britain in the Far East. But public and senatorial opinion would have rejected anything like an alliance, and the most that Hay could do was to invite the powers chiefly concerned with China to agree to respect the open door

principle, hoping, as Monroe and Adams had hoped in 1823, that Great Britain would back the American position.

A suitable occasion for such a proposal was offered by the Russian government in an imperial ukase in mid-August 1899, giving assurance that Russia would not interfere with or control the collection of Chinese customs in her sphere of interest, or place any restrictions on "foreign commerce and trade" in that sphere. Sensing in the unexpected Russian move an excellent opportunity to get general assent to preservation of the open door principle, Hay instructed his chief adviser on Far Eastern matters, W. W. Rockhill, to prepare a memorandum for presentation to the governments concerned. Rockhill and an English friend, Alfred E. Hippisley (an employee, on leave, of the Inspectorate of Maritime Customs in China), had, as a matter of fact, been urging such a course upon the Secretary for weeks, and their memorandum was virtually ready.[17] In the form of similar diplomatic notes, it was presented to the governments of Great Britain, Germany, Russia, France, Italy, and Japan.[18] The note of September 6, 1899, to the United States ambassador in Berlin stated that

. . . the Government of the United States would be pleased to see His German Majesty's Government give formal assurances, and

[17]T. J. McCormick, *China Market: America's Quest for Informal Empire, 1893–1901* (Chicago: Quadrangle Books, 1967), pp. 128, 141–45. McCormick downgrades the importance of Hippisley and Rockhill as progenitors of the Open Door notes, as claimed, for example, in G. F. Kennan, *American Diplomacy, 1900–1950* (Chicago: University of Chicago Press, 1951). Hay, in McCormick's view, needed no prodding and was merely waiting for a sign that his policy might be well received by other governments. The Russian ukase was precisely such a sign.

[18]The notes to Great Britain, Germany, and Russia were dated September 6, 1899; the others were not sent till November. They were addressed to the United States ambassadors or ministers in the respective countries.

lend its cooperation in securing like assurances from the other interested powers, that each, within its respective sphere of whatever influence—

First. Will in no way interfere with any treaty port or any vested interest within any so-called "sphere of interest" or leased territory it may have in China.

Second. That the Chinese treaty tariff of the time being shall apply to all merchandise landed or shipped to all such ports as are within said "sphere of interest" (unless they be "free ports"), no matter to what nationality it may belong, and that duties so leviable shall be collected by the Chinese Government.

Third. That it will levy no higher harbor dues on vessels of another nationality frequenting any port in such "sphere" than shall be levied on vessels of its own nationality, and no higher railroad charges over lines built, controlled, or operated within its "sphere" on merchandise belonging to citizens or subjects of other nationalities transported through such "sphere" than shall be levied on similar merchandise belonging to its own nationals transported over equal distances.

The notes, it will be observed, did not propose the abrogation of spheres of interest; these, Hay and his advisers assumed, would have to be recognized as facts. What they asked was assurance that within those spheres the regular Chinese tariff should continue to be collected and that the trade of all nations should be treated without discrimination as to tariffs, railroad rates, and harbor dues. They asked an opportunity for American trade to expand in China without the American government's being burdened with colonial responsibilities or the obligations of protectorates. "In short, a most interesting hybrid of anti-colonialism and economic imperialism."[19]

Five of the six governments addressed replied that they were willing, in their spheres of interest, to abide by the principles set forth by Secretary Hay if all the other governments concerned would agree

to do the same. The Russian reply was less forthright. It dealt specifically only with the question of tariffs and was equivocal even on that point; it contained a declaration that "the Imperial Government has no intention whatever of claiming any privilege for its own subjects to the exclusion of other foreigners," but in a context which suggested that the promise applied to Chinese territory outside, not inside, the Russian sphere of interest. The Russian Foreign Office, nevertheless, authorized Hay to treat the reply as favorable, and on March 20, 1900, he notified the six governments that the United States regarded acceptance by all as creating a binding agreement. Thus, as Hay's biographer writes, "What began as straightforward diplomacy . . . ended in diplomatic prestidigitation."[20]

John Hay
and the Boxer Rebellion

John Hay had asked only that the powers observe the principles of the open door with respect to foreign trade within their spheres of interest; he had not proposed that they surrender those spheres or agree not to enlarge them. While the diplomats were still debating the significance of the notes and the replies to them, events occurred in China that threatened to provide an excuse for a further partitioning of the empire among the western powers—perhaps even for a final extinction of its independence.

Chinese leaders at the turn of the century were of two minds. A reform party, headed by the well-meaning but weak Emperor, Kuang Hsü, wished to westernize and modernize China in emulation of Japan. A reactionary party, which secured the support of the Dowager Empress, Tzu Hsi

---

[19]McCormick, *China Market*, p. 128.

[20]Tyler Dennett, *John Hay, from Poetry to Politics* (New York: Dodd, Mead & Co., 1933), p. 293.

("Old Buddha" as foreigners called her), advocated the expulsion of the "foreign devils" and the destruction of their influence. The spearhead of the reactionaries was the secret society known to the West as "Boxers," from the emblem of a clenched fist. When the Emperor attempted to institute a reform program, "Old Buddha" came out of retirement and seized the reins of government. With her secret connivance, the Boxers began a campaign of violence, at first directed against foreign missionaries and their Chinese converts in Shantung province, but soon broadened to include the elimination from China of all foreign influence. From Shantung the Boxer hordes advanced against the imperial capital of Peking, took possession of the city, murdered the German minister in the streets, and laid siege to the legation quarter, where foreign diplomats and other foreign residents set up precarious defenses. For weeks in the summer of 1900 the foreigners in Peking were cut off from all communication with the outside world, where it was feared that all might have perished.

The Boxers had persuaded themselves and many others, including the Empress, that they had magic powers which made them invulnerable. Otherwise they could hardly have counted upon a successful defiance of the western nations. The long-run danger was not that western influence in China would be destroyed, but rather that the western powers would seize upon the Boxer outrages as an excuse for partitioning China among them. If China's independence and territorial integrity were thus violated, few would predict a long life for the open door principle. It became the policy of the United States, as voiced by John Hay, to liquidate the Boxer outbreak in a manner that would not involve further seizures of territory by foreign governments.

While, therefore, preparations were being made for the dispatch of an international army for the relief of the legations in Peking, Hay insisted that the powers were not at war with China but only with a rebellious faction within the empire. He kept in contact with friendly groups in China and through them succeeded in reopening communications with the American minister in Peking, thus obtaining the welcome news that the legations were still holding out. Most celebrated, if not most important, of Hay's measures was his circular note to the powers of July 3, 1900, setting forth the aims of American policy. The purpose of the President, he said, was to act concurrently with the other powers in rescuing those in danger in Peking, protecting American lives, property, and legitimate interests wherever they might be imperiled, and preventing the spread of disorders to other provinces of China. In regard to the means for obtaining these results, Hay continued,

> the policy of the Government of the United States is to seek a solution which may bring about permanent safety and peace to China, preserve Chinese territorial and administrative entity, protect all rights guaranteed to friendly·powers by treaty and international law, and safeguard for the world the principle of equal and impartial trade with all parts of the Chinese Empire.

Thus Hay recognized the relationship between the preservation of China's territorial integrity (this term, rather than "entity," came to be generally used) and the maintenance of the open door in China.[21] It was, he said, the policy of the United States "to seek a solution" that would preserve both.

[21]Rockhill's correspondence with Hippisley prior to the issuance of the open door notes of 1899 shows that Rockhill even then wished to speak out for the preservation of China's territorial and administrative integrity. Indirectly he did so in the proposal in those notes that the tariff duties levied at ports in the spheres of interest "shall be collected by the Chinese Government." P. A. Varg, *Open Door Diplomat: The Life of W. W. Rockhill,* Illinois Studies in the Social Sciences, Vol. 33, No. 4 (Urbana: The University of Illinois Press, 1952), pp. 31–32.

Orally or in writing, the governments of France, Great Britain, Germany, Russia, and Italy expressed concurrence with Hay's statement, and on October 29, 1900, Hay could state that the United States had had "the gratification of learning that all the powers held similar views."[22]

A month after the dispatch of the circular note of July 3, an international army of 19,000 men, chiefly Japanese and Russian but including 2,500 American troops from the Philippines, set out from the coast for Peking. The Empress fled from the city disguised as a peasant woman. Resistance collapsed and on August 14 the expeditionary force entered the Chinese capital, bringing succor to the besieged foreigners, among them a future President of the United States, Herbert Hoover. Gradually order was restored, the anti-foreign movement disintegrated, and the Chinese government agreed to the payment of an indemnity for foreign lives lost and property destroyed. Whether or not as a result of Hay's statement of American policy, the governments concerned did not ask additional cessions or leases of territory, and the United States exerted its influence to reduce the amount of money indemnity demanded. A figure of $333,000,000 was finally fixed upon, of which slightly less than $25,000,000 was assigned to the United States. When it was discovered that all American losses could be covered by little more than half of this sum, the United States voluntarily agreed to remit the balance. China thereupon put the remitted portion into a fund for the education of young Chinese in American universities.[23]

[22]*Foreign Relations of the United States, 1900* (Washington, D.C.: Government Printing Office, 1902), pp. 304, 316, 317, 324, 328, 344, 345, 359.

[23]As a consequence of this first remission and a later one in 1924, the United States retained only some $6,000,000 of the Boxer indemnity. Tsing Hua College, designed to prepare Chinese students for American universities, was instituted and supported largely from Boxer indemnity funds. W. W. Willoughby, *Foreign Rights and Interests in China,* 2 vols. (Baltimore: The Johns Hopkins Press, 1927), 2: 986–87, 1012–17.

In addition to the payment of an indemnity, the Chinese government agreed to punish those persons chiefly responsible for the attacks on foreigners and to permit the foreign powers to police the railroad line connecting Peking with the coast near Tientsin, a right that they continued to enjoy until World War II.

While befriending China with respect to the amount of indemnities to be paid, the United States never lost sight of its main objective, the China market. In tariff negotiations that accompanied those on indemnities, the United States was in accord with the European powers in withholding tariff autonomy from China, and the rates were so adjusted as to discourage China from developing "a more balanced, advanced, and sophisticated economy." China must still look to the West for all but the simplest products of the machine age.[24]

What Did Hay Accomplish?

John Hay's Chinese policy—his espousal of the open door and of China's territorial integrity—was hailed in his own day and for many years thereafter as a great achievement in American diplomacy. Later his policy was subjected to criticism, not only as ineffectual, but even as detrimental to the true interests of the United States—as embroiling that nation needlessly in the international strife of a distant continent.

The last criticism seems devoid of substantial foundation. Hay was under steady pressure from American business concerns to protect their current and future interests in China.[25] Certainly the United States had a legitimate interest in keeping the Chinese market open to American trade without adverse discrimination, even though contemporary notions of that market's impor-

[24]McCormick, *China Market,* p. 179.

[25]C. S. Campbell, Jr., *Special Business Interests and the Open Door Policy* (New Haven: Yale University Press, 1951).

tance were exaggerated. And certainly the preservation of China's independence and territorial integrity would be essential to keeping the market open. These objectives, though perhaps not worth fighting for, were nevertheless legitimate and proper objects of diplomacy.

There seems no good reason, therefore, to doubt that Hay's efforts were in the national interest. But we may well question whether they were successful and whether the United States consistently practiced the policy that it asked others to follow. If the United States really believed in an open door policy in the Orient, it could have set an example in its newly acquired possession, the Philippines. It did not do so. At the earliest moment permitted by the terms of the treaty of peace with Spain it established there a preferential system favoring the United States at the expense of other powers.[26]

But, consistency aside, was Hay's policy successful? Could diplomatic notes and ambiguous promises alone preserve China's territory intact and prop open the door? Could incantations subdue greedy imperialism? Such was not the belief of England and Japan, the two powers whose wishes were then most nearly in accord with those of the United States. Japan, anticipating correctly that Russia would seek to strengthen her economic and political hold on Manchuria, inquired what attitude the United States would take if Russia should violate her promises. Hay replied that the United States was not prepared to back up its policy with force, either alone or in concert with other powers. Whatever Hay's personal desires, he had to recognize that neither would the Senate accept a treaty of alliance, nor would public opinion support a war, in defense of the nation's Far Eastern policies. Consequently, when first Russia and later Japan strengthened their hold on Manchuria and violated the spirit of the open door, the United States could do no more than write ineffectual diplomatic protests. That there was no immediate extension of the boundaries of the spheres of interest in China is to be attributed to the balance of power among the governments interested rather than to the notes of the brilliant Secretary of State.

This is not to say that Hay's notes were without effect. They may perhaps have aided in restraining some imperialistic ambitions; they may have made Russia and Japan more cautious and moderate than they would otherwise have been in squeezing foreign trade out of their Manchurian spheres of interest. But that John Hay had struck "a tremendous blow . . . for the triumph of American principles in international society," is, as George F. Kennan has said, largely a "myth."[27] Later attempts to establish the Hay policies by international consent won a number of verbal triumphs, as will subsequently appear, and put some temporary restraints upon Japan; but the sequel was to show that Japan could not be restrained by words.

The Russo-Japanese War

While the United States relied upon words alone, England and Japan looked about for more substantial means of defending their interests in Asia. The British government

---

[26]Hay was not responsible for American economic policy in the Philippines, but in another matter he laid himself open to a charge of inconsistency, though the facts came to light only many years later. In December 1900, at the instance of American military and naval officers, he prepared to request from China permission to establish a naval base in Samsah Bay on the Chinese coast opposite Formosa. He took the precaution, however, of sounding Tokyo first. Japan, which had a nonalienation agreement with China for Fukien province, where Samsah Bay is located, discouraged the project, and Hay dropped it. The correspondence in regard to Samsah Bay was published in *Foreign Relations, 1915* (1924), pp. 113–15, note.

[27]Kennan, *American Diplomacy*, p. 37.

turned first to Germany and in October 1900 concluded an agreement by which both powers promised to respect the integrity of China and the open door, unless aggressions by a third power should compel them to reconsider their decision. This document was so phrased, however, as not to apply to Manchuria, where Germany desired to see Russia have a free hand. But since Russia was England's chief rival in Persia and Afghanistan and Japan's chief rival in the Far East, it was only natural that Great Britain and Japan should draw together in an alliance designed to check Russia. This they did in 1902. By the Anglo-Japanese alliance of that year the two governments, although declaring their devotion to the maintenance of the territorial integrity of both China and Korea, and the open door in both, recognized each other's special interests in China, while Great Britain also recognized the special interests, "politically as well as commercially and industrially," of Japan in Korea. In order to protect those interests in China and Korea from encroachment by a third power, each of the allies promised to remain neutral if the other became involved in war with a third power and to come to the support of the other should it be attacked by two or more enemies.[28]

Within two years the chief purpose of the treaty was revealed—the protection of Japan from attack by other powers while she expelled Russia from the latter's holdings in southern Manchuria. Since the Sino-Japanese war of 1894–1895, the clash of Russian and Japanese interests had been acute. Russia had posed as a friend of China, had taken the lead in forcing Japan to restore the Liaotung peninsula to China, and had been compensated by permission to extend the Trans-Siberian Railway across northern Manchuria to Vladivostok.

With this portion of the line, known as the Chinese Eastern Railway, Russia acquired also extensive economic and policing rights. In 1898, as was noted earlier, Russia exacted from China a twenty-five-year lease of the same Liaotung peninsula which Japan had been required to disgorge. With the lease went also the right to build and police a railroad line (the South Manchuria Railway) from Harbin on the Chinese Eastern south to Port Arthur at the tip of the Liaotung peninsula. Economic and policing rights also accompanied the new concession; and at Port Arthur Russia proceeded to build a great naval base. The Boxer outbreak gave the Czar's government an excuse for moving large numbers of troops into Manchuria. Under pressure from other powers, Russia agreed in 1902 to withdraw these troops but neglected to do so. Russia was obviously transforming Manchuria from a part of the Chinese empire into a Russian colony.

More alarming to Japan than Russia's encroachments in Manchuria were those in Korea, the nominally independent kingdom which since 1895 had come under strong Japanese influence. Korea was, in the words of an old saying, "a dagger pointed at the heart of Japan." Japan could not in safety permit Russia to grasp the hilt of the dagger, nor could she afford to see Korea's economic resources pass into any hands but her own.

In 1903 Japan and Russia opened negotiations in an effort to settle both the Manchurian and Korean questions. Japan demanded in effect a free hand in Korea, although conceding Russia's superior economic interests in Manchuria. Russia demanded a free hand in Manchuria; in return she would recognize Japan's special interests in southern Korea but proposed that Korea north of the 39th parallel be treated as a neutral zone. Neither party would meet the demands of the other. In February 1904 Japan broke off the negotiations and without awaiting a formal decla-

---

[28]The Anglo-Japanese alliance was renewed in stronger terms in 1905 and again renewed for a ten-year period in 1911.

ration of war made a surprise attack on the Russian fleet, which imprudently lay at anchor outside the defenses of Port Arthur.

The Russo-Japanese war, thus begun, lasted for a year and a half and ended in a complete victory for Japan. Russia's Far Eastern fleet, divided between Port Arthur and Vladivostok, was destroyed piecemeal. Her Baltic fleet, after a long voyage from European waters, was annihilated in a one-sided battle in Tsushima straits, May 27, 1905. Meanwhile Port Arthur had surrendered (January 2, 1905) after a long siege, and the main Russian army had been defeated in the battle of Mukden, February–March 1905.

Roosevelt the Peacemaker

The United States, though sympathetic to Japan, adopted a correctly neutral attitude. It assisted in securing from the belligerents an agreement to respect the neutrality of China, with the important exception of the Manchurian provinces, where the land war was fought. Informally, the United States aligned itself with Great Britain in support of Japan, against France, Russia's ally, and Germany, which encouraged Russian adventuring in the Far East. President Roosevelt admired the Japanese and had little but contempt for Russian officialdom. He assured Japan at the beginning that American neutrality would be "benevolent" toward her. He warned Germany and France, so he reported later, that he would intervene if necessary to protect Japan from being robbed of the fruits of a successful war, as she had been in 1895 after defeating China.[29]

If Roosevelt's preferences were partly sentimental, they were also based upon his conception of American interest as affected by the balance of power in the Far East. In 1904, Russia presented the chief threat to that balance and hence to the territorial integrity of China and the open door. Therefore Roosevelt backed Japan against Russia. As the war developed into a series of brilliant Japanese victories, he became apprehensive lest the power pendulum swing too far in Japan's direction. The prospect that, if war continued, Japan might take and hold all of Eastern Siberia he viewed with some alarm.[30] It was perhaps partly for this reason that he welcomed the opportunity to assist in making peace.

Japan, though everywhere victorious, had strained her resources to the limit and was anxious to bring the war to a close. She so intimated confidentially to Mr. Roosevelt in the spring of 1905, asking that he, "on his own initiative," propose a peace conference. This he did, and in August 1905 Russian and Japanese delegates met at Portsmouth, New Hampshire.

The principal obstacle to the conclusion of a peace treaty was Japan's demand for a large money indemnity, six hundred million dollars or more, to cover the cost of the war. This Russia resolutely refused, and over this issue the conference was close to breaking up in failure. At this point, however, President Roosevelt persuaded Japan to drop the indemnity from her list of demands, and a treaty was signed, September 5, 1905. The signing took place in an atmosphere of amity and good will strangely in contrast with the relations of opposing diplomats in some later international con-

---

[29]E. E. Morison, ed., *The Letters of Theodore Roosevelt*, 8 vols. (Cambridge: Harvard University Press, 1951–1954), 4: 1284.

[30]Morison, *Letters*, 4: 1315. The suggestion here that Roosevelt promoted peace in order to prevent an undue predominance of Japan in the Far East is contradicted by his alleged statement to a friend that from the standpoint of pure national interest he would have preferred to see the war continue until both belligerents were completely exhausted; that in taking on the role of peacemaker he bowed to American public opinion against his better judgment. See H. L. Stoddard, *It Costs to Be President* (New York: Harper & Row, Publishers, 1938), pp. 148–52.

troversies. The negotiators clasped hands across the conference table. Baron Rosen, of Russia, then rose, as he said, to "fulfill a most agreeable duty in acknowledging that in negotiating with our hitherto adversaries we have been dealing with true and thorough gentlemen to whom we are happy to express our high esteem and personal regard."[31]

By the treaty of Portsmouth, Russia recognized the paramount interest of Japan in Korea and ceded to her the southern half of the island of Sakhalin, all Russian rights in the Liaotung peninsula, and the South Manchuria Railway extending from Port Arthur and Dairen to Changchun. Both powers agreed to withdraw from Manchuria all troops other than railway guards and to restore Manchuria to Chinese civil administration.

In July 1905, before the delegates met at Portsmouth, Mr. William H. Taft, then Secretary of War in Roosevelt's cabinet, visited Tokyo. In a confidential meeting with the Japanese Premier, Count Katsura, Taft received assurances that Japan would respect United States sovereignty in the Philippines and in return promised American approval if Japan should find it necessary to assume control of the international relations of Korea. President Roosevelt gave his emphatic endorsement to the attitude thus expressed by his emissary. Accordingly, in the following November, when Japan announced that she was taking full charge of Korea's foreign relations, the United States gave immediate approval and promptly closed its legation in Korea. Nor did the United States protest when, five years later, Japan transformed her protectorate over Korea into complete sovereignty.

At the close of the Russo-Japanese war, then, the governments of Japan and the United States enjoyed relations of mutual friendliness and cordiality. The American people, too, had shown overwhelming sympathy for Japan—little David in a struggle with giant Goliath. But the terms of peace were bitterly disappointing to the Japanese public, who had been led to expect much more—a huge money indemnity and the cession of all of Sakhalin, perhaps even Vladivostok and Russia's maritime province. For what they considered the meagerness of the peace terms, the Japanese press and public blamed partly their own government, partly the United States and President Roosevelt. When the terms were announced, angry mobs rioted in Tokyo and other cities, attacking government buildings and the pro-government press, threatening foreigners, and burning Christian churches, most of them American. A regime of martial law put an end to the disorders, but the popular attitude boded ill for the future of Japanese-United States relations. Soon the governments, too, were engaged in controversy.

Japanese Immigration and the "Gentlemen's Agreement"

The United States soon had reason to doubt Japan's devotion to the open door principle, though she had warmly endorsed Secretary Hay's original proposal and had assured President Roosevelt that, if she were victorious in her war with Russia, she would maintain the open door in Manchuria. But once Japan was inside the door, her enthusiasm for keeping it open abated. As early as February 1906, the State Department had cause to complain of discrimination against American trade in Japan's Manchurian sphere of interest. Japan repeated her avowals of adherence to open door policy but continued in subtle ways to violate it. The United States, unwilling now as before to back up words with action,

---

[31]*New York Times,* September 6, 1905, p. 2. For his share in ending the war, President Roosevelt was awarded the Nobel Peace Prize.

could only continue to deliver ineffectual notes of protest.

More dangerous to Japanese-American relations than Japan's light regard for her open door pledges were the manifestations of anti-Japanese sentiment in the United States, particularly in California. The immigration of Japanese, unlike that of Chinese, was not prohibited by American law. Since 1900, it is true, the Japanese government had itself refused passports to Japanese laborers to come to continental United States. Indirectly, however, via Hawaii, Canada, or Mexico, Japanese did enter in considerable numbers, as many as a thousand per month in 1906, and most of them settled in Pacific coast states. Japanese immigrants seem to have been well behaved and to have been objectionable only on grounds of race prejudice and of their willingness to work for a lower wage than their Caucasian competitors.

The most troublesome manifestation of anti-Japanese feeling occurred in October 1906, when the San Francisco school board barred Japanese children—there were only 93 of them and they were generally model pupils—from the city's regular public schools, requiring that they attend instead an Oriental school established long before for Chinese and Korean children. This action fixed upon the Japanese a stigma of inferiority which their nation, having just handily defeated one of the "great powers" of white Europe, regarded as an insult. The Japanese ambassador[32] protested, and the Japanese press, which like the American had its sensational and jingo elements, engaged in warlike talk.

The management of San Francisco schools was a matter outside of federal jurisdiction, unless, which was doubtful, the case was covered by a most-favored-nation clause in the treaty of 1894. Rather

[32] In May 1906 the United States and Japanese legations in Tokyo and Washington respectively were raised to the rank of embassies.

than have the matter tested in the courts, President Roosevelt tried persuasion on the San Francisco officials. The mayor, the superintendent of schools, and the school board were invited to Washington. By pointing to the danger of war (which would fall most heavily upon the Pacific coast) and by promising action to check Japanese immigration, the President secured from the San Francisco authorities a promise to rescind their order for school segregation. He then concluded with the Japanese ambassador a "gentlemen's agreement": Japan would continue to refuse passports to laborers coming to mainland United States; it would make no objection if the United States barred Japanese from coming from intermediate points such as Hawaii, Canada, or Mexico. An executive order put the new immigration policy into effect.

The "gentlemen's agreement" continued in force till 1924, when it was superseded by prohibitive legislation. It worked well except for one loophole. The Japanese government reserved the right to give passports to subjects who had already resided in the United States or to wives and children of residents. This proviso was so interpreted as to permit the entry of "picture brides"—young women married in Japan to bridegrooms *in absentia* residing in the United States. Even this abuse (if such it was) was terminated before 1924.

A Naval Demonstration and a Seeming Diplomatic Victory

The "gentlemen's agreement" of 1907 did not end Japanese-American friction. Later in the year there were anti-Japanese riots in San Francisco, despite the fact that Japan had donated generously to victims of the earthquake and fire of April 1906. Rumors of impending war circulated in the American press and were rife in the capitals of Europe, where bettors placed odds on

Japan to win. Roosevelt was so far disturbed by these rumors that he expressed to Taft an inclination to give independence to the Philippines, which, in a possible conflict with Japan, would "form our heel of Achilles." In October 1907 he sent Taft again to Tokyo, whence the Secretary of War sent home a long cable reporting that Japan's intentions were altogether peaceful.

Roosevelt's handling of relations with Japan exemplified his dictum, "Speak softly, but carry a big stick." On the one hand, he treated all Japanese complaints with courtesy and consideration. On the other hand, he prepared an impressive demonstration of force—no less than sending the entire United States battleship fleet around the world. This, Roosevelt hoped, would convince the Japanese that the United States was no "push-over," like Russia. It would also be excellent advertising for the Navy and might aid Roosevelt in getting adequate naval appropriations from Congress.

The "Great White Fleet"—sixteen battleships attended by colliers and other auxiliary craft—visited Tokyo harbor by invitation of the Japanese government. There were those who, remembering Japan's surprise attacks on China and Russia, predicted that the American fleet would find a watery grave in the bay where Perry, fifty-four years earlier, had wrested a treaty from a reluctant Shogun.[33] The visit passed without untoward incident, however, and with impressive displays of courtesy on both sides. War talk died down, and a few weeks after the fleet had left Tokyo, Secretary of State Elihu Root and Kogoro Taka-

hira, the Japanese ambassador in Washington, by an exchange of notes, agreed to a set of principles in tune with United States policy.

By the Root-Takahira agreement (November 30, 1908) the governments of Japan and the United States declared themselves "firmly resolved reciprocally to respect the territorial possessions belonging to each other" in the Pacific area, and announced their determination

> to preserve the common interest of all powers in China by supporting by all pacific means at their disposal the independence and integrity of China and the principle of equal opportunity for commerce and industry of all nations in that Empire.

Since the text of the Root-Takahira agreement seemed entirely to favor the United States—even adding equality of treatment for industry to that previously asked for trade—historians have searched for some hidden price paid by the United States for these concessions. Some have found it in a clause of the agreement in which the two governments declared it to be their purpose to maintain "the existing status quo" in the region referred to, and have interpreted this language as a tacit recognition by the United States of Japan's special interests in Manchuria. There is no evidence of such an understanding in the records of the Root-Takahira conversations, and the circumstantial evidence is ambiguous. State Department records show that on the day the notes were signed, Root received from Tokyo a report of an official conversation in which Foreign Minister Komura had declared "that South Manchuria constituted Japan's outer line of defense and that Japan no longer considered the principle of China's integrity to include Manchuria." Whether Root had read this report before signing the note by which the United States promised to respect the status quo in the area is not known. If he had done so, his

[33] The Japanese main fleet, with fewer battleships than the American, but with large contingents of cruisers, destroyers, and submarines, all in battle trim, was engaged in maneuvers between Japan and the Philippines during the U.S. visit. In a confrontation the U.S. would have been at a great disadvantage. See R. A. Hart, *The Great White Fleet: Its Voyage Around the World, 1907–1909* (Boston: Little, Brown and Company, 1965).

acceptance of the status quo could be construed as acceptance of the status of South Manchuria as defined by Komura.[34] This interpretation is supported by Roosevelt's action two years later, when he warned his successor, President Taft, against giving the Japanese in Manchuria any reason to feel that the United States was "a menace—in however slight a degree—to their interests."

The Root-Takahira agreement contained no provision to protect the interests of Japanese residing in the United States. Within a week after it was signed, Roosevelt was expressing alarm at the possible effect in Japan of legislation proposed in California that would have excluded Japanese residents from the ownership of land. He was "thankful that our squadron left Japanese waters before California and other Western States began this idiotic procedure, . . ."[35] Roosevelt, working through the Republican governor of California, was able at that time to dissuade the California legislature from enacting discriminatory land laws. Four years later, President Wilson was less successful. Despite his best efforts and those of Mr. Bryan, his Secretary of State, California in 1913 passed legislation forbidding ownership of land to "aliens ineligible for citizenship," that is, Japanese. Despite a protest from the Japanese ambassador so vigorous that the Joint Army-Navy Board incurred Wilson's anger by urging him to put the Navy on guard, California refused to rescind or modify its alien land law, and other western states were soon enacting similar legislation.

"Dollar Diplomacy" in the Far East

In the four-year interval between Roosevelt and Wilson, President William H. Taft and

his Secretary of State, Philander C. Knox, were giving a new turn to the open door policy. John Hay's notes had asked for equal treatment in matters of trade only. Few Americans in 1899 were interested in putting money into the development of Chinese industry or the exploitation of China's natural resources. Taft and Knox became interested in securing entry into China for American capital, particularly in the field of railroad building.

Taft and Knox owed their inspiration chiefly to Willard Straight, formerly United States consul general at Mukden in Manchuria, and for some months in 1908–1909 acting chief of the newly formed Division of Far Eastern Affairs in the State Department. Straight, in turn, was in close touch with the American railroad king, E. H. Harriman, who dreamed of extending his railroad empire to Asia and in the fall of 1905 had received some encouragement from Japan in a plan to purchase the South Manchuria Railway. A Japanese change of heart, the financial panic of 1907, and Harriman's death in 1909 all contributed to the defeat of this particular scheme, but Straight did not abandon the general idea. Straight viewed the investment of American dollars in China, not primarily with the eyes of an investor seeking profits, but rather with those of a statesman pursuing high policy. He believed that only a substantial stake in the country would enable the United States to block Japan's plans for taking over southern Manchuria and perhaps additional slices of the tottering Chinese empire. It was his wish that dollars should be made to serve the ends of diplomacy.

But first diplomacy must open the door for dollars. Acting in this sense, President Taft, in July 1909, took the unusual course of addressing a letter to the Chinese Prince Regent, asking that American bankers be admitted with those of England, France, and Germany to a proposed banking pool to finance Chinese railroad construction. The request, though resisted by the other

[34] R. A. Esthus, *Theodore Roosevelt and Japan* (Seattle: University of Washington Press, 1966), chap. 16.

[35] L. F. Abbott, ed., *The Letters of Archie Butt* (Garden City, N.Y.: Doubleday & Company, Inc., 1924), pp. 220–21.

banking groups, was eventually granted. Still later, Russian and Japanese bankers were also included, thus forming the so-called Six-Power Consortium. Results in railway construction were not large.

Secretary Knox, in the meantime, proposed (November 1909) that American and European banking groups purchase and thus "neutralize" the railroads of Manchuria—the Chinese Eastern, owned by Russia, and the South Manchuria, owned by Japan. A novice in handling delicate international relations, Knox assumed that by thus taking ownership of the railroads out of the hands of Japan and Russia, China would be enabled to recover her complete sovereignty over Manchuria. He was apparently unaware that in 1907 Japan and Russia had formally recognized one another's spheres of interest in southern and northern Manchuria respectively and had secured approval of that arrangement from France and Great Britain and from China herself. Japan and Russia not only regarded themselves as in Manchuria to stay; they had also delimited their spheres of interest in Mongolia: Outer Mongolia for Russia, Inner Mongolia for Japan. No wonder that they received Knox's proposals with cool disapproval; nor did Knox get encouragement from England, which he tried to use as an intermediary. England, allied with Japan, had now settled her differences with Russia. She needed the friendship of both in her growing rivalry with Germany and could not afford to antagonize them by supporting Knox's plans for Manchuria. Thus Knox met complete defeat in his effort to rescue Manchuria from the imperialistic clutches of Russia and Japan.

An opportunity to use the resources of the Six-Power Consortium for a purpose other than railroad construction occurred after the Chinese revolution of 1911, which overthrew the Manchu Dynasty and resulted in the setting up of a republic with Yüan Skih-k'ai as President. In serious financial straits, the new government opened negotiations with the six-power banking group for a loan of $300,000,000 to be used for the reorganization of the administration. The proposed terms involved some control over expenditure and over collection of the salt tax, or gabelle, which was pledged as security.

Arrangements for the loan were pending in March 1913, when Taft surrendered the presidency to Woodrow Wilson. It seems evident that the bankers of the American group did not find loans to China attractive on their merits and were willing to participate only if the United States government desired that they do so for political ends. Five days after Wilson took office, representatives of the American banking group (one of whom was Willard Straight, who had left government service some time previously) had an interview with Secretary of State Bryan. They informed Mr. Bryan that the American bankers would seek their share of the proposed loan only if the new administration should so request.

After discussion in two cabinet meetings, but without consulting the experts in the State Department or the other governments concerned, Wilson issued a statement to the press. The administration, he said, would not request the American bankers to participate in the loan,

> because it did not approve the conditions of the loan or the implications of responsibility on its own part which it was plainly told would be involved in the request.
>
> The conditions of the loan seem to us to touch very nearly the administrative independence of China itself, and this Administration does not feel that it ought . . . to be a party to those conditions. The responsibility on its part which would be implied . . . might conceivably go the length in some unhappy contingency of forcible interference in the financial, and even the political, affairs of that great Oriental State, just now awakening to a consciousness of its power and of its obligations to its people. . . .

Thus Wilson frowned upon this form of

dollar diplomacy and in so doing put an end to the participation of American bankers in the Consortium. Several years later, when he saw that Japan was enjoying a practical monopoly on loans to China and was thus strengthening its influence there, Wilson reversed his position and encouraged American bankers to take part in a new consortium. But before this new turn in American policy, the war in Europe had greatly altered the picture, diverting the attention of the West to problems nearer home and giving Japan a rare opportunity to rivet chains on China. How the United States met Japan's new aggressive moves will be told in a later chapter.

ADDITIONAL READINGS

COHEN, WARREN I., *America's Response to China: An Interpretative History of Sino-American Relations.* New York: John Wiley & Sons, Inc., 1971.

HEALY, DAVID F., *The United States in Cuba, 1898–1902.* Madison, Wis.: University of Wisconsin Press, 1963.

HUNT, MICHAEL H., *Frontier Defense and the Open Door: Manchuria in Chinese-American Relations, 1895–1911.* New Haven, Conn.: Yale University Press, 1973.

SCHMIDT, HANS, *The United States Occupation of Haiti, 1915–1934.* New Brunswick, N.J.: Rutgers University Press, 1971.

SCHOLES, W. and M., *The Foreign Policies of the Taft Administration.* Columbia, Mo.: University of Missouri Press, 1970.

WELLS, S. F., R. H. FERRELL, and D. F. TRASK, *The Ordeal of World Power: American Diplomacy since 1900.* Boston: Little Brown, 1975.

13. The Road to World War I

In the period from 1899 to 1914, between the Spanish-American War and the First World War, while the United States consolidated its hold on the Caribbean and played a prominent rôle in the politics of the Far East, it was also taking an increasing part in the affairs of Europe. In particular it was lending its support to efforts for the peaceful settlement of international disputes.

These fifteen years were the heyday of the peace movement. The peace societies became affluent and respectable; the Permanent Court of Arbitration was established at The Hague; arbitration and conciliation treaties were concluded in dozen lots; and the United States continued its tradition of settling amicably its controversies with other states. Some people who lived through those calm and peaceful years can recall arguing in all seriousness that the day of wars, at least of major wars, was past. It seemed clear that, given the costly and destructive potentialities of modern warfare, even the victors in such a struggle would lose more than they could possibly gain. Man, it was assumed, was a rational animal and could see the folly of squandering his resources in a game of self-destruction.

Prosperity of the Peace Societies

The peace societies had hitherto drawn their membership mainly from the clergy and from idealists who had little standing in the worlds of business and politics. After the turn of the century there was a noticeable increase in the number of prominent and "practical" men who took part in their affairs. The American Peace Society, before 1914, counted among its members the President and the Secretary of State of the United States—Woodrow Wilson and William Jennings Bryan. In 1906 the New York Peace Society chose as its president Andrew Carnegie, the steel king, who had already donated a magnificent "Peace Palace" at The Hague. At a New York Peace Congress, sponsored in 1907 by the society and its president, the participants included "ten mayors, nineteen members of Congress, four supreme court justices, two presidential candidates, thirty labor leaders, forty bishops, sixty newspaper editors, and twenty-seven millionaires." In 1910, the Boston publisher, Edward Ginn, established the million dollar World Peace Foundation, which sponsored numerous publications in the fields of international law and international relations. In the same year, Carnegie, not to be outdone, set up the more wealthy and pretentious Carnegie Endowment for International Peace, which likewise sponsored publications but also granted subsidies to other organizations working for the same ends.[1]

Organizations of businessmen vied with the churches and with such religious groups as the Y.M.C.A. and the Christian Endeavor Society in their apparent zeal for the abolition of war. When President Taft, in 1910, proposed general arbitration

[1]Merle Curti, *Peace or War: The American Struggle, 1636–1936* (New York: W. W. Norton & Company, Inc., 1936), p. 207. Chapter 7 of this work summarizes the nongovernmental aspects of the American peace movement, 1900–1914.

treaties with Great Britain and France, almost three hundred chambers of commerce in as many cities supported him. There was, of course, little that the United States wanted that could be gained by war. Many businessmen, furthermore, had probably reached the same conclusion as the Englishman Norman Angell who in his book, *The Great Illusion,* published in 1910, argued convincingly that no one wins in modern war.

The Hague Peace Conferences

The private sponsors of the peace movement in these years were not only more respectable, better heeled, and more optimistic than their predecessors; they were far more influential in, or at any rate more in accord with, the actual policies of the government. The United States participated, with twenty-five other powers, in the conference on disarmament, generally referred to as the First Hague Peace Conference, called by the Russian Czar in 1899. In its attempt to put limits on military and naval expenditure (the principal object for which it had been called), the conference failed completely. Its efforts in this direction were not aided by Captain A. T. Mahan, one of the United States delegates, who remarked privately to a British representative that the new responsibilities of the United States in the Pacific would require that it have more navy, not less.[2] The conference adopted conventions on treatment of prisoners, including sick and wounded, the status of flags of truce, respect for the Red Cross, the outlawing of such allegedly "inhumane" implements of war as missiles dropped from balloons, poisonous gas, and expanding bullets—in

general, agreements to alleviate the effects of war rather than to prevent it. In practice, even such modest agreements as these were soon to be violated.

The most celebrated achievement of the First Hague Conference was the creation of the Permanent Court of Arbitration—the international body for which, together with the Permanent International Bureau that served as its secretariat, Andrew Carnegie built the famous "Peace Palace." This was not really a court at all but a panel of jurists—four named by each of the twenty-six member nations—from which the parties to a dispute might select the judges if they agreed to arbitration. The signatory governments made no promises to take disagreements between them to the Court for arbitration. They agreed merely to use their best efforts to insure the peaceful settlement of international disputes. The Court, with its panel of jurists, was there for whoever cared to use it.

The Second Hague Peace Conference met in 1907, again at the call of the Czar, who in the interval had engaged in the disastrous war with Japan. At the suggestion of the United States, invitations had been sent to all the republics of Central and South America, with the result that forty-four governments sent representatives. Again, no steps were taken for the limitation of armaments, nor did the Conference agree to the proposal of the United States that a genuine international court of justice be established. Aside from extending most of the conventions agreed to eight years previously, the Conference could point to only two promising achievements, and in neither of these was the promise fulfilled. First, it adopted a modified form of the Drago Doctrine, which, because of the modifications, proved unacceptable to the Latin American states chiefly interested. Second, it provided for the creation of an International Prize Court of Appeals for maritime prize cases; and, since there were differences of opinion about

[2]G. P. Gooch and Harold Temperley, eds., *British Documents on the Origins of the War, 1898–1914,* 11 vols. (London: H. M. Stationery Office, 1926–1938), 1: 231.

points of international law that such a court would administer, it was agreed that a conference should meet in London to codify the international law of maritime war. The London Conference, meeting in 1908–1909, issued its findings in a Declaration of London, but when war began in 1914, neither the Declaration nor the convention creating the International Prize Court had received the necessary ratifications. Nor did they ever do so.

The Root Arbitration Treaties

The existence of a court of arbitration, such as that at the Hague, had little importance if the nations of the world were under no obligation to use it. President Theodore Roosevelt and his two Secretaries of State (John Hay, 1898–1905; Elihu Root, 1905–1909) were willing to accept such obligation for the United States in certain categories of cases. Hay, accordingly, taking a recent Anglo-French treaty as a model, negotiated a number of bilateral arbitration treaties, under which the parties would agree to submit to the Hague Court questions of a legal nature or relating to the interpretation of treaties, not affecting "the vital interests, the independence, or the honor" of the two states, or the interests of third parties. The exceptions listed, which apparently excluded all important questions from the obligation to arbitrate, were broad enough; but the Senate weakened the agreements still further by adding the requirement that every arbitration under the treaties be preceded by a special agreement made with the advice and consent of the Senate, that is, requiring approval by a two-thirds vote.

In Hay's opinion, the Senate amendments made the treaties valueless, and upon his advice President Roosevelt let them die. Secretary Root, on the other hand, considered even such weak treaties better than none. In 1908–1909, accordingly, he negotiated twenty-five treaties similar to Hay's but containing the Senate amendment and having a duration of five years. Of the twenty-five, all but three were ratified by the other parties. Most of them were renewed at five-year intervals until replaced by the Kellogg treaties of 1928–1931.

President Taft's Abortive Arbitration Treaties

Speaking at a peace meeting in New York, March 22, 1910, President Taft voiced his belief that the time had come when even questions affecting national honor could safely be submitted to arbitration. This pronouncement was generally so well received that Taft instructed Philander C. Knox, his Secretary of State, to negotiate general treaties of arbitration with France and Great Britain. The two treaties, signed August 3, 1911, provided for the submission to the Hague Court or other suitable tribunal of all "justiciable" questions, that is, questions "susceptible of decision by the application of the principles of law or equity," which could not be settled by ordinary diplomacy. The treaties provided machinery for determining whether or not questions were justiciable. The Senate, however, amended the treaties to reserve this determination for itself and appended a long list of subjects to which the agreements should not apply. The excluded subjects embraced the admission of aliens to the United States and to the educational institutions of the United States (clearly referring to the Japanese question in California and her neighbor states), the alleged monetary indebtedness of any state (a reference to the Reconstruction debts of the South), and questions involving the Monroe Doctrine. Unwilling to ask the French and British governments to accept the Senate amendments, President Taft pigeon-holed the mutilated treaties.[3]

The Bryan Conciliation Treaties

A final phase of treaty-making in the interest of peace preceded the outbreak of the First World War. Secretary of State William Jennings Bryan, although not a pacifist in the extreme sense, was a staunch opponent of war and had electrified many an audience with his oration, "The Prince of Peace"—second in fame only to his "Cross of Gold" speech of 1896. Soon after taking over his official duties, he began the negotiation of a series of conciliation treaties, popularly known as "cooling-off" treaties because they would have the effect of at least postponing a resort to arms till the parties to a controversy had had time to think it over. Supplementary to the Root arbitration treaties, they provided a procedure in questions which the parties might be unwilling to arbitrate.

Under the Bryan treaties—of which thirty were negotiated and twenty-one ratified and proclaimed—the parties agreed that any dispute which diplomacy should fail to adjust should be submitted for study to an international commission of five persons, two to be chosen by each government (one from among its own citizens and one from a third state) and a fifth to be agreed upon by the two governments. The commission should, within one year, make a recommendation for settlement. The parties were not obligated to accept the recommendation, but they agreed not to declare war or begin hostilities until the commission should have made its report.

Putting the Hague Court to Work

The United States, as was observed in an earlier chapter, had already made a good record in submitting troublesome disputes to arbitration. It soon took advantage of the creation of the Permanent Court of Arbitration at The Hague to lay a dispute before a panel of jurists from that tribunal. At the suggestion of a French visitor that the United States might set a good example by sending a case to the court, President Roosevelt in 1902 persuaded Mexico to agree to the arbitration of the "Pious Fund" controversy—the question of Mexico's obligations to Franciscan missions in California, which before the Mexican War had received their support from a fund in Mexico. The dispute was arbitrated in 1902, and Mexico was directed to pay over $1,400,000 for the support of the missions.[4]

The Alaska Boundary Controversy

A more serious controversy than that over the Pious Fund was the Alaska boundary dispute. President Roosevelt, convinced of the complete justice of the American case, and regarding the Canadian pretensions as "dangerously near blackmail," refused to submit this dispute to the Hague Court or to any tribunal where a neutral might cast the deciding vote. In fact, he denied that the mode of settlement adopted, a procedure by which the United States could not lose, was really arbitration.

The Alaska controversy, involving the boundary between British Columbia and southern Alaska, depended upon the interpretation of the Anglo-Russian bound-

---

[3]J. P. Campbell, "Taft, Roosevelt, and the Arbitration Treaties of 1911," *Journal of American History*, 53 (September 1966), 279–98.

[4]Curti, *Peace or War*, pp. 190–91; F. J. Weber, "The Pious Fund of the Californias," *Hispanic American Historical Review*, 43 (February 1963), 78–94.

ary treaty of 1825. The rights to which Russia was entitled by that treaty were inherited by the United States when it purchased Alaska in 1867. The ownership of certain islands in the Portland Channel was in dispute, but the principal disagreement concerned the location of the boundary line from the head of that estuary to the meridian of 141° west longitude. The treaty prescribed that the line should parallel the

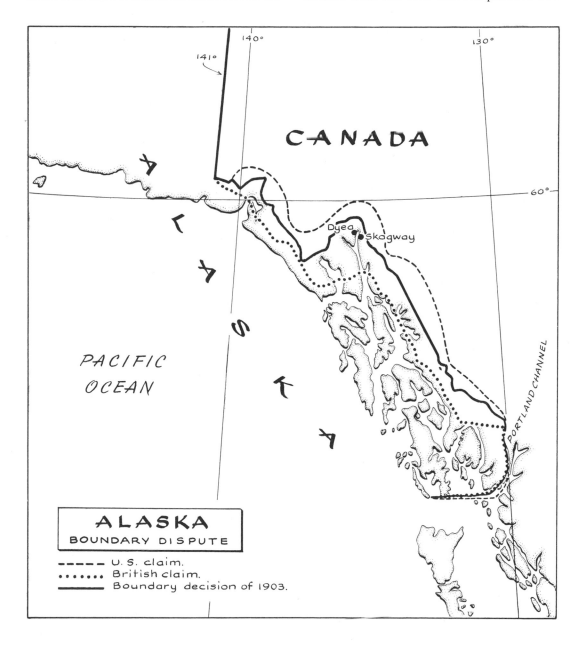

ALASKA
BOUNDARY DISPUTE

----- U. S. claim.
••••••• British claim.
——— Boundary decision of 1903.

coast at a distance of ten leagues (thirty miles) inland. Until the 1890's it was generally assumed that the thirty miles were to be measured from the head of tidewater; but when the gold rush to the Klondike gave sudden importance to the Lynn Canal and the boom towns of Dyea and Skagway at its head, the Canadians produced the theory that the thirty miles should be counted from the outer limits of the irregular coast, in which case Dyea and Skagway would be left on the Canadian side of the boundary.

British attempts to secure concessions by the United States in Alaska in return for British concessions in Panama failed. A *modus vivendi* agreed upon in 1899 left Dyea and Skagway for the time being under American jurisdiction. Not until 1903 did the British and American governments agree on a procedure for final settlement. The treaty of that year provided for submission of the question to the decision of a commission composed of six "impartial jurists," three American, two Canadian, and one British. Here was a possibility, obviously, of a tie vote and no settlement.

The British government named to the commission Lord Alverstone, Lord Chief Justice of England, and two Canadians who, if not wholly "impartial," were at any rate jurists of some repute. President Roosevelt followed the questionable course of appointing his Secretary of War, Elihu Root, and two senators—Lodge of Massachusetts and Turner of Washington. Root was a great lawyer but had presumably formed his opinion of the controversy; the other two could hardly be called either jurists or impartial. In justification of Roosevelt's choice, it may be said, first, that he had tried unsuccessfully to persuade two justices of the Supreme Court to accept appointments; second, that an advance and confidential assurance that "safe" men would be named was perhaps necessary to secure Senate approval of the treaty.[5]

Canadians considered Roosevelt's selections contrary to the spirit of the treaty, if not its letter; and though it cannot be said that the decision reached was unjust to Canada, the episode left a residue of ill will north of the border.

The commissioners met in London in September 1903. So determined was Roosevelt to have the decision his way that he engaged in what sounded definitely like saber-rattling, sending troops to southern Alaska (where they were perhaps needed for the preservation of order) and letting it be known informally to the British ministry that if the commission deadlocked, he proposed, as he put it, "to run the boundary on my own hook." It is to be hoped that Lord Alverstone was not swayed by these hints but rather by the documents in the case, which undoubtedly upheld the American contention. For whatever reason, he voted on the most controversial issue with the three Americans and against the two Canadian jurists. The disputed islands were divided between the contestants, but the mainland portion of the line was established eastward of the heads of the inlets, thus leaving Lynn Canal with Dyea and Skagway securely on the American side.

Arbitration of the Northeast Fisheries Dispute

A better example of genuine arbitration than the Alaska boundary settlement was the submission to the Hague Court of the northeast fisheries controversy. The *modus vivendi* of 1888, extended from time to time, had prevented friction with Canada, but Newfoundland, upon whose ports and inshore waters New England fishermen largely depended for bait, had continued to harass the Americans with a variety of troublesome and unreasonable regula-

---

[5]T. A. Bailey, "Theodore Roosevelt and the Alaska Boundary Settlement," *Canadian Historical Review,* 18, (1937), 123–30. See also P. C. Jessup, *Elihu Root,* 2 vols. (New York: Dodd, Mead & Co., 1938), 1:389–401.

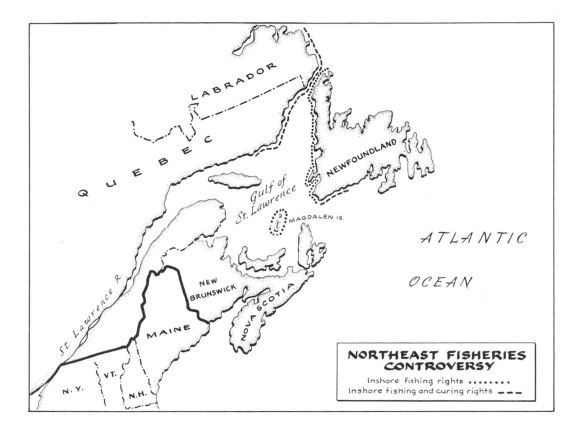

tions, which the United States contended were contrary to the spirit, if not the letter, of the treaty of 1818. Newfoundland would have relaxed her impositions in return for the duty-free admission of her fish to the American market, but a proposal to this effect was rejected by the United States Senate.

After prolonged negotiation, the United States and British governments agreed in 1909 to submit the entire question of the fisheries to a panel of five judges selected from the membership of the Hague Court of Arbitration. The panel was composed of one American and one Candian jurist and one each from Austria, The Netherlands, and Argentina. The panel decided all the principal questions in favor of the United States. The most important feature of the award was the ruling that all local regula-

tions affecting visiting fishermen must be "reasonable" and that their reasonableness should be subject to determination by a mixed commission representing both parties. Certain restrictions that Newfoundland had sought to impose upon American fishing vessels were definitely ruled out by the court.

An interesting question, but one that had long ceased to make serious trouble, was the definition of inshore waters on those coasts where American fishermen were excluded from inshore fishing. Was the three-mile line, beyond which Americans must not go, to follow all the sinuosities of the coast, as Americans claimed, or to be drawn from headland to headland across the mouth of every bay, as was the Canadian contention? Though practical understandings on this point had long since been reached, it was placed before the Hague panel for final determination. The panel adopted the arbitrary rule that when the entrance to a bay did not exceed ten miles in width, the waters of the bay should be counted as inshore waters; in wider bays the three-mile line should mark the limit of the prohibited area. Thus another troublesome dispute, in fact, the longest in American diplomatic history, was finally and amicably disposed of.

The Panama Canal Tolls Question

Still another disagreement with Great Britain, one that might properly have been submitted to arbitration but was handled in a different way, was the controversy over tolls to be charged for use of the Panama Canal. The Hay-Pauncefote Treaty of 1901 had stipulated that the Canal should be "open to the vessels of commerce and of war of all nations . . . , on terms of entire equality." When Congress, in 1912, legislated for the operation of the canal, which was nearing completion, it provided that United States ships engaged only in the coastwise trade, as from New York to San Francisco, should be exempt from the payment of tolls for the use of the canal. This provision was at once attacked by the British as inconsistent with the equality of treatment promised by the treaty. American supporters of the measure contended that, since foreign ships were excluded from the coastwise trade, exemption of American coastwise shipping from payment of tolls was not discrimination. Foreigners replied that the loss of tolls resulting from the exemption of American coastwise shipping would necessitate higher tolls on other shipping, which would therefore suffer discrimination.

The Democratic platform on which Woodrow Wilson won the presidency in 1912 supported the tolls exemption in the recently enacted law. Wilson soon became convinced, however, that the British had good ground for their objections. He believed, as did leading Republicans like Roosevelt, Root, and Lodge, that the question was a suitable one for arbitration. But arbitration could be instituted only through a treaty, and there was little chance that such a treaty would be approved by two-thirds of the Senate. Wilson decided, therefore, to ask Congress for outright appeal of the tolls exemption.

Wilson's case for repeal was strengthened by the fact that Britain had accepted—though disliking—his anti-Huerta policy in Mexico and had removed her minister, who had befriended Huerta. It was America's turn to make a concession, especially in a matter in which Britain appeared to many to have right on her side. Wilson used this argument by implication, without specific mention of Mexico, when on March 5, 1914, he asked Congress to repeal the tolls exemption, "in support of the foreign policy of the administration." Leading Republicans like Root, now a senator from New York, and Lodge gave Wilson their support. The repeal bill became law on June 15, 1914.

Europe Drifts Toward War

The same years that saw so much apparent progress toward the substitution of arbitration for war in the settlement of international controversies saw also a steady intensification in the rivalries of the principal European powers. Europe, in fact, became divided into two mutually antagonistic armed camps.

At the turn of the century a Dual Alliance of France and Russia faced a Triple Alliance of Germany, Austria-Hungary, and Italy. Aside, however, from the French desire to recover Alsace-Lorraine, surrendered to Germany in 1871, the rift between the groups was not too deep. In fact, as appeared in the story of Far Eastern developments, Germany on some occasions cooperated with France and Russia. Great Britain as yet held aloof, not aligning herself with either group of powers. Her chief rivalries in the 1890s were with France in Africa and with Russia in Persia, Afghanistan, and China.

The rise of Germany as a great industrial, commercial, and naval power gave Great Britain a new rival, one more to be feared than France and Russia, her traditional enemies. As a consequence, Great Britain settled her differences first with France and then with Russia. In 1904 England and France composed their colonial rivalries in Africa and the Pacific, forming what was called the *Entente Cordiale.* In 1907 England and Russia came to terms over their conflicting interests in Asia; the *Entente Cordiale* became the Triple Entente of France, Russia and Great Britain—not an alliance (except between France and Russia) but an understanding that the three powers would work for common objectives. Japan, furthermore, was allied with Great Britain after 1902 and in 1907 reached agreement with Russia in regard to Manchuria. Italy, moreover, showed signs of drifting away from her Teutonic allies in the direction of better relations with France.

The chief scenes of rivalry after 1904 were in North Africa, where France and German ambitions clashed, and in the Balkans, where Austria-Hungary, backed by Germany, worked at cross-purposes with Russia.

In North Africa, by the agreement of 1904, France had given up, for the benefit of England, any claim to the Egyptian Sudan, receiving in return from Great Britain a free hand in Morocco. A subsequent agreement with Spain divided Morocco, though still nominally independent, into French and Spanish spheres of interest. Germany resented the partitioning of Africa without regard to German interests and, in particular, took exception to the French assumption of paramount interest in Morocco. Taking advantage of the weakening of the Dual Alliance by Russia's disastrous war with Japan, Germany in 1905 provoked a crisis with France over Morocco, forced the resignation of the ambitious French Foreign Minister, Théophile Delcassé, and brought about an international conference at Algeciras, Spain, in which the United States took part. At Algeciras, Germany secured recognition of her limited economic interests in Morocco and assurances that an open door policy would be followed there. On two later occasions, 1909 and 1911, Germany rattled the saber over the Moroccan question. Unable to break French political predominance in Morocco, Germany exacted, in compensation for her acquiescence, the cession of certain French territories in central Africa.

More perilous to peace than the question of Morocco was great-power rivalry in the Balkan peninsula. Here a German-Austro-Hungarian *Drang nach Osten*—an eastward thrust through the Balkans and Turkey, symbolized by the Berlin-to-Baghdad Railway—ran counter to Russia's traditional desire to control the Bosporus and Dardanelles and her more recent assumption, as leader of a Pan-Slavic movement, of a sort of guardianship over the Slavs of the Balkans, especially the Serbs and Bulgars. Russia, still debilitated by her defeat by Japan, was too weak to resist when Austria-Hungary, in 1908, annexed Bosnia and Herzegovina, Slavic provinces of the crumbling Turkish Empire. But she did nothing to restrain anti-Austrian activities on the part of Serbia. Serbia bitterly resented Austria's seizure of the Slavic peoples of Bosnia-Herzegovina. Among them and among other South Slavic groups living under the Dual Monarchy, the Serbs launched propaganda aimed at liberating their kinsmen from Austro-Hungarian rules as they themselves had been liberated from the tyranny of the Turk.

In the Balkan Wars of 1912–1913, Serbs, Bulgars, Greeks, and Rumanians expelled the Turks from most of the remnants of their European possessions outside the city of Constantinople and then fought among themselves over the spoils. Most significant, however, was the intervention of Austria-Hungary to prevent Serbia from using her victory to secure a port on the Adriatic. This action added fuel to the fire of Serbian hatred for Austria, which was to have its tragic outcome in the assassination at Sarajevo of Archduke Francis Ferdinand, heir to the thrones of Austria and Hungary.

The growing tension between Austria-Hungary and Serbia meant growing tension also between the Dual Monarchy and Russia, friends of Serbia. And since France and Germany were bound by alliances with Russia and Austria-Hungary respectively, while England had at least moral commitments to France and Russia, it was obvious that a spark in the Balkans might set off a general European conflagration. Recognizing the danger, and at the same time increasing it, all continental powers in 1913 enlarged their armies by extending the periods of military service. Great Britain increased her naval budget. Germany and Russia were building strategic railroad lines. The world talked of peace, but Europe prepared for war.

Theodore Roosevelt and the Moroccan Question

Americans in general, although they deplored the signs of increasing tension and growing militarism in Europe, felt little direct personal concern about them. Europeans might foolishly go to war; Americans would remain at peace. Theodore Roosevelt was more aware than most of his countrymen of the realities of European politics and of their implications for the United States. He had a wide circle of acquaintances among Englishmen, French, and Germans. He kept up, as President, a lively correspondence with the German Kaiser, whose vagaries he viewed with an amused condescension. The Kaiser aided Roosevelt in his efforts to make peace between Russia and Japan and in turn appealed to him for support in the Moroccan crisis with France in 1905. Roosevelt responded by urging France to agree to a conference on Morocco but in doing so assured the French government of American support in resistance to any unreasonable German demands. The United States was itself represented at the ensuing conference at Algeciras, January to April 1906. Roosevelt found an excuse for American participation in the fact that a commercial treaty of 1880 with Morocco gave the United States a legitimate interest in keeping the Moroccan door open to American trade. Roosevelt's real purpose, however, was to maintain the balance of power in Europe, with the American weight thrown temporarily into the scale instead of Russia's; to prevent the humiliation of France, to improve Anglo-German relations, and to reduce the chances of a European war.

By the resulting treaty of Algeciras the powers, including the United States, avowed their devotion to the independence and territorial integrity of Morocco, the sovereignty of the native Sultan, and the preservation of the open door in the Sultan's dominions. They devised measures for administrative and financial reform, assured Germany of a substantial share in an International Bank set up at Tangier to handle Moroccan finance, but gave to France and Spain the authority to officer and instruct a native police force. On the whole, France had come out well, German ambitions had been restricted within small bounds, and Roosevelt had succeeded in his aims. The United States had been able, as

Secretary of State Elihu Root phrased it, to "preserve world peace because of the power of our detachment."[6]

Last-Minute Efforts to Prevent War

In participating actively in the Algeciras Conference, Theodore Roosevelt ventured further than any other American President before 1917 into the intricacies of European politics.[7] President Taft and Secretary Knox directed their international activities principally toward the Far East and the Caribbean. By the time Woodrow Wilson entered the White House, European tension had reached an alarming pitch. This fact did not escape the attention of Walter Hines Page, United States ambassador in London, or of Colonel Edward M. House, Wilson's confidential friend and adviser. Both Page and House had ideas for preventing war that they correctly sensed to be just around the corner.

To Page it seemed that the only hope was to find some useful and constructive work in which the great European armies might be employed instead of fighting each other. He suggested a clean-up campaign in Mexico and unspecified tropical countries—"to clean out bandits, yellow fever, malaria, hookworm—all to make the countries healthful, safe for life and invest-

ment and for orderly self-government at last. . . . And the tropics cry out for sanitation, which is at first an essentially military task."[8]

House had something of the same idea. To the German ambassador in Washington he suggested "a sympathetic understanding between England, Germany, Japan, and the United States. . . . They could ensure peace and the proper development of the waste places."[9] In House's conception "the proper development of the waste places" appeared to be not "an essentially military task" but a problem of guaranteed investments at reasonable rates of interest. If Germany could find outlets in this way, if, for example, she could be encouraged to "exploit South America in a legitimate way," tensions might be reduced, and armies also. In the hope of working out such an arrangement—reduction of armaments based upon an internationally accepted program of overseas investments—House visited Berlin and other European capitals in May, June, and July 1914. He received some encouragement, but on June 28, while he was in London, Archduke Francis Ferdinand, heir to the thrones of the Dual Monarchy, was assassinated at Sarajevo, Bosnia, by a young Bosnian under secret Serbian sponsorship.[10] When the colonel sailed for home on July 21, Austria-Hungary was on the point of presenting to Serbia the fateful ultimatum that touched off the First World War.

---

[6]Jessup, *Elihu Root,* 2:59. Quotations from *Elihu Root* reprinted by permission of the publisher.

[7]The Senate, in approving the Algeciras treaty, sought to dispel the impression that American participation in conference and treaty was a departure from standard United States policy. It appended a reservation explaining that the United States had taken part because of its treaty of 1880 with Morocco and adding that participation was "without purpose to depart from the traditional American foreign policy which forbids participation by the United States in the settlement of political questions which are entirely European in their scope."

[8]B. J. Hendrick, ed., *The Life and Letters of Walter H. Page,* 3 vols. (Garden City, N.Y.: Doubleday & Company, Inc., 1923–1925), 1: 272–73. Reprinted by permission of The Odyssey Press.

[9]Charles Seymour, ed. *The Intimate Papers of Colonel House,* 4 vols. (Boston: Houghton Mifflin Company, 1926–28), 1: 239–40. Quotations from *The Intimate Papers of Colonel House* reprinted by permission of the publisher. Walter Millis, *Road to War: America 1914–1917* (Boston: Houghton Mifflin Company, 1935), pp. 21–27.

[10]Vladimir Dedijer. "Sarajevo Fifty Years After," *Foreign Affairs,* 42 (July 1964), 569–84.

American Opinion and the War

Though informed Americans had been aware of the growing tensions in Europe, the actual outbreak of war took both the American public and government completely by surprise. The assassinations at Sarajevo (June 28) made newspaper headlines for a day and then were largely forgotten. For over three weeks there were few hints of serious trouble brewing. Then, on July 23, Austria-Hungary presented to Serbia a forty-eight-hour ultimatum whose terms, if accepted, would have gone far toward extinguishing Serbian sovereignty. Rejecting Serbia's partial acceptance as unsatisfactory, Austria-Hungary on July 28 declared war upon the Serb kingdom. Two days later, Russia mobilized, determined to defend her small protégé. On August 1, Germany declared war against Russia; on August 3, against Russia's ally, France, which had refused to give assurance of remaining neutral; on August 4, against Belgium, which had denied passage to German armies en route to France. On August 4, also, Great Britain declared war upon Germany—ostensibly as a joint guarantor of Belgian neutrality; more realistically, because of moral commitments to France and Russia and unwillingness to acquiesce in the domination of Western Europe by her most dangerous rival. Subsequently, Turkey and Bulgaria entered the war as allies of Germany and Austria-Hungary—the "Central Powers"; while Italy (repudiating her Triple Alliance ties) and Rumania eventually joined the side of the Triple Entente powers—the "Allies," as they were called in American parlance. Meanwhile, Japan had declared war upon Germany on August 23, 1914, and set out to seize for herself German holdings in China's Shantung peninsula and German islands in the North Pacific. Eventually no less than thirty-two nations—including the British Dominions and India—were involved in the war against Germany. To the average American the war in Europe seemed remote—a deplorable tragedy indeed, which might entail inconvenience to his trade or travel but was unlikely to involve him in any more serious way. But some Americans saw it in a different light, as a struggle that might have deep significance for the United States. Elihu Root wrote to an English friend:

> Underlying all the particular reasons and occasions for the war, the principle of Anglo-Saxon liberty seems to have met the irreconcilable conception of the German State, and the two ideas are battling for control of the world.[11]

Robert Lansing, who in July 1915 became Wilson's Secretary of State, took a view similar to Root's and drew from it a practical conclusion:

> . . . Germany must not be permitted to win this war or to break even, though to prevent it this country is forced to take an active part. . . . American public opinion must be prepared for the time, which may come, when we will have to cast aside our neutrality and become one of the champions of democracy.[12]

Still other Americans foresaw a danger to the United States in an upsetting by Germany of the European balance of power. Great Britain and France were "satisfied" powers; so long as they dominated the eastern Atlantic, the United States had nothing to fear. But should their place be taken by imperial Germany, "unsatisfied" and hungry for colonies and colonial markets, the United States might

[11]Jessup, *Elihu Root*, 2:313.

[12]*War Memoirs of Robert Lansing* (Indianapolis: The Bobbs-Merrill Company, Inc., 1935), p. 21. Quotations from *War Memoirs of Robert Lansing* reprinted by permission of the publisher.

have to surrender the Monroe Doctrine or fight to defend it.[13]

But these were the opinions of a select few. To most Americans, though they might sympathize with one side or the other, the war was a European affair. It took the German submarine attacks on American lives and American ships—attacks which, in American eyes, were both inhumane and illegal—to bring the United States to the point of intervention.

President Wilson issued a formal proclamation of neutrality on August 4, 1914. Fifteen days later, in a message reminiscent of Washington's Farewell Address, Wilson appealed to his countrymen to avoid taking sides in the European struggle. Otherwise, he warned, Americans might "be divided in camps of hostile opinion, hot against each other, involved in the war itself in impulse and opinion if not in action."

> The United States [he continued] must be neutral in fact as well as in name. . . . We must be impartial in thought as well as in action, must put a curb upon our sentiments as well as upon every transaction that might be construed as preference of one party to the struggle before another.

Wilson attempted, during the next two and one-half years, to keep the United States "neutral in fact as well as in name," though consciously or unconsciously American interpretations of international law were consistently favorable to the side of the Allies. But no one could compel or persuade the American people to be "impartial in thought," and this lack of impartiality was conspicuous in the President's own official family. Mr. Bryan, Secretary of State until July 1915, was, indeed, as impar-

tial as one could well be, seeing little to commend the British case over the German. Lansing, second man in the State Department in 1914 and Bryan's successor the next year, believed that the United States must enter the war if necessary to prevent a German victory. Walter H. Page, ambassador to Great Britain, saw the war as a crusade in which England and her allies were to Germany as St. George to the dragon. Edward M. House, Wilson's unofficial ambassador to Europe on several occasions, was almost as pro-Ally as Page. Wilson himself, however impartial at first, had come by May 1915 to a belief that "England is fighting our fight." A year later, exasperation at certain British practices had driven him back to a relatively impartial attitude.

Public opinion from the beginning tended to be pro-Ally. Americans had ties of race, language, culture, and political ideals with England and bonds of ancient friendship with France, which had no substantial counterpart in their relations with Germany. Only in communities where the German or Irish heritage was strong was there likely to be much pro-German (or anti-British) sentiment. Both sides in the war made their propaganda appeals to American public opinion. The British had the advantage—in a day when wireless transmission of news was relatively unimportant—of controlling the cables and hence of shaping news from the war fronts to suit their purposes. German "atrocities" were magnified or even invented. Such exaggerated stories were often accepted as sober truth. German propaganda, on the other hand, was more often spotted as such and discounted accordingly.

British propaganda, however, was probably less influential in building anti-German sentiment than authentic words and deeds of German leaders and the German armed forces. Chancellor von Bethmann-Hollweg's injudicious reference, in his closing conversation with the

---

[13]Walter Lippmann, *U.S. Foreign Policy, Shield of the Republic* (Boston: Little, Brown and Company, 1943), pp. 33–39. The various motives for American intervention are discussed in detail in Part Two of R. E. Osgood, *Ideals and Self-Interest in American Foreign Relations* (Chicago: The University of Chicago Press, 1953).

British ambassador, to the treaty neutralizing Belgium as a "scrap of paper" sounded a false note to American ears, as did the actual invasion of neutral Belgium and the destruction of the great library of the University of Louvain. The execution as a spy of the English nurse Edith Cavell by the German armies seemed to the American public an act of wanton cruelty. Later, the German U-boat campaign against merchant ships and cases of sabotage against American suppliers of war material for the Allies—whatever one thinks of them in retrospect—contributed to a popular conception of a Germany careless of neutral rights and of human life.

Such pro-Ally sentiment was stronger along the Atlantic coast than in the interior; stronger among the well-to-do classes than among the less affluent. Many American businessmen had banking and commerical ties with England; many had found a playground in France. Similar links with Germany were relatively few.

The American Economy and the War

The war itself bound the United States with new and powerful bands to France and Great Britain. The initial effect of the war on the American economy was disastrous. German markets were cut off by the British Navy. German merchant shipping was bottled up in port, the Allied ships were in many cases diverted from their customary routes and services. Luxury purchases virtually ceased. American business, already wallowing in the trough of a minor cyclical depression, was still further depressed by these disruptions of the foreign market. Soon, however, relief came in the form of large munitions orders from the Allies, and by the closing months of 1915, the United States was enjoying a war-born prosperity.

The sale of munitions of war to the Allies raised the question of neutral obligations. German sympathizers complained that such sales, being made exclusively to the Allied side, were unneutral. To such critics Mr. Lansing replied:

> If one belligerent has by good fortune a superiority in the matter of geographical location or of military or naval power, the rules of neutral conduct cannot be varied so as to favor the less fortunate combatant.

Such a change in the rules would in itself be unneutral. There was no doubt that this position was correct in law and precedent. Sale of munitions of war to belligerents was no breach of neutrality. That only one set of belligerents could buy was the result of their control of the seas, not of United States policy. The sale of munitions continued, therefore, at a rapidly climbing rate. Exports of explosives, six million dollars in value in 1914, jumped to $467,000,000 in 1916.

In the first few days of the war, it became apparent that the Allies, if their munitions purchases were to continue over a long period of time, would need to finance them by borrowing in the American money market. In August 1914 the New York firm of J.P. Morgan and Company inquired of Secretary Bryan what would be the attitude of the government to such transactions. Bryan replied that loans by bankers to belligerent governments were "inconsistent with the true spirit of neutrality." Whatever the ethics of Bryan's position, it had no legal standing. Loans by neutral bankers to belligerent governments were common enough. Both North and South had borrowed in Europe to finance the American Civil War. Japan had borrowed extensively in England and the United States to pay for her recent war with Russia, and Russia had fought back with money borrowed in France.

Bryan was apparently convinced by the

French ambassador, J. J. Jusserand, that his position was untenable. He disguised his retreat by distinguishing between loans and "credits." In October 1914, with State Department consent, Morgan granted a ten million dollar "credit" to the French government.[14] Other credits followed, but "loans" were still banned when Bryan resigned as Secretary of State. In September and October 1915, Secretary Lansing and Secretary of Treasury William G. McAdoo persuaded Wilson to abandon Bryan's position completely, arguing that without large-scale loans, Allied purchasing would taper off, and the country would face a depression. Thereupon the Morgan firm, which became purchasing agent in the United States for the Allied governments, assisted in floating an issue of a half-billion dollars in Allied war bonds. Before American entry into the war in 1917, the Allied governments had borrowed over two and one-quarter billion dollars in the United States, of which nearly one and one-half billion dollars went to Great Britain.

The loans, and the trade that they supported, made and kept the United States prosperous until its own entry into the war. That prosperity was dependent upon a continuance of Allied purchases in the United States. In 1915–1916, half of American foreign trade was with France and Great Britain. The German submarine campaign of 1917, besides violating the American interpretation of international law threatened to destroy this trade altogether. There is no evidence that President Wilson was swayed by such economic considerations in his decision to accept the German challenge. The most that can be safely said is that the existence of these strong economic ties with the Allies, compared with almost no such ties with Germany, made it easy to break with Germany when occasion arose.

[14]See "A Communication" from Charles A. Beard, *New Republic*, 87 (June 17, 1936), 177.

The British Navy Revives Old Issues

Observance of neutral obligations was a relatively simple matter for the United States in 1914–1917. Enforcement of its rights as a neutral raised more complicated and difficult problems. It embroiled the State Department in long arguments with the leading belligerents on both sides and eventually led to a declaration of war against Germany.

The rights in question were mainly those of trade and travel by sea. Each belligerent attempted, so far as it dared and with the instruments at its disposal, to shut off neutral trade with its antagonist, raising again the old questions of contraband and blockade and new questions of the immunity of commercial vessels, with their crews and passengers, from lethal attack by submarines. Each belligerent denounced the other's methods as illegal, and the United States, as the leading neutral, saw illegalities in both.

The London Naval Conference of 1908–1909, already referred to, had attempted to reach agreement upon disputed points of maritime law and had issued its findings in the Declaration of London. On nearly all controversial points, the declaration would have restricted belligerent activities and thereby would have enlarged the rights of neutrals and also those of the inferior naval power—the belligerent that did not control the sea. For this very reason, the British Parliament had withheld its approval, and at the outbreak of war, the declaration had no legal standing.

Secretary Bryan proposed, nevertheless, that the belligerents agree to abide by the rules laid down in the declaration. Germany and Austria-Hungary expressed their willingness to accept the declaration if their opponents would do so. The British government agreed only with qualifications and reservations that virtually nullified the declaration. In particular, the British rejected the rigid categories of contraband, noncontraband, and conditional contraband[15] commodities set up by the declaration; they made, from time to time, sweeping additions to the contraband lists and in the end wiped out the distinction between contraband and conditional contraband. The British also refused to be bound by the articles of the declaration which provided that blockading forces "must not bar access to the ports or to the coasts of neutrals," and that the doctrine of continuous voyage, although applicable to stoppage of contraband, could not be invoked for enforcement of blockade with respect to noncontraband goods.

It is a fact worth noting that the British government never formally declared a blockade of Germany. It accomplished the same end by other means. The lists of contraband were gradually enlarged until they included not only foodstuffs and cotton but nearly all articles of consequence that Germany was in the habit of importing. By a drastic order-in-council of March 11, 1915, Great Britain announced that thereafter goods "of enemy destination, ownership, or origin" would not be permitted to proceed to or from Germany, directly or indirectly. This was a blockade in all but name. It was a blockade, furthermore, that applied to trade via neutral ports, such as those of Holland and Denmark, as well as trade via German ports. By this order the British carried the doctrine of continuous voyage to its logical conclusion.[16] Neutral states with access to Germany which desired to import goods by sea were required to guarantee, not only that such goods would not be re-exported to Germany, but also that like goods of domestic production, for which the imports might be substituted, would not be so exported.[17]

Against these interferences with its trade—trade with Germany and with Germany's neutral neighbors—the United States from time to time protested. It protested, too, against other and incidental British wartime practices—the taking of American ships into British ports for search, with consequent interminable delays; interference with the mails; the blacklisting of American firms alleged to have some German connections; the flying of the American flag on British ships for purposes of disguise. Although these protests were sometimes strongly worded[18] (to satisfy suffering American shippers and to balance contemporary protests to Germay), they never reached the ultimatum stage. Mr. Lansing never lost sight of the possibility that the United States might become an ally of Great Britain and might then even wish to engage in some of the very practices against which it was protesting. Consequently, as he wrote later:

> The notes that were sent [to England] were long and exhaustive treatises which opened up new subjects of discussion rather than closing those in controversy. Short and emphatic notes were dangerous. Everything was submerged in verbosity. It was done with

---

[15]"Conditional contraband" comprised commodities susceptible of both military and nonmilitary uses, which became "contraband" (and so liable to confiscation) only when consigned to the armed forces or a government department of the enemy state.

[16]In the case of noncontraband neutral property stopped en route to Germany, the British did not assert the right of confiscation, as they could have done for breach of blockade. German property and neutral contraband property were subject to confiscation as such.

[17]In their blockade policy, the British did not always "play fair" with neutrals. To a considerable extent, they allowed British exporters to ship to Scandinavian countries "the very products which they intercepted when bound to such destinations from America." Jessup, *Elihu Root*, 2: 320, and compare M. W. W. P. Consett and O. H. Daniel, *The Triumph of Unarmed Forces* (New York: Brentano's, 1923).

[18]Ambassador Page, who had no patience with his government's objection to British practice, described one of Lansing's notes as "an uncourteous monster of 35 heads and 3 appendices."

deliberate purpose. It insured continuance of the controversies and left the questions unsettled, which was necessary in order to leave this country free to act and even to act illegally when it entered the war.[19]

The United States, as a matter of fact, came close to giving its case away as early as December 26, 1914, when it acknowledged that "imperative necessity to protect their national safety" might justify the Allies in committing acts that would otherwise be illegal. Subsequent protests against British blockade policy, Sir Edward Grey, British Foreign Secretary, was able to answer more or less effectively with the arguments that:

1. The British interference with trade to the European neutrals was based upon, and went little beyond, the practice followed by the United States in the Civil War.
2. New instrumentalities of trade necessitated modifications of international law. With modern steam transportation a blockade of German ports would be futile if trade to Danish and Dutch ports were unmolested.
3. Extension of the contraband lists to cover food and other commodities largely for civilian use was justified by the fact that in modern war the entire nation participates, the factory or railroad worker behind the lines no less than the soldier in the trenches.

Although the United States never accepted this reasoning as satisfactory, it took no steps, beyond making protests, to enforce its conception of maritime rights against Great Britain. In the controversy with Germany over the submarine, Colonel House and Wilson himself assured the German government that in return for German concessions to the American position, the United States would put pressure on England to make corresponding concessions. These promises were never effectively carried out.

[19]*War Memoirs of Robert Lansing*, p. 128.

The German Submarine Raises New Problems

The British practices against which the United States had occasion to protest violated property rights only; they exposed no neutral lives to danger. In this respect they differed radically from the German use of the submarine for warfare upon commerce, which became the chief grievance against Germany. President Wilson made clear the American attitude toward the two kinds of grievance in a speech of September 2, 1916. When American rights became involved, he said,

> this was our guiding principle: that property rights can be vindicated by claims for damages when the war is over, and no modern nation can decline to arbitrate such claims; but the fundamental rights of humanity cannot be. The loss of life is irreparable.[20]

"The fundamental rights of humanity," as Wilson saw them, were violated by the German submarine.

On February 4, 1915, the German government announced that the waters around the British Isles would thenceforth be considered a "war zone" in which enemy merchant vessels would be sunk at sight by German submarines. Furthermore, because the British had adopted the practice of disguising their ships with neutral flags, Germany could not guarantee the safety of neutral vessels that ventured into the war zone.[21]

[20]R. S. Baker and W. E. Dodd, eds. *The Public Papers of Woodrow Wilson: The New Democracy,* 2 vols. (New York: Harper & Row, Publishers, 1926), 2: 282.

[21]The Germans had early begun laying mines in the North Sea. The British had asserted the right to retaliate, and on November 2, 1914, had proclaimed the entire North Sea to be a "war area," which merchant vessels would enter at their own risk. The United States had not seen fit to join the Scandinavian governments in protesting this action. C. C. Tansill, *America Goes to War* (Boston: Little, Brown and Company, 1938), pp. 176–77.

To this unprecedented innovation in maritime warfare the United States replied promptly on February 10. For any loss of American ships or lives as a result of the new policy, the German government would be held to "a strict accountability," and the United States would take any necessary steps "to safeguard American lives and property and to secure to American citizens the full enjoyment of their acknowledged rights on the high seas." So began the controversy that after two years was to involve the United States in the war.

To the use of the submarine as a weapon against enemy naval vessels there could be no objection. The objection to its use as a commerce destroyer arose from the fact that it could not easily conform to established rules for commerce destruction. Recognized practice called for visit and search of the commercial vessel by the enemy warship, inspection of its papers, and, if possible, the bringing of the suspected ship into port—a home port of the captor—for adjudication by a prize court. But when the latter part of this process was impossible—as it obviously was for a German submarine in the face of the British navy—international law permitted the destruction of the prize at sea, *but only if adequate provision was made for safety of crew and passengers.*

A submarine was a small and cramped vessel which could not possibly take on board and care for the noncombatants from a large freighter or passenger ship. The best it could do, if it destroyed the ship, was to give passengers and crew an opportunity to take to the lifeboats and in them to face precariously the perils of the deep. But a submarine was also a weak and vulnerable craft; and since the British armed their merchant ships and instructed them to fire upon or ram enemy submarines, the Germans contended that only by torpedoing such ships without warning could they use the submarine safely and effectively. The United States complained that this practice

violated the principle that noncombatant lives must be protected. The Germans replied that armed merchant ships forfeited their immunity from attack and, furthermore, that old concepts of international law must be adapted to new conditions and the employment of new weapons.

The United States Objects

Opinions differed within the State Department itself on how the United States should meet the new German policy. Bryan, who saw that a challenge to Germany on this issue might lead to war, favored submission; he would warn American citizens who chose to travel on belligerent ships that they did so at their own risk. Lansing, on the other hand, contended that American citizens had a right to travel on British ships, even though the latter were defensively armed, and that the United States government must defend its citizens in the enjoyment of such rights. Lansing was apparently wrong on two counts: (1) persons of whatever nationality traveling on a British ship could properly look only to the British government for protection; (2) an armed merchant vessel, even though the armament was defensive forfeited its immunity from armed attack.[22] Wilson, nevertheless, accepted Lansing's position rather than Bryan's. From then on, the United States contended that its citizens had the right to travel in safety on British ships and to look to their own government for protection in that right. It mattered not that the British ships were armed or that they carried, as most of them did, cargoes of munitions for Allied armies.

[22] E, M. Borchard and W. P. Lage, *Neutrality for the United States,* 2nd ed. (New Haven: Yale University Press, 1940), pp. 87–88, 136–37, 177–83. Tansill, *America Goes to War,* p. 649. There are indications that Lansing later realized he had been wrong but was unwilling to acknowledge it.

Two attempts were made to solve the problem of submarine warfare by compromise. Soon after the original German announcement, the United States proposed that Germany restrict its use of submarines against merchant vessels to legal visit and search, in return for a relaxation of the British food blockade and a British promise to abandon the use of neutral flags. This attempt failed when Germany demanded free access to raw materials for her industry as well as food. The second attempt was made early in 1916. Lansing then proposed that the British give up arming their merchant ships in return for a German agreement that submarines would not attack unarmed ships without warning and without taking precautions for the safety of those aboard. This proposal failed to meet a favorable response in London and Paris. A move in Congress to support it by warning American citizens against travel in armed belligerent ships (the Gore and McLemore resolutions) was blocked at the request of President Wilson, who wrote to the chairman of the Senate Foreign Relations Committee that he could not "consent to any abridgment of the rights of American citizens in any respect."

The Lusitania Crisis

Long before this second attempt at compromise, German-American relations had passed through their first serious crisis, brought on by the torpedoing of the British Cunard liner *Lusitania* off the Irish coast on May 7, 1915. The vessel sank in eighteen minutes. Of the 1,198 persons who lost their lives, 128 were American citizens. Despite the fact that the German embassy had published warnings to Americans to avoid the *Lusitania,* there was apparently no deliberate German plot to "get" that particular ship. The commander of the offending submarine, the *U-20,* had actually begun his homeward voyage when the big liner hove in sight, steaming with culpable disregard of precautions prescribed by the British Admiralty.

The phrase "strict accountability" was now put to the test. Lansing and some others, in or close to the administration wished a declaration of war against Germany but realized that public opinion would not support that course. Over Bryan's protest and finally despite his resignation, President Wilson made and reiterated a demand upon the German government for disavowal of the sinking, reparation for the injury caused, and the taking of "immediate steps to prevent the recurrence" of such acts. The German government, unwilling to make a public surrender but not ready to risk a break with the United States, issued secret orders to submarine commanders not to attack passenger ships without warning. In Washington the German Ambassador, Count von Bernstorff, hard pressed by the State Department, exceeded his authority and permitted publication of his assurance that: "Liners will not be sunk by our submarines without warning and without safety of the lives of non-combatants, provided that the liners do not try to escape or offer resistance." After months of further negotiation the German government conceded its "liability" for the sinking of the *Lusitania.*[23]

Germany Retreats

The continuance of German-American amity was again endangered in March 1916, when the French channel steamer

[23]Tansill, *America Goes to War,* chaps. 13–14. Bernstorff did not present his assurance that liners would not be sunk until September 1, 1915. In the meantime on August 19, the White Star liner *Arabic,* en route from Liverpool to New York, had been sunk without warning, with two American lives lost. For this sinking, which was apparently in violation of orders, the German ambassador expressed disavowal, regret, and offer of indemnity.

Sussex, an unarmed passenger vessel, was torpedoed in the English Channel. The *Sussex* managed to make port, and no American lives were lost, though American passengers were injured. It seems well established that the submarine commander who attacked the *Sussex* mistook her for a type of British mine-layer which in silhouette she closely resembled.[24] At the time, however, the incident appeared to be a deliberate violation of the assurance given after the *Lusitania* sinking. Lansing and House advised breaking off diplomatic relations with Germany. Wilson, not ready to go so far without another attempt at an understanding, presented a vigorous ultimatum to the German government.

> Unless the Imperial Government [Wilson wrote] should now immediately declare and effect an abandonment of its present methods of submarine warfare against passenger and freight-carrying vessels, the Government of the United States can have no choice but to sever diplomatic relations with the German Empire altogether.

Again the German government yielded, giving definite assurance (May 4, 1916) that merchant vessels would "not be sunk without warning and without saving human lives, unless these ships attempt to escape or offer resistance." The note concluded, however, by stating the expectation that, in return for German concessions, the United States would compel England to abandon her allegedly illegal practices, and by warning that unless England should alter her methods, "the German Government would then be facing a new situation, in which it must reserve [to] itself complete liberty of action."

The British Try Wilson's Patience

The eight months following settlement of the *Sussex* crisis were the most satisfactory

[24]Tansill, *America Goes to War,* p. 491.

period of the war in German-American relations. The Germans were on their good behavior. German submarines continued to prey upon Allied commerce but acted within the rules of law and humanity. At the same time the Allies, especially the British, were exasperatingly uncooperative.

During the early months of 1916, Wilson had permitted Colonel House to make an effort to end the war, coupled with a conditional offer of American intervention on the side of the Allies if the effort should fail. The plan was as follows: At a secret signal from the Allies, Wilson was to invite both groups of belligerents to meet in a peace conference. The Allies would accept. If Germany declined, as was expected, or if, after accepting, she refused to make peace on "reasonable" terms (which were to have been agreed upon in advance between Wilson and the Allies), the United States would enter the war against Germany. A memorandum to this effect, agreed upon by House and Sir Edward Grey, was cabled to Wilson from London for his approval. The President, who under the Constitution could not promise a declaration of war, inserted the word "probably" in the clause predicting American action. Whether because of this element of uncertainty or because they hoped for victory without agreeing to terms that would satisfy Wilson's idealism, the Allied governments never signified their readiness for Wilson's invitation.

Apparently Wilson was, like House, chagrined at this cool treatment of a generous offer. It is clear that he was intensely annoyed at a blacklist of American business concerns issued by the British government in July 1916. The blacklist contained the names of nearly one hundred American firms or individuals with which, because of supposed German connections, British subjects and corporations were forbidden to have any business dealings; nor could firms in neutral countries do business with them except at the risk of being themselves blacklisted. Even Ambassador Page considered this British move "tactless and unjust," and the usually pro-Ally *New York Times* characterized it as "quite the most tactless, foolish, and unnecessary act of the British government during the war."

The blacklist, coupled with a contemporary British order-in-council setting aside all that remained of the Declaration of London, and with the British government's ruthless suppression of an Irish rebellion in April 1916, aroused a storm of anti-British feeling in the United States, in which Wilson shared. "I am . . . about at the end of my patience with Great Britain and the Allies," he wrote House. "This blacklist is the last straw." And to Page, home on vacation from the London embassy, Wilson remarked that earlier public sympathy for England and the Allies "had greatly changed. He saw no one who was not vexed and irritated by the arbitrary English course.[25]

Not loving Germany more but Britain less, Wilson reverted at this time to an attitude close to the impartiality in thought that he had advised in August 1914. He allowed his supporters to campaign for his reelection with the slogan "He kept us out of war," carrying the implication that if reelected he would continue to do so. At the same time, he had permitted himself to be won over to a program of military preparedness for the United States—a program for strengthening and improving the Army and greatly increasing the Navy. The naval increases, for whatever reasons, were not in the small, swift ships that would be effective in combating submarines, but in battleships which might be expected to con-

test control of the seas with the British Grand Fleet. To House, with whom in September the President was discussing British relations, he remarked: "Let us build a navy bigger than hers and do as we please."

A Peace by Compromise or a "Knockout Blow"?

Had the German government continued to act with wisdom and moderation, it might well have capitalized upon Wilson's growing irritation at Great Britian, have insured the continued neutrality of the United States, and have won the war on the European continent. For after the collapse of Russia, which began in March 1917, only the entry of the United States could save the Allies from defeat. Chancellor von Bethmann-Hollweg and other civilian elements in the German government desired to hold to a policy of conciliating the United States, but they were under constant pressure from the military and naval leaders, who wished either to make peace at once on their terms, or else to use the full power of the enlarged fleet of submarines to starve Great Britian into surrender.

Victorious against Russia in the east and against Rumania, which had rashly entered the war, in the Balkans, and holding their own on the western front in France and Belgium, Germany and her allies wished to conclude a peace that would reflect their favorable military situation. Through the fall they urged Wilson, as head of the leading neutral state, to invite the belligerents to a peace conference. When he procrastinated (chiefly, perhaps, because Colonel House opposed his taking such a step without Allied approval), the German government itself announced, December 12, 1916, that it was ready to begin peace negotiations.

In England, where a few months earlier proposals for a compromise peace might have got a hearing, David Lloyd George

[25]Congress empowered the President to retaliate for the British blacklist by refusing clearance to the ships of nations that discriminated against American commerce or to ships that refused to carry the products of blacklisted firms. The authority was not used because of advice from the Department of Commerce that British countermeasures might be disastrous to American industry. Tansill, *America Goes to War*, pp. 535–47; A. S. Link, *Woodrow Wilson and the Progressive Era, 1910–1917* (New York: Harper & Row, Publishers, 1954), pp. 219–22.

had replaced Asquith as Prime Minister, and Lloyd George had declared that only the defeat of Germany by a "knockout blow" could ensure a lasting peace. The Allies, therefore, contemptuously rejected the German invitation. When Wilson, hoping still to find a compromise, asked both sides to state their peace terms, the Central Powers refused, explaining that the proper place for such a statement would be the peace conference that they had suggested. The Allies, on the other hand, named terms so extravagant that only complete victory could have justified them.[26]

Wilson was under no illusions in regard to the probable consequences of the failure of these attempts to end the war. He knew that their failure must lead to resumption by Germany of unrestricted submarine warfare; that in that event he would have no course but to break off diplomatic relations with Germany; that severance of diplomatic relations would almost certainly be but a prelude to war. In his desire to halt this chain of events, the President made one last effort at peace. For months there had been forming in his mind the conception of a league of nations which, when the current war should end, would guarantee the world's peace against future wars.[27] The United States, he believed, should be a participant in such a league, but only if the terms of peace, which the league must guarantee, should conform to American ideals. It now occurred to him, apparently, that an outline of the kind of peace that

America would be willing to support might serve as a basis for negotiations.

Accordingly, in an address to the Senate, January 22, 1917, Wilson undertook to state the conditions under which, as he said, the government of the United States "would feel justified in asking our people to approve its formal and solemn adherence to a League for Peace." His conditions were these: The peace must be "a peace without victory," since a peace forced by the victor upon the vanquished sows the seed of future wars. It must be a peace based upon the equality of rights of all nations, upon the principle of government by the consent of the governed, upon access to the sea for "every great people," upon freedom of the seas, and upon a general reduction of armaments. Here was an unprecedented offer to exert the influence and power of the United States for the maintenance of a just peace if the warring governments would but agree to make one.

The Germans Abandon Moderation

Whatever effect Wilson's pronouncement might have had if made earlier, it came too late to be useful. Three days before it was delivered, Ambassador von Bernstorff had been informed of his government's decision to resume unrestricted submarine warfare beginning February 1. Von Bernstorff, knowing better than his masters in Berlin what American entry into the war would mean, labored during the time that remained to persuade them to reconsider their decision. He had Wilson's promise, he reported, that if Germany would adhere to the *Sussex* pledge and offer reasonable peace terms, Wilson would use whatever pressure he needed to bring the Allies into line. His pleas were unheeded, and on January 31 he carried out his orders by announcing to Lansing that, because Great Britain was continuing her illegal

---

[26]Wilson's biographer, Arthur Link, found evidence that Lansing secretly advised the British and French to name impossible conditions in order to insure the renewal of unrestricted submarine warfare and American participation in the war. Arthur S. Link, *Wilson* [5]: *Campaigns for Progressivism and Peace* (Princeton: Princeton University Press, 1965), pp. 221–25.

[27]Wilson had spoken to this effect at a dinner of the League to Enforce Peace, held in Washington, May 27, 1916. Henry Cabot Lodge spoke on the same occasion and in much the same sense.

practices, Germany would resume the "freedom of action" reserved in the *Sussex* note and beginning the next day, would sink all vessels encountered in the seas adjacent to the British Isles and the coasts of France and Italy. Neutral ships that had set out prior to the notification would be spared, and one American steamer weekly, carrying no contraband and painted with red and white stripes to insure identification, might proceed unmolested from New York to Falmouth, England.

On February 3, 1917, von Bernstorff was given his passports, and Ambassador Gerard was recalled from Berlin. Wilson still hoped to avoid war. The mere breaking of diplomatic relations, he hoped, might deter Germany from actually carrying out her threat. Unlike Lansing, he would, at least at this juncture, have stood aside while Germany won the war, provided only that she refrained from destroying American ships and American lives on the high seas.[28]

But Germany had not been bluffing. Her military masters were confident of crushing England by submarine blockade before the United States could take a telling part in the war. Sinkings began at once. Recalling, perhaps, the "armed neutralities" of days gone by, Wilson asked Congress for the authority to arm American merchantmen against submarine attack and to use "any other instrumentalities or methods" to protect American lives and commerce. In the Senate "a little group of willful men" (Wilson's words) filibustered the bill to death in the closing days of the Sixty-fourth Congress; but upon Lansing's

advice that the necessary authority existed anyway, Wilson announced on March 12 that merchant ships would be provided with guns and gun crews.

In the meantime, February 24, the State Department had received from British Naval Intelligence an intercepted note from Herr Arthur Zimmermann, German Foreign Minister, to the German minister in Mexico, proposing that if the United States went to war, Mexico should ally herself with Germany and seek to persuade Japan (Great Britain's ally!) to do the same. For her cooperation Mexico would be rewarded by restoration of her "lost provinces" of Texas, New Mexico, and Arizona. The Zimmermann proposal, absurd though it was, was no more immoral than the secret treaties by which the Allies had agreed to apportion conquered enemy possessions among themselves. Nevertheless, its publication on March 1 created great indignation in the United States, particularly in the Southwest, where anti-German feeling had so far been at a minimum. It also added to Wilson's distrust of Germany and brought him a step nearer to asking a declaration of war.[29]

On the same day (February 26) on which Wilson had asked for authority to arm merchantmen, it had become known that two American women had died when a German submarine sank the Cunard liner *Laconia*

---

[28]In the hearings on the treaty with Germany in 1919, Wilson was asked: "Do you think that if Germany had committed no act of war or no act of injustice against our citizens that we would have gotten into this war?" He replied: "I do think so." *Peace Treaty Hearings (Senate Document* 106, 66 Congress 1 sess.), p. 536. This later opinion is contradicted by what is known of the attitude of Wilson and the country in general in 1917. See The discussion in Link, *Wilson: Campaigns,* pp. 277–81.

[29]Wilson was particularly indignant at the way in which the note had been sent. Because of British control of the cables, von Bernstorff had been permitted, by a technical violation of neutrality, to communicate with his government in cipher through the State Department and the American embassy in Berlin. Zimmermann's proposal to dismember the United States had been sent through this privileged channel to von Bernstorff in Washington and relayed by him to Minister von Eckhardt in Mexico City. British Intelligence, having possession of the German code, caught the communication from the cable and also as sent by wireless. R. S. Baker, *Woodrow Wilson, Life and Letters,* 8 vols. (Garden City: Doubleday & Company, Inc., 1927–1939), 6: 470–79; Hendrick, *The Life and Letters of Walter H. Page,* 3: chap. 12.

on February 25.[30] When to this act was added the torpedoing on March 18 of three American merchant ships, it became fully apparent that the German submarine campaign was on in deadly earnest, and that neither American lives nor American ships would be spared. For Wilson the only choice was between humiliating retreat and war. He chose the latter. In an address, April 2, 1917, to a special session of Congress, he related the history of the submarine controversy with Germany, denounced the current submarine campaign as "a warfare against mankind" and "war against all nations," and advised Congress to "accept the status of belligerent which has thus been thrust upon it." Going beyond the immediate purpose of defeating Germany, he declared it to be the purpose of the United States "to vindicate the principles of peace and justice . . . and to set up amongst the really free and self-governed peoples of the world such a concert of purpose and of action as will henceforth insure the observance of those principles." And again, in his final paragraph, he declared:

> . . . we shall fight for the things which we have always carried nearest our hearts,—for democracy, for the right of those who submit to authority to have a voice in their own Government, for the rights and liberties of small nations, for a universal dominion of right by such a concert of free peoples as shall bring peace and safety to all nations and make the world itself at last free. . . .

Four days later, April 6, 1917, Congress resolved: "That the state of war between the United States and the Imperial German Government which has been thrust upon the United States is hereby formally declared." The vote was 373 to 50 in the House, 82 to 6 in the Senate. On the same date the President proclaimed the existence of war.[31]

---

[30]Samuel R. Spencer, Jr., *Decision for War, 1917* (Peterborough, N.H.: Richard R. Smith Co., Inc., 1953), chap. 2.

[31]Daniel M. Smith and Joseph M. Siracusa, *The Testing of America: 1914–1915* (St. Louis: Forum Press, 1979), chap. 2.

ADDITIONAL READINGS

BAILEY, THOMAS A. and PAUL B. RYAN, *The Lusitania Disaster: An Episode in Modern Warfare and Diplomacy*. New York: The Free Press, 1975.

LEVIN, N. GORDON, *Woodrow Wilson and World Politics*. New York: Oxford University Press, 1968.

MAY, ERNEST R., *The World War and American Isolation, 1914–1917*. Cambridge: Harvard University Press, 1959.

PENLINGTON, NORMAN, *The Alaska Boundary Dispute: A Critical Appraisal*. New York: McGraw-Hill, 1973.

SMITH, DANIEL M., *The Great Departure: The United States and World War I, 1914–1920*. New York: John Wiley & Sons, Inc., 1965.

14. Peace and Its Aftermath

The United States had quarreled with Germany, not with Germany's allies. Following the declaration of war, however, Austria-Hungary and Turkey broke off diplomatic relations with the United States. Bulgaria did not do so, nor did the United States sever relations with Bulgaria or declare war against Turkey. On December 7, 1917, after the disaster to the Italian Army at Caporetto, Congress declared war against Austria-Hungary upon advice that such action would bolster Italian morale.

With the British and French and their allies and associates in the war, the United States made no treaty of alliance. Its relation to them was described as that of an "associated power." The distinction was not important—a mere gesture out of respect to the American tradition against "entangling alliances"—for no ally could have given more complete military cooperation than did the United States.

President Wilson, in his war message, had indicated the forms that American cooperation might take: "the most liberal financial credits"; "the organization and mobilization of all the material resources of the country"; "the immediate full equipment of the Navy in all respects but particularly in supplying it with the best means of dealing with the enemy's submarines"; "the immediate addition to the armed forces of . . . at least five hundred thousand men, . . . and also the authorization of subsequent additional increments of equal force so soon as they may be needed and can be handled in training." The increments to the armed forces, Wilson added, "should, in my opinion, be chosen upon the principle of universal liability to service."

The program thus outlined by Wilson was the program actually followed, with details taking shape as the war progressed. Credits advanced to the Allied powers, exclusive of reconstruction credits granted after the armistice, totaled over seven billion dollars. The industrial resources of the country were, as never before, channeled into the production of goods needed for winning the war. A War Industries Board, created for the purpose, attained the status of an economic dictatorship. Food, rail transportation, and shipping were similarly controlled for the purpose of meeting most effectively the war-connected needs of the United States and its friends in Europe. American shipyards were mobilized and enlarged to produce replacements for the hundreds of ships sunk by submarine attack. The Navy, shelving temporarily its ambitious big-ship program, devoted itself to the war against the submarine. Destroyers and smaller "submarine-chasers" received priority in construction. An effective convoy system was introduced in cooperation with the British; and in the last year of war a great mine-barrage was laid across the narrows of the North Sea as a barrier to the exit of enemy submarines. The Army grew, with selective service as the chief factor in its increase, from two hundred thousand to four million men, of whom half were in Europe before the fighting ended.

In military policy, the United States threw its influence in favor of a united command over all armies on the western front, which was finally agreed to in the spring of 1918, with the French General Foch as supreme commander. General John J. Pershing, commander of the A.E.F.

(American Expeditionary Force), resisted, with government backing, the Allied demand that American troops be brigaded with British and French. He insisted, at the cost of some delay in getting them into the line, that they be employed as a distinct United States Army, and he had his way. His insistence, also, that the United States Army be trained for open fighting, not merely for trench warfare, paid off when the great German retreat began.

Meantime, American ideas, particularly President Wilson's statements of war aims, were helping to win the war. In the war's closing months, airplanes and balloons dropped 100,000 leaflets daily far behind the German lines. These carried translations of Wilson's Fourteen Points and other addresses, which called for no "unconditional surrender" but stressed his concept of a peace that should be fair and just to all, and his insistence that America's quarrel was with the German government, not with the German people, toward whom, he had said in his war message, "we have no feeling . . . but one of sympathy and friendship." Such propaganda, in the opinion of German military leaders, was effective in shattering the war morale of the German people and in preparing the way for both the German surrender and the Kaiser's abdication.[1]

The military history of the war would be out of place in this narrative. Suffice it to say that the withdrawal of Russia from the war after the Bolshevik revolution of November 1917[2] enabled Germany to shift large forces from the eastern to the western front and to launch a succession of formidable offensives in the spring of 1918. With France and England near exhaustion after almost four years of war, only the timely arrival of American reinforcements prevented a German victory in France. With American aid the German drives were halted, and the last one, launched in July, was turned into a retreat that ended only with the signing of the armistice in November. By mid-August the German high command knew that victory was impossible and awaited only some minor success as an occasion for proposing peace. No minor success occurred. While the German armies were pushed back, Germany's allies were succumbing one by one. Bulgaria surrendered September 29; Turkey, a month later. An Austrian proposal for a peace conference (September 16) was rejected by Wilson, speaking for the Allies. Finally, on October 6 and 7, Germany and Austria-Hungary offered, through the neutral Swiss and Swedish governments, to make peace upon the terms previously set forth by President Wilson. Those terms must now be examined.

Wilson's Peace Program: The Fourteen Points

A few weeks before the United States entered the war, President Wilson had described in brief and general terms the kind of peace which, in his opinion, the American people would support. For many months thereafter, the mobilization of the

---

[1] W. P. Slosson, *The Great Crusade and After, 1914 –1928*, Vol. 12 of *A History of American Life* (New York: The Macmillan Company, 1931), p. 65.

[2] The government of the Czar was overthrown in March 1917 and succeeded by a provisional government representative of middle-class elements and headed by Prince Lvov as Premier and Professor Miliukov as Foreign Minister. These leaders tried to continue the war against Germany, as did the socialist Alexander Kerensky, who in July 1917 replaced Lvov as Premier. War weariness among soldiers, workers, and peasants played into the hands of the Communist, or Bolshevik, leaders, Lenin and Trotsky, who on November 7, 1917, overthrew the provisional government and substituted a government of Soviets (working-class committees) headed by themselves. On December 15, 1917, they signed a military armistice with Germany and on March 3, 1918, agreed to the Treaty of Brest-Litovsk.

war machine absorbed his attention, but before the end of the year he felt that a more explicit statement of war aims was desirable. Such a statement might please liberal opinion in the United States and England and commit the Allied governments to a peace of justice rather than a peace of vengeance. It might win support among liberals and socialists in Germany. Most important, perhaps, it might satisfy the Bolshevik leaders in Russia and possibly dissuade them from making a separate peace with Germany.

Immediately after seizing power on November 7, 1917, the Bolshevik leaders had issued an appeal to all the belligerents to make peace on a basis of universal self-determination, a peace without annexations or indemnities. Only Germany and her allies responded favorably to this proposal, offering the prospect of a separate Russian-German peace. Colonel House, in Europe, tried to persuade the Allied leaders to match the Soviets in an idealistic declaration of war aims, hoping thereby to induce the Russians to adhere to the alliance. When the French and Italian Premiers refused to disavow their nationalistic objectives, Wilson resolved to issue a unilateral statement of the war aims of the United States. This he did in the famous Fourteen Points address to Congress of January 8, 1918.

That the address was aimed particularly at Russia was made clear in the introductory paragraphs. Here the President referred to the negotiations then in progress between the Soviet government and the Central Powers and contrasted the reasonable proposals of the former with the imperialistic demands of the latter. He assured the Russian people of the deep sympathy of the people of the United States. ". . . It is our heartfelt desire and hope," he declared, "that some way may be opened whereby we may be privileged to assist the people of Russia to attain their utmost hope of liberty and ordered peace."

The President then came to his statement of American war aims, the object of which, he said, was "that the world be made fit and safe to live in; and particularly that it be made safe for every peace loving nation. . . ." The Fourteen Points, briefly summarized, comprised: "open covenants of peace, openly arrived at," freedom of the seas, removal of economic barriers, limitation of armaments, recognition of the interests of native populations in the adjustment of colonial claims, evacuation and restoration of Allied territory invaded by the Central Powers, readjustment of the boundaries of Italy, the Balkan States, and Turkey on lines of nationality, an independent Poland, opportunity for autonomous development for the peoples of Austria-Hungary, and the creation of "a general association of nations."

Point 6 dealt with Russia. It called for the evacuation of all occupied Russian territory and a sincere welcome of Russia "into the society of free nations under institutions of her own choosing; . . . The treatment accorded Russia by her sister nations in the months to come," the President continued, "will be the acid test of their good will, of their comprehension of her needs as distinguished from their own interests, and of their intelligent and unselfish sympathy."

Wilson's address had no effect on the Soviet-German peace negotiations. Neither did a speech on February 11, in which he specifically endorsed the Russian peace formula of "no annexations, no contributions, no punitive indemnities," nor a special message of friendship to the Russian people a month later. An armistice had been signed in December, and negotiations proceeded, with several interruptions, until March 3, 1918, when the Russians, in the Treaty of Brest-Litovsk, accepted the harsh German terms. In that document, which the Congress of Soviets ratified on March 15, Russia surrendered title to Finland, the Baltic provinces, Lithuania, Russian Poland, and the Ukraine. Consequently, Russia withdrew from the war, and German armies were shifted westward for the spring offensive in France.

But though Wilson's Fourteen Points failed to achieve their purpose in Russia, they did offer an idealistic peace program and gained for it a worldwide hearing. Because the Allied governments did not at the time repudiate or take exception to them, the Fourteen Points were generally accepted as a statement of the war aims of the Allies. Together with principles stated in several later addresses, they became the basis on which Germany offered to make peace.[3]

The Armistice

President Wilson now took it upon himself (despite objections from overseas) to act as

spokesman for "the principal Allied and Associated Powers" in answering the Austrian and German peace overtures. As far as Austria was concerned, the President replied that the Fourteen Points were no longer wholly applicable. Point 10 had declared for the autonomous development of the peoples of Austria-Hungary, but subsequently the United States had recognized a Czechoslovak National Council as a *de facto* government to the South Slavs under Austrian rule in their aspirations for independence. Hence, said the President, it was for those nationalities, not for him, to say what concessions from the Austro-Hungarian government would satisfy them.

To Germany, Wilson specified the conditions upon which the Allies would be willing to enter into peace negotiations. He insisted upon four things: full acceptance of the Wilsonian terms; complete evacuation of Allied territory; abandonment of illegal practices (obviously referring in part to submarine warfare) on sea and land; assurance that the German government which was to conduct the negotiations should represent the people, not "the military masters and the monarchical autocrats," of Germany. The last stipulation was construed in Germany as requiring the abdication of the Kaiser. This occurred on November 9, 1918, and on the same day there was organized a provisional German People's Government, headed by the socialist deputy, Friedrich Ebert.

In the meantime, Germany had accepted Wilson's other conditions. Then, however, it became apparent that Wilson's idealism had outdistanced the more mundane thinking of his European associates. Not until after a protracted argument and even a threat that the United States might make a separate peace with Germany did Colonel House, representing Wilson in Europe, secure acceptance of the Fourteen Points by the governments of England, France, and Italy. And even then, the acceptance was

---

[3]Scholars have detected thirteen additional or supplementary points in Wilson's addresses of February 11, July 4, and September 27, 1918, but nearly all of these are restatements or generalizations of principles (like that of self-determination) already explicit or implicit in the original fourteen. The following may be considered additions: (1) the renunciation of annexations, contributions, and punitive indemnities, cited above; (2) a statement in the same address (February 11, 1918) that "each part of the final settlement must be based upon . . . such adjustments as are most likely to bring a peace that will be permanent"; (3) a designation as an aim of first importance of "the destruction of every arbitrary power anywhere that can separately, secretly, and of its single choice disturb the peace of the world; or, if it cannot be presently destroyed, at the least its reduction to virtual impotence." Since Germany asked for peace on the basis of the Fourteen Points *and subsequent addresses*, these last two broad statements could be cited to justify the imposition of terms that seemed to conflict with the Fourteen Points. See T. A. Bailey, *Woodrow Wilson and the Lost Peace* (New York: The Macmillan Company, 1944), pp. 297–98. The later addresses are found in R. S. Baker and W. E. Dodds, eds., *The Public Papers of Woodrow Wilson: War and Peace*, 2 vols. (New York: Harper & Row, Publishers, 1927), 1, *passim*.

qualified by two reservations. On Wilson's second point, "freedom of the seas," a phrase open to varied interpretations, they reserved complete freedom of decision. Wilson's statement that territory occupied by the enemy should be "restored" as well as freed, they construed as meaning that Germany must pay compensation "for all damage done to the civilian population of the Allies and their property by the aggression of Germany by land, by sea and from the air." With this second reservation, which was to serve as the basis of the large reparations bill presented to Germany, Wilson indicated his complete agreement. The reply of the Allies, including the reservations, was communicated to the Germans on November 5, and they were informed that Marshal Foch would formulate the military terms of an armistice. These included evacuation of all Allied territory and of the German lands west of the Rhine, and surrender of the German fleet, of heavy military equipment, and of large numbers of locomotives and freight cars. Acceptance of these terms would render Germany incapable of renewing the struggle.

German armies were still intact and held an unbroken line on foreign soil. But morale in both the civilian population and the armed forces had so nearly collapsed—witness a mutiny in the High Seas Fleet at Kiel on November 3—that the high command feared to continue the war. To prevent a destructive invasion of the Fatherland, the German government thus accepted Marshal Foch's terms. In a railway car near Compiègne, which served Foch as headquarters, the German commissioners signed the armistice at 5 A.M., November 11, to become effective six hours later. Austria and Italy had signed an armistice on November 3. The Austrian surrender terms did not, strictly speaking, include the Fourteen Points. Morally, however, Austria was entitled to expect that her peace settlement would conform to Wilson's principles.

Wilson Goes to Paris

Before the signing of the armistice, President Wilson had decided to attend the peace negotiations in person. For this decision he has been much criticized. His critics argue, first, that if he had remained in Washington, at a distance from the angry debates in Paris and immune from the compelling persuasiveness of Lloyd George and Clemenceau, he could have held out for a settlement more in accord with his ideals than that actually reached. They argue, in the second place, that in Washington he would have kept in touch with American opinion and might have avoided the collision with the Senate that in the end undid his work at Paris. Neither point can be proved. There is something to be said for Wilson's evident conviction that only his presence would ensure the acceptance of the kind of treaty that he deemed essential. Lloyd George himself, less than two years previously, had urged: "The President's presence at the peace conference is necessary for the proper organization of the world which must follow peace."[4] But whether Wilson's resolve to attend the conference was wise or mistaken, there is no doubt that he showed poor judgment in selecting the other delegates. The men chosen—House, Lansing, General Tasker H. Bliss, and the diplomat Henry White—were all estimable people, but not one of them possessed the kind of political influence that would be useful in seeing the treaty through the Senate. President McKinley, a smaller man but a wiser politician than Wilson, had named three senators, two Republicans and a Democrat, as members of the commission to make peace with Spain. Thus he not only flattered the *amour propre* of the Senate but also ensured bipartisan support for the treaty in that body. Wilson took no senator to Paris,

---

[4]*Foreign Relations, 1917, Supplement 1,* p. 44.

and the only Republican among the delegates was Henry White, a career diplomat who did not count in Republican politics.

Wilson's failure to make a bid for Republican support was particularly imprudent, for the Senate that would pass upon the treaty would be controlled by a Republican majority. Just before the congressional elections of 1918, Wilson had appealed to the electorate to return Democratic majorities in House and Senate in order that he might, as he said, "continue to be your unembarrassed spokesman in affairs at home and abroad." The appeal had failed. Not only did the voters elect Republican majorities in both houses of Congress; Wilson's appeal, at a time when Republicans had supported the war as loyally as Democrats (though they had begun to attack his peace program), offended the party leaders and made it certain that they would view critically any treaty that Wilson might lay before the Senate.[5]

Under these circumstances Wilson would have been well advised to include at least one prominent Republican on his peace commission. Henry Cabot Lodge would, after March 4, 1919, become chairman of the Senate Committee on Foreign Relations. He would have been, for this reason, the logical choice. But if Wilson found Lodge objectionable, Elihu Root, William H. Taft, and Charles Evans Hughes were all prominent Republicans who sympathized generally with Wilson's program for a peace settlement and a league of nations.

Politically, then, the American delegation was weak. The fact that its members lacked detailed knowledge of the intricate problems facing them was not a serious deficiency, for the commission was to have the advice of a group of experts—historians, economists, bankers, geographers, ethnologists—who had been brought together at the insistence of Colonel House. Though Wilson made less use of their advice than he might have done, the members of "The Inquiry" (as the group was called) won the hearty respect of their British opposite numbers and, in collaboration with the experts of other nationalities, actually wrote the less controversial portions of the treaty with Germany.[6]

Could Wilson Put Over His Program?

Wilson's grand purposes at Paris were two: (1) a peace settlement of justice, based, with respect to territorial adjustments, upon the principle of self-determination—a settlement that would leave no sores to serve as centers of infection productive of future wars; (2) the creation of a league of nations to ensure preservation of peace, the covenant of the league to be an integral part of the peace treaties, so that no government could participate in the peace settlement without becoming a member of the league. Adherence to the principles of the Fourteen Points, Wilson believed, would accomplish these objectives.

Wilson had advantages on his side but serious obstacles in his path. His chief advantage was the extraordinary position of moral leadership to which he had risen. His eloquent statements of idealistic war aims had made him a hero to liberals everywhere and had led war-weary or oppressed populations throughout the world to hail him as their deliverer. This moral leadership was fated to decline as ideals were forced to

[5] A factor in the Democratic defeat in 1918 may have been Wilson's consent to parley with the Germans when there was a popular hue and cry for an "On to Berlin" policy. Bailey, *Wilson and the Lost Peace,* pp. 40–41. The defeat has generally been ascribed more to domestic issues. See Selig Adler, "The Congressional Election of 1918," *South Atlantic Quarterly,* 36 (1937), 447–65.

[6] L. E. Gelfand, *The Inquiry: American Preparation for Peace, 1917–1919* (New Haven: Yale University Press, 1963).

compromise with practical considerations and as the aspirations of different national groups—such as Italians and Yugoslavs—proved to be mutually incompatible.

One obstacle to a Wilsonian peace was the group of secret treaties and agreements that the Allies had made among themselves before the United States entered the war. Thus France had been promised by Russia, although not by Great Britain, not only the return of Alsace-Lorraine, but also possession of the Saar Valley and the conversion of German territory west of the Rhine into an independent "buffer state." Italy had been assured of large accessions of Austrian territory in the Trentino or southern Tyrol and about the head of the Adriatic; and Japan had been promised the German islands in the North Pacific and the inheritance of German rights in Shantung. Russia also had been promised Constantinople and other Turkish territory, and still other portions of the Ottoman Empire had been apportioned prospectively among France, Great Britain, Italy, and Greece. The Russian claims were renounced by the Bolshevik government. The other Allies pushed their claims with varying degrees of persistence. The French and Italian claims in Europe and Japan's claim to Shantung were destined to give Wilson more headaches than any other problem of the Conference. The claims derived from the secret treaties conflicted with the principle of self-determination and specifically with Wilson's declaration (February 11, 1918) that "peoples and provinces are not to be bartered about from sovereignty to sovereignty as if they were mere chattels and pawns in a game."[7]

[7]The texts of most of the secret agreements are found in H. W. V. Temperley, ed., *A History of the Peace Conference of Paris,* 6 vols. (London: Henry Frowde and Hodder & Stoughton, Ltd., 1920–1924), *passim.* Most of them were first published by the Bolshevik government of Russia in December 1917, as illustrative of the crimes of imperialism.

Wilson (despite a later denial before the Senate Committee on Foreign Relations) had certainly known of the existence of these treaties, with the exception of that concerning Shantung, since shortly after the United States entered the war. He had made no effort to have them set aside, and he rejected a French proposal for a conference agenda which stated, among other things, that all secret treaties should be suspended. In the showdown the principle of self-determination was in part sacrificed to claims based on these treaties.

A second obstacle in Wilson's path was the vindictive spirit prevalent among the peoples of the Allied countries, not excluding the United States—a spirit which, for the very reason that these countries were democratic, had to be taken into account. Lloyd George, Clemenceau, and Orlando (the Italian Premier) had all made extravagant promises to their electorates—that Germany should be made to pay for the war, the Kaiser should be hanged, and so forth. Now, often against their better judgment, they were under compulsion to exact the pound of flesh from the prostrate foe. Thus the very democracy that Wilson and Lansing thought a safeguard against war proved to be a barrier to a statesmanlike peace.

Still a third obstacle to Wilson's success was the awareness on the part of the other negotiators that he had been in a manner repudiated in the recent congressional elections. He himself, in his pre-election appeal to the voters, had warned: "The return of a Republican majority to either house of the Congress would . . . be interpreted on the other side of the water as a repudiation of my leadership." When the election had given majorities in both houses to the Republicans, Theodore Roosevelt exulted in a public statement: "Our allies and our enemies and Mr. Wilson himself should all understand that Mr. Wilson has no authority whatever to speak for the American people at this time." Under analogous circumstances, Lloyd George or Clemenceau or Orlando would have had to resign his premiership. In their eyes Wilson's loss of the election inevitably lessened his bargaining power.

Treaty of Versailles

President Wilson arrived in Paris on December 13, 1918, but not until the following January 12 did the representatives of the great powers hold their first formal meeting. Since November 1917, the British, French, and Italian Prime Ministers, with the occasional attendance of Colonel House representing President Wilson, had exercised direction of the war as the Supreme War Council. Now the three Prime Ministers—Lloyd George, Clemenceau, and Orlando—President Wilson, and the ranking Japanese delegate, representing the "Big Five" powers, took full charge of the Conference and assumed authority to make all crucial decisions. They determined what states should be represented, the number of delegates allowed to each, and the makeup of the commissions that did the bulk of the work of the Conference.

The Problem of Russia

The Conference comprised the representatives of the thirty-two "allied and associated powers," including the four British dominions and India. Neither the enemy states nor the neutrals had been invited to send delegates, nor had the Bolshevik (or Soviet) government of Russia. None of the states represented at the Conference had recognized that government. France, in particular, held that in making a separate peace with Germany the Soviet leaders had betrayed their allies and had forfeited any right to be represented at the general peacemaking. Wilson's plea in the Fourteen Points for a generous treatment of Russia did not, apparently, comprehend Russia's

current rulers. Both he and Lloyd George, however, believed that the Russian people should be represented at a conference that was to remake the map of Europe, but since Russia was still in the throes of civil war between "Reds" and "Whites," there was no government or party that could speak for the Russian people as a whole.

At Wilson's suggestion, the Conference leaders proposed that all contending Russian factions agree to a cease-fire and send representatives to the island of Prinkipo in the Sea of Marmara to confer with one another and with spokesmen for the Allies and the United States. There was a faint hope that in this way the civil war might be ended, extremist positions moderated, and a delegation representing all Russian factions might be sent to Paris. The plan collapsed, despite qualified Soviet acceptance, when the chief "White" leaders (with French encouragement) refused to cooperate. Later an American secret mission to Russia, approved by Lloyd George and headed by William C. Bullitt, brought back a conciliatory offer from Lenin. News of the mission, meanwhile, had leaked to the press and caused such a furor in conservative quarters that Lloyd George repudiated it, and Wilson refused even to see Bullitt when he returned to Paris.[8]

Soviet Russia, therefore, remained without visible representation at the Peace Conference. The threat of Bolshevism, however, was always present, like Banquo's ghost at the feast, and influenced in various ways the decisions of the Allied statesmen.[9]

[8]G. F. Kennan, *Russia and the West under Lenin and Stalin* (Boston: Little, Brown and Company, 1961), chap. 9.

[9]This thesis is expounded in great detail in A. J. Mayer, *Politics and Diplomacy of Peacemaking: Containment and Counterrevolution at Versailles, 1918–1919* (New York: Alfred A. Knopf, Inc., 1967), and more briefly, with specific reference to American policy in N. G. Levin, Jr., *Woodrow Wilson and World Politics: American Response to War and Revolution* (New York: Oxford University Press, 1968). Levin depicts Wilson's policy as a conscious attempt to steer a middle course between revolution and reaction.

So far as their very limited resources permitted, the British and French gave aid to anti-Bolshevik Russian generals—Denikin in the South, Kolchak in Siberia. They had persuaded President Wilson in July 1918, after months of resistance, to consent to the landing of American troops at Archangel on the White Sea, and, with Japanese contingents, at Vladivostok, in Eastern Siberia. The Allies clearly hoped to use these troops in the fight against Bolshevism but were blocked by Wilson's stipulation that the American forces were to take no part in the contest between Russian factions.[10]

All such attempts at military counter-revolution were destined to failure, as was an American plan to bribe the Soviets into virtual surrender by providing food for the Russian people, reduced as they were to near starvation. As hope for destruction or subversion of the Soviet regime faded, the conservative Allied statesmen in Paris fell back upon "containment" as a second choice. Reliable anti-Communist governments of old and new nations in Eastern Europe—Rumania, Poland, Czechoslovakia—were strengthened by material aid and accessions of territory in order to form a *cordon sanitaire* on Russia's western border.

The problems arising from the prevalence of Communism in Russia and threats of its raising its head elsewhere in Eastern Europe (for example, the short-lived regime of the Communist Béla Kun in Hungary, March to August 1919) were distracting but did not prevent the Conference from getting on with its other work. The Conference held a number of plenary sessions—ten from January to June—but these meetings were mainly ceremonial and served to rubber-stamp decisions already reached by the delegates of the Big Five powers. These, at the beginning of the

Conference, began holding sessions as the so-called Council of Ten, comprising the heads of government and foreign ministers of Britain, France, Italy, and the United States and two of the Japanese delegates. This group became the dominating committee of the Conference and so remained until the latter part of March, when it was replaced by a still smaller group, the Council of Four—Wilson and the three prime ministers, Lloyd George, Clemenceau, and Orlando. During several weeks in April and May, while Orlando was sulking in Italy, the Council of Four became a Council of Three. All crucial questions affecting Europe were decided, up to the signing of the treaty with Germany, by these three or four statesmen. The great bulk of the detailed and routine work of the Conference, however, was done by commissions, composed of delegates and expert advisers. Fifty-two such commissions were organized, and it was they who actually wrote most of the treaty with Germany, subject always to the final decision of the Ten or the Four.

Until sometime in the spring, it was quite generally assumed that the Conference then in session was preliminary; that it would be followed by one in which the defeated powers would be permitted to negotiate, as the French had done at Vienna after the downfall of Napoleon, and perhaps would be allowed to mitigate some of the harsher features of the treaty. Such plans were laid aside. There was no second conference and no negotiation. The victors wrote the treaty and summoned the vanquished to sign on the bottom line.

Wilson's Great Victory— The League of Nations

Wilson's most conspicuous success at the Conference was the adoption of the Covenant of the League of Nations and the decision that it should be made an integral part of each peace treaty. Wilson himself

---

[10]The contention of Levin, *Wilson and World Politics*, pp. 197 ff., that Wilson, contrary to the plain meaning of his words, intended that American troops should be used against the Bolshevik government is doubtful.

was chairman, and Colonel House, a member of the commission, appointed to draft the Covenant. The commission held ten sessions, from the third to the thirteenth of February, and on the fourteenth presented to a plenary session of the Conference the document which, with a few changes, became the Covenant of the League.

With this initial triumph in his pocket, Wilson boarded the steamer *George Washington* to return to the United States, where his presence was necessary at the end of the congressional session, March 4. Supporters and opponents of the League of Nations idea were already busy in the United States. In the Senate, where any treaty must run the gauntlet, partisan opposition was developing, joining hands with opposition that was honestly isolationist. Wilson, having "sold" his plan in Paris, must now attempt to convince his own countrymen.

At Colonel House's suggestion, Wilson had invited the members of the Senate Foreign Relations and House Foreign Affairs Committees to meet with him for discussion of the League Covenant. They dined at the White House (Senators Borah and Fall declining) on February 26. Wilson defended his pet project but won no converts among the doubters. A few hours before Congress adjourned, Senator Lodge read in the Senate a statement signed by thirty-seven Republican senators or senators-elect, declaring that "the constitution of the league of nations in the form now proposed . . . should not be accepted by the United States"; that peace with Germany should be made as soon as possible "and that the proposal for a league of nations to insure the permanent peace of the world should then be taken up for careful and serious consideration."

This famous "Round Robin," signed by four more senators than were needed to block a treaty,[11] Wilson met first by de-

[11]Really six more, for two additional senators signed later.

fiance and later by an attempt at conciliation. In a speech at the Metropolitan Opera House, New York, just before heading back to Paris, he told his opponents that when his work was done, the treaty of peace would be tied with so many threads to the League Covenant that it would be impossible to separate them. It did not occur to him, apparently, that such organic union might result, not in acceptance of the Covenant, but in rejection of the treaty.

On the advice, however, of both Democratic and Republican friends of the League—the latter group including ex-President Taft and President Lowell of Harvard—who warned that without some changes the Covenant would never receive Senate approval, Wilson reconvened the League of Nations Commission and asked that the Covenant be amended. The changes deemed essential to insure Senate approval were four: (1) recognition of the right of members to withdraw from the League; (2) exemption of domestic questions (such as tariff and immigration) from League jurisdiction; (3) a statement that no member would be required, against its will, to accept a mandate over a former enemy colony; (4) a declaration safeguarding the Monroe Doctrine.

On two of these proposed changes—the right of withdrawal and the Monroe Doctrine—Wilson met stiff opposition, particularly from the French delegates, who argued that these changes would weaken the protection that France expected from the League. France, Great Britain, Italy, and Japan all tried to exact *quids pro quo* for their consent to the American amendments. France asked for an international general staff to direct action against new aggressions. Great Britain (outside the League Commission) demanded that the United States give up its ambitious naval building program. Italy stepped up its insistence that its new boundaries include Fiume, a city and port on the Adriatic. Japan revived a proposal, made and discarded earlier, for a recognition of racial equality in the Preamble of the Covenant. After many days of apparent deadlock, Wilson secured the desired amendments without accepting the changes in the Covenant proposed by others. There is no doubt, however, that he paid in concessions in other matters for the acquiescence of his colleagues in his embarrassed effort to placate the United States Senate, or that his insistence upon what appeared to be special privileges for the United States weakened his moral position at Paris. The amended Covenant was adopted at a plenary session of the Conference on April 28.

The Peace and the Fourteen Points

In Wilson's mind the making of the League of Nations was the most important item in the peace settlement. To get the Covenant adopted, incorporated in the treaties with Germany and the other enemy states, and accepted by the very principal Allied governments was an achievement so precious that he was willing to pay for it with concessions in other matters—concessions that in many cases contravened the principles of the Fourteen Points. What did some injustices here and there in boundaries or other particulars matter if the world had, in the League, machinery to prevent war and to correct wrongs by peaceful process? So the Fourteen Points, though not forgotten, were sometimes stretched till they were hardly recognizable. It would be a great mistake, however, to conclude that Wilson yielded on everything except the League. The surprising fact is not that he compromised on some points but that he saved as much of his program as he did.

Apart from the League Covenant, the fruits of Wilson's efforts at Paris may best be estimated by comparing the terms of the peace settlement with the ideals set forth in the Fourteen Points and later addresses.

Wilson was successful in gaining assurances that hereafter international engagements would be "open covenants," as provided by the first of the Fourteen Points.

Article 18 of the League Covenant required that every treaty or international engagement thereafter entered into by any member of the League be registered with the League Secretariat and published as soon as possible. No treaty should be binding unless so registered. By Article 20 all engagements inconsistent with the terms of the Covenant were declared abrogated.[12]

Of point 2, "freedom of the seas," upon which the Allies had reserved freedom of decision, nothing further was heard. Nor was any step taken to implement point 3, removal of economic barriers, beyond the innocuous promise in Article 23 of the Covenant that members of the League would make provision to secure and maintain "equitable treatment for the commerce of all Members of the League."

The Covenant, in Article 8, recognized the necessity for the reduction of armaments (point 4) in the interest of peace and charged the Council of the League with formulating plans for such reduction. But members of the League were not obliged to accept such plans, and in the practice, no armaments were limited except those of the enemy states.

Point 5 had called for "a free, open-minded, and absolutely impartial adjustment of all colonial claims," with a view to the interests of the colonial populations no less than to the rights of the claimants. How was this principle to be applied to the former German colonies in Africa and the Pacific, all of which had been conquered during the war, and to the non-Turkish parts of the Ottoman Empire, which had been occupied by the Allied armies?

Had the precedents of the past and the secret understandings of wartime been followed, these areas would simply have been

[12]The phrase "openly arrived at" in point 1 of the Fourteen "was not meant to exclude confidential diplomatic negotiations involving delicate matters. The intention is that nothing which occurs in the course of such confidential negotiations shall be binding unless it appears in the final covenant made public to the world." *Foreign Relations*, 1918, Supplement 1, I, 405.

annexed by the conquerors, and this was what at least some of the conquerors desired. Such a solution, however, would have violated the spirit of point 5 and would have made ridiculous the professions of high moral purpose by the Allies and the United States. The dilemma was solved by the system of mandates, devised chiefly by one of the American experts, Professor G. L. Beer, and persuasively sponsored by Prime Minister Jan Christiaan Smuts of South Africa. As embodied in Article 22 of the Covenant, it provided that colonies and territories which had been detached by the war from the states that formerly governed them, and which were not prepared for self-government, should be placed under the tutelage of advanced nations which were both competent and willing to undertake the responsibility. The nations accepting such assignments, or "mandates," should exercise authority on behalf of the League and should report annually to an organ of the League, a permanent Mandates Commission.

Wilson had hoped to see the mandates assigned to small neutral countries like Switzerland and the states of Scandinavia. In practice they were given to the victorious Allies—the United Kingdom, the British Dominions, France, Belgium, and Japan—a distribution closely following the provisions of the secret understandings. Different mandatory powers took their obligations with varying degrees of responsibility. That the system was something more than the old imperialism camouflaged is shown by the progress toward, and final attainment of, independence by such of the mandated areas as Iraq, Jordan, Palestine, Syria, and Lebanon, even before the insistent anti-colonial urge of the 1960's.

Japan received the mandate for the former German islands in the North Pacific—the Marshalls, Carolines, and Marianas—but her claim to former German rights in Shantung was not thus disposed of. In 1915, as a feature of the Twenty-One Demands, Japan had forced China to agree in advance to any cession of rights that Japan might exact from Germany at the close of the war. Later she secured British and French promises to support her claim. China, asserting that her promise had been made under duress, now demanded the return to her of all German rights, privileges, and property in Shantung. Wilson was eager to restore to China what German imperialism had wrested from her, but Lloyd George and Clemenceau backed the Japanese claim. Japan played her trump card in a threat that unless humored in Shantung, she would not join the League of Nations. To this menace Wilson yielded. The treaty assigned to Japan the German rights in Shantung, but Wilson did receive from the Japanese their pledge that they would "hand back the Shantung Peninsula in full sovereignty to China retaining only the economic privileges granted to Germany and the right to establish a settlement . . . at Tsingtao."[13] This compromise, though probably representing the greatest concession that Japan could have been induced to make, was rejected by the Chinese delegation, which refused on that account to sign the treaty. Its unpopularity in the United States became one obstacle to approval of the treaty by the Senate.[14]

Self-Determination—for Friends but Not Always for Foes

Wilson's points 6 to 13 were concerned principally with the "restoration" of terri-

[13]R. H. Fifield, *Woodrow Wilson and the Far East: The Diplomacy of the Shantung Question* (New York: Thomas Y. Crowell Company, 1952), treats the subject in great detail. Japan actually returned Shantung to Chinese sovereignty and renounced preferential rights in the province after the Washington Conference of 1921–1922. Japan failed in her attempt to insert in the League Covenant a declaration against racial discrimination.

[14]China became a member of the League of Nations by signing the treaty with Austria.

tory occupied by the enemy and the re-drawing of national boundaries along lines of nationality or self-determination. In this respect the peace settlement registered some significant achievements but also some unfortunate surrenders. (Point 6, on Russia, had presumably been rendered invalid by Russia's defection from the alliance.) Alsace-Lorraine was restored to France. The new states of Poland, Czechoslovakia, and Yugoslavia emerged from the breakup of Austria-Hungary and also from the detaching of Polish territory from Germany and Russia. Germany ceded to Denmark, Belgium, and Czechoslovakia small areas inhabited chiefly by people of those nationalities. Austria and Hungary were separated, and Transylvania was taken from Hungary and added to racially kindred Rumania. These were but the more significant of the changes in the European map made in response to the demands of nationalism. In the Near East, the Arab portions of the Ottoman Empire became independent (like Saudi Arabia) or were put on the road to independence under the mandate system. All this was in accord with the Fourteen Points.

The same can be said of Wilson's unyielding resistance to Italian demands for Fiume and French demands for German territory west of the Rhine. The city of Fiume on the Adriatic had a population more than half Italian, but its hinterland was Slavic and it was the natural outlet to the sea for both Yugoslavia and Austria. Although the secret treaty of London had not assigned Fiume to Italy, Italy now demanded both Fiume and non-Italian portions of the Dalmatian coast to assure her naval control of the Adriatic. Wilson refused. He even issued an appeal to the Italian people over the heads of the Italian delegates. He continued to refuse when those delegates, Orlando and Sonnino, dramatically left Paris and returned after two weeks during which they were enthusiastically acclaimed by the Italian

people and given a vote of confidence by the Italian parliament.[15]

France, for her part, demanded that the Rhineland (German territory west of the Rhine) be separated from Germany to serve as a buffer state and that the Saar basin, valuable for its coal mines, be annexed to France. These demands (which had been agreed to by Russia in a secret exchange of notes in February 1917) the French attempted to justify on grounds of security, reparation for French coal mines flooded by the German armies, and the fact that France had exercised temporary sovereignty over the Saar a century before. In Wilson's mind, the French proposals were plainly in violation of the principle of self-determination. In a compromise solution, the Rhineland, although remaining under German sovereignty, was demilitarized as was a strip of land fifty kilometers wide east of the Rhine, and as additional security, the Allies were given for a period not to exceed fifteen years bridgeheads east of the river. France received title to the Saar coal mines, and for a fifteen-year period the Saar territory was to be administered by the League of Nations. At the end of that time the inhabitants would determine by plebiscite whether they should rejoin Germany, be annexed to France, or continue under international control.[16]

As a means of inducing the French government to abandon its designs upon the Saar and Rhineland—designs motivated by

---

[15]The question of Fiume was not solved in Paris but was left to Italy and Yugoslavia to settle. In September 1919 the city was seized and occupied for Italy by the Italian poet-adventurer, Gabriele D'Annunzio. Late the following year, Italy and Yugoslavia agreed to recognize it as a "free state," and Italian troops expelled D'Annunzio's filibusters. This arrangement proving unsatisfactory, the two governments in 1924 divided it between them, Fiume proper going to Italy and the adjacent Port Baros to Yugoslavia.

[16]In 1935, after a vigorous campaign of Nazi propaganda, the people of the Saar voted overwhelmingly for reannexation to Germany.

an understandable French concern for military security—Wilson consented to a tripartite agreement by which the United States and Great Britain promised to come to the aid of France if she should again be attacked by Germany. The American treaty was duly sent to the Senate but never reported out of committee.

But if Wilson fought for self-determination on the questions of Fiume and the Rhineland, he surrendered without a struggle in some other cases where that principle was involved. At the opening of the Conference, he promised the Italians the strategic frontier of the Brenner Pass (which they claimed under the secret treaty of London), although that involved surrender by Austria of the South Tyrol or Trentino, populated by over 200,000 Austrian Germans. Likewise, with his consent, Austria with its seven million Germans, a small and feeble country since the destruction of the great empire once ruled from Vienna, was forbidden to unite with Germany. Such a natural solution of its problems was ruled out by French fears of an enlarged Germany. It would be easy to mention numerous other violations of self-determination—always in the interest of the victorious powers. Yet, by and large, self-determination won at Paris. "Many more millions of minority groups were released from alien domination than were consigned to alien domination. The result was the closest approximation that modern Europe has ever had to an ethnographic map coinciding with a political map."[17] Whether or not such an order of things is necessarily good, it was what Wilson aimed at.

Reparations

In the light of subsequent events, it may be that Wilson's most serious failure at Paris

[17]Bailey, *Wilson and the Lost Peace*, p. 316.

was his consent to the reparations clauses of the treaty; for, although these brought little benefit to the victor powers and were in the end largely nullified, they created in Germany a feeling of grave injustice, a sense of grievance that boded ill for the future.

In his speech of February 11, 1918, the President had declared that there should be "no contributions, no punitive damages."[18] This speech was one of the "subsequent addresses" which, with the Fourteen Points, had been accepted as the basis of Germany's surrender. This particular stipulation had been qualified by the Allied reservation that Germany's obligation to "restore" occupied territory was to embrace payment "for all damages done to the civilian population of the Allies and their property by the aggression of Germany by land, by sea and from the air." This phrasing seemed to preclude any attempt to levy the cost of the war upon Germany, but Allied statesmen, particularly the British in the parliamentary election campaign of December 1918, had promised to do just that.

When Wilson rejected "war costs" as contrary to the terms of the armistice, Lloyd George brought forward the specious contention that pensions and separation allowances paid to Allied soldiers and their dependents could properly be classified as "damages done to the civilian population." In British eyes this thesis had the merit not only of doubling the aggregate reparations bill but of substantially increasing Britain's share, since actual damage to British civilian property had been comparatively slight. Wilson allowed himself to be convinced by the British argument, apparently under the impression that inclusion of pen-

[18]The account of the reparations settlement is adapted with slight changes from J. W. Pratt, *Challenge and Rejection: The United States and World Leadership, 1900–1921* (New York), pp. 189–91. Copyright 1967 by The Macmillan Company. Selections from *Challenge and Rejection* reprinted by permission of the publisher.

sions would merely increase the British share of a fixed sum based on calculations of Germany's capacity to pay.

The claim based on pensions and separation allowances was in fact added to claims for other losses. It brought the total reparations bill to a sum far exceeding any reasonable estimate of Germany's capacity to pay, particularly when other features of the treaty deprived her of resources that could have facilitated payment. These included her colonies, most of her merchant marine, German-owned property in Allied countries, the coal of the Saar, the iron ore of Lorraine, and a substantial fraction of both her industrial and her agricultural capacity. Wilson and his American advisers would have preferred to fix the sum to be paid then and there. The Allies, unable to agree on a figure, left it to be determined after the Conference by a Reparations Commission. It was eventually set at $33,000,000,000—thirty-three times the indemnity that Germany had imposed on France in 1871. Though only a small part of it was ever actually paid, the enormous bill left Germany, together with a large body of Western liberal opinion, with a sense of having been double-crossed. This feeling was aggravated by the imposition of the "war guilt" clause (Article 231) of the treaty by which Germany was required to accept for herself and her allies responsibility "for causing all the loss and damage" which the Allies and their nationals had suffered "as a consequence of the war imposed upon them by the aggression of Germany and her allies." This thesis of the exclusive responsibility of the Central Powers for the war may have been generally believed by the men who wrote the treaty. Accepted by the Germans under duress, it was not believed by them and is not sustained by history.

There are two prudent ways, thought Machiavelli, of dealing with a defeated enemy: either destroy him altogether or treat him so generously that he will become your friend. Any middle course is perilous. At Paris, Wilson and the Allies had chosen a middle course.

Germany Accepts

When the delegates of the Allied and Associated Powers had finished their wrangling over the terms of peace, they summoned the Germans to Paris—not to discuss the treaty, but to receive and prepare to sign it. At a plenary session of the Conference on May 7, 1919, Premier Clemenceau, as president of the Conference, handed the lengthy document of 440 articles to the German delegation headed by Count Brockdorff-Rantzau. The Germans received the treaty with a display of sullenness and discourtesy and made their reply on May 29 in a similar spirit. Thereby they injured their own case. Had they shown themselves conciliatory, had they singled out only the worst features of the treaty for criticism, they might have found much sympathy and support among the Allies, for many in the Allied delegations, having at last seen the treaty as a whole, were appalled at its severity. It had been written in sections, with the authors of each section largely in ignorance about the proceedings of others. Some of the commissions, furthermore, had worked with the idea that they were preparing "asking terms," which would be whittled down in negotiation. When the sections were assembled and stamped as final, their combined weight surprised even the authors.

Dissatisfaction with the severity of the treaty was especially strong among members of the British delegation. Had the Germans been good diplomats, they might have divided their opponents and have won large concessions. By their resentful attitude and by making a violent attack on all major features of the treaty, they helped to consolidate the Allied delegations around

Clemenceau, who opposed any substantial moderating of the terms. A few concessions were in fact granted—slight modifications of the boundaries between Germany and Poland and Denmark, agreement that the disposition of a part of Upper Silesia should be decided by plebiscite instead of by outright cession to Poland, better German representation on the commissions that were to control German rivers, and assurance that the limitations of armaments imposed on Germany was "also the first step towards that general reduction and limitation of armaments . . . which it will be one of the first duties of the League of Nations to promote." With such minor changes and assurances as these, the Germans had to be content—unless they preferred to renew the war and have the Allied armies march on Berlin.[19]

On June 23, 1919, an hour and a half before the deadline set for the expiration of the armistice, the Germans accepted the treaty. Formal signature by the delegations of thirty-two governments took place on June 28 in the Hall of Mirrors at Versailles—the hall in which the victorious Prussians had in 1871 proclaimed the establishment of the German Empire.[20]

---

[19]The German counter-proposals and the allied reply are printed in *Foreign Relations of the United States: The Paris Peace Conference,* 13 vols. (Washington, D.C.: Government Printing Office, 1942–1947), 6: 800 ff. See also J. T. Shotwell, *At the Paris Peace Conference* (New York: The Macmillan Company, 1937), chap. 4; Temperley, *A History of the Peace Conference of Paris,* 2: 1–20.

[20]The treaty with Germany took effect—but not for the United States—on January 10, 1920. Treaties with the other Central Powers were signed as follows: with Austria at St. Germain-en-Laye, September 10, 1919; with Bulgaria at Neuilly-sur-Seine, November 27, 1919; with Hungary at the Trianon, June 4, 1920. A treaty with Turkey was signed at Sèvres, August 10, 1920, but the Nationalist revolution in Turkey prevented its taking effect. A treaty with the new Turkish government was signed at Lausanne, July 24, 1923. The United States shared in the negotiation of the treaties with Austria, Bulgaria, and Hungary but they were not sent to the Senate. The United States was not represented at Sèvres. At Lausanne an American "ob-

Just before leaving Paris, President Wilson was asked at a press conference: "Mr. President, do you feel that you achieved here the peace that you expected to make?"

"I think," replied Wilson, "that we have made a better peace than I should have expected when I came here to Paris."[21]

The League of Nations and the Senate

Wilson officially laid the treaty before the Senate on July 10, 1919. To the senators the document was not new. Weeks earlier Senator William E. Borah of Idaho, a leading opponent of the League, had procured a copy with the assistance of a Chicago *Tribune* journalist and had read the long text verbatim into the *Congressional Record,* so that not only senators and members of the House, but any of the public who cared to, might peruse it. The general nature of Part I, the League of Nations Covenant, had been known since February and had been debated by both friends and foes alike. The amendments subsequently added to the Covenant had also been published, and Senator Henry Cabot Lodge, who had rebuffed an inquiry from Delegate Henry White as to what changes would satisfy the Senate, had let it be known that Wilson's changes did not satisfy him. From the time that the Senate met in special session in May, Republican opponents of the treaty in its existing form had been planning strategy. Senator Knox (formerly Taft's Secretary of State) introduced a resolution to separate Covenant from treaty so

---

server" negotiated two separate treaties with Turkey—a general treaty and an extradition treaty. The Senate rejected the former and approved the latter only in 1934, but diplomatic and consular relations with Turkey were re-established by executive agreement in 1927.

[21]*The Autobiography of Lincoln Steffens* (New York: Harcourt, Brace & World, Inc., 1931), pp. 788–89.

that the latter could be approved without accepting the League. A more indirect method was adopted. Senator Lodge, who almost certainly desired to see the treaty defeated despite his protestations to the contrary,[22] believed that sentiment for the League was so strong both in the country and in the Senate that the treaty could not be defeated by direct attack. The course adopted was a dual one: first, to delay action by prolonged hearings and debate, giving pro-League enthusasm time to cool; second, to load the treaty down with amendments or reservations and then count upon Wilson and the Democrats to reject it. Such tactics would appear to shift the responsibility for killing the treaty from its opponents to its friends.[23]

Opposition to the treaty stemmed from varied motives. Sincere isolationists feared the League as a "super-state," which would destroy American independence and drag the United States into quarrels with which it had no concern. A resurgent nationalism saw treason in an attempt to subject the will of the American people to any form or degree of international control. "If the Savior of men," said Senator Borah, "would revisit the earth and declare for a League of Nations, I would be opposed to it." The League, he said, was "the first step in internationalism and the sterilization of nationalism." A western "progressive" in domestic politics, Borah charged that the League was designed as a tool of Wall Street bankers and big businessmen. His feeling was shared by many liberals, former supporters of Wilson, who now attacked him for surrendering his principles and selling

out to British, French, and Japanese "imperialists." Socialists of nearly all varieties would have none of the League because, as they charged, it enthroned capitalism.[24] While liberals and radicals were damning the League as an invention of big business, isolationist Senators Knox and Brandegee were obtaining from millionaires Andrew W. Mellon and Henry Clay Frick funds with which to fight the treaty. The battle made strange bedfellows.

Racial groups in the United States stemming from "oppressed" nationalities to whom the Paris settlement had brought neither independence nor self-determination were bitter against the treaty and the League. Most numerous, best organized, and most influential were the Irish, who through their society, "Friends of Irish Freedom," missed no opportunity to damn Wilson and the League for failing to rescue Ireland from British tyranny. Egyptians and Indians, though not numerous in the United States, found many friends who added their voices to those of Erin. American committees were organized to promote freedom for Korea and for Armenia and other neglected nationalities. Italian-Americans resented Wilson's refusal to give Fiume to Italy. German-Americans, of course, deplored the harsh terms imposed on the fatherland. All these groups gave their support to the senators opposing the treaty.[25]

Partisanship and personal feuds made their contributions to the opposition. Republicans, with an eye on the 1920 campaign, even suspecting that Wilson might run for a third term, were reluctant to place such an impressive achievement as the

[22]H. C. Lodge, *The Senate and the League of Nations* (New York: Charles Scribner's Sons, 1925), p. 209. For an opposite view, see especially D. F. Fleming, *The United States and World Organization, 1920–1933* (New York: Columbia University Press, 1938), pp. 19–25; also D. F. Fleming, *The United States and the League of Nations, 1918–1920* (New York: G. P. Putnam's Sons, 1932), pp. 475–87.

[23]Lodge, *Senate and the League of Nations,* p. 164.

[24]The liberals' break with Wilson is well described in Selig Adler, *The Isolationist Impulse: Its Twentieth Century Reaction* (New York: Abelard-Schulman Limited, 1957), chap. 3. Especially illuminating was the defection of the weekly periodicals *New Republic* and *Nation.* Chapter 5 of the same work describes the resurgence of nationalism.

[25]Adler, *The Isolationist Impulse,* chap. 4.

League in Democratic hands. Senatorial jealousy of the executive, and personal dislike for Wilson on the part of some senators were certainly among the motives that stimulated the fight against the League Covenant and the treaty of which it was a part.

Leader and organizer of the Senate opposition was Senator Henry Cabot Lodge, chairman of the Committee on Foreign Relations in the newly elected Senate, which the Republicans controlled by the slender majority of 49 to 47. Lodge found a complex picture in the Senate. Of the forty-nine Republicans, fifteen were bitter-end opponents of the League—"irreconcilables" they came to be called. They would vote with Lodge for any reservations he cared to propose and at the end would vote against the treaty even with reservations. Thirty-four would vote for reservations of varying degrees of strictness and would vote for the treaty with reservations that suited them. Eight to ten of these were "mild reservationists," though strongly pro-League. About eighteen stood with Lodge for strong reservations or amendments. The remainder were somewhere between these and the "mild reservationists." Lodge's first problem was to unite the Republican majority behind a set of reservations strong enough to "make the League safe for the United States" if the treaty passed, or perhaps strong enough to ensure its defeat by the Democrats. The Senate Democrats, too, were divided. Reed of Missouri voted always with the Republican irreconcilables; Gore of Oklahoma and Shields of Tennessee would support the treaty only with strong reservations. Several others, pro-League but not 100 percent pro-Wilson's Covenant, would support Lodge at least part way. The remaining Democrats were divided about equally between those who insisted on the Covenant as it was and those who would take it either with or without reservations.

An Unsympathetic Committee

The first hurdle for the treaty was the Committee on Foreign Relations. Lodge, the chairman, had seen to it that the committee was "packed" with senators unfriendly to the League. Of the ten Republican members, six—a disproportionately large number—came from the irreconcilable group. They included such redoubtable foes of the League as Borah of Idaho, Knox of Pennsylvania, and Hiram Johnson of California. Two others, Harding of Ohio and New of Indiana, were reliable party men. Only McCumber of North Dakota, among the Republicans, could be described as genuinely pro-League. The seven Democrats on the committee were fairly representative of their party in the Senate; even one of them, Shields of Tennessee, agreed more with Lodge than with Wilson.[26]

Officially printed copies of the treaty were available to the committee on July 14. As a part of the strategy of delay, however, hearings were not begun until July 31. Wilson himself was heard—the committee meeting with him at the White House August 19—as was Secretary Lansing. Lansing, who did not share Wilson's enthusiasm for the League, did not betray his skepticism to the committee; but another witness, William C. Bullitt, bared the rift in the American delegation. Bullitt, one of the "experts" attached to the delegation, had resigned in a huff in Paris. He now voluntarily revealed to the committee a confidential conversation with Lansing, in which the Secretary reportedly had described the League of Nations as "entirely useless" and had added that "if the Senate could only understand what this Treaty means, . . . it would unquestionably be defeated." Though Lansing asserted that his language had been distorted, Bullitt's testimony was

[26]Lodge, *Senate and the League of Nations,* p. 151.

damaging to the chances of the League. So also was much of the other testimony, for the committee heard, for the most part, unfriendly witnesses.

An Appeal to the People

Wilson, in his testimony before the committee, had stated that he would not object to interpretative or clarifying reservations, provided these were not incorporated in the resolution of ratification. If they were so incorporated, he explained (inaccurately), he would have to obtain the consent of the other parties to the treaty before ratification could be completed. It now appeared that the committee, and perhaps the Senate, would insist on much more than the interpretative reservations that Wilson was willing to accept.

Wilson, consequently, resolved to appeal to the country over the heads of the Senate, and, like President Andrew Johnson before him, set out on a "swing around the circle." His tour was routed through the Old Northwest, the Upper Mississippi Valley, and the Far West—the sections that furnished much of the opposition to the treaty. Despite the rather academic and "literary" style of his addresses, Wilson roused much popular enthusiasm with his appeal for a League that should make unnecessary a repetition of recent sacrifices and his warning that failure to make the League work would surely open the way for new aggressions in Europe and new necessity for intervention by the United States. His reception was particularly warm and enthusiastic on the Pacific coast and at his last appearance, in Pueblo, Colorado.

But although Wilson had captivated popular audiences, he had no success in winning the needed senatorial support. His references to his opponents were unconciliatory, tactless, and in some instances offensive. He offered no compromise; the Senate, he said, must take the treaty as it

was or have no treaty at all. Senators who would withhold the support of the United States from the peace organization would be, he said, "absolute, contemptible quitters." Isolationist senators trailed his footsteps, giving their side of the argument to the same public he had addressed. Wilson won no votes in the Senate, and his opponents, if they were changed at all, were more bitterly defiant than before.

Practically speaking, the trip was a failure, ending in personal tragedy. The strain of the effort—the thirty-six formal addresses in addition to numerous "whistle-stop" back-platform speeches, the intense heat without benefit of air conditioning, the unrelenting personal interviews and press conferences—was too much for a constitution already weakened by the long struggle in Paris. After the speech at Pueblo, September 29, Wilson's health gave way. He was rushed back to Washington, a very ill man. A few days later came the paralytic stroke that made him for months an almost helpless invalid and from which he never fully recovered. Secluded from friends and shielded from sound advice by the solicitous Mrs. Wilson, the sick man in the White House clung to his conviction that the treaty must be approved as he had written it or not at all. It would have been far better had he stayed in Washington and continued the effort, begun in July and August, to reach an agreement with the "mild reservationists" and the moderate Republicans.[27]

Senator Lodge's Fourteen Points

Meanwhile, the Foreign Relations Committee had completed hearings on the

[27]Kurt Wimer, "Woodrow Wilson Tries Conciliation: An Effort That Failed," *The Historian,* 25 (August 1963), 419–38. Wilson's speaking tour and its results are well described and appraised in T. A. Bailey, *Woodrow Wilson and the Great Betrayal* (New York: The Macmillan Company, 1945), chaps. 6–7.

treaty, and on September 10 the majority made its first report, proposing forty-five amendments and four reservations. This action was too drastic even for many Republicans. About a dozen of them joined the Democrats in voting down the committee's amendments and others offered from the floor. The idea of amending was given up, and on November 6, Lodge proposed a resolution of advice and consent to ratification subject to fourteen reservations. Of these, twelve were accepted by the Senate and two more added, restoring the number to fourteen. In adopting the reservations, the Republicans held together almost solidly and had the aid of a number of Democratic votes, ranging from four to ten on different reservations.[28]

The substance of the reservations thus adopted may be described without taking them up point by point. The majority of them simply made explicit the retention of powers by the United States or by Congress that under the Covenant could hardly have been denied them. They declared, for example, that the United States should judge, in case it withdrew from the League, whether it had fulfilled its obligations. They reserved to the United States the right to decide what questions were (for it) domestic and hence outside the jurisdiction of the League, and they specified as domestic questions immigration, labor, coastwise traffic, the tariff, commerce, and the suppression of traffic in women and children, and in opium, and other dangerous drugs. They reserved to Congress the right to determine whether the United States should accept a mandate or should participate in the International Labor Organization proposed in Part XIII of the treaty; the right to provide by law for the appointment of United States representatives to the

League, to appropriate funds for the American share of League expense, and to give or withhold assent to interference by the Reparations Commission with trade between the United States and Germany. Such provisions as these were comparatively harmless. Much more controversial were those of Article 10 (the mutual guarantee of independence and territorial integrity), the Monroe Doctrine, the multiple votes of the British Empire, and the Shantung section of the treaty.

The second reservation stated:

> The United States assumes no obligation to preserve the territorial integrity or political independence of any other country or to interfere in controversies between nations— whether members of the league or not— under the provisions of article 10, or to employ the military or naval forces of the United States under any article of the treaty for any purpose, unless in any particular case the Congress, which, under the Constitution, has the sole power to declare war or authorize the employment of the military or naval forces of the United States, shall by act or joint resolution so provide.

The fifth reservation declared that the United States would not submit to arbitration or to inquiry by the Assembly or Council of the League any question that in its judgment depended upon or related to "its long-established policy, commonly known as the Monroe doctrine," and announced further, that that doctrine was "to be interpreted by the United States alone" and was "wholly outside the jurisdiction" of the League.

Reservation 6 withheld the assent of the United States from the Shantung settlement.

Reservation 14, alluding to the fact that the four British dominions and India were to be members of the League, announced that the United States assumed no obligation to be bound by any decision of the Council or Assembly in which "any member

---

[28]On the third reservation, declaring that the United States should accept no mandate without consent of Congress, there was no objection and no record vote. Lodge, *Senate and the League of Nations,* p. 185.

of the league and its self-governing dominions, colonies, or parts of empire, in the aggregate have cast more than one vote"; and furthermore that it assumed no obligation to be bound by a decision "arising out of any dispute between the United States and any member of the league if such member, or any self-governing dominion . . . [etc.] united with it politically has voted."

These four were the reservations most likely to cause trouble. The introductory resolution stated that ratification would not take effect until the reservations had been accepted by an exchange of notes by three of the four "principal allied and associated powers"—Great Britain, France, Italy, and Japan. Would Great Britain accept reservation 14 limiting the voting power of the dominions? Would France, already worried about security, accept the qualification to the guarantees of Article 10? Would Japan ratify the treaty in the face of American refusal to recognize her rights in Shantung? Would any three of them agree to the sweeping reservation on the Monroe Doctrine? But these questions were as yet academic. The immediate problem was whether Wilson and his friends in the Senate would accept the Lodge program. Would the invalid in the White House, despite his defiant utterances on the stump, consent to take half a loaf rather than no bread? Would Democratic senators vote to approve the treaty with the Lodge reservations?

The First Defeat

Wilson was not opposed to all compromise. Before setting out on his speaking tour, he had handed to Senator Gilbert M. Hitchcock, minority leader in the Senate, four reservations that he would be willing to accept if such a course were necessary to get the treaty approved. These dealt with withdrawal from the League, Article 10, the Monroe Doctrine, and domestic questions, and differed from the Lodge reservations on the same points more in wording than in substance. They were so similar to proposals made by the Republican mild reservationists as to suggest that the latter and the Democrats could readily have reached a compromise had Wilson encouraged such an effort. But when, in November, Hitchcock introduced the substance of the Wilson reservations, adding a fifth on the British Empire's six votes,[29] the moderate Republicans had committed themselves to the Lodge program and complained with reason that Hitchcock came late with his appeal for compromise.

This far Wilson was willing to go, but no further. The Lodge reservation on Article 10 he had denounced as "a rejection of the covenant." As the day approached for the vote on the treaty with the fourteen reservations, he wrote from his sickbed to Senator Hitchcock that affirmative action would mean not ratification but "nullification of the treaty." "I trust," he added, "that all true friends of the treaty will refuse to support the Lodge resolution."

Hitchcock and the Democrats heeded the word of their stricken leader. Some of them, perhaps, hoped as he did that defeat of the treaty with the Lodge encumbrances would clear the way for a favorable vote on the treaty without, or with only mild, reservations—a vote in which enough moderate Republicans would join the Democrats to provide the needed two-thirds. And so, on November 19, 1919, all but four of the Democrats joined the Republican irreconcilables to defeat the treaty with the reservations by a vote of 39 to 55. A second vote showed a slight shift, 41 to 50. The Senate refused to reconsider the treaty

[29]Wilson's and Hitchcock's reservations are printed in parallel columns in Bailey, *Wilson and the Great Betrayal*, pp. 393–94. Hitchcock did not reveal the source of the reservations.

with Hitchcock's reservations and then voted down, 38 to 53, a resolution to approve with no reservations. Here all breeds of Republicans (with the sole exception of Senator McCumber) joined against most of the Democrats. Neither with the Lodge reservations, nor without any, could the treaty command a bare majority of the Senate, not to mention the required two-thirds. The Senate adjourned *sine die,* or indefinitely.

The Last Chance

By no means all "true friends of the treaty" favored Wilson's uncompromising course. House (no longer in the President's good graces) had urged compromise. Herbert Hoover, a professed friend of the League, had urged acceptance of the Lodge reservations, as had also the League to Enforce Peace and its president, William H. Taft. When the next session of Congress convened in December, new hopes for compromise arose. At the Jackson Day dinner in Washington, January 8, 1920, William Jennings Bryan told his fellow Democrats that democracy required that the President bow to a majority of the Senate. From across the water came word that Great Britain would welcome American ratification with or without the Lodge reservations, although Viscount (formerly Sir Edward) Grey registered a caveat at the reservation on British Empire voting,[30] and Lloyd George hoped that the other governments might be allowed to consent by silence rather than by affirmation.

But Wilson stood firm. To the same Jackson Day dinner that Bryan addressed, he sent a letter saying that the United States must take the treaty "without changes that alter its meaning, or leave it"; that, if there were any doubt as to what the people of the

country thought on this vital matter, the next presidential election should be made "a great and solemn referendum" in which the people's will could be ascertained.[31] He himself was convinced "that the overwhelming majority of the people of this country desire the ratification of the treaty." Long written pleas from Joseph P. Tumulty, his private secretary, urging that he yield gracefully to the majority opinion in the Senate, either did not reach him—for Mrs. Wilson excluded even the faithful Tumulty from his presence—or, if he saw them, failed to budge him from his position.[32]

Nevertheless, attempts at compromise went on. During the latter half of January 1920, Republican and Democratic senators, including Lodge and Hitchcock, in a series of informal meetings sought to find common ground in a modified set of reservations. Reports from the secret conferences were so optimistic that the irreconcilable senators took alarm. A delegation of them, meeting with Lodge and New (a Republican senator from Indiana) were assured, in Lodge's words, "that there was not the slightest danger of our conceding anything that was essential or that was anything more than a change in wording."[33] The confer-

---

[30]Canada had threatened not to join if her voting rights were in any way restricted.

[31]Prior to writing the Jackson Day letter, Wilson had contemplated challenging the opposition senators to resign and stand for re-election on the League issue, promising that, if a majority of them won, he and Vice President Marshall would resign after making way for one of the opposition (through appointment as Secretary of State) to succeed to the Presidency. Kurt Wimer, "Woodrow Wilson's Plan for a Vote of Confidence," *Pennsylvania History, Quarterly Journal of the Pennsylvania Historical Association,* 28, No. 3 (July 1961), 2–16.

[32]J. M. Blum, *Joe Tumulty and the Wilson Era* (Boston: Houghton Mifflin Company, 1951), pp. 230–39.

[33]Lodge, *Senate and the League of Nations,* p. 194. According to Senator Borah's biographer, Borah and his fellow irreconcilables threatened Lodge with deposition from his post of Republican leader if he compromised with the Democrats. C. O. Johnson, *Borah of Idaho* (New York: Longmans, Green & Company, Inc., 1936), pp. 246–48.

ences reached agreement on some minor points but not on the crucial questions of Article 10 and the Monroe Doctrine. Lodge was a prisoner, more or less willingly, of the irreconcilables; the Democrats, or a goodly number of them, were bound hand and foot by Wilson.

On February 10, 1920, Lodge again reported the treaty to the Senate, with a few changes in the November reservations in conformity with tentative agreements reached in the recent conferences. From then until the middle of March, the Senate went over the old ground, readopting the Lodge reservations with changes that were hardly material. One exception should be made to that statement. The resolution of ratification provided, as Lloyd George had suggested, that failure of the allied and associated powers to object to the reservations should be counted as acceptance. But even this apparent gain was balanced by giving the right of objection to all or any of the allied and associated powers, rather than only to the Big Four, as in the original reservation. In the reservations themselves, it is hard to see any change that could have made them more palatable to Wilson; nor were they made more acceptable by the assertion in reservation 14 that if the British Empire had six votes, the United States should have the same, or by the addition of number 15, introduced by Senator Gerry of Rhode Island and adopted by a close vote. This final reservation, more relevant to domestic politics than to ratification of the treaty, affirmed the Senate's interest in the cause of Irish independence and its hope that, once this independence was achieved, Ireland would be promptly admitted to the League of Nations.

Wilson wrote again on March 8, urging his supporters to defeat ratification on Lodge's terms. On the day of the voting, March 19, 1920, members of his cabinet, according to Lodge, were on the floor of the Senate to hold wavering Democrats in line. Such efforts were successful in defeat-

ing the treaty but not, this time, in maintaining an unbroken Democratic front. The vote stood:

	Ayes	Nays
Republicans	28	12
Democrats	21	23
	49	35

Thus the treaty, with the revamped Lodge reservations, received the votes of a majority of the senators but of fewer than two-thirds of those present. Twenty-one Democrats broke away from administration dictation and voted for ratification. Had only seven of the remaining 23 done likewise, the treaty would have been approved, 56 to 28. Such a result, however, would hardly have changed history,[34] for the ill and stubborn President would almost certainly have refused to ratify the treaty with the reservations that he had repeatedly denounced as nullification. In any event, the treaty was dead. On Lodge's motion, it was returned to the President.

Who Was Responsible?

Defeat of the treaty with the Lodge reservations can unquestionably be laid at the door of President Wilson. But what would have been the situation if Wilson and his supporters had consented to take the treaty in that form? Would the other "allied and associated powers" have accepted the reservations? Would the reservations, if accepted, have impaired the strength of the League?

Considering the second question first,

[34]If the Senate had approved the treaty and Wilson had pigeonholed it, the Republican party would have stood committed to ratification with the Lodge reservations. That this would have meant resubmission, reapproval, and ratification by President Harding is possible but hardly seems probable.

the crucial fact was that the Senate had reserved to the United States Congress the right to decide in each case whether, and how, the United States would assist in carrying out the guarantees under Article 10 and other provisions of the Covenant. Such a reservation certainly raised an element of doubt as to the effective operation of the League's enforcement machinery. But in practice, the right of every member of the League to determine what enforcement action it would take came to be recognized very soon anyway.[35] Thus any weakening of the League that would have resulted from the Senate's reservation on Article 10 came about by other means. It seems fair to say, therefore, that the League would have gained much more from having the United States as a member than it would have lost by accepting the Senate's reservations.

But would the other members of the League have accepted the Senate's reservations? To this question there can be no certain answer. Some of the reservations would certainly have presented difficulties, especially when we bear in mind that the March resolution of advice and consent,

unlike that of November, gave a potential veto to each of the other thirty-one signatories of the treaty. It would have been difficult for Japan to accept the reservation on Shantung; for the Latin American republics to accept that on the Monroe Doctrine; for the British Dominions to agree to the restriction on their voting rights. On the other hand, such was the power, the wealth, and the prestige of the United States that any member of the League that hoped to see the world organization function effectively would perhaps have consented to some sacrifice of pride or "face" in order to assure American participation. In the opinion of T. A. Bailey, a recognized authority on the question, the other governments would have ended by reconciling themselves to the American reservations, perhaps with some adjustments.[36] If not, the responsibility for America's failure to join the League would have rested clearly with them and with the Senate.

It seems in retrospect that the ill and stubborn President made a tragic mistake in holding out for the impossible instead of accepting an available second-best.

---

[35]F. P. Walters, *A History of the League of Nations*, 2 vols. (London: Oxford University Press, 1952), 1: 259.

[36]Bailey, *Wilson and the Great Betrayal*, pp. 281–84.

ADDITIONAL READINGS

BIRDSALL, PAUL, *Versailles Twenty Years After*. New York: Reynal & Company, Inc., 1941.

BONSAL, STEPHEN, *Unfinished Business*. Garden City, N.Y.: Doubleday & Company, Inc., 1944.

BOOTHE, LEON, "Anglo-American Pro-League Groups Lead Wilson, 1915–1918," *Mid-America*, 51 (1969), 92–107.

DUFF, JOHN B., "The Versailles Treaty and the Irish-American," *Journal of American History*, 55 (1968), 582–98.

FERRELL, R.H., "Woodrow Wilson and Open Diplomacy," in G. L. Anderson, *Issues and Conflicts*. Lawrence, Kansas: University of Kansas Press, 1959.

KILLEN, LINDA, "The Search for a Democratic Russia: Bakhmetev and the United States," *Diplomatic History*, 2 (1978), 237–56.

PARSONS, EDWARD, B., *Wilsonian Diplomacy: Allied-American Rivalries in War and Peace*. St. Louis: Forum Press, 1978.

TILLMAN, SETH P., *Anglo-American Relations at the Paris Peace Conference*. Princeton, N.J.: Princeton University Press, 1961.

15. The United States Renounces War but Spurns Peace Machinery

The Senate's rejection of the Treaty of Versailles left the United States still technically at war with Germany. When Congress attempted, by a joint resolution of May 21, 1920, to declare the war with Germany and Austria-Hungary at an end, Wilson vetoed the measure as "an action which would place ineffaceable stain upon the gallantry and honor of the United States." It may be well at this point to round out this phase of the story by recording how the United States finally made peace with its former enemies. An act of Congress of March 3, 1921 made that day the date of expiration of all emergency war legislation. Under the new Republican administration, the joint resolution to terminate the state of war was revived, passed, and signed by President Harding on July 2, 1921. Treaties of peace with Germany, Austria, and Hungary, negotiated by the new administration, were approved by the Senate on October 18, 1921. All were ratified and proclaimed before the end of the year. The treaties reserved to the United States, in accordance with the terms of the joint resolution of July 2, all the rights to which it would have been entitled under the treaties of Versailles, St. Germain, and Trianon, while relieving it of all the responsibilities it would have assumed as a party to those treaties. So the United States brought to an inglorious close its crusade in behalf of democracy, international law, and world peace.

The League of Nations in the Campaign of 1920

The events last described took place after the fateful presidential campaign and election of 1920, which must now be considered. Wilson had proposed that the approaching election be made "a great and solemn referendum," in which the voters of the country might declare themselves for or against the League—Wilson's League without paralyzing reservations. It was not possible, of course, to isolate the League issue in the campaign; other questions competed for the voters' attention. Furthermore, the Republican position toward the League was so ambiguous that a vote for the Republican candidate could be counted as a vote either for or against the League.

The Democratic convention took a forthright stand in favor of "immediate ratification of the treaty without reservations that would impair its essential integrity" but disregarded a rather plain hint from the ailing President that he would welcome a renomination and an opportunity to run for a third term with the League as an issue.[1] The nominee, Governor James

[1] J. M. Blum, *Joe Tumulty and the Wilson Era* (Boston: Houghton Mifflin Company, 1951), pp. 239–47; C. W. Stein, *The Third Term Tradition: Its Rise and Collapse in American Politics* (New York: Columbia University Press, 1943), chap. 9; W. M. Bagby, *The Road to Normalcy: The Presidential Campaign and Election of 1920* (Baltimore: The Johns Hopkins Press, 1962).

M. Cox of Ohio, campaigned valiantly for American entry into the League, though suggesting that he would go further than Wilson in the direction of compromise.

The Republican platform declared that the party stood "for agreement among the nations to preserve the peace of the world . . . without the compromise of national independence." It denounced the Covenant signed at Paris as failing "signally to accomplish this great purpose" and commended the senator who had prevented its approval. Threatened with a possible bolt by the irreconcilable minority, the Convention refrained from committing the party to ratification of the treaty with the Lodge reservations. Senator Warren G. Harding, the Republican candidate, had stood with Lodge and had voted for ratification with the Lodge reservations. Early in the campaign he announced that he would support an "association of nations" and added that he would keep the good and reject the bad in Wilson's Covenant. As the campaign progressed, his speeches became more and more anti-League and in a speech at Des Moines, Iowa, October 7, 1920, he said the issue was clear: "In simple words it is that he [Cox] favors going into the Paris League and I favor staying out." It was noticeable that isolationist senators like Borah and Johnson, cool to Harding at first, later came out strongly in his support.

In view of the candidate's anti-League statements, there was cause for surprise when thirty-one prominent pro-League Republicans published, three weeks before election, a statement in support of Harding and the League. The thirty-one, including Elihu Root, Henry L. Stimson, Herbert Hoover, Abbott Lawrence Lowell, and Charles Evans Hughes (soon to be Secretary of State), argued thus: With Harding in the White House, the United States might persuade the other powers to eliminate from the Covenant Article 10, a provision "very objectionable to great numbers of the American people." A Covenant thus modified, the United States could accept.

On the other hand, if Cox were elected and if he held, like Wilson, that Article 10 was "the heart of the Covenant," the deadlock of the previous winter would be repeated.

The perplexed voter who wished to support Harding, therefore, could tell himself either that he was voting with Root and Lowell for American entry into a League without Article 10, or that, with Borah and Johnson, he was voting against American participation in a league of any kind. Under these circumstances there was no justification for interpreting the Republican landslide of November 1920 (16,000,000 for Harding to 9,000,000 for Cox) as a popular mandate against any connection with the League. It was thus interpreted, nevertheless, by the irreconcilables in the Senate and by all opponents of the League, in or out of Congress. Charles Evans Hughes, who became Secretary of State under Harding, hoped at first to carry out the program of the "Thirty-One"—entry into the League without Article 10. But Borah, Johnson, and other isolationist senators threatened, if this were attempted, to retaliate by blocking other parts of the administration's program, and pro-League senators could give no assurance that the Senate would approve a modified Covenant. President Harding decided against making a fight either for the League or for a different "association of nations." He informed Congress, April 12, 1921, that "there will be no betrayal of the deliberate expression of the American people in the recent election . . . the League Covenant can have no sanction by us." Hughes accepted the President's decision. No subsequent administration, Republican or Democratic, attempted to revive the League issue.

Relations of the United States and the League of Nations

The League of Nations became a living organism on January 10, 1920, following the deposit in Paris of the requisite number of ratifications. The United States at this time was represented on the Reparations Commission and was participating in other Allied agencies that would now fall under the aegis of the League. After the Senate's final rejection of the Covenant (March 19, 1920), the Wilson administration withdrew from all association with the League. The American representative on the Reparations Commission was recalled, and the State Department became negligent in replying to communications from the Secretariat or other League organs. This practice continued, apparently unknown to Hughes, for several months after he took office. He then gave orders that League correspondence be treated with ordinary courtesy.

Secretary Hughes did not share, though he did not openly repudiate, the attitude toward the League expressed by George Harvey, the new United States ambassador to Great Britain. Harvey assured a London audience that the United States would not "have anything whatsoever to do with the League or with any commission or committee appointed by or responsible to it, directly or indirectly, openly or furtively." Hughes, on the contrary, attempted to resume official participation in the Reparations Commission and other agencies of the League, but he was blocked by objection from the Senate. That body, now apparently hypnotized by the irreconcilables, approved the separate peace treaty with Germany (October 18, 1921) subject to a reservation declaring that the United States should "not be represented or participate in any body, agency or commission . . . unless and until an Act of the Congress of the United States shall provide for such representation."

Although thus prevented from participating officially in the business of the League, Hughes made increasing use of "unofficial observers," who attended meetings of League commissions and conferences to report their proceedings to Washington. As years passed, the United States, through such "observers" and through conventions signed in common with members of the League, cooperated more and more actively in the social and humanitarian work of the League. It thus took part in the regulation of traffic in opium and other drugs, the suppression of the international white slave traffic, and even in such political matters as the discussion of limitation of armaments. Such cooperation, however, was always with the understanding that the United States assumed no responsibility whatever for the collective security features of the League or for its attempts to settle international disputes. Furthermore, American representatives sat *with*, not *in*, League commissions like those dealing with the opium traffic; they could suggest but, not being members, could not vote. Not until 1934 did the United States officially join the International Labor Organization, which had been set up in pursuance of Part XIII of the Treaty of Versailles. In 1934, also, it finally agreed to submit its treaties to the League Secretariat for registration and publication. The cooperation of the United States with the League in the Manchurian crisis of 1931–1932 will be treated in another place.

The World Court Fulfills an American Dream

No international organization could have been more American in conception or purpose than the Permanent Court of International Justice, or the World Court, as it was usually called. Such a court—a court of law as distinct from a court of arbitration—had been proposed, under instructions from Secretary Hay, by the American delegation at the First Hague Conference in 1899. Secretary Root had repeated the proposal when the Second Hague Conference met in 1907, and that Conference would probably have established such a court if it had been able to find a method of selecting judges that was agreeable to both great and small powers. An international court of justice had been a keystone of the program of the League to Enforce Peace, and Charles Evans Hughes, as the Republican presidential candidate in 1916, had warmly endorsed the idea. Nowhere had the substitution of law for force in international relations had more hopeful advocacy than in the United States.

Of this aspiration the League of Nations Covenant took account in Article 14, which directed the Council to "formulate and submit to the Members of the League for adoption plans for the establishment of a Permanent Court of International Justice." The Council, promptly after its organization, appointed an Advisory Committee of Jurists to formulate plans for the Court and, quite appropriately, named Elihu Root as a member of the Committee. During June and July 1920, the Advisory Committee, meeting at The Hague, drew up a statute for the Court. The statute, amended by the League Assembly, was ratified by the requisite number of members of the League and became effective in September 1921. Judges were elected, rules of procedure were adopted, and on May 12, 1922, the Council declared the Court open to all nations.

Unlike the so-called Hague Court of Arbitration, which was merely a panel of jurists willing to be drawn as arbitrators, the Permanent Court of International Justice was as much a true court as is the Supreme Court of the United States. It was composed of eleven judges and four deputy judges (later, of fifteen judges of equal status) chosen for nine-year terms from a list of nominees presented by the national groups of judges constituting the Hague Court of Arbitration. The problem of election, which had baffled the architects of 1907, was neatly solved through use of the organs of the League of Nations. Election was by majority vote in the Council and Assembly sitting separately. Thus the interests of both great and small powers were safeguarded. No two judges might be of the same nationality.

The jurisdiction of the Court extended to all cases that the parties thereto might refer to it either by special agreement or under general treaties or conventions. By the so-called "optional clause," members *might* agree in advance to refer to the Court any disputes between them which they were unable to settle by diplomacy and which should fall within any of the following categories: (1) interpretation of a treaty; (2) any question of international law; (3) the existence of a fact which, if established, would constitute a breach of such an obligation. The Court was also empowered to give "an advisory opinion upon any dispute or question referred to it by the Council or by the Assembly."

The law to be applied by the Court in making its decisions was to comprise international conventions and custom, general principles of law recognized by civilized nations, judicial decisions, and the opinions of the best authorities on international law. Hearings and arguments before the Court were to be public (unless otherwise by special decision or upon demand of one of the parties). The Court would hold its deliberations in secret. Decisions would be by majority vote, and the basis of the Court's conclusions must be announced. English and French were the official languages of the Court.

Isolationists Block American Participation in the World Court

Although created pursuant to an article of the League Covenant and tied through the process of election to the League organs, the Court owed its legal existence to ratification of the statute by the member states acting individually, and membership in it was open to states not members of the

League. In rejecting the League, therefore, the United States had not debarred itself from participation in the Court, of which it had been the original promoter. Under urging from Secretary Hughes, President Harding on February 24, 1923, sent to the Senate a proposal that the United States adhere to the statute of the Court with four reservations proposed by Hughes. The reservations stipulated: (1) that in joining the Court the United States contracted no legal relationship with the League of Nations; (2) that the United States should participate equally with members of the League in the election of judges; (3) that the United States should pay a fair share of the expenses of the Court, to be determined and appropriated by Congress; (4) that the statute of the Court should not be amended without the consent of the United States.

Unfortunately for the plans of Harding and Hughes, the Senate Foreign Relations Committee, through which any such proposal had to pass, was still dominated by the irreconcilables who had defeated the Treaty of Versailles; for many years they and their equally isolationist successors were able to control it. Lodge, who had practically moved over into the isolationist camp, died in 1924, but his place as chairman was taken by Borah, a man of great integrity but one of the extreme isolationists in the Senate. Such men professed belief in *an* international court of justice but held that the only such court in existence was contaminated by its connection with the League. It was a "League Court" and hence one to be avoided by the United States.

Tactics of delay, which had helped to defeat the League, were again resorted to. Hearings were postponed from time to time. Impractical schemes for divorcing the Court from the League were advanced. Thus action was delayed for nearly three years, and this in spite of evidence of overwhelming popular approval of membership in the Court.

When at last public pressure became too strong to be further withstood, the Foreign Relations Committee reported, and the Senate passed (January 27, 1926), a resolution of adherence to the protocol of the Court, embodying not only the four Hughes reservations but three in addition. One required the consent of the Senate for the submission of any case to the Court. A second reaffirmed the "traditional attitude" of the United States "toward purely American questions." A third, expressing a newly aroused isolationist alarm at one of the functions of the Court, stipulated that the Court should not, without the consent of the United States, "entertain any request for an advisory opinion touching any dispute or question in which the United States has or claims an interest."[2]

The Senate resolution required that this last reservation, as well as the four Hughes reservations, be agreed to individually by all other members of the Court, now forty-eight in number, before the completion of United States ratification. This requirement led to objections, compromise proposals, and more delay, for which the Coolidge and Hoover administrations must share responsibility with isolationist senators. Finally, under a compromise formula devised by Elihu Root and acceptable to other members of the Court, the protocol of adherence came to a vote in the Senate on January 29, 1935. This was the dawn of the neo-isolationism of the 1930's. A veritable storm of adverse propaganda assailed the Senate before the vote, and despite an urgent appeal in behalf of the Court from President Roosevelt, the protocol went down to defeat with 52 votes for to 36 against —a majority but, like the final vote

---

[2] An advisory opinion may be defined as an opinion of the legality or constitutionality of an action that has not yet been taken, as contrasted with a judgment in regard to a completed action. Advisory opinions are not given by the U.S. Supreme Court but are given by the highest courts of a number of States. The United States could not be bound but might be embarrassed by an adivsory opinion of the World Court.

on the Treaty of Versailles, seven votes short of the necessary two-thirds.[3]

The Kellogg-Briand Pact

The decade following its participation in World War I, the United States rejected membership in the League of Nations—the organization through which it might have taken an active part in the promotion of international justice and the preservation of peace. It held for years at arms' length and finally rejected, chiefly because of its connection with the League, the Permanent Court of International Justice, a tribunal embodying an old American ideal and built almost to American specifications. While it rejected these opportunities to work with other nations in the interest of peace, it revived the old habit—possibly to ease a guilty conscience—of signing arbitration treaties qualified by conditions that made them worthless, and concluded a new series of "cooling-off" treaties of the kind dear to Mr. Bryan.[4] It also took a leading,

though at first reluctant, part in promoting the most grandiose project of the period, the Kellogg-Briand Pact, or Pact of Paris, by which it joined the other nations of the world in renouncing war as an instrument of national policy.

In spite of multitudes of such arbitration and conciliation treaties as the United States had sponsored, in spite of the obligation assumed by members of the League to submit disputes between themselves to arbitration or judicial settlement[5], or to study by the Council or the Assembly, the possibility of "legal" war—war not in violation of the Covenant—still remained. The more earnest and idealistic advocates of peace sought means to make all war illegal, to "outlaw war," in the hope that no nation would risk being branded by the rest of mankind as a criminal. Salmon O. Levinson, a Chicago lawyer, became the leading propagandist for the "outlawry of war."[6] He found a convert, surprisingly, in Senator Borah. A foe of all positive collective security measures, Borah was not averse to the plan to call all war, except war in self-defense, illegal. Even less objectionable from Borah's point of view would be a gen-

---

[3]The story of the long fight over the Court is told in D. F. Fleming, *The United States and the World Court* (Garden City, N.Y.: Doubleday & Company, Inc., 1945). Failure of the United States to join the Court did not prevent American jurists from serving as judges. John Bassett Moore, Charles Evans Hughes, Frank B. Kellogg, and Manley O. Hudson were in turn elected to the bench.

[4]Secretaries of State Frank B. Kellogg (1925–1929) and Henry L. Stimson (1929–1933) negotiated sixteen new conciliation treaties on the Bryan pattern. Kellogg replaced Root's arbitration treaties with "Kellogg treaties" and concluded a number of treaties of the latter type with states with which the United States had previously had no arbitration treaties, including new states that had emerged from the war. The Kellogg treaties differed from the Root treaties chiefly in dropping the "vital interests and honor" escape clause and substituting domestic questions and questions involving the Monroe Doctrine. Of these treaties, 27 were in effect by 1936. With the American republics, the United States negotiated multilateral treaties of conciliation (1923 and 1929) and arbitration (1929).

The conciliation treaty was similar to the Bryan bilateral treaties. The arbitration treaty obligated the parties to arbitrate disputes arising from justiciable questions with the exception of (a) domestic questions, (b) questions affecting a state not a party to the treaty. By 1942 the conciliation treaty had been ratified by 18 and the arbitration treaty by 16, of the American republics, including the United States in each case.

[5]The phrase "judicial settlement" was introduced into Articles 12, 13, and 15 of the League Covenant after the World Court had been established.

[6]J. E. Stoner, *S. O. Levinson and the Pact of Paris* (Chicago: University of Chicago Press, 1943). The most authoritative account of the origin of the Pact of Paris is still R. H. Ferrell, *Peace in Their Time; The Origins of the Kellogg-Briand Pact* (New Haven: Yale University Press, 1952). See also D. H. Miller, *The Peace Pact of Paris* (New York: G. P. Putnam's Sons, 1928); J. T. Shotwell, *War as an Instrument of National Policy* (New York: Harcourt, Brace & World, Inc., 1929).

eral renunciation of war—a promise not to resort to it. Levinson, Borah, and others had prepared a partly sympathetic climate in the United States for the proposal that came from Aristide Briand, French Foreign Minister, in the spring of 1927.

Briand's message to the American people, communicated through the Associated Press on April 6, 1927, was inspired by—was in fact written by—Professor James T. Shotwell of Columbia University. A disappointed proponent of American entry into the League of Nations, a believer that civilization and modern war are incompatible, Shotwell took advantage of an interview with Briand to suggest that the latter take a first step toward a general renunciation of war by proposing a treaty renouncing it between France and the United States.

Briand apparently saw in the suggestion a chance to tie the United States even in a negative way, to the system of alliances that France was building as protection against a feared renewal of German aggression— treaties with Belgium, Poland, Czechoslovakia, Rumania, and Yugoslavia. A treaty with the United States mutually renouncing war would at least insure the benevolent neutrality of the United States in a future conflict between France and Germany.[7] Whether that was his purpose or not, Briand chose April 6, the tenth anniversary of the American war against Germany, to publish an open letter to the people of the United States. France, he said, "would be ready publicly to subscribe, with the United States, to any mutual engagement tending, as between those two countries, to 'outlaw war,' to use an American phrase." The signatories to the Covenant of the League of Nations, he continued, were already familiar with the concept of

> the renunciation of war as an instrument of national policy. . . . Any engagement subscribed to in the same spirit by the United States with another nation such as France would greatly contribute in the eyes of the world to broaden and strengthen the foundation upon which the international policy of peace is being raised.

Both Secretary Kellogg and President Coolidge were somewhat annoyed at Briand's disregard of diplomatic niceties in making his appeal to the American people instead of the State Department. They were annoyed also because France at this time was acting uncooperatively in regard to war debts and naval arms limitation. Kellogg, furthermore, was cool to the proposed treaty with a single European state as looking too much like an alliance. He at first ignored Briand's proposal, but under prodding from President Butler of Columbia University,[8] *The New York Times,* and other sources, he finally indicated a willingness to discuss the proposal. Thereupon Briand, on June 20, 1927, handed the United States ambassador in Paris a draft treaty, which supplied the wording for the multilateral pact finally adopted.

For over six months, however, Briand's proposal remained unanswered. Kellogg did not like it, but public opinion, stirred by Briand's friendly appeal and cultivated by Levinson and his circle, demanded that something should be done. Meeting with the Senate Foreign Relations Committee, December 22, 1927, Kellogg learned that the committee would not support the

---

[7]That such was Briand's purpose is the well-reasoned conclusion of R. H. Ferrell in *Peace in Their Time,* especially pp. 73–74. Professor Shotwell, on the other hand, insists that Briand had no such hidden motive.

[8]N. M. Butler, *Across the Busy Years,* 2 vols. (New York: Charles Scribner's Sons, 1930–1940), 2: 202–12. Butler had hitherto ridiculed the "outlawry" idea. Charles A. Lindbergh's dramatic solo flight from New York to Paris, May 20–21, 1927 stimulated popular interest in closer United States-French relations.

proposed treaty if made with France alone but would support it if it were converted into a general multilateral treaty for the renunciation of war.[9] Accordingly, on December 28, he dispatched the latter proposal to France.

Briand was reluctant to accept an arrangement so different from the intimate bilateral treaty that he had proposed, but Kellogg, now grown quite enthusiastic over the plan, pushed it with vigor. Having secured from Briand a tentative acceptance, he invited the governments of Great Britain, Italy, Japan, and Germany to join in the discussions. Agreement was reached in July, and on August 27, 1928, the treaty was ceremoniously signed in Paris by representatives of the six governments already named and of nine others—fifteen in all.[10] The Kellogg-Briand Pact, or Pact of Paris, was thrown open to general signature and was eventually signed and ratified by nearly all the nations of the world. Its signers included Germany, Italy, Japan, and the Soviet Union. It was approved by the Senate with but one dissenting vote and was proclaimed in effect by President Hoover on July 24, 1929.

The essential portions of the Pact are the following:

Article I. The High Contracting Parties solemnly declare in the names of their respective peoples that they condemn recourse to war for the solution of international controversies, and renounce it as an instrument of national policy in their relations with one another.

Article II. The High Contracting Parties agree that the settlement or solution of all

disputes or conflicts of whatever origin they may be, which may arise among them, shall never be sought except by pacific means.

The Senate approved the Pact without reservation. Secretary Kellogg had said, in fact, that he would have no "reservations," although he did not object to "qualifications" or "interpretations." Of these there had been a number. The French had made it plain, with Kellogg's consent, that the Pact did not prohibit wars of self-defense or wars in pursuance of France's obligations under the League Covenant, the Locarno treaties, or her postwar treaties of alliance, and that breach of the Pact by one party would release others from its obligations. Kellogg had not objected when Sir Austen Chamberlain, speaking for the British government, pointed out that

there are certain regions of the world the welfare and integrity of which constitute the special and vital interest for our peace and safety. His Majesty's Government have been at pains to make it clear in the past that interference with these regions cannot be suffered. Their protection against attack is to the British Empire a measure of self-defense. It must be clearly understood that His Majesty's Government in Great Britain accept the new treaty upon the distinct understanding that it does not prejudice their freedom of action in this respect.

Now the Senate Committee on Foreign Relations in reporting the treaty favorably to the Senate, stated its understanding that: (1) the treaty did not impair the right of self-defense, of the necessity of which each nation is the sole judge; (2) since the Monroe Doctrine was an element in American self-defense, the treaty did not rule out armed support of the Monroe Doctrine; (3) the United States assumed no obligation to enforce the treaty against signatories that might violate it—"the treaty does not provide sanctions, express or implied."

[9]There is disagreement as to whether the idea of a multilateral treaty originated in Kellog's mind or was suggested by Senator Borah in the committee hearing, or had still other sources. Apparently the same idea occurred to several people. See Ferrell, *Peace in Their Time*, pp. 138–41, and sources there cited.

[10]The other original signatories were Belgium, Poland, Czechoslovakia, Ireland, India, Canada, Australia, New Zealand, and South Africa.

Though none of these interpretations was attached to the treaty in the form of a reservation, there is no doubt that they determined the meaning of the Pact of Paris,[11] or perhaps, indeed, rendered it meaningless. The latter was the opinion of Senator Carter Glass of Virginia. Though he proposed to vote for its ratification, he said,

> I am not willing that anybody in Virginia shall think that I am simple enough to suppose that it is worth a postage stamp in the direction of accomplishing permanent international peace. . . . it is going [he added] to confuse the minds of many good and pious people who think that peace may be secured by polite professions of neighborly and brotherly love.

The minds of senators were not so confused. Having approved with one dissenting vote (that of Senator John J. Blaine of Wisconsin) the treaty renouncing war, the Senate turned to the next item of business —the appropriation of $270,000,000 for fifteen 10,000-ton cruisers for the United States Navy. The bill was duly passed and signed by President Coolidge within less than a month from the day when he had ratified the Pact of Paris.

The Washington Conference and its Sequel

One notable success in international understanding stands out amid the diplomatic futilities of the 1920's. A nine-power conference in Washington in 1921–1922 disposed, for the time being, a number of troublesome controversies in the Pacific and the Far East and halted a costly and dangerous competition in armaments between the world's three leading naval powers.

[11] Ferrell, *Peace in Their Time*, chap. 13.

Though the United States and Japan had fought on the same side in the recent war, the partnership had been productive of discord rather than concord between them. Japan took early advantage of the war in Europe to press demands upon China that she would have hesitated to make under normal circumstances. In January 1915 she presented secretly her Twenty-one Demands to President Yüan Shih-k'ai. These were arranged in five groups, of which the first four were mainly economic, while the fifth was political and military. Most important in the first category were demands that China agree to Japan's acquisition of German rights in Shantung and grant to Japan new rights of exploitation in Manchuria and adjoining eastern Inner Mongolia. The proposals in Group V would require China to employ Japanese advisers in financial, political, and military matters, to accept joint administration of the police in the principal Chinese cities, to procure munitions in Japan, and to establish a joint Chinese-Japanese arsenal under the direction of Japanese technical experts. Group V, if accepted, would have gone far toward making China a protectorate of Japan.

The Chinese government shrewdly permitted the secret demands to "leak." The European powers were in no position to offer support to China, but from Washington came a warning (May 11, 1915) drafted by Lansing and signed by Secretary of State Bryan, that the United States

> cannot recognize any agreement or undertaking . . . between the Governments of Japan and China, impairing the treaty rights of the United States and its citizens in China, the political or territorial integrity of the Republic of China, or the international policy relative to China commonly known as the open door policy.

As a result of such pressure from the United States and resistance from China,

Japan shelved, temporarily at least, the demands in Group V, while China agreed to most of the others. Japan fortified her position by a secret treaty with Russia in 1916, by which the two powers delimited their spheres of interest in Manchuria and Inner and Outer Mongolia, and by understandings of the next year with Great Britain and France, who agreed to support Japan's claims in Shantung and in the Pacific islands that she had seized from Germany.

The Lansing-Ishii Agreement

After the United States entered the war, Japan sent a special envoy, Viscount Ishii, to Washington to seek an understanding with regard to China. By an exchange of notes (November 2, 1917), known as the Lansing-Ishii agreement, the two governments declared their continued adherence to the policy of respecting the independence and territorial integrity of China and the preservation there of the open door for commerce and industry. These phrases embodied the traditional policy of the United States, but they were preceded by a statement scarcely in harmony with them and giving Japan a reasonably free hand in China.

> The Governments of the United States and Japan [the statement read] recognize that territorial propinquity creates special relations between countries, and consequently the Government of the United States recognizes that Japan has special interests in China, particularly in the part to which her possessions are contiguous.

Even though this declaration was qualified by a secret protocol (not published until 1938) in which the two governments promised that they would "not take advantage of the present conditions to seek special rights or privileges in China which would abridge the rights of the subjects or citizens of other friendly states," the recognition of Japan's "special interests" in China represented a clear retreat for the United States. It is partly to be explained, as are the earlier agreements with Japan on the part of Great Britain, France, and Russia, by discreet hints that Japan, unless treated generously, might desert the allied and associated powers and cast her lot with Germany.[12] China, quite aware of the fact that Japan was being paid in Chinese coin, informed the United States that "the Chinese Government will not allow herself to be bound by any agreement entered into by other nations."

At the Paris Peace Conference, as noted, Wilson reluctantly agreed to the transfer to Japan of Germany rights in Shantung, accompanied by a Japanese promise to restore sovereignty of the province to China. But since China refused to sign the treaty and the United States did not ratify it, the Shantung settlement had the consent of neither government. The Shantung question remained, therefore, as a sore spot in the relations of Japan with both China and the United States.

The Japanese Mandate and Yap

By its failure to ratify the Versailles Treaty the United States had also withheld its assent from the transfer of the former German islands, the Marshalls, Carolines, and Marianas, to Japan as a mandate. These island groups formed a perfect screen between the Hawaiian and Philippine islands and quite surrounded the little American outpost of Guam in the Marianas. That Japan's seizure of them early in the war did not alarm the United States is to be explained, first, by confidence in Japanese assurances that occupation was temporary;

[12]F. W. Iklé, "Japanese-German Peace Negotiations During World War I." *American Historical Review,* 71 (October 1965), 62–76.

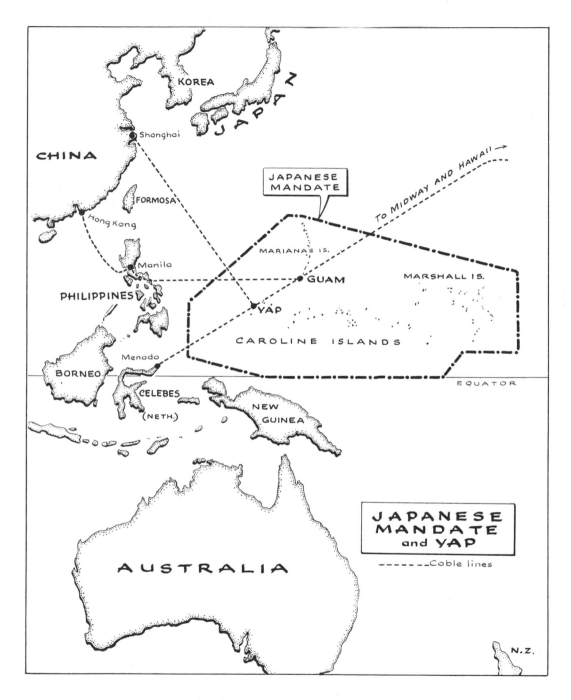

JAPANESE MANDATE

TO MIDWAY AND HAWAII →

KOREA

JAPAN

CHINA

Shanghai

FORMOSA

Hong Kong

Manila

PHILIPPINES

MARIANA'S IS.

GUAM

YAP

MARSHALL IS.

CAROLINE ISLANDS

EQUATOR

BORNEO

Menado

CELEBES
(NETH.)

NEW
GUINEA

**JAPANESE
MANDATE
and YAP**

------- Cable lines

AUSTRALIA

N.Z.

and second, by Wilson's belief that the Philippines were ready for independence and hence that the United States need no longer concern itself over defending them. Before the Peace Conference met, it was evident that Japan intended to keep the islands. Wilson insisted that they should not pass under Japanese sovereignty but acquiesced in Japan's receiving the mandate to administer them.

Wilson did not, however, acquiesce in the inclusion under the mandate of the little island of Yap in the Carolines. Yap was a cable station of importance, the meeting-point of cables from Guam, Shanghai, and Menado in the Dutch East Indies. For the United States it commanded the only cable connection with the Dutch East Indies and the best connection with China.[13]

At Paris Wilson insisted emphatically that Yap must be internationalized. He claimed subsequently that such had been the understanding when the Council of Four gave the mandate for the Carolines to Japan. The Japanese, on the other hand, maintained that Yap was embraced in the mandate, and in this claim they were backed by the British. A heated controversy over the disposition of Yap arose in the closing months of the Wilson administration.

When Secretary Hughes inherited the controversy in March 1921, he broadened it to include the whole question of the islands mandated to Japan. Without the consent of the United States as one of the conquerors of Germany, he argued, German possessions could not be legally disposed of, and that consent could only be given in a treaty properly ratified. Thus Hughes called in question the right of Japan to control, not only Yap but all the mandated islands. The position was a good one for bargaining purposes.[14]

Japanese Imperialism in Siberia

Still another source of friction with Japan was the Japanese occupation of Eastern Siberia and northern Sakhalin. Japanese and American troops had entered Siberia through Vladivostok in 1918, after the Soviets' surrender to Germany. Their ostensible purpose was to guard military supplies (which it was feared might fall into German hands) and to assist in the escape across Siberia of the Czechoslovak legion, a body of troops formerly prisoners of Russia but now liberated and moving along the Trans-Siberian railroad toward Vladivostok. The American troops, in reality, had been sent partly to keep an eye on the Japanese, who were rightly suspected of having imperialistic designs on the mainland. When the ostensible aims had been accomplished, however, the United States troops, commanded by General William S. Graves, were withdrawn (April 1920), but the Japanese, who had far outnumbered the Americans, stayed on. Japanese newspapers began to speak of the Sea of Japan as "the new Inland Sea," and it was evident that Japanese imperialists were intent upon permanent occupation of Eastern Siberia.

Although the United States had not recognized the Russian Soviet government, Secretary Hughes opposed Japanese expansion at the expense of Russia no less than at the expense of China. He warned Japan that the United States would not recognize "any claim or title arising out of the present occupation" nor acquiesce in any action that "might impair existing treaty rights or the political or territorial integrity of Russia."[15]

Three-Cornered Naval Rivalry

Thus in Shantung, in Siberia, in Yap, in the mandated islands, American and Japanese policies were in conflict. Furthermore, despite the promises of the Lansing-Ishii agreement, the menace of Japanese domination still hung over China as a whole; the

[13]R. L. Buell, *The Washington Conference* (New York: Appleton-Century-Crofts, 1922), pp. 52–53.

[14]M. J. Pusey, *Chas. Evans Hughes*, 2 vols. (New York: The Macmillan Company, 1951), 2: chap. 43.

[15]Pusey, *Chas. Evans Hughes*, 2: 524.

fifth group of the Twenty-one Demands had been shelved for the time being but not renounced, and Japanese promises to observe the open door principle in her sphere of interest had been found not wholly dependable. War clouds darkened the relations of the two countries. In 1919 the United States moved the major part of its battle fleet to the Pacific and announced that it would remain there. This move and the American program of naval expansion, initiated in 1916 and resumed at the end of the war, were countered by a new Japanese program calling for a fighting fleet of eight battleships and eight battle cruisers with annual replacements of one ship of each type. Here was naval rivalry that involved not only the United States and Japan but Great Britain also, for Great Britain would not willingly surrender her traditional mastery of the sea, and this mastery was threatened by the naval program of the United States.

The naval expansion bill passed by Congress in 1916 called for an unprecedented amount of naval construction—ten battleships, six battle cruisers, and over one hundred smaller types, to be built over a five-year period. The war with Germany diverted American shipyards from battleship construction to the turning out of destroyers and "sub-chasers" for use against the U-boat, but in July 1918 Congress ordered the resumption of the program of 1916, and later in the year the Navy Department proposed a second five-year plan similar to the first, which would have given the United States a fighting fleet equal to the existing strength of all other navies combined.[16] This prospect naturally alarmed the British, and at the Paris Conference Lloyd George, in return for support of Wilson's amendments to the League

Covenant, received assurances that the President would not push the Navy's second five-year plan. But even at that, England's traditional naval supremacy was threatened and could be maintained, if at all, only by an expensive building program that the British pocketbook could ill afford.

The Anglo-Japanese Alliance

That Americans should feel it necessary to compete, not only with Japan, but also with England in naval building was due to several causes. With Germany removed from the scene, the United States would be England's chief commercial rival, and such rivalry might breed hostility. British attempts to monopolize the petroleum resources of the Middle East were particularly alarming to Navy men. More serious, however, was the continued existence of the Anglo-Japanese alliance. The alliance had been renewed in 1911 for a ten-year period. To placate the United States the British had then inserted a clause to the effect that neither party to the alliance should be obligated to go to war with a third power with which it had "a treaty of general arbitration." This phrase alluded to the "Taft treaty" of arbitration then under negotiation between Great Britain and the United States. Taft's refusal to ratify the amended treaty nullified the escape clause in the alliance, for it was doubtful whether either a "Root treaty" or a "Bryan treaty" could be described as a "treaty of general arbitration."

A possibility existed, therefore, that if friction between the United States and Japan should lead to war, Great Britain might have to side with Japan. This possibility was highly distasteful not only in the United States but in Canada as well. At a British Imperial Conference in London in June 1921, Canadian Prime Minister Arthur Meighen opposed renewal of the Anglo-Japanese alliance, which was due to

---

[16]This program was inspired, at least in part, by the surrender of the German High Seas Fleet to the British and uncertainty as to its future disposition. This particular problem was solved when the German crews scuttled the ships at Scapa Flow in June 1919.

expire that year, and won the Conference to acceptance of his position over the initial opposition of Australia and New Zealand. This move placed Lloyd George in a difficult position. If he were to remain on good terms with Japan, he must find something to offer her as a substitute for the alliance she was asked to give up. Such a substitute could be found, if at all, only through an understanding with the United States in regard to the Far East and the Pacific. A conference for that purpose seemed called for.

Limiting the World's Navies

Already moves were on foot for a conference to end the naval armaments race. In Washington, Congress adjourned in March 1921 without appropriating funds for naval expansion, and the new Congress passed, almost unanimously, a resolution introduced by Senator Borah calling upon the President to invite Great Britain and Japan to a conference on the subject. In England, a spokesman for the Admiralty expressed a willingness to accept naval parity with the United States instead of the "two-power standard" that Britain had long maintained. An exchange of communications between Washington and London, in which the United States, for obvious reasons, proposed including Far Eastern questions in the agenda, enabled President Harding to announce, July 11, 1921, that the powers concerned (Soviet Russia excepted) were being invited to a conference on naval armaments and the Far East, to meet in Washington on the following November 11, Armistice Day. Included, in addition to the United States, the British Empire, and Japan, were France and Italy (naval powers of lesser rank), Portugal, The Netherlands, Belgium, and China, all with interests in the Far East. Sponsors of the Conference hoped to end the threat of a three-power race in naval armaments and, as a means to that end, to compose the disputes in the Far East which stimulated the naval competition. They were, in the short run, highly successful.

Three major treaties and a number of minor treaties and agreements emerged from the Washington Conference, which met from November 11, 1921, to February 6, 1922. Most dramatic was the Five-Power Treaty on naval limitation (signed February 6, 1922), which Secretary of State Hughes and the delegation that he headed steered through the Conference with great skill. Taking as a basis the tonnage of capital ships (battleships and battle cruisers) built and under construction,[17] the American delegation proposed a ratio of 5-5-3 for the United States, Britain, and Japan respectively. All construction (and numerous obsolescent craft) were to be scrapped. At the end of ten years, the parties might begin building replacements for their older ships, but the new battleships were to be limited to 35,000 tons displacement and to mount no guns of more than 16-inch bore. When all older ships had been replaced by the new type prescribed, the United States and Great Britain would each have fifteen battleships of an aggregate 525,000 tons and Japan, nine of 315,000 tons. The much

[17]This basis was chosen as most favorable to the United States. On the basis of complete ships, Great Britain would have had a much larger quota than the United States. On the basis of ships built, building, and projected, Japan would have been only slightly below the United States. G. T. Davis, *A Navy Second to None* (New York: Harcourt, Brace & World, Inc., 1940), pp. 277–78. Other excellent accounts of the Washington Conference are found in Pusey, *Chas. Evans Hughes;* Harold and Margaret Sprout, *Toward a New Order of Sea Power* (Princeton: Princeton University Press, 1940); Buell, *The Washington Conference;* Thomas Buckley, *The United States and the Washington Conference, 1921–1922* (Knoxville: University of Tennessee Press, 1970); Merze Tate, *The United States and Armaments* (Cambridge: Harvard University Press, 1948), chap. 9. The Davis and Tate volumes are also useful for the later conferences described in this chapter.

smaller French and Italian navies would each be limited to five battleships totaling 175,000 tons.

Japan was reluctant to accept a figure less than that of the United States or Britain and consented only when those powers agreed not to build new fortifications or to strengthen those existing in the Western Pacific—west of Hawaii for the United States, north of Singapore for Britain.[18] Japan also agreed not to fortify her outlying possessions, but the ban on American or British bases within thousands of miles of Japan presumably made her militarily the equal of either of the others in the area of her principal concern.

Outside the category of capital ships, only aircraft carriers were limited: 135,000 tons each for the United States and Britain, 81,000 tons for Japan, 60,000 tons each for France and Italy. Carriers were normally not to exceed 27,000 tons displacement, but as an exception to this rule, the United States was permitted to convert into carriers two vessels that had been begun as battle cruisers and that as carriers would displace 33,000 tons each. These ships became the *Lexington* and *Saratoga,* famous flattops of World War II.

Hughes had hoped to limit also the building of smaller types of ships—cruisers, destroyers, and submarines—but met with refusal from France and achieved nothing more than a "qualitative" limitation, stipulating that no cruiser should exceed 10,000 tons in displacement or carry larger than 8-inch guns.

The Five-Power Treaty was to remain in force until December 31, 1936, and there-

after was subject to termination by two years' notice by any one of the signatories.

The Nine-Power Treaty on Policy in China

Signed by all the participating delegations, also on February 6, 1922, the Nine-Power Treaty was something of an achievement for the United States. It gave solemn treaty form for the first time to the traditional policies of the United States with relation to China. The signatories, other than China herself, agreed "to respect the sovereignty, the independence, and the territorial integrity of China," to allow China the fullest opportunity "to develop and maintain for herself an effective and stable government," and to use their influence for establishing and maintaining the open door for commerce and industry throughout China. Borrowing the language of the secret protocol attached to the Lansing-Ishii agreement, Hughes planted it in the new treaty in the pledge of the signatories:

> To refrain from taking advantage of conditions in China in order to seek special rights or privileges which would abridge the rights of subjects or citizens of the friendly States, and from countenancing action inimical to the security of such States.

The signatories, other than China, agreed not to do anything, nor to support their subjects or citizens in doing anything, that would infringe the principles here stated, or that would tend to create spheres of influence or exclusive opportunities in any part of China. China, on her part, agreed not to discriminate in any way between nationals of different countries. Other governments having treaty relations with China and recognized by the signatory powers would be invited to adhere to the treaty.

---

[18]U.S. Military Intelligence had broken the Japanese diplomatic codes and supplied the State Department with translations of confidential messages between Tokyo and the Japanese delegation. Hughes knew, therefore, just how far the Japanese would retreat. H. O. Yardley, *The American Black Chamber* (Indianapolis: The Bobbs-Merrill Company, Inc., 1931), chap. 16.

Ending the Anglo-Japanese Alliance: The Four-Power Treaty

One purpose of the Washington Conference, as indicated, was to terminate the Anglo-Japanese alliance by finding some substitute that would be acceptable to Japan. Hughes had made his dislike of the alliance clear to the British ambassador before the Conference met. Now that Germany and Russia had ceased to be obstacles in Japan's path, he remarked, Americans regarded the alliance as aimed at the United States. The secretary feared, too, that the alliance with Great Britain tended to encourage Japan to undertake imperialist adventures in Asia that she would otherwise avoid. Discussions with Arthur James Balfour, head of the British delegation, led to agreement on a formula proposed by Hughes that was then accepted by Japan, and, at Hughes's suggestion, by France. In a Four-Power Treaty, signed on December 13, 1921, the signatories agreed to respect one another's rights in their Pacific insular possessions, to consult with one another if any controversy should arise between any two of them with respect to such rights, or if such rights should be "threatened by the aggressive action of any other Power." The Anglo-Japanese alliance would terminate upon ratification of the new treaty, which would remain in effect for ten years and thereafter until terminated by any one of the parties giving one year's notice.

For the United States the Four-Power Treaty had a double value: it abrogated the Anglo-Japanese alliance, and it reaffirmed, in treaty form and with British and French endorsement, Japan's promise to respect the United States sovereignty in the Philippines. Of all the Washington treaties, however, it alone met serious opposition in the Senate, where isolationist senators suspected that a commitment to consult implied further obligations. The Senate approved it by a vote of 67 to 27 but only after attaching a reservation asserting that the treaty involved "no commitment to use armed force, no alliance, no obligation to join any defense."

Other Treaties and Understandings

In addition to the Four-Power, Five-Power, and Nine-Power Treaties, the Washington Conference made other contributions to the settlement of Pacific and Far Eastern problems. A treaty between China and Japan (February 4, 1922), negotiated with the assistance of Hughes and Balfour, provided for the restoration of Chinese sovereignty in Shantung, the withdrawal of Japanese troops, and the purchase by China from Japan of the principal railroad in the province. Thus Japan carried out her promise made to President Wilson in Paris in 1919. In a statement to the Conference, the Japanese delegation announced the surrender of special privileges in China obtained under the Twenty-one Demands and abandoned Group Five of those demands, which in 1915 had been "postponed for future negotiations."

A treaty between the United States and Japan (February 11, 1922) assured the United States of free access to the island of Yap for purposes connected with cable and radio communications, rights of residence and property-holding for American citizens, and freedom of cable and radio communications from censorship and taxes. By the same treaty, the United States gave its consent to the exercise by Japan of its mandate over the Caroline, Marshall, and Mariana islands, while Japan promised the United States freedom for missionary enterprise and respect for property rights in the islands and application there of the provisions of existing Japanese-American commercial treaties. Among the stipulations of the mandate, which thus became part of the agreement between Japan and the United States, was Japan's promise that "no military or naval bases shall be established or fortifications erected in the territory." Japan also agreed to submit to the United States a duplicate of each annual report to the League of Nations on the administration of its mandate.

One other subject of friction, the Japanese occupation of Russian territory in Siberia and northern Sakhalin, was not disposed of by treaty, but Baron Shidehara, one of the Japanese delegates, gave assurance, in a speech before the Far Eastern Committee of the Conference, that the Japanese troops would soon be withdrawn. The process was not a rapid one, but the Japanese did in fact evacuate Siberia later in 1922 and northern Sakhalin in 1925.[19]

Work of the Conference Appraised

The Washington Conference was hailed in its own day as a brilliant achievement in American diplomacy. In the short run that acclaim was justified. From the point of view of the national interest alone, the United States gained acceptance by the powers concerned,[20] and for the first time in treaty form, of its traditional policy toward China. It secured the withdrawal of Japan from Shantung and a promise to withdraw from Siberia. It gained assurances of use, on satisfactory terms, of cable and radio facilities on the island of Yap and of freedom of missionary enterprise and most-favored-nation commercial treat-

ment in the remainder of the mandated islands. It acquired naval parity with England, five-to-three naval superiority over Japan, and relief for ten years from the burdens of an expensive competition in capital ships. It effected an easing of tensions with Japan and termination of the objectionable Anglo-Japanese alliance.

These were substantial gains. They were not secured without a price, but the price, measured in realistic terms, appears trifling. The United States agreed to scrap a large number (twenty-eight to be exact) of battleships and battle cruisers, of which the majority were obsolete and the remainder under construction with little prospect that Congress would provide money for their completion. It surrendered the right to improve its position in bases and fortifications in the Philippines and other islands west of Hawaii. But here again, although the right existed on paper, Congress had shown no disposition to exercise it. If the United States erred in limiting its Navy and forgoing the building of bases, if by the two measures combined, it conceded supremacy to Japan in the waters bordering Asia, the fault was that of Congress and public opinion, not of the diplomats in Washington. The price paid by the United States for termination of the Anglo-Japanese alliance was adherence to a consultative pact that entailed no obligation to follow consultation with material of any kind. All things considered, the contemporary impression that Secretary Hughes had served his country well seems quite justified. In the words of one authority writing in the 1930s, "the treaties went as far as pen and ink could go to preserve a peace founded on such antithetical elements as those inherent in the *status quo* of the Far East."[21] Time was to show that pen and ink could not restrain those antithetical elements for more than a decade.

[19]Under pressure from Hughes, but not until more than a year after the Conference, Japan agreed to set aside the Lansing-Ishii agreement of 1917 in which the United States had recognized the "special interest" of Japan in China. J. C. Vinson, "The Annulment of the Lansing-Ishii Agreement," *Pacific Historical Review*, 27 (February 1958), 57–69.

[20]The one exception was Russia, whose Soviet government was not recognized by the participating powers and not invited to send representatives to Washington. The Soviet government resented its exclusion and served notice that it would not be bound by any decision made in its absence.

[21]A. W. Griswold, *The Far Eastern Policy of the United States* (New York: Harcourt, Brace & World, Inc., 1938), p. 331.

The Sequel to Washington

The failure of the Washington Conference to limit the building of auxiliary naval vessels—cruisers, destroyers, and submarines—was not regarded too seriously at the time. The American expectation was that, without express agreement, strength in these categories would be limited in approximately the same ratio as that set for capital ships. But although the United States, where both Congress and President Coolidge were economy-minded, refrained for several years from building new cruisers, both Great Britain and Japan embarked upon building programs in the unrestricted categories. The United States, therefore, found actual parity with Great Britain slipping from its grasp and its superiority over Japan being whittled down. In the hope of correcting this situation by fixing limits for auxiliary craft, President Coolidge invited the other four naval powers to meet in Geneva in the summer of 1927.

The Geneva Conference of 1927 was as conspicuous for its failure as that at Washington had been for its success. France and Italy refused to attend. The American and British delegations were at odds over large versus small cruisers. The United States, which had few naval bases outside home waters, had a preference for 10,000-ton cruisers (armed with 8-inch guns), which had a long cruising radius, and wished to be free to include in its total tonnage as many of this type as it saw fit. The British, on the other hand, with their great network of commercial lanes and strategically placed naval stations in the seven seas, had little need of large cruisers. What they needed was a large number of smaller vessels with guns no larger than 6-inch. They did not wish the United States left free to build a large fleet of big cruisers, whose fighting power, ton for ton, exceeded that of the small ships. They proposed that the number of such ships be limited to fifteen for each navy, the remainder of a suggested total of 600,000 tons to be made up of 6-inch-gun cruisers of not over 7,500 tons displacement. Of the latter, they wanted a larger number than the Americans thought reasonable. What the British really wanted was parity in battle fleets and their essential auxiliaries, and *in addition* enough light cruisers to guard their commerce, whereas the United States insisted on mathematical parity. The Conference adjourned on August 4, 1927, after six weeks of futile argument.

Failure at Geneva and subsequent revelations brought out the fact that elements in the British government, including Winston Churchill, then Chancellor of the Exchequer, were not really willing to concede full naval parity to the United States. The United States, on the other hand, had a growing commerce and no guarantee of neutral rights in future wars. Its naval strategists were intent upon having a navy capable of defending its sea-borne trade against potential belligerent interference from Great Britain. A new acrimony entered British-American relations. President Coolidge, in his 1928 Armistice Day address, complained, alluding to a tentative Anglo-French understanding, that "foreign governments made agreements limiting that class of combat vessels in which we were superior, but refused limitation in the class in which they were superior." He urged the passage of a bill authorizing the building of fifteen 10,000-ton cruisers, which in the last session of Congress the House had passed but the Senate had rejected. The bill was passed and signed in February 1929, a few weeks after the United States, by ratifying the Kellogg-Briand Pact, had "renounced war as an instrument of national policy."

The London Conference of 1930

The inauguration, March 4, 1929, of President Herbert Hoover, who had both a keen desire for peace and an understanding of British problems, was followed within three months by the ousting of the British Conservatives and the installation of a Labour government headed by Ramsay MacDonald. Statesmen on both sides of the water deplored the naval rivalry and asked why British and Americans should build against each other, now especially, when both had subscribed to the Kellogg-Briand Pact. This new spirit quickly dissolved the differences that at Geneva had seemed insoluble. In the fall, MacDonald visited Hoover in the White House and at the President's rural retreat in Virginia. "On a log by the Rapidan," the two statesmen came to a full understanding on the naval problem, and a new conference was called for the following year in London.

At the London Naval Conference of 1930, the American delegation was headed by Secretary of State Henry L. Stimson, who fully shared Hoover's desire for Anglo-American understanding. Anglo-American harmony was restored. France and Italy were again represented. Japan brought an insistent demand for improved ratios in auxiliary vessels.

The dispute that had broken up the Geneva Conference was easily disposed of. The United States had dropped its demand for twenty-one 10,000-ton cruisers. The United States agreed that it might have either eighteen of these and an overall cruiser tonnage some 15,000 tons below Great Britain's, or fifteen of the big cruisers and parity (339,000 tons) with Great Britain in all cruiser categories. A rather complicated formula gave Japan a cruiser strength approximately seventy percent of that of the United States and Great Britain. Destroyer and submarine tonnage was also limited—Japan receiving a 7 to 10 ratio in the former and parity with England and the United States in the latter. Replacement of capital ships, which by the Washington treaty was to begin in 1931, was deferred until 1936, thus saving many millions of dollars for all participants. Of the capital

ships then in commission it was agreed that Great Britain should destroy five, the United States three, and Japan one, leaving capital ship strength at fifteen, fifteen, and nine respectively. France and Italy, being unable to agree on cruiser ratios, accepted only parts of the treaty. An "escalator clause" reserved to the three principal signatories the right to exceed the quotas agreed upon if their security should be threatened by new naval construction by a power not a party to their agreement. The five participants, and later all other important naval powers, agreed that the submarine should in future be used against commerce only in accordance with the rules of international law and humanity. This provision was to be of indefinite duration; other portions of the treaty would expire December 31, 1936.

The End of Naval Limitation

The London Conference of 1930 was the last successful attempt to limit the size of navies by international agreement. The period of peace and comparative harmony following World War I was ended in 1931 by Japanese aggression in Manchuria. Japanese militarists, who had always resented the inferior naval ratios accepted by Japan at Washington and London, gained control of the government. In 1934, Japan served notice that for her the limitations of the Washington and London treaties would terminate December 31, 1936. An attempt to reach agreement was made at another conference in London in 1935–1936, but the Japanese delegation withdrew when British and Americans refused their demand for parity in all categories. The only agreement reached on that occasion was a treaty for "qualitative" limitation between Great Britain, France, and the United States. It placed no limit upon the number of ships in any category but limited the size of battleships to 35,000 tons and the bore of guns to 14 inches instead of the 16 inches allowed by the Washington treaty. It limited the size of other vessels also, declared a six-year holiday in the building of heavy cruisers, and provided for exchange of information regarding any new naval construction. Another "escalator clause" released the signatories from these restrictions upon receipt of evidence that any other power was exceeding the dimensions named.

The Washington Five-Power Treaty, consequently, came to an end on the last day of 1936. Thereafter there was no treaty limit on the number of naval vessels to be built by any government. Rumors that Japan was building 45,000-ton battleships, and the Japanese government's refusal to confirm or deny such reports, led the United States, Great Britain, and France in 1938 to invoke the "escalator clause" of the treaty of 1936. Thereafter,"the sky was the limit" in number, size, and armament of the world's navies.

Economic Foreign Policy
During the Interwar Period

A consequence of the First World War whose significance was little recognized was the sudden transformation of the United States from a debtor to a creditor nation. Like other new countries, the United States had hitherto been consistently a borrower. Its canals, railroads, and industry had been built, in large measure, with capital borrowed in Europe, which it had been enabled to service by an excess of exports over imports. By the end of the century, the United States was also lending or investing money abroad (for example, some $50,000,000 invested in Cuba before 1898), but in 1914 it was still on balance a debtor, owing Europe from 4½ to 5 billion dollars against 2½ billion American dollars invested abroad, chiefly in Canada, Mexico, and Cuba.[22]

[22]B. H. Williams, *The Economic Foreign Policy of the United States* (New York: McGraw-Hill Book Company, 1929), p. 17.

Early in the war large quantities of American securities held abroad were sold in New York in order to finance purchases of American war materials by the Allied governments. By the fall of 1915, those governments found it necessary to float a bond issue of $500,000,000 in the United States through the agency of J. P. Morgan and Company, and such borrowings continued until the United States entered the war. The role of lender was then assumed by the United States government, which advanced to friendly governments over 7 billion dollars before the armistice of November 11, 1918, and 3¼ billions in subsequent months. Without counting interest, therefore, the United States government at the close of the war was a creditor of its wartime associates to the extent of $10,350,000,000. The war also, although it impoverished Europe, brought sudden wealth to the United States and thereby created a large fund of surplus capital ready to seek investment abroad. By 1928 private investments in foreign lands totaled between 11½ and 13½ billions of dollars. Deducting the still-existing American indebtedness to foreign investors, we find the United States, ten years after the armistice, a net creditor, on both public and private account, to the extent of well over 20 billion dollars.

Acceptance of the new creditor role should have entailed changes in policy, especially tariff policy, which American statesmenship proved incapable of making. But before considering this problem of adjustment, it will be well to glance at the American attitude toward the war debts and toward investment in and trade with foreign countries.

Settling the War Debts

The 10⅓ billion dollars advanced by the United States to friendly governments during and immediately after the war had unquestionably been regarded as loans by both lender and receivers. In the United States Congress, it is true, a few voices were raised in support of the thesis that the advances should be viewed simply as part of America's contribution to the war, as a means of enabling others to do what, for the moment, the United States could not do with its own Army and Navy. There were warnings, too, of the ill will that might result from an American effort to collect the debts from governments which the war would leave close to bankruptcy. But such pleas and warnings went almost unnoticed, and President Wilson and his advisers rebuffed all proposals for cancellation of the debts or for discussing them at the Paris Peace Conference.[23]

In June 1921 President Harding proposed that Congress empower the Secretary of the Treasury to negotiate with the debtor governments adjustments of the war debts as to terms, interest rates, and dates of maturity. Congress responded by an act (February 9, 1922) creating the World War Foreign Debt Commission with the Secretary of the Treasury as chairman, and authorizing it to negotiate settlements upon terms defined by the act. No portion of any debt might be cancelled; the interest rate must not be less than 4¼ percent; nor the date of maturity later than 1947. The commission found no debtor government willing to settle on these difficult terms. The procedure it adopted, therefore, was

to make with each debtor the best terms possible (taking into account in the later settlements "capacity to pay") and then to ask Congress in each case to approve the departure from the formula originally prescribed.

In this way, between May 1923 and May 1926, the World War Foreign Debt Commission negotiated settlements with thirteen governments. Settlements with Austria and Greece were later made by the Treasury Department. With the exception of Austria, which received special treatment, all the settlements provided for annual payments over sixty-two years. In theory, no part of the principal (which included accrued interest to the date of settlement) was cancelled; in practice, the rates of interest were so adjusted downward that varying portions of the debts were actually forgiven. Comparing the total amounts to be paid under the settlements with the amounts that would have been paid at the interest rate of 4¼ percent originally prescribed by Congress, we find effective cancellations ranging from 19.3 percent for Finland and 19.7 percent for Great Britain to 52.8 percent for France and 75.4 percent for Italy. The amounts of the principal funded, the rates of interest to be paid, and the portions of the debts that were, in effect, cancelled, are shown in the table on p. 290.

The Reparations Problem

Throughout the debt settlement negotiations, the European debtor governments argued that payments on the debts should be dependent upon the collection of reparations from Germany. The United States refused consistently to recognize any relation between the two transactions. In American eyes, the Allied governments that had borrowed from the United States—had "hired the money," as President Coolidge put it—were under obliga-

[23]Great Britain, which had loaned to its allies more than it had borrowed from the United States, and which had cancelled debts owed to it at the close of the Napoleonic wars, suggested twice in 1920 a general cancellation of inter-Allied debts in the interest of European recovery. The British were advised that neither Congress nor public opinion in the United States would sanction cancellation in whole or in part. The United States, it was pointed out, had gained no territory or other advantages from the war, and the American taxpayer would not willingly shoulder the burden of paying off the Allied indebtedness. H. G. Moulton and Leo Pasvolsky, *War Debts and World Prosperity* (Washington: Brookings Institution, 1932), pp. 52–70.

Country	Principal	Rate of Interest	Percentage of Cancellation
Austria	$ 24,614,885	—	70.5
Belgium	417,780,000	1.8	53.5
Czechoslovakia	115,000,000	3.3	25.7
Esthonia	13,830,000	3.3	19.5
Finland	9,000,000	3.3	19.3
France	4,025,000,000	1.6	52.8
Great Britain	4,600,000,000	3.3	19.7
Greece	32,467,000	0.3	67.3
Hungary	1,939,000	3.3	19.6
Italy	2,042,000,000	0.4	75.4
Latvia	5,775,000	3.3	19.3
Lithuania	6,030,000	3.3	20.1
Poland	178,560,000	3.3	19.5
Rumania	44,590,000	3.3	25.1
Yugoslavia	62,850,000	1.0	69.7
Total	$11,579,435,885		

tion to repay their borrowings without regard to what they might be able to collect from Germany. In actual fact, however, it was obvious that the ability of the Allied governments to pay their debts would be affected by their success or failure in collecting reparations, and the United States took a sympathetic attitude toward efforts to solve the reparations problem.

The Peace Conference had left to the Reparations Commission the determination of the amount to be paid by Germany. In May 1921 the Commission set the figure at 132 billion marks, or approximately 33 billion dollars. Germany accepted the figure under threat of occupation of additional German territory. Annual payments of a minimum of 2 billion marks were to begin at once, later payments to be adjusted in the light of estimates of capacity to pay and evaluation of payments in kind already made.

Within fifteen months of the settlement, Germany was in default on the required payments, whether willfully or through inability to meet the schedules. Over British objection (backed by that of the American observer) the Reparations Commission authorized occupation of the great German industrial area of the Ruhr. French and

Belgian armies carried out the mandate in January 1923 and held the Ruhr till September 1924. Germany met the occupation with passive resistance. The German economy suffered a prolonged and disastrous inflation. Reparations payments stopped entirely.

In the meantime, Secretary of State Hughes (in an address to the American Historical Association in New Haven, December 29, 1922) had proposed that a committee of experts study Germany's capacity to pay and devise a plan to facilitate payments. Late in 1923 all the governments concerned agreed to the suggestion, and the Reparations Commission appointed two committees to study different aspects of the problem. One of the committes was headed by the Chicago banker, Charles G. Dawes, and the arrangement adopted is known on that account as the Dawes Plan.

The Dawes Plan, in effect September 1, 1924, was admittedly a temporary expedient, providing a rising scale of reparations payments over a period in which it was hoped the German economic and monetary system could be restored to a healthy condition. Germany received an international loan of $200,000,000. She agreed to make reparations payments beginning at 1 billion gold marks the first year and rising to 2½ billions the fifth year and thereafter. Payments would be made in German currency to an Agent General for Reparations. Thereupon Germany's responsibility would cease. The problem of converting the marks into foreign currencies would be the responsibility of an inter-Allied Transfer Committee. No attempt was made to reassess the total or to set a date for the termination of payments.

During the prosperous years 1924 to 1928, the Dawes Plan worked satisfactorily, and by the latter date, the time appeared ripe for an attempt at a final settlement. A new committee headed by another American, the New York financier Owen D. Young, proposed the Young Plan, which was agreed to by Germany and her creditors in January 1930. By the new arrangement, which was intended to make a final disposition of the reparations problem, Germany agreed to make thirty-seven annual payments averaging a little over $500,000,000 followed by twenty-two annual payments averaging slightly under $400,000,000. By the end of the fifty-nine years, Germany would have paid altogether about 9 billion dollars of principal and 17 billions of interest—a drastic reduction from the 33 billions of principal at first demanded by the Reparations Commission. Furthermore, the Young Plan clearly recognized the relationship between reparations and war debts through a concurrent agreement (not participated in by the United States) that any scaling down of the debts would bring about a corresponding reduction in reparations. The annuities to be distributed under the plan were so proportioned as to cover the war debt payments to be made by the recipients. So long as Germany continued to pay the Young Plan annuities, the debtor governments would have the wherewithal to satisfy their creditors, of whom the chief was Uncle Sam. If general prosperity continued, the plan would be workable.

Emigrant Dollars

No one foresaw, apparently, that Uncle Sam himself would supply a large share of the funds which would be used by Germany to pay reparations and then be the recipient of reparations to pay war debts to the United States. But such was the case. The schedules of both the Dawes and the Young Plans were in theory adjusted to Germany's estimated capacity to pay. But Germany, with her credit established, found it easier to pay by borrowing abroad than out of her own resources. The German government, governments of states and municipalities, and German industry all engaged in borrowing. By purchasing the securities of German government, German municipalities, business enterprises, and the like, American investors, supplied the dollars that the Germans could then use for reparation payments. In the period 1924–1931, while the German government was paying some 2¾ billion dollars in reparations, the same government, local German governments, and industry were borrowing abroad about 4½ billion dollars, of which approximately half came from the United States. In the same years, the United States received some 2 billion dollars in payment on the war debts. Thus the United States government (and in the last analysis, the taxpayer) was receiving indirectly[24] from Germany 2 billion dollars while American investors were supplying Germany with 2¼ billions. Since, after the world economic depression began in 1929, the German securities acquired shrank in value to nearly zero, the American taxpayer was really paid, not without some irony, by the American investor.

The American private funds invested in

[24]The United States received directly from Germany a small amount of reparations—3.2% of the Young Plan payments. The figures here given, translated from marks to dollars, are from Moulton and Pasvolsky, *War Debts,* p. 300.

German securities were but a part of the flood of dollars that went abroad in the 1920's. American dollars were plentiful, and rates of interest obtainable abroad were generally higher than those at home—by 1 or 2 percent, sometimes more. The United States government encouraged such foreign investments or, more accurately, did not discourage them so long as they were not in conflict with some national policy. The State Department, through expressions of disapproval, in effect, vetoed loans to governments unrecognized by the United States, such as that of Soviet Russia. It similarly discouraged loans to France until the French government had agreed to settle its war debt. Although it frowned upon loans for military purposes, it did not obstruct loans designed to enlarge and modernize heavy industry in Germany, Italy, and Japan. Thus, as one writer has phrased it, "our financial mechanism was busily creating future targets for our bombers."[25] But, in general, the American administrations of the 1920s—those of Presidents Harding, Coolidge, and Hoover—regarded foreign lending and investment by the American public as a healthy activity. With such encouragement, American private investments abroad grew mightily, from a mere 2½ billion dollars in 1914 to an estimated 11½ to 13½ billion dollars in 1928. Such investments and loans, like the war debts, were economically sound only if foreign governments and other foreign borrowers could find means to pay the interest on them and over the years to repay the principal. In the long run, they could pay only by exporting their products, or selling their services, to the United States.

Adjusting the Tariff— in the Wrong Direction

It becomes relevant, therefore, to inquire

[25]Herbert Feiss, *The Diplomacy of the Dollar: The First Era, 1919–1932* (Baltimore: The Johns Hopkins Press, 1950), p. 43.

into the attitude of the United States toward the acceptance of foreign goods and services as payment of interest and principal on the war debts and the private investments abroad and in exchange for the goods and services that the United States itself desired to dispose of abroad. In particular, was the United States tariff policy appropriate to a nation that had become a large-scale international creditor?

At this point it may be useful to glance at the course of United States tariff policy since the turn of the century. Traditionally, the Republican party was committed to a high-tariff policy, and the Republicans were in full control of the presidency and Congress from 1897 to 1911. Throughout those years they adhered, with minor exceptions, to their traditional policy. The Dingley tariff of 1897 raised again the protective rates that the Democrats had lowered in 1894. By 1908 popular discontent with rising prices—the "high-cost-of-living"—induced the Republicans in the presidential campaign of that year to promise tariff revision, presumably downward revision. But the Payne-Aldrich tariff, passed in 1909, failed to make significant changes, leaving import duties, on the average, close to what they had been before. The Republicans, in consequence, were charged with repudiating their campaign promises and in the elections of 1910 lost their majority in the House of Representatives. During their years of control the Republicans had made one small breach in the tariff wall through a reciprocity agreement of 1903 with Cuba. Designed primarily to aid the struggling economy of the liberated island, the agreement admitted Cuban products (notably sugar) to the United States at rates of duty 20 percent below the prevailing rates, while American products exported to Cuba received reductions of 20 to 40 percent. Republican Congresses had also instituted free trade with the new territories of Hawaii and Puerto Rico, both of which were brought within the United States tariff wall, and had provided a preferential arrangement, which eventually became full free trade, with the Philippines. Thus the United States failed to practice, in its new possessions, the open door principle that it asked other powers to observe in China.

After the passage of the unpopular Payne-Aldrich tariff, President Taft and Canadian Premier Sir Wilfred Laurier, both in search of means to improve their popularity with their respective electorates, hit upon the old idea of a reciprocal trade agreement between the two countries. The idea was popular in the farm country of the Canadian west, in manufacturing areas in the United States, with American newspapers that wished free importation of wood pulp and pulpwood from Canada, and generally with Democrats, who by tradition and interest looked with favor upon low tariffs. It proved unpopular in the western farm belt of the United States and in the Canadian east. An agreement was signed in January 1911, to be put in effect not by treaty but by concurrent legislation. It provided generally for free trade in raw materials and reduction of duties on a substantial list of manufactured products. President Taft, after many months of effort, and with the support of Democrats and eastern Republicans, got the measure through Congress. In Canada the proposal was attacked less on economic than on nationalistic grounds. Some unfortunate remarks in the United States, especially by Speaker Champ Clark of the House of Representatives and by the Hearst press, had pictured reciprocity as a step toward annexation. Canadian opponents of reciprocity made the most of these slips, warning their countrymen that their status in the British Empire was at stake. From England the imperialist poet Rudyard Kipling warned: "It is her own soul that Canada risks today." Reciprocity became a party issue between Laurier's Liberals and the opposing Conservatives. Sir Wilfred was forced to dissolve Parliament and appeal to the electorate. In the ensuing election the

Conservatives swept the country, and reciprocity was dead.[26]

The Democrats, who in 1912 won the presidency and majorities in both houses of Congress, signalized their victory by passing in 1913 the Underwood tariff, the lowest since the Civil War. Wartime conditions, which followed soon after, made it impossible to estimate the normal results of a low tariff on the national economy. A postwar economic slump and the sweeping Republican victory in the 1920 elections produced an outcry for restoration of high protective duties. An emergency tariff bill was passed in the closing days of the expiring Congress and vetoed by President Wilson in one of his last papers, March 3, 1921. Calling attention to the necessity of accepting the products of Europe if Europe were to settle her debts and to buy from the United States, the President remarked: "Clearly, this is no time for the erection here of high trade barriers."

Wilson's influence was at an end, however, and a few weeks after his veto message, a special session of Congress passed, and President Harding signed (May 27, 1921), an emergency tariff imposing high duties on a number of staple farm products. A year later (September 19, 1922) the President approved the Fordney-McCumber tariff "with rates higher than any in the long series of protective measures of the whole period."[27]

Completely fantastic as the policy of a nation that was seeking to collect its huge debts and to increase its exports, the high

[26]The story of this ill-fated proposal is exhaustively treated in L. E. Ellis, *Reciprocity 1911: A Study in Canadian-American Relations* (New Haven: Yale University Press, 1939).

[27]F. W. Taussig, *The Tariff History of the United States*, 8th ed. (New York: G. P. Putnam's Sons, 1931), chap. 10. Taussig ascribes the postwar revival to protectionism to two causes: (1) a war-induced craving for economic self-sufficiency; (2) a short fall in agricultural prices and a belief, especially in the western states, that higher duties would ensure higher prices. Asking protection for themselves, the western agrarians could not well refuse it to eastern industry.

rates of the tariff of 1922 were immediately less injurious than might have been expected. Their consequence was postponed as long as the United States remained able and willing to loan to foreigners the money that they needed to pay their debts and to purchase American exports. So, during the boom years of the 1920's, the United States continued to insist upon payment of the war debts, to invest in what were assumed to be profitable ventures in foreign countries, to exert every effort for expanding its exports, to enlarge its merchant marine. All these activities logically implied a hospitality to imports from abroad. That such hospitality was belied by contemporary tariff policy was concealed by the piling of foreign loan upon foreign loan.

This process could not go on indefinitely, and a halt came with the stock market crash of October 1929. Easy American money disappeared, practically overnight, and with it vanished the ability of the foreign world to pay its debts to the United States and to buy American products. A lowering of the tariff wall would have been at least a partial remedy. Instead, Congress raised it still higher. Called in special session to pass a tariff for the hard-pressed farmer, Congress got out of hand and in the Hawley-Smoot tariff of 1930 raised rates all across the board. President Hoover approved the bill (June 17, 1930) despite a protest signed by 1028 American economists, pointing out that an increase in rates would impede the export trade, place obstacles in the way of debt collection, incur retaliation in kind from other countries, and create worldwide ill will toward the United States.

All these gloomy predictions were realized. Thirty-four foreign governments lodged official protests against the increase in rates, and many of them followed the American example, raising their own tariff rates or fixing quotas on imports. International trade declined disastrously. There seems no reason to doubt that the American tariff deepened the depression. It helped to raise anew the thorny questions of reparations and war debts.

President Hoover's Moratorium

An already unsound and dangerous economic and financial situation in Europe was aggravated in March 1931 by an announcement that Germany and Austria had agreed to form a customs union. This move was denounced in France as a first step toward *Anschluss*—union of Germany and Austria—which was forbidden by the peace treaties. Eventually the proposed customs union was ruled out by the World Court as contrary to treaty obligations, but in the meantime French banks had brought pressure upon both Germany and Austria by demanding of banks in those countries payment of short-term loans to an estimated amount of three hundred million dollars. "It was the last push against an already tottering economic structure in Europe."[28] The strain was too much for the banks involved. In June the *Creditanstalt*, largest of Austria's private banks, was saved from collapse only by the intervention of the Austrian government. The panic spread to Germany, which seemed again, as in the early 1920s, on the brink of national bankruptcy.

To President Hoover in Washington it appeared that a temporary suspension of the payment of reparations and war debts might alleviate sufficiently the strain on Germany and her neighbors to permit recovery and stave off worldwide financial disaster. After consulting congressional leaders of both parties (Congress not being in session), he announced on June 20, 1931, that (subject to confirmation by Congress)

---

[28] *The Memoirs of Herbert Hoover:* [3] *The Great Depression, 1929–1941* (New York: The Macmillian Company, 1952), p. 62.

the United States would waive all inter-governmental payments during the year beginning July 1 if other governments would do the same. The American people, he said, should "be wise creditors in their own interest and be good neighbors."

Other governments were prompt to accept the proposed moratorium (an agreed-upon period of delay in meeting an obligation). France alone held out for three weeks before consenting, thereby contributing to the closing of practically all banks in Germany and Austria. To Congress, when it met in December 1931, the President recommended approval of the moratorium and also the re-creation of the World War Foreign Debt Commission with authority to re-examine the debt situation and report on it to Congress. Congress gave its consent to the one-year moratorium but refused to call the commission back to life. In fact, it declared it to be "against the policy of Congress that any of the indebtedness of foreign countries to the United States should be in any manner canceled or reduced." Congress expected, in other words, that the regular schedule of payments would be resumed on December 15, 1932, the first payment date after the expiration of the moratorium.

The End of Reparations— and of War Debts

Such optimism proved unfounded. An appeal from Germany for more substantial relief than that afforded by the one-year postponement led to a meeting with her European creditors at Lausanne, Switzerland, in June and July, 1932. It was there agreed that Germany might liquidate her reparations obligation by depositing with the Bank for International Settlements bonds to the amount of three billion gold marks (approximately $715,000,000). The bonds would not bear interest for the first

three years, nor thereafter until sold by the bank. At the end of three years the bank should offer them for sale to the public, and such bonds as proved unsalable on reasonable terms at the end of 15 years would be cancelled.

In thus forgiving nine-tenths or more of Germany's remaining reparations bill, the European governments expected to get corresponding relief from their own creditors. Ratification of the Lausanne agreement was in fact made contingent upon the securing of such relief. This meant, of course, that the United States, as the end creditor, was invited to bear the principal cost of the cancellation of reparations. But Congress had already shown that it was in no mood to consent to even partial cancellation. President Hoover was more aware than Congress of the realities of the situation. He feared that by insisting on all, the United States might lose all. He sought in vain the support of President-elect Roosevelt, victor in the November 1932 election, in a second effort to persuade Congress to reconstitute the War Debt Commission. Congress would do nothing, and the President had no choice but to send to the debtor governments notices of the payments due December 15. Most of the debtors paid on this occasion, but thereafter, with the exception of Finland (which had a small debt and an export surplus which provided her with dollar exchange), none of them made more than token payments. Even these ceased after the Attorney General of the United States ruled that token payments did not save the debtor governments from being held in default.

For all practical purposes, therefore, payments both on reparations and on war debts (Finland's excepted) came to an end with the Hoover moratorium. Payments that had not been too burdensome in prosperous times and with the aid of American loans became too much for human nature to bear in the depths of the great depression. The United States, by its tariff policy, had doubtless contributed to the difficulty, but Congress, unconscious of any responsibility in the matter, proceeded to "punish" the recalcitrant debtors. By the Johnson Act of April 13, 1934 (sponsored by isolationist Senator Hiram Johnson of California) it forbade within the jurisdiction of the United States the making of loans, by sale of securities or in any other way, to any government which was in default upon its debts to the United States. The Johnson Act stimulated no resumption of debt payments but added appreciably to the stock of international ill will. It seems safe to say that both the United States and the world at large would have been better off if the former had consented in the beginning to consider its loans in the light of contributions to the common war effort.

President Roosevelt Torpedoes the World Economic Conference

Before the end of the Hoover administration the United States had joined in plans for a World Economic Conference, to meet in London for a concerted attack on the worldwide depression. A commission of experts appointed to prepare the agenda of the conference found that barriers to trade, the failure to reach agreement on the war debts, the cessation of foreign loans, and the departure of some governments—notably the British—from the gold standard, all contributed to the prolongation of the depression, and that each of these factors aggravated the others. The best hope for recovery, the commission believed, lay in a concerted international attempt to remove or alleviate these malign influences, not singly but all together.[29]

[29]W. O. Scroggs, *The United States in World Affairs, 1933* (New York: Harper & Row, Publishers, 1934), pp. 7–8.

The date for the conference was finally set for June 1933. During the spring, representatives of eleven governments visited Washington to discuss conference plans with President Roosevelt. All seem to have agreed, and Roosevelt with them, that stabilization of currency exchanges should have high priority at the conference. As late as May 16, 1933, Roosevelt announced that the conference "must establish order in place of the present chaos by a stabilization of currencies."

In the meantime, however, the United States had itself gone off the gold standard, and as the dollar had declined in relation to gold, commodity prices had risen. To Roosevelt, the restoration of prices to predepression levels, in the interest of hard-pressed debtor groups, was an objective of the utmost importance. If this could be achieved domestically by currency manipulation, then the right to manipulate the currency was not to be surrendered, and hence the United States should not for the present enter into any international agreement to stabilize currencies. Unfortunately, Roosevelt seems to have come to this conclusion only after the American delegation, headed by Secretary of State Cordell Hull, had departed for the London Economic Conference, and the members of the delegation were not adequately informed of the change in policy. The "gold bloc" at the conference—the gold standard countries led by France, Italy, Switzerland, Belgium, and The Netherlands—insisted that stabilization of currencies and a return to the gold standard by those who had left it were measures essential to recovery. To meet them halfway, the United States and British delegations agreed to an innocuous declaration. Espousing eventual return to gold and agreement to discourage speculative fluctuations in currencies, the statement left the United States and Great Britain free to determine when and at what level the dollar and pound should be stabilized.

This declaration was cabled to President Roosevelt for approval. His rejection of it, July 2, 1933, has been referred to both as a "bombshell" and as the "torpedo" that sank the conference. He would regard it as a great catastrophe, said the President,

> if the great conference of nations, called to bring about a more real and permanent financial stability and a greater prosperity to the masses of all nations, should . . . allow itself to be diverted by the proposal of a purely artificial and temporary expedient affecting the monetary exchange of a few nations only. . . .

The President's complete repudiation of an effort to achieve one of the principal objectives for which the conference had been called ended whatever slim chances for achievement the meeting may have had. The delegations of Great Britain and the gold bloc favored immediate adjournment, putting the blame for failure at the President's door. The urging of Hull and his colleagues, backed by the delegates from the British dominions, kept the conference in session for three weeks longer, but it could do nothing beyond passing resolutions on some minor subjects and acknowledging disagreement on others more important. The American delegates had been forbidden to discuss the intergovernmental debts. Secretary Hull, whose chief enthusiasm was for the lowering of trade barriers, had hoped to negotiate reciprocal trade agreements, but Congress had adjourned without passing the necessary legislation. The conference adjourned, July 27, with nothing substantial to show for six weeks of labor. On the part of the United States it was a sad example of poor preparation, lack of understanding between President and delegates and among the delegates themselves, and changing of the target after the arrow left the bow.

The Hull Reciprocal Trade Agreements Program

The authority to negotiate reciprocal tariff agreements that Secretary Hull had failed to get at the time of the London Conference was given him a year later. Hull, imbued with the traditional low-tariff views of a southern Democrat, also had a fervent belief that the lowering of economic barriers was a cornerstone of international peace.

> . . . To me [he wrote] it seemed virtually impossible to develop friendly relations with other nations in the political sphere so long as we provoked their animosity in the economic sphere. How could we promote peace with them while waging war on them commercially?[30]

For many years, as a representative and senator from Tennessee, he had fought consistently for lower tariffs. As Franklin Roosevelt's Secretary of State, and with a Congress overwhelmingly Democratic, he saw an opportunity to realize a lifelong objective.

The first year of the New Deal, however, was not propitious for a lowering of tariff rates. President Roosevelt, intent upon raising domestic prices through the NRA and AAA, foresaw the possibility that higher rates on imports might be necessary to offset higher prices of home products. Nevertheless, at the Inter-American Conference at Montevideo in December 1933, Hull won great acclaim by his proposal for the reciprocal lowering of rates. This success, in part, won the President to his program, and with presidential support, Con-

[30]*The Memoirs of Cordell Hull,* 2 vols. (New York), 1: 355. Copyright 1948 by The Macmillan Company. Quotations from *The Memoirs of Cordell Hull* reprinted by permission of the publisher. Hull's account of the beginning of the reciprocal trade program is in ibid., 1: chaps. 26, 27. See also Pratt, *Cordell Hull,* 1: chap. 5.

gress passed the Reciprocal Trade Agreements Act of June 12, 1934.

The purpose of the law, as stated officially in the preamble, was that "of expanding foreign markets for the products of the United States (as a means of assisting in the present emergency . . .)"; essentially, it was an anti-depression measure. Technically an amendment to the Hawley-Smoot tariff of 1930, it empowered the executive to negotiate with other governments agreements lowering (or raising) by as much as 50 percent the existing rates on imports from those countries, or "freezing" existing rates or import restrictions, in return for reciprocal concessions on American products imported into the foreign countries. Due notice must be given and hearings must be held before the opening of negotiations for lower rates on any commodity, so that domestic interests might have their say; and the President must seek (though he need not follow) the advice of the Tariff Commission and the Departments of State, Agriculture, and Commerce. But once made, the agreement required no action either by the Senate or by Congress as a whole to put it into effect. Thus agreements under the new act escaped the pitfalls that had been fatal to most attempts at such agreements in the past.

Another novel feature of the act of 1934 was its directive that the trade agreements embody the most-favored-nation principle in its unconditional form. The United States had, as a matter of fact, made the shift from the conditional to the unconditional form of treaty in 1923, but it now appeared for the first time in reciprocal trade agreements. It meant that when an agreement with Brazil, for example, lowered the duties on certain imports from Brazil, the same reduction took effect on similar goods imported from other countries, provided only that the countries in question did not discriminate against the

trade of the United States. Thus each agreement had the effect of lowering duties on a wide front, not only between the two parties to the pact. In practice, agreements would normally be negotiated for commodities of which each of the negotiators was principal supplier to the other.

Every agreement under the act was to be effective for three years and thereafter until one party terminated it by giving six months' notice. The power to conclude agreements conferred upon the President was of three years' duration, but its term was extended from time to time for periods of three years or less. The three-year renewal of July 5, 1945, was particularly significant in that it permitted a 50 percent reduction in the rates of January 1, 1945, instead of those of the 1930 tariff. Thus rates that had already been reduced by 50 percent could now be lowered by an additional 50 percent, making a total reduction of 75 percent from the 1930 rates.

From 1934 to 1947 the executive negotiated bilateral reciprocal trade agreements with twenty-nine countries, resulting in the reduction or binding of duties on commodities constituting about 70 percent of all dutiable imports. In 1947, at Geneva, Switzerland, the United States negotiated with twenty-two other countries the General Agreement on Tariffs and Trade (GATT), by which numerous bilateral agreements were combined into a multilateral program. By 1963, membership in GATT had expanded to forty-four countries, while some thirty others enjoyed some form of affiliation with it. Together they accounted for well over four-fifths of the world's international trade.

As a consequence of tariff reductions under the Reciprocal Trade Agreements Act, the average rate on dutiable goods imported into the United States had dropped from 46.7 percent in 1934 to 12.5 in 1951; while the average rate on all imports, dutiable and free, had fallen from 18.4 percent to 5.6 percent. These figures, based upon the value of all imports and the duties collected thereon, are misleading, since rates so high as to be prohibitive do not enter into the calculations at all. Part of the reduction, furthermore, is accounted for by increases in the prices of articles on which the duties are specific, that is at rates of so much per pound or per yard, instead of *ad valorem.* Thus a rate on sugar of two cents a pound will be 40 percent when sugar sells for five cents a pound, but only 20 percent if the price advances to ten cents. But when allowance is made for these elements in the picture and for other barriers to trade, such as quotas, which the United States Congress often resorted to, the reciprocal trade program had done much to facilitate the flow of international commerce and the payment of international debts. As Secretary of State Acheson stated to the House Ways and Means Committee in 1951, "Tariffs have been reduced over a wider area of world trade than ever before."

Though more popular with big business than with agriculture, and with Democrats than with Republicans, the reciprocal trade program in the end received a measure of the bipartisan support for which Secretary Hull had labored. It was repeatedly extended, though in some instances with weakening amendments, by both Democratic and Republican Congresses, with the support of President Eisenhower as well as with that of the Democratic Presidents who preceded and followed him. In order to enable the President to bargain effectively with the European Common Market, Congress, in the Trade Expansion Act of 1962, gave the Executive tariff-cutting powers much more comprehensive than those bestowed by the Act of 1934 or its various extensions.

ADDITIONAL READINGS

ADLER, SELIG, *The Isolationist Impulse: Its Twentieth Century Reaction.* New York: Abelard-Schuman Limited, 1957.

———, *The Uncertain Giant: American Foreign Policy Between the Wars.* (New York: Macmillan, 1965.

DINGMAN, ROGER, *Power in the Pacific: The Origins of Naval Arms Limitation, 1914–1922.* Chicago: University of Chicago Press, 1976.

GARDNER, LLOYD C., *Economic Aspects of New Deal Diplomacy.* Madison, Wis.: University of Wisconsin Press, 1964.

KNEESHAW, STEPHEN J., "The Kellogg-Briand Pact and American Recognition of the Soviet Union," *Mid-America,* 56 (1974), 16–31.

MADDOX, ROBERT J., *William E. Borah and American Foreign Policy.* Baton Rouge, La.: Louisiana State University Press, 1969.

PELZ, STEPHEN E., *Race to Pearl Harbor: The Failure of the Second London Naval Conference and the Onset of World War II.* Cambridge: Harvard University Press, 1974.

SMITH, DANIEL M., *Aftermath of War: Bainbridge Colby and Wilsonian Diplomacy, 1919–1921.* Philadelphia: American Philosophical Society, 1970.

16. The Manchurian Crisis and the Rise of the European Dictators

The peace system set up by the Treaty of Versailles in 1919, reinforced by the Washington treaties of 1921–1922 and the Pact of Paris of 1928, suffered its first serious breach in 1931. The peace-breaker then was Japan, and the scene was Manchuria.

For almost a decade after the successful Washington Conference of 1921–1922, Japan was on her good behavior, and Japanese-American relations were generally cordial. Such friction as existed was the result of American rather than Japanese action. Americans, it is true, contributed generously to relief of the victims of the destructive Japanese earthquake of September 1, 1923. But the good will thus won was largely dissipated by the Johnson Immigration Act of 1924. By this measure Congress prohibited the immigration of Japanese and other Orientals—aliens ineligible for citizenship—instead of admitting them on a quota basis as in the case of Europeans. To the Japanese, who had in good faith carried out the Gentlemen's Agreement of 1907, this discrimination was a needless affront—needless, because Japan's quota of immigrants, had she been given one, would have been so small as to be negligible. President Coolidge and Secretary of State Hughes both disapproved of the ban on Japanese immigration. Their efforts to dissuade Congress from imposing it were hindered rather than helped by a protest from Japanese Ambassador Hanihara. The ambassador warned Secretary Hughes that such discriminatory treatment would bring "grave consequences . . . upon the otherwise happy and mutually advantageous relations between our two countries." The implied threat angered Congress and hastened passage of the bill containing the offensive provision.

Passage of the Johnson Act produced a new flurry of anti-American pronouncements in the Japanese press, but the excitement soon subsided. On the American side there was a growing appreciation of Japan's point of view, and by 1931 there was good reason to hope that Congress would repeal the exclusion provision of the Johnson Act and permit Japanese immigration under the quota system. This possibility was destroyed when the Japanese army launched its campaign for the conquest of Manchuria.

Sino-Japanese Rivalry in Manchuria

The motives of the army in its Manchurian adventure are clear enough. Since 1922 and especially since 1924, the Japanese armed services had been losing ground to the civilian elements in government. This was a period of rising democracy at home and conciliatory behavior abroad. Baron Kijuro Shidehara, Foreign Minister 1924–1927 and 1929–1931, followed a policy of treaty observance, friendliness with the West, and moderation toward China, where the rising tide of nationalism endangered both Japanese and western interests and treaty rights. Shidehara and Premier Hamaguchi, leaders of the Minseito, the more moderate Japanese party, were responsible for Japan's signing the London Naval Treaty of 1930, by which Japan continued to accept naval limits inferior to those of the United States and Great Britain. Their success in persuading the Emperor to ratify the treaty despite the opposition of his military and naval advisers seemed to the armed services to imperil their privileged position in the Japanese government. Their resentment was shown in the assassination of Premier Hamaguchi in November 1930, but Shidehara continued as Foreign Minister, and the new Premier, Wakatsuki, had been one of the negotiators of the London treaty. Only some drastic action, it seemed, could save the armed services from being subjected to civilian control.

They found an occasion for drastic action in Manchuria. Still nominally the "Three Eastern Provinces" of China, Manchuria had long since been divided into Japanese and Russian spheres of interests. Russia's hold upon the northern portion had weakened as a result of the Soviet Revolution. Japan, holding the Liaotung peninsula (embracing Port Arthur and Darien) and the zone of the South Manchurian Railway, had come to regard all of Manchuria as her economic "life-line," to be controlled by her in the future. The Japanese, therefore, were understandably disturbed when the new Nationalist government of China began to reassert Chinese authority in Manchuria. China, since the revolution of 1911, had been di-

vided and almost powerless. Its reunification under Chiang Kai-shek and the Kuomintang (Nationalist People's Party) began in 1926 when Chiang's armies swept north from Canton to the Yangtze Valley, where a new seat of government was established at Nanking. In 1928 the drive was extended northward and Peking, the old imperial capital, now rechristened Peiping ("Northern Peace" instead of "Northern Capital"), was brought under the nationalist government. In the same year Marshal Chang Tso-lin, the autonomous war lord of Manchuria, was killed when his train was blown up (supposedly by Japanese agents). His son, Chang Hsüeh-liang, the "Young Marshal," inheriting his father's position, declared his allegiance to the Nationalist government, which was thus put in a position to reassert Chinese authority over Manchuria. Japan, therefore, faced the prospect of a China reunified and strong, extending its control over Japan's Manchurian "lifeline." China, moreover, was disposed to regard lightly (as accepted under duress) certain treaties of 1915 and earlier, by which she had recognized Japan's special interest in Manchuria and had agreed, among other things, not to build railroads to compete with the Japanese-owned South Manchurian line.

Out of this situation, friction inevitably developed between Japan and China. In the summer of 1931 the Japanese press published sensational accounts of an attack by Chinese upon a group of Korean farmers (Japanese subjects) engaged in peaceful pursuits in Manchuria. A more serious incident was the killing by Chinese troops of Captain Nakamura, a Japanese army officer in disguise, who was pursuing a mysterious mission in central Manchuria. The Japanese government under Wakatsuki and Shidehara sought a peaceful settlement of such incidents. The Army hoped to make them an excuse for seizing control of Manchuria and reasserting its authority in the government. It is significant that on

September 17, 1931, the Nakamura case was reported to be on the verge of amicable adjustment.[1] With this incident about to slip out of its grasp, the Army seized—more probably created—another.

The September Eighteenth Incident

Japan was entitled to keep troops in the Liaotung leased territory and as railway guards along the line of the South Manchurian Railway. On the night of September 18, 1931, a Japanese patrol north of Mukden, according to report, heard an explosion on the railway and, upon investigation, discovered that a section of rail had been broken off by a mine. The damage was so slight that an express train passed over the spot without injury a few minutes later, and it seems probable that the occurrence was a synthetic one. At any rate, Chinese soldiers were charged with an attempt to blow up the track, and with a speed and efficiency that bespoke careful planning, Japanese troops surrounded the Chinese barracks at Mukden, captured the garrison and military stores, and within a few hours seized other key points on or near the railway line. All this was done by the Army on its own initiative without the consent of the Premier or the Foreign Office.[2]

The Chinese government at Nanking appealed at once both to the United States and to the League of Nations for protection against Japan. Japan's action, as inter-preted by all parties concerned except the Japanese themselves, appeared to be in violation of Japan's obligations as a member of the League, in violation of the Nine-Power Treaty of 1922 (by which she had promised to respect the independence and territorial and administrative integrity of China), and in violation of the Kellogg-Briand Pact or Pact of Paris. The United States, not a member of the League, was a party to the two treaties mentioned. If, through invoking any or all of these international engagements, Japan could be stopped, the cause of peace would have won a notable victory. If Japan got away with her act of aggression, her success would be an example to other ambitious and unscrupulous governments. Civilization had reached a turning point.

The United States Joins Hands with the League

The Council of the League, meeting in Geneva, promptly took up China's appeal. A proposal to send a commission of inquiry to the scene of the dispute was dropped upon the objection of Japan, backed by disapproving comment from the United States. In a resolution adopted September 30, the Council took note of a Japanese promise to withdraw all troops to the railway zone as soon as safety should permit and called upon both parties to do nothing that would tend to aggravate the dispute. It then adjourned until October 14.

In Washington, Henry L. Stimson, Secretary of State, was perplexed by conflicting opinions in his own department, where there were pro-Japanese as well as pro-Chinese experts. Stimson wished, within limits, to cooperate with the League. He was, however, inclined at first to be sympathetic to Japan and was anxious not to appear more anti-Japanese than the members of the League Council. For reasons of

[1] S. R. Smith, *The Manchurian Crisis, 1931–1932; A Tragedy in International Relations* (New York: Columbia University Press, 1948), p. 127. See also Armin Rappaport, *Henry L. Stimson and Japan, 1931–1933* (Chicago: University of Chicago Press, 1963); R. N. Current, *Secretary Stimson: A Study in Statecraft* (New Brunswick: Rutgers University Press, 1954).

[2] R. H. Ferrell, "The Mukden Incident: September 18–19, 1931," *Journal of Modern History,* 27 (March 1955), 66–72.

domestic politics, too, he wished to make it plain that the United States was making up its own mind and not merely following the League's lead. These considerations induced a caution that made Stimson's protests to Japan in conjunction with the League appear dilatory and half-hearted.[3]

Stimson, furthermore, fell at the beginning into the natural error of believing that if he treated the Japanese government, that is, Wakatsuki and Shidehara, gently, he would strengthen their hands in putting restraints on the Army, whereas "tough talk" addressed to them would unify popular sentiment behind the militarists. For this reason, during the early stages of the controversy, he "pulled his punches," and even when he did speak firmly, he withheld his notes from publication. Thus both the Japanese and the American public got the impression that Stimson was more inclined to condone Japanese action than actually was the case.

To both the United States and the League Council, Shidehara replied in a conciliatory spirit, promising that the unruly soldiers would be called back within the limits of the railway zone. Probably these promises were made in good faith, but they were not kept. Such was the nature of the Japanese government that neither the Premier nor the Foreign Office had any effective control over the Army. Disillusion first came on October 8, 1931, when Japanese planes bombed Chinchow in southwestern Manchuria. It was here that

Chang Hsüeh-liang, the "Young Marshal," had set up his government after being expelled from Mukden. General Honjo, commanding the Japanese forces in Manchuria, had resolved to drive Chang and his government from that area without regard to promises given by the Foreign Minister.

The bombing of Chinchow led Stimson, with President Hoover's approval, to instruct an American representative, Consul Prentiss Gilbert in Geneva, to sit with the League Council when next it discussed the Manchurian question. Gilbert, however, was directed to participate in the proceedings only when the bearing of the Kellogg-Briand Pact was under discussion. His joining the circle at the Council table was hailed with enthusiasm in Geneva (except by the Japanese representative, who had opposed inviting him). It was viewed with misgivings by isolationists in the United States. His presence, though symbolizing the unity of purpose of the League and the United States, had little practical effect.

The Council, meeting from October 14 to October 24, finally passed a resolution calling upon Japan to withdraw her troops into their legitimate zone by November 16. Stimson, nearly two weeks later, sent a note with a similar request but setting no deadline date. The Japanese Army showed its contempt for the polite notes from Geneva and Washington by launching a campaign for control of northern Manchuria. On November 18, two days after the date set by the Council for withdrawal, Japanese forces occupied Tsitsihar, north of the Chinese Eastern Railway.

The Council of the League met again on November 16, this time in Paris. Charles G. Dawes, United States ambassador to Great Britain and formerly Vice President under Coolidge, was directed to go to Paris to cooperate with the Council; whether he should sit with it, as Gilbert had done at Geneva, was left to his discretion. He chose not to attend the Council meetings either as

---

[3]Smith, *Manchurian Crisis,* emphasizes the ineffectual character of Stimson's cooperation with the League. Much the same view is taken in D. F. Fleming, *The United States and World Organization, 1920–1933* (New York: Columbia University Press, 1938), chap. 13, and in F. P. Walters, *A History of the League of Nations,* 2 volumes (New York: Oxford University Press, 1952), 2: chap. 40. For Stimson's own view, see H. L. Stimson, *The Far Eastern Crisis: Recollections and Observations* (New York: Harper & Row, Publishers, 1936), and H. L. Stimson and McGeorge Bundy, *On Active Service in Peace and War* (New York: Harper & Row, Publishers, 1948), chap. 9.

a participant or as an observer. Setting up his quarters at the Hotel Ritz, he held sessions with the Japanese and Chinese representatives and tried to contribute to a settlement. But what the Council could not do, neither could Dawes.

It was apparent by this time that Japan would not yield to persuasion or to diplomatic pressure. That she should be forced to yield seemed to Secretary Stimson a matter of great importance to the United States. To permit Japan to have her way in Manchuria, he believed, would impair American prestige in China, would injure American trade and endanger its Pacific possessions, and, most serious, would be a blow to the cause of world peace. Stimson had by now lost hope that conciliatory treatment would enable the Japanese moderates to bring the military to heel and, in contrast to his early posture of foot-dragging, he now took the lead in seeking collective measures to halt Japan. Yet what could he do? Economic sanctions were discussed, though not publicly, both in Washington and in the League Council in Paris. But in Washington President Hoover was unalterably opposed to American participation in such measures, which he believed to be a step toward war. Hence, while Stimson could cheer for economic sanctions by the League, he could promise none by the United States, saying only that this country would not interfere with any that the League might impose. And as for the League, while delegates of the small powers could talk of sanctions, the British and French governments felt more than a little sympathy for Japan and would not go beyond words in criticism of her policy.

The Council, therefore, could do little but repeat its hope that Japan would remove her troops. It did, however, resolve—this time at Japan's suggestion—to appoint a commission of inquiry to visit the Far East, examine the issues between China and Japan, and recommend a solution which would reconcile the interests of both parties. From this resolution came the Lytton Commission, so called from the English Earl of Lytton who became its chairman.

The Hoover-Stimson Doctrine

With economic sanctions ruled out on both sides of the Atlantic, President Hoover and his Secretary of State discussed means of subjecting Japan to purely moral pressure. It was apparently Hoover who suggested reviving the device first used by Secretary Bryan in 1915,[4] namely, a declaration that the United States would not recognize any situation brought about by action in violation of its treaty rights. The idea was held in reserve so long as there was any faint hope that Japan would draw back from her career of aggression in Manchuria. Such hope did not long persist. On December 11, 1931 (the day after the adjournment of the League of Council in Paris), the Wakatsuki cabinet resigned. It was replaced two days later by a cabinet of the Seiyukai party, a party more amenable than the Minseito to Army influence. On January 3, 1932, the Japanese army occupied Chinchow at the southwestern extremity of Manchuria. Four days later, Secretary Stimson addressed to Japan and China identical notes setting forth what became known as the Stimson Doctrine (more accurately the Hoover-Stimson Doctrine). In these notes the Secretary informed the governments of China and Japan that the government of the United States

can not admit the legality of any situation de facto nor does it intend to recognize any treaty or agreement entered into between these governments, or agents thereof, which may

---

[4]Current, *Secretary Stimson*, pp. 79–80; *The Memoirs of Herbert Hoover:* [2] *The Cabinet and the Presidency, 1920–1933* (New York: The Macmillan Company, 1952), pp. 362–78.

impair the treaty rights of the United States or its citizens of China, including those which relate to the sovereignty, the independence, or the territorial and administrative integrity of the Republic of China, or to the international policy relative to China, commonly known as the open-door policy; and that it does not intend to recognize any situation, treaty, or agreement which may be brought about by means contrary to the covenants and obligations of the pact of Paris of August 27, 1928, to which treaty both China and Japan, as well as the United States, are parties.

Nonrecognition, if practiced by the United States alone, would clearly have little value as a weapon. Before publishing his notes, Stimson had informed Great Britain and France of his plan and invited them to adhere to his declaration; he had hoped that other governments would follow suit. France made no response. The British government, in a communiqué released to the press, announced that it relied on Japan's promises to keep the door open to trade in Manchuria and saw no need for adopting the American position.

The British attitude changed somewhat when, late in January, 1932, the Japanese attacked the Chinese section of Shanghai. The purpose of this maneuver was to compel the Chinese to drop their boycott of Japanese goods, the peaceful yet potent weapon with which they had retaliated for aggression in Manchuria. The attack on Shanghai endangered the populous and important International Settlement (which, with the French concession, constituted the foreign area of the city); it was also a blow at the heart of the British sphere of interest in the Yangtze Valley. Now the British joined the Americans in protesting the Japanese aggression and in promoting direct negotiations between Chinese and Japanese. These negotiations, also sponsored by the League of Nations, resulted in March in a suspension of hostilities in the Shanghai area and on May 5 in the signing of an armistice. Between March and May,

Japanese troops at Shanghai were reduced to the small number normally kept in the International Settlement.[5]

Manchuria Becomes "Manchukuo"

But while at Shanghai Japan yielded to stubborn Chinese resistance and to international pressure, she was consolidating her gains in Manchuria. As each portion of Manchuria was occupied by Japanese troops, the civil administration was reorganized with Japanese in key positions. Japanese civil and military officials, in close touch with aggressive militarists in Tokyo, "made use," in the words of the Lytton Report, "of the names and actions of certain Chinese individuals, and took advantage of certain minorities among the inhabitants, who had grievances against the former administration," to organize an independence movement. Such a movement, said the Report, "had never been heard of in Manchuria before September 1931." On February 18, 1932, the independence of Manchuria was proclaimed, the country henceforth to be known as "Manchukuo," the Country of the Manchus.

This was a plain challenge to the American doctrine of nonrecognition. Stimson responded in a letter of February 23, to Senator Borah, chairman of the Senate Foreign Relations Committee. He invited other governments to adhere to the nonrecognition policy and added, by way of warning to Japan, that, since the Wash-

---

[5]Secretary Stimson attributed the Japanese surrender to international pressure at Shanghai in part to the presence of the United States battleship fleet in the Pacific, whither it had come for previously scheduled maneuvers centered at Hawaii. Current, *Secretary Stimson*, p. 103. As a further warning to Japan, he persuaded Hoover to keep the battle fleet at Hawaii and with it the scouting force, which otherwise would have returned to the Atlantic. Rappaport, *Stimson and Japan*, pp. 161–62.

ington treaties of 1922 were all inter-related, a violation of one of them by one signatory released other signatories from their obligations under other treaties in the group. In other words, if Japan violated the territorial or administrative integrity of China, protected by the Nine-Power Treaty, the United States was no longer bound by the limitations on her naval strength and her fortifications in the Pacific imposed by the Five-Power Treaty. This warning made no more impression upon Japan than the earlier nonrecognition note. Nor did the United States carry out the implied threat.

But if Stimson was unable to deflect Japan from her course, he did have the satisfaction of seeing his (or Hoover's) doctrine officially adopted by the League of Nations. On February 12, 1932, China had requested the transfer of her appeal from the Council of the League to the Assembly. The latter body, on March 11, 1932, adopted a resolution in effect endorsing the nonrecognition doctrine and declaring it incumbent upon members of the League not to recognize any situation "brought about by means contrary to the Covenant of the League of Nations or to the Pact of Paris."

The League and the Lytton Report

The five-man Commission of Enquiry, or Lytton Commission, with the British Earl of Lytton as chairman and General Frank R. McCoy as the American member, arrived in Tokyo on February 29, 1932, and spent six months in Japan, China, Manchuria, and Korea. Its report, dated September 4, 1932, although recognizing that Japan had legitimate rights in Manchuria that had been endangered by Chinese policy, concluded, nevertheless, that Japan's military action, initiated on September 18, 1931, had not been justified, as Japan claimed, as legitimate self-defense. It concluded that

the establishment of independent Manchukuo did not represent the wishes of the population of Manchuria but had been engineered by Japan as a part of her program of expansion. The government of Manchukuo, it found, was dominated by Japanese, of whom there were nearly two hundred in the central government alone.

The Commission did not, however, recommend a return to the status quo before September 1931, a status that had not adequately protected Japanese interests. It proposed, instead, a special administration for the Three Eastern Provinces (Manchuria), under Chinese sovereignty, but with a large degree of autonomy in local affairs. Both Chinese and Japanese troops would be withdrawn, and a special gendarmerie would be entrusted with the maintenance of order. Japanese interests would be safeguarded in a treaty to be negotiated between Japan and China. The Commission recommended also that Japan and China negotiate a commercial treaty and a treaty of arbitration and conciliation, nonaggression and mutual assistance. The essence of the proposal was reconciliation of Chinese sovereignty in Manchuria with protection of legitimate Japanese economic interests.[6]

The Lytton Report, conscientious and reasonable as it appears to an unprejudiced eye, was spurned by Japan. In fact, without awaiting its publication, Japan on September 15, 1932, officially recognized her puppet state of Manchukuo. The League Assembly, on the other hand, approved the Commission's recommendations and at the same time (February 24, 1933) advised all League members not to recognize Manchukuo "either *de jure* or *de facto*." Japan's response was to give the required two-year notice of withdrawal from the League.

Neither the Stimson doctrine nor the letter to Borah, the retention of the Pacific fleet in Hawaiian waters, nor an address by

[6]*Lytton Report, passim.*

Stimson declaring that the United States could not remain neutral in a war between aggressor and victim[7] had the slightest effect upon Japanese policy—partly, perhaps, because the Japanese knew that Stimson's threats were a bluff. Stimson had taken a high moral position, but the chief practical effect had been to incur Japanese ill will by making the United States appear the chief opponent of Japanese expansion in Asia.[8]

A More Cautious Policy

A few days after the League Assembly rendered its verdict against Japan and the puppet state of Manchukuo, Franklin D. Roosevelt entered the White House in Washington, and Cordell Hull replaced Stimson in the State Department. Stimson had conferred at length with Roosevelt during the winter and had been assured that in the Far East the new administration would continue the policy of old.[9] The United States, accordingly, persisted in refusing recognition to Manchukuo and accepted a nonvoting membership in an Advisory Committee on the Far East set up by the League of Nations. Roosevelt also kept the battleship fleet in the Pacific, where it had been since 1932, and announced that the Navy would be built up to treaty limits.

Yet the diplomacy of the new administration toward Japan was in a much lower key than Stimson's. There had, in fact, been a change in priorities. "In particular," observed Dorothy Borg, "the emphasis which had been placed upon the necessity of supporting the peace system began to be shifted to another objective: the avoidance of a conflict between the United States and Japan."[10] Having announced that it would not recognize the new situation in Manchuria, the United States gave up protesting against it. The change was noted by the Japanese and called forth appreciative comments.[11]

Actually, Japanese military aggression came to a pause soon after Roosevelt and Hull took office. In February and March 1933 the province of Jehol (pronounced ray-hō), adjoining Manchuria and formerly a part of Inner Mongolia, was annexed to Manchukuo. Japanese troops engaged in this operation penetrated south of the Great Wall into the Chinese province of Hopei. Here they met firm resistance, and here, on May 31, 1933, they signed the Tangku truce, which established a demilitarized zone south of the Great Wall in Hopei. Chinese troops were to withdraw to a line just north and east of the cities of Peiping and Tientsin; Japanese were to retire beyond the Great Wall. The truce ended active hostilities between Japanese and Chinese forces for four years and appreciably reduced United States-Japanese tension.

Closing the Open Door

Tension was kept alive, however, by other Japanese actions. Japan was quietly promoting disregard of the open door principle by the puppet government of Manchukuo. Intermittently during 1934, Hull was protesting to Tokyo over discriminations against American trade in that area. Japan had initially given assurances that the open door principle would be respected in Manchukuo, but in April 1935 the British and American ambassadors were told by

---

[7]Rappaport, *Stimson and Japan*, p. 169.

[8]Rappaport, *Stimson and Japan*, pp. 176–77, 202–3.

[9]Current, *Secretary Stimson*, chap. 6.

[10]Dorothy Borg, *The United States and the Far Eastern Crisis of 1933–1938* (Cambridge: Harvard University Press, 1964), p. 522.

[11]Hull, *Memoirs*, 1: 270, 274.

Foreign Minister Hirota that these assurances

> had been given on the understanding that "Manchukuo" would be recognized by other nations and that until the existence of "Manchukuo" was recognized "no dispute whatever could be entertained with regard to that country."

On another occasion Ambassador Joseph Grew was informed that since Manchukuo was an independent country, protests should be addressed to Hsinking, the Manchukuo capital,

> but that if foreign countries claim that Manchuria is still a part of China they should protest to Nanking, . . .

The Foreign Office spokesman added that "Japan does not consider that the Nine Power Treaty applies to 'Manchukuo.'"[12]

Thus Japan evaded all responsibility for discrimination against non-Japanese trade in Manchukuo. The United States rejected the Japanese evasions but for the time being limited its opposition to rather mild protests and to moralizing upon the virtue of keeping promises.

In other ways Japan was making clear its determination to establish its supremacy in the Far East, free from either American or European interference. In April 1934, Eiji Amau, spokesman for the Foreign Office, told a press conference that because of Japan's "position and mission," she alone had the duty "to keep peace and order in East Asia." Japan objected, he said, to "any joint operations, even in the name of technical or financial assistance," such as the League of Nations had proposed for China. Japan would also object to aid or advice of a military or political nature furnished to China by foreign nations acting individually.[13] Secretary Hull protested mildly. Nevertheless, the United States cancelled current plans for aid to China.[14]

A few weeks after the Amau statement, Hiroshi Saito, the new Japanese ambassador, proposed to Hull an eight-point agreement between Japan and the United States. The heart of the agreement was to be recognition of American and Japanese spheres in the Pacific and an undertaking on the part of the two governments, "so far as lies within their proper and legitimate power to establish a reign of law and order in the regions geographically adjacent to their respective countries." This proposal for what the Japanese sometimes referred to as a "Japanese Monroe Doctrine"—a proposal that would have given Japan a free hand in China with no compensating gain to the United States—was politely rejected by Secretary Hull. It turned up from time to time in the Japanese press as a rumor of an accord about to be reached.[15]

By 1935 the Japanese had become dissatisfied with their gains. Economically, Manchukuo had been disappointing, and Japan coveted the markets and raw materials of northern China. Seeking a less expensive and less offensive method than conquest, Japanese agents undertook to stimulate native autonomy movements in five provinces, three in China proper and two in adjoining Inner Mongolia. These

---

[12] Joseph C. Grew, *Turbulent Era: A Diplomatic Record of Forty Years, 1904–1945,* ed. Walter Johnson, 2 vols. (Boston: Houghton Mifflin Company, 1942), 2: 970, 979–80. Quotations from *Turbulent Era* reprinted by permission of the publisher.

[13] *Foreign Relations, Japan, 1931–1941,* 1: 224–25. League of Nations experts had been at work on plans for the economic reconstruction of China. The United States, Germany, and Italy were assisting in different ways in the building of a Chinese air force. H. M. Vinacke, *A History of the Far East in Modern Times,* 5th ed. (New York: Appleton-Century-Crofts, 1950), p. 548.

[14] Borg, *The U.S. and the Far Eastern Crisis,* p. 523.

[15] Hull, *Memoirs,* 1: 281–84; Grew, *Turbulent Era,* 2: 997. One report expanded the accord to include Great Britain, which was to keep peace in a European sphere.

attempts had little success, and though the Japanese Army was disposed to insist on "independence" for those five provinces, the Foreign Office preferred another path. During 1935 and 1936, it pressured the Nanking government for a diplomatic settlement on the basis of three principles: (1) cessation of anti-Japanese activity in China, (2) tacit *de facto* recognition by China of Manchukuo, (3) cooperation between China and Japan for the suppression of Communism in the Far East. Such a settlement, in the opinion of American diplomats in Tokyo and Peiping, would eventually mean domination of China by Japan without the need of military conquest, and apparently Washington was prepared, however reluctantly, to acquiesce in such an outcome.[16]

The negotiations were complicated by sporadic Sino-Japanese "incidents," usually attacks by Chinese on Japanese subjects, and by an invasion of the province of Suiyuan by Manchukuoan and Japanese forces. The repulse of this invasion stiffened Chinese resistance, and in December 1936 the Japanese moderated their demands. The Nanking government was being advised by the British to make reasonable concessions,[17] but any chance of agreement was lost when, following the

---

[16]Borg, *The U.S. and the Far Eastern Crisis,* chaps. 5–6, and p. 528. Cordell Hull stated in his *Memoirs* (1, 290–91) that after Japan's refusal to renew the Washington and London naval treaties and their expiration at the end of 1936, he and the President reached a decision "to continue to insist on the maintenance of law, on our legitimate rights and interests in the Far East, and on observance of the treaties and declarations that guaranteed an independent China." It appears from Borg's study that no such fateful decision was made at this time. Even after the outbreak of Sino-Japanese hostilities in 1937, the United States avoided a course that might lead to a military showdown. Only after Japan aligned itself with the Axis and proclaimed its Greater East Asia program did the U.S. government resolve that Japan must be stopped whatever the cost.

[17]The various stages in these negotiations are reflected in Grew, *Turbulent Era,* 2: 1003–14, *passim*.

"Sian incident,"[18] Chiang Kai-shek came to an understanding with the Chinese Communists for a common front against Japan. Negotiations with Japan ceased. The following July was to witness the opening of full scale hostilities between Japan and China. These events will be treated in a subsequent chapter.

European Dictators and American Neutralism

While the Japanese militarists and nationalists were seizing control of their government and launching Japan upon an aggressive career of expansion in the Far East, similar developments were taking place in the politics of two of Europe's leading states. Fascism rose to power in Italy and Nazism in Germany. Both movements were anti-Communist but also anti-democratic and totalitarian. German Nazism was, in addition, violently anti-Semitic. Both set up one-party states, in which all opposition was suppressed. Freedom of speech, of the press, of teaching, of association were abolished. Control of the national economy was assumed by the government. Both Fascism and Nazism were nationalistic to the point of chauvinism. Benito Mussolini, the founder of Fascism, aspired to re-establish for Italy something of the grandeur of imperial Rome, at least to make Italy supreme in the Mediterranean. Adolf Hitler, who built his National Socialist Party (Nazis for short), upon the Italian model, sought not only to make Germany supreme in Europe, bringing

---

[18]In December 1936 Chiang Kai-shek was kidnapped at Sian by the forces of Marshal Chang Hsüeh-liang, who instead of fighting the Chinese Communists were fraternizing with them. No agreement was put in writing, but before his release Chiang evidently reached an understanding with the Communists for cessation of the civil war and a united front against Japan.

into the Reich all German populations living under other sovereignties, but also to conquer for Germany *Lebensraum* (living space) at the expense of her eastern neighbors, to recover the German colonies lost in World War I, and to elevate Germany to a position of world leadership superior to that which she had held under Kaiser Wilhelm II. Such purposes, which Hitler set down in writing in his book *Mein Kampf (My Struggle),* published in 1924, could be attained only by tearing up the peace settlement of 1919.

Mussolini came to power in Italy, following the Fascist "march on Rome" in October 1922. Most Americans were not greatly concerned with the anti-democratic features of his domestic regime, the strong-arm measures of his "Black Shirts," or the elimination, even by assassination, of parliamentary opponents. That he had suppressed Communism and socialism (though himself formerly a socialist), put an end to strikes, and "made the trains run on time," seemed, to the average American visitor, to justify his unconventional methods. Not until the middle 1930s, when he set out to conquer an empire, did Mussolini's activities seriously affect American thought or American policy.

Hitler followed Mussolini by a decade. His first bid for power, the Munich beer hall *Putsch* of 1923, failed completely. Not until 1930 (when the German Republic was hard hit by depression and unemployment) did his National Socialist followers make a respectable showing at the polls, and not until January 30, 1933 (five weeks before the accession of Franklin Roosevelt) was Hitler named Chancellor of the Reich by President von Hindenburg. In March, following new elections, the Reichstag gave Hitler dictatorial powers for four years. When President von Hindenburg died in 1934, Hitler united in himself the powers of President and Chancellor, though preferring his Nazi title, *der Führer* (the Leader), to that of President.

Although acting promptly to suppress opposition parties, deprive Jews of citizenship, and substitute a centralized for the federal state—in other words to set up his totalitarian, anti-Semitic system within Germany—Hitler moved more cautiously in foreign policy. In fact, his early moves in the international field were more conciliatory than had been expected. The tragic significance for the whole world of his rise to power was not at once perceived, certainly not in the United States.

The General Disarmament Conference Fails

One of the first international problems to confront both Hitler and Roosevelt as they took up their new duties was the question of disarmament by international agreement. The General Disarmament Conference, which had first convened a year earlier, was sitting at Geneva in the spring of 1933.

The history of this attempt at a general limitation of armaments goes back to the Treaty of Versailles and the League of Nations Covenant. Article 8 of the latter had made it a responsibility of the Council of the League to "formulate plans for . . . reduction [of armaments] for the consideration and action of the several Governments." The treaty had strictly limited Germany's armed forces but placed no restriction upon those of the victors. In 1926 the Council appointed a Preparatory Commission for the Disarmament Conference. Included were representatives of Germany and the United States, and ultimately of the Soviet Union, as well as representatives of the League powers. The Commission sat intermittently from 1926 to 1930 and at length drew up an outline for a treaty on disarmament, details of which the conference itself would have to fill in.

The General Disarmament Conference first met in Geneva, February 2, 1932, with representatives from sixty nations, including Germany (now a member of the League), the United States, and the Soviet Union. The most serious obstacle to agreement lay in the relations between France and Germany. Germany was now insisting upon her right to "equality" in armaments instead of the Versailles limitations. France, with bitter memories of 1870 and 1914, insisted upon some new guarantees of security before she would consent to German rearmament. Attempts of President Hoover to break the deadlock failed to satisfy France.

Upon Hitler's accession to power, Germany's insistence upon equality in armament grew more urgent. In May 1933, President Roosevelt made a new attempt to bring about agreement. Urging the Conference to adopt a compromise plan for progressive disarmament offered by the British, he proposed a solemn nonaggression pact by which the signers would promise, during the implementation of the disarmament program, not to send their armed forces outside their own territory. A few days later (May 22, 1933), through an address by Delegate Norman H. Davis at the Conference, Roosevelt offered an agreement to consult with other governments in the event of a threat to the peace and to refrain from interfering with League sanctions against an aggressor if the judgment of the United States as to the aggressor coincided with that of the League. These promises of cooperation with the League, which went beyond any previously offered by the United States and which were given in the hope of satisfying the French craving for security, were conditional upon the adoption of a general plan for disarmament—a plan that should include abolition of offensive weapons and reduction of others.[19]

[19]The President's proposal and Davis's address are printed in U.S. Department of State, *Peace and War: United States Foreign Policy, 1931–1941* (Washington: Government Printing Office, 1943), pp. 179–82, 186–91.

Meanwhile, on May 17 (the day after Roosevelt's proposal of a nonaggression pact), Hitler addressed the Reichstag, which he had convoked in special session. Germany was willing, he said, to go as far as her neighbors in disarmament. She was even willing to defer for five years the attainment of equality. But she would not be bound by majority votes in the Conference and would sign no document perpetuating her inferiority in armaments.

In spite of these good omens of success, the Conference recessed in June without agreement. Before the date set for reconvening in October, Hitler's fleeting interest in cooperation had dissolved. On October 14, 1933, Germany announced her withdrawal from both the Disarmament Conference and the League of Nations. The German secession ended any hope for an agreement on disarmament. The meeting of the Conference planned for October was postponed until May 1934. After two weeks of futility, it adjourned June 11, never to meet again.

Hitler Repudiates Versailles

Hitler's withdrawal from the Disarmament Conference and the League of Nations was a prelude to the rearmament of Germany in total disregard of the Versailles Treaty. On March 16, 1935, the Führer announced that Germany was resuming compulsory military service (forbidden by the treaty) and increasing her army to 500,000 men (five times the treaty limit). The treaty limitations on Germany's armament, he argued, were nullified by the failure of other powers to carry out the plan for general disarmament; but he assured an anxious world that Germany would continue to observe all other articles of the Versailles Treaty, including those on boundaries and the demilitarization of the Rhineland.

Great Britain joined with France and Italy, both in the League Council and outside, in condemning Hitler's violation of treaty engagements; but in June 1935, the British government condoned Hitler's action by formally consenting to the building of a German navy 35 percent the size of Britain's—far beyond the limit set by the Versailles Treaty.

In March 1936, when Mussolini's invasion of Ethiopia had driven a wedge between Italy and her former allies, England and France, Hitler seized the occasion to proclaim his repudiation of the entire Treaty of Versailles and also of the Locarno Pact of 1925, by which Germany had joined in guaranteeing the frontiers of her western neighbors. Simultaneously he announced the remilitarization of the Rhineland and occupied it with thousands of German troops. The League Council and the signers of the Locarno Pact condemned the German action as in violation of treaty obligations. The possibility of sanctions was discussed but failed to receive adequate support in the Council. Hitler "got away with" his breach of the peace system as Japan and Italy had been permitted to do with theirs.

The United States Is Warned of Hitler's Purposes

What was known in the United States about Hitler's aggressive plans, and what, if anything, did Americans propose to do about them? American representatives in Europe were fully aware of the trend in German policy, and from 1934 on, they were sending alarming reports to the State Department. As early as April 1934, the acting American commercial attaché in Berlin, Douglas Miller, thus described German purposes:

> The fundamental purpose is to secure a greater share of the world's future for the Germans, the expansion of German territory and growth of the German race until it constitutes the largest and most powerful nation in

the world, and ultimately, according to some Nazi leaders, until it dominates the entire globe.

Elsewhere in the same report, Miller predicted: "Germany is to engage in a gigantic struggle with the rest of the world to grow at the expense of its neighbors." And, eleven months before Hitler announced his plans for rearmament, Miller reported that the Nazis were "building a tremendous military machine" and were "determined to secure more power and more territory in Europe. If this is voluntarily given to them by peaceful means," he continued, "well and good, but if not, they will certainly use force. That is the only meaning behind the manifold activities of the movement in Germany today."[20]

Similar warnings were passed along from time to time during the next two years by Ambassador William E. Dodd in Berlin. In April 1935, he reported German opinion as holding that American intervention had prevented Germany from dominating Europe in 1918, and as now believing: "Since American intervention will not be repeated the Third Reich will at a strategic moment seize the [Polish] corridor of Austria and if war follows win what was lost in 1918 . . ."[21] Chancellor Hitler, Dodd reported a few months later, had "repeatedly said that he could make no arrangement with any Powers which might deny German advances into Lithuania, Latvia and Esthonia—'barbaric peoples,' he said to Sir John Simon." Hitler looked to those states as part of a plan to encircle Russia.[22] Dodd assured the State Department, furthermore, that Hitler could count on the sup-

[20]U.S. Department of State, *Peace and War*, pp. 211–14.

[21]*Foreign Relations, 1935*, 2: 320–21. At almost the same time that Dodd was reporting thus, the German ambassador in Washington was declaring to Secretary Hull that Germany had no designs on the Polish corridor, Austria, or portions of Czechoslovakia; in fact, no aggressive designs whatever. Ibid., p. 318.

[22]*Foreign Relations, 1935*, p. 337

port of "an overwhelming majority of the German people in any venture he might undertake," even if it were "one of outright conquest."[23]

The United States Chooses Neutrality

By 1935 it was apparent that the postwar system of peace and collective security, already ruptured by Japan in Asia, was further imperiled by the aggressive designs of Germany and Italy in Europe. New wars in Europe seemed certain, unless the "peace-loving" states in the League could act more energetically to preserve the peace than they had done to suppress Japanese aggression or to prevent Germany from tearing up the Versailles Treaty. This they were not likely to do; certainly they would not do it without the active support of the United States. The United States faced a choice between active support of collective security to prevent war on the one hand, and, on the other hand, an attempt to insulate itself from whatever war might come. The United States chose the latter course. Assuming that new wars were inevitable, it set up safeguards against being drawn into them as it had been drawn in in 1917.

Whether this decision was right or wrong, the reasons for it are clear. The basic one was disillusionment with the results of World War I. Woodrow Wilson had justified that war to the American people, and to himself, with idealistic arguments. The war was to "make the world safe for democracy," to end secret diplomacy, to ensure the self-determination of peoples, to set up a League of Nations that should suppress aggression and prevent wars in the future. Having been led to expect too much, the American people were doomed to be disappointed with the practical realities of the postwar world. Idealists had been shocked by some of the compromises

of the Paris peace settlement, and their opposition had helped to prevent ratification of the treaty. At Paris and in the subsequent years, much had been accomplished for democracy, for self-determination, and for open diplomacy. Even the League of Nations had been successful in settling many minor disputes, besides making useful contributions in the economic and social fields. But Americans were characteristically prone to emphasize its weaknesses rather than its successes, and their skepticism about the League was reinforced by its failure to take vigorous action against Japan and Germany. Few of them paused to reflect that American membership in the League might have closed the gap between failure and success.

After 1931, furthermore, Americans were impatient with the refusal of their former associates to settle their war debts. Not always appreciative of Europe's problems, such as the French passion for security, they resented the expenditure on new European armaments of money which might have been used to pay back to Uncle Sam the generous loans that had saved Europe from conquest by Germany.

All in all, as the average American saw it, the United States had participated in World War I for altruistic reasons and at great cost. Then its former associates had used the war and the peace settlement for their own selfish advantage, had repudiated the ideals for which America had fought, and had shown neither gratitude for American aid nor a disposition to pay their just debts. This was a partial and a distorted view of history. It took no account, for example, of the perils that German victory would have held for the United States, and of the idea that hence, in aiding to defeat Germany, the United States had been effectively safeguarding its own future.[24] But it was a

---

[23]*Foreign Relations, 1936,* 2: 152.

[24]Cf. Walter Lippmann, *U.S. Foreign Policy: Shield of the Republic* (Boston: Little, Brown and Company, 1943), pp. 33–39; R. E. Osgood, *Ideals and Self-Interest in America's Foreign Relations* (Chicago: University of Chicago Press, 1953), pp. 397–400.

widespread and a popular view, in Congress no less than with the general public. It pointed unmistakably to the conclusion: Our entry into World War I was a grave mistake: we must never repeat it.

If the interest of the United States was in keeping out of future wars in other continents, the investigation of a Senate committee beginning in the fall of 1934 suggested how that end might be attained. The committee, headed by Senator Gerald P. Nye of North Dakota, was organized for the purpose of investigating the operations of manufacturers of, and dealers in, arms and munitions of war. In months of sensational public hearings, the committee convinced itself and a large share of the public that a hidden reason for American entry into the war in 1917 had been to protect its trade in munitions with the Allies and the loans made to those same Allies by American bankers. It was no news that the presence in the war zones of American citizens traveling on ships of the belligerents had also contributed in an important way to drawing the United States into the war. The conclusion was obvious: If the activities of bankers, munitions-makers, and citizens traveling in war zones dragged the country into war in 1917 against its own best interests, such activities should be prohibited in connection with future foreign wars.[25]

Congress Legislates Neutrality

By the summer of 1935 a foreign war was clearly imminent. In the preceding December, Italian and Ethiopian troops had clashed at a place called Wal Wal near the boundary of Ethiopia and Italian Somaliland. When Italy, although professing to desire a peaceful settlement, obstructed all attempts at arbitration and conciliation and began mobilizing her war machine, it was evident that Mussolini was bent upon conquering an African empire. Some senators and congressmen thought now was the time for legislation that might protect the United States against a repetition of the mistake of 1917.

Here the aims of Congress and the administration diverged. President Roosevelt and Secretary Hull wished legislation flexible enough to empower the President to forbid the exportation of arms and munitions to an aggressor government while permitting their sale to the victim of aggression. A bill to this effect had been prepared by the State Department. Such discretionary power would have enabled the President to cooperate with the League of Nations in withholding arms from a nation adjudged the aggressor. Such action, however, would have meant taking sides in a conflict and possible involvement in war. This Congress did not wish to risk. The Senate set aside the administration bill and passed a substitute requiring the President, in the event of a foreign war, to forbid arms shipments to both belligerents without distinction. A joint resolution in this form, usually referred to as the First Neutrality Act, was passed by both houses of Congress and became law on August 31, 1935. President Roosevelt signed it reluctantly because of its failure to permit any discrimination between attacker and attacked in cutting off war material.[26]

The new law directed the President, upon the outbreak of war between two foreign countries, to proclaim the existence of such a war and prohibited thenceforth the exportation from the United States of arms, ammunition, and implements of war to or for either belligerent. It also forbade American ships to carry such articles from any point to or for a belligerent; and it

[25] Osgood, *Ideals and Self-Interest,* pp. 365–66. Secretary Hull believed the Nye Committee was unrivaled in its unfortunate effects on American foreign policy, except by the committee that prepared the way for rejection of the League of Nations. Hull, *Memoirs,* 1: 398.

[26] Hull, *Memoirs,* 1: chap. 29.

empowered the President, at his discretion, to warn American citizens that they would travel on belligerent ships only at their own risk. Another selection of the Act created a National Munitions Control Board, with the Secretary of State as chairman. Every person engaged in manufacturing, exporting, and importing arms, ammunition, or implements of war was required to register with the Secretary of State and to obtain a license for every transaction by which such commodities were exported from, or imported into, the United States.

The Italo-Ethiopian War and American Neutrality

This was the legislation governing President Roosevelt's action when Italy, without formally declaring war (she had renounced war by signing the Pact of Paris), invaded Ethiopia early in October 1935. The President acted promptly. In a proclamation of October 5, he announced that actual war existed between Italy and Ethiopia, even though there had been no declaration. He therefore prohibited the exportation of arms, ammunition, or implements of war to or for either country. In this instance, the necessity of including both belligerents in the embargo did not displease the President. Ethiopia, a completely landlocked country with poor overland communications, could not have imported significant amounts of material from America in any case; the practical effect of the embargo was, therefore, felt less in Ethiopia than in Italy, the aggressor power.

But what Italy needed most was oil, and since oil was not classified as ammunition or an implement of war, the President had no authority to forbid its export. He and Secretary Hull did, however, resort to a "moral embargo" on oil and other commodities, appealing to American exporters to hold

their shipments to Italy to normal prewar levels.[27]

In the meantime, the Council of the League of Nations, acting with more vigor than it had yet shown, declared Italy an aggressor and imposed sanctions. It forbade the shipment to Italy, by members of the League, of arms, ammunitions, or implements of war; forbade loans to Italy, either to the government or to private parties; prohibited acceptance of imports from Italy; and embargoed shipments to Italy of various commodities produced chiefly by League powers.[28] Omitted from this list were oil, iron and steel, coal and coke, which were obtainable in non-League countries.

Great Britain also made an impressive show of force, moving her Mediterranean fleet to the vicinity of the Suez Canal and her home fleet to Gibraltar.

These, and similar French gestures, however, turned out to be principally bluff. Great Britain and France were now deeply concerned over the plans of Hitler's Germany. Anxious to divide Mussolini from Hitler and retain the friendship of the former, they agreed between themselves not to push sanctions to a point that might provoke Italy to war. In December, the British and French Foreign Secretaries, Sir Samuel Hoare and Pierre Laval, proposed a settlement that would have given Italy most of what she desired at the expense of Ethiopia. This proposal for appeasement was so strongly condemned in England that Hoare resigned, and Anthony Eden became Foreign Secretary.

A proposal for an embargo on oil—really the key commodity in the Italian campaign—was then seriously made and discussed; but before a decision could be

[27] Hull, *Memoirs*, 1: chap. 31.

[28] Walters, *A History of the League of Nations*, 2: chap. 53, gives a good account of League policy in the Italian crisis. See also Herbert Feis, *Seen from E.A.* (New York: Alfred A. Knopf, Inc., 1947), pp. 193–283.

reached, Hitler proclaimed the end of the Treaty of Versailles and marched his legions into the Rhineland. These events stole the spotlight from Italy and added to France's reluctance to take drastic action against a power that she might need as a friend. They ended talk of an oil embargo and virtually assured an Italian victory, since Great Britain declined to take the one other step that might have been effective—closing the Suez Canal. On May 5, 1936, an Italian motorized column entered Addis Ababa, the Ethiopian capital. Four days later, Mussolini decreed the annexation of all Ethiopia to the Italian empire. Resistance to the invaders collapsed, and in July the League Assembly voted to put an end to the sanctions against Italy. For the third time, collective security had failed to restrain the aggression of a major power. Italy, angered by the League's attempt to curb her and by the Assembly's refusal to unseat the Ethiopian delegation, withdrew from membership, as had Japan and Germany before her. The Assembly failed to take a stand against recognition of the conquest, as it had done in Manchuria, and one by one, members of the League recognized Italy's sovereignty in Ethiopia.

The attitude of the United States toward the League in its battle with Mussolini was sympathetic but not very helpful. The "moral embargo" on oil and other commodities not on the prohibited list was, said Hull, "reasonably successful." An attempt to give the President discretionary authority to impose a legal embargo on such commodities was defeated in Congress before passage of the Second Neutrality Act of February 29, 1936 (the date on which most provisions of the original act were due to expire). The League powers knew, therefore, that if they should impose an embargo on oil, the President of the United States would have no authority to join in it, except insofar as he could persuade American exporters to restrict voluntarily their oil shipments. This situation was certainly a deterrent to an oil embargo by the League.

The Second Neutrality Act, furthermore, contained a new feature that was hardly encouraging to those who might consider using stronger sanctions against Italy. The act of 1935 *authorized* the President, when a new belligerent entered an existing war, to extend the embargo to cover dealings with the new entrant. The act of 1936 *directed* him to do the same. This meant, for example, that if imposition of sanctions upon Italy should lead her to attack Great Britain, the latter, as a belligerent, would be cut off from "arms, ammunition, and implements of war" produced in the United States. It cannot be said that such misgivings about the attitude of the United States to possible sanctions were *the* reason for the halfheartedness of League action; they may well have been *one* of the reasons.[29]

The Second Neutrality Act contained two other provisions not found in its predecessor. It forbade loans to belligerent governments, through purchase of their securities or otherwise, by "any person within the United States." This was clearly an application of the Nye Committee's thesis that loans to the Allies by American bankers had been a factor in seducing the United States into war in 1917. The other new provision, which might be regarded as a corollary of the Monroe Doctrine, exempted from the bans on munitions, loans, and the like, an American republic engaged in war with a non-American state, "provided the American republic is not cooperating with a non-American state or states in such war."

Except for these modifications, the Second Neutrality Act extended the provisions of the First to May 1, 1937.

---

[29]Feis, *Seen from E.A.,* pp. 280–81. As a matter of fact, the League had no positive assurance that the U.S. would submit to a complete or partial blockade of Italy should the League impose one.

The Spanish Civil War and American Neutrality

The neutrality regulations were applicable to wars between foreign states; they made no mention of civil wars. A new problem was raised, therefore, when, in July 1936, General Francisco Franco launched his insurrection against the Republican government of Spain. The Spanish Civil War, thus begun, was fought bitterly for nearly three years, finally ending in victory for Franco and his so-called Nationalists. What was to be the American policy with regard to the sale of arms to the opposing Spanish groups? If the United States had followed the practice that had been customary in dealing with civil wars in Latin America, the legitimate government of the Spanish Republic would have been permitted to purchase freely in the American market, while that privilege would have been denied to the insurgents. But Europe adopted a different course, and the United States conformed to it. The Spanish Civil War contained the germ of a possible international conflict. It was known that Germany and Italy sympathized with Franco, while Russia, France, and to a less degree Great Britain were friendly to the Republican or Loyalist side. Intervention by these powers in behalf of the opposing parties in Spain might bring them into armed collision with one another and set off a new world war. In August 1936, therefore, upon French initiative, the European governments agreed upon a policy of nonintervention in Spain and set up a committee in London to supervise its operation and to prevent assistance to either side from the cooperating powers.

That Germany and Italy would violate their nonintervention agreement on a large scale, and so ensure Franco's victory, could not be foreseen.[30] It seemed best to Messrs. Roosevelt and Hull in Washington to adopt a policy parallel to that of Europe. In August 1936, accordingly, the Secretary of State announced that though the President had no authority to institute an arms embargo in a civil war, he hoped nevertheless that American exporters would refrain from shipping war material to either side in Spain. Thus they would be conforming to the spirit of the Neutrality Acts.

This "moral embargo" was not observed in all instances, and early in January 1937, the President asked Congress to make it legal. Accordingly, in a joint resolution signed on January 8, 1937, Congress prohibited the export of any arms, ammunition, or implements of war to either of the opposing forces in Spain. The wisdom of thus shutting off war materials from the Loyalist government in Spain has been much debated pro and con.[31] In retrospect, it appears certain that American policy, like British and French nonintervention policy, played into the hands of Hitler and Mussolini, enabling them to assist in establishing a friendly Fascist government in Spain.

---

[30]Russia, too, violated the agreement, sending what aid she could to the Loyalists, who included an influential Communist contingent, but for geographical reasons Russia was not able to match the aid given by the Fascist powers.

[31]Hull, *Memoirs*, 2: chap. 34, vigorously defends the policy. Congress recognized, he said, that American aid to the Spanish government might lead to a spread of the war "and that our peace and security required our keeping aloof from the struggle" (p. 491). On the other hand, Sumner Welles, Assistant Secretary of State at the time, believed that the Roosevelt administration committed "no more cardinal error [in foreign policy] than the policy adopted during the civil war in Spain." *The Time for Decision* (New York: Harper & Row, Publishers, 1944), pp. 60–61. Welles wrote under the erroneous impression that Roosevelt reluctantly signed the law, whereas in reality he strongly urged it. Basil Rauch, *Roosevelt from Munich to Pearl Harbor* (New York: Creative Age Press, 1950), pp. 34–41, also believes the Spanish policy was a mistake, a reversal of Roosevelt's policy toward Italy. He attributes it in part to the influence of the Catholic Church, which was incensed at the anticlerical policy of the Spanish Republicans.

There is, on the other hand, a strong probability that a Loyalist victory would have meant eventually a Spain under Communist domination.

Making Neutrality "Permanent"

The new neutrality had now become established American policy. The new neutrality, in essence, was a waiving of rights that had been claimed under the old neutrality—rights of doing business with belligerents, especially on the high seas,—because insistence upon those rights meant a risk of war. The laws of 1935 and 1936 had been experimental; their provisions would expire May 1, 1937. Before that date Congress undertook to put them in permanent form, with various modifications and improvements. The result was the Third Neutrality Act, signed May 1, 1937. The new act (technically, like the others, a joint resolution) extended indefinitely the main features of the acts of 1935 and 1936. Its provisions were to be applied whenever the President should find that a state of war existed between two or more foreign states. They might also be applied in a foreign civil war if the President should find that export of arms and munitions "would threaten or endanger the peace of the United States." American citizens were now forbidden to travel on belligerent ships instead of being merely warned that such travel was at their own risk. A temporary "cash and carry" provision (to expire May 1, 1939) empowered the President, at his discretion, to prohibit the export to or for a belligerent of commodities not included in the lists of arms, ammunition, and implements of war, (a) in any American vessel, and (b) until ownership had been transferred to the foreign purchaser. The obvious intent was to prevent "incidents" that might arise from destruction of American property by one of the belligerents; but since this portion of

the act expired before there was any occasion to use it, it was of no practical importance.

The United States was now fortified, or so it seemed, against being drawn into any "foreign war" through such violations of "freedom of the seas" as had involved it in 1812 and 1917. Freedom of the seas, as earlier understood, had been surrendered, or at least waived for the time being. The legislation had the merit of reserving to the United States itself the decision whether it should enter a "foreign war." Such entry was no longer to be dependent on the decision of a foreign government, as war or peace in 1917 had hung upon whether Germany did or did not resort to unrestricted submarine warfare. The United States could now make its own decision, based upon national interests more vital than the right of American ships or citizens to sail the oceans unmolested, or the right of American munitions-makers to sell their products to belligerent governments.

But if the new neutrality had this merit from the point of view of the United States alone, from a broader view it did a disservice to the cause of peace. It was notice to well-armed dictators like Hitler and Mussolini, that if they chose to attack their democratic neighbors, the latter could get no aid from the United States, either in direct war material or in loans of money or credit. Had such laws been on the books in 1914, the Kaiser's Germany would have won the First World War. Should these laws remain on the books, Hitler's Germany might expect to win the next war, for the American "arsenal of democracy" would be closed to the democracies of Europe. To President Roosevelt and Secretary Hull, who had accepted this policy reluctantly, it was evident that it encouraged aggression. But the American Congress was so intent upon keeping America out of the next war that it deliberately passed legislation which, by encouraging aggression, made that war more probable.

ADDITIONAL READINGS

ADLER, SELIG, *The Isolationist Impulse: Its Twentieth-Century Reaction.* New York: Abelard-Schuman Limited, 1957.

DIVINE, ROBERT A., *The Illusion of Neutrality.* Chicago: University of Chicago Press, 1962.

OFFNER, ARNOLD A., *The Origins of the Second World War: American Foreign Policy and World Politics, 1917–1941.* New York: Praeger Publishers, 1975.

THOMAS, HUGH, *The Spanish Civil War.* New York: Harper & Row, Publishers, 1961.

WILSON, JOAN HOFF, *American Business and Foreign Policy, 1920–1933.* Boston: Beacon Press, 1973.

17. A Good Neighbor Policy for the New World

While the United States was setting up safeguards against involvement in the wars of Europe and Asia, it was acting to reduce friction and to improve friendly relations with its neighbors of the New World. Relations with the other American republics had suffered as a consequence of the policy of intervention in the Caribbean and Central America practiced under Presidents Theodore Roosevelt, Taft, and Wilson. The role of international policeman assumed by Uncle Sam had not endeared him to his neighbors, and the neighbors could not forget that in the Panama episode of 1903 the policeman had participated in what many of them thought an act of larceny. Woodrow Wilson, as was noted before, tried to allay the fear of "Yankee imperialism" that flourished south of the border, but his reassuring words were contradicted by his vigorous acts of intervention in Haiti and the Dominican Republic. Wilson's Republican successors, Harding, Coolidge, and Hoover, made varying contributions to an improvement of relations with Latin America, but it remained for Franklin D. Roosevelt to go the whole way in surrendering the policy of intervention that his Republican cousin had instituted.

First Withdrawals from the Caribbean[1]

Warren G. Harding, while campaigning for the presidency in 1920, had criticized President Wilson's policy of intervention in the Caribbean. As President (1921–1923) he took steps to liquidate the most objectionable of the protectorate regimes—that in the Dominican Republic. In 1922 a native provisional government was installed as successor to the United States Navy's military regime. Two years later regular elections were held, and as the elected government began to function, the last United States marines left the island. A new treaty provided for continuance of the customs receivership instituted in 1907 until bond issues authorized by the new agreement should have been retired.

President Calvin Coolidge (1923–1929), under whose administration the restoration of self-government in the Dominican Republic was completed, also called home the legation guard of marines from Managua, the capital of Nicaragua. Since 1912 this small force had effectively deterred the Nicaraguan opposition from resorting to arms to overthrow the pro-United States government of Adolfo Díaz and his successors. Peaceful habits seemed so well established that in 1925 Coolidge deemed it safe to remove this symbol of American power. Within a few months, civil war broke out between rival claimants to the presidency. Díaz, the Conservative and a friend of the United States, again held the office. Sacasa, a Liberal, had some basis of claim to it and had the backing of the government of Mexico. Díaz appealed to the United States

---

[1]The account of the withdrawal from the protectorates in the Caribbean and Central America is

adapted from chapter 8 of J. W. Pratt, *America's Colonial Experiment* (Englewood Cliffs, N.J.: Prentice-Hall, Inc., 1950). Source citations are given in that chapter.

for aid. Early in 1927 the marines were sent back, not to fight for Díaz, but to neutralize certain areas and to protect American and other foreign lives and property.

The renewed intervention in Nicaragua provoked widespread criticism in both the United States and Latin America. President Coolidge defended the intervention as warranted by "the proprietary rights of the United States in the Nicaraguan canal route" and "the obligations flowing from the investments of all classes of our citizens in Nicaragua." The United States, he said, could not

> fail to view with deep concern any serious threat to stability and constitutional government in Nicaragua tending toward anarchy and jeopardizing American interests, especially if such a state of affairs is contributed to or brought about by outside influences or by any foreign power.

But when it appeared that President Díaz, even with the advantage of arms supplied by the United States, was unable to suppress his Liberal opponents, and that Nicaragua faced the probability of a prolonged civil war, the United States undertook to bring about a compromise settlement. For this purpose Coolidge requested Colonel Henry L. Stimson, who had served as Secretary of War under President Taft, to go to Nicaragua as a special representative of the United States and to confer with the leaders of both factions.

Stimson's mission was successful. Díaz was, as usual, willing to accept United States intervention on almost any terms. He readily agreed to Stimson's proposal that both sides be disarmed by the United States forces. So did General Moncada, the Liberal commander, when informed that the United States proposed to disarm forcibly those who would not disarm voluntarily. An agreement known as the "peace of Tipitapa," was signed after a month of negotiation. The national army was to be replaced by a National Guard, to be trained and temporarily officered by United States

marines. Díaz was to continue in office, with Liberals admitted to his cabinet, until the 1928 elections, which were to be supervised, and their fairness guaranteed, by the United States.

The arrangement committed the United States to further intervention in Nicaragua. The occupation forces, it turned out, supervised not only the elections of 1928 but also those of 1930 and 1932 as well. The fairness of those elections is sufficiently attested by the fact that all three were won by the Liberals—traditionally the anti-American party—Moncada being elected to the presidency in 1928 and Sacasa in 1932. One Liberal leader, Sandino, had refused to abide by the terms of the peace and carried on for three years a guerrilla warfare against the marines, thus keeping the bloody aspects of intervention steadily before the American public. By February 1931, peace was so far restored that Mr. Stimson, now Secretary of State under Herbert Hoover, announced that the marines would be gradually withdrawn, leaving the further suppression of guerrillas to the National Guard, and that the intervention would be terminated after the elections of 1932. This decision was not altered when a new outbreak of guerrilla warfare occurred in the interior in April 1931. In January 1933, the last of the marines were withdrawn, leaving as the only element of American control the customs receivership agreed upon in 1911 and modified in 1917.

The End of the Roosevelt Corollary

The withdrawal of the marines from Nicaragua, and especially the refusal to augment the existing force during the disturbances of 1931, typified the new Hoover-Stimson policy toward Latin America. The "new policy toward Latin American countries" was described in the *New York Times* on "high authority" as representing "a determination on the part of the United States not to intervene in the internal affairs of any of those countries."[2] The policy was exhibited in the prompt abandonment of the Wilsonian practice of refusing recognition to revolutionary governments—a form of intervention—and a return to the traditional American policy of recognizing any government that was *de facto* in control and able and willing to observe its international obligations.[3] It was supported by the publication in 1930 of a *Memorandum on the Monroe Doctrine,* prepared in 1928 by Under Secretary of State J. Reuben Clark. Though never actually made official doctrine, it amounted to a repudiation of the Roosevelt Corollary.

> The [Monroe] doctrine [it declared] states a case of United States *vs.* Europe, not of United States *vs.* Latin-America.
>
> Such arrangements as the United States has made, for example, with Cuba, Santo Domingo, Haiti, and Nicaragua, are not within the Doctrine as it was announced by Monroe.[4]

It is to be noted that the Clark *Memorandum* did not repudiate the right of the United States to intervene in the affairs of neighboring states when its interests were endangered. It merely denied that such right found any basis in the Monroe Doctrine. Arrangements such as those with Cuba and the other states mentioned, it stated, "may be accounted for as the expression of a national policy which . . . originates in the necessities of security or self-preservation." Here was no admission that the United States had done wrong in intervening in the states of Central America and the Caribbean, no promise that it would not intervene again in the interest of "security or self-preservation." But since virtually all the interventions after 1904 had been given a basis in the Roosevelt Corollary of the Monroe Doctrine, and since that basis was now discarded, the issuance of the *Memorandum* was an important step in the direction of complete nonintervention. Taken with other features of the Hoover-Stimson Latin American policy, it warrants the assertion that those two statesmen laid the basis of the "good neighbor policy" of the 1930s.[5]

Changing American Opinion

Franklin Roosevelt, as Assistant Secretary of the Navy under Woodrow Wilson, had played a small part in the American interventions in Haiti and the Dominican Republic; he boasted, in fact, during the cam-

[2]*New York Times,* April 16, 1931.

[3]Early occasion for the application of the new policy was afforded by an epidemic of revolutions occurring in 1929–1930 in Argentina, Bolivia, Brazil, Dominican Republic, Panama, Peru. Until 1934, when the five Central American republics terminated the treaty binding them mutually not to recognize revolutionary governments, the United States made for those republics an exception to its general policy of recognizing *de facto* governments. For Secretary Stimson's defense of this feature of his foreign policy, see H. L. Stimson, "The United States and the Other American Republics," *Foreign Affairs,* 9 (1931), No. 3, Special Supplement.

[4]U.S. Department of State, *Memorandum on the Monroe Doctrine,* prepared by J. Reuben Clark (Washington: Government Printing Office, 1930), p. xix. Secretary of State Hughes had anticipated the Clark interpretation in 1923, declaring that the Monroe Doctrine afforded no support for any idea of superintendence or overlordship in the Western Hemisphere on the part of the United States. Perkins, *History of the Monroe Doctrine,* pp. 333–36.

[5]In fact, Hoover repeatedly used the term "good neighbor" in the "good will tour" of Latin America that he made between his election and his inauguration. Alexander De Conde, *Herbert Hoover's Latin American Policy* (Stanford: Stanford University Press, 1951), chap. 2. Cf. Bemis, *Latin American Policy,* pp. 218–23. On the other hand, Latin Americans blamed Hoover for the Hawley-Smoot tariff, which had disastrous effects on their economy. Sumner Welles, *The Time for Decision* (New York: Harper & Row, Publishers, 1944), pp. 190–91. It is one of the ironies of this period of history that a chief motive of Hoover's new Latin American policy was to build up trade by removing political antagonism, whereas the tariff bill that he signed had just the opposite effect.

paign of 1920, that he not only had "had something to do with running" those two republics but had himself written Haiti's constitution of 1918. Before reaching the presidency, however, he had come to repent of these actions and to feel that the United States should renounce "for all time" its practice of "single-handed intervention . . . in the internal affairs of other nations." If intervention should be necessary to put an end to disorder in some American state, it should be carried out as a joint enterprise by the American republics, not by the United States alone.[6]

This attitude, which Roosevelt shared with Secretary of State Cordell Hull and Assistant Secretary Sumner Welles, prepared the way for acceptance by the United States of a doctrine of nonintervention which for some years Latin American governments and jurists had been advocating as a principle of American international law, but which the United States hitherto had declined to accept. One of the chief reasons for the exercise by the United States of the right of intervention had now vanished, however, with the elimination of German naval power in World War I. American naval supremacy in the Western Hemisphere was now unchallenged. There was no longer the fear that a rival power might seize a foothold near the Panama Canal if disorder or nonpayment of debts furnished an excuse. To be a "good neighbor" was easier and safer for the United States than it had been before 1914. The trend toward nonintervention, which had begun under Harding and accelerated under Hoover, reached its high point under the second Roosevelt.

A Policy "Opposed to Armed Intervention"

President Franklin D. Roosevelt's original "good neighbor" declaration had no special

[6]F. D. Roosevelt, "Our Foreign Policy: A Democratic View," *Foreign Affairs,* 6 (July 1928), 573–86.

reference to Latin America and was quite innocuous in any event.

> In the field of world policy[he announced in his first Inaugural Address, March 4, 1933] I would dedicate this Nation to the policy of the good neighbor—the neighbor who resolutely respects himself and, because he does so respects the rights of others.

More significant was his declaration at a Woodrow Wilson Foundation dinner, December 28, 1933, that "the definite policy of the United States from now on is one opposed to armed intervention." This statement, while it went much further than the Clark *Memorandum,* was, like it, unilateral. It was a statement of policy that could be altered or revoked at will; it was in no sense a contract with other governments.

Two days before Roosevelt's speech, however, the United States delegation at the Seventh International Conference of American States at Montevideo had signed a Convention on the Rights and Duties of States that declared, in Article 8: "No state has the right to intervene in the internal or external affairs of another." Thus the United States acquiesced in a renunciation of the right of intervention that was more sweeping than that which it had rejected five years before at Havana.

The Montevideo Conference was one of the high points in the diplomatic career of Secretary Cordell Hull, who headed the United States delegation. By accepting the Latin American position on intervention and by his tactful and self-effacing behavior, Hull not only removed a large share of the distrust that Latin Americans felt for the United States; he even won the friendly cooperation of the Argentine Foreign Minister, Carlos Saavedra Lamas, the leading opponent of the United States among Latin American statesmen. Saavedra Lamas had attempted to blanket the achievements of the Conference by proposing his own antiwar treaty, containing a declaration against intervention, whether by arms or diplomacy, and by getting it signed, a few weeks before the Conference opened, by five South American states and Mexico. Hull, instead of treating Saavedra Lamas as a rival, offered to sign his treaty on behalf of the United States and persuaded him to introduce a resolution (which Hull seconded) calling upon all the American republics that had not done so to ratify not only the Argentine peace treaty but the inter-American conciliation treaties of 1923 and 1929, the inter-American arbitration treaty of 1929, and the Kellogg-Briand Pact of 1928. Saavedra Lamas, in turn, agreed to support a resolution calling for the lowering of trade barriers, which Hull introduced and which was a prelude to adoption of the reciprocal trade agreement program mentioned in a previous chapter.

Unlike the earlier Fifth and Sixth Inter-American Conferences (Santiago, 1923; Havana, 1928), which had featured ill-natured attacks on the United States, the Montevideo meeting resembled a love feast. The nonintervention article had been the goal for some years of the Latin American governments. Its acceptance by the United States caused surprise and gratification. None of the delegations, apparently, recognized the full significance of proscribing intervention in "the external affairs" of any American state. If in the future some American state should develop affinity for a Fascist or Communist regime in the Old World, would Article 8 of the Montevideo convention bar its neighbors from acting against it in their own defense? The question was not even asked at Montevideo. Unvoiced there, it was to become crucial twenty years later.[7]

At any rate, the United States Senate approved the convention without a record vote, appending only a mild reservation

___

[7]Bemis, *Latin American Policy*, pp. 272–73. It was not clear from the wording of Article 8 whether or not collective intervention was admissible in the event of such danger as is suggested.

that Hull had injected at the Conference. The gist of this was a statement that the United States reserved its rights under "the law of nations as generally understood." Even this was omitted when nonintervention was reaffirmed at Buenos Aires three years later. The protocol then signed by Hull and approved without reservation by the Senate proclaimed:

> The High Contracting Parties declare inadmissible the intervention of any one of them, directly or indirectly, and for whatever reason, in the internal or external affairs of any other of the Parties.

Nonintervention in Practice

Meanwhile Roosevelt and Hull were giving evidence of their sincerity by liquidating those protectorates where the right of intervention had formerly been exercised— in Haiti, the Dominican Republic, Nicaragua, Cuba, and Panama.

In Haiti, where Hoover had already gone far in returning control of government and services to the Haitian people, Roosevelt accomplished by executive agreement (August 7, 1933) the last step which had eluded Hoover through Haitian rejection of a treaty. The native *Garde d'Haiti* was made completely Haitian, the United States marines were withdrawn, and responsibility for payment of Haiti's bonded indebtedness was conferred first upon a "fiscal representative" nominated by the President of the United States, and after 1941, upon the National Bank of Haiti, with representatives of both the Haitian government and the bondholders on its board of directors. Thus the United States government withdrew from the picture altogether. By a somewhat similar arrangement, the United States relinquished the right to name the general receiver of customs in the Dominican Republic. In Nicaragua the last of the American loans secured by the customs revenue were paid off in 1944, and the collector general was thereafter responsible only to the government of Nicaragua.[8]

In the case of Cuba, the right of intervention embodied in the Platt Amendment of 1901 and the treaty of 1903 was surrendered through a new treaty signed in May 1934. This abandonment of the right of intervention, however, was preceded by an act of diplomatic, not military, intervention, by which Sumner Welles, serving temporarily as United States Ambassador, secured the resignation of the harsh and oppressive Cuban dictator-president, Gerardo Machado, and the election of a successor acceptable to the United States, with whom the new treaty was negotiated. The treaty abrogated the Platt Amendment, reserving to the United States only the right to use the naval base at Guantanamo Bay until that right should be set aside by mutual consent. Thus the United States surrendered all claim to financial control of Cuba and all right to intervene in its affairs.

By a treaty with Panama, signed March 2, 1936, replacing that of 1903, the United States dropped its guarantee of Panama's independence and renounced its right to intervene in Panamanian affairs and to acquire, by eminent domain, additional lands in Panama needed for operation of the canal. The Senate approved the treaty after a three-year delay, upon being assured that in an emergency the United States might utilize positions on the soil of Panama for defense of the canal, with consultation between the two governments to follow instead of preceding such action.[9]

Thus in the 1930's the United States divested itself of all the protectorates in the Caribbean area which it had assumed under the administrations of Theodore Roosevelt, Taft, and Wilson. It thereby accepted, in theory, the principle of the sovereign equality of all independent states. The American control or supervision had provided a degree of stability previously unknown in the states affected. Unfortunately, it had not induced habits of democratic behavior, as evidenced by the flock of dictators that followed withdrawal of American control: Trujillo in the Dominican Republic, the Somozas, in Nicaragua, "Papa Doc" Duvalier in Haiti, Batista and Castro in Cuba.

"Continentalizing" the Monroe Doctrine

When the Montevideo Conference met in December 1933, there was no apparent threat from without to the security of the Western Hemisphere. Hitler had been in power less than a year and had not yet fully revealed his aggressive proclivities. Mussolini's conquest of Ethiopia was still in the future. Japan was quietly digesting her first big bite of Chinese territory. The chief problems confronting the American republics were the elimination of the distrust that the Latin members felt for "the Colossus of

---

[8]Under the Bryan-Chamorro treaty of 1916, the United States still retained its exclusive rights to the Nicaraguan canal route and to bases near the termini. These concessions were resented by Nicaraguan nationalists, but not until March 1970 did the United States offer to reexamine the treaty. *Department of State Bulletin,* 62 (April 27, 1970), 560–61.

[9]In keeping with the abandonment of the protectorate over Panama, was the conclusion in 1937 of a new treaty with Mexico abrogating Article 8 of the Gadsden Treaty of 1853. This never-used article had guaranteed to the United States the use of a proposed plank-and-rail road across the Isthmus of Tehuantepec for its citizens, its mails, its property, and its troops, and had authorized the United States to extend its protection to the route whenever it should feel such protection "sanctioned and warranted by the public or international law."

the North"; the freeing of trade, and the halting of such quarrels as prevailed among the Latin sister republics themselves—notably the destructive war between Bolivia and Paraguay over possession of the Gran Chaco. Something was achieved in all these directions.

Normally, the next Inter-American Conference would have met in 1938, but alarming developments in Europe—the increasing aggressiveness of Nazi Germany and Fascist Italy, the penetration of German and Italian influence and trade into Latin America, and later, the Italo-Ethiopian War—seemed to menace the peace of the New World as well as the Old. They led President Roosevelt to suggest the calling of a special conference to consider how best to safeguard the peace of the American republics. Feelers put out in 1935 brought favorable responses, Argentina stipulating that her acceptance was conditional upon the choice of Buenos Aires as the site of the Conference. Consequently, the Inter-American Conference for the Maintenance of Peace convened in the Argentine capital on December 1, 1936. Again Secretary Hull headed the United States delegation, and to emphasize the importance of the occasion, President Roosevelt made the long voyage to Buenos Aires and addressed the opening session of the Conference.

Apart from the adoption of a strengthened declaration of nonintervention, the most important achievements, of the Buenos Aires Conference were a consultative agreement, officially labeled the Convention for the Maintenance, Preservation and Re-establishment of Peace; and a Declaration of Principles of Inter-American Solidarity and Cooperation. The convention provided that the governments of the American republics should consult together upon methods of peaceful cooperation, (a) "in the event that the peace of the American Republics is menaced," (b) "in the event of war, or a virtual state of war between American States," or (c) "in the

event of an international war outside America which might menace the peace of the American Republics." In the last named contingency, which under the circumstances was the most important, the consultation should "determine the proper time and manner in which the signatory States, if they so desire, may eventually cooperate in some action tending to preserve the peace of the American Continent."[10]

The other principal document emanating from the Buenos Aires Conference, referred to in brief as the Declaration of Solidarity, proclaimed four principles as "accepted by the international American community." These were: (1) nonrecognition of territorial acquisitions by conquest, (2) nonintervention, (3) illegality of the collection of debts by force, and (4) peaceful settlement of all disputes among American states. In subscribing to the declaration, the United States once more endorsed the nonintervention dogma and also accepted, in point 3, the Drago Doctrine without qualification. The heart of the declaration, however, was the assertion

That every act susceptible of disturbing the peace of America affects each and every one of them [the American nations], and justifies the initiation of the procedure of consultation provided for in the Convention . . . executed at this Conference.

It is this paragraph of the declaration, coupled with the convention's provision for consultation, that has given rise to the statement that the Buenos Aires Conference "continentalized" the Monroe Doctrine. That doctrine was not mentioned in the documents, it is true, but henceforth any threat from Europe (or Asia) to the peace or independence of any part of

[10]Of the expression "if they so desire," Hull remarks that the Argentines "were able to emasculate this resolution by inserting four words." Hull, *Memoirs,* 1: 500.

America—any threat that would have led the United States to invoke the Monroe Doctrine—was now declared to affect "each and every one" of the American nations and to justify their consulting together. Consultation, of course, did not guarantee action, but neither did the Monroe Doctrine.

A weak spot in the Buenos Aires program was the failure to define how and through whom consultation should take place. The cog thus omitted from the machinery at Buenos Aires was inserted at the Eighth International Conference of American States at Lima, Peru, in December 1938. The Conference convened shortly after the Munich settlement in Europe, but few of the delegates shared Neville Chamberlain's faith that Munich assured "peace in our time." The likelihood of war in Europe spurred the American statesmen to action. The Declaration of Lima proclaimed any threat to "the peace, security, or territorial integrity of any American Republic" to be the concern of all and provided that to consult upon methods of meeting any such threat, the Foreign Ministers should meet together upon the call of any one of them.

Thus before the war began in Europe, the twenty-one American republics were prepared, to a degree without precedent, to present a common front to danger from abroad. The outbreak of war led to a series of conferences of Foreign Ministers, under the Lima plan, at Panama (September–October 1939), at Havana (July 1940), and after the United States was attacked by Japan, at Rio de Janeiro (January 1942). Eventually all the American republics followed the United States into the war, though Argentina, which harbored an ill-disguised sympathy for the Axis powers, hung back to the last possible moment. Argentina was the weakest spot in the Pan American united front. A state which cooperated in that front, but which in the 1920s and 1930s had sorely tried the patience of the United States, was Mexico.

Mexico Tests the Good Neighbor Policy

In considering United States relations with Mexico in the interwar period, it is necessary to remember that in those years Mexico was passing through the tremendous social revolution that had been launched by Carranza with the issuance of the Constitution of 1917. This was Mexico's "New Deal," a reform movement much more radical than the "Roosevelt Revolution" in the United States. Its theoretical aims were the betterment of the lot of peasant and worker in Mexico and, as a necessary preliminary of such betterment, recovery by Mexico of control of important elements in its resources that had passed into the possession of foreigners. Thus the Revolution took on a "Mexico for the Mexicans" coloration.

This attitude toward foreigners was a reversal of the policy that had prevailed under Porfirio Díaz (1877–1911). Díaz had welcomed foreign capital to Mexico. Foreigners, chiefly Americans and British, had invested in Mexican agricultural, grazing, and timber lands, in Mexican mines, and, especially after 1900, in Mexican oil fields. Without accepting the Mexican thesis that such investments had amounted to "exploitation" of the Mexicans, it can readily be admitted that foreign ownership stood in the way of parts of the new Mexican reform program.

The two aspects of that program that chiefly collided with American property rights were land reform and the nationalization of subsoil properties, especially petroleum.[11] The common lands, or *ejidos*, that had once been appurtenances of Mexican villages had to a large extent been absorbed in private landed estates, some

[11] A third aspect of the program that aroused much antagonism in the United States, though not on economic grounds, was anticlericalism. The campaign against the Roman Catholic Church, especially against its control of education, was deplored by Catholics in the United States.

owned by Mexican, some by foreign land-lords. It became a major object of the Revo-lution to restore the *ejidos* to the peasantry. In the earlier and more conservative phase of the Revolution (1920–1934), dominated by the "Northern Dynasty"[12] of Álvaro Obregón and Plutarco Elías Calles, the lands were distributed in individual hold-ings; under the more leftist Lázaro Cár-denas (1934–1940), the favored system was communal ownership. In obtaining the lands for distribution, the Mexican gov-ernment resorted to expropriation (the tak-ing of property with compensation) rather than confiscation (uncompensated sei-zure). Trouble with foreign owners and their governments arose when compensa-tion was long delayed or inadequate.

The *ejidos* made less international trou-ble than the petroleum properties. Article 27 of the Mexican Constitution of 1917 nationalized subsoil resources. Petroleum or gold or silver, that is, was the property of the nation, not of the person or corporation who owned the surface above it. This was the common rule in Spanish countries and had been the rule in Mexico until 1878. During the Díaz period, however, purchas-ers of Mexican lands had acquired subsoil as well as surface rights, and in this way large petroleum properties had come into the possession of United States and British corporations.

No one denied the right of Mexico to nationalize petroleum deposits not already in private hands. The crucial question was: is Article 27 retroactive? Will oil men who acquired their properties from Díaz now be required to obtain permits and pay fees for the privilege of removing the oil that they

[12]The phrase "Northern Dynasty" is applied to this phase of the Revolution by H. F. Cline in his study, *The United States and Mexico* (Cambridge: Harvard Univer-sity Press, 1953). Obregón (1920–1924), Calles (1924–1928), and the "puppet presidents" (1928–1934) who took orders from Calles all came from northern Mexico and were less socialistic in outlook than many of the southern leaders.

claim is theirs? Carranza had promised pri-vately that Article 27 would not be applied retroactively to American-owned proper-ties and then had broken his promise. Obregón, who in 1920 overthrew Carranza and was then duly elected to the presidency of Mexico, repeated the promise but re-fused the request of Secretary of State Hughes to put it in a treaty. Hughes, there-fore, withheld recognition from Obregón.

The Mexican Supreme Court, in a series of oil cases, enunciated the "positive acts" principle: if the owner of an oil property had before 1917 performed some "positive act," such as drilling a well, his full owner-ship could not be questioned. If he had performed no such act, he forfeited subsoil rights. This was a compromise acceptable to the State Department if its permanency could be guaranteed. Obregón, fearful of domestic repercussions if he yielded too much to Washington pressure, still refused to make a treaty. He did, however, sub-scribe to an "extra-official pact," known as the Bucareli agreement, which embodied the "positive acts" principle and made other concessions to the United States. On this basis the United States accorded Obregón *de jure* recognition, August 31, 1923. In the following year, when he faced a formidable rebellion, arms and airplanes supplied by the United States helped him to rout his enemies.

Under Obregón's successor, Calles (1924–1928), the Mexican Congress evi-dently regarded the Bucareli agreement as no longer binding. It passed legislation limiting to fifty years the ownership of pe-troleum rights acquired before 1917. This apparent breach of faith, aggravated by at-tacks on the Catholic Church in Mexico and by open Mexican support of the Sacasa in-surrection in Nicaragua, produced a crisis in United States—Mexican relations. The Hearst press, the oil companies, and other interested parties, agitated for interven-tion. President Coolidge sent to Congress on January 10, 1927, a special message on

Nicaragua, in which he complained that Mexico alone had recognized Sacasa's insurrectionary government, and that Sacasa had been supplied with arms belonging to the Mexican government through the active agency of Mexican officials. A few days later Secretary of State Kellogg released to the press a statement attempting to link the Mexican government and its interference in Nicaragua with the Communist party in the United States and hence with Russian Bolshevism. Communist Russia, he charged, was seeking footholds in Latin America.[13]

These alarmist pronouncements were received coolly in Congress and in the country at large. On January 18, Senator Joseph T. Robinson of Arkansas introduced a resolution urging arbitration of the controversies with Mexico. The Senate passed it a week later by a vote of 79 to 0. President Coolidge took his cue from the Senate. In an April 25 address to the United Press, he reported friendly assurances from the Mexican ambassador and avowed his conviction that "it will surely be possible to reach an amicable adjustment."[14] Soon thereafter he sent to Mexico a new ambassador, Dwight W. Morrow, with instructions to do whatever was necessary to prevent war. Morrow, though a Wall Street banker, a member of the Morgan firm, showed great sympathy for Mexico and an aptitude for cultivating Mexican good will. From the first he got on well with Calles. Under the latter's influence, the Mexican Supreme Court again entered the picture, reaffirming the principle that "positive acts" before 1917 conferred full ownership. In December 1927, the Mexican Congress adopted a new Petroleum Code, following the court decision and embodying the terms of the Bucareli agreement. The State Department expressed itself as satisfied that American interests could thenceforth rely for protection upon the Mexican courts.

So matters rested, as far as petroleum was concerned, until 1938. Lázaro Cárdenas, who came to the Mexican presidency in 1934, was the first non-northern President since the overthrow of Díaz. Though he owed his rise to Calles, he was more socialistic in his thinking than the "Northern Dynasty" and soon showed that he was no one's puppet. Somewhat like the contemporary Roosevelt, he catered to the small farmer and the working man and placed new emphasis upon the slogan "Mexico for the Mexicans." In his attitude to American interests he may have drawn courage from Roosevelt's acceptance of the nonintervention principle at Montevideo and Buenos Aires.[15] In any event, he stepped up the expropriation of agricultural lands to a new tempo and brought about the effective organization in one union of the scattered employees of the foreign oil companies. Extravagant demands of this union, for increased wages and "fringe benefits," some of which would have amounted almost to management of the businesses, were rejected by the companies. The demands were found "reasonable" by a not wholly impartial commission and ordered into effect by a Federal Board of Arbitration. When the companies again refused, Cárdenas, in a decree of March 18, 1938, ordered their properties expropriated.[16]

---

[13]*Congressional Record,* 68 Cong. 2 sess., pp. 1649–51.

[14]*Foreign Relations, 1927,* 3: 217.

[15]S. F. Bemis emphasizes the effect of nonintervention on Cárdenas' policy in *Latin American Policy,* pp. 345–50. See also the same author's long chapter on Mexico in *A Diplomatic History of the United States,* 4th ed. (New York: Holt, Rinehart & Winston, Inc., 1955), chap. 30.

[16]Cline, *The U.S. and Mexico,* pp. 229–38, believes that Cárdenas did not premeditate the act of expropriation, that he was on the point of accepting a compromise proposal by the companies when their request that he put his promises in writing seemed to him a reflection upon his own and the nation's honor and touched off the decree of March 18.

The Mexican Settlement of 1941

The expropriation of the American and British oil properties involved Mexico in new arguments with both governments concerned. British protests were so strong that Mexico responded by breaking off diplomatic relations. In Washington, Cárdenas' highhanded action and his refusal to submit the American claims for expropriated property to international arbitration exhausted the patience of Secretary Hull. He would have taken as strong a position as the British, and presumably with similar results, had he not been dissuaded by Josephus Daniels, the sympathetic American ambassador in Mexico, and by President Roosevelt. Roosevelt, no great friend of corporations, announced that he felt more concern for expropriated American farmers in Mexico than for the oil companies. The latter, he said, could rightly expect payment for the amount of their invested capital but not for the value of oil still in the ground, which formed a large part of their claim. The United States acknowledged the right of the Mexican government to expropriate private property and ultimately consented to leave the amount and method of compensation to negotiation rather than arbitration.[17]

The American companies negotiated directly with the Mexican government. Their claims totaled $260,000,000. Compromises were suggested, but no agreement was reached. Subsequently, one of the companies, Sinclair Oil, negotiated apart from

the others and accepted $8,500,000 in settlement of its claims.

By this time the clouds of World War II were drifting over the New World. In Mexico, friction with the United States and Great Britain was assisting Nazi infiltration, which was not welcomed either by Cárdenas or by his successor, Manuel Avila Camacho (1940–1946). The United States was anxious both to eliminate the Nazi influence and to close the rift in the Inter-American front before the war actually reached American shores. The situation was favorable for compromise, which was shortly arranged.

An agreement signed November 19, 1941, settled all outstanding controversies between the United States and Mexico and assured Mexico of all the benefits of good neighborliness. The United States promised a reciprocal trade treaty, credits through the Export-Import Bank, continued purchases of Mexican silver at the world price, and help toward modernization of Mexico's obsolete military establishment. In return Mexico agreed to pay a total of $40,000,000 for agrarian and other American claims, exclusive of those derived from oil properties. Of this total, six millions had already been paid; the remainder was to be paid in annual installments of $2,500,000. The task of evaluating the expropriated oil properties and recommending a method of compensation for them was assigned to two commissioners, one from each country, who were to report within five months. Mexico made a down payment of $9,000,000 on the debt that was thus to be adjudicated. The commissioners valued the expropriated properties, exclusive of Sinclair's, at just under $24,000,000. They recommended that one-third of the sum in excess of the $9,000,000 already advanced be paid July 1, 1942; the remainder, in five equal annual installments. The companies protested but were told the State Department would not support them in asking more. They accepted, and payments

---

[17]Bryce Wood, *The Making of the Good Neighbor Policy* (New York: Columbia University Press, 1961), chaps. 8–9. Hull argued that under the inter-American arbitration treaty of 1929, Mexico was obligated to accept arbitration of such claims as those of the oil companies. The position of Mexico and other Latin American governments was that compensation for expropriated property was a domestic matter not subject to arbitration. The United States accepted this position rather than jeopardize the fruits of the Good Neighbor Policy.

were made on schedule. By 1949 the American oil claims had been liquidated.

In all, including principal and interest, the payments to Sinclair, and the purchase price of a few small companies that were not expropriated but were bought out, Mexico paid about $42,000,000 for oil properties owned in the United States. The British, who waited until after the war for a settlement, secured somewhat better terms. By an agreement of 1947, Mexico agreed to pay to the expropriated British companies a principal of $81,250,000, with·interest, in annual installments to end in 1962.[18]

There is no doubt that in accepting this settlement with Mexico the government of the United States sacrificed the interests of some of its citizens. How far the claims that were surrendered or abated were ethically

[18]Cline, *The U.S. and Mexico,* pp. 239–51.

justifiable is a problem too complicated to be attacked here. How those claims could have been collected in full without armed intervention and conquest is not easy to see. Of American policy toward Mexico, as of the voluntary grant of independence to the Philippines, history will perhaps record that the United States was first among western powers to recognize that the sun had gone down upon old-fashioned imperialism, whether political or economic. At any rate, in applying the Good Neighbor Policy to Mexico under trying circumstances, the United States made good the pledges given at Montevideo and Buenos Aires and assured itself of cordial Latin American support in the impending war. Three weeks after the signing of the Mexican agreement, Japanese bombs fell upon Pearl Harbor.

ADDITIONAL READINGS

Dozer, Donald M., *Are We Good Neighbors? Three Decades of Inter-American Relations, 1930–1960.* Gainesville, Florida: University of Florida Press, 1960.

Gellman, Irwin F., *Roosevelt and Batista: Good Neighbor Policy in Cuba, 1933–1945.* Albuquerque, New Mexico: University of New Mexico Press, 1973.

McCann, Frank D., Jr., *The Brazilian-American Alliance, 1937–1945.* Princeton: Princeton University Press, 1974.

18. The Coming of World War II

The three powers, whose initial acts of aggression were described in earlier chapters, operated until 1936 quite independently of one another. It was natural, however, that Germany, Italy, and Japan should be drawn together. All three were "dissatisfied" powers, revisionists not content with the territorial heritage left them by the last war and the peace settlement. They could realize their ambitions only by destruction of the status quo established in 1919 and sanctified by the treaties of Washington and Locarno and the Pact of Paris. All three, furthermore, were ideologically compatible. In all, the governing cliques held democracy in contempt and paid little respect to treaty obligations. An alliance or understanding between them should have surprised no one.

Up to 1936 there had been one point of serious rivalry between Germany and Italy. Hitler was anxious to annex Austria, his native land, to Nazi Germany. Mussolini had no wish to face a powerful Germany at the Brenner Pass. In 1934, when Austrian Nazis murdered Chancellor Dollfuss and tried, unsuccessfully, to take over the government, with *Anschluss* (union with Germany) as an objective, Mussolini mobilized Italian troops on the Austrian frontier and, in effect, served notice that he would defend Austria's independence. But by 1936, the situation had changed. Hitler had maintained a sympathetic attitude to Italy during the war in Ethiopia, when the League powers were trying to halt Italy with sanctions. The outbreak of the Spanish Civil War found the two dictators benevolently disposed to Franco. In July, Hitler promised to respect Austria's independence and to abstain from interfering in her internal politics. On October 25, 1936, Hitler and Mussolini signed an accord pledging collaboration in their policy toward Spain and in the defense of Europe against Communism, and arranging for economic cooperation in southern Europe. Hitler recognized Mussolini's Ethiopian empire and was rewarded with economic privileges there and in other Italian colonies. The "Rome-Berlin Axis" had become a reality.

Just a month after the Rome-Berlin accord, Germany and Japan signed (November 25, 1936) an Anti-Comintern pact. Ostensibly aimed at the Communist International, or Comintern, and pledging the signatories to consultation and cooperation in measures to combat Communism, the pact contained a secret addendum providing for political, or even military, cooperation against the Soviet Union. When Italy signed the document a year later, the combination was referred to as the Rome-Berlin-Tokyo Axis. Henceforth each of the three could expect the sympathetic understanding of the others in its efforts to break down the status quo.

Beginning of the "China Incident"

When Mussolini adhered to the Anti-Comintern pact (November 6, 1937), Japanese troops were already engaged in large-scale operations against China. What the Japanese called the "China Incident" or "China Affair" (but never the China war!) began with a seemingly unpremeditated clash between Chinese and Japanese troops at Lukouchiao, or the Marco Polo bridge, near a village just outside Peiping, on the night of July 7, 1937. The Japanese troops involved were in Hopei province by virtue of the Boxer protocol of 1900, which permitted guards along the Peiping-Tientsin railway. The Japanese had made excessive use of that privilege, but there is no convincing evidence that the collision of armed forces was planned, and there seems to have been a real effort to settle the resulting controversy through negotiations between the local commanders.[1] New fighting broke out, however, both in the Peiping area and at Shanghai. A Chinese proposal made through the British embassy in Tokyo, that hostilities cease and that all troops withdraw to the lines held before the clash, was not answered by the Japanese government.[2] After three weeks of futile negotiations, during which Japanese civilians were warned to leave China and Japanese reinforcements were sent to the mainland, the Nipponese opened a full-scale offensive.

Whatever were the intentions of the Japanese Premier (Prince Konoye) and Foreign Office, it is hard to escape the conclusion that the Army found in the incident of July 7 an excuse to secure by force its main objective in China, the control of the five northern provinces. Since 1933 the objective had been sought in vain by negotiation and by the encouragement of autonomy movements in the northern provinces. Time was strengthening China's hands. Chiang Kai-shek had put down a rebellion in the south and as a result of the "Sian incident," had agreed to join with the Chinese Communists in a united front against Japan. Japanese expansionists must have felt, as they had felt in 1931, that it was now or never for their plans in China.

The United States and the China Incident

The United States took at first an impartial attitude toward the two belligerents. This was in accord with the ideas of Ambassador Joseph C. Grew, who advised a threefold policy: (1) noninvolvement in the conflict, (2) protection of American lives, property, and rights in China, (3) maintenance of friendship with both parties. In the protection of American citizens and their properties and rights in China, the United States adopted what was described as a "middle-of-the-road" policy, neither abandoning its nationals and their rights nor resorting to intervention for their protection. Additional American marines were sent to Shanghai for the protection of the International Settlement, but Americans in China who could leave were advised to do so. The governments of both Japan and China were notified that the United States reserved all its treaty rights in China and the right to compensation for damages inflicted.

Since there had been no declaration of war, the President refrained from invoking the Neutrality Act, though advised to invoke it by Ambassador Grew and by numerous peace societies in the United States. The President thus reversed the policy that he had followed in the similarly undeclared war between Italy and Ethiopia. His reason was, presumably, that application of the act would be more injurious to China than to Japan; it would cut off arms and the use of American ships, both of which China needed and Japan did not. The President did, however, forbid the use of government-owned ships to carry arms, ammunition, or implements of war to either party, and he warned private shipowners that they would engage in such trade at their own risk.[3]

[1] F. C. Jones, *Japan's New Order in East Asia: Its Rise and Fall, 1937–1945* (New York: Oxford University Press, 1954), pp. 30–49.

[2] J. C. Grew, *Turbulent Era: A Diplomatic Record of Forty Years, 1904–1945,* 2 vols. (Boston: Houghton Mifflin Company, 1952), 2: 1049–50, 1052.

[3] On September 16 the S.S. *Wichita,* operated by the U. S. Maritime Commission, was required to unload at San Diego, California, a cargo of airplanes that it was transporting from Baltimore to China.

Early in October 1937, the United States departed from its policy of impartiality to join with the League of Nations in labeling Japan a treaty-violator. On October 5, in a speech in Chicago, President Roosevelt deplored the fact "that the epidemic of world lawlessness is spreading" and suggested a "quarantine" for those nations infected with it. Although the President mentioned no nation by name, he was clearly alluding to Japan. What he meant by a "quarantine" he did not spell out, but there is good evidence that he had in mind complete severance of relations with a nation adjudged to be an aggressor.[4]

The "quarantine" speech met with a mixed reaction in the United States. There was much favorable comment, but the President, apparently more impressed by the very vocal isolationist criticism, did not pursue the idea. On the day after the speech, however, the League of Nations Assembly, sitting in Geneva, adopted a report holding that Japan's invasion of China violated both the Nine-Power Treaty and the Pact of Paris. The State Department announced its concurrence on the same day (October 6, 1937). Thus the United States stood committed in behalf of China and against Japan. This series of events came as a shock to Ambassador Grew in Tokyo. For five years Grew had striven to build a firm structure of Japanese-American friendship; he was convinced of the "hopelessness of deterring aggression by moral judgments." The United States had, he feared, "chosen the road which might lead directly to involvement . . . in the Far Eastern mess."[5]

The Brussels Conference

The League Assembly, at the same time that it charged Japan with treaty violation, suggested that the signers of the Nine-Power Treaty undertake a settlement of the dispute. Accordingly, the Belgian government issued invitations to a conference to be held at Brussels. Invitations went to the original and subsequent signers of the treaty and also to Germany and the Soviet Union.[6] Japan declined the invitation, on the grounds that the League had already condemned Japan without hearing its side of the case and, furthermore, that the quarrel was one purely between Japan and China and in no way concerned the other Nine-Power Treaty powers. Germany also declined to attend. Italy sent a representative, who, as it turned out, supported the views of Italy's axis partner.

The Brussels Conference, attended by delegates from nineteen nations, met from November 3 to November 24, 1937. In Japan's absence and in the face of her refusal to consult with representatives of any of the participating powers, no attempt at composing the conflict was feasible. President Roosevelt, seemingly made cautious by the reaction to his "quarantine" speech, had ruled out any mention of sanctions. The Conference, therefore, could do little more than reaffirm (Italy dissenting) that the principles of the Nine-Power Treaty were applicable to the controversy and serve notice that any settlement of the conflict must be consistent with those principles.[7]

[4]W. L. Langer and S. E. Gleason, *The Challenge to Isolation, 1937–1940* (New York: Harper & Row, Publishers, 1952), p. 19; Dorothy Borg, "Notes on Roosevelt's Quarantine Speech," *Political Science Quarterly*, 72 (September 1957), 405–33; T. B. Jacobs, "Roosevelt's Quarantine Speech," *Historian*, 24 (August 1962), 483–502.

[5]Grew, *Turbulent Era*, 2: 1167–68.

[6]Bolivia, Denmark, Mexico, Norway and Sweden had signed the Nine-Power Treaty subsequent to its negotiation. To the Brussels Conference, Canada, Australia, New Zealand, South Africa, and India, which had been represented in the British Empire delegation at Washington in 1922, sent independent delegations. In all, nineteen nations were represented.

[7]*The Conference of Brussels, November 3–24, 1937, Convened in Virtue of Article 7 of the Nine-Power Treaty of Washington of 1922*, Department of State Conference Series 37 (Washington: Government Printing Office, 1938).

On Japanese policy this notice had no effect whatever. In justification of her course in China, Japan kept insisting: (1) that she was acting in self-defense against Chinese violence and Chinese infringement of Japanese rights; (2) that the Nine-Power Treaty was obsolete and the Pact of Paris inapplicable to the Far East; (3) that the dispute concerned only Japan and China and that intervention of third parties was inadmissible.

The Panay Bombing

A few weeks after the Brussels Conference, Japanese-American relations were imperiled when young Japanese aviators, on December 12, bombed and sank the American gunboat *Panay*, escorting American tankers in the Yangtze River. Two American crew members were killed and many injured. The attack occurred under conditions of excellent visibility and could not be explained away as a mistake. The Japanese government was deeply perturbed. The Foreign Minister came in person to the American embassy in Tokyo to offer abject apologies and a promise of reparations for the injured and the families of the killed, and Japanese civilians contributed generously to a fund for the same purpose. American public opinion took the matter calmly—in contrast to the "Remember the *Maine*" furor of 1898. Within two weeks the Japanese apology was accepted and the crisis passed.[8]

[8]The United States government preferred not to pass on the private donations to the American sufferers. Arrangements were therefore made to have the fund devoted to "some constructive purpose in the interests of Japanese-American friendship." Grew, *Turbulent Era*, 2: 1205. See also M. T. Koginos, *The Panay Incident: Prelude to War* (Lafayette, Ind.: Purdue University Studies, 1967).

The "New Order" in East Asia

In the meantime Japan was pushing the war in an effort to destroy Chinese resistance and compel the government of Chiang Kai-shek to make peace on Japan's terms. In so doing, the Japanese did not hesitate to bomb Chinese cities from the air—a practice to which they had resorted at Chinchow in 1931, which had been followed by Italian and German aviators serving Franco in the Spanish Civil War, but which was still regarded with abhorrence by the democracies. The bombing of Nanking in September 1937, and of Canton and other cities later, led the United States, in July 1938, to place a "moral embargo" on sales of airplanes to Japan. This took the form of a letter from Secretary Hull to American airplane manufacturers stating that the government was "strongly opposed" to the sale of such equipment to nations guilty of bombing civilian populations. This request was, for the most part, adhered to by the companies concerned.[9]

The bombings were in part preparatory to land campaigns against the Chinese cities. Nanking was taken December 15, 1937. The Chinese government had withdrawn to Hankow. In October 1938, Hankow and Canton were occupied, and the government retreated to Chungking on the upper Yangtze. All principal ports, the coast cities, and the main railway lines were now in Japanese hands and, by the ordinary rules of the game, China should have acknowledged defeat and have made peace on Japan's terms. But the Chinese armies, though beaten, had not been destroyed, and the government of Chiang Kai-shek fought stubbornly on.

Since Chiang would not negotiate, the Japanese conquerors set up puppet governments in the occupied area. A Peking Provisional Government was established

[9]*New York Times*, January 10, 1939, pp. 1, 8.

in the north in December 1937; a Reformed Government of the Chinese Republic at Nanking in March 1938. Two years later a once prominent Kuomintang politician, Wang Ching-wei, was persuaded to head the latter, which Japan recognized as the government of China.

While extending her military control over eastern China, Japan was consolidating her economic hold upon the country and following a policy of restricting the activities of foreign business firms, if not forcing them out altogether. At the same time, American and other foreign missions in China found that Japanese bombs had a more than chance affinity for their churches, schools and hospitals. The "open door" was being closed to both the business and the culture of the West.

The opposing Japanese and American positions were clearly stated late in 1938. A Japanese Foreign Office statement, issued on November 3, 1938, proclaimed that Japan was inaugurating a "new order" that would "insure the permanent stability of East Asia," a new order having "for its foundation a tripartite relationship of mutual aid and co-ordination between Japan, Manchukuo and China in political, economic, cultural and other fields."[10] American complaints that the "new order" might infringe treaty rights met with the declaration that no useful purpose would be served by "an attempt to apply to present and future conditions without any changes, concepts and principles which were applicable to conditions prevailing before the present incident."[11]

To this statement Ambassador Grew, speaking for Secretary Hull, replied that the United States was aware that conditions had changed and was willing to adapt existing treaties to new conditions through orderly "processes of negotiation and agreement" but could not assent to "the abrogation of any of this country's rights or obligations by the arbitrary action of agents or authorities of any other country." As for the "new order," the United States could not admit the right of any one power to "prescribe . . . the terms and conditions of a 'new order' in areas not under its sovereignty and to constitute itself the repository of authority and the agent of destiny in regard thereto."[12]

Thus by the end of 1938 the United States and Japan seemed to have reached a complete impasse in regard to China. During the course of that year, however, the center of international tension had shifted from the Far East to Europe.

Hitler Opens His Drang nach Osten

During 1938 Hitler took the first two steps in his *Drang nach Osten* or drive to the east. He annexed Austria and the predominantly German sections of Czechoslovakia. In order to win Italian support, Hitler had, as noted above, promised to respect Austrian independence and to refrain from interfering in the small republic's internal politics. At heart, he had never abandoned his hope of uniting the land of his birth with his adopted fatherland, a feeling not unreciprocated by some Austrians themselves, and by the spring of 1938 he felt strong enough to cast his promises to the winds.

In February he summoned Schuschnigg, the Austrian Chancellor, to a conference at Berchtesgaden, the Führer's mountain retreat in Bavaria, and demanded the admission of prominent Austrian Nazis to the cabinet. Schuschnigg complied but called for an immediate plebiscite, which he felt sure would demonstrate popular opposition to union with Germany. The Nazis were apparently of the same opinion, for

---

[10]*Foreign Relations, Japan, 1931–1941,* 1: 478.

[11]*Foreign Relations, Japan, 1931–1941,* 1: 800.

[12]U. S. Department of State, *Peace and War; United States Foreign Policy, 1931–1941* (Washington: Government Printing Office, 1943), pp. 445–47.

they at once demanded the resignation of Schuschnigg and a postponement of the plebiscite, threatening invasion by German troops as the alternative. Schuschnigg resigned on March 11. His successor as Chancellor, the Nazi Seyss-Inquart, immediately called in German troops, allegedly to suppress disorders in Austria. On March 12 the German government proclaimed Austria to be a state of the German Reich, and two days later Hitler entered Vienna amid a great show of rejoicing. *Anschluss* was complete. France and Great Britain protested, but no one raised a hand in resistance, least of all Mussolini, who had blocked the way in 1934.

Chamberlain Goes to Berchtesgaden

Hitler next turned to "rescue" what he termed the "tortured and oppressed" Germans of Czechoslovakia, the most democratic state of Central Europe. Of Czechoslovakia's 14,500,000 people, about 3,500,000 were Germans. These lived for the most part in the Sudeten area that fringed the western end of the republic, facing German territory to the north, west, and south. The Sudeten Germans, comprising one of numerous racial minorities in Czechoslovakia, had shown little dissatisfaction with their government until 1932, when the Nazi movement first gained some strength among them. From then on to 1938, the Sudeten Nazis, led by one Konrad Henlein, kept up a growing agitation, first for complete cultural and political autonomy within Czechoslovakia, finally for union with Nazi Germany.

The Czechoslovak government made a succession of compromise offers, but these were one by one rejected by Henlein, who consulted Hitler at each step. By September 1938 it was evident that nothing less than cession of Sudetenland to Germany would satisfy the Führer. The Czechoslovak government did not propose to yield to dismemberment without putting up a fight. It had a relatively good army and a defensible frontier. It also had defensive alliances with France and Russia. If it were attacked by Germany, and if its allies fulfilled their obligations, a general European war was certain. This would, in all probability, involve England also.

In an effort to find a peaceful settlement for the Sudeten problem, Prime Minister Neville Chamberlain of Great Britain paid two visits to Hitler, at Berchtesgaden and at Godesberg. In the first (September 15, 1938) Chamberlain ascertained that the Führer would take nothing less than surrender of the Sudetenland to Germany. In the second, a week later, he submitted to Hitler a plan for the prompt and peaceful transfer to Germany of the areas of Czechoslovakia with population more than 50 percent German, the fixing of the new frontier by an international commission, and an international guarantee of the independence of a Czechoslovakia shorn of these important segments of her territory and population. These terms the Czech government had agreed to under combined British and French pressure.

To Chamberlain's consternation, Hitler rejected this proposal as too slow. Instead, he demanded the immediate withdrawal of all Czech military and official civilian personnel from areas that he specified, with plebiscites to follow in other areas where the percentage of German population was doubtful. German troops, he said, would occupy the specified areas October 1, whether or not Czechoslovakia accepted his ultimatum.

Czechoslovakia at once rejected this proposal and mobilized its army of 1,500,000 men. France followed with partial mobilization, as did Belgium. France and Britain made it clear that they would assist Czechoslovakia if it were attacked, while Mussolini announced his intention of standing by his Axis partner. The threat of war was very real.

The United States Has a Finger in Appeasement

At this point (September 27, 1938) President Roosevelt entered the picture. Urging Hitler to lay the controversy before an international conference, he added:

> Should you agree to a solution in this peaceful manner I am convinced that hundreds of millions throughout the world would recognize your action as an outstanding historic service to all humanity.

Roosevelt also joined with Chamberlain and French Premier Daladier in a plea to Mussolini to persuade Hitler to accept a peaceful settlement that would give him substantially all he asked for. Hitler yielded to the extent of agreeing to meet with Mussolini and the French and British Premiers at Munich. There, on September 29, Hitler and Mussolini, Chamberlain and Daladier agreed on a plan that the Czech government perforce accepted. It differed little from Hitler's ultimatum of a week before, merely allowing slightly more time for Czech withdrawal from the surrendered area. Thus, it was assumed, war had been averted.[13] Prime Minister Chamberlain told the people of England that he had

---

[13]There is some reason to believe that Hitler was bluffing at Godesberg and Munich. His Chief of Staff, Marshal Keitel, was asked after the war whether Germany would have attacked a Czechoslovakia backed by France and Great Britain. He replied: "Certainly not. We were not strong enough militarily." The object of the Munich settlement, he said, "was to get Russia out of Europe, to gain time, and to complete the German armaments." Quoted by Winston S. Churchill, *The Gathering Storm*, Vol. 1 of *The Second World War* (Boston: Houghton Mifflin Company, 1948), p. 319. Quotations from *The Second World War* are reprinted by permission of Houghton Mifflin Company and Cassell & Co. Ltd., London. That American policy in the Munich crisis weakened the French spirit of resistance to Hitler is the conclusion of John McV. Haight, Jr., "France, the United States, and the Munich Crisis," *Journal of Modern History*, 32 (December 1960), 340–58.

brought back "peace with honour. I believe," he added, "it is peace in our time."

The Munich settlement proved to be but the prelude to the complete extinction of Czechoslovakia as an independent nation. Hungary and Poland at once demanded and received slices of territory where Magyars and Poles were numerous. Internal dissension between Czechs and Slovaks afforded Hitler an excuse for taking control of the destinies of those two ethnical divisions of the former republic. In March 1939, Bohemia-Moravia and Slovakia became German protectorates.

While Hitler was helping himself to territory in Central Europe, Mussolini seized the occasion to strengthen Italy's position in the Mediterranean. On April 7, 1939, Italian troops occupied the independent state of Albania, which was, a few days later, added to the realms ruled over by Mussolini in the name of King Victor Emmanuel III.

The Threat to Poland

Hitler had declared at Munich: "This [Sudetenland] is the last territorial claim which I have to make in Europe."[14] His absorption of Czechoslovakia had given the lie to that declaration, and by April 1939 he was pressing Poland for consent to annexation of the free city of Danzig and a sort of German corridor across the Polish Corridor to give Germany freer access to East Prussia. By this time even Mr. Chamberlain had lost faith in Hitler's promises. He abruptly abandoned appeasement and, with France, gave guarantees of aid against aggression to Poland and later to Rumania and to Greece, the latter threatened by Italy's April occupation of Albania. Geography would make it difficult to implement these guarantees effectively, but they at least served notice on the Axis powers that further aggression against their small

---

[14]Churchill, *The Gathering Storm*, p. 345.

neighbors would mean war with the great western democracies.

The United States Tries to Shake Off Its Fetters

In Washington, the sympathies of the administration were unequivocally on the side of the European democracies and against the Fascist and Nazi dictatorships. In his annual message to Congress, January 4, 1939, Mr. Roosevelt remarked that although the United States had no intention of using other than peaceful methods to discourage aggressors, there were "many methods short of war, but stronger and more effective than mere words, of bringing home to aggressor governments the aggregate sentiments of our own people." But "methods short of war," if that phrase meant material aid, were barred by the neutrality law which, as the President complained in the same message, "may actually give aid to an aggressor and deny it to the victim." Thus began a long campaign to have the neutrality law repealed or revised.[15]

On April 15, a week after the Italian invasion of Albania, Roosevelt addressed a surprise message to Hitler and Mussolini. Referring to the fear of war that hung over the world, he suggested that the two dictators could dispel it by giving a ten-year nonaggression guarantee to their neighbors in Europe and the Near East—the President named thirty-one. He believed that he could, in return, secure similar promises from the governments named. Could this be accomplished, he promised, the United States would gladly participate in discussions aimed at easing the burden of armaments and freeing the channels of international trade.

To this communication Mussolini made no reply. Hitler answered it two weeks later, in a speech to the Reichstag. He had, he said, inquired of all the thirty-one governments named by Mr. Roosevelt as to whether they feared aggression by Germany and therefore felt the need of such promises as the President had proposed. In each case, he said, the answer had been negative. Any fear of German aggression, he implied, must exist only in President Roosevelt's imagination.[16]

As spring turned to summer and as European tension built up over the Polish question, President Roosevelt and Secretary Hull became more and more convinced that the neutrality law, especially the arms embargo, served as an encouragement to aggression. It assured Hitler that in a general European war, Great Britain and France could purchase no arms, ammunition, or implements of war in the United States. Repeal of the arms embargo, the administration reasoned, would make Hitler think twice before inviting war with the democracies. During June and July, therefore, administration leaders in Congress made an attempt to secure repeal of that provision, while leaving the remainder of the law intact or slightly modified. The House passed a bill so mutilated as to be worthless. In a final effort, the President and Secretary Hull met with leading senators and sought to impress upon them the danger of war in Europe, and the perils that would confront the United States if the Axis won, as it might well do. The surest road to security for America, they argued, lay in taking action that would assure Great Britain and France of access to American materials and so deter Hitler from starting a war. Senator Borah, always the isolationist, replied that he had sources of information in Europe more reliable than those of the State Department, and that his

---

[15]Langer and Gleason, *Challenge to Isolation,* pp. 46–48.

[16]Langer and Gleason, *Challenge to Isolation,* pp. 83–90.

sources assured him that there would be no war. Isolationist sentiment was strong in the Senate, and the administration's friends were forced to admit that they did not have the votes to pass the repeal bill. Congress adjourned without taking action.[17]

Hitler Precipitates War

While Roosevelt asked in vain for legislation to strengthen the hands of the democracies, the British and French were seeking the only available means of making effective their guarantees to Poland and Rumania; namely, the support of the Soviet Union. Though Russia had been ignored at Munich, Stalin in April 1939 offered to make with France and Great Britain a defensive alliance against further German aggression. Negotiations began in April and dragged on into August. The stumbling block was the refusal of Poland, Rumania, and the Baltic States to accept a Russian guarantee of their territory, which would imply a right to occupy it for protection against German aggression. To the Russians this right seemed an essential element in their plans for defense. To the small states lying between Germany and Russia, the eastern giant was at least as great a peril as the western. When the British and French balked at forcing Russia's attentions upon its neighbors against their will, the Kremlin secretly opened parallel negotiations with Germany. On May 3, Maxim Litvinov, a friend of the West and of the League of Nations, was replaced as Foreign Commissar by that diplomat of ill omen, Vyacheslav M. Molotov. For three months Molotov shrewdly kept two paths open, one to Berlin, one to Paris and London. The first clue to the outcome was the an-

nouncement on August 20 that Russia and Germany had signed a trade agreement. Immediately thereafter Nazi Foreign Minister Joachim von Ribbentrop flew to Moscow and on August 23 signed with Molotov a nonaggression pact that assured Hitler of Russian neutrality if he invaded Poland. Accompanying it was a secret agreement for the partition of Poland between Germany and Russia and for delimitation of their spheres of influence in the Baltic States.[18]

Hitler now pressed peremptorily his territorial demands on Poland, hoping to avoid war with England and France but willing to face it rather than retreat. Last minute efforts at settlement by negotiation broke down. On September 1, 1939, German armies crossed the Polish frontier, and German airplanes rained bombs on Polish cities. Two days later (September 3), Great Britain and France declared war against Nazi Germany. It was the beginning of World War II.

The United States
as a Nonbelligerent

In Washington, the President issued on September 5, 1939, the customary proclamation of American neutrality. In this instance, with war having been formally declared by all the principal belligerents, he had no choice but to invoke the provisions of the neutrality law whose amendment he had earlier sought from Congress. The arms embargo and other features of the act were applied against both belligerent camps. There was, however, no repetition of Wilson's appeal for impartiality in thought, nor was there any pretense of impartiality on the part of the administration.

An analysis of President Roosevelt's posi-

---

[17]Langer and Gleason, *Challenge to Isolation,* pp. 136–47. It is the opinion of these authors that repeal of the arms embargo at this time would probably not have altered Hitler's course.

[18]Germany claimed only Lithuania, conceding paramount Russian interest in Finland, Estonia, and Latvia.

tion is appropriate at this point. His first priority was to prevent an Axis victory, which in his mind would present a deadly peril to the United States. This he felt from the first but even more keenly after the German victories of 1940 revealed the frightful power of the Nazi war machine. An Axis victory, he believed, would mean eventual encirclement of the United States by the Berlin-Rome-Tokyo combination, followed by economic strangulation if not by military disaster.

Secondly, there seems no good reason to doubt that he sincerely desired to keep the United States out of the war, unless American participation should become necessary to prevent an Axis victory. In that event, as he saw it, better war now with dependable allies than war later when those allies should have been crushed by the Axis. At some point along the way, probably in the summer of 1941, he became convinced that only American entry into the war could insure Allied victory. It should be added that, although believing participation in the war might be necessary to American security, Mr. Roosevelt never took the American people fully into his confidence.

Thirdly, unless or until America should enter the war, the President believed that it should give all possible material and moral aid to the opponents of the Axis. Only thus was there hope of an Allied victory without American participation. This program meant scrapping the neutrality legislation so laboriously written in the 1930s. It meant also complete disregard of the old rules of neutrality, which prescribed impartial treatment of the belligerents and forbade a neutral government to give aid to a belligerent. Justification for this departure from old-fashioned neutrality was found in (a) the argument that the Pact of Paris had made neutrality obsolete, (b) Germany's complete disregard of international law and treaty promises, (c) the imperative needs of national security. Thus the United States moved from a status of neutrality to a

newly recognized status known as nonbelligerency—the status of a nation not at war but giving active aid to one belligerent.

In President Roosevelt's open stand for all-out aid for the Allies short of war, and in his unpublicized belief that war itself would be a lesser evil than an Axis victory, he had important segments of public opinion both with him and against him. The isolationist sentiment that had promoted the neutrality laws was still strong. It opposed aid to the Allies as a step toward war, and it felt that America's sharing in "Europe's wars" was the greatest of evils. It was organized most effectively in the America First Committee, with General Robert E. Wood of Chicago as president and Colonel Charles A. Lindbergh as leading orator. It received the support of, among other journals, the *Chicago Tribune* and the Hearst newspapers. The America First Committee was "going strong" up to the afternoon of the Pearl Harbor attack.

On the other side, the most important organized vehicle for the expression of public opinion was the Committee to Defend America by Aiding the Allies, headed for some time by the well known Kansas editor, William Allen White, and often referred to as the White Committee. Organized in the spring of 1940, it stood for all material aid to the Allies short of war; part of its membership favored outright participation in the war. Some persons sharing this latter view, from both within and without the White Committee, formed the Fight for Freedom Committee in April 1941. They held that, in asking others to do all the fighting, America was playing an ignoble role, and urged that America take its place as a full-scale belligerent in the "fight for freedom."[19]

[19]The story of the two opposing committees is told in two useful monographs: W. S. Cole, *America First: The Battle against Intervention* (Madison: University of Wisconsin Press, 1953); Walter Johnson, *The Battle against Isolation* (Chicago: University of Chicago Press, 1944).

From Neutrality to "Shooting War"

We may now trace the principal steps by which the United States moved away from neutrality and nearer to war with the Axis powers.

Repeal of the arms embargo. The first step was a modification of the neutrality law along the lines earlier proposed by the administration. Roosevelt called Congress to meet in special session on September 21 and asked legislation to permit the sale of arms to the Allies. After six weeks of debate and by safe majorities, Congress passed a Fourth Neutrality Act, which became law on November 4, 1939. It repealed the embargo on arms, ammunition, and implements of war and placed sales to belligerents of goods of all kinds on a cash and carry basis. It empowered the President to designate "combat areas," which American ships and American citizens would be prohibited from entering. Other restrictions of the earlier legislation were generally retained. The great importance of the new law was in opening the American market in war goods to the French and British, since they alone, of the European belligerents, could buy and carry away.

The promise of aid to "the opponents of force." In Europe, a lightning German campaign against Poland was followed by months of comparative inactivity—the *Sitzkrieg* (sitting war) or "phony war." But in April, 1940 the *Sitzkrieg* suddenly became a *Blitzkrieg* (lightning war). Denmark, Norway, the Netherlands, and Belgium were quickly overrun by German airborne troops and motorized columns. The French armies were crushed, the Maginot Line taken in the rear. The British Expeditionary Force escaped, as by a miracle, from Dunkirk, but left on the beaches all its heavy equipment and most of its small arms. On June 10, Mussolini, who hitherto had preserved a nonbelligerent status in his partner's war, declared war upon stricken France. On June 22 France surrendered. All of northern and Western France became occupied territory. The south and east Hitler left to a government established by Marshal Pétain at Vichy.

President Roosevelt's response to these events was prompt and emphatic. Speaking at Charlottesville, Virginia, June 10, he remarked, with reference to Mussolini's attack on France: "The hand that held the dagger has struck it into the back of its neighbor." More important was his declaration:

> In our American unity, we will pursue two obvious and simultaneous courses: we will extend to the opponents of force the material resources of this nation, and at the same time we will harness and speed up the use of those resources in order that we ourselves in the Americas may have equipment and training equal to the task of any emergency and every defense.

The beginning of rearmament. During the summer of 1940, Congress, at Roosevelt's request, took important steps toward strengthening the armed forces of the United States and stepping up production of war material for the use of the "opponents of force." The Army was to be enlarged from an authorized strength of 280,000 men to 1,200,000 as soon as the men could be raised and trained, with other increments to follow. Army and Navy air strength was to be augmented by over 18,000 planes, and a production goal of 50,000 planes annually was set. Authorization of an unprecedented naval increase of 1,325,000 tons laid the basis for a "two-ocean Navy." The total defense appropriation of over 5 billion dollars, more than the President had asked, broke all peacetime records while authorizations for future construction contracts brought the grand total to some 16 billions. In September, Congress passed the first peacetime selective service act in American experience. Fear of Hitler had stimulated a tardy but impressive drive for rearmament.

The destroyer-bases deal.   The surrender of France soon after the President's Charlottesville speech left only two active "opponents of force" in the world, Great Britain in the west, China in the east. Roosevelt's most immediate concern was with Great Britain, now assailed from the sea and air by victorious Germany. If Britain should fall, if her fleet should be destroyed or pass into hostile hands, the future for America would look dark indeed. Britain's most pressing need at the moment was for swift naval vessels for antisubmarine patrol and convoy duty. The United States had fifty overage destroyers, which in the President's mind would serve the United States better if put to active use by the British than laid up "in moth balls" in American harbors. Attorney General Robert Jackson found ingenious paths for the President through both domestic and international law, and on September 2 Mr. Roosevelt agreed to turn over the destroyers to the British Navy in return for the right, over a 99-year period, to set up and maintain American military bases in eight British possessions stretching from Newfoundland to British Guiana.[20] The bases made possible a naval and air screen covering the approaches to the Atlantic coast of the United States and to the Caribbean. In announcing the deal to Congress (he had not asked their consent), the President claimed: "This is the most important action in the reinforcement of our national defense that has been taken since the Louisiana Purchase." Congress and public opinion, for the most part, acquiesced in the President's startling *fait accompli.* The transfer of the destroyers to Great Britain was, as Winston Churchill later wrote, "a

decidedly unneutral act by the United States." But though it would, in Churchill's words, "according to all the standards of history, have justified the German Government in declaring war,"[21] Hitler did not waste time in making official protests.

President Roosevelt's re-election, 1940.   In July the Democratic party had broken precedent by nominating Mr. Roosevelt for a third term as President. The President's prior move of inviting into his cabinet two prominent Republicans, Henry L. Stimson as Secretary of War and Frank Knox as Secretary of the Navy, did nothing to appease the Republican party. But the Republican candidate, Wendell L. Willkie, shared the President's belief in the importance of aid to Britain. Isolation, therefore, was not an issue in the campaign. Neither was its antithesis of joining in the war, for both platforms and both candidates declared emphatically against participation in "any foreign war," though the Democratic platform added the qualification "except in case of attack." The Republicans, however, painted Roosevelt as the war candidate, and the President found it expedient, as the campaign climaxed, to reiterate, "again and again and again," the assurance: "Your boys are not going to be sent into any foreign wars." Roosevelt won the election easily, though with a majority much reduced from that of 1936.

"The arsenal of democracy": lend-lease.   After re-election the President received from Prime Minister Churchill a long letter setting forth Great Britain's financial straits. That nation was scraping the bottom of the barrel to pay for goods already ordered and would need "ten times as much" for the extension of the war. Churchill hoped that Roosevelt would regard his letter "not as an appeal for aid, but

---

[20]The other base sites were Bermuda, the Bahamas, Jamaica, Antigua, St. Lucia, and Trinidad.

[21]Winston S. Churchill, *Their Finest Hour,* Vol. 2 of *The Second World War* (Boston: Houghton Mifflin Company, 1949), p. 404.

as a statement of the minimum action necessary to achieve our common purpose."[22] The problem, as Roosevelt saw it, was how to aid England in the common cause without incurring such a breeder of ill will as the war debt problem after World War I. After brooding over the matter for days during a Caribbean cruise on the cruiser *Tuscaloosa,* he came up with the ingenious idea of lending goods instead of money. He wanted, as he told a press conference, to get away from that "silly, foolish old dollar sign," and he compared what he proposed to do to lending a garden hose to a neighbor to put out a fire that might otherwise spread to one's own house.[23]

In a "fireside chat" on December 29, 1940, he pictured the United States as the "arsenal of democracy," and in his message to Congress a few days later he made officially the proposal that resulted in the Lend-Lease Act of March 11, 1941.

The Lend-Lease Act was the complete negation of old-fashioned neutrality. It empowered the President to make available to "the government of any country whose defense the President deems vital to the defense of the United States" any "defense article," any service, or any "defense information." "Defense articles" might be manufactured expressly for the government that was to receive them, or they might (after consultation with top military and naval advisers) be taken from existing stocks in the possession of the United States. Launched on a modest scale, the lend-lease program eventually conveyed goods and services valued at over $50,000,000,000 to the friends and allies of the United States in World War II; and it left in its wake no such exasperating war debt problem as that of the 1920s.[24]

Planning for joint military action. From January to March, 1941, while Congress was debating the lend-lease proposal, British and American military and naval officers were holding secret staff conferences in Washington. Their purpose was to plan coordination of the American and British effort, (a) on the basis of lend-lease while the United States remained nonbelligerent; (b) in joint military and naval operations if and when the United States entered the war. The conferences reached the fundamental decision that if Japan entered the war, Germany was still to be regarded as Enemy Number One and her defeat to be given priority over that of Japan. One reason for this decision was fear that the German scientists, if given time, might perfect new super-weapons. There was no such apprehension as to Japanese achievement.[25] After conclusion of the conferences, American officers went to England to select sites for future naval and air force bases.

---

10 billions in so-called reverse lend-lease from its allies. After the War the United States negotiated settlement agreements with most of the recipients. These were in general on the theory that lend-lease materials not used in the war should be returned or paid for, but the settlements were also shaped by the proviso written into the original lend-lease agreements, that final settlement terms should "be such as not to burden commerce but to promote mutually advantageous economic relations . . . and the betterment of world-wide economic relations." As of December 31, 1953, settlement agreements totaling over $1,557,000,000 had been negotiated on which $477,000,000 had been paid. The U.S.S.R., which had received over $11,000,-000,000, was the only large debtor that had failed to agree to a settlement. *Thirty-fifth Report to Congress on Lend-Lease Operations* (Washington: Government Printing Office, 1954).

[25]S. E. Morison, *The Battle of the Atlantic, History of United States Naval Operations in World War II,* Vol. 1 (Boston: Little, Brown, & Company, 1947), pp. 46, 47; Winston S. Churchill, *The Grand Alliance,* Vol. 3 of *The Second World War* (Boston: Houghton Mifflin Company, 1950), pp. 137–38; Maurice Matloff and E. M. Snell, *Strategic Planning for Coalition Warfare, 1941–1942* in *United States Army in World War II: The War Department* (Washington: Department of the Army, 1953), chap. 3.

---

[22]The letter and comment are printed in Churchill, *Their Finest Hour,* pp. 555–67.

[23]*Harbor* (New York: Creative Age Press, 1950), p. 296.

[24] Against the 50 billions of lend-lease aid furnished by the United States, it received approximately

Coordinating the defense program with Canada's.   Akin to this tie-up with belligerent Britain were contemporary arrangements with belligerent Canada. In August 1938, a year before the outbreak of war, President Roosevelt and Prime Minister Mackenzie King had exchanged assurances of mutual assistance in case of need; the President declaring that the United States would not "stand idly by if domination of Canadian soil is threatened by any other empire."[26] Meeting at Ogdensburg, N.Y., August 17, 1940, while the battle of Britain still hung in the balance, the two statesmen agreed to set up a Permanent Joint Board of Defense for the protection of their two countries. After the passage of the Lend-Lease Act they met again at Roosevelt's home at Hyde Park, April 20, 1941, and took steps to gear together the production facilities of the United States and Canada for their own defense and that of Britain. A Joint Defense Production Committee was established on November 5, 1941. Thus months before the United States became a belligerent, it was working closely with Canada for a common objective: defeat of the Axis powers.

The Atlantic Charter.   In August 1941, the Prime Minister of belligerent Great Britain and the President of the nonbelligerent United States met secretly for their first conference at Argentia, Newfoundland. In explaining his desire for such a meeting, Mr. Churchill wrote afterwards that "a conference between us would proclaim the ever closer association of Britain and the United States, would cause our enemies concern, make Japan ponder, and cheer our friends."[27] The two statesmen discussed a variety of topics connected with the war, including means of deterring Japan from attacking the British or Dutch

possessions in the Far East. But the most famous if not the most important achievement of the conference was the production of the document known as the Atlantic Charter.[28] This pronouncement, which came chiefly from Churchill's pen, may be compared roughly to Wilson's Fourteen Points in World War I. Like Wilson's formulation, it set up idealistic objectives that might be expected to appeal to liberals everywhere. That it brought the United States a step nearer to war was clearly seen and appreciated by Churchill, who wrote:

> . . . The fact alone of the United States, still technically neutral, joining with a belligerent Power in making such a declaration was astonishing. The inclusion in it of a reference to "final destruction of the Nazi tyranny" . . . amounted to a challenge which in ordinary times would have implied warlike action. . . .[29]

Patrolling the Atlantic sea lanes.   The lend-leasing of "defense articles" to Great Britain was worse than useless unless the articles could be delivered. The protection against German submarines of convoys from North American to British ports strained the resources of the British and Canadian navies. The problem was further complicated when Hitler attacked the Soviet Union, June 22, 1941, and the United States determined to make the U.S.S.R. a beneficiary of lend-lease. The northern sea route to Russia stretched around the northern tip of Norway to its terminus at Murmansk. The British navy could not protect the Murmansk convoys unless it got relief elsewhere.

---

[26]E. W. McInnis, *The Unguarded Frontier: A History of American-Canadian Relations* (Garden City, N.Y.: Doubleday & Company, Inc., 1942), pp. 355–56.

[27]Churchill, *The Grand Alliance,* p. 427.

[28]The text of the Atlantic Charter is in Joseph M. Siracusa, *The American Diplomatic Revolution: A Documentary History of the Cold War, 1941–1947* (Port Washington, N.Y.: Kennikat, 1977), pp. 7–9. Also see Daniel M. Smith and Joseph M. Siracusa, *The Testing of America: 1914–1945* (St. Louis: Forum Press, 1979), p. 203.

[29]Churchill, *The Grand Alliance,* p. 444.

For the United States to convoy British shipping carrying lend-lease "defense articles" would have been stretching nonbelligerency to a point that even Roosevelt thought inexpedient. But a substitute method was found. A Conference of American Foreign Ministers at Panama in September–October 1939 had proclaimed the neutrality of a wide belt of the western Atlantic and had warned the belligerents against acts of war in these waters. Though neither England nor Germany had paid any heed to this declaration, Roosevelt decided, in the spring of 1941, to have the navy "patrol" not only the waters so defined, but the entire North Atlantic west of 26° west longitude and to "publish the position of possible aggressor ships or planes when located in the American patrol area."[30] Thus British convoys would be warned of the positions of Nazi submarines located by the United States Navy.

Patrolling was facilitated by the American occupation of Greenland under an agreement made with the Danish minister in Washington, April 9, 1941. German aerial activity had been observed over Greenland's east coast and German weather stations had been set up on the island. To these activities the United States now put a stop. Three months later, July 7, 1941, United States forces occupied Iceland, by agreement with the local government and with the British authorities, who had previously landed troops there as a precautionary measure. The United States now had a legitimate reason for convoying its own supply ships to Iceland. On July 19, 1941, Admiral E. J. King, Commander in Chief, Atlantic Fleet, directed a naval task force to "escort convoys of United States and Iceland flag shipping, *including shipping of any nationality which may join such . . . convoys, between United States ports and bases, and Iceland.*"[31] Thus the United States

[30]Churchill, *The Grand Alliance*, p. 140.

[31]E. J. King and W. M. Whitehill, *Fleet Admiral King: A Naval Record* (New York: W. W. Norton & Company, 1952), p. 343 (italics inserted).

Navy, in company with that of Canada, began actually escorting British lend-lease convoys as far as Iceland, where the British navy picked them up.

A "shooting war" begins. Such "nonbelligerent" activity could not continue for long without bringing on clashes with German U-boats. On September 4, 1941, the destroyer *Greer,* while trailing a submarine and signaling its position to a British plane, was made a target for two torpedoes from the U-boat, both of which missed their mark. A week later President Roosevelt, without describing the circumstances of the incident, denounced the German attack as "piracy" and warned "German or Italian vessels of war" that they entered American waters at their own peril; he had, he said, issued orders to "shoot on sight" at such craft.

Other torpedoings followed. On October 17, the destroyer *Kearny,* doing convoy duty on the Iceland run, was hit by a torpedo with the loss of eleven men. On October 31 the *Reuben James* lost 96 men in a similar attack. Speaking October 27, after the attack on the *Kearny,* the President told the country: "We have wished to avoid shooting. But the shooting has started. And history has recorded who fired the first shot. . . ."

Reclaiming "freedom of the seas." While the country was still excited over the "attack" on the *Greer,* the President thought the time had come to get rid of as many as possible of the troublesome remaining restrictions of the neutrality law. On October 9, 1941, he asked Congress for repeal of the section forbidding the arming of merchant vessels. "We intend," he said, "to maintain the policy of protecting the freedom of the seas against domination by any foreign power which has become crazed with a desire to control the world." In spite of large anti-interventionist blocs in both houses of Congress, in spite of warnings that repeal meant war, Congress passed and the President signed on November 17, 1941, a law that went further than he had asked. It not only permitted the arming of American merchantmen, but also repealed the cash-and-carry and combat area provisions of the law of 1939. American merchant ships were now free to arm themselves and to sail anywhere on the globe, carrying, if their owners wished, arms, ammunition, and implements of war for the British, the Russians, or the Chinese.[32] American destroyers and German submarines were already trading depth charges for torpedoes in the North Atlantic. With all restrictions removed from American merchant ships, it is any one's guess how long the country would have waited before an accumulation of "incidents" would have drawn a declaration of war from a reluctant Congress—or a reluctant Führer. The Japanese eliminated any such period of waiting.

Hitler Declines a Challenge

There can be little doubt that by the fall of 1941 Roosevelt wished war with Germany, and that he had concluded that only through active participation by the United States could Germany and Italy be defeated. He never said so publicly nor, so far as the records have revealed, privately. He exasperated the more war-minded of his advisers, like Secretary Stimson, by his failure to share frankly with the American people his apparent conviction that the road to national security lay through war. He feared, we may assume, to call for a declaration of war as long as the response of Congress and the public was in doubt. As late as November 5, 1941, a poll conducted by the American Institute of Public Opin-

ion showed 63 percent noes to 26 percent yeses in answer to the question: Should Congress pass a resolution declaring that a state of war exists between the United States and Germany?[33] In Congress, the bill for arming merchant ships had carried by a vote, in the two houses, of 262 in favor, 231 against. To a declaration of war a still more formidable opposition might be expected. A defeat on this crucial issue would, from the President's point of view, have been disastrous. A victory by such a slender margin would have been an inauspicious beginning of a war for survival.

So, it would appear, the President tried to provoke Hitler into declaring war or into committing an overt act that would silence American opposition to war. The President's words and actions toward Germany, from August to November 1941, were not the words or actions of a man who wished peace. He committed himself, in the Atlantic Charter, to "the final destruction of the Nazi tyranny," he sent the navy out to "shoot on sight" at German U-boats, and declared "The shooting has started." In reverting to a defense of "freedom of the seas," in sweeping away virtually all the safeguards against war in the neutrality legislation, he was inviting collisions with Germany that must surely lead to war.

Why, in the face of American unneutrality, did Hitler shun war with the United States? From the time of the destroyer deal in September 1940, the United States had committed one unfriendly act after another. It was overtly aiding Hitler's foes in ways that a belligerent would hardly have stood for in any prior war. Yet Hitler issued no ultimatum, threatened no reprisals. He

---

[32]The bill passed Congress by votes of 50 to 37 in the Senate, 212 to 194 in the House. Its passage left intact the National Munitions Control Board, the section forbidding Americans to travel on belligerent ships, and the ban on loans to belligerent governments. The last-named provision had been rendered academic by the lend-lease policy.

[33]Hadly Cantril, ed., *Public Opinion, 1935–1946* (Princeton: Princeton University Press, 1951). p. 1172. It is interesting to compare this result with that of another poll taken after the Japanese attack on Pearl Harbor but before the German declaration of war. To the question: Should President Roosevelt have asked Congress to declare war against Germany as well as Japan? 90 percent answered yes; 7 percent, no. Ibid., p. 1173.

said merely, after Roosevelt's shoot-on-sight order, that German submarines would defend themselves. The reasons for Hitler's forbearance are clear enough. However irrationally he may have acted in other matters, in this one he was realistic and rational. He well knew the result of American participation in the war of 1914. Germany had lost that war by inviting attack from the United States. The Führer was determined to avoid repeating that mistake if possible, until he had won his war in Europe. When he had crushed Russia and defeated or cowed Britain, there would be time enough to reckon with America.

The Road to Pearl Harbor

While the United States was drifting into an undeclared naval war with Germany in the Atlantic, it was approaching a crisis in its relations with Japan in the Pacific. Japan followed up its announcement of the "New Order for East Asia" by seizing, in February 1939, the large island of Hainan off the south China coast, and, a month later, the Spratly Islands in the South China Sea. Hainan, a Chinese island, was in the French sphere of influence; it also lay in close proximity to the British shipping lane between Singapore and Hong Kong. The Spratly Islands, claimed by France, were uncomfortably close to French Indochina and the American Philippines. Japan, in other words, while ostensibly fighting only China, was moving southward into an area where her forces constituted a potential threat to the possessions of France, the United States, and Great Britain, and even to those of the Netherlands. At the same time she continued her policy of gradually closing the door of China to western trade and western culture.

Ambassador Joseph C. Grew, at home in the United States during the summer of 1939, found, as he wrote, "an unmistakable hardening of the Administration's attitude toward Japan and a marked disinclination to allow American interests to be crowded out of China."[34] This hardening attitude took tangible form when, on July 26, 1939, the United States gave the required six months' notice of the abrogation of its 1911 commercial treaty with Japan; thus it would be free, early in 1940, to restrict Japan's trade with the United States in any way it might deem expedient. "Methods short of war" were in the making.

Upon returning to his post in Tokyo, Grew publicly warned the people of Japan that the policy of their government was alienating the friendship of the United States. In a speech (October 19, 1939) to the America-Japan Society of Tokyo, which he described as coming "straight from the horse's mouth," the ambassador pointed out that the American people

have good reason to believe that an effort is being made to establish control, in Japan's own interest, of large areas on the continent of Asia and to impose upon those areas a system of closed economy. It is this thought, added to the effect of the bombings, the indignities, the manifold interference with American rights, that accounts for the attitude of the American people to Japan today. . . .[35]

When this speech was delivered, Europe had been at war for seven weeks. The "phony war" of the following months had little effect on the Far Eastern situation, but the spring and summer of 1940 seemed to open magnificent opportunities to the ambitious Japanese. First the Netherlands and then France succumbed to German might; only the English Channel and the Royal Air Force and Navy barred Hitler from the conquest of Great Britain, and how long those barriers would hold, no one could foretell. French Indochina, the Nether-

[34]Grew, *Turbulent Era*, 2: 1211–12.
[35]Grew, *Turbulent Era*, 2: 1219–20.

lands East Indies, and British Malaya appeared as tempting prizes to Hitler's Asiatic partner. A new Japanese ministry, headed, like that of 1938, by Prince Konoye, proclaimed on August 1 a "New Order for Greater East Asia." This enlargement of Japan's prospective empire, also called the "Greater East Asia Co-prosperity Sphere," was chiefly the plan of the new Foreign Minister, Yosuke Matsuoka. Aggressive, boastful and garrulous, pro-Axis and anti-United States, Matsuoka was described by Secretary Hull as being "as crooked as a basket of fishhooks." The Greater East Asia Co-prosperity Sphere was defined, under Matsuoka's inspiration, by a Liaison Conference (cabinet and Army and Navy leaders) in Tokyo, September 19, 1940, as comprising the former German islands under mandate to Japan since 1920 (the Carolines, Marianas, and Marshalls), French Indochina and French islands in the Pacific, Thailand, British Malaya and Borneo, the Dutch East Indies, Burma, Australia, New Zealand, and India, "with Japan, Manchuria, and China as the backbone." An item conspicuously missing from this list, no doubt out of temporary deference to the United States, was the Philippines. To take care of such omissions, Matsuoka had added an "etc." at the end of his enumeration and in addition had commented that "this sphere could be automatically broadened in the course of time."[36]

In April, after the fall of Holland, Secretary Hull had put up a no-trespassing sign on the Netherlands East Indies, warning that any alteration of their status by other than peaceful means "would be prejudicial to the cause of stability, peace, and security . . . in the entire Pacific area." The Japanese heeded the caution for the time being, but in August submitted to the local officials in Indochina a demand for access to the ports, cities, and airfields of the northern part of the French possession. These were important to the Japanese because they commanded a principal supply route to the Chinese at Chungking. Pressure by Hitler on the Vichy regime forced the French to give way. Representatives of Vichy continued in office in the colony, but on September 22 key centers in the Tonkin area were occupied by Japanese forces. They could now halt supplies to China via the railroad from Hanoi, and their planes could threaten traffic over the Burma Road.

The Tripartite Pact

Matsuoka, in the meantime, had opened negotiations for an outright alliance with Germany and Italy.[37] On September 27, 1940, representatives of the three powers signed in Berlin a Tripartite Pact, comprising mutual recognition by the three partners of the "new orders" instituted by them in Europe and Greater East Asia respectively, and also a defensive alliance. By the latter (Article Three) Germany, Italy, and Japan agreed:

> to assist one another with all political, economic and military means when one of the three contracting powers is attacked by a power at present not involved in the European war or in the Chinese-Japanese conflict.

This article was obviously aimed at the United States, since another article excluded Russia from its application. Its purpose was to deter the United States from entering the war against either Germany or Japan by the warning that by so doing it would have to fight all three Axis powers. With American interference thus fended off, Matsuoka believed, Japan could readily take possession of French,

---

[36]Herbert, Feis, *The Road to Pearl Harbor: The Coming of the War Between the United States and Japan* (Princeton: Princeton University Press, 1950), pp. 114, 120.

[37]The Anti-Comintern Pact had become a dead letter upon Hitler's entering his partnership with Stalin in August 1939.

Dutch, and British colonies in Greater East Asia. He hoped, too, that the pact would enable Japan to improve her relations with the Soviet Union and, by isolating China, to compel Chiang Kai-shek to make a peace satisfactory to Japan.[38] This was the bright mirage that dazzled Yosuke Matsuoka and led Japan along the road to disaster.

The United States Applies Pressure

Far from intimidating the United States, the Tripartite Pact still further stiffened the American attitude toward the Axis. The threat of encirclement made the two wars one in American eyes, and, in the mind of President Roosevelt at any rate, strengthened the determination to aid Britain. Roosevelt followed up his re-election in November by proposing the lend-lease policy, which became law in March 1941. In a letter to Ambassador Grew he explained the "global strategy" that he thought imperative in the interest of American security. The President wrote, January 21, 1941:

> Our strategy of giving them [the British] assistance toward ensuring our own security must envisage both sending supplies to England and helping to prevent a closing of channels of communication to and from various parts of the world, so that other important sources of supply will not be denied to the British and be added to the assets of the other side.[39]

[38]Jones, *Japan's New Order in East Asia, 1937–1945,* pp. 195–202; Feis, *Road to Pearl Harbor,* pp. 111–17. By a secret exchange of notes at the time of signing the pact, the parties agreed that any question of whether one of the powers had been attacked within the meaning of Article Three would be decided by consultation between them. The Soviet Union had signed a non-aggression treaty with Nationalist China in August 1937 and from that time until attacked by Germany in 1941, sent to China large quantities of military supplies, including several hundred airplanes.

[39]Grew, *Turbulent Era,* 2: 1259–66.

The President referred specifically in this connection to the Dutch East Indies and British Malaya, sources of rubber, petroleum, and tin. A few weeks later (February 14, 1941), Mr. Dooman, of the American embassy in Tokyo, passed on this idea to the Japanese Vice Minister for Foreign Affairs. He added that the United States had a direct as well as an indirect interest in the products of Malaya and the N.E.I. and that "a Japanese threat to occupy areas from which the United States procured essential primary commodities would not be tolerated."[40]

As the fateful year 1941 dawned, friction between the United States and Japan was increasing. Resentful of Japan's assaults upon China's independence and of violations of the open door, the United States was now seriously concerned about Japan's affiliation with the European Axis and her threatened appropriation of the rich raw materials of Southeast Asia. During 1940, the United States had begun to exert economic pressure upon Japan. The launching of the rearmament program in the spring and summer furnished a pretext for cutting off supplies from Japan on the ground that they were needed at home. On July 25, 1940, the President prohibited the export without license of petroleum, petroleum products, and scrap metal. Six days later he placed an embargo upon the export of aviation gasoline to all countries outside the Western Hemisphere, except for the use of American planes in the service of foreign countries. As an answer, presumably, to the Japanese landings in Indochina and the advance news of the signing of the Tripartite Pact, the President on September 26, placed a similar embargo on exports of scrap iron and steel, making shipments to Great Britain the only exception. Other gestures designed as warnings to Japan were a $25,000,000 loan to China through the Export-Import Bank, and a

[40]Grew, *Turbulent Era,* 2: 1307.

notice to all American citizens in the Far East urging that they return to America.

Deadlocked Negotiations

Such measures as these, and the possibility of still more drastic ones, without doubt, gave Japan pause, for her industry and her ability to make war were heavily dependent upon her trade with the United States. Japanese policy in the winter and spring of 1941 apparently had a three-fold purpose: (1) to reach agreement with the United States if this were possible at not too great a cost; (2) to bring the Netherlands East Indies into the Co-prosperity Sphere, peaceably if possible, forcibly if necessary; (3) to remove the danger of an attack from the Soviet Union if Japan's southward expansion should involve her in war with the United States or Great Britain.

Serious negotiations with the United States began in April, following the arrival in Washington of a new Japanese ambassador, Admiral Kichisaburo Nomura. Nomura's negotiations with Hull were complicated by the presence in Washington of two Roman Catholic clerics, Bishop James E. Walsh and Father James M. Drought of the Maryknoll Society, who had returned from a visit to Japan bringing what they thought to be an offer from the Japanese government. Japan, they reported, was ready to recall Japanese troops from China and to nullify the Tripartite Pact insofar as it was a threat to the United States. The source of this supposed offer is unknown.[41] Hull soon discovered that it misrepresented Japanese intentions.

[41]John H. Boyle, "The Drought-Walsh Mission to Japan," *Pacific Historical Review,* 34 (May 1965), 141–61. See also R. J. C. Butow, "The Hull-Nomura Conversations: A Fundamental Misconception," *American Historical Review,* 65 (July 1960), 822–36, and W. L. Langer and S. E. Gleason, *The Undeclared War, 1940–1941* (New York: Harper & Row, Publishers, 1953), pp. 314–15, 321, *et passim.*

Actually, as the conversations with Nomura revealed, Japan was asking the United States to press Chiang Kai-shek to accept Japan's terms (including merger of his government with the puppet government in Nanking, and retention of some Japanese troops in North China and Inner Mongolia). Should he refuse, the United States should deprive him of any further aid. The United States was also to restore normal trade with Japan (insofar as articles needed by Japan were available) and to assist Japan in obtaining raw materials from Southeast Asia to meet her needs. In return, Japan would promise to use only peaceful means in seeking her ends in Southeast Asia and would reserve to herself the right to interpret her obligations under the Tripartite Pact; in other words, if the United States went to war with Germany, Japan would decide independently whether she was bound to assist her Axis partner.

The United States, for its part, asked Japan's acceptance of four general principles set forth by Secretary Hull: (1) respect for the sovereignty and territorial integrity of all nations; (2) noninterference in the internal affairs of other countries; (3) the open door, or equality of commercial opportunity; (4) no disturbance of the status quo in the Pacific except by peaceful means. Specifically the United States asked that Japan withdraw her armed forces from China and Indochina, accept the government of Chiang Kai-shek as the only legitimate government of China, and disavow the Tripartite Pact as aimed at the United States. Each government adhered inflexibly to its set of demands, and by June 1941, an impasse had been reached.

By June, also, Japan had been rebuffed in her attempt by negotiation to take over practical control of the Netherlands East Indies. The Netherlands government, in exile in London, proved more intractable than had the Vichy government of France, and a Japanese mission, which had gone to

Batavia in September 1940 in quest of special concessions, returned home empty-handed in June 1941.

With Russia the Japanese government was more successful, though the success there was illusory. On April 13, 1941, in Moscow, Matsuoka signed with Molotov a five-year treaty of neutrality, pledging each party to remain neutral if the other should become involved in war. Russia agreed to respect the territorial integrity of Manchukuo, and Japan gave a similar promise with respect to Outer Mongolia, which had fallen under Soviet influence. Matsuoka, believing that Japan's southward drive might bring conflict with Great Britain or the United States or both, thought the promise of Russia's neutrality worth a price. He promised surrender of Japanese economic concessions in North Sakhalin (a promise that was not carried out). He did not know, though he had just come from Berlin, that Hitler was preparing to attack the Soviet Union. When that event took place, on June 22, 1941, the neutrality pact was of more value to the U.S.S.R. than to Japan.

Japan Moves South and is Rebuked

Matsuoka, as a matter of fact, wished to violate the pact that he had just made and to join Germany in war against the Soviets, but he was overruled. His cabinet colleagues and the top military men preferred a southward drive combined with neutrality in the Russo-German war. An Imperial Conference on July 2 decided upon an advance into southern Indochina and Thailand, even at the risk of war with the United States and Britain. Indochina would serve as a takeoff point for attacks on Singapore and the Netherlands Indies. A cabinet reorganization eliminated Matsuoaka from the Foreign Office. On July 24, with the reluctant consent of the Vichy government, Japanese troops landed in southern Indochina. An accord with Vichy, signed a few days later, permitted the Japanese to establish air and naval bases in the colony, while Japan promised to respect French political and territorial rights there.

This renewal of aggressive action by Japan, clearly designed as a prelude to armed attack upon Malaya and the Netherlands Indies,[42] brought quick response from the United States, Great Britain and the Netherlands. The Japanese excuse—that the occupation was a defensive measure against alleged British designs—was answered by President Roosevelt with a proposal that Indochina be neutralized. This suggestion was refused by Japan. In the meantime, the United States had broken off the discussions with Nomura that had been proceeding since April, and had announced, July 25, the freezing of all Japanese funds in the United States. Within a few days Great Britain and the Netherlands took similar action. This was the final stroke in cutting Japan off from her most important markets and sources of raw material. Would Japan submit or fight, or was some compromise still possible?

There were those in both England and the United States who believed that Japan would retreat before a united front of the democracies. With this idea in mind, Winston Churchill, at the Atlantic Conference in August, urged President Roosevelt to warn Japan that an attack on British or Dutch possessions in the Far East would compel the United States "to take counter-measures, even through these

---

[42] U. S. Naval Intelligence had broken one of the principal Japanese codes and in the operation known as "Magic" was regularly intercepting and translating Japanese broadcasts to diplomatic representatives abroad. Thus the United States and, through it, the British government, knew in advance not only of the plan against Indochina but also of the proposed further moves against British and Dutch possessions. Jones, *Japan's New Order,* p. 263.

might lead to war between the United States and Japan." These fighting words, which Roosevelt had apparently agreed to, were toned down at the urging of the State Department, and the warning that the President read to the Japanese ambassador on August 17 was as follows:

> This Government now finds it necessary to say to the Government of Japan that if the Japanese Government takes any further steps in pursuance of a policy or program of military domination by force or threat of force on neighboring countries, the Government of the United States will be compelled to take immediately any and all steps which it may deem necessary toward safeguarding the legitimate rights and interest of the United States and American nationals and toward insuring the safety and security of the United States.

The warning was accompanied by an offer to reopen the interrupted conversations and to institute a helpful economic program for the Pacific area if Japan were willing "to suspend its expansionist activities . . . and to embark upon a peaceful program for the Pacific . . ."[43]

Konoye Seeks a Meeting with Roosevelt

Upon Roosevelt's return from the Atlantic Conference with Churchill, he had found awaiting him a proposal for a Pacific Conference with Prince Konoye, the Japanese Premier. Konoye had suggested that a personal meeting of the two statesmen might settle controversies that seemed otherwise insoluble. The proposal was heartily endorsed by Ambassador Grew. Grew believed that Japan was ready to make impor-

tant concessions. As he saw it, the inconclusive and costly war in China, economic pressure from the democracies, and growing distrust of Germany had combined to convince the cabinet, the Emperor, and many top military men that Japan was following a ruinous course. Retreat would be difficult and would meet strenuous opposition, but Grew believed, and the entire embassy staff shared his view, that a dramatic meeting of Premier and President, productive of a promising economic program, even though at the cost of important concessions, would catch the popular imagination and overwhelm the opposition. Confidence in this outcome was strengthened by the assurance that such a program would have the full support of the Emperor. Specifically, Grew believed that Konoye was ready to satisfy the United States in regard to the Tripartite Pact and to withdraw Japanese troops both from Indochina and from China, "with the face-saving expedient of being permitted to retain a limited number of troops in North China and Inner Mongolia temporarily."[44]

President Roosevelt was at first quite taken with the suggestion of a Pacific Conference. Secretary Hull, however, threw cold water on the idea. He doubted the ability of the Premier, whatever his intentions, to gain the consent of the militarists to a program acceptable to the United States; and he insisted that the general lines of an acceptable agreement be sketched out before the meeting. Otherwise, he feared the meeting would result in a fiasco, which Japanese propaganda would then turn against the United States. On the necessity of a preliminary agreement, the President accepted Hull's position, and Konoye was asked to state Japan's terms.

---

[43]Langer and Gleason, *The Undeclared War*, pp. 670–77, 694–95; Winston S. Churchill, *The Grand Alliance*, pp. 440, 446.

[44]Grew, *Turbulent Era*, 2: 1355. This whole question is treated in much detail in ibid., pp. 1262–1375, with valuable footnotes by the editor, Walter Johnson. Grew continued to believe after the war, as he believed in 1941, that a Roosevelt-Konoye meeting might well have succeeded in averting war.

In a talk with Grew on September 6, Konoye stated that he accepted "conclusively and wholeheartedly" (the Foreign Office later added the weasel words "in principle") the four principles of international behavior previously set forth by Secretary Hull. But on specific concessions that they were willing to make, the Japanese refused to commit themselves, possibly, as Grew believed, because they feared that leaks in the Foreign Office would reveal such proposals prematurely to Matsuoka and other extremists. In the absence of specific advance commitments by Japan, President Roosevelt was unwilling to meet the Premier. On October 16 the Konoye ministry resigned, and whatever chance there was for an agreement at the top level was lost.

Was Grew right in thinking there was a chance for agreement? Konoye's memoirs, published after his postwar suicide, reveal at least part of what was in his mind. In seeking the consent of the Army and Navy to his plan, Konoye assured the War and Navy Ministers that Japan would "insist, of course, on the firm establishment of the Greater East Asia Co-prosperity Sphere," while American claims would be based on the Nine-Power Treaty. The two were incompatible; but, Konoye pointed out, the United States had stated its readiness to discuss revision of the treaty "through legal means," while Japan could not expect immediate fulfillment of her "ideal" of the Co-prosperity Sphere. There was, in other words, enough flexibility in each program to enable Konoye to say: "I do not believe that Japanese-American talks are an impossibility if they are carried out with broadmindedness. . . ."

But Konoye was ready with an alternative plan if the meeting did not result in an agreement. If the President did not "understand," Konoye would

> be fully prepared to break off the talks and return home. It is, therefore [he added] an undertaking which must be carried out while being fully prepared for war against America. [If the talks should fail] the people will know that a Japanese-American war could not be avoided. This would aid in consolidating their determination. The world in general, also, would . . . know that great efforts were made [by Japan] in behalf of maintaining peace in the Pacific. . . .[45]

It seems a fair supposition that Konoye had real hopes of coming to an agreement with Roosevelt but at the same time had in mind the propaganda value of a meeting that failed—blame for the failure, of course, to be saddled upon the United States. In view of the reluctance, certainly of the Navy, possibly of the Army, to face a war with the United States (to be mentioned below), it seems at least possible that a Roosevelt-Konoye meeting might have produced an agreement. One may question whether such a meeting would have involved any risks for the United States serious enough to justify the American refusal.

Final Negotiations

The discussions of a possible Roosevelt-Konoye meeting were carried on simultaneously with Japanese planning for war if no agreement with America were reached. An Imperial Conference on September 6 had decided upon war with the United States, Great Britain, and the Netherlands if by the beginning of October the negotiations did not show promise of a satisfactory outcome. The Emperor had accepted this decision unwillingly, and, though the Supreme Command ("top brass" of the Army and Navy) had proposed it, levelheaded men in both services had misgivings. Early in October, General Tojo, Minister of War, intimated to Konoye that if the Navy would state explicitly its opposition to war with

---

[45]Quoted in Grew, *Turbulent Era,* 2: 1303n.

America, "the Army would have to reconsider its position." When the Navy refused to take the odium by advertising its reluctance, Tojo advised that the cabinet resign and proposed that Prince Higashikuni, a member of the royal family, become Premier and take the responsibility of reversing the decision of September 6.[46] This solution proved unfeasible, and on October 18 General Tojo himself became Premier. Halfhearted attempts were made, by the Emperor and others, to avoid a war that few responsible people wanted, but Japan had got herself "out on a limb" and could not crawl back without serious loss of face, as well as possible assassination of officials responsible for a retreat.

Upon Tojo's taking office it was announced that the change in cabinets meant no change in policy and that negotiations with the United States would continue. An Imperial Conference of November 5 resolved to continue the negotiations still further. A few concessions were agreed to, and another ambassador, Saburo Kurusu, was sent to assist Nomura in Washington. The Emperor requested that efforts at a peaceful agreement with America be redoubled. At the same time, the Conference resolved that preparations for war should be completed by early December. Time was running out.

During the next two weeks, operation "Magic"—the decoding and translation by Naval Intelligence of intercepted Japanese messages—picked up a steady stream of messages passing back and forth between Tokyo and the Japanese embassy in Washington. It was thus known that the Japanese envoys had been given two sets of proposals to lay before the American government, Plan A and Plan B, the latter to be presented if the former were rejected. Plan

B represented the greatest concessions that Japan was willing to make. It was known, too, that Japan had set a deadline, first November 25, later November 29, by which time the negotiations must be completed. "After that," ran one intercepted message, "things are automatically going to happen." Pleas from the ambassadors (Kurusu arrived in Washington November 15) for more time and further concessions met with blunt refusals in Tokyo. Washington knew, therefore, that unless by November 29 the United States accepted Japanese Plan B, or persuaded Japan to take something less, "things" were "going to happen." Washington did not know what or where, but Japanese concentrations of troops and transports pointed to attacks on British Malaya, Thailand, the Dutch East Indies, or possibly the Philippines.

It was assumed in Washington that an attack on the British or Dutch possessions would, or at least ought to, bring the United States into the war. President Roosevelt had, in fact, given secret assurances to this effect to the British. Such a course was in line with Roosevelt's "global strategy" and had been made plain to Japan. But neither the Army nor the Navy was prepared for war in the Pacific; both desperately needed time. Secretary of War Stimson, in particular, believed that in three months he could build up a force of B-17s (flying Fortresses) in the Philippines that could block Japan's southward expansion. So the Army and Navy pleaded for a postponement of the showdown, for three months at least, and there was talk of a possible temporary *modus vivendi* if no permanent agreement could be reached.

Japanese Plan A having been presented piecemeal and rejected by Secretary Hull, the envoys brought in on November 20 their Plan B, which they described as a *modus vivendi,* or way of getting along, presumably only temporarily. The proposals were as follows: (1) neither government to send armed forces into the Southeast Asia or South Pacific area, except Indochina; (2)

[46]This is the course of events described by Toshikazu Kase, a Foreign Office official, in *Journey to the Missouri* (New Haven: Yale University Press, 1950), pp. 46–64. On the attitude of the Navy see also Jones, *Japan's New Order,* pp. 290–91.

the two governments to cooperate to secure needed commodities from the Netherlands Indies, (3) commercial relations to be restored to their status before the freezing of funds, the United States to supply Japan with "the required quantity of oil"; (4) the United States "not to resort to measures and actions prejudicial to the endeavors for the restoration of general peace between Japan and China"; (5) Japan to move its troops in southern Indochina into the northern portion upon the conclusion of this agreement, and to withdraw all troops from Indochina upon the making of peace with China "or the establishment of an equitable peace in the Pacific area."

In regard to Japan's relations with Germany, not mentioned in the document, Kurusu had said to President Roosevelt on November 17 that Japan could not openly abandon the Tripartite Pact but "had no intention of becoming a tool of Germany nor did she mean to wait until the United States became deeply involved in the battle of the Atlantic and then stab her in the back."[47]

These proposals the United States rejected. Acceptance of them, as Cordell Hull wrote later, "would have placed her [Japan] in a commanding position later to acquire control of the entire western Pacific area. . . . It would have meant abject surrender of our position under intimidation. . . ." But since the Army and Navy were pressing for time, Hull prepared a *modus vivendi* of his own. This he thought of proposing to the Japanese as a basis for a three months' truce, during which either a permanent agreement might be reached or, if not, the armed forces would have had that much more time to prepare for war. The new proposals comprised mutual pledges of peaceful policy; promises that neither would advance further in the Pacific area by means of force or threat of force; withdrawal of Japanese forces from

southern to northern Indochina and limitation of those in that area to 25,000; resumption of trade with Japan on a limited scale; sale of petroleum to Japan for civilian use only; any settlement between Japan and China to be "based upon the principles of peace, law, order, and justice."

The difference between these proposals and Japan's Plan B was not so wide as to rule out possible agreement. On the other hand, they provided so little for China (nothing but a "pious hope," in fact), that China, which, with the United Kingdom, the Netherlands, and Australia, was consulted about them, protested bitterly. Since neither the British nor the Dutch greeted them with enthusiasm, and since their publication at home was sure to bring charges of "appeasement," Hull decided reluctantly, and after consulting with Roosevelt, to discard the *modus vivendi* entirely and to submit instead a ten-point program for a permanent settlement along strictly American lines. Since this program called for withdrawal of all Japanese troops from China and Indochina and for a virtual disavowal of the Axis Pact, Hull must have known when he presented it on November 26 that Japan would spurn it and that "things" would begin to happen. He made this clear next day by telling Stimson: "I have washed my hands of it, and it [the situation] is now in the hands of you and Knox, the Army and Navy."

Would the United States Fight if Not Attacked?

The note of November 26, sometimes referred to as an ultimatum, was, more accurately, a rejection of Japan's ultimatum of November 20. As far as the United States was concerned, it left the door open for further negotiation. In fact, the Army and Navy still hoped for at least a postponement of hostilities. Intercepted messages, however, directing Japanese envoys

[47]Jones, *Japan's New Order*, p. 304.

in the democracies to burn their codes and destroy their code machines and referring to war as imminent, made it plain that Japan was bent on war. The movement of a large Japanese convoy down the China coast in the direction of Indochina pointed surely to a southern campaign. Its objective might be Thailand, British Malaya, the Netherlands Indies, or the Philippines—any or all of these. Prevailing opinion in Washington in these last days of peace held that Japan would not deliberately attack United States territory, and the problem that most exercised the minds of the President and his advisers was whether American opinion, in Congress and out, would support the administration in making war if the Japanese attack should fall only upon British or Dutch or Thai territory.

To meet this contingency the President set his advisers to work drafting a message to Congress for the purpose of demonstrating to the legislators that any further Japanese advance in Southeast Asia would threaten the vital interests of the United States and thus justify armed resistance. But this message to Congress was to be preceded by a last ditch attempt to dissuade Japan from aggression—a direct appeal from the President to the Emperor. The idea of an appeal to the Emperor was threshed over for at least a week before the message was sent. One draft revived the idea of a *modus vivendi,* with a ninety-day truce between Japan and China, as well as between Japan and the western powers. The message actually sent, on the evening of December 6, too late to have any effect, contained no such proposal. It reviewed the long friendship between Japan and the United States and the current threats to it, and described the occupation of Indochina as a threat hanging over the peoples of Malaya, the Netherlands Indies, Thailand, and the Philippines. It offered guarantees that no other power would occupy Indochina if Japan withdrew and promised: "Thus a withdrawal of the Japanese forces

from Indo-China would result in the assurance of peace throughout the whole of the South Pacific area." It is notable that this last appeal to Japan placed all the emphasis upon Southeast Asia, none upon China. This final attempt to stave off hostilities reached Ambassador Grew in Tokyo too late for delivery to the Emperor until almost the moment of the fateful Pearl Harbor attack.

The Japanese reply to the American note of November 26—a long complaint against American policy in the Far East ending with notice of the breaking off of the negotiations—was presented by the ambassadors to the Secretary of State at 2:20, Washington time, on Sunday afternoon, December 7, 1941. The hour set for its delivery had been one o'clock, a few minutes before the first bombs were to fall on Pearl Harbor. Delay in decoding postponed the envoys' call upon Secretary Hull. When they reached his office, he knew, as they did not, of the Japanese surprise attack. After glancing at the note (of whose content he was already apprised through "Magic"), Mr. Hull castigated it as "crowded with infamous falsehoods and distortions," and showed the ambassadors the door. Later in the day came word that Japan had formally declared war, some two hours after the Pearl Harbor attack. Congress responded the next day (December 8) with a declaration of war against Japan. The British government had done the same a few hours earlier. On November 29 Japan had received assurance that Germany would join her if she went to war with the United States. On December 11 Germany and Italy declared war. The United States was in the war "up to its neck," in Europe and in the Pacific.

Post-Mortem on Pearl Harbor

The naval task force under Admiral Nagumo that launched the surprise attack on Pearl Harbor had been assembled behind a perfect screen of secrecy at Hitokappu Bay on Etorofu Island in the Kuriles. It had set out for the vicinity of Hawaii on November 25 with orders to launch the attack at dawn December 7 (December 8, Tokyo time), but with the understanding that it would be recalled if a settlement were reached in the meantime. Its assignment was performed with complete success but with results disastrous for Japan. Nothing could have so unified sentiment in the United States as the "sneak attack" at Pearl Harbor.

The phrase "sneak attack," however, was a convenient rationalization which helped to divert attention from the culpable negligence that made the surprise possible. There were several reasons why the attack should have been anticipated. In the "war games" of 1932, American carriers had launched a successful Sunday morning attack on the defending force at Pearl Harbor. This exploit gave the Japanese a perfect pattern but had apparently been forgotten by responsible Americans. As early as January 1941, Ambassador Grew reported to the State Department, Tokyo rumors that Japan would open hostilities with an air attack on Pearl Harbor. From September 1941 to the eve of the attack, intercepted Japanese instructions to the Japanese consul general in Honolulu showed a suspicious curiosity about the exact location of ships at Pearl Harbor. In November, when negotiations were approaching a climax, Ambassador Grew warned that hostile Japanese action might come "with dangerous and dramatic suddenness"; and Secretary Hull remarked to a meeting of the "War Cabinet" at the White House that the Japanese "might make the element of surprise a central point in their strategy," that "they might attack at various points simultaneously. . . ." The Japanese habit of striking first and declaring war later was well known. Why was Pearl Harbor asleep?

In answering that question, we may discard at once the discredited theory that President Roosevelt deliberately enticed the Japanese to attack Pearl Harbor in order to get the United States into the European War by the "back door."[48] That Roosevelt would voluntarily have invited destruction of a major weapon, the Pacific Fleet, as a means toward involvement in a two-front war which he did not want, stands the test neither of reason nor of the evidence. The explanation for the disaster lies, not in a conspiracy of FDR and a few close advisers, but in complacency and negligence, both in the administration in Washington and in the high command in Hawaii.

Certainly Washington was remiss in its failure to alert the Hawaiian commanders more emphatically to the possibility of surprise attack. "War warnings" were sent to the Army and Navy commanders there and in the Philippines on November 27, the day after the final note was handed to Japan. The warnings were not followed up as it seems clear they should have been when intercepted messages revealed that the zero hour was approaching. For reasons of security, knowledge of the "Magic" intercepts was limited to a very few persons in Washington. Their content was not communicated to the commanders in Hawaii or the Philippines. Even if it had been, there is no certainty that Admiral Husband E. Kimmel and General Walter C. Short in Hawaii would have acted with more foresight than they actually exhibited. The intercepts showed unmistakably that war was coming—somewhere. The only item that pointed specifically to an attack on the fleet at Pearl Harbor was the display of Japanese interest in the precise location of the ships there; and, as Roberta Wohlstet-

[48]The most formidable presentation of this conspiracy theory is C. C. Tansill, *Back Door to War: The Roosevelt Foreign Policy* (Chicago: Henry Regnery Co., 1952).

ter has shown in her impressive study of the shortcomings of American intelligence operations in 1941, the Japanese were showing similar curiosity about ship locations in Panama, San Diego, San Francisco, Portland, Vancouver, and elsewhere.[49] Washington intelligence failed to see any special threat to Pearl Harbor (even though Pearl Harbor sheltered the prime target for Japanese attack). With the same information, Kimmel and Short might well have similarly failed in its interpretation. In the absence of more specific warnings from Washington, Admiral Kimmel and General Short took measures for protection against submarine attack and sabotage respectively. These measures apparently satisfied their superiors in Washington. They were not told to, nor did they, take special precautions against attack from the air.

Neither in Washington nor in Hawaii, it seems in retrospect, was there the alert imagination that imminent war with a tricky enemy called for. For Washington, the rather obvious explanation (certainly not a justification) of the blind spot is the fact that all eyes were fixed so intently on the Far East that earlier warnings of danger to Hawaii were forgotten. Japanese concentrations in Formosa (threatening the Philippines), large Japanese convoys heading for Malaya, other concentrations in the Carolines pointing toward the Netherlands Indies—all these were known, were real, were watched with anxiety. No one had spotted Admiral Nagumo's task force, plowing through the North Pacific toward Hawaii. No one dreamed, apparently, that Japan could be aiming another major blow in addition to the several for which preparations were visible.

There are other intriguing questions. Why did Roosevelt keep the Pacific Fleet at Pearl Harbor when its former commander, Admiral James O. Richardson, had advised that it would be both safer and more effective if operated from Pacific Coast bases? The probable answer is that Roosevelt, though realizing the military soundness of Richardson's advice, took a calculated military risk rather than withdraw the fleet in a move which both the Japanese and their Chinese victims would have viewed as a retreat by the United States.

Why did the Japanese, aware of the greatly superior material and human resources of the United States, initiate a war in which the long-range odds were so heavily against them? The answer lies partly, of course, in their reliance upon the prowess of their German ally, but also in their drawing a false lesson from history. Records of prewar military discussions suggest that Japanese optimists expected to repeat the achievements of their fathers against Russia in 1904–1905. In that conflict, a succession of early and impressive victories had worn down the determination of a stronger foe and led to a favorable peace. Would not the same strategy work against America?[50]

Finally, why did the United States think it necessary to oppose Japan's program of expansion up to the point where Japan had either to abandon it or to fight for it? American policy may have been right or wrong, but it had historical roots and a logical pattern. The United States had objected from the beginning to Japan's step-by-step domination of China. It began to talk of forcible resistance only after Japan allied herself with Germany and threatened to absorb in her Greater East Asia Co-prosperity Sphere areas considered vital to the free world. There may have been errors of judgment and missed opportunities for compromise, as Ambassador Grew be-

[49]Roberta Wohlstetter, *Pearl Harbor: Warning and Decision* (Stanford: Stanford University Press, 1962), p. 390. A judicious brief summary of the mistakes and mischances that contributed to the Pearl Harbor disaster is M. S. Watson, *Chief of Staff: Pre-War Plans and Preparations* (Washington: Department of the Army, Historical Division, 1950), especially pp. 518–19.

[50]Nobutaka, Ike, ed., *Japan's Decisions for War: Records of the 1941 Policy Conferences* (Stanford: Stanford University Press, 1967), p. xxv.

lieved; but the fact remains that Japan was bent upon expanding its empire in ways incompatible with Roosevelt's "global strategy," with his commitments to Great Britain, and with his moral commitments, at least, to Chiang Kai-shek. The United States did not choose to fight; it blocked Japan's path and left the choice to her.

ADDITIONAL READINGS

BUTOW, R. J. C., *The John Doe Associates: Backdoor Diplomacy for Peace, 1941.* Stanford: Stanford University Press, 1974.

COLE, WAYNE. *Charles A. Lindbergh and the Battle against America in World War II.* New York: Harcourt Brace Jovanovich, 1973.

DIVINE, ROBERT A., *Roosevelt and World War II.* Baltimore: Johns Hopkins University Press, 1969.

DOENECKE, JUSTUS, D., "General Robert E. Wood: The Evolution of a Conservative," *Journal of the Illinois State Historical Society*, 71 (1978), 162–75.

EDWARDS, JEROME E., *The Foreign Policy of Colonel McCormick's Tribune, 1924–41.* Reno, Nevada: University of Nevada Press, 1971.

TREFOUSSE, H. L., *Germany and American Neutrality, 1939–1941.* New York: Bookman Associates, 1951.

WOHLSTETTER, ROBERTA, *Pearl Harbor: Warning and Decision.* Stanford: Stanford University Press, 1962.

19. The Grand Alliance and the Ending of the War

Upon entering World War II, the United States did not, as in 1917, hold itself aloof from its associates. In 1917–1918 the United States had described itself as an "associated power," not one of the Allies. In the later war, although it made no formal treaty of alliance, it took the lead in drawing up and signing, January 1, 1942, the Declaration by United Nations, which for practical purposes amounted to the same thing. Other signatories were the United Kingdom, the Soviet Union, and China; the five nations of the British Commonwealth, the governments in exile of eight European countries overrun by the Axis powers; and nine states of Latin America that had followed the United States into the war. The original signers numbered twenty-six; before the war's end the number had grown to forty-seven.[1]

The signatory governments, endorsing the "program of purposes and principles embodied in the . . . Atlantic Charter," and avowing their conviction "that complete victory over their enemies is essential to defend life, liberty, independence, and religious freedom, and to preserve human rights and justice," declared:

1. Each Government pledges itself to employ its full resources, military or economic, against those members of the Tripartite Pact and its adherents with which such government is at war.
2. Each Government pledges itself to cooperate with the Governments signatory hereto and not to make a separate armistice or peace with the enemies.

In signing this declaration, with its pledge to employ the nation's full resources for war and its promise not to make a separate peace, President Roosevelt, as one authority has remarked, "virtually contracted an alliance, and this without the consent of any legislative body, and indeed almost without a voice raised in criticism."[2]

The members of this "grand alliance" contributed to the common cause in proportion to their ability, combined with their enthusiasm, the contributions of many being purely nominal. The brunt of the fighting was borne by the "Big Three," the

---

[1]The original signers, in order of signing, were the United States, the United Kingdom, the U.S.S.R., China, Australia, Belgium, Canada, Costa Rica, Cuba, Czechoslovakia, Dominican Republic, El Salvador, Greece, Guatemala, Haiti, Honduras, India, Luxembourg, Netherlands, New Zealand, Nicaragua, Norway, Panama, Poland, Union of South Africa, Yugoslavia. Subsequent signers were Bolivia, Brazil, Chile, Colombia, Ecuador, Egypt, Ethiopia, France, Iran, Iraq, Lebanon, Liberia, Mexico, Paraguay, Peru, Philippines, Saudi Arabia, Syria, Turkey, Uruguay, Venezuela. All of these governments declared war against one or more of the Axis powers. Argentina declared war on March 27, 1945, but did not sign the Declaration by United Nations. *Documents on American Foreign Relations*, 7; July 1944—June 1945, pp. 301, 344–45. The text of the Declaration is in ibid., 4: 203, 218.

[2]Dexter Perkins, *The American Approach to Foreign Policy* (Cambridge: Harvard University Press, 1952), pp. 138–39.

United States, the United Kingdom, and the Soviet Union, with China a poor fourth. The British Dominions, the Yugoslav guerrillas, and the Free French under General Charles de Gaulle did their full share. All the allies that contributed to the war, and some that did not, received the benefits of the lend-lease program of the United States.

The United States and Great Britain

The most intimate cooperation was that between the United States and the United Kingdom. This cooperation originated at the highest level. Within a few hours after receiving the news from Pearl Harbor, Winston Churchill was planning a visit to Washington. He spent several weeks at the White House in December and January (with excursions to Ottawa and to Palm Beach). This conference (which was given the code name of "Arcadia") was the first of a notable series of meetings in which the President and the Prime Minister and their advisers made decisions on matters of high strategy, both political and military.[3] Not always did they see eye to eye, but they always resolved their differences amicably. The President, commanding the greater resources in men and matériel, had his way more often than did the Prime Minister.

On one basic matter there was never any difference of opinion between the two men: Hitler's Germany was Enemy Number One. This decision had been reached, it will be recalled, in staff confer-

[3] In addition to the Atlantic Conference of August 1941 and the "Arcadia" Conference, meetings of the President and the Prime Minister occurred as follows: Washington, June 1942; Casablanca, January 1943; Washington, May 1943 ("Trident"); Quebec, August 1943 ("Quadrant"); Cairo, November 1943 (with Chiang Kai-shek); Teheran, November–December 1943 (with Stalin); Cairo, December 1943; Quebec, September 1944; Yalta, February 1945 (with Stalin).

ences nearly a year before the United States entered the war. Germany was a more dangerous foe than Japan, and her defeat must have priority. From the British point of view this was an obvious truth. To an American, after Pearl Harbor, it was less obvious, particularly to American commanders like General MacArthur and Admiral King, who had the task of fighting Japan. Even General Marshall, the Chief of Staff, sometimes wavered. Yet Roosevelt adhered consistently to the Germany-first policy and would have had the satisfaction, had he lived, of seeing Japan surrender three months after the defeat of Germany.

On some other important aspects of the war there were differences. Roosevelt rated much more highly than Churchill the importance of China and of assisting Chiang Kai-shek, perhaps because he expected that China would follow the American lead in international policy. This difference was not of too great practical importance, since available aid for Chiang was severely limited. The war against Japan was won, not on the Chinese mainland, but by sea and air attacks upon the Japanese homeland and its communications.

In the strategy of the war in Europe, such differences as arose were between the two men's military advisers rather than between Roosevelt and Churchill themselves. The Americans, anxious to deliver a knockout blow at Germany at the earliest possible moment, urged a crossing of the English Channel by Anglo-American forces in the spring of 1943, with a possible preliminary crossing still earlier. The British, with tragic memories of the trench warfare of World War I, would not agree to such a crossing until assured of possession of overwhelming force and adequate landing equipment, and until Germany had been further worn down by blockade, bombing, and attrition on the Russian front. Nineteen forty-three, they insisted, was too early. In the face of this refusal, General Marshall proposed shifting the main American effort to the Pacific. Roosevelt at once vetoed this suggestion. A compromise was found in TORCH, the North African landing, in November 1942, followed by the advance into Sicily and Italy in 1943, and OVERLORD, the Normandy landing, in June 1944. The dispute had been over timing, not over the final objective. A proposal of Churchill's in 1944 that troops in Italy, earmarked for southern France, be sent instead across the Adriatic into Yugoslavia and perhaps as far as Vienna and Hungary (where they might have anticipated the Russian armies) was vetoed by Roosevelt. Churchill, disturbed by the advance of the Red armies was more concerned for the political future of Central Europe than were Roosevelt and his advisers, who tended to think in strictly military terms.

One real difference in outlook between the two men is deserving of a paragraph. Roosevelt, an anti-imperialist, had no enthusiasm for preserving or restoring the colonial holdings of the French or the British, and occasionally urged upon Churchill the claims to independence of India or other British possessions. Churchill not unexpectedly, took a dim view of such ideas. Proud as Rudyard Kipling of his nation's imperial achievements, he proclaimed in the House of Commons, soon after the Anglo-American landing in North Africa: "I have not become the King's First Minister in order to preside over the liquidation of the British Empire."[4]

The anticolonialism of Roosevelt and Cordell Hull was traceable in principle to Woodrow Wilson's preaching of self-determination, to carry it no further back, but it had, too, an important economic significance. Colonial empires, even the liberal British Commonwealth, were associated with "imperial preference," with partially closed economic systems. These were contrary to the nondiscriminatory, or "open door," principle which Hull had tried to promote through the reciprocal trade treaties and the terms of the lend-lease agreements; but the best assurance of the end of "imperial preference" would be the end of empires. Here, as in some other matters, American principles were in harmony with American economic interests.

Between conferences Roosevelt and Churchill kept in touch through frequent letters, telegrams, and telephone conversations. Roosevelt's friend, Harry Hopkins, was frequently in England and was in Churchill's confidence. In these various ways, regular diplomatic channels were largely bypassed.

As one consequence of the Arcadia Conference there was set up in Washington in January 1942 a body known as the Combined Chiefs of Staff. This was made up of the Joint Chiefs of Staff of the United States (the Army, Navy, and Air Force Chiefs, together with, later on, the Chief of Staff to the President) and deputies of the corresponding British Chiefs, the deputies being quartered in the Pentagon in offices adjacent to those of the American Chiefs. This body was charged with making and executing plans for the strategic conduct of the war, for meeting war requirements in matériel, for allocating munitions and transportation facilities, all, of course, under the general direction of the President and the Prime Minister.

Further machinery for Anglo-American collaboration took the form of a number of Combined Boards, of which the most important were those for Raw Materials, Munitions Assignments, Shipping Adjustment, Production and Resources, and Food. These were all created in 1942, with American and British members. On the last two, Canada also was represented. The purpose was to direct all materials and services available to the United Nations into

---

[4]R. E. Sherwood, *Roosevelt and Hopkins: An Intimate History* (New York: Harper & Row, Publishers, 1948), p. 656.

channels where they would contribute most to winning the war.

There was, of course, friction between Americans and British at various levels, but on the whole, the branches of the English-speaking world cooperated with gratifying smoothness and success.

Wartime Relations with Russia: The Background

With the third member of the Big Three, the Soviet Union, such close and mutually trustful relations proved impossible, despite an undoubted wish on Roosevelt's part to create them. It would, indeed, have been miraculous if the sudden partnership in the war against Hitler had produced friendship and confidence where incompatible ideologies had long bred hatred and suspicion.

It will be well at this point to summarize briefly the story of prewar relations between the United States and the Soviet Union. The United States had hailed with enthusiasm the overthrow of the Czar in March 1917 and the establishment of a liberal provisional government in Russia, but enthusiasm had turned to dislike and suspicion when the Bolshevists, led by Lenin and Trotsky, seized power in November, made a separate peace with Germany, and adopted a program of world revolution. Communist Russia was excluded from the Paris Peace Conference and was long refused recognition by the United States. The reasons for withholding recognition (after an initial period when the permanence of the new regime was in doubt) were: (1) refusal of the U.S.S.R. to recognize the financial obligations of its predecessors; (2) its refusal to recognize claims of American citizens for damages sustained as a result of the revolution; (3) its denial of the validity of international agreements; (4) the subversive activities of the Communist Inter-

national, the propaganda agency of the Moscow government, operating through Communist parties in the United States and other capitalist countries.

For a brief period in 1918–1919 American troops joined British and French forces in Archangel in futile cooperation with Russian anti-Bolshevik elements. The Siberian expedition of 1918–1920, on the other hand, was designed partly to safeguard Russian territory against Japanese expansionism. At the Washington Conference of 1921–1922, though Russia was not invited to participate, the United States took the position that no action injurious to Russia must be taken and was successful in persuading Japan to evacuate Siberia and return northern Sakhalin to Russia. The United States again took Russia's part in 1929, when Nationalist China undertook to oust Russia from the Russian-built and Russian-owned Chinese Eastern Railway. In other words, the United States, although withholding recognition from the Soviet government, took action repeatedly to protect the interests of the Russian people.

By 1933, some of the arguments against recognition had lost a part of their force. In Russia, Leon Trotsky, chief apostle of world revolution, had been expelled from the Communist party and from the country, and Stalin had adopted the slogan "Socialism in one country." To a considerable extent, the Soviet government had settled the claims of American individuals and corporations, as the price of doing new business with them. The economic depression of the early thirties aroused a hope that official recognition of Russia would expand the Russian market for American products. The Manchurian crisis had re-emphasized the common interest of Russia and the United States in opposing Japanese expansion on the Asiatic mainland. Finally, the Roosevelt administration was not, like its predecessor, committed to a policy of nonrecognition. Consequently, at Roosevelt's invitation, the Soviet government sent

Maxim Litvinov to Washington, and on November 16, 1933, the United States established regular diplomatic relations with Moscow.

By an exchange of notes prior to recognition, the Soviet government agreed not to sponsor, nor to permit within its jurisdiction, propaganda or other activity aimed at the overthrow of the government of the United States; to allow religious freedom and protection in the courts of American nationals residing in Russia; and to negotiate for a settlement of debts and claims. The results were disappointing. No agreement on claims was reached. Moscow-sponsored Communist activity in the United States continued. Trade figures were far below expectation; and there was no cooperation in opposing Japan.

If a lack of cordiality characterized Russian-American relations until 1939, the events of that year and of 1940 turned American sentiment violently against the Soviets. Stalin's pact with Hitler was quickly followed by Russia's occupation of eastern Poland. The Baltic states of Lithuania, Latvia, and Estonia were first required to admit Russian troops for their "protection" and then quietly incorporated into the Soviet Union.[5] When Finland refused to grant in full the Kremlin's demand for bases on Finnish territory and was attacked and invaded in consequence, it put up a brave but hopeless fight, which won the sympathy of the democracies and led to the expulsion of Russia from the League of Nations—the League's last, futile gesture against aggression. All of these Russian acts alienated whatever sympathy American non-Communists may have felt for the U.S.S.R. and were poor preparation for partnership.

[5]The Molotov-Ribbentrop pact of 1939 had assigned Lithuania to the German sphere of influence. Lithuania was later shifted by agreement to the Russian sphere, but friction arising from Russia's absorption of it was a contributing cause of Germany's break with Russia in June 1941.

Wartime Relations with Russia: Strains and Stresses

When Hitler turned his arms against his former partner on June 22, 1941, the United States joined Great Britain in welcoming Russia into the fellowship of the nations engaged in combating totalitarianism. Secretary Hull, ill at home, phoned the President: "We must give Russia all aid to the hilt. We have repeatedly said we will give all the help we can to any nation resisting the Axis."[6] Roosevelt stated at once that the United States was prepared to give all possible assistance to the Soviet Union.

Convinced through on-the-spot investigations by Harry Hopkins, Averell Harriman, and others that Russia would hold out if adequately supplied, he informed Stalin on October 30 that military equipment and munitions to the value of one billion dollars would be supplied under lend-lease. A week later he instructed the Lend-Lease Administrator that he had "today found that the defense of the Union of Soviet Socialist Republics is vital to the defense of the United States," and that defense supplies were therefore to be transferred to the Soviets under lend-lease. This was the first installment of lend-lease goods to the amount of $11 billion to be supplied to the Soviet Union during the war. Shipments went via Murmansk, via Vladivostok (under the noses of the Japanese), and via the Persian Gulf and Iran.

In return, the Russian armies and people, through their heroic resistance, played an indispensable role in defeating Nazi Germany. Apart from this, the Soviet government made certain gestures of good will. Speaking through the Soviet ambas-

[6]Hull, *Memoirs*, 2: 967. Others in the State Department were less sympathetic to the Soviets. See Daniel M. Smith and Joseph M. Siracusa, *The Testing of America: 1914–1945* (St. Louis: Forum Press, 1979), pp. 202–203.

sador in London, it endorsed the liberal principles of the Atlantic Charter, though with a qualification that provided a loophole; namely, "Considering that the practical application of these principles will necessarily adapt itself to the circumstances, needs, and historic peculiarities of particular countries."[7] The Soviet Union was one of the original signers of the Declaration by United Nations, January 1, 1942. In May 1943, furthermore, the Communist International, or Comintern, was dissolved by the action of its own governing body, and all former supporters of the Comintern were called upon "to concentrate their energies on the whole-hearted support of and active participation in the war of liberation of the peoples and the states of the anti-Hitlerite coalition . . ."[8] Thus was soft-pedaled, for the time being, the basic antagonism of Soviet Communism for the capitalist world.

On the American side there was much wishful thinking, to the effect that the cooperation of wartime would survive the destruction of Hitler. Neither Roosevelt nor his advisers, whether civil or military, seemed aware of the danger of a too powerful postwar Russia; or, if the danger occurred to them, their remedy was to integrate Stalin's aims with those of the West's. If faith in Russia's good intentions wavered, there was another reason for "being nice to Russia"—fear: fear that Russia might turn again to Hitler and make a separate peace, or fear that Russia would not aid in defeating Japan after Germany had been crushed. The idea prevailed in Washington that the United States needed Russia more than Russia needed the United States. Therefore Stalin could name his price and sometimes got even more than he asked. Lend-lease aid, for example, was some-

times pressed upon indifferent Russian recipients.

The Soviet Union, for its part, showed no such naive trust in its Western allies. It was not without grounds for suspicion, for a common British hope had been to see Germany and Russia tear each other to pieces while the West stood by. So now, almost from the time the United States entered the war, Stalin demanded the opening without delay of a second front in Europe, to relieve the pressure on the Russian armies. Misleading assurances about a second front in 1942 were given Molotov on a visit to Washington in May and June of that year, and Churchill later had difficulty in persuading Stalin that the landing in North Africa (November 1942) was the only offensive possible to the Western Allies at that stage. Up to the Normandy landing in June 1944, there were periodic complaints from Moscow that the Anglo-American forces were dragging their feet. And as late as March 1945, Anglo-American negotiations looking to the surrender of German troops in northern Italy brought from Stalin angry accusations that his allies were planning a separate peace.

In the meantime there was endless friction in negotiation over comparatively minor matters—over the use of bases in Soviet territory, over liberated prisoners of war, even over the details of lend-lease, where the Russians were given to haggling over prices of goods for which they would never be called upon to pay. One difficulty arose from the almost invisible amount of discretion allowed to Soviet negotiators at all but the top levels; virtually all decisions had to be referred to higher authority. And when Soviet authorities made concessions on paper, they too often failed to implement them in practice. When the President and the Secretary of State met with their Russian opposite numbers, as they did on several occasions, superficial harmony was generally achieved; but in these meetings the Russians generally had their way, and

[7]*Documents on American Foreign Relations*, 4: 216. All quotations from *Documents* . . . reprinted by permission of Council on Foreign Relations.

[8]Ibid., 5: 527–30.

such concessions as they made to the American or British point of view were too often forgotten when the time came to apply them. Since the conferences with Stalin and Molotov dealt largely with postwar matters, an account of them is deferred until later.

China as an Ally

In its character of nonbelligerent (rather than neutral), the United States had been assisting China against Japan for some time before December 1941. China, that is, the government of Chiang Kai-shek, had received, since 1937, loans or credits to the amount of $120 million from the Export-Import Bank in Washington. It had been made eligible for lend-lease assistance. Its principal air force, the American Volunteer Group (A.V.G.) or Flying Tigers, was commanded by a retired United States Air Force officer, Claire L. Chennault; the planes were American planes, and they were flown and fought by American Air Force pilots, who had been permitted to resign or take leave with the object of serving in China. An American military mission was in China for the purpose of instructing and training Chinese personnel in the use of American equipment.[9] Since all Chinese seaports were in Japanese hands, material aid from the United States was sent by way of Rangoon and the Burma Road into southwest China.

The Japanese attack at Pearl Harbor at last made China and the United States full-fledged allies. American policy toward China, as defined by Secretary Hull, now assumed two purposes: (1) to ensure

Chinese cooperation in waging effective war against Japan; (2) to raise China to the status of a great power, not only for the better prosecution of the war, but also that she might serve as a stabilizing factor in the postwar Far East.[10]

In pursuance of the policy of elevating China to great-power status, the United States granted to the Chinese government and people an equality that had been denied them since the first entry of the West into Chinese affairs. By a treaty with China signed January 11, 1943, the United States surrendered the extra-territorial rights that it had enjoyed since 1844, as well as the policing rights accorded at the time of the Boxer Rebellion, and its political and jurisdictional rights in the Diplomatic Quarter at Peiping and in the International Settlements at Shanghai and Amoy. The British signed a similar treaty on the same day. Thus, in theory, China recovered jurisdiction over her territory and over foreigners residing in China. The last of the "unequal treaties" were abrogated by the voluntary action of the United States and Great Britain.[11] Later in the same year Congress repealed the Chinese exclusion laws which, in some form or other, had been on the statute books since 1882. By the same act it placed Chinese immigration on the same quota basis as immigration from Europe and made Chinese immigrants eligible for naturalization.

By these measures the United States removed the taint of inequality that had always marked its relations with China. It went further in bringing about the association of China with itself, Great Britain, and

[10]Hull, *Memoirs,* 2: 1583–87.

[11]The treaty and related documents are printed in *Documents on American Foreign Relations,* 5: 485–501. By an exchange of notes at the time of signing the treaty the United States also surrendered special rights formerly enjoyed by United States shipping in the coastal trade of China and special rights that had been accorded to United States naval vessels in Chinese waters.

[9]Herbert Feis, *The China Tangle: The American Effort in China from Pearl Harbor to the Marshall Mission* (Princeton: Princeton University Press, 1953), p. 4; C. L. Chennault, *Way of a Fighter: The Memoirs of Claire Lee Chennault,* edited by Robert Hotz (New York: G. P. Putnam's Sons, 1949).

the Soviet Union, as one of the "Big Four" powers. With the other three, China signed the Moscow Declaration on General Security, of October 30, 1943, sponsored the call for the United Nations Conference on International Organization at San Francisco in 1945, and became one of the five permanent members of the United Nations Security Council.

These important reforms, accomplished by the approving and signing of certain documents, were relatively easy to achieve. Giving effective military support to Chiang Kai-shek was a more difficult matter and was never accomplished to the Generalissimo's satisfaction.

The early decision to give the European war priority over that in Asia limited the amount of aid available for China. The amount was further limited when the Japanese, early in 1942, overran Burma and closed the Burma Road. Until the Ledo (or Stilwell) Road from India to Yunnan was opened in the fall of 1944, all material for China had to be flown in "over the hump" from bases in northeast India. What could be done was done, however. The "Flying Tigers" evolved into the Fourteenth Air Force, which fought the enemy effectively in southern China. General Joseph W. Stilwell, who had had previous experience in China, was sent in to command United States ground forces, to serve as Chief of Staff to Chiang Kai-shek, and to act in part under the direction of the British commander of the China-Burma-India theater. He was effective as a trainer and commander of Chinese troops. He succeeded in recovering northern Burma from the Japanese and in opening the road from Ledo, that was named in his honor. Unfortunately, he disagreed with General Chennault, commander of the Fourteenth Air Force, about the relative importance of air and ground action; and he developed a strong dislike for Chiang Kai-shek, to whom he referred contemptuously as "the Peanut." His demand that he be entrusted with full command of all Chiang's armies and be permitted to amalgamate with them the Communist armies in north China led to his recall at Chiang's peremptory request in the fall of 1944. By that time the approach to Japan by way of the Philippines and the Marianas was deemphasizing the importance of the war in China, and there was a consequent tapering off in the effort to build up Chiang's military power. This change in policy had its bearing on Chiang's later defeat by the Communists.[12]

Good Neighborliness Is Reciprocated

By its Good Neighbor Policy of the 1930s, the United States had laid the basis for New World solidarity in confronting Axis aggression. Axis sympathizers were influential in Argentina and, to a lesser degree, in Chile. The rest of Latin America cordially supported the United States during both its nonbelligerency and its participation in the war.

Following the outbreak of war in Europe, the Foreign Ministers of the American Republics met in conference at Panama in September and October 1939. There they approved a General Declaration of Neutrality of the American Republics and announced rules of neutral conduct which, like the United States Neutrality Act of 1939, favored the European democracies. In the Declaration of Panama they undertook to prohibit any belligerent act in the waters adjacent to the American continents (south of the Canadian boundary) and delimited those waters as extending on the average three hundred miles to sea. It was in this declaration that President Roosevelt found justification for patrolling North Atlantic waters for the detection of Axis submarines.

[12]Feis, *The China Tangle*, p. 196.

The German victories over the Netherlands and France in the spring of 1940 raised the question of the fate of the French and Dutch possessions in the Caribbean. The possibility that they might be claimed or seized by Germany called forth reassertions by the Secretary of State and by Congress of the non-transfer principle long associated with the Monroe Doctrine. It led also to another conference of American Foreign Ministers at Havana, in July 1940. There, by the Act of Havana, the Foreign Ministers provided that an "emergency committee," one member from each republic, might set up a "provisional administration" for any European colony in the American area that might be threatened with a change of sovereignty. In urgent cases, a single American republic might act without waiting for a meeting of the committee. Upon the ending of the danger, the colony in question should either become independent or return to its former status. A convention, giving permanent form to the provisions of the act, also signed at Havana, was ratified and proclaimed early in 1942.

Such drastic action as that contemplated in the Act and the Treaty of Havana proved unnecessary. The landing of American troops in Greenland and Iceland was done with the consent of the Danish minister in the first case and the Iceland government in the second. By arrangement with the Netherlands government, United States and Brazilian troops aided in the protection of the bauxite mines in Surinam, whence came 60 percent of the ore for the American aluminum industry. In the spirit of Havana, however, the United States informed the American republics of its action in Surinam, and declared open to the use of any of them the bases acquired from Great Britain in the destroyer deal and any that it might establish in Greenland.

The attack on the United States at Pearl Harbor and the declarations of war by the Axis powers brought the real test of inter-American solidarity. The results were in the main gratifying. All of the Central American and Caribbean republics (many of them former objects of intervention by the United States) promptly declared war against the Axis powers and were on hand to sign the United Nations Declaration, January 1, 1942. Mexico, Colombia, and Venezuela severed diplomatic relations with the Axis. The other republics without exception sent friendly messages to the United States. Not one subjected it to the restrictions that normally would have been imposed upon a belligerent.

For a third time the Foreign Ministers or their deputies met in January 1942, this time at Rio de Janeiro. Here they declared that an act of aggression against one is aggression against all and recommended that all member states that had not yet severed relations with the Axis powers do so without further delay. This recommendation met with prompt compliance, except by Chile, which delayed until January 1943, and Argentina, which continued to harbor Axis diplomats until January 1944.

Eventually all the American republics declared war against Germany or Japan or both—Argentina not until March 27, 1945. All except Argentina and Panama received lend-lease assistance. Brazil sent an expeditionary force to Europe. Brazil, Cuba, Ecuador, and Panama permitted the United States to establish military bases within their territory. Otherwise, except in the furnishing of raw materials at good prices, their positive contributions to the war effort were not great. But the assurance that enemy agents would not find harborage in neighboring territory was an advantage of no small consequence to the United States.

The European Neutrals and the War

A number of European countries remained neutral or nonbelligerent throughout the war or until near the end. Eire, Sweden, and Switzerland kept out of it entirely, as did Turkey until February 1945, when it joined the United Nations. Portugal, too, did not enter the war but in October 1943 made an air base in the Azores available to Great Britain and the United States. The government of Spain, headed by General Franco, made no effort to disguise its pro-Axis sympathy, though the practical expressions of that sympathy faded and disappeared at the same rate as the prospects for Axis victory. France, after June 1940, had two governmental entities, each professing to speak for the French people. The government of Marshal Pétain at Vichy was a prisoner of Hitler, and of such pro-Hitler Frenchmen as Pierre Laval. General Charles de Gaulle, head of the Free French movement and claiming to be the spokesman of the true France, carried on the war against the Axis from foreign shores. Of these countries, the wartime relations of the United States with France and Spain were important.

Marshal Pétain's government broke off relations with Great Britain in July 1940, when the British navy attacked a portion of the French fleet at Oran in Algeria, to end all possibility of its falling into German or Italian hands. The break with England made it the more important for the United States to maintain relations with Vichy. Such contact, it was hoped, could reduce Hitler's influence to a minimum, prevent the surrender to the Axis of the French fleet or French bases in Africa, and serve as a channel of information in regard to Axis plans and activities. For American ambassador to Vichy, Roosevelt picked a distinguished naval officer, Admiral William D. Leahy, who held the office from January 1941 to May 1942.[13] His presence there was

a reminder of both the friendliness and the power of the United States. It made possible the negotiation of the Murphy-Weygand agreement, by which the United States undertook to provide French North Africa with essential food supplies and other commodities, and was authorized to supervise their distribution. The presence of American agents in Algiers and French Morocco, ostensibly for that purpose, was of importance in preparing the way for the Anglo-American landings of November 1942. At the news of those landings, Marshal Pétain broke off relations with the United States, though reportedly sending secret directions to Admiral Darlan, in Algiers, to stop resistance to the invaders.[14]

While maintaining relations with Vichy, the United States had recognized the Free French National Committee of General Charles de Gaulle, to the extent of granting lend-lease aid to forces operating under its direction and dealing with colonial regimes that accepted its authority, such as the government of New Caledonia. At a conference at Casablanca, Morocco, soon after the landings in North Africa, Roosevelt and Churchill brought about a meeting of de Gaulle and General Henri H. Giraud, who had been their choice to command French forces in North Africa. Some months later de Gaulle and Giraud joined in setting up a Committee of National Liberation, which from then on served as a sort of French government in exile. Giraud was soon eased out, and de Gaulle became the un-

---

[13]Leahy's story of his ambassadorship and other wartime activities is told in W. D. Leahy, *I Was There* (New York: Whittlesey House, 1950). See also W. L. Langer, *Our Vichy Gamble* (New York: Alfred A. Knopf, Inc., 1947); D. C. McKay, *The United States and France* (Cambridge: Harvard University Press, 1951), chap. 6.

[14]Admiral Jean Francois Darlan, French Minister of Marine and powerful Vichy politician, had been sympathetic to the Axis cause but before the North African landings had sent secret intimation of his readiness to cooperate with the Anglo-Americans. His offer was not accepted, and his presence in Algiers at the time of the landings was accidental. It was also fortunate, since French commanders in North Africa obeyed his cease-fire order; they refused to recognize the authority of General Giraud, who had landed with the Americans and British. American embarrassment at having to deal with a man of Darlan's reputation was ended when, on December 24, 1942, Darlan was assassinated by a young French fanatic. Langer, *Our Vichy Gamble*, 321–23, 345, 352–54, 379.

questioned head of the Committee. Unfortunately, General de Gaulle had antagonized Secretary Hull and had failed to ingratiate himself with President Roosevelt. The United States, therefore, held back when Churchill proposed to recognize de Gaulle's Committee of National Liberation as the provisional government of France. Only after the Allies had taken Paris in the summer of 1944 was such recognition finally granted.

With the Spain of General Franco, the leading problem of both American and British diplomacy was to prevent nonbelligerency from slipping into belligerency. The pro-Axis sympathies of Franco were well known. Serrano Suñer, his brother-in-law and, from October 1940 to September 1942, his Foreign Minister, was even more of a Germanophile than Franco himself. Spain, though a poor and weak nation, held a vitally important strategic position. Should she, with or without German aid, capture Gilbraltar, she would be able to forbid access to the Mediterranean from the west. Thus she might have prevented the North African offensive; or, had she intervened after that campaign was launched, she might have frustrated it by severing its communications with the Atlantic.

The means of preventing this course, first devised by the British, was to take advantage of Spain's economic weakness, supplying just enough essential raw materials, especially petroleum, to meet her day-to-day needs but none for stockpiling. The United States, where Franco was much detested and where emotion often interfered with the expedient course, was slow in adopting this policy, but eventually did so. Thus Spain was made to feel keenly her dependence upon British and American good will.

How far Franco's decision not to enter the war was influenced by British and American pressure is not easy to determine. He was nearest to intervention in the fall of 1940, when he had a personal meeting with Hitler at Hendaye, France. An agreement that Spain should join the Axis seems then and there to have been reached, but the time for the move was not set. Thereafter Franco, aware of Spain's weakness and more and more convinced that the war would be a long one, postponed the date of entry and raised his price. Hitler abandoned his plan for a campaign through Spain and turned east to strike Russia. Franco cooperated by sending the "Blue Division" to fight Communism on the eastern front, by conniving at the supplying of German U-boats from Spanish ports, and by facilitating the purchase of wolfram (tungsten ore) from Spanish mines by German agents. The tungsten purchases went on, despite Anglo-American protests and preclusive buying, until April 1944.

But Franco did nothing whatever to interfere with the Allied landings in North Africa or to hamper the ensuing campaign; and as the prospects of the Axis victory faded, he became more and more cooperative with the Allies. Instead of moving from nonbelligerency into war (as Mussolini had done, to his sorrow), Franco moved from nonbelligerency to neutrality—a neutrality that became increasingly benevolent to the Allies as their prospects of victory brightened.

Ending the War

Plans for ending the war and arranging for the peace to follow it began many months before the United States became a belligerent. The chief planners were the United States and the Soviet Union. American plans were highly publicized in the pronouncements of Franklin Roosevelt, idealistic in the main but not altogether neglectful of American material interests, Stalin talked little but moved quietly to safeguard the Russian future. Winston Churchill, a poor third in the possession of power, accepted the American program with skepticism and watched the Russian strategy with misgiving.

Roosevelt, in proposing the lend-lease program to Congress, January 6, 1941, described the kind of world that the program was designed to make secure—"a world founded upon four essential human freedoms." These were freedom of speech and expression, freedom of religion, freedom from want, and freedom from fear, the last to be achieved by a worldwide reduction of armaments to such a point that no nation would be able to commit an act of aggression against a neighbor. Seven months later, in the Atlantic Charter, Roosevelt and Churchill joined in a declaration of their objectives, Churchill as head of a government at war, Roosevelt as head of a nonbelligerent government committed to all aid short of war. Notable among those objectives were the "desire to see no territorial changes that do not accord with the freely expressed wishes of the people concerned"; respect for "the right of all peoples to choose the form of government under which they will live"; and the "wish to see sovereign rights and self-government restored to those who have been forcibly deprived of them." The Charter contemplated also "the establishment of a wider and permanent system of general security."

The fourth point of the Charter, proposing for all states "access, on equal terms, to the trade and to the raw materials of the world which are needed for their economic prosperity," committed the signers to the principle of elimination of economic barriers, or the "open door," which Secretary of State Cordell Hull had considered vital to the preservation of world peace. While nominally idealistic, this principle was also undoubtedly conducive to the economic prosperity and growth of the United States. It was rarely lost from sight in American planning for the postwar world.[15]

The principles of the Atlantic Charter were, as recorded above, endorsed by the Soviet Union, with an interpretative qualification, and were accepted by the governments signing the Declaration by United Nations of January 1, 1942. Thus they became, at least in theory, a part of the program of the nations allied against the Axis powers.

Stalin, in the meantime, was working toward ends that directly contradicted the principle of self-determination so prominent in the Atlantic Charter. Anthony Eden, British Foreign Secretary, visiting Moscow in December 1941, was confronted with a demand that Great Britain recognize Russia's annexation of the Baltic States and a slice of Finland. Eden agreed to pass on the Russian proposal to Great Britain and the United States. The United States rejected this demand as in conflict with the Atlantic Charter, despite Churchill's argument in favor of expedient concessions to the Kremlin.[16] Both powers, furthermore, refused to accede to Molotov's demand, a few months later, that they recognize Russia's claims to eastern Poland and a part of Rumania. Molotov settled for a twenty-year treaty of alliance with Great Britain, in which both governments agreed to "act in accordance with the two principles of not seeking territorial aggrandizement for themselves and of non-interference in the internal affairs of other States."[17] This phraseology accorded well with the Atlantic Charter, but at the Teheran Conference (November–December 1943) Stalin informed Roosevelt that the status of the former Baltic States was not open to discus-

---

[15]For very different views of the "open door," which tend to exaggerate the role of economic motiva-

tion in wartime and postwar policy, see W. A. Williams, *The Tragedy of American Diplomacy*, rev. ed. (New York: Dell Publishing Co., Inc., 1962); and Gabriel Kolko, *The Politics of War: The World and United States Foreign Policy, 1943–1945* (New York: Random House, Inc., 1968).

[16]Winston S. Churchill, *The Hinge of Fate*, Vol. 4 of *The Second World War* (Boston: Houghton Mifflin Company, 1950), p. 327.

[17]*Documents on American Foreign Relations*, 4: 254–57.

sion, since they had voted to join the Soviet Union. At the same conference the Western powers agreed to the Russian proposals for the boundaries of Poland. Here as elsewhere, the principles of the Atlantic Charter yielded, first, to the urgent need of holding Russia as an ally, and later, to the persuasive presence of victorious Russian armies.

"Unconditional Surrender"

The frequent meetings of Roosevelt and Churchill were concerned very largely with the conduct of the war. As military prospects improved, however, their meetings and those that they held with Stalin and Chiang Kai-shek dealt increasingly with the shape of the peace and with postwar problems.

In January 1943, two months after the successful landings in North Africa, the President and the Prime Minister met at Casablanca, on the Atlantic coast of Morocco. Premier Stalin was invited to attend the meeting but, in the words of the official communiqué, "was unable to leave Russia at this time on account of the great offensive which he himself, as Commander-in-Chief, is directing." The principal business of the conference was the planning of campaigns to come, in the Mediterranean theater and elsewhere, but in his remarks to the press correspondents at the close of the conference (January 26, 1943) the President used a momentous expression. Recalling the phrase, "unconditional surrender," used by General Grant in the American Civil War, Roosevelt informed the reporters: "The democracies' war plans were to compel the 'unconditional surrender' of the Axis." The use of this phrase, which had been approved in advance by Churchill and the British War Cabinet, was apparently designed to convince the Russians that America and England were determined to fight the war to

a finish. In the opinion of most analysts, it had the unintended and unfortunate effect of stiffening enemy resistance and postponing the day of surrender, certainly of Germany and Japan, perhaps of Italy. Conducive to the complete destruction of German and Japanese military potential, it helped to ensure the collapse of the balance of power and the military ascendancy of the Soviet Union in Europe and Asia.

Similarly unfortunate in its hardening effect on German resistance was the endorsement by Roosevelt and Churchill, in September 1944, of the so-called "Morgenthau Plan" for the postwar treatment of Germany. In the words of the memorandum signed by the two heads of government at Quebec, September 16, 1944:

> This programme for eliminating the war-making industries in the Ruhr and in the Saar is looking forward to converting Germany into a country primarily agricultural and pastoral in its character.

This program was the work of Henry Morgenthau, Jr., Secretary of the Treasury. It was vigorously opposed by Secretaries Hull and Stimson in Washington, but Roosevelt invited Morgenthau to Quebec, where he had an opportunity to present it to the President and the Prime Minister. Roosevelt later explained lamely to Stimson that he must have signed the document "Without much thought," but that "England was broke" and that under the Morgenthau Plan she "might inherit Germany's Ruhr business." Churchill recalled that he had "at first . . . violently opposed the idea,"

> but the President, with Mr. Morgenthau— from whom we had much to ask—were so insistent that in the end we agreed to consider it.

The suggestion here is that British acceptance of the plan was looked upon as a price to be paid for postwar loans from the

United States. In any event, both Roosevelt and Churchill soon had their eyes opened to the preposterous nature of a program that would have eliminated the most productive industrial workshop in Europe, leaving a void in the European economy and starving millions in western Germany. The plan was quietly shelved, but not before it had "leaked." To Joseph Goebbels, Minister of Information in Berlin, it had obvious propaganda value.[18]

The Foreign Ministers' Conference at Moscow

Roosevelt was to meet Stalin for the first time in November 1943. But a month before that, Secretary Hull, despite his seventy-two years and frail health, had flown to Moscow to confer with Molotov and Anthony Eden. Italy had surrendered to Anglo-American forces in September, and the German divisions that still held much of the peninsula were being steadily pushed back. The Russian armies, too, had taken the offensive. The tide of war had turned, and it was none to soon to consider postwar arrangements.

At the close of a twelve-day conference (October 19–30, 1943) the Foreign Ministers of the Big Three issued a communiqué and a number of declarations. They had agreed upon setting up in London a European Advisory Commission (EAC) to study and make recommendations upon questions that might arise as the war developed. An Advisory Council for Italy, to include a representative of the French Committee of National Liberation, and eventually representatives of Greece and Yugoslavia, was to make recommendations for coordinating Allied policy in Italy. A Declaration regarding Italy promised a government "made more democratic by the introduction of representatives of those sections of the Italian people who have always opposed Fascism." It also promised to the Italian people restoration of freedom of speech, the press, political belief, public meeting, and religious worship. A Declaration on Austria promised liberation from German domination and recorded the wish of the three governments "to see reestablished a free and independent Austria."

At the urging of Secretary Hull, China was invited to join in what thus became a Declaration of Four Nations on General Security. In this the four governments pledged that the united action of wartime would be "continued for the organization and maintenance of peace and security" and recognized "the necessity of establishing at the earliest practicable date a general international organization" for that purpose. Here was the first definite international commitment to the idea of a postwar substitute for the League of Nations. In Secretary Hull's mind, the fact of having secured a Russian pledge to cooperate with the Western powers in a postwar security organization was an important achievement. In reporting on the work of the conference to a joint session of Senate and House of Representatives, he prophesied:

As the provisions of the Four-Nation Declaration are carried into effect, there will no longer be need for spheres of influence, for alliances, for balance of power, or any other of the special arrangements through which, in the unhappy past, the nations strove to safeguard their security or to promote their interests.[19]

---

[18]H. L. Stimson and McGeorge Bundy, *On Active Service in Peace and War* (New York: Harper & Row, Publishers, 1948), pp. 568–83 (the memorandum is on pp. 576–77); Winston S. Churchill, *Triumph and Tragedy*, Vol. 6 of *The Second World War* (Boston: Houghton Mifflin Company, 1953), pp. 156–57; Chamberlin, *America's Second Crusade*, pp. 301–10; Hull, *Memoirs* 2: chap. 115; Henry Morgenthau, Jr., *Germany Is Our Problem* (New York: Harper & Row, Publishers, 1945).

[19]Hull, *Memoirs*, 2: 1314–15 (chaps. 92–94 for full account of conference); Winston S. Churchill, *Closing the Ring*, Vol. 5 of *The Second World War* (Boston: Houghton Mifflin Company, 1951), Book 1, chap. 16. Also see, Joseph M. Siracusa, *The American Diplomatic Revolution: A Documentary History of the Cold War*,

"While Six Million Died"

The Foreign Ministers at Moscow also issued a declaration on German atrocities over the signatures of Roosevelt, Churchill, and Stalin. This promised punishment for crimes committed against nationals of the countries occupied by German armed forces but said nothing about Nazi atrocities against their own Jewish nationals. Merciless persecution of German Jews had begun immediately upon Hitler's accession to power in 1933. It had been promptly extended into the countries annexed or occupied by the Third Reich.

While such racial persecution was deplored in the United States, the American people, with some millions unemployed, showed no disposition to make places for refugees from the Nazi terror, and the State Department, partly out of fear that spies might slip in as refugees, displayed a surprising indifference to the sufferings and death of millions of European Jews and to the plight of thousands of Protestant and Catholic Christians who were also victims of Nazi persecution. Contrary to precedent, the Department, with Roosevelt's approval, took the position that the United States had no right to interfere with the German government's policy toward its own nationals. Even after receipt in August 1942 of conclusive evidence that Hitler's "final solution" of the Jewish question was the extermination of all European Jews, the State Department declined to protest.[20]

Omission of all mention of the plight of the Jews from the Moscow Declaration aroused deep indignation among Jews in the United States and Britain. In the ensuing month, however, Secretary of the Treasury Henry Morgenthau, Jr., and members of his staff were able to convince Roosevelt that some effort should be made to save those European Jews who had not yet been sent to the gas chambers. On January 20, 1944, the President set up the War Refugee Board, which acted vigorously and with some success to save many thousands of Jews remaining in satellite countries. In a strong statement two months later, Roosevelt described Nazi treatment of the Jews as "one of the blackest crimes of all history" and gave assurance of American determination that none who participate in these acts of savagery shall go unpunished."[21]

The new policy bore some fruit. It should have been tried years earlier, although the threats of punishment owed their efficacy to the growing conviction that Hitler was doomed to defeat.

Cairo and Teheran

During the Moscow Conference, arrangements had been perfected for a meeting of Roosevelt, Churchill, and Stalin at Teheran, the capital of Iran or Persia. This was as far as the Russian dictator could be induced to journey from his own borders. Chiang Kai-shek, on the contrary, did not hesitate to fly to Cairo to confer with Roosevelt and Churchill as they stopped there en route to Teheran. From Cairo the three statesmen issued a declaration (released December 1, 1943) of importance for the postwar Far East.

. . . It is their purpose [said the declaration] that Japan shall be stripped of all the islands

---

1941–1947 (Port Washington, N.Y.: Kennikat Press, 1977), pp. 31–36, for Hull's report to Congress.

[20] Arthur D. Morse, *While Six Million Died: A Chronicle of American Apathy* (New York: Random House, Inc., 1968); David S. Wyman, *Paper Walls: America and the Refugee Crisis 1938–1941* (Amherst: University of Massachusetts Press, 1968).

[21] Morse, *While Six Million Died*, p. 337. President Roosevelt had voiced at least one earlier public denunciation of Nazi anti-Semitism. After the massacre of the "Night of Broken Glass" in November 1938, he recalled the U.S. ambassador from Berlin and remarked at a press conference: "I myself could scarcely believe that such things could occur in a twentieth century civilization." Ibid., p. 231.

in the Pacific which she has seized or occupied since the beginning of the first World War in 1914, and that all the territory Japan has stolen from the Chinese, such as Manchuria, Formosa and the Pescadores, shall be restored to the Republic of China. Japan will also be expelled from all other territories which she has taken by violence and greed. The aforesaid three great powers, mindful of the enslavement of the people of Korea, are determined that in due course Korea shall become free and independent.

At Teheran, where the Big Three leaders and their advisers conferred from November 28 to December 1, 1943, Roosevelt, as he reported to Congress, "'got along fine' with Marshal Stalin," and on the basis of this experience predicted "that we are going to get along well with him and the Russian people—very well indeed." The meeting was, in fact, quite harmonious. Important military decisions were reached; notably that the cross-Channel invasion, known as OVERLORD, should be launched in May or June 1944, with a supporting landing on the south coast of France and a simultaneous Russian offensive in the east. Stalin repeated the promise, made to Hull at Moscow, that as soon as Germany was defeated, Russia would enter the war against Japan. He mentioned no price for such intervention, but Churchill expressed sympathy with the Russian desire for an ice-free port, and Roosevelt suggested that access to Dairen in South Manchuria would meet that need. It was agreed that in Yugoslavia all aid should be given to Tito and his partisans—a decision that insured Communist, though not necessarily Russian, domination of that country.

On the political side, the most important questions debated were the boundaries of Poland and the future of Germany. The three leaders were in general agreement that Poland's eastern boundary should be the Curzon Line, a supposedly ethnographical demarcation proposed in 1919.

Poland would thus lose some White Russian and Ukrainian areas that she had held from 1921 to 1939. For these losses in the east she was to be compensated in the west by accessions of German territory up to the Oder River. Neither Churchill nor Roosevelt betrayed any moral scruple about these territorial changes, to be made, contrary to the promise of the Atlantic Charter, without "the freely expressed wishes of the peoples concerned," though Churchill did insist upon Polish boundaries that he could defend to the Polish government in exile in London.

Nor did either Roosevelt or Churchill reveal any uneasiness over the proposed elimination of Germany as a military factor and the consequent destruction of the balance of power in Europe. Both agreed with Stalin that the revival of German military might must be made impossible. Roosevelt proposed that Germany be partitioned into five independent states, excluding the Ruhr-Saar and Kiel areas, which should be internationally controlled. Churchill preferred to isolate Prussia on the one hand, and, on the other, to construct a Danubian Confederation along lines resembling those of the former Austro-Hungarian Empire. Stalin preferred Roosevelt's solution to Churchill's. No decision was reached, but the debate showed to what an extent the Nazi peril had blinded Roosevelt, and even Churchill, to the menace of a strong Communist Russia.

Churchill at Moscow

Roosevelt and Stalin did not meet again until the celebrated Yalta Conference in February 1945. In the interval, Churchill paid a visit to Moscow, in October 1944, (code-named "Tolstoy") with the principal object of seeking an understanding on the affairs of Poland and the Balkan States.

The latter problem proved the easier to solve temporarily and superficially. It existed because of the advance of the Russian armies into Rumania and Bulgaria and a threatened conflict between Russian and British interests, especially in Greece and Yugoslavia. A temporary arrangement of the previous June, giving to Russia predominance for three months in Rumania and to Britain the same in Greece, had been acceded to by President Roosevelt over the objections of the State Department. Now Churchill proposed and Stalin accepted (at least he made a blue check mark on Churchill's memorandum) an extension of this arrangement on a mathematical formula. According to Churchill's notation, as amended by Molotov, Russia should have 90 percent predominance in Rumania, and Great Britain (presumably in accord with the United States), 90 percent in Greece. Russian influence should predominate 80 to 20 percent in Bulgaria and Hungary, while in Yugoslavia the proportion was to be 50–50.[22] It seems clear that this exercise in arithmetic had no binding force, particularly since Roosevelt had cautioned Stalin that he would not be bound by any tête-à-tête agreement made in his absence; but it is useful in indicating the thinking of Stalin and Churchill at the time.

At Churchill's urging, Stanislaw Mikolajczyk, head of the Polish government in exile in London, came to Moscow during the conference. There he and several of his colleagues met with representatives of a Russian-sponsored Polish government set up at Lublin. The two groups failed to agree as to their respective shares in a new government for Poland. Mikolajczyk finally consented to urge his London colleagues to accept the Curzon Line, but the outcome was in doubt. Because of the exigencies of American poli-

tics, the unsatisfactory status of the Polish negotiations was kept quiet until after the presidential election of November 7.[23]

Europe at the Yalta Conference

Re-elected for a fourth term, Roosevelt proceeded with preparations for another meeting with Churchill and Stalin, this time at Yalta in the Russian Crimea, recently liberated from the German invader. Here the three statesmen, with their diplomatic and military staffs—seven hundred British and Americans were flown in a night from Malta to Yalta—met from February 4 to 11, 1945. Four principal subjects occupied the time of the conference: (1) details of the proposed United Nations Organization; (2) the treatment of defeated Germany; (3) restoration of self-government in the countries of eastern Europe, now occupied in whole or in part by Russian armies; (4) the terms of Russia's entry into the war against Japan. The first of these subjects is deferred to the next chapter; the others are considered here.

Treatment of defeated Germany. The future of Germany was left undecided. The governments of the United Kingdom, the United States, and the Soviet Union were declared to possess "supreme authority" to "take such steps, including the complete disarmament, demilitarization and dismemberment of Germany as they deem requisite for future peace and security." Study of the procedure of dismemberment was referred to a committee consisting of the British Foreign Secretary and the American and Russian ambassadors in London, who might at their discretion bring in a French member. In the meantime, Germany was to be divided into four zones of military occupation, a French zone to be formed out of previously agreed upon American and British zones.

[22]Churchill, *Triumph and Tragedy,* pp. 227, 232; also see, Sir Llewellyn Woodward's *British Foreign Policy in the Second World War* (London: Her Majesty's Stationery Office, 1971), pp. 146–53.

[23]Churchill, *Triumph and Tragedy,* pp. 235–43.

Germany was to pay reparations in kind, in the first instance to the nations that had borne the main burden of the war, suffered most heavily, and "organized victory over the enemy." Reparations were to be of three categories: (1) removal, over a two-year period, of capital goods located either within or without German territory, "chiefly for the purpose of destroying the war potential of Germany"; (2) "annual deliveries of goods from current production for a period to be fixed"; (3) "use of German labor." A reparations commission representing the three governments was to be set up in Moscow. The American and Soviet delegations agreed in recommending that the commission should take, "as a basis for discussion," a total reparations figure of twenty billion dollars, one-half to go to the Soviet Union. The British delegation was opposed to naming any figure, pending consideration by the commission.

The question of punishment of major war criminals was left for inquiry and later report by the three Foreign Secretaries.

Poland and liberated Europe.   The Conference agreed that a new Polish Provisional Government of National Unity should be established, constituted by including with the existing (Communist) Provisional Government at Lublin "democratic leaders from Poland itself and from Poles abroad." The new government should be "pledged to the holding of free and unfettered elections as soon as possible on the basis of universal suffrage and secret ballot." The "three heads of Government" considered that Poland's eastern boundary should be the Curzon Line, with some deviations in favor of Poland, and that Poland should receive "substantial accessions of territory in the north and west." These accessions were not defined.

For other portions of liberated Europe and for former Axis satellites (such as Hungary, Rumania, and Bulgaria) the three statesmen promised assistance in the establishment of internal peace, in relief of suffering, in the setting up of interim governments "broadly representative of all democratic elements," and in "the establishment through free elections of governments responsive to the will of the people."

The Far East at the Yalta Conference

Both the American and British governments had for some time considered Russian aid indispensable against Japan if the war in the Far East were to be brought to an early conclusion. Stalin had promised such aid to Hull in Moscow, to Roosevelt at Teheran, and to Churchill during his visit to Moscow in October 1944. Beyond specifying that he would need to stockpile over a million tons of lend-lease goods for the campaign in the Far East, Stalin had hinted in October 1944 that there were political questions that should be "clarified" before Russia entered the war. In an interview between Stalin and Ambassador Averell Harriman in December 1944, the questions became demands. These demands Harriman telegraphed to Roosevelt on December 15. The President knew of them, therefore, six weeks before setting out for Yalta and had ample time to consider them.[24] They were embodied almost word for word in the Yalta agreement.

By that agreement Stalin promised that the Soviet Union would enter the war against Japan "in two or three months" after the German surrender, upon the following conditions:

1. Preservation of the status quo in Outer Mongolia; that is, continuance of the Soviet-sponsored Mongolian People's Republic in an area long claimed by China.

2. Restoration of "the former rights of Russia violated by the treacherous attack of Japan in 1904"; namely: (a) return to the Soviet

[24]Feis, *The China Tangle,* pp. 232–33.

Union of southern Sakhalin; (b) internationalizing of the port of Dairen, with safeguards for the "preeminent interests of the Soviet Union," and restoration to Russia of the lease of Port Arthur for a naval base; (c) the Chinese Eastern and South Manchurian Railroads to be operated by a joint Soviet-Chinese company, with safeguards for "the preeminent interests of the Soviet Union" and retention of Chinese sovereignty in Manchuria.

3. Cession of the Kurile Islands to the Soviet Union.

President Roosevelt undertook to obtain the concurrence of Chiang Kai-shek in the provisions in regard to Outer Mongolia and the Manchuria ports and railroads, but all three heads of government agreed that the conditions should be "unquestionably, fulfilled" after the defeat of Japan. Stalin, for his part, expressed a readiness to conclude a treaty with Chiang's government for the purpose of aiding in "liberating China from the Japanese yoke."[25]

Criticism of the Yalta Agreements

No single act of President Roosevelt's career has been more harshly criticized than this group of agreements with Stalin at Yalta. One of his principal critics, William Henry Chamberlin, stated this point of view in the following:

These agreements grossly violated the Atlantic Charter by assigning Polish territory to the Soviet Union and German territory to Poland without plebiscites. They violated the most elementary rules of humanity and civilized warfare by sanctioning slave labor as 'reparations.' And the whole historic basis of American foreign policy in the Far East was upset by the virtual invitation to Stalin to take over Japan's former exclusive and dominant role in Manchuria.[26]

In weighing these criticisms, several basic facts must be borne in mind: (1) Russian armies had overrun all or nearly all of Poland, Rumania, Bulgaria, Hungary, and Yugoslavia. The Western Allies, in consequence, had little bargaining power with regard to eastern Europe. They could ask but not demand. (2) Both Roosevelt and Churchill, especially the former, still relied on the good will and trusted the promises of the Soviet Union, and they were sure that they required its cooperation for the peace no less than for the war. (3) No one, at that stage, was disposed to be very tender toward the Germans. "Unconditional surrender," as Churchill had remarked, excluded the enemy from any claim to the benefits of the Atlantic Charter. (4) The opinion prevailed in influential quarters that Japan was capable of prolonged resistance, that she had a powerful army in Manchuria, and that Russian participation might greatly shorten the war and reduce the cost of victory to the United States by perhaps a million casualties. Therefore Russia's price must be paid. No doubt, also, a tortured sense of justice made it seem right to restore to the Soviets what Japan had once taken from the Czar.

The student of history who wishes to understand the Yalta agreements must try to put himself into the mood and the state of knowledge of the men who made them. He will then perhaps regard both the men and the agreements with more indulgence than

---

[25]The Yalta agreements are printed in *Documents on American Foreign Relations*, 8: 919–24. The best appraisal of the conference is J. L. Snell, ed., *The Meaning of Yalta* (Baton Rouge: University of Louisiana Press, 1956). See also E. R. Stettinius, Jr., *Roosevelt and the Russians: The Yalta Conference* (Garden City, N.Y.: Doubleday & Company, Inc., 1949); Leahy, *I Was There*, chap. 18; Sherwood, *Roosevelt and Hopkins*, pp. 850–69; Feis, *The China Tangle*, chaps. 22, 23; Diane Shaver Clemens, *Yalta* (New York: Oxford University Press, 1970).

[26]W. H. Chamberlin, *America's Second Crusade* (Chicago: Henry Regnery Company, 1950), p. 220. Reprinted by permission of the publisher.

has been shown by some critics equipped with 20–20 hindsight. The Polish boundaries had been previously agreed upon at Teheran. For the Curzon Line (with deviations in favor of Poland) there were sound ethnographical arguments, and Mikolajczyk had reluctantly agreed to recommend it to his London colleagues. This cannot be called a decision in "accord with the freely expressed wishes of the people concerned," but it was the best that the Soviets were willing to concede. The compensation of the Poles with German territory, and likewise the inclusion of German labor as a form of reparations, cannot be justified; they can be understood only as manifestations of the hate-engendered thesis that Germans had forfeited all claim to humane treatment. The promises of free elections open to all democratic elements in Poland and liberated Europe sounded fair and generous. No one as yet recognized that the Russians would equate democracy with acceptance of Communism and would enforce this view ruthlessly in areas that they held vital to their security.

The least excusable of the agreements made at Yalta was that concerning the Far East. The pretense that it restored to Russia rights of which Japan had robbed her was hollow. Russia had been the most active aggressor in the Far East between 1895 and 1904, and her moral claim to Dairen, Port Arthur, and the Manchurian railroads was no better than Japan's. All had been exacted from China by the threat of force. To restore to Russia these rights and properties, with recognition of her "preeminent interest" in Manchuria, was a contradiction of American policy since John Hay's time. It was paying Russia for her assistance with Chinese coin. Yet on the assumption that Russian assistance might save the lives of a million American soldiers, would another President in Roosevelt's place have refused it?

The tragic irony of this part of the story is that Russian aid was not needed. The postwar U.S. Strategic Bombing Survey concluded that without Russian entry into the war, without invasion of the homeland, and without use of the atomic bomb, Japan would have surrendered before December 31 and probably before November 30, a month after the date set for the first Anglo-American invasion of the home islands. This estimate, of course, was not known to Roosevelt or his advisers at Yalta, but it is to be noted that both the Navy and the commander of the Strategic Air Force were skeptical about the need for invasion or Russian assistance. It was the Army that misjudged the situation and was chiefly responsible for Roosevelt's decision to pay Stalin's price.[27]

To say that the agreement on the Far East was both unnecessary and morally hard to justify is not to endorse all that has been written of its evil results. Critics have charged that it betrayed Chiang Kai-shek, made the Soviet Union a Pacific power, and paved the way for the triumph of Communism in China, Indochina, and northern Korea. This reasoning seems to betray a naive view of the power of paper agreements, particularly as they affect the Soviet Union. It is difficult to believe that, had there been no agreement, the Soviet Union would have abstained from attacking Japan or from taking what it wished in the Manchurian area. The only way to prevent it would have been to follow a course more Machiavellian than President Roosevelt was willing to follow or the American public to endorse—such as making an easy peace with Japan that would have left her, though shorn of her conquests, still a formidable military power. Shrewd American statesmanship would have aimed at preserving a balance of power in both Asia and Europe, but both Roosevelt and Hull had repudiated the balance of power concept as one of the techniques of an evil and war-ridden past.

[27] Herbert Feis, *The Atomic Bomb and the End of World War II* (Princeton: Princeton University Press, 1966), pp. 190–93.

The German Collapse

Events moved swiftly after the Yalta Conference. Russia was soon displaying a callous disregard of her Yalta pledges, in both Poland and Rumania. She did, however, give warning of her intention to join in the war against Japan by serving notice, on April 5, 1945, that she would not renew the neutrality treaty of 1941 upon its expiration. Russia would thus be freed to attack Japan but only—if she kept faith—after April 13, 1946. On April 12, President Roosevelt died of a cerebral hemorrhage at Warm Springs, Georgia. Meanwhile, Allied armies were pouring into Germany from east and west, and the German front in Italy was collapsing. On May 1 it was reported that Russian forces had entered Berlin and that Hitler had died in the Reichchancellery. Admiral Karl Doenitz headed a short-lived provisional government. On May 7, representatives of the German Army signed surrender terms at Reims, and on the following day President Truman and Prime Minister Churchill proclaimed V-E (Victory in Europe) Day. On May 9 the formalities of surrender were completed in Berlin, and Stalin announced the end of the war to the Russian people. Early in June an Allied Control Committee for Germany began functioning in Berlin. It consisted of General Eisenhower and Marshals Montgomery and Zhukov.

Japan Surrenders

The war in Europe was ended; that in the Pacific went on, but Japanese surrender was nearer than most responsible Allied statesmen supposed. From the time of the first Japanese naval reverses in the Coral Sea and at Midway, in May and June 1942, there had been a peace party in Japan, headed by certain ex-Premiers, and this group had gained in strength with every Japanese defeat. It was not, however, until the appointment of a cabinet headed by the octogenarian Admiral Suzuki, in April 1945, that the peace group felt strong enough to oppose the Army, which favored resistance to the bitter end. But even the peace-minded men of the Suzuki cabinet found an obstacle in the "unconditional surrender" formula. Loyalty to the Emperor and the dynasty prescribed that as a minimum the Emperor system must be preserved.[28] Beginning in June, Japan made a series of attempts to secure Russian mediation in getting a peace with at least this face-saving condition. The Soviet government, for understandable reasons, turned aside these proposals.

In Washington, meanwhile, the War Department was planning an invasion of Japan's home islands, to begin November 1. At the same time, those who believed that there was a responsible peace party in Japan were seeking ways to make surrender easy and avoid the frightful costs of invasion. A beginning was made by President Truman on V-E Day, in his proclamation announcing the German surrender. Calling upon the "Japanese military and naval forces"—not the Japanese government—to "lay down their arms in *unconditional surrender,*" he added the assurance: "Unconditional surrender does not mean the extermination or enslavement of the Japanese people." On the same day, Captain Ellis M. Zacharias, the Navy's leading expert on Japan, began a series of

[28]The best account of the events leading to the Japanese surrender is R. J. C. Butow, *Japan's Decision to Surrender* (Stanford: Stanford University Press, 1954). See also F. C. Jones, *Japan's New Order in East Asia: Its Rise and Fall, 1937–1945* (New York: Oxford University Press, 1954), pp. 420–49; Toshikazu Kase, *Journey to the Missouri* (New Haven: Yale University Press, 1950), chaps. 6–11; J. C. Grew, *Turbulent Era: A Diplomatic Record of Forty Years 1904–1945*, 2 vols. (Boston: Houghton Mifflin Company, 1952), 2: chap. 36; Stimson and Bundy, *On Active Service in Peace and War,* chap. 23; R. N. Current, *Secretary Stimson: A Study in Statecraft* (New Brunswick: Rutgers University Press, 1954), pp. 220–37.

Japanese-language broadcasts designed to show the Japanese that they could surrender without loss of honor, sovereignty, or "national structure."[29] Former Ambassador Joseph C. Grew, now Under Secretary of State, wished to tell the Japanese in plain language that the United States would not object to their retaining a constitutional monarchy, and he was supported by Secretary of War Stimson. A Proclamation to the People of Japan, containing such an assurance, was prepared under their joint direction; but before it was issued from Potsdam, July 26, 1945, over the signatures of Truman, Attlee (who had succeeded Churchill), and Chiang Kai-shek, that particular assurance was deleted.

This document, often referred to as the Potsdam Declaration, called, as had Truman earlier, for the unconditional surrender of the Japanese armed forces, for the complete elimination of militarism and militarists, the setting up of "a new order of peace, security and justice," the removal of obstacles to democratic tendencies, the punishment of war criminals, and the carrying out of the terms of the Cairo Declaration. The Japanese, it promised, would not be "enslaved as a race or destroyed as a nation." Allied forces would occupy designated points in Japanese territory until the objectives were accomplished and until there should have been "established in accordance with the freely expressed will of the Japanese people a peacefully inclined and responsible government."[30]

This declaration held out enough hope to encourage the peace party in Japan, but since the government had not yet despaired of securing Russian mediation, the Foreign Minister advised that no response be made until a reply was received from Moscow. Premier Suzuki gave the Cabinet the impression that he accepted this advice, but under pressure from the military he told the press that Japan would "ignore" the declaration.[31] This unfortunate note of defiance led to the decision in Washington to drop atomic bombs on Hiroshima and Nagasaki (August 6 and 9).[32] It also allowed time for Russia to enter the war, as she did on August 8, sending armies into Manchuria and Korea. From Tokyo on August 10 there came by way of Switzerland an acceptance of the Potsdam terms, but with the understanding that the declaration "does not comprise any demand which prejudices the prerogatives of His Majesty as a Sovereign Ruler." To the request for an "explicit indication" that this understanding was warranted, James Byrnes, now Secretary of State, replied that during the occupation the authority of the Emperor would be subject to the Supreme Commander of the Allied Powers, and that the ultimate form of Japan's government should be determined "by the freely expressed will of the Japanese people."

On the question of whether to surrender on the basis of the Potsdam Declaration thus interpreted, the Supreme War Direction Council divided three to three—the Premier, Foreign Minister, and Navy Minister for, the Army Minister and the two Chiefs of Staff against. In the face of this deadlock, the Premier appealed to the Emperor to make the decision (as he had already done in a similar situation in the preliminaries). The Emperor chose peace. Japan's surrender was proclaimed by President Truman on August 14. The formal signing of surrender terms took place on the battleship *Missouri*, in Tokyo Bay, September 2, 1945.

[29] E. M. Zacharias, *Secret Missions: The Story of an Intelligence Officer* (New York: G. P. Putnam's Sons, 1946), chap. 31.

[30] *Documents on American Foreign Relations*, 8: 105–6.

[31] Butow, *Japan's Decision to Surrender*, pp. 143–49; Feis, *The Atomic Bomb and the End of World War II*, pp. 107–10.

[32] A recent, critical assessment of American policy in this regard is Martin J. Sherwin, *A World Destroyed: The Atomic Bomb and the Grand Alliance* (New York: Alfred A. Knopf, 1975). For an equally critical view of Sherwin's work, consult Joseph M. Siracusa, "Atomic Diplomacy Revisited," essay review of Martin J. Sherwin's *A World Destroyed: The Atomic Bomb and the Grand Alliance*, in *Review of Politics*, 38 (1976), pp. 627–31.

ADDITIONAL READINGS

BURNS, JAMES MACGREGOR, *Roosevelt: The Soldier of Freedom.* New York: Harcourt Brace Jovanovich, Inc., 1970.

GADDIS, JOHN LEWIS, *The United States and the Origins of the Cold War, 1941–1947.* New York: Columbia University Press, 1972.

HARRIMAN, W. AVERELL, "Our Wartime Relations with the Soviet Union," *Department of State Bulletin,* 25 (September 3, 1951), 371–79.

———— and ELIE ABEL, *Special Envoy to Churchill and Stalin, 1941–1946.* New York: Random House, 1975.

HERRING, GEORGE C., JR., *Aid to Russia, 1941–1946: Strategy, Diplomacy, and the Origins of the Cold War.* New York: Columbia University Press, 1973.

HOPKINS, GEORGE E., "Bombing and the American Conscience during World War II," *Historian,* 38 (1966), 451–73.

LOEWENHEIM, FRANCIS L., HAROLD D. LANGBY, and MANFRED JONES, eds., *Roosevelt and Churchill: Their Secret Wartime Correspondence.* New York: Saturday Review Press/E. P. Dutton & Co., 1975.

LOUIS, WILLIAM ROGER, *Imperialism at Bay: The United States and the Decolonization of the British Empire, 1941–1945.* New York: Oxford University Press, 1978.

MASTNY, V., "Stalin and the Prospect of a Separate Peace in World War II," *American Historical Review,* 77 (1972), 1365–88.

O'CONNOR, RAYMOND G., *Diplomacy for Victory: FDR and Unconditional Surrender.* New York: W. W. Norton, 1971.

SMITH, GADDIS, *American Diplomacy during the Second World War, 1941–1945.* New York: John Wiley & Sons, Inc., 1965.

20. The United Nations, the United States, and the Onset of the Cold War

The Japanese attack at Pearl Harbor, and the German and Italian declarations of war that followed, silenced, if they did not kill, isolationalism in the United States. The elaborate neutrality legislation of the 1930's had failed to insulate the United States from war in Europe and Asia. To many Americans it appeared that in the future the United States could hope to avoid war only by joining in a system of collective security capable of preventing war. To such people American membership in an improved and strengthened League of Nations seemed the only hope of peace.

Almost from the outbreak of war in Europe, Secretary Hull and his State Department subordinates began planning for a new world organization, of which the United States should be a leading member. In January 1940 Hull announced the appointment of an Advisory Committee on Problems of Foreign Relations, with subcommittees to study political, economic, and security questions. In addition to State Department personnel, members of the House and Senate, both Democrats and Republicans, were brought in, as were experts from private life. Notable among these were Isaiah Bowman, well known geographer and president of Johns Hopkins University, and Hamilton Fish Armstrong, editor of the influential quarterly, *Foreign Affairs*. As time went on, a number of nongovernmental organizations were brought into consultation with the State Department, among them the Federal Council of Churches of Christ in America and the Council on Foreign Relations. The latter, aided by a grant from the Rockefeller Foundation, conducted several series of studies by experts in close liaison with the Department, to which it sent 682 memoranda in the period 1939–1945.[1]

Hull, a former follower of Woodrow Wilson and advocate of the League of Nations, was acutely aware of Wilson's mistakes and determined to avoid them. In particular, he was careful to take Republicans as well as Democrats into his confidence. No one would be able to charge this time that the administration's plans for the postwar world were tinged with partisanship.

Franklin Roosevelt, though he may have shared the belief of his Secretary of State that the United States must lead in the preparation for a new League of Nations, at first feared the political reaction to public announcement of such a view: At the Atlantic Conference in August 1941, he rejected a declaration, proposed by Church-

---

[1] Hull, *Memoirs*, 2: 1625–1713; Pratt, *Cordell Hull*, 2: chap. 22; U. S. Department of State, *Postwar Foreign Policy Preparation, 1939–1945* (Washington: Government Printing Office, 1950), *passim; The War and Peace Studies of the Council on Foreign Relations* (New York: Council on Foreign Relations, 1946).

ill, for a peace that would, "by effective international organization . . . afford to all States and peoples the means of dwelling in security." Such an expression, he feared, would rouse the suspicion of the isolationists, in Congress and out. But he let himself be persuaded by Churchill and Harry Hopkins into accepting a statement of the same idea in different words. Paragraph 8 of the Atlantic Charter proposed the disarmament of aggressor nations, "pending the establishment of a wider and permanent system of general security."[2]

By the fall of 1943, the political hazards of advocating American participation in a collective security organization had been eliminated. By large majorities, the Senate and the House of Representatives, respectively, had passed the Connally and Fulbright Resolutions, declaring that the United States, acting "through its constitutional processes," should participate in international machinery to prevent aggression and preserve the peace of the world. A Republican Post-War Advisory Council, meeting at Mackinac Island in September, adopted a resolution of similar purport.

In the spring of 1944, speeches by the Secretary of State, by Assistant Secretary Breckinridge Long, and by the President himself informed the public that the State Department was making plans for a postwar international organization to keep the peace. They even sketched out its general lines: an assembly representing all members of the organization, a smaller body with power to act against aggression, and an international court of justice. The structural similarity to the League of Nations is obvious. The planners hoped to avoid the weaknesses of the League, first, by including all the great powers in the membership; secondly, by vesting in the enforcement agency power of vigorous action.

The Dumbarton Oaks Conference

Hull relates that in State Department discussions he emphasized the belief that

> there was no hope of turning victory into enduring peace unless the United States, the British Commonwealth, the Soviet Union, and China agreed to act together.[3]

The Four Nations' Declaration, issued at Moscow, October 30, 1943, was a good omen for such agreement. In order to make sure of a plan that would be acceptable to the governments of these four powers, the United States invited the other three to send delegations to Washington in August 1944 to cooperate in producing a tentative charter for a permanent United Nations Organization. The conference was held at Dumbarton Oaks (a Washington estate owned by Harvard University), from August 21 to October 7. The Soviet Union, still at peace with Japan, refused for that reason to confer with belligerent China. Hence the conference had two phases: the United States, Great Britain, and Russia, August 21 to September 28; the United States, Great Britain, and China, September 29 to October 7. For the most part, the Chinese delegation accepted the work already done by the other three.

The Dumbarton Oaks Proposals, published October 9, 1944, contained most of the provisions that took lasting form in the United Nations Charter. They proposed the creation of a permanent organization to be known as the United Nations, open to "all peace-loving states" and based on the "sovereign equality" of such states. Its purposes should be: (1) to maintain peace and security through collective measures; (2) to develop friendly relations between states; (3) to effect cooperation in the solution of international economic, social, and humanitarian problems; (4) to afford a

[2]R. E. Sherwood, *Roosevelt and Hopkins: An Intimate History* (New York: Harper & Row, Publishers, 1948), pp. 359–60.

[3]Hull, *Memoirs,* 2:1651.

center for harmonizing the action of nations for their common ends. The principal organs would be a General Assembly, a Security Council of eleven members (four permanent, the others chosen for two-year terms), a Secretariat, an Economic and Social Council (subsidiary to the General Assembly), and an International Court of Justice. It was the hope of the architects of the plan that the General Assembly and the Economic and Social Council would remove or alleviate causes of friction, the International Court would settle peaceably any disputes susceptible of judicial determination, and the Security Council would assist in the peaceful settlement of disputes and suppress any acts of aggression or breaches of the peace that might unfortunately occur.

On several questions the delegations at Dumbarton Oaks had failed to reach agreement. When and where should a general meeting be held to write the charter with the proposals as a starting-point? What nations should be invited to that meeting and thus become original members of the United Nations? What should be done with the former Japanese mandated islands, most of them certain to be in United States possession at the end of the war? Should the constituent republics of the U.S.S.R., or any of them, have separate membership in the United Nations? Most crucial of all, should each of the great powers, permanent members of the Security Council, have the right to veto its decisions? These questions were taken up by Roosevelt, Churchill, and Stalin, when they met at Yalta in February 1945.

The Yalta Decisions

The three heads of government reached agreement on these pending problems without great difficulty. The date for the conference on world organization was set at April 25, 1945, and the place at San Fran-

cisco. The governments invited to participate would be those already cooperating as the United Nations and such others as might declare war "on the common enemy" by March 1, 1945. Stalin had once intimated that all sixteen republics of the U.S.S.R. should be separately represented—bringing from Roosevelt the rejoinder that in that case he would ask separate membership for all forty-eight states of the U.S.A. The Russian dictator now moderated his demands, asking separate membership in the San Francisco Conference and in the proposed world organization only for the Ukraine and White Russia. Roosevelt and Chruchill agreed to support this request at the Conference. Stalin, in return, offered to support the United States if it should ask for three votes in the General Assembly to balance Russia's three. In theory, at least, these proposed multiple votes were intended to offset the six votes of the British Commonwealth of Nations. (It may be noted here that when the time came, the United States did not ask for or receive extra votes.)

It was tentatively agreed to replace the Mandate System of the League of Nations with a system of territorial trusteeships—much the same thing under a different name. It was to apply to (a) existing mandates of the League of Nations, (b) territories taken from the enemy in the current war, (c) any other territory that a sovereign power might voluntarily place under trusteeship.

On the question of voting in the Security Council—in other words, the right of veto—the State Department had prepared a formula. Some members of the Department, notably former Under Secretary Sumner Welles, had opposed granting any power the right, in Welles's words, "to veto action against itself if it undertook to pursue policies of aggression."[4] To Secretary Hull, however, it was clear that neither the

[4]Sumner Welles, *Where Are We Heading?* (New York: Harper & Row, Publishers, 1946), pp. 24–25.

Soviet Union nor the Senate of the United States would accept a charter that failed to vest the right of veto in the permanent members. The great-power veto was a practical necessity. The hope was that it would not be abused.

The formula devised by the State Department, approved at Yalta, and eventually adopted at San Francisco, permitted decision in procedural matters by the votes of any seven of the eleven members of the Security Council. In all substantive matters, however, the seven affirmative votes must include the votes of all five[5] permanent members, with the unimportant qualification that a member that was a party to a dispute should not vote if the question were one merely of investigation or of recommending peaceful methods of settlement. Thus a permanent member could veto the use of sanctions against itself or even a motion finding it guilty of an act of aggression. If a dispute concerned not itself but one of its satellites, it could even veto a proposal for an investigation.

The price of securing the adherence of the Soviet Union, and of ensuring a favorable vote by the United States Senate, was thus a veto provision that would paralyze the Security Council in any controversy between two or more of the Big Five powers. It was frankly recognized at the time, and became tragically apparent later, that only through friendly cooperation of the Big Five could the United Nations operate successfully as a security organization.

President Roosevelt, however, returned from Yalta in a mood of confidence. Reporting to Congress on March 1, 1945, he said:

> The Crimean Conference was a successful effort by the three leading nations to find a common ground for peace. It spells the end of the system of unilateral action and exclusive alliances and spheres of influence and

balances of power and all the other expedients which have been tried for centuries—and have failed.

> We propose to substitute for all these a universal organization in which all peace-loving nations will finally have a chance to join.[6]

The San Francisco Conference

The members of the American delegation to the San Francisco Conference (officially the United Nations Conference on International Organization, or UNCIO) were named by President Roosevelt before his death. In choosing the delegates, as in other aspects of preparation for the U.N., Roosevelt profited from Woodrow Wilson's errors. Headed by the Secretary of State, Edward R. Stettinius, Jr., the delegation was bipartisan and contained distinguished members of both Senate and House: the chairmen and ranking minority members of the Senate Committee on Foreign Relations and the House Committee on Foreign Affairs. No one could make the charge that Roosevelt had slighted either the Senate or the Republican party, as Wilson had been accused of doing. Of special importance was the selection of Senator Vandenberg. A trusted Republican leader and long an outspoken critic of Roosevelt, he did effective work at San Francisco and conjured away Republican opposition when the Charter came before the Senate.

The nations originally invited to send delegations to San Francisco were forty-six—the forty-seven that had signed the United Nations Declaration by March 1, 1945, minus Poland, whose government had not yet been reconstituted according to the Yalta formula. In fulfillment of Roosevelt's promise at Yalta, the United States delegation helped to secure from the Conference the admission of delegates

---

[5]It was agreed at Yalta to include France as one of the permanent members of the Council.

[6]*Documents on American Foreign Relations,* 7: 28.

from the Ukraine and White Russia. The Latin American republics consented reluctantly to this action and in return asked for and obtained the admission of Argentina, which had been a laggard in breaking with the Axis. Denmark, now liberated from Axis occupation, was also admitted, raising to fifty the number of nations participating. These became "charter members" of the United Nations. It was agreed that Poland, though not admitted to the Conference, should also be considered an original member. In future, membership in the organization was to be open to "all other peace-loving states" that should accept the obligations contained in the Charter and should be judged able and willing to carry these out.

The United Nations Charter

The Conference labored for two months, from April 25 to June 26. The charter, signed by the delegates on the latter date, followed closely the Dumbarton Oaks Proposals in general structure. To the four "principal organs" orginally proposed—General Assembly, Security Council, Secretariat, and International Court of Justice—the Conference added two: the Economic and Social Council (raised from subsidiary level) and a Trusteeship Council.

It will be useful here to comment briefly upon some of the ways in which the Charter of the United Nations altered, added to, or elaborated upon the plan sketched out at Dumbarton Oaks.

Idealistic phraseology. In the Preamble, the statement of Purposes and Principles, and elsewhere, the charter is profuse in such expressions as "fundamental human rights," "the equal rights of men and women," "social progress and better standards of life," and the like. Senator Vandenberg considered it an achievement to have obtained the insertion of the word "justice" as

expressing one of the objectives of the organization.

A more important role for the General Assembly. The original proposals had lodged almost all power in the Security Council, which would be dominated by the Big Five and was expected to function partly through the use of force, economic or military. Senator Vandenberg, believing that in the long run moral force—mobilized world opinion—might count more than material force, led a movement to make the General Assembly "a town meeting of the world" by giving it practically unrestricted freedom to debate and to make recommendations upon any matter of international concern. This was finally accomplished over strenuous opposition from the Russian delegation.

Restriction of the veto in the Security Council. The right of the permanent members to veto *action* by the Security Council had been generally accepted as inescapable, whether desirable or not. At San Francisco, however, it became apparent that the Russians conceived of the veto power as extending also to discussion. No subject, they claimed, could be brought before the Security Council for consideration without the consent of all five permanent members. To the Americans, and apparently to all other delegations not under Soviet influence, this seemed an intolerable infringement of free speech. This issue very nearly broke up the Conference. An appeal to Stalin, through Harry Hopkins and Ambassador Averell Harriman in Moscow, finally brought about a Russian retreat.

Action through regional organizations. A conference of the American States in Mexico City in February and March 1945, had adopted the Act of Chapultepec, which declared an act of aggression against one American state to be aggression against all and obligated the several states to consult, in such a case, "upon the measures it may be desirable to take." A provision (Article 53), however, had been incorporated in the

United Nations Charter forbidding enforcement action by regional agencies without the authorization of the Security Council. It was plain to the Latin American delegations, and to Nelson Rockefeller, United States Assistant Secretary of State for Latin American Affairs, that a Council veto, by Russia, for example, could, under this article, prevent the American republics from taking any action under the Act of Chapultepec; could, in fact, make impossible action to uphold the Monroe Doctrine. To meet this situation the American delegation made a proposal that eventually took the form of Article 51 of the Charter. This reserved to member nations "the inherent right of individual or collective self-defense" in case of attack, until the Security Council should have taken "measures necessary to maintain international peace and security." It would be difficult to exaggerate the importance of this article, which like the guarantees of free discussion in the Assembly and Council, was accepted only after prolonged Russian opposition. Its recognition of the right of "collective self-defense" served to reconcile with the charter not only the inter-American security arrangements but the later North Atlantic Treaty Organization and mutual defense treaties between the United States and Australia, New Zealand, the Philippines, Japan, Nationalist China, and the Republic of Korea, and the later Southeast Asia pact.

The International Court of Justice. This was a new tribunal, not a revised form of the World Court established in 1922. The reason for making it so was the practical one that revision of the statute of the old World Court would have required the consent of all its members, several of which were in the enemy camp. It was simpler to let it die (as the League of Nations died) and set up a new body.[7] The new Court was in most respects similar to the old one. The chief difference was that it was an organic part of the United Nations, not separate, as the World Court had been from the League. The Statute of the Court was an annex of the U.N. Charter, and all members of the U.N. were *ipso facto* members of the "I.C.J."

The Economic and Social Council. This wholly new body was given considerable powers of initiative in sponsoring studies, making recommendations, and preparing draft conventions in relation to international economic, social, cultural, educational, and medical matters. It might "make recommendations for the purpose of promoting respect for, and observance of, human rights and fundamental freedoms for all." In addition, it was made the coordinating body for various "specialized agencies," some old, some new, such as the International Labor Organization, the International Bank and Monetary Fund, the World Health Organization, the Food and Agricultural Organization, the United Nations Educational, Scientific and Cultural Organization (UNESCO), and others.

Trusteeship arrangements. Aims and principles for the administration of non-self-governing territories were set forth in some detail, and a Trusteeship System was made the successor to the Mandate System of the League, with a Trusteeship Council as the supervising body. In the United States, the Army and Navy had objected strongly to placing under trusteeship the former mandated islands taken from Japan at great cost. The armed services would have preferred outright annexation. But the United States had forsworn territorial aggrandizement as an object of the war and had sponsored the trusteeship system. It could not consistently annex the islands. The American delegation at San Francisco worked out a compromise, which was embodied in Articles 82 and 83 of the charter. These specified that any area in a trust territory might be declared a "strategic area"

[7]F. P. Walters, *A History of the League of Nations,* 2 vols. (New York: Oxford University Press, 1922), 2: chap. 67.

and that all United Nations functions relating to such an area should be exercised under direction of the Security Council. The United States, having a veto in that body, could block any attempt that it might make to interfere with American administration of any "strategic area" under its charge. Eventually the former Japanese mandated islands—the Marshalls, Carolines, and Marianas—were assigned to the United States as a trust territory and were designated a "strategic area."[8]

The United States Accepts the U.N.

The action of the Senate and the Congress on the United Nations Charter contrasts strikingly with the Senate's mutilation and final rejection of the Covenant of the League. The Second World War had changed the senatorial attitude, but, as has been remarked before, Roosevelt, Hull, and their successors had learned much from Wilson's mistakes.

The Senate gave its approval of the charter on July 28, 1945, by a vote of 89 to 2, the two nays being cast by Senators Langer of North Dakota and Shipstead of Minnesota. Congress later provided that after contingents of American armed forces had been designated for use at the call of the Security Council, the President might use them at the Council's call without awaiting special permission by Congress. The Senate, which had rejected membership in the original World Court, now, by a vote of 60 to 2, accepted compulsory jurisdiction of the International Court of Justice in certain types of cases by approving the "optional clause" in the Statute of the Court. One may well

[8] J. W. Pratt, *America's Colonial Experiment* (Englewood Cliffs, N.J.: Prentice-Hall, Inc., 1950), pp. 362–67. For nonstrategic territories the Trusteeship Council was responsible to the General Assembly, where there was no veto.

wonder how the history of the world might have been changed if the United States had entered the League of Nations in a spirit of international cooperation such as that which it initially showed toward the United Nations.

Beginnings of a Rift

The fundamental purpose of the United Nations was, of course, the prevention of acts of aggression, whether these were accomplished by force or the threat of force. Its chief function was a policing function. For this purpose the Security Council was empowered, if efforts at peaceful settlement of a controversy failed, to call upon members of the U.N. to sever diplomatic relations with an offender and to apply economic sanctions. If such measures proved inadequate, the Security Council was to have at its disposal armed force contingents made available to it in advance by the members, and might use these as it saw fit against the offender. Immediate direction of such forces would be in the hands of a Military Staff Committee, made up of the chiefs of staff of the permanent members of the Council, or representatives of those chiefs of staff. But all action by the Security Council, it must be remembered, must have the concurrence of the five permanent members; it was subject to veto by any one of them.

In reality, this enforcement machinery, so impressive on paper, was paralyzed from the beginning by the rift between the Soviet Union and the West. No contingents of armed forces were made available to the Security Council, because the Military Staff Committee could not agree on their composition. The British and Americans wished specialized forces: they would furnish the principal naval and air contingents and expect the U.S.S.R., with its huge army, to provide most of the land forces. The

Russians insisted upon equal and similar contributions from all five of the major powers. This disagreement was never composed.

A similar fate befell attempts at disarmament, notably the effort at international control of atomic energy and prevention of its use for warlike purposes. After August 1945, the specter of atomic war hung over the world. The United States, having for the time being an advantage in atomic knowhow and the possession of atomic weapons, took the lead, in company with Great Britain and Canada, in proposing international control. In January 1946, the U.N. Assembly established a United Nations Atomic Energy Commission. To this Commission, on June 14, 1946, the American member, Bernard Baruch, submitted a proposal thereafter generally referred to as the Baruch Plan. It called for the creation of an International Atomic Development Authority, to have complete control over the primary production of fissionable materials and over all dangerous forms of atomic energy development, as well as licensing and inspection authority over nondangerous forms. It should have unrestricted rights of inspection, aerial and otherwise. As soon as the proposed system of control and inspection was set up and functioning, the United States would dispose of its stockpile of atomic weapons, and the production of such weapons would thereafter be strictly prohibited. Any violation of this or other prohibitions would be subject to prompt and severe punishment; and here the Baruch Plan emphasized the point that no veto must stand in the way of punishment for this one type of offense.

The Baruch Plan was rejected by the Soviet Union, which would neither surrender national control of atomic activities, submit to effective inspection, nor waive the veto. It insisted, on the other hand, that existing atomic bombs be at once destroyed and the manufacture and use of others be strictly prohibited. The impasse, which de-

veloped in 1946, had not been resolved in September 1949, when it was revealed that the Soviet Union had perfected the technique of constructing atomic weapons, nor in August 1953, when both the United States and the U.S.S.R. had succeeded in producing the still more potent and frightful hydrogen bomb.

Europe and the Cold War

The rift in the United Nations between the Soviet Union, backed by its satellites, and the United States, generally supported by the other democracies, reflected a mounting antagonism between the two groups. The origin of this antagonism and of the resulting contest, dubbed the "cold war," has itself been a subject of controversy. One interpretation, until recently generally accepted in the United States, finds the origin of the strife in the supposed determination of the Soviet leaders to make the whole world Communist, by force if necessary. They had, according to this theory, used the alliance with the West for the destruction of Nazism. That accomplished, the alliance had lost its value to them, and they quickly abandoned it to pursue their goal of world revolution. In violation of the promises subscribed to at Yalta, they set up Communist regimes in "liberated Europe" and only awaited a favorable occasion to impose such regimes on the nations of the Western Europe, allies of the United States. The cold war began when the United States resisted such Communist expansion through the "containment" policy described below.

Alternative Theories

One school of historians, commonly referred to as New Left revisionism, offers a directly opposite interpretation, placing the chief blame for the cold war upon the United States. Viewing economic motives as determinative, historians of this group interpret American foreign policy since 1945, like that of the preceding half-century, as "imperialistic" and counterrevolutionary. The cold war, they say, began when President Harry Truman, apprised of the prospect of American possession of a potent secret weapon, the atomic bomb, resolved to require Stalin to relax his grasp of the nations of Eastern Europe and permit them to enjoy an "open door" (to American capitalism). In this plan he had the hearty support of James F. Byrnes, who became his Secretary of State in July 1945. In this general framework, these scholars cite specific actions by the United States which, at best, were less than gracious toward a wartime ally: the abrupt termination of lend-lease to Russia after the German surrender; denial of a reconstruction loan to Russia on terms acceptable to the Kremlin, while making a postwar loan of 3¾ billion dollars to Britain; the withholding from Russia of the secret of the atomic bomb, and so forth.[9] Thus, in their view, Stalin was driven into an antagonistic position by the aggressive policies of "American imperialism."

The New Left's explanation of the cold war has on balance, had a salutary effect in correcting some of the excessively nationalistic and moralistic views popular in the United States, but like other monocausational interpretations of history, it goes much too far. With the passage of time, it will probably contribute to a more balanced historical perspective of the era.

A third interpretation takes account of American materialistic motives and ungracious actions toward the Soviet Union as contributing factors in producing the cold

war but finds the main cause elsewhere. It acknowledges that American fears of Soviet expansionism were genuine but believes that they were largely ill-founded. This theory, accepted today by many students of Soviet policy, holds that the Soviet leaders were less interested in spreading Communism than in safeguarding Russia against further attacks from the West, such as those delivered by Germany in 1914 and 1941, to say nothing of Napoleon in 1812. Thus, in discussing the fate of Poland at Yalta, when Churchill remarked that for Britain the question of Poland was one of honor, Stalin replied that for Russia the question was "one of life and death. . . . Throughout history," he added, "Poland has been the corridor for attack on Russia." The Soviet leaders, in other words, put national security ahead of world revolution and sought security, much as the Czars had done, by establishing firm control over the small states on their western frontier.

In accord with this theory was Stalin's agreement with Churchill in October 1944 conceding British or British-American predominant influence in Greece in return for predominant Soviet influence in Rumania, Bulgaria, and Hungary, with a fifty-fifty split in Yugoslavia. Why Stalin seemingly abandoned this position at Yalta, accepting Roosevelt's proposal for an assurance of democracy and self-determination in Poland and "liberated Europe," is not clear. At any rate, he secured a loophole in unofficial assurances at Yalta that those neighbor states should have "friendly" governments, which the Russians interpreted to mean Communist governments.

Put in different words, the Soviets were insisting on a sphere of influence in Eastern Europe while conceding a similar sphere to the Western Allies in Greece, Italy, and Western Europe in general and also, a little later, reluctantly, in occupied Japan. Unfortunately for the future of East-West harmony, Stalin made promises at Yalta which, if taken literally, could not be recon-

[9]For a discussion of the origins, impact and significance of the New Left, see Joseph M. Siracusa, *New Left Diplomatic Histories and Historians: The American Revisionists* (Port Washington, N.Y.: Kennikat Press Corp., 1973), particularly, pp. 76–103.

ciled with his sphere-of-influence agreement with Churchill. Churchill, in fact, was the first Allied statesman to object to the Soviets' riveting their control on Rumania and Bulgaria. As for the United States, it could not cheerfully accept Soviet domination of those states, which violated the American dogma of self-determination and the American economic prinicple of the "open door." Its adherence to principle was no doubt reinforced by the presence in the electorate of several million persons of Polish and other East European ancestry.

Eventually the United States did recognize the Russian-imposed Communist governments in Eastern Europe, thus, in effect, accepting Russia's sphere of influence in that area, but it did so with such ill grace and with such persistent demands for fulfillment of the Yalta promises, that the Kremlin suspected its former ally of planning to "liberate" Eastern Europe once more, this time from its Soviet "liberators." Meanwhile, the Western powers were equally suspicious of Stalin's purposes, which they assumed to embrace the subjection of all Western Europe to Communism, if need be by the use of the huge Russian armies.

Soviet suspicion of Western intentions (as distinct from wishes) had no basis in fact; and it seems probable today that Western suspicions of Soviet purposes were almost equally unfounded. But suspicion bred suspicion, and each defensive measure taken by one party was viewed by the other as aggressive and so calling for more defense. Hence the spiral of escalation in fears and in armaments. In this theory, the "cold war" was a product of exaggerated mutual suspicion, which in turn derived partly from a failure of communication, perhaps inevitable between parties harboring such antipathetic ideologies.

If this interpretation is correct, Stalin's decision to abandon cooperation with the West did not come at once as a consequence of the German surrender. There is good reason to believe that for some time after May 1945 he expected that cooperation to continue. This can be inferred from the advice that he was giving to Communist leaders in the Far East and in Europe: Mao Tse-tung should accept the supremacy of Chiang Kai-shek; Tito should welcome King Peter back to Yugoslavia; the French and Italian Communists should avoid "adventurism." Not, apparently, until some time in 1946 or early 1947 did he take a wholly uncompromising position on the chief issues that divided the former Grand Alliance.[10]

The Future of Germany

The rift that began over the fate of Eastern Europe was widened when the Allied governments undertook to determine the fate of Germany—a matter of the first importance for the future peace of Europe. The statesmen at Yalta had reached no decision on what its ultimate fate should be. Germany was, it is true, to be de-Nazified and demilitarized and to pay a large (but as yet undetermined) amount of reparations. Whether it was to remain one nation or to be dismembered, and if so, how, had not been decided, but arrangements had been made for temporary military occupation by the victor powers. A European Advisory Commission established by the Big Three in London, drew the boundaries of the German zones that were to be occupied, after the German surrender, by Russian, British, American, and later, French armies. The zone assigned to Russia, includ-

[10]Joseph R. Starobin, "Origins of the Cold War: The Communist Dimension," *Foreign Affairs*, 47 (July 1969), 681–96. James McGregor Burns, in *Roosevelt: The Soldier of Freedom* (New York: Harcourt Brace Jovanovich, Inc., 1970), pp. 373–74, finds the origin of the cold war in Russian resentment at the postponement of the Anglo-American second front in Europe until 1944.

ing Mecklenburg-Pomerania, Branden-burg, Saxony-Anhalt, Thuringia, and all to the eastward, contained 40 percent of the territory, 36 percent of the population, and 33 percent of the productive resources of pre-1937 Germany. This no doubt seemed a fair division at the time, but it had, as was learned later, two great disadvantages: it brought the advanced posts of the Russian occupation within less than one hundred miles of the Rhine, and it placed Berlin far within the Soviet zone, distant a hundred miles or more from the nearest point in the British zone. State Department representa-tives saw the danger in the latter arrange-ment and proposed reserving a corridor into Berlin from the western zones, but were told by the War Department that this was a question for the military only. The consequence was that, except by air, American and British access to Berlin was at the mercy of the Russian occupiers.

The zones were not designed to limit the areas of initial military operations but those alone of subsequent occupation. The un-expectedly rapid advance of the Anglo-American armies brought them into the Soviet zones of Germany and Austria and also into western Czechoslovakia, which the Russians viewed as within their sphere. Prime Minister Churchill, convinced, as he wrote later, "that Soviet Russia had become a mortal danger to the free world,"[11] wished to take advantage of Western mili-tary success by seizing Berlin and holding all the territory occupied until Stalin could be induced to live up to the promises made at Yalta. Otherwise, Churchill warned, the "iron curtain" which the Russians had al-ready "drawn down upon their front," would descend over a much wider area, and "a broad band of many hundreds of miles of Russian-occupied territory will isolate us from Poland."[12] But Eisenhower, sup-ported by Roosevelt and then by Truman, declined to pay the cost of what he thought a useless advance to Berlin, and Truman refused to postpone the withdrawal of American troops from the Russian zone beyond July 1. The Russians took Berlin, Prague, and Vienna—the three great an-cient capitals of Central Europe.

The Potsdam Conference

The Big Three heads of government held their last wartime meeting, code-named "Terminal," at Potsdam, just outside the ruins of Berlin, July 17 to August 2, 1945. Truman replaced Roosevelt, and midway through the Conference the victory of the Labour party in the British elections re-moved Churchill and Eden and substituted Clement Attlee and Ernest Bevin as Prime Minister and Foreign Secretary respec-tively.

The atmosphere was friendly and the discussions were generally good-tempered, but many controversial issues were passed over with no agreement. Such issues were Western complaints of one-party domina-tion in Bulgaria and Rumania, and the Russian request for British and American recognition of the governments of these countries;[13] Soviet desire for control of the Dardanelles and a trusteeship over former Italian possessions in the Mediterranean; and American interest in the international-ization of such waterways as the Darda-nelles and the Danube.

---

[11]Winston S. Churchill, *Triumph and Tragedy,* Vol. 6 of *The Second World War* (Boston: Houghton Mifflin Company, 1953), p. 456.

[12]Churchill, *Triumph and Tragedy,* p. 573.

[13]The government of Poland was for the time being removed from the field of controversy. At the end of May, Truman had sent Harry Hopkins to Mos-cow to seek agreement on Poland. Stalin had then consented to the admission of Mikolajczyk and other non-Communist Poles to the Provisional Government of National Unity, which had then been recognized by the United States and the United Kingdom. Also see Daniel M. Smith and Joseph M. Siracusa, *The Testing of America: 1914–1945* (St. Louis: Forum Press, 1979), pp. 220–22.

Map legend and labels:

NORTH SEA

DENMARK

BALTIC SEA

AMERICAN ZONE

Hamburg

Bremen

Stettin

Danzig

Berlin

NETHERLANDS

BRITISH ZONE

G E R M A N Y

RUSSIAN ZONE

Elbe

Oder R.

Neisse R.

Administered by Poland

POLAND

BELGIUM

Cologne

Breslau

Oder R.

LUX.

FRENCH

Rhine R.

Prague

CZECHOSLOVAKIA

FRANCE

Rhine R.

ZONE

Danube R.

AMERICAN ZONE

RUSSIAN ZONE

Linz

Vienna

Munich

AMERICAN ZONE

LIECHTENSTEIN

FRENCH ZONE

A U S T R I A

BRITISH ZONE

HUNGARY

ALLIED OCCUPATION IN GERMANY AND AUSTRIA

SWITZERLAND

ITALY

YUGOSL.

International occupation.

Area occupied by U.S. and British forces and released to the Russians.

Adapted from a map in Winston S. Churchill, *Triumph and Tragedy,* with the permission of Cassell and Company, Ltd., London, and Houghton Mifflin Company, Boston.

On a number of important matters there was agreement, superficial though it was. The task of drawing up treaties with Italy and with the Axis satellites, Hungary, Bulgaria, Rumania and Finland,[14] was as-

[14]Finland, having been defeated and despoiled of part of her territory by Russia in 1939–1940, had joined Germany in the war against the Soviets after June 1941.

signed to a Council of Foreign Ministers of the American, British, French, and Russian governments, which was to meet in London. China would also be represented but would not participate in European settlements.

The three leaders agreed that supreme authority in Germany should rest in the hands of the commanders of the four occupying armies, each in his own zone, and acting together in Berlin as a Control Council in matters affecting Germany as a whole. Germany was to be demilitarized, de-Nazified, and democratized. War criminals were to be punished. Local German governments were to be established. Though for the time being there was to be no central German government, certain central administrative departments were to be set up in such fields as finance, transport, communications, foreign trade, and industry. As this last provision suggests, Germany was to be administered as an economic unit, with establishment of common policies in all major fields of economic activity. Production policies were to be adjusted to meet the needs of the occupying forces and displaced persons, and to maintain for the German population a standard of living no higher than the average for other European countries, exclusive of the United Kingdom and the Soviet Union.

As *faits accomplis* the President and Prime Minister accepted the Polish occupation of German territory up to the Oder-Neisse line (except the Königsberg area of East Prussia, which was claimed by the Soviets) and the expulsion from that area of the German population, though nominally the fixing of Germany's eastern boundary was reserved for the future treaty of peace.

For reparations, the Potsdam agreement authorized each occupying power to remove property from its own zone and to seize German assets abroad. In order to balance the predominance of industry in the Western zones against that of agriculture in the East, Russia was entitled to 10 percent of industrial equipment taken from the Western zones, plus another 15 percent which was to be exchanged for products of the East, chiefly coal, raw materials, and foodstuffs. What remained of the German merchant marine and the German navy was to be divided equally among the United States, the United Kingdom, and the Soviet Union.

The Satellite Treaties

The Council of Foreign Ministers met in London (September 1945), Moscow (December 1945), Paris (April–May and June–July 1946), and New York (November–December 1946), in prolonged and finally successful efforts to make treaties with the former so-called "Axis satellites."

The first meeting of the Council, to which Secretary Byrnes went "with the atomic bomb in his pocket," produced nothing but an unseemly wrangle. Though the agenda was limited to Europe, Molotov complained repeatedly of the exclusion of the Soviets from a share in the control of Japan. At Moscow, three months later, a better spirit prevailed. Concessions were made on both sides. The Soviet Union consented to the holding of a conference of the Big Five with the sixteen other nations that had made more than nominal contributions to the war in Europe. This Conference sat in Paris from July 29 to October 15, 1946. It could only recommend. All final decisions were made by unanimous vote of the Council of Foreign Ministers. Agreement was reached in New York in December 1946, and the treaties were signed in Paris on February 10, 1947.

The treaties imposed monetary indemnities upon all the former Axis satellites, Finland, Hungary, Rumania, and Bulgaria, as well as upon Italy. They required Finland and Rumania to cede territory to the Soviet Union, and Italy to surrender her African conquests; and they imposed strict limits upon the armed forces of all. Unable to agree upon the disposition of Italy's former African possessions—although the Soviet Union dropped its demand for a trusteeship over Libya—the Foreign Ministers turned over the problem to the U.N. General Assembly, which put Libya and Italian Somaliland on the road to independence and federated Eritrea with Ethiopia.

The most difficult problem faced by the

Foreign Ministers in connection with the satellite treaties was the conflict over Trieste between Yugoslavia and Italy. The Yugoslav claim was backed by Russia; the Italian claim, by the Western powers. The compromise solution was to place the territory of Trieste temporarily under the Security Council of the United Nations. In practice, the Security Council could never agree on the appointment of a governor for Trieste, and until 1954 the territory remained under military occupation, the city and northern portion (Zone A) by Anglo-American forces, the remainder (Zone B) by the Yugoslav Army. Efforts of the United States and Great Britain to bring about a settlement were at long last rewarded. By an agreement signed on October 5, 1954, Italy received Zone A, with slight adjustments in the boundary; Zone B was retained by Yugoslavia. The Soviet Union, more flexible since Stalin's death (1953), created general surprise by announcing that it approved the settlement.

The United States was a party to, and in due time ratified, all these treaties except that with Finland. By signing the treaty with Bulgaria, the United States recognized the Communist-dominated government of that country, as it had already done in the case of Rumania. At Moscow, in December 1945, Stalin had promised a relaxing of one-party control in Rumania and Bulgaria. The United States had recognized Rumania without waiting for the promise to be fulfilled, and Bulgaria, after waiting a year in vain. In so doing it tacitly acquiesced in Soviet domination of these two countries, in plain disregard of the promises of Yalta.

Austria Regains its Independence

Austria presented problems more complicated than those of the satellite states. At Moscow in 1943, the Big Three Foreign Ministers had promised that Austria, as "the first free country to fall a victim to Hitlerite aggression," should be "liberated from German domination" and re-established as "free and independent;" and that the way should be opened for the Austrian people to find "political and economic security." The statesmen at Potsdam had declared Austria exempt from the payment of reparations. Yet this little country, with the area of South Carolina and the population of Michigan, was subjected, like Germany, to a four-power occupation, with Vienna a divided city. The most productive agricultural and industrial districts were governed by the Soviet element.

In November 1945, the Austrians were permitted to elect their own Parliament, which was, and remained thereafter, overwhelmingly anti-Communist and pro-Western. Negotiations for a treaty, which should liberate the country from military occupation, were begun in 1946 but were endlessly prolonged by the Russians. Not until the spring of 1955, two years after Stalin's death, did the Russians cease their obstruction. On May 15, 1955, a treaty was signed which ended the occupation and re-established Austria as a free and independent state. Separate agreements with the Soviet Union and the Western powers guaranteed its neutralization.

Deadlock in Germany

But relations between East and West in Austria appeared harmonious when compared with their relations in Germany. There, the Four-Power Control Council, established in Berlin, soon reached a condition of chronic deadlock, resulting from the requirement that all decisions be by unanimous vote. The French, miffed at their exclusion from Yalta and Potsdam, were guilty of some of the most flagrant obstructionist tactics in the early months of the occupation; but in the end it was the Russians who sabotaged attempts at a common policy for the four zones by repudiating in practice the Potsdam agreement that Germany should be treated as an economic unit.

The consequence was that each of the four powers applied its own ideas in its own zone. The Americans undertook to build democracy, starting from the grass roots, combined with a system of free enterprise. The Russians, finding German Communists too few to rule their zone, forced a union of Communists and Social Democrats to form the Socialist Unity Party, which became their instrument of government. Large landed estates were broken up, and large industries were nationalized. The French and British were less zealous for democracy than the Americans, and the British, under a Labour government, talked little of free enterprise and much of nationalizing the giant Ruhr industries, located in their zone. But policies in the three Western zones were sufficiently alike to make their economic and political union an easy matter.

The Russians' independent course on reparations—taking from their zone whatever they wished in capital goods and current production without giving an accounting to their allies—and their refusal to send food and raw materials to the Western zones led to an abandonment of the reparations policy in the latter in the spring of 1946 and, a few months later, to the economic union of the American and British zones. The Russians refused an invitation to merge their zone with the "Bizonia" thus formed, denouncing it as a step toward a permanent division of Germany. France, unwilling to offend the Soviets, also held aloof.

The trend of events was clearly in the direction of a Germany divided by the iron curtain. In order to prevent such division, and to put an end to the necessity of economic support that weighed heavily upon the Western powers, Secretary of State James F. Byrnes, in a speech at Stuttgart, September 6, 1946, proposed that Germany be reunited, not only economically but politically, with a central government on a federal pattern. To quiet French or Russian fears of a revived and rearmed Germany, Byrnes repeated an earlier offer on the part of the United States, to sign a twenty-five- or even forty-year four-power treaty to keep Germany disarmed and to leave American troops in Germany as long as any armed occupation should be necessary.[15]

This offer of American participation in a treaty to guarantee German disarmament was rejected by the Soviet government. It was rejected again in March 1947, when George Marshall, then Secretary of State, went to Moscow for another meeting of the Council of Foreign Ministers. The West made another bid for German unification, economic and political—a bid the failure of which was to lead to the organization of West Germany as a separate entity. The Soviets would agree to economic union on two conditions: a share in control of the industry of the Ruhr and recognition by the West of Russia's claim to 10 billion dollars in reparations, a claim that had been waived at Potsdam and revived later. On neither point would the Western powers yield. The two camps were equally far apart on political organization, the Western allies proposing a rather loose federal system, the Russians insisting on a strongly centralized government. The former, it was felt, would be a barrier against Communism; the latter might facilitate the communizing of the entire German state. The Moscow Conference adjourned without agreement on any significant point. "Moscow really marked the end of the road which began at Teheran and Yalta."[16]

[15]*Documents on American Foreign Relations*, 8: 210–18. This was a startling offer in the light of President Roosevelt's statement to Stalin that American troops would remain in Europe no longer than two years.

[16]*U.S. in World Affairs, 1947–1948*, p. 78.

The Policy of Containment: The Truman Doctrine

The antagonism that disrupted the Moscow Council of Foreign Ministers in March 1947 had been building up through the preceding year. Two speeches early in 1946 sounded like unofficial declarations of war. Stalin, on February 9, restated the Marxist-Leninist dogma of inevitable war between Communism and capitalism and called for three five-year plans to prepare the Soviet Union for the struggle. A month later Winston Churchill—not then a member of the British cabinet, be it noted—delivered at Fulton, Missouri, his famous denunciation of the "iron curtain" and urged "a fraternal association of English-speaking peoples" to defend the free world.

Stalin followed this speech with a tightening of the Kremlin's hold upon the governments of Eastern Europe, an intensified suppresion of human liberties in the Soviet Union, and a campaign of propaganda directed against the West, especially the United States.[17] Actions on both sides contributed to the growing tension: final breakdown of negotiations for an American loan to Russia; Soviet rejection of Secretary Byrnes' Stuttgart offer; disruption of the reparations program; pressures of Russia or Russian satellites upon Greece and Turkey; and replacement of negotiations by propagandist oratory in the meetings of the Council of Foreign Ministers (opened to the press and public in April).

Yet to the end of 1946, hope of accommodation was not wholly ended. The satellite treaties were made and ratified. Soviet troops, whose presence in Iran contravened wartime promises, were finally withdrawn, and Stalin sometimes talked affably with visitors from the West of peaceful coexistence between opposing sys-

[17]Starobin, "Origins of the Cold War."

tems. Not until the spring of 1947, with the failure of the Moscow Conference and the simultaneous announcement by the United States of the policy of "containment," did the break become clearly irreparable and the cold war begin in earnest.

The new American policy was based upon the thesis that the Soviet Union had a persistent tendency to expand the boundaries of its empire wherever possible but would not undertake to do so at the risk of major war. The United States, therefore, by exerting counterpressure, should "contain" the U.S.S.R. and its Communist satellites within their existing bounds, hoping that time and internal strains would eventually sap the strength of the Red Empire.[18]

The first notice of the new policy came on March 12, 1947. While the Foreign Ministers were wrangling in Moscow, President Truman went before Congress to ask for $400 million in military and economic aid for Greece and Turkey. Since 1945 the royal government of Greece had been struggling against Communist forces within, aided by heavy infiltrations from Greece's three northern neighbors, all

[18]Authorship of the "containment" policy is often attributed to George F. Kennan, a Foreign Service officer who, after spending some years in Russia, became head of the new Policy Planning Staff in the State Department in the Spring of 1947. Kennan expounded the general philosophy of "containment" in an anonymous article (signed "X"), "The Sources of Soviet Conduct," in *Foreign Affairs,* 25 (July 1947), 566–82; republished in G. F. Kennan, *American Diplomacy, 1900–1950* (Chicago: University of Chicago Press, 1951), pp. 107–28. He was, however, critical of Truman's message of March 12. He disapproved military aid to Greece and Turkey and the later military emphasis on containment. He and his staff, on the other hand, played an important part in formulating the Marshall Plan, as did also Under Secretaries of State Dean Acheson and William L. Clayton. See G. F. Kennan, *Memoirs, 1925–1950* (Boston: Atlantic Monthly Press, 1967), chaps. 14–15: Joseph M. Jones, *The Fifteen Weeks (February 21–June 5, 1947)* (New York: Viking Press, 1955), pp. 154–55, 255; Dean Acheson, *Present at the Creation: My Years in the State Department* (New York: W. W. Norton & Co., Inc., 1969), chaps. 24–26.

satellites of the Soviet Union. Turkey was reported to have been pressed by Moscow to yield control of the Dardanelles and to surrender the districts of Kars and Ardahan at the eastern end of the Black Sea, which Russia had surrendered at the end of World War I. Great Britain, which had been aiding both Turkey and Greece, informed the United States in February 1947 that she would no longer be able to do so. Truman promptly accepted the responsibility for the United States. In asking authority and funds to assist Greece and Turkey, he propounded a general principle that came to be referred to as the "Truman Doctrine."

> I believe [said the President] that it must be the policy of the United States to support free peoples who are resisting attempted subjugation by armed minorities or by outside pressures . . .

President Truman's proposal met a generally favorable response in the United States, though some critics thought its scope too broad. Congress acted after two months of debate. An act of May 22, 1947, authorized the expenditure of $100 million in military aid to Turkey and, for Greece, $300 million equally divided between military and economic assistance. The act also empowered the President to send military and civilian experts as advisers to the Greek and Turkish governments. American aid, thus begun and continued from year to year, proved effective as a means of "containment" in that quarter. But the Truman administration moved quickly on to assume broader responsibilities.

The Marshall Plan

Greece and Turkey might thus be strengthened against armed aggression or the threat of it. But to Europe as a whole the danger from Communism lay principally in the economic stagnation that had followed the war. Western Europe in the spring of 1947 was facing catastrophe after an exceptionally severe winter. Food and fuel were in short supply, and foreign exchange, notwithstanding the large dollar loan to England, would be exhausted by the end of the year. Large Communist parties in France and Italy stood ready to profit from the impending economic collapse and human suffering.

The best protection against the spread of Communism to Western Europe would be economic recovery. So, at least, it appeared in Washington, and on this theory Secretary of State George Marshall, speaking at the Harvard Commencement, June 5, 1947, offered American aid to such European nations as would agree to coordinate their efforts for recovery and present the United States with a program and specifications of their needs. Marshall drew no distinction between Communist and non-Communist Europe, but the Soviet Union spurned the proposal as a new venture in "American imperialism," a threat to the sovereignty of small nations that might accept it. The satellite governments obeyed the dictum from Moscow, as did Finland and Czechoslovakia, which dared not offend the Soviet giant. They had been tempted, as had Poland, by Marshall's proposal, and all three declined it with regret. Rejection of the offer by the Soviet bloc no doubt contributed greatly to its endorsement by Congress.

The other sixteen nations of Europe (excluding Spain, which was not invited, and Germany, which as yet had no government) formed a "committee of European Economic Cooperation, which, in September 1947, presented to the United States a report proposing the achievement by 1951 of a self-sufficient European economy, at an estimated cost to the United States of $19.3 billion. In December, President Truman laid the proposal before Congress, with a request for $6.8 billion for the first fifteen months of the program and $10.2 billion for the succeeding three years—a total of $17 billion. In explaining the motive for his request, the President said:

> I am proposing that this Nation contribute to world peace and to its own security by assisting in the recovery of sixteen countries which, like the United States, are devoted to the preservation of free institutions and enduring peace among nations.

Congress slashed the figure somewhat, but on April 3, 1948, established the Economic Cooperation Administration to handle the program and at the end of June appropriated an initial $4 billion for the purpose, which might be spread over either twelve or fifteen months at the discretion of the administrator of the program. So was launched the Marshall Plan, or European Recovery Program, which was to continue for three years, to cost the United States $10¼ billion, to contribute to an impressive economic recovery in Europe, and to be broadened to serve many non-European countries.[19] Unlike later programs of military assistance, the Marshall Plan has had few critics from the American New Left.

Point Four

The Marshall Plan was designed to aid in the recovery of nations with advanced economies that had been dislocated by the war. By increasing production and trade, by alleviating unemployment and poverty, its authors expected it to halt the growth of Communism among the working classes of Europe. But Communism was also a threat among the poverty-stricken masses in countries of Asia, Africa, and Latin America, where the modern economy had made little or no impress. The "containment" of Communism called for measures to raise the standard of living in countries such as these.

It was with this purpose in mind that President Truman, in his second-term Inaugural Address, January 20, 1949, proposed his "Point Four," or Technical Assistance program.

> . . . we must [he said] embark on a bold new program for making the benefits of our scientific advances and industrial progress available for the improvement and growth of underdeveloped areas.[20]

The Point Four program got under way in 1950, with a modest appropriation of $35 million. Authorized expenditures for the three years 1951–1954 totaled nearly $400 million. In 1953 the program was placed, with other forms of foreign aid, under the Foreign Operations Administration (FOA).

The West German Republic

In the meantime there had been important developments in Germany. Failure of the Foreign Ministers to reach agreement at Moscow in March 1947, and at London in November and December of the same year, led to moves by the Western powers toward the creation from their three zones of a unified and self-governing West Germany. The British and Americans had already taken one step in that direction in the

---

[19]Nominally, the program lasted four years and cost approximately $13,350,000,000, but virtually all the aid in the fourth year went for defense or defense support under the Mutual Security Agency, which in 1951 supplanted the E.C.A.

[20]*Documents on American Foreign Relations*, 11: 10. This was the fourth point in the foreign policy program outlined by the President. The first three were support of the United Nations, continuation of the European Recovery Program, and the strengthening of "freedom-loving nations against the dangers of aggression." The last referred especially to the North Atlantic Treaty then under negotiation.

economic merging of their zones. Consultations in London in the spring of 1948 by representatives of France, Great Britain, the United States, and the three Benelux countries (Belgium, the Netherlands, and Luxembourg) resulted in agreements, announced June 7, proposing the creation of a West German government and, as a safeguard against a too strong Germany, control of the Ruhr industries by an international authority representing the six states and West Germany. The Germans of the Western zones would elect members of a constituent assembly. This body would then draw up a constitution for a federal state, which might eventually include the Eastern zone. The new government would exercise sovereignty over its domestic affairs and limited control over foreign relations; but the ban on rearmament would remain, and the military occupation would continue "until the peace of Europe is secured."[21]

The West German Constituent Assembly met in Bonn, September 1, 1948, and proceeded with its work of preparing a constitution. A German Federal Republic, comprising the three Western zones, was inaugurated at Bonn in September 1949. Military government terminated, although occupation forces remained. Allied authority was exercised through a High Commission, to which the United States, France, and the United Kingdom each appointed one member. The Federal Republic was soon made eligible for Marshall Plan aid and was given a voice in the international control of the Ruhr. Under its first Chancellor, Konrad Adenauer (1949–1963), it showed a spirit of willing cooperation with the West.

Divided Germany

The Russians had not viewed these developments without protest and counter-

---

moves. The Marshall Plan they interpreted as an aggressive scheme of the United States, aimed eventually at "liberating" the satellite states of Eastern Europe. Their response was the holding of a conference of nine East European states in Warsaw (September 1947), which resolved to do everything possible to defeat the program of "American imperialism." Communist-inspired strikes in France and Italy sought in vain to deter these countries from accepting Marshall Plan aid. The Communist Information Bureau, (Cominform), a successor of the Comintern, dissolved in 1943, was set up at Belgrade. Treaties of defensive alliance linking the Soviet Union with Bulgaria, Finland, Hungary, and Rumania were added to treaties previously negotiated with Czechoslovakia, Poland, and Yugoslavia.

More violent reaction accompanied the early steps toward the unification of West Germany. In February 1948 a Communist coup overthrew the democratic government of Czechoslovakia and installed one firmly attached to Moscow. This blow to the West was partly compensated for later in the year, when Yugoslavia, under Tito's leadership, broke with the Cominform and with Moscow. The government remained firmly Communist but ceased to take orders from the Kremlin and took a basically neutralist position. With the opening of the six-power talks on Germany in London, the Soviets complained that the Western powers were destroying the four-power control of Germany agreed to three years before, and hence that they had no further business in Berlin. The Western Allies, on the other hand, maintained that they were in Berlin by virtue of their part in the defeat of Germany.

At any rate, the Russians now began an attempt to squeeze the Western Allies out of Berlin, which, it will be recalled, lay wholly within the Soviet zone with no guaranteed surface corridor communicating with the West. Restrictions upon movement to and from the city were first imposed in April 1948. In June all surface transportation between Berlin and the Western zones was halted. The Western powers must now either withdraw their garrisons from Berlin in admitted defeat or find means of supplying not only them but the two million people of West Berlin. Rejecting advice that he "call the Russian bluff"—open the roads by military force —President Truman (and the British) resorted to air transport, the only means for which they had signed agreements with the Russians. The "air lift" started at once, and by September 1, American and British planes were flying in four thousand tons of supplies daily. Russian planes occasionally threatened the air lift but never ventured to attack. Allied persistence and patience eventually paid off. In May 1949, the Soviet Union agreed to end the blockade and to participate in another meeting of the Big Four Foreign Ministers. The meeting achieved no agreement, but the blockade was ended.

In October 1949, after the inauguration of the German Federal Republic at Bonn, a so-called People's Council in Berlin proclaimed a new government for the Soviet zone of Germany. Styled the German Democratic Republic, it rested upon a constitution designed, like that at Bonn, to unite all of Germany. Two Germanys had come into being, one totalitarian, the other democratic; one under the domination of the Soviet Union, the other closely tied to Western Europe and America.

Collective Self-Defense

The Communist coup in Czechoslovakia and the Berlin blockade alarmed the Western powers. Though the blockade had been beaten, there was no guarantee that the Russians might not make a new attempt to oust the Western Allies from Berlin or to prevent the formation of the German Federal Republic. It was true that the Soviets,

since 1945, had reduced their armed forces from eleven and a half million men to fewer than three million,[22] but they still far outnumbered those available in the West. Their numerical, as well as qualitative, superiority, it was feared, might tempt the Russians to commit some aggressive act against a weak spot in the fragile Western armor. "Containment" of Russia, till now dependent chiefly upon economic and political means, appeared to need military backing. If the Soviet Union could be warned that an act of aggression against any one of the free nations of Western Europe would mean a conflict with the others and also with the United States, it might be deterred from such acts. The United Nations, because of the Soviet veto, could not supply such a deterrent, but Article 51 of the U.N. Charter legalized "collective self-defense" by groups within the U.N., and to agreements under Article 51 the free world now turned.

In the Americas, the Rio Pact of September 2, 1947, had already invoked Article 51 in a hemispheric collective security agreement. In Europe a beginning was made in March 1948, when Great Britain, France, and the Benelux countries signed at Brussels a fifty-year treaty of economic, social, and cultural collaboration and collective self-defense. But in order to constitute an impressive warning, such a treaty needed the backing of the United States. Such backing was promptly proposed by President Truman in an address to Congress on March 17, 1948. In the same address, the President spoke frankly of the danger from Russia; in order to enable the United States to meet it, he called for adoption of a universal military training program and temporary re-enactment of selective service legislation. The United States had allowed its military might to disintegrate since 1945. It must grow strong

[22]Adam B. Ulam, *Expansion and Coexistence: The History of Soviet Foreign Policy, 1917–1967* (New York: Praeger Publishers, 1968), p. 404.

again and must show its willingness to pool its strength with that of like-minded nations.

The build-up of American armed strength began with the enactment by Congress of a new selective service, or draft, law in June 1948. With the aid of this and under the stimulus of war in Korea, which began in June 1950, the strength of the Army, Navy, and Air Force grew from 1,350,000 in 1948 to 3,630,000 in June 1952.

The way for collective action was cleared when the Senate, in the Vandenberg Resolution of June 11, 1948, voiced the opinion that the United States should, among other measures for promoting peace, associate itself, "by constitutional process, with such regional and other collective arrangements as are based on continuous and effective self-help and mutual aid, and as affect its national security." The United States ought also, the resolution declared, to make clear "its determination to exercise the right of individual or collective self-defense under article 51 should any armed attack occur affecting its national security."[23]

The North Atlantic Treaty Organization

The Vandenberg Resolution was the prelude to the North Atlantic Treaty, an important and ambitious venture in search of collective security. The treaty—a pronounced break with the principle of "no permanent alliances"—was signed April 4, 1949, by twelve nations of the North Atlantic and Western European areas. This number was increased to fifteen by the accession of Greece and Turkey in 1952 and

West Germany in 1955.[24] The parties agreed to settle peacefully all disputes between themselves and to develop their capacity to resist armed attack "by means of continuous and effective self-help and mutual aid." But the heart of the treaty was Article 5, which declared that an armed attack upon any one of the members in Europe or North America would be considered an attack upon all and pledged each member in case of such an attack to assist the party attacked "by such action as it deems necessary, including the use of armed force." Thus began the North Atlantic Treaty Organization, or NATO. Its directing body was a North Atlantic Council, made up of the Foreign, Defense, and Finance Ministers of the member states.

The United States now took the lead in providing and organizing the military deterrent envisaged by the framers of the North Atlantic Treaty. The American position was ably stated in a top secret document labeled NSC68, prepared at President Truman's request by the State and Defense Departments in the spring of 1950. The document's substance had been revealed by, among others, Dean Acheson, who, as Secretary of State, played an important part in its adoption.

NSC 68 started from an assumption as to Soviet intentions which, as Acheson admits, was opposed by the most prominent Soviet experts in the State Department though accepted by the Planning Staff. In this analysis the Russian threat, in Acheson's words, "combined the ideology of communist doctrine and the power of the Russian state into an aggressive expansionist drive, which found its chief opponent, and, therefore, target in the antithetical ideas and power of our own country." The threat to Western Europe, he thought, seemed "singularly like that which Islam had posed

[23]*Documents on American Foreign Relations*, 10: 302; A. H. Vandenberg, Jr., ed., *The Private Papers of Senator Vandenberg* (Boston: Houghton Mifflin Company, 1952), pp. 403–11.

[24]The twelve original signers were the United States, Canada, Iceland, the United Kingdom, France, Belgium, the Netherlands, Luxembourg, Denmark, Norway, Portugal, and Italy.

centuries before, with its combination of ideological zeal and fighting power."[25]

Such being the perceived threat to Western Europe and ultimately to the United States, NSC 68 recommended that the United States "strike out on a bold and massive program of rebuilding the West's defensive potential to surpass that of the Soviet world, and of meeting each fresh challenge promptly and unequivocally." With the security of the free world at stake, costs of such a program were immaterial. The country could afford to spend, if necessary, 20 percent of its gross national product on defense. President Truman approved NSC 68 in September 1950, and it thereby became official government policy.

The assumption of NSC 68 as to Moscow's aggressive purposes seemed to Acheson and others to be borne out by events in the Far East and by the revelation in September 1949 that the U.S.S.R. had exploded its first atomic bomb. The Communist conquest of all mainland China was completed in the summer of 1949, and the government of the People's Republic of China was proclaimed at Peking on October 1. The Chinese Communists were thus regarded as puppets of Moscow and their victory, as a major triumph in the Kremlin's program of world revolution. Then on June 25, 1950, several months before the approval of NSC 68, Communist North Korea invaded the South. What part the Kremlin played in launching the Korean aggression we do not know, but in official circles in Washington in 1950 it was generally assumed that this was yet another Soviet blow for world conquest. Here was a

"fresh challenge" of the kind which NSC 68 had said should be met "promptly and unequivocally;" in another way, the North Korean attack made the task of "selling" NSC 68 to the American public easier than had been anticipated.

While that challenge was being met, the United States, working now through NATO, was building defenses in Western Europe against supposed Soviet plans for a Communist conquest of that incomparably important area. Early in 1951 the North Atlantic Council set up military headquarters near Paris, known as SHAPE (Supreme Headquarters, Allied Powers in Europe), with General Eisenhower as Supreme Commander. Its purpose was to build a defense force in Western Europe, not equal to the huge army maintained by the Soviet Union (175 Russian divisions and 60 or more divisions from the satellite states), but strong enough to make the Russians think twice before going to war, and, if war should come anyway, strong enough to hold the Russian armies in check until (it was hoped) the strategic air power of the United States could destroy the centers of Soviet strength.

American aid to Europe now began to shift from economic to military. The Mutual Security Agency in 1951 replaced the Economic Cooperation Administration and was in turn, in 1953, succeeded by the Foreign Operations Administration. From October 1949 to the end of 1953, the United States supplied nearly $6 billion worth of arms and military equipment to its European allies, as well as $1.7 billion worth to other countries. The United States also increased its divisions stationed in Germany and Austria from two to six, following a "great debate" in which the Senate approved this increase but advised against sending additional troops abroad without the consent of Congress. The European allies in the same period spent over $35 billion in building up their military forces and installations. The result was an encourag-

[25]Dean Acheson, *Present at the Creation*, pp. 375–77, 752–53. Reprinted by permission of W. W. Norton and Hamish Hamilton, Ltd., London. "The Report by the Secretaries of State and Defense on 'United States Objectives and Programs for National Security,' April 7, 1950," which is usually referred to by its serial number, NSC 68, was declassified in February 1975. It has been reproduced in *Naval War College Review* (May–June 1975), 51–108.

ing increase in the troops, planes, and airfields available for NATO service.

Throughout this period, the United States was pressing strongly for the inclusion of West German units in the defense forces. The prospect of a rearmed and nationalistic Germany was almost as alarming to France and the Benelux countries as the Russian danger. A French proposal for a European Defense Community (E.D.C.), which would make it possible to use and yet control German troops by integrating them with those of France, Italy, and the Benelux states, was finally rejected by the French Assembly in August 1954, in spite of urgent pleas by U.S. Secretary of State John Foster Dulles. A substitute was found in a set of treaties constituting Western European Union (W.E.U.), an alliance rather than an organic union as E.D.C. would have been. The treaties became effective on May 6, 1955. Under this arrangement, Italy and the Federal Republic of (West) Germany were admitted to the Brussels Pact alliance of 1948 with Britain, France, and the three Benelux countries. West Germany recovered its sovereignty and was permitted to rearm, though pledging itself to manufacture no atomic, chemical, or bacteriological weapons. United States, British, and French troops were to remain in West Germany for its defense and that of the North Atlantic area until the Bonn government could provide its own defense forces. West Germany became a member of NATO, and the armed forces of the Western European Union, with certain exceptions, became subject to the NATO supreme command, referred to as SACEUR (Supreme Allied Commander, Europe). To quiet French fears of a rearmed Germany, Great Britain and the United States agreed to maintain substantial military forces on the continent, four ground divisions and a tactical air force for Britain, six divisions or the equivalent for the United States. To the British, American, and French forces and the smaller contingents to be furnished by Belgium and the Netherlands were to be added, it was hoped by 1960 but actually not until 1963, twelve divisions from the German Federal Republic. Such an army, centrally commanded from SHAPE, should be able to put on a strong first line defense against aggression from the east.

Beginnings of an Arms Race

The Russians had watched with misgivings the formation of NATO and the Western European Union, and especially the plans for rearming West Germany, and had tried to halt the process by threats, persuasion, and offers of compromise, but none that the Western leaders felt safe in accepting. What the Russians feared most was the rearming of West Germany, especially the possibility that German troops, as NATO forces, might acquire atomic weapons. Having failed in their attempts to block these measures of the West, they turned to countermeasures. At Warsaw on May 14, 1955, the Soviets negotiated an alliance of eight Communist states—a sort of Eastern European Union—professedly for defense against the allegedly aggressive intentions of NATO.

We may well ask today: was this inauguration of rival alliances and rival military build-ups necessary? Did the Soviet leaders of a country slowly recovering from a frightfully devastating war, actually plan armed aggression against Western Europe? There is no doubt that Truman and Acheson and their fellow planners in England and France perceived the threat to be real. On the basis of what they believed, their precautions were justified. But it is to be remembered that the Soviet experts in the State Department in 1950 were skeptical of Russia's aggressive intentions, and some careful students of Soviet policy many years later were convinced that Russia was too weak, and knew she was too weak, to attempt a takeover in Western Europe and a resulting confrontation with the United States. For their part, the Russians seem to have believed, partly as a result of such rhetoric as that of the Republican platform of 1952, that this country was determined to "liberate" the states of Eastern Europe from Soviet control. Thus, in the words of historian Adam Ulam:

> The Russians knew that they would not and could not move against the West. What, then, was the purpose of NATO, if not to push them from the positions they had secured in Eastern Europe between 1944 and 1947? Contrariwise, the Western statesmen, at least in 1949 and 1950, knew that they would not and could not reverse the *faits accomplis* in Poland, Rumania, etc. Why, then, did the Russians try to sabotage NATO unless they wanted a disarmed and weak Western Europe as their prey?[26]

The inevitable result of this atmosphere of mutual suspicion and fear was, in the words of political Hans J. Morgenthau, "a drastic militarisation of the Cold War in the form of a conventional and nuclear armaments race, the frantic search for alliances, and the establishment of military bases."[27]

Admitting, however, that neither alliance had any ambitious designs upon the territory or the sovereignty of the other, there remained the possibility that war might begin by accident or miscalculation. Berlin was the chief danger spot. Should the Russians or their puppets, the East Germans, try to seize the Western sector or to resume the blockade, the West would have to choose between surrender and conflict. Faced with this possibility and the Russian superiority in number of troops available, the West could hardly do otherwise

than arm for defense. To a large degree, therefore, it might be said that the escalation of the cold war stemmed from the mistake of 1945 which left the West so vulnerable in Berlin.

The hopes of 1955 for a NATO army were never completely realized. The gain in strength from the addition of the West German army to NATO forces was largely offset by losses elsewhere. The nationalist rebellion against the French in Algeria, which had begun in 1954, drew off the greater part of the French forces that had been committed to NATO. Pressure for economy, doubt as to the efficacy of conventional forces in an age of nuclear weapons and long-range ballistic missiles, and occasional relaxation in East-West tensions, led to reductions in other national contingents. The goal of ninety-six divisions, set at the Lisbon meeting of the North Atlantic Council in 1952, was abandoned, and the "irreducible minimum" of thirty divisions, announced year after year by American Supreme Commanders at SHAPE was never attained. Shortages of manpower, indeed, were compensated for by increases in firepower, as NATO troops in Europe were gradually equipped with tactical (low yield) atomic weapons. These were supplied by the United States, and their atomic warheads were kept under American custody, as required by the Atomic Energy Act. Any satisfaction afforded by this modernization of weaponry was qualified, however, by the reflection that the Russians were undoubtedly effecting similar improvements.

The weapons picture, in fact, had changed radically since the NATO treaty was signed in April 1949. Then the West held a monopoly of atomic weapons, and the United States, with the long-range bombers of the Strategic Air Command (S.A.C.), presumably possessed the capability of destroying Russian centers of population and industry without suffering comparable injury. Later in the same year,

[26] Adam B. Ulam, *Expansion and Coexistence:* p. 511. Reprinted by permission of Praeger Publishers and The Pall Mall Press, Ltd., London.

[27] Hans J. Morgenthau, "Arguing about the Cold War," *Encounter,* May 1967, p. 39.

however, the U.S.S.R. exploded its first atomic bomb. Four years later it followed the United States by only a few months in setting off its first hydrogen, or thermonuclear device, thus closing the gap between the nuclear-weapon capabilities of the two major powers. The Russian success in launching the rocket-propelled satellites, Sputnik I and Sputnik II (October 4, November 3, 1957), ushered in the age of the intercontinental ballistic missile (ICBM) and its less potent relative, the intermediate-range ballistic missile (IRBM), which soon largely supplanted the slower and more vulnerable airplane as prospective carriers of nuclear destruction. By the early 1960s the Russians had developed, in the ICBM, means of delivery at least equal to those of the United States and also (as demonstrated in their tests in the fall of 1961) nuclear weapons of many megatons in potency.

Something like a stalemate in nuclear weapons between the United States and the U.S.S.R. had been reached. Since each had the unquestioned power to destroy the other, nuclear war between them had become "unthinkable." The terms "balance of terror" or "mutual deterrence" described the relationship. Each government, however, was in constant search of more powerful and reliable weapons, and the search often took the form of exploding nuclear devices in the atmosphere with the resulting fallout of radioactive particles that created worldwide hazards to health. An unofficial moratorium on such tests was instituted in 1958, but in 1961 the Soviet Union resumed testing, and Britain and America felt it necessary to follow suit. Finally, on August 5, 1963, the three powers signed the Test Ban Treaty, by which they agreed to abstain from exploding nuclear devices in the atmosphere, in outer space, and underwater. Underground tests were not banned. The treaty, which could be terminated by any signatory at three months' notice, was promptly ratified by the signers and adhered to by most of the governments of the world, excluding France, Communist China, and Cuba.[28]

[28]Text of treaty in *Documents on American Foreign Relations, 1963,* pp. 130–32.

ADDITIONAL READINGS

ARKES, HARDLEY, *Bureaucracy, the Marshall Plan and the National Interest.* Princeton, N.J.: Princeton University Press, 1972.

DIVINE, ROBERT A., *Second Chance: The Triumph of Internationalism in America during World War II.* New York: Atheneum, 1967.

————, *Blowing on the Wind: The Nuclear Test Ban Debate, 1954–1960.* New York: Oxford University Press, 1978.

GRAEBNER, NORMAN A., *Cold War Diplomacy: American Foreign Policy, 1945–1975* (2nd ed.). New York: D. Van Nostrand Company, Inc., 1977.

MEE, CHARLES L., JR., *Meeting at Potsdam.* New York: M. Evans and Co., 1975.

MISCAMBLE, WILSON D., "Anthony Eden and the Truman-Molotov Conversations, April 1945," Diplomatic History, 2 (1978), 167–80.

PATERSON, THOMAS G., *Soviet-American Confrontation: Postwar Reconstruction and the Origins of the Cold War.* Baltimore: Johns Hopkins Press, 1978.

RICHARDSON, J. L., "Cold War Revisionism: A Critique," *World Review,* 24 (1972), 579–612.

ROSE, LISLE A., *After Yalta: America and the Origins of the Cold War.* New York: Charles Scribner's Sons, 1973.

————, *Dubious Victory: The United States and the End of World War II.* Kent, Ohio: Kent State University Press, 1973.

SIRACUSA, JOSEPH M., *The American Diplomatic Revolution: A Documentary History of the Cold War, 1941–1947.* Port Washington, N.Y.: Kennikat Press Corp., 1976.

———— and GLEN ST. JOHN BARCLAY, eds., *The Impact of the Cold War: Reconsiderations.* Port Washington, N.Y.: Kennikat Press Corp., 1977.

WALTON, RICHARD J., *Henry Wallace, Harry Truman, and the Cold War.* New York: The Viking Press, 1976.

21. From Peaceful Coexistence to Détente

Long before the major antagonists in the cold war had reached agreement on the test-ban treaty, important changes in personnel and in techniques had taken place in the Soviet Union. The death in March 1953 of Marshal Josef Stalin, the Russian dictator, was the prelude to the rise to power in Moscow of a leader whose aims were the same as Stalin's but whose methods were more flexible, more seductive, and more dangerous. Stalin's first successor as Premier, Georgi M. Malenkov, was quickly thrust aside to make way for Nikolai A. Bulganin, while Communist Party Secretary, Nikita S. Khrushchev, emerged as the man who really held the reins. In March 1958 Khrushchev took over the Premiership from Bulganin.

The new regime was more tolerant at home than its predecessor. With few exceptions its defeated opponents were relegated to obscure posts rather than liquidated in Stalinesque fashion, and the terrorism of the secret police largely disappeared. In foreign policy, the new rulers undertook to entice the uncommitted nations instead of frightening them. With a great show of affability, Bulganin and Khrushchev—popularly referred to as "B. and K."—paid friendly visits to India, Burma, and Afghanistan in 1955. There followed, for those countries and others, substantial grants or loans of economic and technical aid, to which, the Russians boasted, no political strings were attached.

When the Twentieth Congress of the Communist Party of the Soviet Union convened in Moscow in February 1956, Khrushchev, in a secret speech, roundly denounced Stalin's bloodthirsty methods and inaugurated a process of de-Stalinization calculated to degrade the dictator's name from its hitherto honorable place in Soviet history. It was at this time, too, that Khrushchev enunciated his policy of "peaceful coexistence," repudiating the Leninist doctrine of inevitable war between the Communist and capitalist societies, and declaring that Communism could achieve its victory by peacefully demonstrating its superiority. "We will bury you," he informed the capitalist world on a later occasion, but he meant that he would bury the system, not the people who lived under it. The Soviet government, meanwhile, having negotiated the Warsaw Pact in response to Western European Union, showed a spirit of conciliation by signing (May 15, 1955) the treaty ending the occupation of Austria and accepting on the same day an invitation from the United States, Great Britain, and France for a summit meeting of the Big Four heads of government at Geneva in July.

At Geneva, July 18 to 23, 1955, President Eisenhower, Prime Minister Anthony Eden (who had recently succeeded Winston Churchill), French Premier Edgar Faure, Russian Premier Bulganin, their Foreign Ministers, and other dignitaries (including, of course, Party Secretary Khrushchev), met face to face in an effort to resolve critical East-West difficulties. The meeting had been heralded from Moscow and Washington as promising agreement, and its sessions were conducted in a tone of cordiality which gave rise to the phrase, "spirit of Geneva." On substantive matters, however, no agreement was achieved. On the reunification of Germany, the Western proposal that it be effected by free elections won temporary assent from the Russians, but this assent was repudiated when the Foreign Ministers met later to work out details. This was not surprising, since it was well understood that a Germany unified by free elections would be anti-Communist and pro-West.

On disarmament, the West considered effective inspection essential; the Soviets held it inadmissible. President Eisenhower's generous proposal that East and West exchange "blueprints" of their armed forces and permit mutual "open skies" aerial inspection of their territory found no favor with the Russians. On European security, Russian insistence that NATO be disbanded and American troops withdrawn from Europe was equally unacceptable to the West. Only on such matters as freer cultural exchanges was there any real meeting of minds. The questions unresolved "at the summit" were referred to the four Foreign Ministers, who met late in October, also in Geneva. Their failure to agree on anything significant left no doubt that East and West had reached a new impasse.

Tragedy in Hungary

From 1955 to 1963 relations of the United States and its NATO Allies with the Soviet bloc, so far as Europe was concerned, involved a series of alternating crises and détentes, with the status of West Berlin eventually taking a prominent place as a factor in the crises. The first serious crisis after the Geneva summit meeting of 1955, however, did not concern Berlin. The crisis of 1956 was a dual one produced by Russian sup-

pression of an attempted anti-Communist revolution in Hungary and an attack on Egypt by Israel, France, and Great Britain. The Egyptian crisis will be dealt with elsewhere. The Hungarian tragedy is considered here.

An important characteristic of Soviet policy after Stalin was a degree of relaxation in Moscow's control of Communist parties and governments in neighboring states. The dissident Marshal Tito of Yugoslavia, after playing host to Khrushchev, was welcomed on a visit to Moscow and assured that the Kremlin accepted the principle of "national Communism" which he espoused. Encouraged by this display of conciliation toward Yugoslavia, the Polish Communists installed a pronounced anti-Stalinist, Wladyslaw Gomulka, as Party Secretary and dissuaded Khrushchev from interfering. Still Communist to the core and continuing to adhere to the Warsaw Alliance, the Polish regime had successfully defied the dictatorship of the Kremlin.

In Hungary, dissatisfaction took a more radical turn. Anti-Soviet and antigovernment riots in Budapest led to the installation, October 24, 1956, of a new government headed by Imre Nagy. A few days later, Nagy, though a Communist, admitted non-Communists to his government. On November 1 the government repudiated the Warsaw Alliance, declared Hungary a neutral state, and appealed to the United Nations for assistance.

This was more than the Soviet Union could let pass. Success in Hungary's secession from the Communist bloc could well lead to a complete breakup of Moscow's circle of satellites. Moscow reacted violently. After temporarily withdrawing its tanks and troops from Budapest, it sent them back in force, suppressed the popular uprising in the city, and connived at the installation of a new Communist government headed by János Kádár, which invited Russian assistance. Imre Nagy took refuge in the Yugoslav embassy. Enticed out by hints of office in the new government, he was seized, abducted to Rumania, and later executed. Weeks of fighting followed, but a virtually unarmed populace was no match for Russian tanks. No aid came from the West, and the collapse of an heroic struggle for independence was inevitable.

In Washington President Dwight D. Eisenhower had been elected in 1952 after a campaign in which the Republican Party had condemned the "containment" policy of the Democrats as "negative, futile, and immoral" and promised to "again make liberty into a beacon light of hope that will penetrate the dark places." "Liberation" of peoples under the Communist yoke was to replace "containment" of Communism. How far the Hungarians and other captive peoples had been encouraged to hope for aid by these campaign declarations and by broadcasts from the official Voice of America and its unofficial American counterpart, Radio Free Europe, it is impossible to say. It is certain that neither President Eisenhower nor Secretary of State John Foster Dulles intended to encourage a popular rebellion against impossible odds or to assist such a rebellion at the risk of war with the Soviet Union. Even if the United States, or NATO, had wished to intervene in Hungary, it would have been seriously hampered by contemporary events in the Middle East. But it seems clear that no such desire existed. Action by the United States was limited to the expression of sympathy for the Hungarian people, the sponsoring of resolutions by which the U.N. General Assembly futilely called upon the Soviet Union to withdraw its troops, and the offering of asylum in the United States to Hungarian refugees.

It should be added that the United States welcomed such varying degrees of independence from Moscow as were represented by Yugoslavia since 1948 and Poland under Gomulka's once restive government. America had for several years been supplying economic and even military aid to Yugoslavia and now began providing aid to Poland, chiefly in surplus food products. Such aid was based upon the theory that any measure which lessened the dependence of these regimes upon Moscow served the interests of the West.[1]

Berlin and Camp David

The next serious crisis in NATO-Warsaw Pact relations concerned Berlin. In a speech of November 10, 1958, and in notes to the United States, Great Britain, and France on the 27th, Khrushchev demanded an end to the occupation of West Berlin by the three Western powers. In the notes, he insisted upon a solution within six months, threatening otherwise to make a peace treaty with East Germany and leave the Allies to negotiate their rights in Berlin and their access thereto with the East German government which they did not recognize. Any attempt to maintain their position against East Germany by force, Khrushchev warned, would be met by all the power of the Warsaw Alliance.

The Soviet ultimatum—for that is what it appeared to be—received a unified response from the Western powers. In Paris, December 14, the Foreign Ministers of the United States, Great Britain, France, and West Germany joined in an unqualified rejection of the Soviet ultimatum, and their position was endorsed two days later by the NATO Council. The reply of the United States to the Russian note of November 27 was dispatched on December 31. Briefly stated, the Western argument was that the Soviet Union had no right by unilateral action to cancel the rights of the Western Al-

[1] For a different, official view, and one that suggests that the policy of the U.S. should be to make the relationship between Eastern Europe and the U.S.S.R. natural and "organic," see David Binder, "A Modified Soviet Bloc Is Avowed as U.S. Policy," *New York Times*, April 6, 1976, pp. 1, 14.

lies in West Berlin, which were theirs by virtue of the common victory over Germany. The Allies also emphasized their obligation to maintain the freedom of the more than two million people of West Berlin. They expressed their desire to see the Berlin question settled as a part of the German question as a whole and repeated their proposal that Germany be unified through the holding of free elections in both parts of the divided country.

Faced by determined and united Western opposition, Mr. Khrushchev softened the ultimative tone of his demand by letting it be known that the six months time limit need not be taken literally. It was then agreed that the Big Four Foreign Ministers should meet in Geneva in May to discuss Berlin, Germany, European security, and disarmament. It was further understood that if they should make progress toward an accord, their sessions would be followed by another summit meeting, which might perhaps end the cold war. From May 11 to June 30 and again from July 13 to August 5, 1959 the Foreign Ministers met at Geneva. They considered possible compromise solutions for the Berlin question but reached no agreement on this or on any of the other major issues before them. President Eisenhower, who had at first made some preliminary agreement a prerequisite of another summit meeting, now waived that requirement. He invited Nikita Khrushchev—now Chairman of the Council of Ministers of the U.S.S.R., or Premier—to visit him at Camp David, his mountain retreat in Maryland.

The meeting at Camp David, September 25 to 27, 1959, climaxed ten days in which Khrushchev's touring of the United States and his sensational proposal in the United Nations General Assembly of general and complete disarmament had enjoyed continuous spotlight. His conversations with Eisenhower were marked by cordiality on both sides, giving rise to talk of a "spirit of Camp David." The joint communiqué is-

sued at the close of the meeting stated that while the talks were not undertaken to negotiate issues, they had been useful in mutually clarifying the positions of the two leaders and should thus contribute "to the achievement of a just and lasting peace." The two had agreed that the question of general disarmament was "the most important one facing the world today." On the Berlin question they had agreed that, subject to the approval of the other parties concerned, negotiations should be reopened in the hope of reaching a satisfactory solution. It was also agreed, Eisenhower told a news conference and Khrushchev concurred "that these negotiations should not be prolonged indefinitely but there could be no fixed time limit on them." The leaders rejected the use of force in settling "outstanding international questions," and finally they agreed that President Eisenhower should visit the Soviet Union in the following spring, at a date to be arranged through diplomatic channels.

Explosion at the Summit

In December, after the Camp David meeting, Great Britain and France joined the United States in proposing a summit meeting of the Big Four for the following spring. The Russians accepted, and the date was fixed at May 16, 1960, the place, in Paris. Eisenhower's visit to the Soviet Union was to follow in June.

In the months prior to the Paris meeting, the "spirit of Camp David" was clearly deteriorating. There were renewed threats from Khrushchev of drastic action if the Berlin question were not soon settled, and equal assurances from Washington that the United States would never desert the people of West Berlin. Prospects of agreement, growing dim already, were completely destroyed by the Russian reaction to the U-2 incident early in May.

On May 1 a high-flying U.S. reconnaissance plane of the U-2 type was shot down while on a flight across Russia from Pakistan to Norway. The pilot, Francis Gary Powers, was captured unharmed, along with his photographic and other equipment. Khrushchev adroitly held back details while the State Department tried to explain the presence of the U-2 over Russia as the result of a navigational error. But when it became apparent that the Russians "had the goods" on Powers and his flight, Secretary of State Christian A. Herter admitted that the flight of the U-2 was but one of a number of such flights, conducted for the purpose of photographing installations in the Soviet Union. The President confirmed Herter's admission, and both men defended this type of espionage as a means of guarding against surprise attack, necessitated by Russian secretiveness, and as in no way more culpable than other forms of espionage notoriously practiced by the Soviet Union.

It seems evident that Khrushchev and his associates in the Kremlin seized upon the U-2 incident as an excuse for wrecking a summit conference in which they realized the West would never accept their terms for Berlin or Germany. Khrushchev came to Paris and in brutal and boorish language refused to negotiate unless President Eisenhower would, among other things, apologize for the U-2 flight and agree to punish those responsible for it. He also withdrew the invitation to Eisenhower to visit the Soviet Union. He was not mollified by the President's assurance that there would be no more U-2 flights during his term of office or by the conciliatory efforts of President de Gaulle and Prime Minister Macmillan. The summit conference ended abruptly on May 17, one day after its opening.[2]

[2] Powers told the story of his flight and imprisonment in Francis Gary Powers and Curt Gentry, *Operation Overflight: The Story of U-2 Sky Pilot, Francis Gary Powers* (New York: Holt, Rinehart and Winston, 1970).

Khrushchev and Kennedy

In spite of his violent diatribes in Paris, Chairman Khrushchev did not follow up his threat to conclude a peace treaty with the East German regime. On the contrary, he told an audience in East Berlin that the existing situation would have to be preserved until there could be another summit conference, perhaps after six or eight months. It was plain that he hoped to find Eisenhower's successor more yielding.

It was not, however, until June 1961 that Khrushchev and President John F. Kennedy met for a two-day conference in Vienna. Although this meeting was on the surface friendly and courteous, the *aide-mémoire* which Khrushchev handed to the President resurrected the Berlin crisis in much the same terms as before and again with a six months time limit. Unless within that time the four governments could agree on a peace treaty or treaties with Germany, united or divided, the Soviets would conclude a separate treaty with what they called the German Democratic Republic, and occupation rights in West Berlin would terminate. West Berlin might continue as a "free city," and either neutral U.N. troops or "token forces" of the three Western powers and the Soviet Union might be stationed there, but it seemed clear that the city's contacts with the West would be at the mercy of the G.D.R.[3]

The United States replied to the *aide-mémoire* in a note of July 17. The United States had, it averred, together with its British and French Allies, "a fundamental political and moral obligation" to "maintain

For documents on the U-2 flight and the summit conference, see *Documents on American Foreign Relations, 1960*, pp. 106–67. Herter had succeeded John Foster Dulles as Secretary of State upon the latter's resignation in April 1959. Dulles had died of cancer a month later. Macmillan had succeeded Eden after the Suez crisis.

[3] *Documents on American Foreign Relations, 1961*, pp. 137–41.

the freedom of over two million people in West Berlin." Any attempt to hinder the fulfillment of that obligation "would have the gravest effects upon international peace and security and endanger the lives and well-being of millions of people." In a nationwide broadcast, July 25, the President told the country: "We cannot and will not permit the Communists to drive us out of Berlin, either gradually or by force." Remarking that "we do not want to fight, but we have fought before," Mr. Kennedy announced that he was asking Congress for a $3.25 billion increase in the defense budget, for increase in Army, Navy, and Air Force manpower, and for authority to call various reserve units to active duty. By increasing the conventional forces at home and in Europe, the President intended "to have a wider choice than humiliation or all-out nuclear action."[4]

Congress gave the President what he asked for, and an additional force of 45,000 men was moved to Europe. France and West Germany also strengthened their NATO forces. All in all, General Norstad, NATO Supreme Commander, now had twenty-five divisions or the equivalent, most of them in markedly improved fighting condition. Whether or not because of these warlike gestures, Mr. Khrushchev again removed the time limit from his demand for a Berlin settlement. For a time in the early months of 1962, there was Russian harassment of Western planes in the air corridors from West Germany to Berlin, accompanied by other forms of pressure, but after March, the Berlin front was relatively quiet.

But if such concessions relaxed tension at one point, other moves by Khrushchev or his henchmen had the reverse effect. On August 13, 1961, the East German regime began construction of the wall separating

East from West Berlin, thus effectively putting an end to West Berlin's important role as an "escape hatch" from Communist East Germany. The United States responded by protest only. At the end of August, Khrushchev announced the early beginning of a new series of nuclear tests in the atmosphere, ending an informal moratorium begun in 1958, and necessitating further tests by the United States and Great Britain. In December the Soviet government announced a 10 percent increase in its defense budget for 1962, acknowledging at the same time that the original estimates for 1961 had already been increased by nearly one-third. The following year, 1962, was marked by the most dangerous confrontation since 1945—Khrushchev's audacious planting of nuclear missiles in Cuba and his retreat when faced by American firmness. More of this will be discussed later.

The Quest for a Détente with the Soviet Union

After the settlement of the Cuban missile crisis, there seemed some hope for a real improvement of relations between the United States and the U.S.S.R. Both had, apparently, accepted the nuclear stalemate as a reality. The questions of Germany and Berlin were by no means settled; but the successors of Chancellor Adenauer, who retired in October 1963, were less insistent than he upon German reunification as an immediate goal, while on the other hand, the Soviets refrained from creating further crises over Berlin. There were, it is true, sporadic threats and some harassing of transportation into and out of West Berlin on occasions when the West German Bundestag (Parliament) or its committees chose to meet there—illegally from the East German and Russian point of view; but these interferences were short-lived and did not

[4]The note of July 17 and the broadcast of July 25 are printed in *Documents on American Foreign Relations, 1961,* pp. 141–49 and 95–105, respectively.

threaten the life of the city or the security of its Western garrisons.

Under these circumstances Presidents Lyndon B. Johnson (1963–1969), Richard M. Nixon (1969–1974), Gerald R. Ford (1974–1977) and Jimmy Carter (1977–) sought to improve relations with the Soviet Union and, as Johnson phrased it, to "build bridges" of trade and understanding with the smaller nations of Eastern Europe.

Johnson's efforts to improve trade relations with the Communist bloc were hampered by a reluctant Congress, while the war in Vietnam and Soviet support of the Arabs against Israel in the Six-Day War of 1967, and subsequently in the Yom Kippur War of 1973, kept tensions alive between the United States and the U.S.S.R. Until the collapse of American policy in Indochina in 1975, Moscow viewed the war in Vietnam as a "war of national liberation" on one side and a war of United States "aggression" and "imperialism" on the other. The Soviets, therefore, provided war equipment on a generous scale to the armies of North Vietnam, and Premier Kosygin, who together with Communist party chief Leonid I. Brezhnev had replaced Khrushchev in 1964, told the editors of *Life* (February 2, 1968) that "we [the Soviets], for our part will do all we can so that the U.S. does not defeat Vietnam. American aggression," he added, "will be met with growing rebuff." Accordingly, attempts by both Johnson and Nixon to persuade Moscow to assist in bringing Hanoi to accept United States peace terms were, on the whole, futile.

In the Arab-Israeli Six-Day War of June 1967 the Soviet Union, if it did not instigate hostile moves by the Arabs, certainly did not restrain them.[5] It furnished no military aid to the Arabs during this particular round of warfare but was quick, after the ceasefire, to replace the immense stores of military equipment destroyed or captured by the Israelis.

---

[5]The story was much the same in the Yom Kippur War of 1973. See the chapter on the Middle East.

The war gave the Soviets an excuse to move a large naval presence into the Mediterranean, where it monitored the movements of the American Sixth Fleet. This naval force, together with the then-unquestioned friendship of most of the Arab states, gave the Soviet Union a foothold in the Middle East which the most powerful of the Czars would have envied. Conversely, American influence in the area declined.

Eventually the U.S.S.R. and the United States agreed on the Security Council resolution of November 22, 1967, recommending terms of settlement of the Arab-Israeli War, but differed as to interpretation and implementation. Meanwhile, a meeting of President Johnson and Premier Kosygin at Glassboro, New Jersey (June 23, 25, 1967), produced amicable discussion but no agreement on either the Middle East or Vietnam.

President Nixon entered office, January 20, 1969, with high hopes for, as he put it, substituting "negotiations" for "confrontation" in relations with the Soviet Union and for securing Soviet aid in bringing peace to both the Middle East and Vietnam. And though Nixon himself would not survive the Watergate scandal that brought him disgrace and resignation in 1974, it can be argued that progress toward settlement had been made in both areas. For one thing, and for better or worse, America's commitment to Vietnam was liquidated in 1973 with the signing of the Paris Peace Accords. For another, and while it would require an additional and tragic war between Arabs and Israelis—the Yom Kippur War of 1973—the United States would find itself in the enviable position of having displaced Soviet influence in such places as Egypt.

Even before the Nixon Presidency, considerable headway had been made in the negotiation of desirable treaties, both bilateral, between the United States and the Soviet Union, and multilateral, including both as signatories. The Nuclear Test Ban

Treaty of 1963 has already been discussed. A U.S.—Soviet convention was signed in 1964 and ratified four years later. In July 1969 reciprocal arrangements were made for the opening of consulates in San Francisco and Leningrad. A multilateral treaty on the peaceful uses of outer space, signed in January 1967, went into effect later in the year. A treaty to prohibit the placing of nuclear weapons on the seabed beyond any nation's twelve-mile limit, sponsored jointly by the United States and the U.S.S.R., was approved by the U.N. General Assembly's Political Committee in November 1970 and became effective with the ratification of 22 governments. A treaty to halt the spread of nuclear weapons (The Nuclear Nonproliferation Treaty), prepared by the United States and the Soviet Union and overwhelmingly approved by the U. N. General Assembly, was signed by the United States, U.S.S.R., and Britain, and approved by the United States Senate on March 13, 1969. It received the necessary ratifications and went into effect on March 5, 1970, its importance limited by the nonparticipation of France and Communist China.

The hope at the close of 1969 that the long-sought treaty halting competition in nuclear strategic weapons between the superpowers might at last be in sight was premature. The banning of nuclear tests in the atmosphere[6] had not halted the race in nuclear weapons. During 1966 the United States learned that the Soviet Union was pushing the development of both offensive missiles and defensive anti-ballistics missiles (ABMs) in an effort to overcome assumed American superiority, or even a quest for "first strike" capability—the ability to destroy the retaliatory power of an enemy by a surprise attack. In the United States, the Nixon administration, after a long debate in the Senate, resolved to begin laying down a "light" ABM system, known as "Safeguard," theoretically for defense of

missile sites. Both governments, also, were experimenting with the latest offensive improvement, the MIRV (multiple independently targetable re-entry vehicle), an ICBM armed with not one but a number of nuclear warheads, which could be aimed at as many separate targets, cities or missile sites, in the enemy country.[7] Given the enormous costs and potential destructiveness of such weapons systems, common sense and interests behooved the United States and the Soviet Union to stop the race.

The prospect of the deployment of MIRVs by both parties made the need to halt the race particularly urgent. The number and location of ICBMs could be checked by satellite photography, which each party was now assumed to employ as a matter of course. Each party to a limitation agreement would thus be able to check on the performance of its rival as to the number of missiles deployed. But once the deployment of the hydra-headed MIRVs began, there would be no way of determining the number of warheads per missile and hence the total number of the rival's nuclear armaments. If the arms race could not be halted before the deployment of MIRVs had proceeded very far, there was slim chance of halting it at all.[8]

In June 1968 the Kremlin, reacting to a four-year old American proposal, had offered to begin talks on the subject in Geneva in September. The United States promptly agreed, but backed off when Russia invaded Czechoslovakia in August, and the question of arms talks was left to the Nixon administration.

Richard Nixon, who in his campaign for the presidency in 1968 had talked of negotiating "from a position of superiori-

---

[6]France, Communist China, and, more recently, India reserve the right to test in the atmosphere.

[7]American nuclear power rests, essentially, on a "triad" of ICBMs, submarine-launched ballistic missiles on nuclear-powered submarines, and the Strategic Air Command.

[8]The U.S. began MIRVing its ICBMs in 1970 and has since spread the network. In 1975 the U.S.S.R. successfully flight-tested missiles with multiple warheads that could be directed to separate targets.

ty," spoke after his inauguration of "sufficiency" in nuclear arms as an acceptable basis for talks.[9] The change was encouraging, since each of the nuclear giants already had weapons "sufficient" to destroy each other many times over. Nixon showed no haste to begin the talks, however, and delayed action until he was assured Congress would approve deployment of the ABM "Safeguard," which he felt would give him, in the terminology of Henry Kissinger, an added "bargaining chip."[10]

After the Senate's narrow approval of "Safeguard" in August 1969, the administration apprised the Soviets of its readiness to talk, with the result that the Strategic Arms Limitation Talks (SALT) opened at Helsinki, Finland, on November 17, 1969, in a mood of unusual cordiality and unguarded optimism. As it turned out, the optimism was unfounded. Alternating between Helsinki and Vienna and after several years of tough bargaining on both sides, SALT I, as these talks came to be called, did not bear fruit until May 26, 1972. At that time President Nixon and General Secretary Leonid Brezhnev, both committed to a policy of détente,[11] affixed their signatures to two epochal agreements: the Treaty on the Limitation of ABMs and the Interim Agreement on Strategic Offensive Missiles. The ABM treaty, with its protocol of July 1974, stipulated that neither government should deploy more than two ABM systems, a limit subsequently reduced

to one. The Interim Agreement on Strategic Offensive Missiles, on the other side of the coin, sought to limit, among other things, the construction of additional fixed land-based ICBMs, as well as submarine-launched ballistic missiles (SLBMs), the consequence of which was a temporary five-year ceiling on a broad range of offensive missiles.

SALT II talks were aimed at converting the interim agreement into a permanent treaty. Needless to say any treaty that sought to deal with the more delicate problem of placing a limit on the number of strategic offensive weapons each nation was to possess, not to mention determining how many may be armed with multiple warheads, was bound to run into difficulties.[12] To try to break the deadlock, President Gerald Ford, the erstwhile Congressman from Michigan, met with Brezhnev in November 1974 in the so-called Vladivostok Summit. Essentially, the superpowers reached a tentative agreement that SALT II should put a ceiling of 2,400 each on the total number of ICBMs, SLBMs, and heavy bombers and limit the number of missiles that can carry multiple warheads, in this case of each side's total of 2,400, 1320 could be so armed. But no binding treaty had as yet been concluded, although there had been much speculation that then President-elect Jimmy Carter expected negotiations to be completed by October 1977 when the first such agreement expired.[13]

In any case, Brezhnev reciprocated Nixon's trip to Moscow in 1972 with a trip to the United States in June 1973 at which time both leaders initialed an accord titled The Prevention of Nuclear War, in which it was hoped that each side would avoid increasing tensions and would consult in dangerous situations. This together with

---

[9]Comparable expressions include "strategic parity" and "essential equivalence."

[10]Henry Kissinger was President Nixon's National Security Adviser until August 1973 at which time he replaced William P. Rogers as Secretary of State.

[11]While generally aimed at a reduction of tensions, the policy of détente has become to mean different things to each side. For a comparison of these meanings on the Soviet and American side, see respectively Brezhnev's comments at the 25th Congress of the Soviet Communist Party in February 1976, *New York Times*, February 25, 1976, p. 14 and Secretary of State Kissinger's interview in *U.S. News and World Report*, March 15, 1976, pp. 24–28.

[12]See Paul H. Nitze, "Assuring Strategic Stability in An Era of Détente," *Foreign Affairs*, 54 (January, 1976), 207–232.

[13]The new agreement covers the period from October 1977 to December 1985.

other progress in the field of commercial and economic relations,[14] peaceful uses of atomic energy, and cultural exchanges seemed to augur well for Soviet-American relations. With the coming of the Yom Kippur War in October and the resulting great power confrontation, however, many began to ask, undoubtedly in both countries, what, if anything, détente was all about.

In many respects, one of the most significant advances in American-Soviet cooperation was in the area of limiting underground atomic tests. In May 1976 the United States and the U.S.S.R. signed a treaty limiting the size of the underground nuclear explosions for peaceful purposes, including, for the first time, provisional on-site inspection of compliance. The treaty, scheduled to run for five years, complemented a 1974 pact limiting the yield of underground tests of nuclear weapons. Both treaties set upper limits of 150 kilotons—the impact of 150,000 tons of TNT—for single detonations, the 1976 treaty also allowing for a series of detonations up to 1.5 megatons—1,500 kilotons. On-site inspection became obligatory in the case of explosions of more than 150 kilotons, though neither country had as yet gone above that mark. These treaties still await ratification.

NATO in Trouble

The relations of the United States with the Soviet Union were not separable from those of NATO with the Warsaw Alliance. NATO in its second and third decades had lost much of its cohesiveness and at least some of its importance. As the apparent danger of Soviet aggression declined, so did the bond that held the diverse members of the alliance together, and rifts appeared in the structure. Many of these were minor. Europeans, understandably, resented an American habit of making unilateral decisions on defense and other matters. Americans, in turn, felt that the NATO nations of a newly prosperous Europe were carrying less than their fair share of the burden of common defense. Some Americans deplored the failure of most of the NATO allies to sympathize with and support American policy in Vietnam, Communist China, Cuba, and more recently the Middle East. The United States furthermore found its neighbor to the north, Canada, less than cooperative in continental defense policy during the prime ministership of John Diefenbaker (1957–1963), though this trend reversed itself somewhat under Pierre Trudeau. Portugal, for its part, resented its allies' faultfinding with its colonial policy in Africa and threatened to deny them the use of bases in the Azores. In the mid-1970s Portugal's domestic upheavals caused the United States no small concern. Greece and Turkey continued to quarrel over Cyprus, thereby rendering NATO's right flank vulnerable. And Italy, which increasingly relied on the support of the Italian Communists to function,[15] caused NATO to pause over the prospect of bringing local Communists into policy making with its attendant access to classified material.

De Gaulle Sabotages NATO

These misunderstandings and problems seemed of minor importance as compared with the aftermath of the partial defection

---

[14]Soviet expectation of U.S. loans and most-favored-nation status for imports was stalled in the U.S. Senate when concessions were linked to a freer Russian emigration policy.

[15]See Vincent P. DeSantis's "Italy and the Cold War," in *The Impact of the Cold War: Reconsiderations,* edited by Joseph M. Siracusa and Glen Barclay (Port Washington, N.Y.: Kennikat Press Corp., 1977), pp. 26–39.

of France under Charles de Gaulle (1958–1969). Called to power in France in June 1958 as the successor to a series of weak governments, de Gaulle quickly restored stability to French political life and ended the exhausting colonial war in Algeria, much to the satisfaction of the United States. But de Gaulle, the wartime leader of the Free French, was dissatisfied with France's relatively minor role in world politics compared with that of the "Anglo-Saxons" as he was fond of saying. When President Eisenhower rejected his proposal for a three-power directorate—France, Britain, and the United States to guide the policies of NATO—de Gaulle repeatedly took positions antagonistic to the United States—recognizing Communist China, condemning American policy in Vietnam, catering to anti-Americanism in Latin America, encouraging French separatism in Quebec, siding with the Arabs against Israel in the Six-Day War of 1967, and rebuffing the United States as well as England in barring the United Kingdom from the European Economic Community (Common Market), a situation remedied in 1973, three years after de Gaulle's death.

Most serious, however, was de Gaulle's policy toward NATO, a policy characterized by his fervent nationalism. In opposition to American policy, he insisted that France must have, at great expense, her independent nuclear force, or *force de frappe*. To justify the enormous costs involved, he warned the French people and their European allies that the United States would not defend Western Europe at the cost of a nuclear exchange with the Soviet Union.[16] He gave assurances that France would fulfill her obligations under the North Atlantic Treaty but rejected, so far as

he was concerned, the idea of a unified command—a fundamental concept of NATO. Measures of partial withdrawal from the command structure—detachment of the French Mediterranean fleet, denial of base and air rights to nuclear-armed American planes, and so forth,—climaxed in March 1966, when the French President served notice to all NATO military installations, including headquarters at SHAPE, that they must leave French soil by April 1, 1967. Even before that date French officers were withdrawn from all SHAPE's planning committees.

NATO headquarters, civil as well as military, were moved to Belgium within the time allowed. France continued as an ally and made no move to withdraw when NATO's first twenty years ended in 1969. But the armed forces of France, the geographical and military keystone to the defense of Western Europe, could no longer be counted upon to take orders from SHAPE, and the problems of the Supreme Commander in the event of an attack from the East were greatly complicated. De Gaulle's passing from the scene failed to improve matters, as his successors continued to pursue an independent nuclear force replete with atomic bombers, second generation ICBMs, and a modest nuclear submarine fleet. Furthermore, the French made no secret that they would respond to a threat of Soviet invasion with the immediate use of tactical nuclear weapons in contrast to NATO's policy of "flexible response," which relies in the first instance on conventional warfare rather than on nuclear weapons.[17]

In the late 1960s other nations followed France, not in detaching their forces from SHAPE but in reducing the number of forces readily available. The United States, where the maintenance of 350,000 troops in Europe contributed (with the war in Vietnam) to a chronic foreign exchange

---

[16]It was partly to counteract de Gaulle's influence and to assure the German people that they could count upon American protection that President Kennedy visited Bonn and West Berlin in June 1963, declaring in the latter city: "Today, in the world of freedom the proudest boast is *'Ich bin ein Berliner.'* "

[17]*New York Times*, December 23, 1973.

deficit, transferred 35,000 troops from Europe to American soil in 1967, though these troops were still committed to NATO and could be returned to Europe on short notice. Britain took similar action with 6,500 of her 51,000 troops on the continent. Canada, two years later in 1969, announced that it would cut its ground troops and air force in Europe by almost 50 percent. And West Germany reduced her projected contribution to NATO forces from 508,000 to 400,000 men.[18]

As Democratic Senate Leader Mike Mansfield called year after year for a "substantial reduction" of American forces in Europe, the further reduction of NATO troops seemed likely. This move was successfully resisted by Presidents from Johnson to Nixon, and the Senate defeated Mansfield's amendment in May, 1971, by a vote of 61–36. By mid-1976, and in the face of a new set of circumstances—the steady buildup of Soviet military power—the United States pledged to increase its army in Europe from 13 to 16 divisions, with the intention of stationing a new army brigade on the critical sector of the North German plain. This decision combined with the work of America's European allies in the area of standardization and interoperation of common forces, suggests that NATO still held the imagination, if not always the allegiance, of its many parts.[19]

The Road to Helsinki

Weakening and revival of commitments to NATO were the result, actually, of fluctuating skepticism as to the reality of the danger of Soviet aggression. Such doubts grew as tension over Berlin relaxed and the

[18]*U. S. in World Affairs,* 1967, pp. 201–204; *New York Times,* September 20, 1969, pp. 1, 4.

[19]Secretary of State Henry Kissinger's Alistair Buchan Memorial Lecture, London, June 25, 1976. Courtesy of the United States Information Service.

U.S.S.R. became more deeply involved in her quarrel with Communist China in the 1960s. Western fears were reawakened, however, when Russian-led Warsaw troops invaded Czechoslovakia in 1968 to suppress a liberalizing program in that Communist state. In justification of this action, General Secretary Brezhnev proclaimed, in what came to be known as the Brezhnev Doctrine or in party jargon "defense of proletarian internationalism," the right of the Soviet Union to intervene in any state of the Communist bloc to preserve the integrity of the socialist system.

More alarming than the Brezhnev Doctrine were the arrival on the Czechoslovak-West German frontier of five Russian divisions and a statement from Moscow that Articles 53 and 107 of the U.N. Charter gave the Soviet Union the right to intervene in West Germany, a former enemy state. Not surprisingly, the threat brought about a more cooperative attitude on the part of France and led the governments of France, Britain and the United States to warn the Kremlin to keep hands off the German Federal Republic. The Moscow threat was probably bluff; it was not followed up, and the relaxation of tensions was resumed.

In March 1969, at Budapest, the Warsaw Pact powers proposed a conference on security by nations of East and West Europe, the consequence of which would be an official endorsement of Soviet territorial gains from World War II in exchange, presumably, for a more accommodating attitude on the part of the Communist nations. Nothing came of the proposal, and in October of that year the Warsaw Pact powers tried again, proposing Helsinki as a meeting place and—a novel feature in such proposals—leaving open the possibility that the United States and Canada might be included. NATO's reply came from Brussels at the end of a three-day meeting at the Council. The communiqué issued in December, declared that the NATO governments were "receptive" to suggestions on "measures to reduce tension and promote cooperation in Europe," but stipulated that "prospects of concrete results" would be essential to their consent to the proposed conference. Listed as such "concrete results" were free access to West Berlin, a working agreement between East and West Germany, and an agreement on reduction of armed forces in Europe. It was reported that these preconditions for a conference were insisted upon by the United States over the objection of a number of European allies, leading one American commentator to deplore Washington's attitude "that we can't enter a conference unless we know in advance what its outcome will be."[20]

But while NATO as a whole hesitated, Chancellor Willy Brandt was making promising moves toward détente with the Communist bloc directly. As Foreign Minister in the coalition cabinet of Chancellor Kurt Georg Kiesinger (1966–1969), he had refrained from pushing for reunification of Germany as an immediate goal and had dropped the demand of the previous regime of Ludwig Erhard (1963–1966) for access to nuclear weapons. He had also violated an unofficial West German taboo by offering to recognize the Oder-Neisse line as Germany's eastern boundary, thus surrendering claims to the formerly German territory occupied since 1945 by Poland and the U.S.S.R.

As Chancellor, after the victory of the Social Democrats in the German elections of September 1969, Brandt proposed to negotiate agreements renouncing the use or threat of force with the nations of Eastern Europe, agreements that would also guarantee mutual respect for the territorial integrity of the signers, thus in effect assuring Poland and Czechoslovakia against any

German irredentist claims. While still unwilling to recognize East Germany as a sovereign state and insisting that all Germany was really one, Brandt stated his government's willingness to work for "contractually agreed cooperation" with East Germany and to abandon attempts to interfere with East Germany's economic and cultural relations with other nations.[21]

Meetings between Chancellor Brandt and East German Premier Willi Stoph, in March and May 1970, met an obstacle in Stoph's insistence that Bonn accord full diplomatic recognition to East Germany as an independent sovereign state. The meetings were not resumed until December, but meanwhile talks by Bonn with Warsaw and Moscow were more productive. The Moscow talks reached a culmination on August 7, when the Soviet and West German Foreign Ministers initialed a treaty by which both governments renounced the use of force in their mutual relations and agreed to respect existing national boundaries. In accompanying notes, the Bonn government reserved the right to seek the unification of Germany by peaceful means and assured the Western Allies that the treaty in no way infringed their rights in Berlin.

Three months later, in a treaty with Poland, West Germany accepted the Oder-Neisse line as Poland's border with Germany. And while treaties with Czechoslovakia and Hungary were expected to follow, Chancellor Brandt made it perfectly clear that neither the Soviet nor other treaties would be submitted to the Reichstag until East Germany agreed to relax tensions in Berlin and to ease restrictions on intercourse between Berlin and West Germany.

Additional hopes for relief of these tensions were found in the resumption, in Berlin, after twenty-two years, of amicable discussions of the Berlin question between

---

[20]*New York Times*, December 6, 1969, pp. 1, 14. Brzezinski, "Détente in the 70s," *The New Republic*, January 3, 1970, pp. 17–18.

[21]*New York Times*, October 29, 1969, p. 10.

delegates of the four occupying powers. Beginning in March 1970, these talks took place with increasing frequency from late June until at the 33rd meeting on August 23, it was officially announced that the draft text of the settlement, known as the Quadripartite treaty, had been agreed upon. The four ambassadors—the British, French, and United States ambassadors to West Germany on the one side and the Soviet ambassador to the German Democratic Republic on the other—signed the first part of the agreement and initialed the last part on September 3 at the former Allied Control Council building. The heart of the treaty was the section dealing with the critically-exposed Western access to Berlin, the U.S.S.R. pledging to make traffic unimpeded between them and the Federal Republic of Germany.

In the meantime talks between East and West Germany on mutual relations, which had begun in November 1970 bore fruit in December 1971 with the conclusion of a number of agreements aimed at implementing the terms of the Quadripartite treaty. In January 1972 the two governments then proceeded to open negotiations with a view to concluding a traffic treaty between the two German states. Successfully concluded in April of that year, the treaty was signed in East Berlin on May 26. Furthermore, the Quadripartite treaty itself came into effect with the signature of the final protocol by the foreign ministers of the four occupying powers on June 3, the same day, it should be noted, as the exchange of instruments of ratification of the treaties between West Germany and the U.S.S.R. and Poland. Thus, despite animosities that were never very far below the surface, the principals in a changing concept of the Cold War were able to come to terms on what had once been the world's premier flashpoint.

On another front, and after much preparation, the heads of the 35 nations of Europe, plus the United States and Canada

but minus Albania, came together in Helsinki in late summer 1975 to sign the so-called "final act" of the Conference on Security and Cooperation in Europe, the Helsinki Conference for short. The high-water mark of détente, the Helsinki Conference declared the current frontiers of Europe "inviolable," thereby endorsing the Soviet Union's postwar territorial gains and its hegemony in Eastern Europe, but not excluding the alteration of borders by "peaceful agreement."[22] This latter agreement thus left open the prospect of a German reunification in the future, though here again the West had few illusions. In return, the NATO countries hoped to induce Moscow and the Warsaw powers to open themselves to a freer flow of people and ideas and a reaffirmation of the dignity of the individual. Needless to say, there was no shortage of critics to point out that Communist-dominated police states do not work this way.[23] Only the future will tell.

Whatever the merits of détente,[24] none could doubt that the decade of the 1970s had witnessed profound changes in the character, if not the conduct, of United States foreign policy. The Vietnam experience had left its mark on Presidents and Congress alike, the result being a less idealistic but, at the same time, a more pragmatic attitude toward the outside world and its problems. More importantly, the traditional adversary relationship that

[22]*New York Times*, August 2, 1975. Parallel negotiations, which originated with a NATO offer in May 1970 to discuss "mutual and balanced force reductions" with the Warsaw Pact powers, had stalled in the meantime and had achieved little by the end of 1978.

[23]For example, George F. Kennan's remarks in *Encounter*, 47 (September 1976), p. 42; and Alexander Solzhenitsyn's *Warning to the Western World* (London: The Bodley Head and British Broadcasting Corporation, 1976).

[24]Interestingly, during the 1976 Presidential campaign President Ford felt compelled to remove the word "détente" from his political vocabulary for fear that the word had become identified with being "soft" on the Soviet Union, and thereby a political liability.

had animated American-Soviet relations since 1945 had undergone a fundamental shift away from ideology to practical problems. Perhaps no one statement of the period illustrates the point more than President Nixon's commencement address at the U.S. Naval Academy in June 1974. At the height of Congressional efforts to block the proposed Soviet-American trade treaty with its most-favored-nation status for Russian imports, the President put the Cold War to rest, at least in the form that it had originally been conceived. Nixon observed that while "We can never acquiesce in the suppression of human liberties. . . . [and] do all that we reasonably can to promote peace," there were limits to America's "capability to change the domestic structure of other nations." Holding that the primary responsibility of the nation was to prevent nuclear catastrophe, the President concluded that "We would not welcome the intervention of other countries in our domestic affairs, and we cannot expect them to be cooperative when we seek to intervene directly in theirs." Thus, officially, ended the spirit of one age and began the beginning of a new one.[25] Or, so it was hoped.

[25]Joseph M. Siracusa, "Lessons of Vietnam and the Future of American Foreign Policy," *Australian Outlook: Journal of the Australian Institute of International Affairs,* 30 (1976), pp. 230–31.

ADDITIONAL READINGS

BRANDON, HENRY, *The Retreat of Power.* New York: Doubleday, 1973.

BUCHAN, ALISTAIR, *NATO in the 1960's.* New York: Praeger Publishers, Inc., 1960.

FRYE, ALTON, "Strategic Restraint, Mutual and Assured," *Foreign Policy,* 27 (Summer, 1977), 3-26.

KENNAN, GEORGE F., *Cloud of Danger.* Boston: Little Brown, 1977.

KUBÁLKOVÁ, V., and A. A. CRUICSHANK, *Marxism-Leninism and the Theory of International Relations.* London: Routledge & Keegan Paul, 1979.

McLELLAN, DAVID S., "The Changing Nature of Soviet and American Relations with Western Europe," *Annals of the American Academy of Political and Social Science,* 372 (1967), 16-32.

MORRIS, ROGER, *Uncertain Greatness.* New York: Harper & Row, Publishers, 1977.

OSGOOD, ROBERT E., *The Entangling Alliance.* Chicago: University of Chicago Press, 1962.

POLMAR, NORMAN, *Strategic Weapons: An Introduction.* New York: Crane, Russak & Co., 1975.

ROBERTS, CHALMERS M., *The Nuclear Years: The Arms Race and Arms Control.* New York: Praeger Publishers, Inc. 1970.

STEIBEL, GERALD L., *Détente: Promises and Pitfalls.* New York: Crane, Russak & Co., 1975.

22. The Postwar Far East, I: Beginnings—The Korean War

For the postwar Far East the United States had, if not a program, at least a rather clear ideal. This ideal may be defined as anticolonialism or, more affirmatively, nationalism. Japan, in the first place, was to disgorge all the territories that she had taken at the expense of other nationalities. She was, furthermore, to be so thoroughly demilitarized and democratized that she would have neither the power nor the will to begin a new career of conquest. China, freed from the inequalities that she had endured for a century, was to be recognized as one of the great powers and to be assisted in becoming strong, united, and democratic. Korea, as had been promised at Cairo, was to become, "in due course," free and independent. In Southern and Southeast Asia, where Japanese conquest had weakened the fabric of European colonialism and given an impetus to nationalistic movements, progress toward independence was to be encouraged. Determined to carry out its prewar promise of independence for the Philippines in 1946, the United States was anxious to push other colonial powers—Great Britain, France, the Netherlands—along the path it had chosen for itself. Anticolonialism was, in fact, an old American ideal, which the nation had repudiated only partially and temporarily at the turn of the century.

If the general purpose was fairly clear, the performance was inconsistent and faltering, and the result more failure than success. The aim for China had been compromised in the agreement at Yalta, by which the Soviet Union was to be restored to the privileged position in Manchuria which Russia of the Czars had enjoyed before 1904. The Soviets, it is true, later surrendered most of these special privileges, but only after, in a major defeat for American policy, China had become a Communist state. The victory of home-grown Communism in China and China's subsequent alliance with the Soviet Union increased the danger that the Asiatic colonies of European powers might be added to the Communist empire instead of becoming free nations on the Western pattern, for Communism was skillful in allying itself with Asiatic nationalism against the remnants of Western imperialism. The break between Peking and Moscow, which began in the late fifties and reached the brink of war in 1969, destroyed once and for all, the image of a monolithic world Communism, widely accepted in the United States, but the fact that Russia and China were now rivals instead of partners in spreading their gospel to the former colonial lands did not end the threat. There was danger, therefore, that in southern Asia, as in China, the victory of nationalism would be accompanied by subversion to Communism. The American conviction that here, as in Europe, Communism must be "contained" produced an Asiatic phase of the cold war, which, unlike that in Europe, became sporadically a hot war, as in Korea and later in Vietnam.

Thirty-two years after Japan's surrender Western imperialism in Asia was dead, but Communism had made impressive gains.

China, Indochina, and parts of Korea had slipped behind the Iron Curtain, or the "Bamboo Curtain," as it was sometimes called in this area. Great Britain had granted independence to India, Pakistan, Ceylon, Burma, Malaya, Singapore, and other minor colonies. All except Burma had elected to remain within the British Commonwealth. In 1963, Singapore, North Borneo, and Sarawak were federated with Malaya to form Malaysia, but Singapore resumed its independence two years later. India, Ceylon, and Burma preferred neutralism to alignment with the West in the cold war. The states of former French Indochina had won their independence, but North Vietnam was Communist, and the ill-fated U.S.-South Vietnamese war to save South Vietnam from Communism had spilled over into nominally neutral Cambodia and Laos and had involved independent Thailand. Indonesia, with U.S. encouragement, had won its independence from the Netherlands. Its demagogic leader, Sukarno, was on the verge of forming an alliance with Communist China when the Army (following an abortive premature attempt at a Communist coup, September 30, 1965) seized power and steered the nation back onto a neutral course, though friendly to the West. In Indonesia, in the former British colonies, in the Philippines, and in Japan, the United States could see some realization of its hopes of 1945.

Toward a Democratic and Peaceful Japan

Japan escaped the divided control that frustrated reconstruction in Germany and Austria. General Douglas MacArthur, bearing the title Supreme Commander for the Allied Powers (SCAP), received his orders from Washington. A Russian request to share in the occupation was refused. This refusal and the assumption by the United States of unilateral control over Japan offended the Russians and may have contributed to their uncooperative attitude in Europe and China. At the Foreign Ministers Conference in Moscow (December 1945), the United States made concessions in form rather than substance. Thereafter, a four-power Allied Council for Japan, representing the United States, the Soviet Union, the British Commonwealth, and China, sat in Tokyo; it could advise the Supreme Commander but not compel him. A Far Eastern Commission in Washington, speaking for the eleven powers that had fought against Japan,[1] in theory made policy for the Occupation; in reality it acquiesced in SCAP's decisions.

General MacArthur's regal bearing and magisterial language appealed to the same Japanese traits that accounted for Emperor-worship. The people of the islands submitted to his rule with surprising docility and accepted, at least superficially, reforms that revolutionized their way of life. Japan's once great empire was cut down to the four islands that had formed her domain at the time of Commodore Perry's visit in 1853. Her armed forces were abolished, her war industries liquidated. In the new constitution, prepared by SCAP and put into effect May 3, 1947, the Japanese people "forever renounce[d] war as a sovereign right of the nation" and agreed that "land, sea, and air forces, as well as other war potential, will never be maintained. The right of belligerency of the state will not be recognized." War criminals were punished; some, such as the war Premier, General Tojo, with the death penalty. Political life was purged of those individuals who could be held most responsible for Japan's war policy. On the theory that democracies are pacific, the new con-

[1]The U.S., the U.S.S.R., the United Kingdom, China, France, the Netherlands, Canada, Australia, New Zealand, India, the Philippines. The Commission was enlarged to thirteen, November 17, 1949, by the addition of Burma and Pakistan.

stitution, although retaining the monarchy, placed all power in the representatives of the people. These were to be chosen by extremely democratic procedures, including the novelty of female suffrage. The Emperor conformed to the new spirit. In his New Year's Rescript, January 1, 1946, he repudiated "the false conception that the Emperor is divine and that the Japanese people are superior to other races and fated to rule the world." By dissolving the great industrial and commercial combines, the Zaibatsu, and by consigning all but the smallest landed estates to peasant proprietorship, the Occupation attempted to democratize economic life. Educational reform accompanied these political and economic transformations. The dissolution of the Zaibatsu did not long outlast the military occupation: the other reforms promised to be more permanent.

The complete demilitarization of Japan, like that of Germany, was undertaken in the naive faith that the Soviet Union would continue friendly and cooperative with the West. Discovery that that faith was false suggested an entirely different approach to the Japanese problem. The change became imperative when China was drawn into the Soviet orbit.

First Postwar Steps in China

At the Yalta Conference, Stalin, in return for concessions given him at China's expense, had offered to make a treaty of alliance with the Nationalist government of China and to assist in liberating China from the Japanese invaders. To United States Ambassador Hurley, who stopped in Moscow on his way to Chungking, and to Messrs. Hopkins and Harriman later, Stalin gave assurances that he wished to see China unified under Chiang Kai-shek, that he would not support the Chinese Communists, that he would respect Chinese sovereignty in Manchuria and the open-

door principle.[2] When the secret of the Yalta agreement was revealed to Chiang Kai-shek, qualified with these assurances, he expressed disappointment but did not seem greatly perturbed. He sent T. V. Soong to Moscow to negotiate an agreement with the Soviet Union. The treaty and agreements which Soong signed August 14, 1945, were generally in accord with the Yalta promises.

The treaty was one of friendship and alliance against Japan. Both parties promised cooperation to bring about Japan's defeat and to prevent a repetition of her aggression. They promised respect for each other's sovereignty and territorial integrity and noninterference in each other's internal affairs. Notes and agreements signed at the same time as the treaty provided for independence of Outer Mongolia if a plebiscite showed this to be the desire of the people; status of Dairen as a free port; joint use of Port Arthur as a naval base by the Soviet Union and China; the establishment of Chinese civil administration in Manchuria *pari passu* with the completion of Soviet military operations; joint ownership and management of the Chinese Changchun Railway, comprising the former Chinese Eastern and South Manchurian Railways. Reassuring to the Chinese were a reaffirmation by the Soviet Union of respect for "China's full sovereignty" over Manchuria and, especially, a promise that support and assistance would "be entirely given to the National Government as the central government of China." The last promise, if observed, would eliminate the danger of Soviet support for the Chinese Communists.[3]

[2] Herbert Feis, *The China Tangle: The American Effort in China from Pearl Harbor to the Marshall Mission* (Princeton: Princeton University Press, 1953), pp. 284–89, 309–12.

[3] The texts of all these agreements are printed in *United States Relations with China,* Department of State Publication 3573. (Washington: Department of State, 1949), pp. 585–96.

Publication of this group of agreements was well received in the United States, the *New York Times* hailing it as a "victory for peace as great as any scored on the battlefield." With Sino-Soviet relations apparently harmonized, the United States could proceed with the development of its policy for the creation of a "strong, united, and democratic China." American postwar policy toward China was based on the fallacious belief, common at the time, that Communists and Kuomintang men could work together in a democratic government, not unlike Republicans and Democrats in the United States. General Stilwell had sought during the war to bring the two groups together for united opposition to the Japanese invaders. With the war over, the peaceful unification of China became an immediate aim of United States policy. In the fall of 1945, United States Ambassador Patrick J. Hurley brought the Communist leader, Mao Tse-tung, to Chungking, where he spent six weeks in negotiations with Chiang Kai-shek. The two parted on apparently friendly terms, announcing that they had reached agreement on the majority of points in dispute and were not too far apart on the remainder.

In the meantime, while Chiang's Nationalist forces, with American aid, were reoccupying the coastal area of China and most of its large cities, Communist armies continued to hold large areas of the interior in the Northwest and North and were filtering into Manchuria. Here they took over arms and supplies from the surrendering Japanese and were soon receiving, *sub rosa*, assistance and cooperation from the Russians in direct contravention of recent Russian promises.[4] Armed clashes between Nationalists and Communists occurred with increasing frequency. It was evident that only energetic action by the United States could save China from disastrous civil war.

The Marshall Mission

To carry out this delicate mission, and to replace Ambassador Hurley who resigned in November 1945, President Truman picked General George C. Marshall, who had just retired as Army Chief of Staff. Marshall was directed to seek, first, a truce in the fighting; and second, political unification through a conference of Nationalists, Communists, and other groups. He was given considerable discretion in the use of persuasion and pressure, but it was made plain that the existing Nationalist government, "the only legal government in China," was to form the foundation of the new political structure. That government, President Truman stated publicly, "is the proper instrument to achieve the objective of a unified China."[5]

Marshall's China mission lasted throughout the year 1946. After a promising beginning, during which the Communists apparently agreed to accept a minority position in a unified government and a subordinate position in a unified army, the two factions fell to fighting again, and nothing that Marshall could do could halt the drift into full-scale civil war. Marshall came home in December. His report, dated January 7, 1947, blamed the failure of his mission on "extremist elements on both sides." Between the Communists, who "frankly state that they are Marxists," and the conservative leaders of the Kuomintang, Marshall saw no hope of a compromise settlement.[6]

[4]There is reason to believe that Stalin at first intended to keep his promise not to aid the Communists. He is reported to have told the Yugoslav Vice Premier later that he had directed the Chinese Communists to drop their opposition to Chiang Kai-shek and take part in his government, but that they disobeyed his directive. Vladimir Dedijer, *Tito* (New York: Simon & Shuster, Inc., 1953), pp. 331–32.

[5]Feis, *The China Tangle*, chap. 37; *U.S. Relations with China*, pp. 607–9.

[6]*U.S. Relations with China*, pp. 686–89. Marshall was immediately appointed Secretary of State.

The Downfall of Chiang Kai-shek

The end of Marshall's mission meant also the end of the American effort at mediation in China's internal politics. The United States continued to recognize the government of Chiang Kai-shek as the legitimate government of China but was unwilling to give Chiang the massive military aid and cooperation that alone might have enabled him to win his war against the Communists.[7] The United States government had lost faith in Chiang's ability to solve China's problems. It was now, furthermore, committed to fostering European recovery under the Marshall Plan and to succoring Greece and Turkey with both economic and military aid. As during the war, Europe came first and China was relegated to a secondary position.

There followed a rapid deterioration in the position of the Nationalist government and a series of victories by the Communists that gave them control of all mainland China by the end of 1949. In December Chiang withdrew to Formosa (Taiwan), where he set up his new capital at Taipei. Incompetent military leadership and a collapse in morale, rather than lack of military supplies, accounted for the débacle. In fact, great quantities of American-made military matériel were surrendered to the Communists.[8]

The People's Republic of China

In September 1949, a Chinese People's Consultative Conference met at Peiping (to which the Communists now restored its ancient name of Peking) and produced a constitution for the People's Republic of China. The constitution followed closely the Soviet pattern. There was window dressing indicative of democratic character, but all real power was lodged in the Communist party or its leaders. The new government was inaugurated October 1, with Mao Tse-tung holding the office equivalent to the presidency and Chou En-lai as Premier and Foreign Minister. The Soviet Union and its satellites promptly recognized the new government as that of China, and a new treaty, signed in Moscow February 14, 1950, sealed an alliance between the Soviet Union and Communist China— a defensive alliance against aggression "by Japan or states allied with it."[9]

The People's Republic of China was recognized not only by the Soviet Union, its satellites, and Yugoslavia, but (after Chiang's flight from the mainland) by Great Britain and a number of other non-Communist governments in both Europe and Asia. The United States was one of numerous governments that withheld recognition from Peking and continued to regard the Nationalist government on Formosa as the government of China. Certainly by the arrest and barbarous treatment of American consular officers, businessmen, and missionaries, and by its denunciation of "American imperialism," the People's Republic of China did nothing to invite recognition by the United States.

But although withholding recognition and opposing admission of "Red China" to the United Nations, the United States had apparently reconciled itself, at least at the beginning of 1950, to the prospect of Red China's taking over Formosa as well as the

---

[7]General Albert C. Wedemeyer, sent to China on a tour of investigation in the summer of 1947, advised that the United States give "moral, advisory and material support to China" on a large scale. He believed an advisory group of 10,000 officers and other qualified persons would be needed to effect the necessary reforms in Chiang's military establishment. *U.S. Relations with China*, p. 814. The text of Wedemeyer's report, not made public till 1949, is in ibid., pp. 764–814.

[8]*U.S. Relations with China*, pp. 299–300.

[9]After signing the treaty of alliance with the Peking government, the Soviet Union agreed to withdraw Russian troops from the Port Arthur area and to surrender to China its share in the Chinese Changchun Railway. It later agreed to assist in building two new railroads connecting China with Siberia and with Soviet Central Asia.

mainland. To congressional proposals that the United States should occupy, or at least defend, Formosa, President Truman responded in a statement of January 5, 1950, that the United States had no intention of establishing bases on Formosa or of providing "military aid or advice" to the Chinese forces there. A week later, in a speech defining the "defensive perimeter" of the United States in the Far East, Secretary of State Dean Acheson omitted Formosa (as well as Korea) from the areas that the United States considered it necessary to defend. Then, within a few months, the picture was changed by the war in Korea.

The Two Koreas

Primarily for the purpose of receiving the surrender of Japanese troops, Korea was divided at the 38th parallel into a Russian and an American zone. There was no thought, on the part of the United States, of a permanent division. The two parts of the country were complementary: the north supplied the electric power and most of the industry; the south was agricultural. The Russians, however, lowered the Iron Curtain at the 38th parallel. North of the line, local government was organized on a Communist basis; south of it, provisional organs of government had a rightist tinge. The American and Soviet Foreign Ministers, at Moscow in December 1945 and again in March 1947, agreed to direct the military commanders in Korea to confer upon setting up a government for a united Korea. The conferences failed because of disagreement as to the Korean groups that were to be represented in the proposed government. Finally, the United States placed the issue before the General Assembly of the United Nations. That body, in November 1947, appointed a Temporary Commission on Korea and directed it to hold elections for a constituent assembly.

Excluded from the Russian zone, the Commission held elections in southern Korea. The assembly thus chosen drew up a constitution for the Republic of Korea, which was inaugurated at the old capital of Seoul in August 1948. Dr. Syngman Rhee, who had been educated and had long resided in the United States, became President.

North of the 38th parallel the Russians organized a Democratic People's Republic of Korea, with seat of government at Pyongyang and with Kim Il Sung as President. Thus there were two Korean governments, one recognized by the U.S.S.R. and its satellites; the other, by the United States and the U.N. Assembly, though a Russian veto in the Security Council blocked its admission as a U.N. member. Each government aspired to extend its rule over the entire peninsula. Each had its army, that in the north trained and supplied by the Russians, that in the south by the Americans. But the Russians had equipped the northern army with tanks and heavy artillery; the Americans— largely because of Syngman Rhee's unconcealed ambition to conquer the north—had provided defensive weapons only, mostly small arms and light artillery. When the occupying armies withdrew, therefore— the Russians in 1948, the Americans by June 1949—the People's Republic in North Korea had a decided military advantage over its southern rival.

Hot War in Korea

The withdrawal from Korea of United States armed forces (with the exception of a military advisory group of about 400) perhaps created the impression that the United States would not defend the Republic of Korea against attack from the north. Such an impression would have been strengthened by certain pronouncements from Washington. In particular, Secretary of State Acheson, in an address to the National Press Club, January 12, 1950, described the "defensive perimeter" of the United States in the Pacific (as had General MacArthur) as running through the Aleutians, Japan, the Ryukyus, and the Philippines. Areas beyond that line, he said, could not be guaranteed against military attack. Should an attack occur in such an area (for example, Korea),

> the initial reliance must be on the people attacked to resist it and then upon the commitments of the entire civilized world under the Charter of the United Nations which so far has not proved a weak reed to lean on by any people who are determined to protect their independence against outside aggression.[10]

The Acheson statement, though certainly not a "green light" for aggression, did hold out the rather vague prospect of United Nations action instead of a warning that the United States would regard an attack on South Korea as a threat to its own security.

Whatever the reasoning behind the Iron Curtain, the North Koreans, on the morning of June 25, 1950 (Korean time), launched a well organized attack along the entire width of the 38th parallel. Within a few hours of receiving the news, President Truman requested a meeting of the U.N. Security Council, and on the afternoon of June 25 (New York time) that body adopted a resolution, introduced by the United States, declaring the North Korean action a "breach of the peace," demanding that the aggressors withdraw beyond the 38th parallel, and calling upon all members of the U.N. "to render every assistance to the United Nations in the execution of this res-

olution and to refrain from giving assistance to the North Korean authorities."[11]

The resolution passed the Security Council by a vote of 9 to 0, Yugoslavia not voting. This temporary relief from the Council's chronic paralysis was due to the absence of the Russian delegate. Since January the Soviet Union had boycotted the Council and other U.N. agencies because of their refusal to seat the representatives of Communist China in place of those of the Formosa regime. Until Soviet delegate Yakov A. Malik returned on August 1 to take his turn as chairman, the Security Council was able to act with vigor. It followed the resolution of June 25 with another on the twenty-seventh, recommending that U.N. members "furnish such assistance to the Republic of Korea as may be necessary to repel the armed attack and to restore international peace and security in the area." On July 7 the Council requested the United States to name a commander for all U.N. forces serving in Korea. The President named General MacArthur.

President Truman had acted promptly in throwing the weight of the United States into the struggle. On June 27 he announced that he had ordered American air and sea forces "to give the Korean Government troops cover and support." Three days later, on the advice of General MacArthur in Tokyo, he authorized the use of United States ground troops in Korea, ordered a naval blockade of the Korean coast, and directed the air force to attack targets in North Korea "wherever militarily necessary."

In his announcement of June 27, President Truman revealed other action that constituted a distinct change of policy by

[10]*Documents on American Foreign Relations,* 12: 431–32. A similar remark was made in May by Tom Connally, chairman of the Senate Committee on Foreign Relations.

[11]This and numerous other documents illustrative of the Korean policy of the United States are printed in U.S. Congress, Senate, *The United States and the Korean Problem: Documents, 1943–1953,* Senate Document 74, 83 Cong. 1 sess. (Washington: Government Printing Office, 1953).

the United States. It was now evident, he said, that "communism has passed beyond the use of subversion to conquer independent nations and will now use armed invasion and war." Under these circumstances, the occupation of Formosa by Communist forces would be a threat to the security of the Pacific area and to United States forces performing their duties there. He had, therefore, "ordered the Seventh Fleet to prevent any attack on Formosa." To obviate excuse for such an attack, he had called upon the Chinese on Formosa to cease all attacks on the mainland and had instructed the Seventh Fleet to "see that this is done." He was also accelerating military assistance to the Philippines and Indochina, the scenes of other armed conflicts with Communist forces. The stretching of the "defensive perimeter" to include Formosa very naturally antagonized Communist China, which claimed the island as part of its domain. It also resulted in friction with other U.N. members, many of whom had recognized the Peking government and endorsed its claim to Formosa.

Response to the Security Council's call for support was spotty. In all, fifteen nations, other than the United States and South Korea, sent armed forces to participate in the fighting.[12] As of February 1951, the others were supplying only 9 percent of the manpower, as compared with 48 percent by the United States and 43 percent by the Republic of Korea. Overall troop contributions for the period of the war were: Republic of Korea, 500,000; United States, 300,000; others, 40,000. Of 411,000 casualties (killed, wounded, captured, missing), the Republic of Korea suffered 63 percent, the United States 33 percent, others 4 percent.[13] It should be said in this connection,

however, that Great Britain and France were actively fighting Communism on other fronts, Malaya and Indochina respectively, and that their exertions in those theaters must be counted as part of their contribution to the global struggle.

Such was the superiority of the North Korean troops in equipment and preparation that they were able to push back the South Koreans and the few U.N. troops at first available into the extreme southeast corner of Korea, an area that fortunately included the important port of Pusan. The tide turned suddenly on September 15, when General MacArthur in a risky maneuver landed U.N. forces at Inchon, far behind the North Korean lines. Large elements of the North Korean army were destroyed or captured, and the remainder driven beyond the 38th parallel. Backed by the authority of a General Assembly resolution reiterating the objective of "a unified, independent and democratic Korea," U.N. forces crossed the 38th parallel on October 7 (Korean time) or October 8 (3:14 A.M. EST—U.S. time) twelve hours before the U.N. resolution was passed and pushed on toward the Yalu River, Korea's northern boundary.

Too little heed had been given to warnings, over the Peking radio and through the Indian delegate in the U.N. Assembly, that Red China might feel called upon to prevent the extinction of the Korean People's Republic. After a skillful build-up whose portentous significance eluded the American command, Chinese armies, late in November, launched a massive attack which in a few weeks threw the Allied armies back below the 38th parallel and recaptured Seoul, the South Korean capital.[14] By mid-January 1951, however, the line had been stabilized and the U.N. forces were ready for a counterattack, which even-

---

[12]The fifteen as listed in U.S. Congress, *The U.S. and the Korean Problem,* pp. 149–51, were: Australia, Belgium, Canada, Colombia, Ethiopia, France, Greece, Luxembourg, Netherlands, New Zealand, Philippines, Thailand, Turkey, United Kingdom, Union of South Africa.

[13]*New York Times,* July 5, 1953.

[14]A vivid account of the Chinese surprise attack is given in S. L. A. Marshall, *The River and the Gauntlet: The Defeat of the Eighth Army by the Chinese Communist Forces* (New York: William Morrow & Company, Inc., 1953).

tually pushed Chinese and North Koreans again beyond the 38th parallel.

In the meantime, efforts by a U.N. committee to arrange a cease-fire agreement brought from the Chinese the declaration that they would make peace only on three conditions: withdrawal of all "foreign troops" from Korea, abandonment of Formosa by the United States, and admission of Red China to United Nations membership instead of the Nationalist government on Formosa. Such terms were unacceptable to the United States as the principal U.N. participant in the war.

In November the General Assembly of the U.N. had adopted the "United Action for Peace" plan, proposed by Secretary Acheson. At the urging of the United States, the Assembly now (February 1, 1951) adopted a resolution declaring Red China an aggressor and appointing two committees: one to consider additional measures to be used against the aggressors, the other to continue efforts for a peaceful settlement. On the advice of the former, the Assembly on May 18, 1951, recommended that member states prohibit the shipment to Communist China and North Korea of "arms, ammunition, and implements of war, atomic energy materials, petroleum, transportation materials of strategic value, and items useful in the production of arms, ammunition, and implements of war." These actions by the Assembly were taken, over the opposition of the Soviet bloc and with abstentions that showed considerable dislike of American policy, particularly on the part of the Asian and Arab members.

General MacArthur Comes Home

On April 11, 1951, President Truman relieved General Douglas MacArthur of his dual position as commander of U.N. forces in Korea and of the occupation forces of the United States in Japan. Growing friction between the general and the administration had resulted from MacArthur's impatience at the restraints placed upon his military activities and his habit of publicly voicing his disagreements with administration and U.N. policy. In particular, MacArthur had complained at the prohibition upon bombing enemy sources of supply and communications in what he termed the "privileged sanctuary" of Manchuria. His recall set off a violent debate in the United States, which continued in muted tones till well after the Korean War had been halted by an armistice. The issue was whether to limit the war to Korea or to go all out for victory against Red China at the risk of bringing in the Soviet Union. The arguments were epitomized in General MacArthur's assertion, "There is no substitute for victory," and the warning of General Omar N. Bradley, chairman of the Joint Chiefs of Staff, that a full-scale war against Red China would be "the wrong war at the wrong place, at the wrong time and with the wrong enemy." The administration's policy gave Europe first place and deferred to the opinion of Allies in the U.N.; MacArthur believed Asia to be the decisive theater in the struggle with Communism and would have the United States "go it alone if necessary." A long investigation by two Senate committees ended inconclusively, and the administration adhered to its policy of limited war.[15]

The Korean Armistice

On June 23, 1951, in New York Mr. Yakov A. Malik, head of the Soviet delegation in

[15]*Military Situation in the Far East* (Hearings before the Committee on Armed Service and the Committee on Foreign Relations, United States Senate, 82 Cong. 1 sess. In five parts. Washington: Government Printing Office, 1951). The case for Truman is stated in lively fashion in R. H. Rovere and A. M. Schlesinger, Jr., *The General and the President* (New York: Farrar, Straus and Young, 1951). The same questions, with particular reference to later phases of the war, were revived by General James A. Van Fleet in an article entitled "Catastrophe in Asia," *U.S. News and World Report*, September 17, 1954, pp. 24–28.

the United Nations, responded to a secret feeler from the United States by stating publicly that the Korean conflict could be settled if both parties so desired. His statement led to the opening of armistice negotiations on July 10, 1951, at Kaesong, just north of the 38th parallel. There, and later at Panmunjom, the negotiations proceeded with a number of interruptions till July 27, 1953. The Chinese dropped their earlier demands in regard to Formosa, admission to the U.N., and withdrawal of foreign troops as indispensable conditions. The questions that proved most troublesome were the location of the cease-fire line, machinery for enforcing the armistice terms, and repatriation of prisoners. By the spring of 1952 agreement had been reached on all points but the last. The Communists demanded that all prisoners of war be repatriated, willy-nilly. The U.N. spokesmen would not agree to compulsory repatriation of thousands of Chinese and North Korean prisoners who were unwilling to return to Communism.

On this issue the negotiations stuck until after the 1952 presidential elections in the United States. The successful Republican candidate, General Eisenhower, after a visit to the Korean front in December, let it be known that he supported the U.N. stand on prisoners of war. He was determined to bring the war to an end and after his inauguration permitted the word to leak to the enemy that if an armistice were not soon agreed to, the United States might find it necessary to use atomic weapons against China. To this covert threat, and to his removal of President Truman's ban on operations from Taiwan (Formosa) against the mainland, the new President later attributed the decision of the Communists to accept U.N. terms.[16] In April 1953, armistice negotiations were resumed after a

suspension of six months. The Communists were ready to make concessions on the prisoners of war issue, and in spite of the violent opposition of President Syngman Rhee, an armistice agreement was signed at Panmunjom on July 27, 1953.

The agreement provided for a cease-fire and withdrawal of the armies two kilometers from the existing battle-line. This ran northeasterly from a point just below the 38th parallel on the west coast to a point some thirty miles above it on the east. A neutral commission (Sweden, Switzerland, Czechoslovakia, Poland) would supervise enforcement of the armistice terms. Willing prisoners were to be exchanged and repatriated within sixty days. Disposition of others who still remained unwilling after a period of persuasion was to be settled by a political conference, but when plans for this fell through, the U.N. on January 24, 1954, began releasing the 22,000 Chinese and North Korean prisoners who had refused repatriation. Most of the Chinese were transported to Formosa. Three hundred fifty U.N. prisoners, including twenty-one Americans, refused repatriation and took their chances behind the Iron Curtain.

The Big Four Foreign Ministers, meeting in Berlin in January and February 1954, agreed that a conference on the Korean question should be held in Geneva in April. There the Republic of Korea and fifteen of the United Nations that had participated in the war confronted North Korea, Communist China, and the Soviet Union. A U.N. proposal for the unification of Korea after supervised free elections throughout the country was rejected by the Communists, and no agreement was reached. The United Nations had no stomach for Syngman Rhee's demand that Korea be unified by force, and armistice conditions—neither peace nor war—continued to prevail. A treaty of mutual defense, similar to others being negotiated by the United States in the Pacific area, was signed by representatives of the United

[16]Dwight D. Eisenhower, *The White House Years: Mandate for Change, 1953–1956* (New York: Doubleday & Company, Inc., 1963), pp. 178–91.

States and the Republic of Korea on October 1, 1953. Korea consented to the stationing of United States armed forces "in and about" its territory. Two American army divisions remained in Korea, nominally as part of a U.N. force, and the United States continued to provide the Republic of Korea with economic aid of some $200 million annually and to help arm and sustain the Korean army at unspecified cost.

No War, No Peace, in Korea

President Syngman Rhee, the 85-year old patriot, was forced to resign in April 1960 as a consequence of unsavory methods employed in his re-election to a fourth term. His constitutionally elected successor, John M. Chang, was overthrown by a group of young army officers in May 1961. The United States recognized the junta as the *de facto* government. Its head, General Chung Hee Park, later laid aside his uniform and as a civilian candidate for the presidency was elected in a close and apparently fair election on October 16, 1963. He was re-elected in May 1967 and in a popular referendum on October 18, 1969, won approval of a constitutional amendment that would permit him to seek a fourth four-year term as President. To the credit of the Park administration were a substantial upturn in the national economy and a treaty with Japan, signed June 22, 1965, which established normal relations between the two governments for the first time since 1945 and in addition provided for $800 million in grants and credits from Japan for Korea's further economic development—a kind of reparations for past injuries.

Relations between the Republic of (South) Korea and the U.S.–U.N. military command on the one hand and the People's Democratic Republic of (North) Korea on the other remained on the unsatisfactory armistice basis of 1953, with both parties guarding their respective sides of the demilitarized zone (DMZ) that straddled the cease-fire line. The neutral commission charged with supervising enforcement of the armistice terms was unable to function. It found its mission was obstructed in North Korea, whereupon its Communist members (Polish and Czech) were expelled from South Korea. Military build-up and modernization of equipment, contrary to armistice terms, proceeded on both sides. Spokesmen of the two military commands, U.S.–U.N. and North Korean, constituting the Military Armistice Commission, met from time to time in Panmunjom on the armistice line. They met, ordinarily, to make and to hear complaints of violation of armistice terms, but actually in most instances to berate and insult each other, not to negotiate.

Each Korean government aspired to unite the country on its own terms. South Korea's endeavors to that end were limited, by U.N. resolution and by its dependence on the United States, to peaceful means. North Korea was not so restricted. When the United States became deeply involved in the Vietnam war, Premier Kim Il Sung apparently saw an opportunity to move toward his goal by force, perhaps in part by stirring up in South Korea the kind of guerrilla warfare that gave the United States so much trouble in South Vietnam. Beginning late in 1966, at any rate, there was a sharp stepping up of infiltrations through the DMZ and around it by water, culminating in a series of dramatic incidents in 1968–1969, which could easily have brought renewal of the war.

On January 21, 1968, a suicide squad of thirty-one North Korean terrorists penetrated the DMZ and reached Seoul with the acknowledged mission of assassinating President Park. Their leaders were captured less than a mile from the presidential palace. Two days later the U.S. naval intelligence ship *Pueblo* was attacked and captured with its officers and crew while in

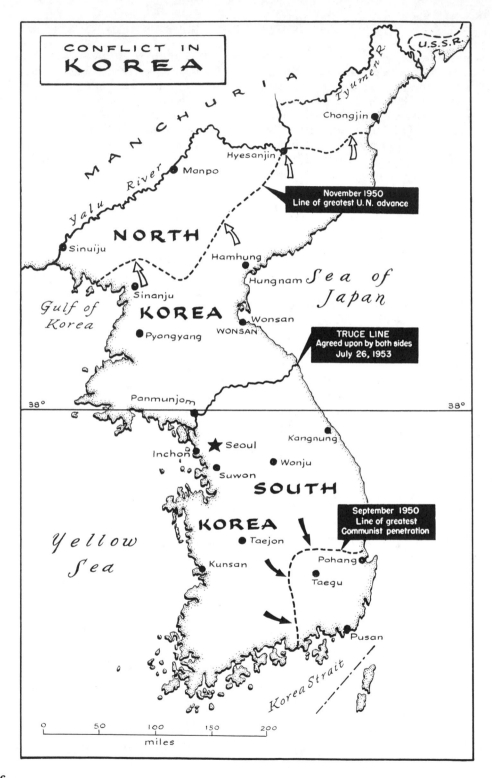

CONFLICT IN
KOREA

MANCHURIA

U.S.S.R.

Tyumen R.

Chongjin

Yalu River

Manpo

Hyesanjin

November 1950
Line of greatest U.N. advance

NORTH

Sinuiju

Hamhung

Hungnam

Sea of
Japan

Gulf of
Korea

Sinanju

KOREA

Pyongyang

Wonsan

WONSAN

TRUCE LINE
Agreed upon by both sides
July 26, 1953

38°

Panmunjom

38°

Seoul

Kangnung

Inchon

Wonju

Suwon

SOUTH

Yellow
Sea

KOREA

Taejon

September 1950
Line of greatest
Communist penetration

Kunsan

Pohang

Taegu

Pusan

Korea Strait

0   50   100   150   200
miles

international waters in the Sea of Japan. The North Korean claim that the *Pueblo* had entered national waters (within the twelve-mile limit) was denied by the United States. After eleven months of negotiations of the Panmunjom type, the eighty-two officers and men of the *Pueblo* (and the body of one killed at the time of the capture) were released to the United States. As a *quid pro quo* the U.S. commander had agreed to sign a confession and apology prepared by the North Koreans, but with the consent of the North Koreans that he should repudiate the document before signing it![17]

Before President Richard Nixon (inaugurated January 20, 1969) had been three months in office, there was another crisis. On April 14, 1969 (Washington time) an unarmed United States naval intelligence plane with a crew of thirty-one was shot down by North Korean planes over the Sea of Japan at an estimated distance of ninety miles from the Korean coast. President Nixon's first impulse was reported to have been to retaliate with air strikes upon North Korean targets. If so, he thought better of it and confined his response to a strong protest to the commission at Panmunjom and the dispatch of a large naval task force into the Sea of Japan, where, however, it remained only briefly. The President stated such aerial reconnaisance as the lost plane had been conducting, which he described as essential to the safety of United States troops in South Korea, would be continued and that the planes engaged in it would be protected in the future. The point apparently made, there was no repetition of the incident.

There was, furthermore, a distinct tapering off of Communist infiltration and other encounters along the DMZ. And though talk of war was still in the air, there were indications that Premier Kim Il Sung had

---

[17]*New York Times*, December 23, 1968, pp. 1–2. The commander of the *Pueblo* describes the incident in Commander Lloyd M. Bucher, U.S.N., *Bucher: My Story* (Garden City, N.Y.: Doubleday and Company, 1970).

adopted a new approach, although his basic objective, the reunification of the Korean peninsula, remained the same. In 1972 the North Korean leader opened negotiations with the South and made proposals aimed at a peaceful political reunification and had actually moved on to bargaining about the reuniting of families. Reflective of the changed atmosphere, American casualties dropped dramatically in numbers along the DMZ between 1970 and 1973, the United States Army going so far as to notify troops in August 1973 that they would no longer be eligible for combat pay for being stationed in Korea.

Unfortunately, as American policy began to crumble in Vietnam and as the Watergate scandal lessened the seeming credibility of the President to act, North Korean tactics changed. American personnel were set upon, elaborate tunnels were dug below the DMZ presumably for invasion purposes, commando raids were initiated, and Kim Il Sung traveled to Peking to secure military assistance. The Chinese, for their own reasons, preferred "the peaceful reunification" of the peninsula. From this point, the North Koreans took their case to the United Nations and won an endorsement from the General Assembly on a resolution calling for the withdrawal of all foreign forces under the U.N. Command (300 troops) and American troops under the South Korean-United States Defense Treaty of 1954. Shortly afterwards the same General Assembly accepted a contradictory resolution on behalf of the United States and other supporters of South Korea. At the United Nations in September 1975, Secretary of State Kissinger proposed that America and the South Koreans meet with the other parties directly concerned—the People's Republic of China and North Korea—to discuss ways of preserving the Armistice Agreement and of reducing tensions in the area. Kissinger noted that in such a meeting the United States would be ready to explore possibilities for a larger conference to negotiate more fundamental arrangements to keep the peace. This invitation was not accepted then and was dismissed altogether by the North Koreans in early August 1976. At the same time, the North Korean leadership embarked upon a major intensification of its effort to force the withdrawal of the United States by depicting the presence of American forces as a source of tension to the stability of the peninsula. Thus, the stage was set for one of the most bizarre incidents of the Cold War.

On August 18, 1976, a United Nations work crew of five Korean laborers accompanied by three U.N. Command officers (two Americans and one South Korean) and a seven-man security force arrived in the joint area at Panmunjom. Their assignment was to prune a tree believed to be obstructing the line of sight between two U.N. Command guardposts in the joint security area.[18] Shortly after the party began work, two North Korean officers and several guards arrived at the scene. After some discussion, in which the North Koreans posed no objection to the tree-pruning, they demanded the work be stopped. The U.N. work crew refused, the North Koreans called for reinforcements, and at this juncture thirty North Koreans attacked the U.N. forces with axes and metal pikes. The incident lasting less than five minutes, caused a number of American casualties, including the deaths of two United States Army officers.[19]

The United States response was swift and unequivocal. President Ford ordered the deployment of the F-4 aircraft from Okinawa, and the F-111's from Idaho, to Korea; the despatching of the Midway task force to the region; the raising of the nation's alert status; and the initiating of daily B-52 flights from Guam to Korea. Moreover, and in spite of Kim Il Sung's decision to put the forces at his disposal on a state of combat readiness, President Ford, who was fighting for his political life at the Republican nominating convention in Kansas City, ordered that the tree in question be cut down on August 21. Impressed with the American show of force, North Korea's leader conveyed an expression of regret to the United Nations command at a meeting of the Military Armistice Commission at Panmunjom several days later, and the crisis was weathered. Subsequent meetings of the Military Armistice Commission designed to draft new agreements for security arrangements in the joint security area suggest that tension would remain high in the DMZ for some time to come.[20]

President Carter's policy toward Korea remained to be revealed. The new President was determined to further reduce the number of American ground troops in South Korea "on a phased basis over a time span." Troop levels were decreased to 42,000 from 60,000 in 1970. Carter also made it clear to the South Korean Government that its internal oppression was repugnant to American traditions and that its continuation could only undermine the support of United States commitments there.[21]

[18]The joint security area was a small, roughly circular area of the DMZ some 800 yards in diameter in which the Military Armistice Commission meetings were held; it was a neutral area maintained and patrolled by both sides.

[19]This account of the incident is derived from a statement made by Ambassador Arthur W. Hummel, Jr., Assistant Secretary of State for East Asian and Pacific Affairs before the Subcommittees on International Organizations and International Political and Military Affairs of the House International Relations Committee, September 1, 1976. Courtesy of the United States Information Service.

[20]*New York Times,* September 5, 1976, p. 6.

[21]Governor Carter's speech before the Foreign Policy Association, Waldorf Astoria Hotel, New York, June 23, 1976. Courtesy of the United States Information Service.

ADDITIONAL READINGS

GEORGE, ALEXANDER L., "American Policy-making and the North Korean Aggression," *World Politics,* 7 (1954–55), 209–32.

GREY, ARTHUR L., JR., "The Thirty-eighth Parallel," *Foreign Affairs,* 29 (1950–51), 482–87.

KIRKENDALL, RICHARD S., *Harry S. Truman, Korea, and the Imperial Presidency.* St. Charles, Missouri: Forum Press, 1975. (pamphlet)

MUELLER, JOHN E. "Trends in Popular Support for the Wars in Korea and Vietnam," *American Political Science Review,* 65 (1971), 358–75.

PAIGE, GLENN D., *The Korean Decision.* New York: The Free Press, 1968.

REISCHAUER, EDWIN D., *The United States and Japan* (rev. ed.). Cambridge: Harvard University Press, 1965.

SIMMONS, ROBERT R., *The Strained Alliance: Peking, Pyongyang, Moscow and the Politics of the Korean Civil War.* New York: The Free Press, 1975.

SMITH, GADDIS, "After 25 Years—the Parallel," *New York Times Magazine,* June 22, 1975, 15ff.

23. The Postwar Far East, II: Japan and Communist China

The outbreak of war in Korea in June 1950 led to a stiffening of American resistance to the spread of Communism in the Far East. President Truman's announcement of his intention to defend Formosa and to speed up assistance to anti-Communist forces in the Philippines and Indochina was noted above. The protection of the Nationalist regime of Chiang Kai-shek on Formosa and refusal to recognize Communist China or to consent to her admission to the United Nations became settled policies of the United States, emphasized even more under the Eisenhower administration (from January 1953) than under its predecessor. President Eisenhower, indeed, went one step beyond President Truman. He withdrew the ban upon Nationalist attacks against mainland China, while continuing to offer protection to the Nationalists against invasion from the mainland.

Japan as an Ally

The Korean War, too, accelerated a movement already begun to negotiate a peace treaty with Japan and to build up that former enemy country as a bulwark against Communism in Asia, as Germany was built up as a bulwark against Communism in Europe. John Foster Dulles, as a consultant to the Secretary of State, began in 1950 the delicate task of finding treaty terms acceptable to Japan and to as many as possible of the nations of the U.N. The Soviet Union was invited to share in the proceedings but took no part in making the treaty. After reaching agreement with Japan, the United Kingdom, France, and other states, the United States invited fifty-four nations to a conference in San Francisco, opening on September 4, 1951, not to negotiate but to sign a treaty already agreed upon. India, Burma, and Yugoslavia declined the invitation. Russia, Poland, and Czechoslovakia attended. When blocked in their efforts to amend the treaty, they refused to sign. The representatives of the other forty-nine governments signed the treaty.[1]

Described as a "Peace of Reconciliation," the Japanese treaty (signed September 8, 1951) well deserved the name. Other than loss of her outlying territories, which was a foregone conclusion, it imposed no penalties and no disabilities on Japan. The question of reparations was left to negotiation between Japan and neighbors like the Philippines, Burma, and Indonesia, which had suffered heavily from Japanese invasion. By recognizing that Japan, as a sovereign state, possessed the right of self-defense, the Allies implicitly consented to her rearming. Some troublesome disputes were avoided by having Japan relinquish her colonial possessions (Formosa, Sakhalin, the Kuriles) without designating the re-

[1]The text of the treaty and background material are printed in *Documents on American Foreign Relations*, 13: 458–79. For intimate details of treaty-making and the conference, see Dean Acheson, *Present at the Creation: My Years in the State Department* (New York: W. W. Norton & Company, Inc., 1969), chaps. 46, 56.

cipients. Japan agreed that the United States should continue to occupy the Ryukyu and Bonin Islands, with the understanding that they might be placed under trusteeship with the United States as administrator. China not being represented at the Conference, Japan was left nominally free to make a treaty with whichever Chinese government she should choose to recognize. Japan acted in accordance with American policy in negotiating a treaty, on April 28, 1952, with the Chinese Nationalist government on Formosa. It established no official relations with the Communist government in Peking.

A Security Treaty, signed at the same time as the other, permitted United States armed forces to remain in Japan "to contribute to the maintenance of international peace and security in the Far East and to the security of Japan." The right was to continue as long as it was needed to assure those objectives.[2] Upon the entering into force of the two treaties with Japan, April 28, 1952, the war in the Pacific came officially to an end,[3] and Japan regained her sovereignty. As a sequel to the Security Treaty, the United States and Japan on March 8, 1954 signed a mutual defense assistance agreement providing for progressive Japanese rearmament with American military and economic aid.

Some Pacific states were less pleased than the United States by the "Peace of Reconciliation" with Japan. The Philippines, which had been so recently a victim of Japanese aggression, Australia and New Zealand, which had narrowly escaped a similar tragedy—these three governments especially wished guarantees against possible dangers from a rearming Japan. To alleviate their fears, the United States signed, a few days before the Japanese treaties, a security treaty with the Philippines and another jointly with Australia and New Zealand. These treaties, less definite in their commitments than the NATO treaty, promised consultation in the event of any threat to the independence, territorial integrity, or security of any of the parties. Each party recognized that an armed attack on either of them "would be dangerous to its own peace and safety" and declared that "it would act to meet the common dangers in accordance with its constitutional processes."[4]

Refusal of the Soviet Union to sign the peace treaty with Japan left those two powers nominally in a state of war. So long as that situation obtained, the Soviet Union continued to block Japan's admission to the U.N. In 1956, however, an agreement though actually not a treaty, was signed terminating the state of war and providing for the resumption of diplomatic relations. Upon its ratification in December, the Russians withdrew their objection to Japan's admission. Japan became a member of the U.N. on December 18, 1956. In the following October it was elected to one of the nonpermanent seats in the Security Council.

The aim of American policy toward Japan after 1951 was to treat Japan increasingly as an equal and to promote its prosperity through facilitating its international trade. Above all, the United States was determined to attach Japan, the one industrially advanced nation of Asia, securely to the West and to circumvent the contrary designs of Japan's neighbors, Communist China and the Soviet Union. In the last-named undertaking the United States had

---

[2]*Documents on American Foreign Relations,* 13: 266–67.

[3]President Truman had proclaimed an end of hostilities December 31, 1946, thereby ending the life of many kinds of wartime legislation. On October 19, 1951, he signed a joint resolution formally ending the state of war with Germany. *New York Times,* January 1, 1947; October 20, 1951.

[4]For a discussion and related documents concerning the U.S., Australia, New Zealand Tripartite Security Treaty, see Glen St. J. Barclay and Joseph M. Siracusa, eds., *Australia-American Relations since 1945* (Sydney: Holt, Rinehart and Winston, 1976), 28–34.

the full support of a succession of Japanese cabinets and of the Liberal-Democratic majority in the Japanese Parliament. The Socialist party, on the other hand, which with other opposition groups controlled over one third of the seats in Parliament, preached a policy of neutralism, recognition of the Peking government, and the cultivation of trade relations with China and the Soviet bloc.

Liberal-Democratic premiers, however, while conforming to United States policy in refusing recognition to the Peking government, were unwilling to join in the American boycott of trade with mainland China, a natural and traditional Japanese market. Unofficial delegations of Japanese businessmen visited China from time to time, with so much success that by 1966 Japan's annual trade with China was over $600 million, exceeding that with Formosa by more than 50 percent.[5]

Japan had also developed a considerable trade with the Soviet Union, in which, however, Japan's imports far exceeded her exports. Japan was also being urged by Moscow to invest heavily in the economic development of Eastern Siberia, but on terms which so far had attracted little Japanese capital.[6]

The bulk of Japan's growing foreign trade however, was with the "free world." In 1955 the United States was instrumental in securing Japan's admission to the General Agreement on Tariffs and Trade (GATT). Its efforts to open markets for Japanese exports were hampered by discriminations practiced by some other governments and by demands in the United States for protection against certain exports from Japan, especially cotton textiles. The latter problem was met in part by persuading Japan to limit "voluntarily" her textile exports to the United States. Trade restric-

tions on both sides, as well as Japanese barriers to foreign investments, remained chronic irritants. In order to alleviate them, the two governments agreed in 1961 to establish at cabinet level a Joint U.S.—Japan Committee on Trade and Economic Affairs (patterned on a similar U.S.—Canadian committee), whose function was to seek solutions for economic problems through periodic discussions.

The United States, at any rate, remained Japan's best customer, and Japan was surpassed only by Canada as a market for American exports. Japan attained unprecedented prosperity in the two decades after the peace treaty. Her gross national product, minimal at the close of the war, reached $37.8 billion in 1960 and $140 billion in 1969. Japan's economy thereby replaced West Germany's as third strongest in the world.[7] Japan's foreign trade in 1968 reached a total value of almost $26 billion, of which over one-fourth was with the United States.[8]

United States Troops and Bases in Japan

More serious sources of friction between the two countries were the continued presence of American troops in Japan and the American occupation, for strategic purposes, of the Bonin and Ryukyu Islands. In accordance with the Security Treaty of 1951, American troops remained in Japan in order to maintain the security of that nation and to preserve international peace and security in the Far East. Their presence and their requirements of more and more land for improved air bases incurred popu-

---

[5] Jerrold L. Schecter, "Japan's New Bid for Leadership," *The Reporter,* May 18, 1967. Cf. *New York Times,* February 16, 1968.

[6] *New York Times,* January 19, 1968; July 14, 1969.

[7] Takashi Oka in the *New York Times,* January 5, 1970, p. 12.

[8] Increased trade with the U.S. had not been without its drawbacks, as Japan's traditional surplus in American trade reached $5.3 billion in 1976 and was even higher in 1977.

lar resentment. Their presence was needed, however, since Japan's capacity for self-defense was limited by the pacifist provisions of the "MacArthur Constitution," which could be amended only by an as yet unattainable two-thirds majority in each House of Parliament. Under a liberal interpretation of the Constitution, the Japanese government did organize "Defense Forces," but these, as of 1977, numbered not over 250,000, a force inadequate to protect Japan in the event of attack from China or the Soviet Union.

In a visit to Washington in June 1957, Premier Nobusuke Kishi secured an agreement that responsibility for Japan's defense should be transferred as rapidly as possible from the United States to Japan and a promise that American ground combat troops should be promptly withdrawn. Navy and Air Force contingents remained.

Premier Kishi also initiated negotiations that resulted in a new Security Treaty, signed January 19, 1960. The new treaty, terminable by either party after ten years, replaced that of 1951. It was designed to raise Japan from a position subordinate to the United States to that of an equal partner. The key provision, not in the treaty itself but in an accompanying exchange of notes, specified that consultation with Japan should precede any new deployment of American forces into Japan, any major changes in equipment (such as the introduction of nuclear weapons), or any use by American forces of bases in Japan for combat operations for any purpose other than the defense of Japan itself. The wording did not specifically give Japan a veto on such American activities, but President Eisenhower assured Kishi that the United States had no intention of acting contrary to Japan's wishes in the matters specified. Subject to these restrictions, American forces were to retain their base facilities in Japan.[9]

The treaty was approved by both Houses of the Japanese Parliament, in spite of riotous demonstrations against it in June, led by students and workers and motivated, in part at least, by fear that the alliance with the United States might drag Japan into nuclear war. It went into effect on June 23, 1960. Premier Kishi, whose high-handed tactics in pushing the treaty through Parliament had aroused much opposition, resigned in July. In the November elections his Liberal-Democratic successor, Hayato Ikeda, easily won a safe majority in the House of Representatives.

Return of the Bonins and Ryukyus

Removal of the other principal source of friction—American occupation of the Bonin and Ryukyu Islands—was reserved for Premier Eisaku Sato, who succeeded Ikeda in November 1964. Premier Sato and his first Foreign Minister, Takeo Miki, struck a new note in Japan's postwar foreign policy by calling for Japan's leadership, in collaboration with the United States, in what Miki described as "the grand task of developing Asia."[10] This proposed role for Japan, reminding some critics of Japan's aggressive prewar program of a "Greater East Asia Co-prosperity Sphere," was in accord with an American wish to see cooperation among the non-Communist nations of East and Southeast Asia for both economic development and security. Japan was contributing to the economic develop-

---

[9]*Documents on American Foreign Relations, 1960*, pp. 416–31. In 1968, in response to growing popular and minority-party agitation for removal of American bases, the United States reached an agreement with the Japanese government for the surrender, joint use, or relocation of 50 of the 148 military base facilities still occupied in Japan. These would constitute about one-half of the area still held, much of it on choice land near urban areas. These changes, it was reported, could be made without detriment to the military capability of the United States. *New York Times,* December 24, 27, 1968; June 23, 1969.

[10]*New York Times,* August 13, 1967, p. 11. Miki, a rival of Sato for the leadership of the Liberal-Democratic Party, was replaced as Foreign Minister in 1968 by Kiichi Aichi.

ment of the region through payment of reparations to the victims of her prewar aggression, through her participation as a large investor in the Asian Development Bank established in Manila in 1966, and through her membership in a series of regional economic conferences, initiated in South Korea in June 1966. Her participation in any security arrangements, however, was prevented by the provisions of the "MacArthur Constitution" as well as by pacifist and neutralist popular sentiment.

Premier Sato's policy was gratifying to the United States, not only in his determination to have Japan share in the economic development of East Asia, but also in his personal endorsement—in the face of strong adverse public opinion—of United States policy in South Vietnam. This cooperative attitude strengthened his hand when he asked the United States for the return to Japan of the Bonin and Ryukyu Islands. The Bonins (with the nearby Volcano Islands, including Iwo Jima) presented no serious problem. Though conquered in 1945 at great sacrifice, they were not important in American postwar strategy. Their chief significance was sentimental. During a visit to Washington in November 1967, Premier Sato secured President Johnson's promise that they should be returned. In subsequent negotiations the Japanese agreed that the American flag on the summit of Mount Suribachi on Iwo Jima should be replaced by a permanent copper reproduction at the top of a stone monument, and below it a bronze replica of the famous photograph of the flag-raising by six dust-covered marines should commemorate the victory of February 23, 1945. On these terms the American flag on Iwo Jima was lowered at 12:05 P.M. on June 26, 1968, and replaced five minutes later by the Rising Sun flag of Japan. The Bonin and Volcano Islands were thereby returned to Japanese administration.[11]

The Ryukyus presented an altogether different problem, for there, on Okinawa, scene of one of the toughest campaigns of the Pacific War, the United States had built its chief military base—sometimes referred to as "the Gibraltar"—of the Western Pacific. Okinawa was, in effect, "an unsinkable aircraft carrier," from which American B-52 bombers could range as far as Korea on the north and Vietnam and Thailand on the south, to say nothing of Taiwan and the nearby Chinese mainland. Okinawa was also, it was well understood, stocked with nuclear weapons, which were barred by agreement from United States bases in Japan. The island was, in the words of Tom Wicker of the *New York Times,* "a general's dream," but at the same time it was a "politician's nightmare"—"a political time bomb ticking away at the heart of the Japanese-American security arrangement, which in turn is the central pillar of the United States position in the Pacific and East Asia."[12]

The time-bomb element was a dual one, comprising the Japanese Okinawans (slightly under a million in number), who had grown increasingly restive under American administration, and, more serious, a rising popular demand in Japan itself for the restoration of Japanese rule in the Ryukyus. So strong had this sentiment become that Premier Sato, after his party's success in elections to the Upper House of Parliament in July 1968, felt it necessary to stake his political future on the return of Okinawa by 1972, though at the same time acknowledging that continuance of the American bases on the island was vital to Japan's security.[13]

The United States faced a difficult dilemma. It had to choose between surrendering political and administrative control of the island harboring its most vital military base in the Western Pacific as well as presumably, the right to arm it with nuclear

---

[11]*New York Times,* November 16, 1967, pp. 1–2; March 18, p. 4; June 27, 1968, p. 3.

[12]*New York Times,* May 27, 1969, p. 46, Cf. Takashi Oka, "Okinawa Mon Amour," *New York Times Magazine,* April 6, 1969, pp. 30, 89–92.

[13]*New York Times,* July 14, 1968, pp. 1, 31.

weapons, and, on the other hand, risking the loss of the friendship and cooperation of the one industrially advanced and politically stable nation of non-Communist Asia, a nation still weak militarily but possessing great military potential. Specifically, the continuation of the 1960 Security Treaty beyond 1970 might depend upon Washington's decision as to Okinawa.

A visit to Washington by Foreign Minister Kiichi Aichi in June 1969 prepared the way for a three-day visit by Sato in November. An agreement reached by Sato and President Nixon was published in a complicated and somewhat ambiguous communiqué of November 21. The President and the Prime Minister agreed that the two governments should at once enter into consultations with a view to the reversion of Okinawa to Japan during 1972, "without detriment to the security of the Far East, including Japan," and "with the necessary legislative support." Japan would "assume gradually the responsibility for the immediate defense of Okinawa" as part of her own territories, but in the meantime the United States would retain "such military facilities and areas in Okinawa as required in the mutual security of both countries." The Security Treaty of 1960 should remain in force and should be applicable to Okinawa. Nuclear weapons would be removed from Okinawa. Whether they might, in emergency, be returned there under the treaty's provision for "prior consultation," was not clear. American officials maintained that they might, whereas Sato upon his return to Japan assured a news conference that Okinawa would remain free of nuclear weapons after its reversion to Japan. Elsewhere in the communiqué Sato stated that it was the intention of the Japanese government "to accelerate rapidly the reduction of Japan's trade and capital restrictions."[14]

Both statesmen expressed the hope that the war in Vietnam would end before the reversion of Okinawa, but declared that if that should not be the case the two governments would consult with each other "so that reversion would be accomplished without affecting the United States efforts" in behalf of the people of South Vietnam.

Thus the most serious issue between the United States and Japan had been placed on the road to final settlement. That the agreement was approved in Japan was demonstrated by the elections of December 27, 1969, which gave the Liberal-Democratic party an increased majority (but still short of two-thirds) in the House of Representatives. Premier Sato interpreted the victory as "a mandate for continual close ties with the United States."[15] Indicative of his cooperative attitude was Japan's signing, February 3, 1970, of the nuclear nonproliferation treaty, sponsored by the United States, Great Britain, and the Soviet Union.

Despite the outcome of the Vietnam conflict, and the shock produced by President Nixon's unexpected announcement in 1971 that he had accepted an invitation to travel to the People's Republic of China (an issue of much importance in Japanese politics), and even though there was electoral damage done to the ruling Liberal-Democratic party as a consequence of the Lockheed aviation bribery scandal, the course of Japanese-American relations continued to run smoothly. As an indication that the Japanese Government sought to close the books, once and for all, on World War II, and as a sign of the untroubled nature of their relationship with the United States, the Japanese Emperor Hirohito, in response initially to a request from President Ford, visited America in October 1975, the first Japanese monarch to set foot on American soil. In 1976, moreover, the Japanese White Paper on

---

[14]Text of communiqué and analysis by Richard Halloran in the *New York Times*, November 22, 1969, pp. 1, 14; summary of Sato's news conference by Takashi Oka in ibid., November 27, 1969, p. 6.

[15]*New York Times*, December 28, 1969, pp. 1, 5; December 29, p. 11. The reversion of Okinawa to Japan took place in 1972 as scheduled.

Defense, the first since 1970, reaffirmed the Japan–United States joint security treaty as an integral part of the basic framework of international relations in Asia. Equally significant, the White Paper noted that while Japan would continue to observe its non-nuclear principles, it would depend on the credibility of the American nuclear deterrent against nuclear threat.[16]

Cold War with Peking

While Japan, the wartime foe of the United States, was becoming her postwar friend and ally, mainland China, her wartime ally, had become her cold war foe. American policy, during the war and just after it, had aimed at the emergence of "a strong, united and democratic China," which could be counted on to help keep the peace of the Far East. Mainland China had indeed emerged strong and united (if not in spirit, at least under despotic central control). It was also "democratic" according to the Communist lexicon. But instead of the friendly and cooperative China that Roosevelt, Hull, and Truman had envisaged, it was a China which aspired to make all East Asia Communist and which never tired of proclaiming its undying enmity to "American imperalists." The United States was seen as Enemy Number One (at least until, strangely enough, Russia entered the competition), generally as the stronghold of world capitalism and "imperialism," more especially as the power which, by shielding the Nationalist government on Taiwan,[17] prevented the unification of China under Communism. This, as the Peking government viewed it, was aggression, interference in China's domestic affairs.

[16]*Sydney Morning Herald,* June 5, 1976.

[17]The island long known to the West as Formosa was coming to be spoken of more and more by its Chinese name, Taiwan.

Reprinted from *The United States in World Affairs 1958,* Council on Foreign Relations, by permission of the publisher.

As the central purpose of American postwar policy in Europe was to prevent the expansion of Soviet Communism, so the containment of Chinese Communism became after 1950 the central purpose of American policy in Asia. Theoretically, the Communist camp was indivisible. Actually, rifts soon appeared between Peking and Moscow, and even before that, the chief pressure in each area was exerted by the nearer of the two Communist giants.

The containment policy in Asia had been implemented in a costly war in Korea, in the treaties with Japan, the Republic of Korea, and the Philippines, and in other treaties

gress, upon Eisenhower's recommendation, passed a joint resolution, signed January 29, 1955, authorizing the President to defend Taiwan and the Pescadores and such other positions as he might judge to be necessary for the defense of those islands. This left any future decision as to defending the off-shore islands entirely in the President's hands.

The British government and important segments of opinion in the United States held that the Nationalist stand on the off-shore islands was weak both politically and militarily, and that Chiang Kai-shek should be persuaded to evacuate them and fall back to a more defensible line. Chiang did, under American pressure, consent to withdraw from the Tachens but refused to give up either Quemoy or Matsu. Communist pressure on Quemoy slackened and was not revived until August 1958, when a new bombardment was opened. On this occasion Secretary of State Dulles made it plain that the United States was not in sympathy with the retention of a large Nationalist garrison on Quemoy, but he refrained from pressuring Chiang to remove it, and the Seventh Fleet aided the garrison to the extent of escorting supply convoys to the vicinity of the island, though the escort vessels halted at the three-mile limit.

The incident ended in a curious kind of truce. Chiang Kai-shek, after a visit from Dulles, announced that the Nationalists' "sacred mission" of restoring freedom to mainland China would be carried out not primarily by force but through propagation of the Three Principles of Dr. Sun Yat Sen—"nationalism, democracy, and livelihood." Thereupon the Communist army command made known that henceforth Quemoy would be bombarded only on odd days of the month. On even days, island activities and even the arrival of convoys would not be disturbed, provided the latter were not under American protection.[19]

Later the shells were sometimes filled with propaganda leaflets instead of shrapnel or high explosives.

The United States had repeatedly proposed to Communist China a mutual renunciation of the use of force with special reference to the Taiwan Strait between Taiwan and the mainland. These proposals had been made through diplomatic contacts that the United States had intermittently maintained with the Peking government since 1954, in spite of American adherence to a policy of nonrecognition of Peking. First on the consular, then on the ambassadorial level, at Geneva and later at Warsaw, these contacts had been initiated for the purpose of securing the release of some scores of Americans, military and civilian, held in Communist China. By the end of 1961 all but four of the detained Americans had been released; in return, 129 Chinese who had been denied exit visas from the United States because of nuclear or other technological skills gained here were allowed to depart if they so desired. When the American negotiators turned from this subject to the suggestion of a formal cease-fire in the Taiwan Strait, they were met with demands that the United States in return abandon Taiwan, withdraw the Seventh Fleet, and lift its embargo on trade with China. On some occasions the Chinese spokesman also demanded a meeting of the two Foreign Ministers—a step toward recognition. Since the majority of these demands were unacceptable to the United States, there was no cease-fire agreement, and the intermittent bombardment of Quemoy continued. Tension in this area was relaxed but could be revived whenever Peking might wish.[20]

[19]*U.S. in World Affairs, 1958*, pp. 313–32.

[20]In June 1962, reports of large movements of Chinese Communist forces to the mainland facing Quemoy led President Kennedy to reaffirm the position taken by President Eisenhower as to the defense of the offshore islands. *New York Times*, June 28, 1962, pp. 1–2.

yet to be described. Giving substance to the treaties were American armed forces stationed in Japan, Korea, Okinawa, Taiwan, the Philippines, and South Vietnam, the presence of the Seventh Fleet in Asiatic waters, and great quantities of economic and military aid around the perimeter from Japan and Korea to Thailand and Pakistan. Aspects of the same policy were the American refusal to recognize the government of Communist China and opposition to the seating of that government in the United Nations.

The assurances given Chiang Kai-shek by Presidents Truman and Eisenhower that his regime on Taiwan would be protected against attack from the mainland were put in binding form in a treaty signed in Washington. December 2, 1954. The treaty resembled closely the treaties with the Philippines and Japan. Each party agreed to regard an attack on the territories of the other in the West Pacific area as dangerous to its own peace and safety and to "act to meet the common danger in accordance with its constitutional processes." The territory of "the Republic of China" (the name still claimed by the Nationalists) was defined as meaning Taiwan and the Pescadores Islands. Other territories might be included by mutual agreement. This definition left in doubt the question whether the United States would help to defend certain small islands near the mainland—notably the Quemoy, Matsu, and Tachen groups. The United States was given the right to station its armed forces "in and about Taiwan and the Pescadores as may be required for their defense." By an exchange of notes following the signing of the treaty, the parties agreed that military operations should be conducted from territory of the Republic of China only by joint agreement (except in cases of emergency self-defense). This agreement evidently debarred President Chiang Kai-shek from undertaking an invasion of the mainland without the consent of the United States. In

other words, if Chiang had been "unleashed" by President Eisenhower in 1953, he was now leashed again.[18]

For the immediate future, however, the Chinese Communists seemed more likely than the Nationalists to initiate invasion. Communist Premier Chou En-lai had declared in August 1954 that it was "imperative that the People's Republic of China liberate Taiwan and liquidate the traitorous Chiang Kai-shek group," which, he charged, had turned Taiwan into a United States colony and military base. But since the U.S. Seventh Fleet barred the way to Taiwan, the Communists began their offensive, September 3, with an artillery bombardment of the islands of Quemoy and Little Quemoy, situated near the entrance to the port of Amoy. These islands and the Matsus and Tachens farther north, though geographically appertaining to the mainland, had been held by the Nationalists when they withdrew to Taiwan. Some of them had been fortified, with American encouragement, and Quemoy at least was strongly garrisoned with some of Chiang's best troops. The usefulness of the islands for the defense of Taiwan was doubtful; they appeared better suited as stepping stones for a Nationalist invasion of the mainland—an enterprise which Chiang Kai-shek never ceased to cherish.

The bombardment of Quemoy and the resulting death of two American officers stationed there as advisers confronted President Eisenhower with a difficult decision. Should the United States regard itself as obligated to defend Quemoy against Communist attack? Overruling the majority of the Joint Chiefs of Staff, the President decided that the United States would aid in defending Quemoy only if the attack on that island was clearly preparatory to an attack on Taiwan. The treaty of the following December left the question open. Con-

[18]*Documents on American Foreign Relations, 1954,* pp. 360–64.

The Two Chinas

In consenting to the diplomatic contacts just mentioned the State Department had made it plain that it was by no means departing from its settled policy of refusal to extend diplomatic recognition to the Peking government. There were, after 1949, two governments, one in Peking, one in Taipei on Taiwan, each claiming to be the government of China. The Nationalist government in Taipei governed an area about equal to that of New Jersey and Connecticut, with a population of some thirteen million people, but claimed to be the legitimate government of all China, which it designated as the "Republic of China." The Communist government at Peking, ruling over the "People's Republic of China," controlled an area larger than the United States with a population thought to exceed seven hundred million. It claimed Taiwan as a province of China and would in all probability have taken it had not the Korean War brought American intervention in support of the Nationalist government at Taipei.

The reason first given by the United States for nonrecognition of the Peking government was its refusal to observe generally accepted standards of international behavior, exemplified in its brutal mistreatment of American nationals in China when it came to power. Such mistreatment of both civilian and military personnel continued during and after the Korean War. Another reason, cited in 1951 by Dean Rusk, then Assistant Secretary of State for Far Eastern Affairs, was the conviction that the Nationalist government more authentically represented "the views of the great body of the people of China."[21] Secretary Dulles, some years later, asserted his belief that Communist rule in China, as elsewhere, was "a passing and not a perpetual phase," and that nonrecognition would contribute to its passing. Recognition on the other hand, Dulles believed, "would be a well-nigh mortal blow to the survival of the non-Communist governments in the Far East." Recognition, followed by admission to the U.N., would so increase the prestige and influence of the Chinese Communists in the Far East, "and so dishearten our allies there, that the Communist subversive efforts would almost surely succeed."[22]

The arguments against the seating of the Peking government in the U.N. were much the same as those against recognition. Here there was the further consideration that that government had been branded an aggressor by the U.N. General Assembly and had never purged itself of the charge. "You can't shoot your way into the U.N." was a common way of stating it; or as Secretary Dulles liked to put it: "The U.N. is not a reform school for delinquent governments." This line of reasoning was reinforced by Communist China's ruthless suppression of dissent in Tibet in 1959 and its undeclared war against India over a border dispute in 1962.

The situation was further complicated by American responsibility to the Nationalist regime on Taiwan. The question was not one of admitting a new member to the U.N. but of choosing between rival governments of a nation which under the Charter was entitled not only to membership but also to one of the five permanent seats on the Security Council. If the Peking regime were seated, what would become of Chiang Kai-shek and his government? For the United States, which had fully committed itself to Chiang's support and had won his cooperation in carrying out impressive economic and social reforms in Taiwan, this was a vital question of the time.

Since admission of a new member was

---

[21]*U.S. in World Affairs, 1951,* p. 115.

[22]*Documents in American Foreign Relations, 1957,* p. 343; *U.S. in World Affairs, 1958,* p. 339.

not involved, recommendation by the Security Council was not needed. In the General Assembly, year after year, the proposal was made to seat representatives of the People's Republic of China in place of those of the Nationalist government. Sponsored at first by the Soviet Union and by India (even in 1962, in the midst of the Chinese invasion of the latter country), the motion always had the support of the Communist bloc, a majority of the Asian and varying proportions of the African delegations, and the Scandinavian countries, which had earlier recognized the Peking regime. Year after year until 1961 the United States tactic was to move for a postponement of the issue, and each year it won by a majority of those voting, though the majorities steadily diminished. In 1961, however, the United States delegation resolved to let the question come up for debate and a vote. Having first resolved that the proposal was an important one, requiring a two-thirds vote for passage, the General Assembly rejected it by a comfortable margin in 1961 and repeated the performance in the next two years.

There was no vote in 1964, but in 1965, 47 states voted to seat the Peking government, 47 voted not to, while 20 abstained. Though the yes vote was far short of the necessary two-thirds, there were many predictions that the next Assembly would override American opposition and admit Communist China. But this did not occur. In 1966 the pro-Peking vote declined to 46 whereas the opposition rose to 57, with 17 absentions, and the ratio varied only slightly from these figures in the next three years, standing at 48–56–21 in 1969. Peking's support in the U.N. had peaked in 1965.

The explanation for the decline in the following years is to be found primarily in developments within China. The year 1965 had marked the beginning of the "Great Proletarian Cultural Revolution," an intense and nationwide struggle between the radical followers of Mao Tse-tung and more moderate elements in the Communist party, in which the Maoists sought to stamp out alleged bourgeois tendencies in the Chinese populace and in the party itself. At the height of this convulsive movement, hundreds of thousands of teen-age Red Guards roamed the country, invading homes, offices, and factories, assaulting suspected reactionaries, destroying books, and disrupting industry. Schools and universities were closed while their students participated in the Revolution, finding answers to all problems in the little Red Book containing *The Thoughts of Mao Tse-tung.*

If such near anarchy detracted from the prestige of the Peking government, policies of the government itself tended to make enemies, rather than friends, among the uncommitted nations. Premier Chou En-lai, on visits to Africa in 1963–1964 and again in 1965, had proclaimed that continent, along with Latin America and parts of Asia, to be "ripe for revolution"—a proclamation that antagonized some independent African governments which wanted no revolution imported from China. Chou's excursion, against the background of the Cultural Revolution, presumably accounted for many of the sixteen African votes cast against Red China's admission in 1966.

Then, in 1970, Peking staged an impressive recovery. The Cultural Revolution had ended, and China was approaching stabilization under Mao Tse-tung and the army. Universities reopened. The government re-established its diplomatic ties abroad, deliberately neglected during months of anarchy at home. Reward came in new recognitions of the Peking regime, by Canada in October and Italy in November 1970, and in a markedly improved showing when the new test came on seating Red China in the U.N. The vote on November 20, 1970, was 51 in favor, 49 opposed, with 25 abstentions. For the first time a majority of the votes cast favored Peking. Though the pro-Peking vote was far below the required two-thirds, there was widespread opinion that it portended the early defeat of the American policy of denying China's seat in the U.N. to the Peking government.

The Sino-Soviet Quarrel

Associated with the Cultural Revolution was Communist China's bitter quarrel with the Soviet Union, with which it had once sworn "eternal friendship." Begun in the late 1950's, when Moscow had refused aid in producing nuclear weapons and had started to withdraw Russian technicians from China, it developed into a dispute over ideology and conflicting territorial claims. Ideologically, the Chinese professed to be the true upholders of the doctrines of Marx and Lenin and charged the Russians with "revisionism" and even with conspiring with the United States against Peking. Peking and Moscow thus became rivals for the leadership of world Communism.

Territorially, China laid claim to enormous areas in Eastern Siberia and Central Asia which Czarist Russia had acquired by questionable means in the nineteenth century. Local disputes in two of those areas—an island in the Ussuri River and a spot on the Sinkiang-Kazakhstan border—led to armed clashes in March and August 1969 and to talk of war, even nuclear war, between the two formerly fraternal nations. A visit of Premier Kosygin to Peking in September paved the way for negotiation of the territorial dispute, which had not, nevertheless, been settled by 1977.[23]

Under such circumstances the Soviet Union had ceased to be an active sponsor of Red China for membership in the U.N. and gave its candidacy only perfunctory support. Moscow was even suspected of encumbering the proposal for seating Peking with conditions certain to ensure its defeat.

The United States Has Second Thoughts

It is interesting to note that in this period when Communist China was losing friends both within and without the Communist bloc, the United States was feeling gingerly for a chance to improve relations. Cut off from its alliance with Russia, China posed less of a threat than in the days of the "Communist monolith." Furthermore, both the Kennedy and Johnson administrations recognized the fallacy of the Dulles assumption that Communist rule in China was but a passing phase, soon to disappear. Mainland China was evidently to remain Communist for some time to come. Its 700 million people constituted one-fifth of the human race. To ignore their existence, or to boycott all trade and cultural relations with them, as the United States had done since 1951, was coming to be recognized as an unrealistic policy that neither weakened the Peking government nor produced any benefit for the United States. Informed American opinion was urging an opening of commercial and cultural channels with mainland China, if not formal recognition of the Peking government. Senate hearings in 1966 gave currency to the popular formula, "containment but not isolation."[24]

Another stimulus to American rethinking of its China policy was Communist China's unexpectedly rapid progress in nuclear and missile technology. The Atomic Energy Commission reported that China's first atomic explosion took place, probably in the desert area of Sinkiang Province, on October 16, 1964. This was followed by others on May 14, 1965, and May 8, 1966.

[23]*New York Times*, March 1, 1977, p. 2.

[24]*U.S. in World Affairs, 1966*, pp. 276–82.

The last of these was estimated to have been of 300 kilotons potency, fifteen times the strength of the bomb that destroyed Hiroshima. On October 27, 1966, according to the same authority, China fired a 20-kiloton bomb an estimated distance of 400 miles on a rocket missile, thus entering the IRBM class. Her first thermonuclear (hydrogen) bomb, estimated at three megatons was exploded on June 17, 1967. By the end of September 1969, China had exploded at least ten atomic or thermonuclear devices and was presumably well on the way to ICBM capability.

If China, as a nuclear power, was to be governed by the restraints that other nuclear powers except France had accepted —the test ban treaty and the nuclear nonproliferation treaty—she must obviously be brought onto speaking terms with the others; yet she was excluded from the U.N. and quarreling with Russia, while with the United States she had only the vestigial diplomatic contacts of the meetings at Warsaw—and even these the Peking government discontinued after January 8, 1968. Genuine diplomatic relations between Peking and Washington were precluded as long as the United States recognized and supported the Nationalist government on Taiwan.

A Two-Chinas Policy?

A much-talked-of solution to the U.N.-membership problem was a "two Chinas" policy. What this phrase inaccurately denoted was recognition of the Peking government as the government of China (with China's rights in the U.N.) and a downgrading of the Nationalist government to the government of an independent Republic of Taiwan. The latter would abandon its pretensions to being the government of China and any hopes of returning to the mainland. Taiwan would then become a mem-

ber of the U.N. on a par with other small nations. The fatal weakness of the plan, for the time being at any rate, was its unacceptability to both Peking and Taipei. The Communists would not surrender their claim to Taiwan, nor the Nationalists, their pretension to being the legitimate government of China.

"Ping Pong Diplomacy"

Under these circumstances there was little that the United States could do toward bettering relations, other than offering in minor matters to open channels of communication on its side of the "bamboo curtain," and this it did despite Peking's dedicated support of Hanoi against the United States in the war in Vietnam. In late 1965 and the spring and summer of 1966, the United States relaxed the ban on travel to China by doctors and medical scientists, congressmen, businessmen, athletes, and some tourists, and offered permission for Chinese newspapermen, and for Chinese scientists and other scholars invited by American universities, to visit the United States. All of these gestures, obviously, depended for results upon cooperative action by the Peking government, and none was forthcoming. The American feelers were rebuffed. After January 1968, also, as stated earlier, Peking repeatedly postponed further meetings at Warsaw as a way of protesting the American War in Vietnam.

Then, toward the end of 1968, came signs that Peking desired a lessening of tensions. As some China-watchers guessed, the Chinese may have been alarmed by the Czechoslovak incident and the Brezhnev Doctrine (which might have been thought applicable to China), and may have hoped for a change in American policy under President Nixon. Whatever the reason, the Peking government, on November 26,

1968, proposed that American and Chinese diplomats meet in Warsaw on February 20, 1969, to seek an agreement "on the five principles of peaceful coexistence."[25] The proposal for renewed talks was welcomed by the new administration in Washington, but two days before the meeting was to take place, the Chinese suddenly canceled it, and Chinese officialdom resumed its customary diatribes against both the United States and the Soviet Union.

The United States, on the other hand, where President Nixon and his advisers genuinely desired a normalization of relations with China, made its attitude clear in statements from the White House and by the Secretary of State and through announcing significant relaxation in the restrictions on travel to China. These American gestures of good will apparently bore fruit when a chance social meeting of American and Chinese diplomats in Warsaw in December 1969 led to agreement on resumption of the suspended diplomatic meetings. Such meetings were held, in an atmosphere of apparent cordiality, on January 20 and February 20, 1970, but a further meeting scheduled for May 20 was called off by the Chinese, presumably because of the American invasion of Cambodia on April 30.

After the vote in the U.N. General Assembly in November 1970 showed a majority in favor of seating the Peking government, President Nixon ordered a review of American policy toward China. The President himself, in his second "state of the world" message, February 25, 1971, broke precedent by referring to the Peking government by its official title, the "People's Republic of China." Almost equally novel

was his declaration that an important challenge to the United States in the 1970's would be the drawing of China "into a constructive relationship with the world community."[26]

These and other conciliatory moves from Washington, including a further relaxation of the ban on American travel to China, were reciprocated in an unexpected manner when an American table tennis team, participating in an international meet in Tokyo, was suddenly, early in April 1971, invited to visit China. Three American newsmen were invited to accompany the team, and a few days later *New York Times* correspondent Tilman Durdin, a knowledgeable pre-1949 "China hand," was given a 30-day visa by the Chinese government. Speculation on the significance of "ping pong diplomacy" was heightened when Premier Chou En-lai greeted the visiting team affably in person and observed that their visit had "opened a new page in the relations of the Chinese and American people," as indeed, it had.[27]

President Nixon responded to this unexpected show of friendliness from Peking by announcing at once an easing of the embargo on trade with China and informing a news conference some days later that he himself fully expected to visit mainland China, but at what time and in what capacity he declined to say.

Authorities on Sino-American relations pointed out that in spite of all this euphoria, nothing had been said or done that touched the main obstacle to the improvement of those relations—American support of the Chinese Nationalist regime on Taiwan. Even on this difficult problem, however, there were signs of a new flexibility in Washington. On April 26, 1971, a presidential commission, appointed months be-

[25]*New York Times*, November 27, 1968, pp. 1, 6. The "five principles of peaceful coexistence, the formula of an earlier agreement between Communist China and India, comprised respect for territory and sovereignty, nonaggression, noninterference in one another's internal affairs, equality and mutual benefit, and peaceful coexistence.

[26]*New York Times*, February 26, 1971, p. 13. See also first-page story by Terence Smith, ibid., March 10, 1971.

[27]*New York Times*, April 15, 1971, p. 1.

fore to review American policy in the United Nations, submitted a recommendation that the United States seek, "as soon as practicable," the admission to the United Nations of the People's Republic of China.[28] The appended qualification that the United States should continue to oppose expulsion from the U.N. of the Nationalist government on Taiwan would almost certainly make the proposal in that form unacceptable to Peking, but it was clear that neither the commission (chaired by former Ambassador Henry Cabot Lodge) nor the President accepted the apparently outworn fiction that the Taipei government was the legitimate government of mainland China.

If world opinion was startled by President Nixon's hint in April that he hoped to visit the People's Republic of China, it was electrified, or in some capitals stunned, by his announcement on July 15, 1971, that he had received and accepted an invitation to visit Peking at some time before May 1972. The announcement, made simultaneously in Peking and in a special broadcast from the Western White House in California, followed a perfectly screened mission to Peking by the President's Assistant for National Security Affairs, Dr. Henry Kissinger, who had spent twenty hours in conference with Chou En-lai.

In the United States, the surprising news got a generally favorable reception, except in strongly conservative circles. It was recognized as a major step toward Nixon's well-known goal of normalization of relations with mainland China, an achievement which, it was supposed, might strengthen the position of the United States internationally and of President Nixon politically.

Abroad, the announcement had a mixed reception. It was generally hailed as realistic by allies like England and France, which had long since recognized the Peking re-

gime themselves. But the President's reassurance that the search for a new relationship with Peking would "not be at the expense of our friends" and was "not directed against any other nation" was received in some quarters with skepticism. The ambassador of the Chinese Nationalist government delivered a strong protest at the State Department. Japanese Premier Eisaku Sato, who, like his predecessors, had consistently followed the American lead in his China policy, expressed resentment at not having been consulted before the announcement of this radical reversal of policy. The Soviet government, which could hardly be happy over a prospective rapprochement of its two chief rivals, withheld official comment for ten days. Then, in an article in *Pravda,* July 25, it took what may be described as a cool and "watchful waiting," rather than a hostile, attitude.[29]

Speculation that the proposed American state visit to Peking augured well for the almost certain and early admission of Communist China to the United Nations proved accurate. For, even while the agenda was being worked out, on October 25, 1971, the General Assembly approved, by a margin of 76 to 35, a resolution calling, simultaneously, for the seating of the People's Republic of China and the expulsion of Taiwan. Thus was signaled the end of one era in the U.N. and the beginning of another.

Accompanied by an army of television crews and newspaper reporters, representatives from the Department of State, and the President's national security advisor, then Henry Kissinger, Mr. Nixon was for over a week hosted and toasted by Premier Chou En-lai, Chairman Mao, and a succession of Chinese dignitaries. From a viewing standpoint, it was a global spectacular, replete with the President's walk on the Great Wall of China.

[28]*New York Times,* April 27, 1971, pp. 1, 16. The Lodge commission also suggested possible U.N. membership for the two Germanys, the two Koreas, and the two Vietnams.

[29]*New York Times,* July 16, 1971, pp. 1–3; July 18 (sec. 4), p. 1; July 25 (sec. 4), p. 1; July 26, 1971, p. 5.

Atmospherics aside, the actual substance of the talks was contained in the text of the so-called Shanghai Communiqué released at the conclusion of the final meeting between President Nixon and Premier Chou En-lai. After expressing their respective positions and attitudes toward the general international situation then obtaining, and especially in Vietnam, the two sides reaffirmed that progress toward the normalization of relations between China and the U.S. would be in the interest of all countries. The main barrier, of course, continued to be Taiwan. The Taiwan question, according to the communiqué, remained the crucial question obstructing Sino-American diplomatic ties. Moreover, the liberation of Taiwan, it went on, is China's internal affair in which no other nation has a right to interfere. For its part, the American side acknowledged that Taiwan was indeed an internal problem for the Chinese people to work out for themselves although it was expected that the final solution would be a peaceful one. With this as a goal, the President affirmed the ultimate objective of withdrawal of American forces and installations from that island, while in the meantime progressively reducing existing forces as tension in the area diminished. Finally, the two sides agreed that they would stay in contact through various channels, including the sending of a senior U.S. representative to Peking from time to time later established as a liaison mission, for concrete consultations with regard to further normalization of relations.[30]

For more than seven years the principles contained in the Shanghai communiqué continued to remain the basic set of groundrules governing the relations between the United States and China. Not even President Gerald Ford's trip to Peking in December, 1975, added anything new to the dialogue. Suggestive of this was the decision at the conclusion of his state visit not to issue a joint communiqué at all. If anything, the welcome that former President Nixon received on his return trip as a "private visitor" in February 1976 indicated to what extent the Chinese still relied on the outcome of the initial talks.

A more significant change, perhaps, was the disappearance of the major actors in the China-Taiwan tangle. Mao,[31] Chou En-lai, and Chiang Kai-shek were dead. Who replaced them, and to what extent their successors would follow their predecessors' policies might largely shape the course of Chinese-American relations for decades to come.

[30]*New York Times*, February 28, 1972, pp. 1, 14.

[31]Mao was succeeded, after apparent internal troubles, by Hua Kuo-feng as Chairman of the Communist Party.

ADDITIONAL READINGS

BARNETT, A. DOAK, *Communist China and Asia: Challenge to American Policy.* New York: Harper & Row, Publishers, 1960.

CARY, JAMES, *Japan Today: Reluctant Ally.* New York: Praeger Publishers, Inc. 1963.

CLUBB, O. EDMUND, *China and Russia: The 'Great Game'.* New York: Columbia University Press, 1971.

DUNN, F. S., *Peace-Making and the Settlement with Japan.* Princeton: Princeton University Press, 1963.

GIBNEY, FRANK, *Japan, the Fragile Superpower.* New York: W. W. Norton & Company Inc., 1975.

HALPERIN, MORTON H., *China and the Bomb.* New York: Praeger Publishers, Inc. 1965.

Japan in Current World Affairs, ed. Kajima Institute of International Peace. Tokyo: Japan Times, 1971.

LARKIN, BRUCE D., *China and Africa, 1949–1970: The Foreign Policy of the Peoples' Republic of China.* Berkeley: University of California Press, 1971.

REISCHAUER, EDWIN O., *The Japanese.* Cambridge, Mass.: Belknap Press, Harvard University Press, 1977.

SNOW, EDGAR, *The Other Side of the River: Red China Today.* New York: Random House, Inc. 1962.

TAVARES DE SA, HERMANE. *The Play within the Play: The Inside Story of the U.N.* New York: Alfred A. Knopf, Inc., 1966.

TERRILL, ROSS, *800,000,000: The Real China.* Boston: Little, Brown, 1972.

24. The Postwar Far East, III: Southeast Asia—The War in Indochina

The war in Vietnam, into which the United States was gradually drawn during the 1960's, was, like the Korean War, a part of the program for containing Asiatic Communism. It differed from the Korean War in that it began not as invasion from the Communist North but as subversion in the non-Communist South. The Viet Cong (Vietnamese Communists) were actually participants in a civil war in South Vietnam. They were supported and eventually backed militarily by the Communist government of North Vietnam in Hanoi. How far they were initially instigated by Hanoi is in some doubt.

Also in doubt is the weight of the role played by Vietnamese nationalism as distinct from Communism in the resistance to France and later to the United States. Ho Chi Minh, who led the war against France and, until his death in 1969, against the United States, was a convinced Communist, but nationalism—his insistence upon independence for Vietnam—seems to have been his major motivation at least in the struggle with France, and the dedication of his followers must certainly be ascribed in part to hatred of foreign domination, whether by Japan, France, or the United States.

These are but a few of the questions that made the war in Vietnam extraordinarily hard to understand for the American public and for many of those called to serve in it.

The French in Indochina

Present-day Vietnam, Laos, and Cambodia were known before World War II as French Indochina.[1] They had come under French rule by stages from the 1860s to the 1880s. The entire area was occupied by the Japanese, with the reluctant consent of the Vichy authorities, on the eve of World War II. The Japanese permitted the French officials to function until March 9, 1945. By a coup of that date they arrested the French officials and interned French troops, except for a few who escaped to the mountains or to China. The Japanese took direct control of southern Vietnam (Cochin China) but returned Cambodia, Laos, and northern and central Vietnam (called by the French Tonkin and Annam) to their native rulers—in Vietnam, to Bao Dai, Emperor of Annam. Thus things remained until the Japanese surrender, August 14, 1945.

Should Indochina be restored to French rule? To this question President Roosevelt, a foe of colonialism in general, had replied with an emphatic No. The French, he

[1]Vietnam under French rule was divided into, from north to south, Tonkin, Annam, and Cochin China. The people of all were predominantly Vietnamese. Cochin China, comprising the Mekong Delta and Saigon, was a colony. Annam, Tonkin, Laos, and Cambodia were protectorates with native rulers guided by French advisers.

charged, had "milked" the country for nearly a hundred years, and the native people were worse off than at the beginning of the period. He proposed that Indochina be put under trusteeship in preparation for independence.[2] After Roosevelt's death, however, such intentions were disavowed by the State Department; the Allied High Command designated Britain and China to receive the surrender of Japanese troops in southern and northern Indochina respectively, and the British and Chinese, in turn, withdrew in favor of the French.

The French, however, met formidable resistance from the Viet Minh (Vietnam Independence League), a native nationalist organization headed by Ho Chi Minh. Ho was a Communist, but the Viet Minh at this stage was a united front of Communists and other nationalist elements, whose common objective was an independent Vietnam. The Viet Minh leaders persuaded Emperor Bao Dai to abdicate and on September 2, 1945, at Hanoi, Ho Chi Minh proclaimed the independence of the Democratic Republic of Vietnam, comprising, it was claimed, Tonkin, Annam, and Cochin China.

An independent Vietnam was not in accord with French plans. For reasons of both economics and prestige, France was determined to keep her prewar colonial empire, though modified to bear a distant resemblance to the British Commonwealth. Negotiations between French authorities and Ho Chi Minh led to an agreement (March 6, 1946) by which France recognized Vietnam as a "free state" within the French Union, on condition (1) that Viet-

nam would be a member of an Indochinese federation, with Laos and Cambodia, which had again accepted the status of French protectorates, and (2) that a plebiscite in Cochin China should determine whether the latter would be included in Vietnam or constitute a separate "free state" in the Union.

The agreement broke down primarily over Cochin China, the most highly developed and productive section of Indochina. So intent were the French upon keeping it in their hands that they ignored the provision for a plebiscite (as did Ngo Dinh Diem ten years later) and set up a puppet "Cochin Chinese Republic." This and other disputes led to an outbreak of hostilities between the French and the Viet Minh under Ho Chi Minh in November 1946—a war which, with a brief interruption and a change in participants raged until 1975. A principal stake at the end as at the beginning of those twenty-nine years was whether the Communist Democratic Republic of Vietnam should dominate former Cochin China, constituting the then vital part of South Vietnam.

The French Fight a Losing War

The French, having broken with Ho Chi Minh, set up a rival Vietnamese government and induced the former Emperor, Bao Dai, to head it as chief of state. To this subservient government they gave the privilege, denied to Ho Chi Minh, of extending its rule over Cohin China. The Bao Dai government gained recognition from Britain and the United States, but since France still refused to grant full rights of self-government, the Bao Dai regime made little appeal to Vietnamese nationalism.

The Viet Minh, meanwhile, was abandoning Ho's united front policy, purging its non-Communist elements, and aligning itself with world Communism. The "Demo-

[2]For a discussion on this subject, see Joseph M. Siracusa, "The United States, Vietnam, and the Cold War: A Reappraisal," *Journal of Southeast Asian Studies,* 5 (1974), pp. 82–101; and, more recently, "FDR, Truman, and Indochina, 1941–1952: The Forgotten Years," in *The Impact of the Cold War: Reconsiderations,* ed. by Joseph M. Siracusa and Glen St. John Barclay (Port Washington, N.Y.: Kennikat Press Corp., 1977), pp. 163–83.

cratic Republic of Vietnam" thereby gained recognition and some material support from China and Russia but, in the words of one authority, "blundered across the no-man's land of the cold war into a position where it found itself confronted by the Communist-containment policy newly formulated by the United States."[3] France and the government of Bao Dai, as opponents of world Communism, could now count upon large-scale aid from the United States. Such aid was stepped up after the Korean War began, until by 1954 the United States was bearing some 70 percent of the cost of the French military effort in Vietnam.

In spite of such massive material aid, the war went badly for the French. It reached a crisis in the spring of 1954 when a French and Vietnamese army of 20,000 men was surrounded and cut off by a superior force of Viet Minh troops in the frontier fortress of Dienbienphu. The French government, in appeals to Washington, warned that without direct military aid from the United States, Dienbienphu was doomed and that its fall might pave the way for Communist conquest of all Indochina, perhaps all of Southeast Asia.

To President Eisenhower, who likened the situation to the falling of a row of dominoes, and even more to Secretary of State John Foster Dulles, such a challenge to the containment policy had to be met at almost any cost. When consultation with congressional leaders revealed strong opposition to American unilateral intervention, Dulles tried unsuccessfully to persuade the British government to join with the United States, France, and minor states in an alliance to save the French in Vietnam and to contain Communism in Southeast Asia. An international conference was about to meet in Geneva to deal with the problem of Korea and also with that of Indochina, and the British were unwilling to take action that might prevent the success of the conference. Consequently nothing was done to save Dienbienphu, which fell on May 7.

The Geneva Conference of 1954

The Geneva Conference (April 26 to July 21, 1954), having failed to reach agreement on Korea, turned to Indochina, where it was more successful.[4] The United States, however, played little more than an observer's role in this phase of the Conference. Dulles, reluctant to meet the Chinese delegate Chou En-lai (whose government the United States did not recognize) and to subscribe to the inevitable cession of territory to the Communist Viet Minh, took little part in the Conference personally, and his deputy, Under Secretary Walter Bedell Smith, attended only intermittently. The United States signed no conference documents.

The armistice terms agreed upon, July 20, ended the fighting in Cambodia and Laos (which had also been invaded by the Viet Minh) and in Vietnam, and divided Vietnam at the 17th parallel of north latitude. The Viet Minh, officially the Democratic Republic of Vietnam, was to take the north, including the cities of Hanoi and Haiphong. The State of Vietnam, soon to be known as South Vietnam, still nominally under Bao Dai, was to take all south of the line. The division, however, was to be temporary. The country was to be united on the basis of free general elections in July 1956. An international commission, com-

[3]Ellen J. Hammer, *The Struggle for Indochina* (Stanford: Stanford University Press, 1954), p. 247. Also see, Gary R. Hess, "The First American Commitment in Indochina: The Acceptance of the 'Bao Dai Solution,' 1950," *Diplomatic History,* 2 (1978), 331–50.

[4]Participants in this phase of the Geneva Conference were the United States, the U.S.S.R., Britain, France, Communist China, Cambodia, Laos, the Democratic Republic of (North) Vietnam, and the State of (South) Vietnam.

posed of representatives of Canada, India, and Poland, was to supervise the carrying out of the armistice terms.

The United States acquiesced in the terms of settlement without being a party to them and gave assurance that it would "refrain from the threat or use of force to disturb them" and would view any attempt by others to do so "as seriously threatening international peace and security." The State of (South) Vietnam also withheld approval from the settlement and protested against many of its terms, including the provision for elections. Under a new premier, Ngo Dinh Diem, the South Vietnamese government was acting independently of the French. Before the end of the year, in fact, France had agreed to the complete independence of all three states of Indochina.[5]

The SEATO Alliance

Since it appeared that only international action could prevent the further advance of Communism in the area, Secretary Dulles took the initiative in the creation of a Southeast Asia Treaty Organization (SEATO) to serve as a "container" of Communism in Southeast Asia, as NATO served in Europe. Unfortunately, several of the most important nations of Southeast Asia—India, Burma, Ceylon, and Indonesia—were so thoroughly committed to neutrality in the struggle between Russia and the West that they would have no part in such an organization. The states of Indochina—Vietnam, Cambodia, and Laos —were prevented from participation by the terms of the Geneva armistice. The Nationalist Chinese government on Taiwan, unrecognized by Great Britain, could not be included for that reason. Japan had no

[5]*Documents on American Foreign Relations, 1954,* pp. 283–318.

contribution to make to a defense organization. The Philippines, Thailand, and Pakistan were the only Asiatic nations that could be counted upon. Delegates of these three met in Manila on September 6, 1954, with representatives of the United States, Great Britain, France, Australia, and New Zealand. Thus five of the eight participating governments were of the West (in culture if not in geography); four were of the English-speaking world.

Such a gathering was certain to be denounced as "imperialist" by Communist spokesmen. Partly, at least, to head off this charge, the delegates adopted a proposal of President Ramón Magsaysay of the Philippines for a "Pacific Charter." The signatories of this document affirmed their faith in "the principle of equal rights and self-determination of peoples" and promised to

strive by every peaceful means to promote self-government and to secure independence of all countries whose peoples desire it and are able to undertake its responsibilities.

Having thus answered the charge of "imperialism," the eight delegations proceeded to their principal task, agreement upon a treaty, which was officially titled the "South-east Asia Collective Defense Treaty" and signed at Manila on September 8, 1954. The treaty followed the pattern of the Australia, New Zealand, and Philippines treaties rather than the NATO model. That is to say, instead of declaring an attack upon one to be an attack upon all, it stated that an attack upon one would be recognized as dangerous to the peace and safety of the others. Each member agreed, in such an event, to "act to meet the common danger in accordance with its constitutional processes." The treaty also provided for consultation and collective action if threats to any member developed in the form of subversion rather than armed attack from without. It provided for

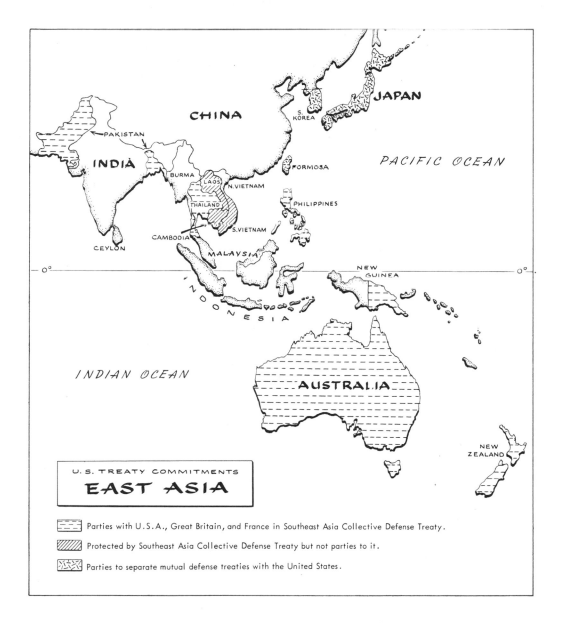

U.S. TREATY COMMITMENTS

EAST ASIA

Parties with U.S.A., Great Britain, and France in Southeast Asia Collective Defense Treaty.

Protected by Southeast Asia Collective Defense Treaty but not parties to it.

Parties to separate mutual defense treaties with the United States.

economic cooperation, including technical assistance, "to promote economic progress and social well-being"; and it declared, through an attached protocol, that Laos, Cambodia, and "the free territory under the jurisdiction of the state of Vietnam" should be eligible for both the protective features and the economic benefits that the treaty provided. To consider matters concerning the implementation of the treaty and to provide for military or other necessary planning in connection with it, the treaty called for the establishment of a council on which all parties should be represented, so organized as to be able to meet at any time.[6]

SEATO, with its annual Council meetings and its occasional joint military maneuvers, may have exercised some deterrent influence upon potential Communist aggression in Southeast Asia, but any such influence was plainly dependent upon the power and the determination of the United States. It was in Laos and South Vietnam that those factors were to be tested.

Upon French acknowledgment of the independence of Cambodia, Laos, and divided Vietnam, the United States promptly accredited ambassadors to the first two and to the State of (South) Vietnam and initiated programs of economic and military aid with a view to enabling them to maintain their independence. American influence soon overshadowed French. It was, in fact, deliberate American policy to supplant the French as supplier of aid and advice to the three states. America, Dulles believed, would not be subject to the suspicion that the native people would feel for their former "imperialist" masters. By thus replacing French influence in the area, the United States also took over from France, morally at least, responsibility for seeing that the Geneva terms were observed by the former protégés of France. Of the three states, Cambodia took an outspokenly neutralist position, seeming at times more suspicious of the West than of the Communist powers. The government of South Vietnam was uncompromisingly anti-Communist and pro-Western. Laos was in danger of being torn apart between leftist, neutralist, and rightist elements. On the morrow of the Geneva Conference, however, the most critical situation was that in South Vietnam.

[6]*Documents on American Foreign Relations, 1954,* pp. 318–23. The United States delegation incorporated in the treaty a statement that the obligations assumed by the United States to act against aggression applied to Communist aggression only, but that the United States agreed to consult with other signers "in the event of other aggression or armed attack."

The long struggle in Vietnam had called forth one interesting personality in the anti-Communist ranks. Ngo Dinh Diem, hitherto little known, had become Premier in June 1954, nominally under the absentee Emperor, Bao Dai. A Catholic Christian, a celibate, an ascetic, a nationalist patriot, he was uncompromising in his opposition to Communism and also to a continuance of French rule. It was he who, along with the United States, had refused to sign the Geneva agreement. Faced with apparently insuperable obstacles—remnants of the Viet Minh and other hostile armed factions at home, antagonism of the Riviera Emperor, hostility of the French, the problem of resettling nearly a million refugees from north of the 17th parallel—the Premier overcame them all, thanks partly to American aid but primarily to his own shrewdness and determination. When the Emperor sought to remove him, he refused to relinquish his post. In October 1955 he held a plebiscite in which the people of South Vietnam were asked to choose between him and Bao Dai. Victor by an enormous majority in an election allegedly "rigged" by his unscrupulous brother, Ngo Dinh Nhu, Diem declared the state a republic—henceforth the Republic of Vietnam—and himself President. By the end of the year he seemed to have the situation well under control. Already in evidence was the reliance on his family which, with the autocratic quality that he displayed later, was to be his undoing.

Compromise in Laos

In the kingdom of Laos the history of the period from 1954 to 1963 is too complicated to permit of more than summary treatment in this narrative. The Geneva settlement had left the Communist Pathet Lao ("Lao nation") forces in occupation of two northeastern provinces adjoining North Vietnam and Communist China. Attempts of the neutralist Premier, Prince Souvanna

Phouma, to integrate these forces and their political leaders into the Laotian army and government aroused rightist opposition and replacement of Souvanna Phouma (repeatedly, though never for long) with Premiers representing the right. Successive attempts of such rightist governments to suppress the Pathet Lao led to armed resistance, supported, so the Laos government claimed, by Communist troops from North Vietnam. An appeal by Laos to the United Nations for action against such aggression in 1959 led the Security Council, over Russian objection, to send a subcommittee to investigate, whereupon the rebellion subsided. In 1960, on the other hand, Souvanna Phouma's renewed effort to come to terms with the Pathet Lao led to rebellion on the right, the flight of the Premier to Cambodia, the choice of still another rightist Premier by the Assembly, and civil war between right and left. Since the United States (which had assumed the task of training and supplying the Royal Laotian Army) was aiding the right and the U.S.S.R. was flying in military equipment for the Communists, there was danger that the civil war might escalate into a major conflict.

As the Royal Army proved unable to stay the Communist offensive, it became apparent in Washington that only some kind of intervention from outside could preserve even a neutral Laos. The SEATO Council, meeting in Bangkok, March 27–29, 1961, failed to take decisive action in spite of the urging of its three Asiatic members and presumably of the United States.[7] President Kennedy now accepted a British proposal that the co-chairmen (Britain and Russia) of the 1954 Geneva Conference call upon it to reconvene to consider an attempt to settle the Laotian muddle.

Accordingly, a fourteen-nation Conference met at Geneva in May 1961.[8] Its ef-

forts were stimulated by the joint statement of President Kennedy and Premier Khrushchev from Vienna, June 4, reaffirming "their support of a neutral and independent Laos." It became apparent that the only neutralist solution for Laos would be found in a coalition government headed by neutralist Prince Souvanna Phouma and his rivals of the right and left, Princes Boun Oum and Souphanouvong respectively. The Conference, therefore, could not conclude its work until the three Princes had reached agreement. This required a year of hard bargaining, during which a new Communist offensive threatened to overflow into Thailand, a SEATO ally of the United States. The landing in Thailand of 1,800 marines from the Seventh Fleet, followed by token forces from Great Britain, Australia, and New Zealand, headed off any such danger and perhaps expedited agreement on Laos.[9]

At any rate, on June 11, 1962, the three Princes reached agreement. Souvanna Phouma became Premier, Prince Souphanouvong and General Phoumi Nosavan (for whom Prince Boun Oum had stepped aside), Deputy Premiers. On questions of foreign policy, defense, and police, decisions were to be concurred in by the three. In a statement of July 9 the new government guaranteed its neutrality and renounced the protection of "any alliance or military coalition" (i.e. SEATO). The transaction was completed at Geneva on July 21, 1962, when the fourteen nations of the Conference signed documents undertaking to respect the independence, sovereignty, neutrality, and territorial integrity of the Kingdom of Laos and setting forth rules for the International Commission that was to supervise the settlement.[10]

---

[7]*U.S. in World Affairs, 1961,* pp. 197–98; *Documents on American Foreign Relations, 1961,* pp. 296–99.

[8]The governments taking part in the Conference were those of Burma, Cambodia, Canada, Communist China, France, India, Laos, Poland, Thailand, the U.S.S.R., the United Kingdom, the United States, North Vietnam, South Vietnam.

[9]*U.S. in World Affairs, 1962,* p. 197.

[10]*New York Times,* June 12, pp. 1, 14; June 13, p. 3; July 10, p. 4; July 22, pp. 1, 14, 1962.

Since the Commission (Canada, India, Poland), like the Laotian government, operated on the "troika" principle except on procedural questions, its efficacy as a bulwark against further Communist encroachment was dubious. During the next year, in fact, intermittent pressure of Communist forces upon neutralist and rightist elements made it plain that the Laotian settlement would never be more than a shaky armistice.

Diem Faces Guerrilla War

Many months before the Laotian settlement was reached, the United States found itself confronted by a crisis in South Vietnam (the usual appellation for the Republic of Vietnam, with its capital at Saigon). The Communist government of North Vietnam (the Democratic Republic of Vietnam) at Hanoi had never abandoned its intention to "liberate" the South and thus unify the country under Communist rule. Ho Chi Minh had expected to accomplish this through the elections to be held in July 1956, and such was Ho's prestige as a nationalist patriot that there is good reason to believe that he could have won in a fair election in Vietnam as a whole. President Ngo Dinh Diem of South Vietnam, however, maintained, with reason, that no election in the Communist North could be fair, and since neither he nor the United States, which backed him in this argument, had signed the Geneva agreement, Diem was within his rights in refusing to hold the elections. In refusing to carry out this part of the Geneva settlement, however, it has been argued that he forfeited any right to be protected by the armistice, another part of the same complex agreement.

At any rate, Diem's refusal meant that no elections were held in 1956, and Ho Chi Minh's hope for unification of Vietnam by that process was frustrated. Here we reach

a very controversial point in the narrative. Was the campaign of terrorism that began in the South in 1957—chiefly in the form of assassination of village officers, killing or kidnapping of schoolteachers, etc.— instigated by Hanoi, or did it spring from local grievances in South Vietnam— abolition of village elections, collection of back rent for absentee landlords, persecution of former Viet Minh and other opponents of the regime? The U.S. State Department has maintained consistently that the campaign of subversion was from the beginning engineered from Hanoi with the object of taking over the country. Some reputable scholars, both French and American, have concluded, on the contrary, that the rebellion against the Saigon government of Ngo Dinh Diem was indigenous to the South and that the Hanoi government came to its support only in 1960 when implored to do so by southern veterans of the former Viet Minh. The answer to this question, if it could be given with certainty, would have an obvious bearing on the character of the war. Was it a war of aggression of the North against the South? Or was it a civil war in the South with the North coming to the aid of one faction? American policy had of course been based on the former hypothesis.[11]

By 1958, at any rate, Diem's government had a guerrilla war on its hands, with the Viet Cong establishing control in many rural areas. Both Diem and his American military advisers, however, were slow in facing the facts. With guerrilla war "breaking out all over," American military advisers provided the native army with training only for conventional war, on the Korean pattern, while political advisers were unable to persuade Diem to adopt economic and social reforms that might have held the loy-

[11]The official interpretation is set forth in the State Department White Paper *Aggression from the North,* Department of State Publication 7839 (Washington: Government Printing Office, 1965).

alty of the peasantry. In December 1960 the formation of the National Liberation Front (NLF) of South Vietnam was announced. This body, which seems clearly to have owed its inspiration to Hanoi, was designated as the political arm of the movement in which the Viet Cong were the military. By 1961, Southerners who had withdrawn to the North at the time of the partition were returning to the South on a large scale and joining in the resistance. By the end of that year the Viet Cong had extended their influence to perhaps 80 percent of the South Vietnamese countryside.

The United States to the Rescue

President John F. Kennedy had been in office only a short time when he received from President Diem an appeal for increased military aid. In May 1961 Kennedy sent Vice President Lyndon B. Johnson on a fact-finding mission to Vietnam and elsewhere in Asia. Johnson, who as Senate Leader had opposed intervention to save Dienbienphu in 1954, found the Communist threat in Vietnam serious, and his report echoed the "domino theory" of President Eisenhower. Unless Communism was successfully fought in Southeast Asia, he told the President, "the United States, inevitably, must surrender the Pacific and take up our defenses on our own shores." The United States must decide whether "to attempt to meet the challenge of Communist expansion now in Southeast Asia by a major effort in support of the forces of freedom in the area, or throw in the towel." An affirmative decision would involve heavy costs "in terms of money, of effort, and of United States prestige" and might lead to the necessity of making "the further decision of whether we commit major United States forces to the area or cut our losses and withdraw should our efforts fail. . . . I recommend," Johnson added,

"we proceed with a clear-cut and strong program of action."[12]

President Diem did not at this time ask for U.S. troops. General Maxwell D. Taylor, whom Kennedy sent on a similar mission a few months later, found that Diem, while not asking for combat troops, would welcome American military personnel to assist in logistics and communications.

President Kennedy responded to Diem's request and Taylor's report in a letter of December 14, 1961. He was convinced, he assured Diem, "that the campaign of force and terror now being waged against your people and your Government is supported and directed from the outside by the authorities at Hanoi." Since these activities on the part of Hanoi violated the provisions of the Geneva settlement, and since the United States viewed such violations "with grave concern," the United States, said the President, would "promptly increase our assistance to your defense effort."[13]

Now began a new phase of American aid to South Vietnam, which for the period 1955–1962 exceeded $2 billion in cost and by 1963 was at the rate of nearly $500 million annually. A dramatic indicator of the new policy was the arrival at Saigon, December 12, 1961, of an American escort carrier bearing over thirty helicopters, four single-engine training planes, and operating and maintenance crews to the number of about four hundred men. This event was a prelude to the "helicopter war," in which United States personnel were to participate throughout the next three years, flying Vietnamese troops over jungles and rice fields in attempts, sometimes successful, sometimes not, to detect, intercept, and destroy units of the Viet Cong, or Communist

[12]Rowland Evans and Robert Novak, *Lyndon B. Johnson: The Exercise of Power* (New York: The New American Library, Inc. 1966, © 1966 by Rowland Evans and Robert Novak), pp. 321–23.

[13]*Documents on American Foreign Relations, 1961*, pp. 323–24.

guerrillas. In addition to a reliance on this mode of transport, the United States had undertaken to train the Vietnamese army in guerrilla tactics and had persuaded President Diem's government to launch a program of isolating the peasantry from the guerrillas by resettling them in fortified villages—a procedure which the British had found successful in fighting Communist guerrillas in Malaya. The number of American troops in South Vietnam increased steadily, reaching some 16,500 before the end of 1963. Technically they were engaged only in transportation, training, and advice, but these activities inevitably exposed them to combat conditions. At first ordered to retaliate if fired upon, they were later authorized to shoot first if obviously about to be attacked. By the end of May 1964 more than two hundred Americans had been killed, about half of them in battle, since the beginning of the new program. A number of American planes had been shot down.[14]

The Fall of Diem

The American task in South Vietnam was rendered more difficult by a growing rift between President Ngo Dinh Diem and non-Communist elements in the population. His rule had become increasingly authoritarian. Members of his family, it was charged, exercised too much influence. This criticism applied especially to his younger brother, Ngo Dinh Nhu, who had become his principal adviser, and the latter's attractive and outspoken wife. The President grew intolerant of criticism, whether voiced by his own people or by

foreigners. He resented, as outside interference, American suggestions for alleviating popular discontent or improving his administrative structure and techniques.

The war against the Viet Cong dragged along with no end in sight. A Senate subcommittee, visiting Southeast Asia late in 1962, found little ground for optimism. It warned, on the one hand, that any sudden termination of the aid programs in the area "would open the region to upheaval and chaos" and probable Chinese domination. On the other hand, it pointed to the danger that the war in Vietnam might be converted "primarily into an American war, to be fought primarily with American lives." "*In present circumstances,*" the report observed, no interest of the United States in Vietnam would justify such a war. Primary responsibility for the survival of the Republic of Vietnam should rest with the Vietnamese government and people, and any further effort necessary to assure it should come from that source.[15]

Dissatisfaction, both native and American, with the rule of the Ngo Dinh family reached boiling point in the summer and fall of 1963. A basic cause of trouble was antagonism between the Catholic ruling family and the Buddhist majority (commonly stated at 70 percent) of the population. A bloody suppression, in May 1963, of a Buddhist procession in Hué (where a brother of Diem was the archbishop) led to Buddhist demonstrations, including a series of spectacular suicides by fire, in the capital, and in turn to government raids on Buddhist pagodas and the imprisonment of scores of Buddhist monks, or bonzes. Native resentment of the oligarchy became so intense that President Kennedy and his advisers were convinced that without a change in policies, if not in personnel, the

---

[14]*Viet Nam and Southeast Asia.* Report of Senator Mike Mansfield et al. to the Committee on Foreign Relations, United States Senate. Printed for the use of the Committee on Foreign Relations (Washington: Government Printing Office, 1963), pp. 3–9; *New York Times,* November 3, 1962, Sec. 4, p. 1; November 15, 1963, p. 13.

[15]*Viet Nam and Southeast Asia,* op. cit., pp. 2, 8–9. The italics are the subcommittee's. What different circumstances might justify a primarily American war in the area it did not explain.

war against the Viet Cong would hopelessly bog down. A new ambassador, Henry Cabot Lodge (grandson and namesake of Woodrow Wilson's antagonist) was sent to Saigon, and Diem was subjected to pressure by cuts in American aid. Lodge was unsuccessful in persuading Diem to part with his brother or to reform his administration. On November 1, a group of army officers,

headed by General Duong Van Minh, carried out a carefully planned revolution, seized the royal palace, and captured the brothers Diem and Nhu, who had taken refuge in a church. Both were killed.

The military junta set up a civilian figure-head as Premier, promised free elections, released political prisoners, declared the press free, and began making disposi-

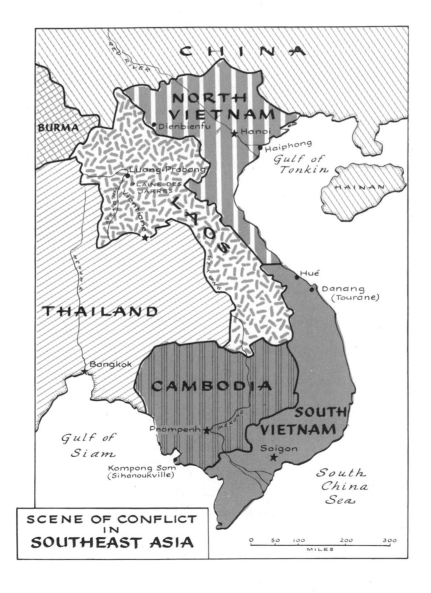

SCENE OF CONFLICT IN SOUTHEAST ASIA

tions for the more effective conduct of the war. The United States promptly recognized the new provisional government, hoping that it might save Washington from the dilemma suggested by Senator Mansfield's subcommittee: make the war in Vietnam "primarily American" or let the Viet Cong take the country.

Escalating the War

The otherthrow and death of President Diem was followed in less than three weeks by the assassination of President Kennedy. Lyndon B. Johnson, the new President, was explicit in assuring the Saigon government of continued American support. In a letter of December 31, 1963, to General Duong Van Minh, chairman of the Military Revolutionary Council in Saigon, Johnson wrote: "The United States will continue to furnish you and your people with the fullest measure of support in this bitter fight."

The stability and efficiency that had been hoped for from the new government did not materialize, however. General Minh was overthrown in January 1964 by another general, and military coups followed one another at frequent intervals until June 1965, when General Nguyen Van Thieu became Chief of State with Air Vice-Marshal Nguyen Cao Ky as Premier. This pair continued to head the government until its collapse in April, 1975. Under a new constitution prepared by a popularly elected convention in 1966 and effective the next year, Thieu was elected President and Ky, Vice President, both for four-year terms. A Senate and House of Representatives were also elected by popular vote under the new constitution, and the government of South Vietnam took on the appearance of a democracy, though opponents of the regime who showed any inclination to compromise with Hanoi or the NLF were denied political rights and often their liberty.

In their relations with the United States, Thieu and Ky were more cooperative and more amenable to suggestion than some of their predecessors had been. Some real progress was made in pacifying the villages and hamlets of the rural areas—winning their allegiance to the government and providing protection from further incursions of the Viet Cong. By September 1967, when elections were held, over 60 percent of the population of voting age were in areas where registration was possible without undue interference from the Viet Cong.

During the year and a half after Diem's fall, however, the war had gone badly for the government, and President Johnson eventually found it necessary to make the decision that he had forseen in 1961— "whether we commit major United States forces to the area or cut our losses and withdraw." He chose the former course, though the decision was made known in stages, each stage usually triggered by an allegedly provocative act by the enemy.

The first such episode was an attack by North Vietnamese PT-boats on American destroyers cruising in international waters in the Gulf of Tonkin (August 2, 1964, and again, so it was claimed, on August 4). The government retaliated by bombing North Vietnamese naval stations, and Congress, at the President's request, passed a joint resolution authorizing the President "to take all necessary measures to repel any armed attack against the forces of the United States," or "to assist any member or protocol state" (for example, South Vietnam) of the SEATO treaty "requesting assistance in defense of its freedom."[16] This Tonkin Gulf Resolution, as it came to be called, passed the House of Representatives unanimously, the Senate by a vote of 82 to 2. Described by the State Department as "a functional equivalent of a declaration of

---

[16]*Documents on American Foreign Relations, 1964*, pp. 216–17.

war," it gave President Johnson congressional backing for such escalation of the war as he might choose to carry out. Its passage was later bitterly regretted by some of its sponsors, notably Senator Fulbright, chairman of the Committee on Foreign Relations, who came to believe that the provocative incidents had been distorted or magnified and used by the President to secure a wide grant of powers.[17]

The Gulf of Tonkin incident, as it happened, came in the thick of a presidential campaign in which the Republican candidate, Senator Barry Goldwater, was urging a more vigorous participation in the war by the United States. In defending his more restrained course, Lyndon Johnson gave repeated assurances that American boys would not be sent "nine or ten thousand miles away from home to do what Asian boys ought to be doing for themselves."[18] His sweeping victory in the election was presumably due in part to such assurances.

By January 1965 there were some 23,000 United States troops in South Vietnam, but these were still "advisers," only incidentally exposed to risks of combat. On February 7, however, at Pleiku, and three days later at Quinhon, attacks by Viet Cong on American barracks caused heavy casualties. In each instance the United States retaliated by bombing military targets in North Vietnam. Beginning as retaliation for specific hostile acts, bombing from American carriers or land bases became more and more frequent until by the summer of 1965 it had become a regular campaign against North Vietnamese military targets. It continued to escalate and to broaden the range of targets, including oil installations at Hanoi and Haiphong, port facilities at Haiphong, iron works and railroad yards, and the railroad from Hanoi to China to within ten miles of the Chinese border.

Such a campaign took risks. Two Russian cargo ships were hit. Bombing so near the Chinese border might have resulted in hostile encounters with the Chinese. The danger of widening the war was evident. Bombing close to or within cities inevitably killed civilians, bringing charges of "war crimes" upon the United States abroad and among critics at home. U.N. Secretary-General U Thant repeatedly called upon the United States to stop the bombing, and President Charles de Gaulle of France declared it "detestable" for "a great nation to ravage a small one."[19] The bombing went on, nevertheless, until 1968, except for occasional pauses, of which it was hoped (in vain) that Hanoi would take advantage by indicating a desire for peace negotiations.

In the meantime, "American boys" were taking over an increasingly heavy share of the war on the ground. To counter the deterioration of the South Vietnamese military position in the interregnum after Diem's fall, the United States put ashore two Marine battalions at Danang (the former Tourane) on May 6, 1965—the first American troops to be actually deployed for combat in Vietnam. Thereafter the

---

[17]Joseph C. Goulden, *Truth Is the First Casualty: The Gulf of Tonkin Affair—Illusion and Reality* (Chicago: Rand McNally & Co., 1969); *The Gulf of Tonkin, The 1964 Incidents.* Hearing before the Committee on Foreign Relations, United States Senate, 90th Congress, 2d session, February 20, 1968 (Washington: Government Printing Office, 1968). There was no question about the attack on August 2. Evidence for that reported on August 4 was less conclusive. Some senators questioned whether the attacks had really been unprovoked and thought that, in any event, the U.S. response (64 air sorties) was excessive. On June 24, 1970, the Senate voted, 81 to 10, to repeal the Tonkin Gulf Resolution. The House of Representatives later concurred in their action, and President Nixon signed on January 12, 1971, an arms sale bill to which the repeal was attached. *Buffalo Evening News,* January 13, 1971. The President had not opposed the repeal, arguing that his actions in Vietnam and Cambodia "are validated by the President's constitutional power to protect the lives of American troops." *New York Times,* June 25, 26 (editorial), 1970.

[18]Quoted, with other similar expressions, in A. M. Schlesinger, Jr., *The Bitter Heritage: Vietnam and American Democracy, 1941–1966* (Boston: Houghton Mifflin Company, 1967), p. 29.

[19]*U.S. in World Affairs, 1966,* p. 94.

number grew rapidly: 180,000 by the end of 1965, 380,000 a year later, 542,000 in February 1969. Combat deaths at the end of 1970 exceeded 44,000.

Hawks versus Doves

The conflict had become a major American war, and yet there had been no declaration of war by Congress. How did the President justify carrying on a war of this scale without that supposedly essential formality? There was, of course, the Tonkin Gulf Resolution, but that resolution, apart from its assertion of the right to defend U.S. forces, found its basis in the SEATO treaty. Each party to that treaty had agreed that an armed attack in the area against any other party or against any state which they had unanimously designated (for example, South Vietnam), "would endanger its own peace and safety" and that it would "act to meet the common danger in accordance with its constitutional processes." The State Department contended that South Vietnam had become an independent state and that infiltration from North Vietnam across the cease-fire line constituted armed aggression, which called for action under the SEATO treaty and also justified it as "collective self-defense" under Article 51 of the U.N. Charter. "Constitutional processes," according to the State Department, had been taken care of by the Tonkin Gulf Resolution.[20]

On grounds of national interest, furthermore, the President and the State Department viewed the defense of South Vietnam as essential to the containment of Chinese Communism, as a test of Lin Piao's theory of the inevitable success of Communist guerrilla war. A Communist victory in South Vietnam would be but a prelude to the conquest of Laos and Cambodia. Then would come the threat to Thailand, Malaysia, Indonesia, the Philippines, Taiwan, and Japan. If Communism were not stopped in this small country, only a much greater war could stop it later. There must not, then, be another Munich in Southeast Asia.

The United States, it was argued further, had promised protection to the government and people of South Vietnam. To ignore that promise would not only expose thousands of its friends and supporters in South Vietnam to bloody reprisals; it would also impair the prestige of the United States and destroy its credibility in the eyes of all its allies. There was some truth in all of these.

Americans who thus argued for continuing the war or, as some of them did, for waging it more relentlessly, were called "hawks." Those who opposed it were "doves," and among them, to name but a few, were such notable figures as Senators J. W. Fulbright, Mike Mansfield, and Wayne Morse, former diplomat George Kennan, journalist Walter Lippmann, and political scientist Hans Morgenthau. In agreement with them were many public men of both political parties, such newspapers as the *New York Times* and *Washington Post,* and an overwhelming majority of the vocal youth of America, especially college youth.

Many doves saw the war in Vietnam, not as an international war of aggression, but as a civil war in which Vietnamese revolutionary nationalism fought a reactionary and corrupt government supported by a foreign power, yesterday France, today the United States. On this kind of war the SEATO treaty had no bearing. The United States had no obligation to intervene under that treaty.[21] It was intervening, further-

---

[20]*Aggression from the North U.S. in World Affairs, 1967,* p. 375.

[21]Was the United States more obligated to defend South Vietnam than other SEATO signatories? England, France, and Pakistan denied any such obligation. Australia, New Zealand, and Thailand sent small military contingents, and Thailand supplied air bases for American planes. The Philippines sent a 2,000-man construction battalion (paid for by the United States). The only nation that sent significant military support (some 50,000 troops) was South Korea, not a member of SEATO.

more, on behalf of an unpopular government and against a popular revolutionary movement. Furthermore, said some doves, the United States could not win, but in the effort to do so, it was destroying the society which it professed to be saving. The war had outraged world opinion. It had divided the American people. It was wasting American resources, starving vital reform programs at home, and cutting down on salutary aid to the developing countries abroad.

A victory of North Vietnam, the doves conceded, might make all Vietnam Communist. But a Communist Vietnam would not be a puppet of China. The Vietnamese people had for centuries hated and feared China. A Communist Vietnam might well be a Yugoslavia of the Far East, Communist but unaligned. In any event, the Communist world was no longer a monolith. Rent by the deep fissure between Peking and Moscow, it was no longer the awesome giant of Stalin's day. Let the United States stop fighting a frightfully costly and destructive war, which it could not win, against a danger of greatly shrunken proportions.

The debate went on, in Congress and out, and the longer the war dragged on with no end in sight, the stronger grew the appeal of the doves to the badly disillusioned public.

The War a Stalemate

Despite the enormous American effort, supplemented by the operations of some 700,000 South Vietnamese troops and the smaller contingents from other allies, the war by 1968 had reached a condition of stalemate. The Viet Cong and North Vietnamese troops (of the latter, some 45,000 were estimated to be committed) obviously could not force the Americans out or destroy the Saigon government. The Americans and their allies, on the other hand, could not destroy the Viet Cong or, despite heavy bombing, prevent North Vietnamese

supplies and reinforcements from reaching the battle area via the Ho Chi Minh Trail through Laos or through Cambodia. Nor could they prevent attacks on South Vietnamese cities by rocket-borne bombs or by occasional infiltration or invasion.

A tragic illustration of the vulnerability of the government-held area of South Vietnam was the Tet (Lunar New Year) offensive of January–February 1968. In November 1967 Ambassador Ellsworth Bunker and General William C. Westmoreland, commander of U.S. troops in Vietnam, were brought from Saigon to report in Washington. Both were optimistic on the pacification program as well as on the war. The general was quoted as saying, "We are winning a war of attrition" and as predicting that within two years the United States would be able to begin a slow withdrawal of its forces, turning over a progressively larger share of the responsibility to the Vietnamese.[22]

Yet barely two months later, in the early morning of January 31, 1968, the Viet Cong made simultaneous surprise attacks on twenty-six or more provincial capitals and, as the *New York Times* reported, "uncounted numbers of district towns and American and Vietnamese air fields and bases." The most dramatic episodes were the seizure and six-hour occupation by twenty suicidal Viet Cong of the American Embassy compound in Saigon, and the capture of the old Annamese capital of Hué, including the ancient citadel, from which the intruders were driven only after weeks of fighting. The Viet Cong took advantage of their occupation of Hué to murder an estimated 3,000 or more Vietnamese citizens, presumably supporters of the Saigon regime.

The Viet Cong were eventually expelled with heavy casualties from all the towns and cities that they had seized, and President Johnson proclaimed the Tet offensive "a complete failure," which it was, in military terms. Yet it had quite destroyed the opti-

[22]*New York Times*, November 26, 1967, Sec. 4, p. 2.

mism produced by the reports of Bunker and Westmoreland, set back the pacification program many months, and shown the war to be truly a stalemate. From this point on, talk of "victory" in the war largely ceased. "Peace," a compromise peace, by negotiation, became the declared objective.

The Search for Peace

In fact, the offer of peace negotiations was as old as active American participation in the war. In a speech at Johns Hopkins University, April 7, 1965, President Johnson had stated the essence of the American peace terms in a few words: "an independent South Vietnam—securely guaranteed and able to shape its own relationships to all others—free from outside interference—tied to no alliance—a military base for no other country." If peace were assured, he added, the United States would be ready to invest a billion dollars in development of the Mekong River area—a development in which he hoped North Vietnam would share.[23]

The Hanoi government responded next day with a four-point peace program comprising: (1) complete withdrawal of all U.S. troops from South Vietnam and cancellation of the alleged U.S.-South Vietnam "military alliance": (2) observation of the 1954 Geneva agreement pending the unification of Vietnam: (3) settlement of the internal affairs of South Vietnam by the people of South Vietnam in accordance with the program of the NLF; (4) peaceful unification of Vietnam "to be settled by the Vietnamese people in both zones, without any foreign interference."[24] Later Hanoi

[23]*Department of State Bulletin*, 52 (April 26, 1965), 606–10.

[24]M. G. Raskin and B. B. Fall, eds., *The Viet-Nam Reader: Articles and Documents of American Foreign Policy and the Viet-Nam Crises* (New York: Vintage Books, 1965), pp. 342–43. Matters included in the NLF program and not mentioned in that of Hanoi were removal of the Saigon government, agrarian and educational reform, improved living conditions, equal treatment of the minorities in Vietnam. Text in ibid., pp. 216–21.

imposed a fifth requirement or precondition: all bombing of North Vietnam must stop before negotiations could begin.

President Johnson was now under pressure from peace-minded persons and organizations at home and abroad to pave the way for negotiations by stopping the bombing of North Vietnam. Secretary-General U Thant, in particular, gave repeated assurances that Hanoi would negotiate if only the bombing were called off. Official and unofficial feelers were tried in efforts to learn Hanoi's real intentions. Responses to some of these seemed promising, and the administration was accused in some quarters of being unreceptive to pacific suggestions from Hanoi.

At any rate, Johnson was willing to experiment with the possible results of a bombing halt. A five-day cessation in May 1965 was criticized as being too short to give Hanoi a chance to respond. This criticism did not apply to a respite from Christmas Eve, 1965, to January 31, 1966. During these thirty-seven days of nonbombing, Johnson made a spectacular peace gesture by sending Vice President Hubert Humphrey, U.N. Ambassador Arthur Goldberg, Ambassador-at-Large Averell Harriman, and other less exalted personages on special missions to forty foreign capitals, to convince those governments of Washington's desire for peace and to enlist their aid in bringing Hanoi to the conference table. When this appeal failed and the bombing was resumed, the President, through Ambassador Goldberg, submitted the problem of finding a road to peace to the U.N. Security Council, which took no action.

The bombing continued through 1966 and 1967, hitting targets in North Vietnam and along the Ho Chi Minh Trail in Laos. The Joint Chiefs of Staff considered the bombing essential in both areas to inhibit the movement of supplies and men from North Vietnam to the scene of fighting, though Secretary of Defense Robert S. McNamara was skeptical about its efficacy for that purpose. Johnson now took the position that he could not halt the bombing without some corresponding de-escalation by the other party. In a speech in San Antonio, Texas, September 29, 1967, he set forth what came to be known as the San Antonio formula:

The United States is willing to stop all aerial and naval bombing of North Vietnam when this will lead promptly to productive discussions. We, of course, assume that while discussions proceed, North Vietnam would not take advantage of the bombing cessation or limitation.[25]

The San Antonio formula was an offer to stop the bombing and begin negotiations on the basis of an assumption, rather than a promise, that the enemy would not utilize the respite to strengthen his position. Another concession was offered on November 2, 1967. Hitherto the United States had made it plain that it would not be willing, in any peace negotiations, to meet representatives of the National Liberation Front as a separate entity, though it would talk with them as a part of a North Vietnamese delegation. This position had been an obstacle to agreement with Hanoi. On November 2, however, Ambassador Goldberg stated—and the State Department concurred—that the United States would not resist participation of the NLF as a party in a peace conference.

The response of Hanoi and the NLF to these invitations was the Tet offensive, described above. Despite President Johnson's description of that enemy effort as "a complete failure," it produced deep disillusionment with the war in the United States. Opposition to Johnson's war policy became formidable within the Democratic party. On March 12, Senator Eugene McCarthy, running on an antiwar platform, won 42 percent of the vote in the New Hampshire Democratic presidential primary. Four days later, Senator Robert F. Kennedy, a more formidable critic of the war policy,

entered the presidential race. Meanwhile, a ferment was working within the administration, apparently set off by an estimate of General Westmoreland that he needed an increase of 206,000 men in Vietnam and by the reaction of a new Secretary of Defense, Clark M. Clifford, who succeeded McNamara on March 1, 1968. Formerly known as a "hawk," Clifford now became convinced that it was useless to press for military victory in Vietnam and that the bombing should be halted as a step toward a negotiated peace. His arguments ultimately prevailed with Johnson. In a television address on the night of March 31, 1968, the President announced that the bombing would be ended on the following day over all of North Vietnam except the sparsely populated southern portion which contained the access routes to South Vietnam. In the same address the President announced that he would not seek or accept renomination for the Presidency.

Negotiations Begin

To the surprise of many, the Hanoi government responded to Johnson's announcement by agreeing to negotiate. After weeks of wrangling about a place for the talks, both sides accepted Paris, and there on May 10, 1968, delegations headed by veteran diplomat W. Averell Harriman for the United States and Xuan Thuy (pronounced "Swan Twee") for North Vietnam met at last. The results were disappointing, though not surprising, for now the North Vietnamese refused to discuss terms of settlement until the United States stopped all bombing of the North. The United States refused, on the ground that to stop bombing the access routes would increase the peril to U.S. troops south of the line. Not until October 31, five days before the presidential election, did Johnson yield, announcing the end of all bombing of North Vietnam.

Now it was the turn of the Saigon government to stall, this time over the status of

[25]*New York Times,* September 30, 1967, p. 8.

the NLF delegation at the talks, symbolized by the shape of the table. Finally, on January 16, 1969, the delegations agreed that the table should be a round one, signifying equality of all participants. Four days later the new Nixon administration took office. Henry Cabot Lodge, twice U.S. Ambassador in Saigon, replaced Averell Harriman as chief negotiator.

When the four delegations met, January 25, 1969, for an actual beginning of negotiations, Lodge proposed as an eventual goal the withdrawal of all foreign (including North Vietnamese) troops from South Vietnam, but as an immediate objective the restoration of the neutralized character of the Demilitarized Zone (DMZ), which had been virtually taken over by the Communists for artillery and other installations. Five days later the North Vietnamese and NLF delegations rejected Lodge's proposal as an attempt to camouflage "American aggressive designs." The rejection was announced in a seven-hour session in which, as described by a *New York Times* reporter, "most of the proceedings were devoted to propaganda, recriminations and occasionally rough language."[26] The parties drew no nearer together in the weekly sessions that followed.

It seemed evident that confrontations in this spirit could hardly produce meaningful negotiation, and it was for this reason, presumably, that Nixon observed in March that only through secret talks with Hanoi could progress toward peace be expected. At the same time President Thieu revealed that he was ready to begin private talks with spokesmen of the NLF or Viet Cong.[27] Such secret talks were said soon thereafter to have begun, but, if so, they were no more

productive than the open sessions, and there were no signs of progress until early May, when both the NLF and President Nixon set forth their peace objectives.

On May 8 the NLF made public a ten-point peace proposal. Six days later President Nixon, in a television address to the nation, stated the American objectives.[28] A comparison of these two sets of proposals reveals the points of incompatibility which, in spite of some optimism at the time, were for many months to stand in the way of any agreement. First, Nixon called for the phased withdrawal of all non-South Vietnamese troops, the evacuation of the forces of the United States and its allies and of those of Hanoi to be completed at the same time. The NLF demanded the unconditional withdrawal of the forces of the United States and its allies but left the question of North Vietnamese forces in South Vietnam to be settled "by the Vietnamese parties among themselves."

Second, Nixon called for elections under the supervision of an international body to replace the existing governmental personnel, who would continue to function until the elections were held. The NLF proposed, on the other hand, that between the restoration of peace and the holding of elections a provisional government should be set up to include all parties in South Vietnam "that stand for peace, independence and neutrality." This provisional government, from which by definition the Thieu-Ky party was excluded, would supervise the American withdrawal and hold the general elections.

In fewer words, President Nixon was demanding, as the Johnson administration had demanded, that Hanoi withdraw its troops from South Vietnam and leave the South Vietnamese people to settle their own affairs in peace. Hanoi refused. Hanoi and the NLF were demanding the unilat-

---

[26]*New York Times*, January 26, 31, 1969, p. 1.

[27]*New York Times*, March 26, 1969, p. 3. These proposals were in accord with an earlier suggestion of parallel negotiations offered by Mr. Nixon's national security adviser. See Henry A. Kissinger, "The Viet Nam Negotiations," *Foreign Affairs*, January 1969, pp. 211–34.

[28]*New York Times*, May 9, 1969, pp. 1, 6; May 15, 1969, p. 16.

eral withdrawal of Allied troops and the creation of a South Vietnamese coalition government from which Thieu and Ky and their faction would be excluded. President Nixon was standing by Thieu and Ky until their successors should be chosen in general elections. If these positions were not clear in May 1969, they became so in succeeding months. They were not changed when the NLF transformed itself in June into the Provisional Revolutionary Government of South Vietnam or when the veteran leader Ho Chi Minh died on September 3, 1969. Negotiations dragged along without result. Ambassador Lodge resigned in frustration on November 20, 1969. President Nixon neglected to replace him with another equally high-ranking spokesman, whereupon the head of Hanoi's delegation ceased to attend meetings, and Hanoi and the NLF all but boycotted the conference. Formal meetings continued to be held but to no purpose.

Finally, July 1, 1970, after the completion of the military campaign in Cambodia, the President announced that he was appointing David K. E. Bruce, a distinguished diplomat and a Democrat, to head the American negotiating team in Paris. Bruce, he said, would take charge on August 1. The President restated the American peace terms. There was nothing new in the formula offered here, but the President promised that Ambassador Bruce would have "great flexibility." He hoped that this move would be reciprocated by the North Vietnamese.[29]

Actually, the chief Viet Cong negotiator, Mme. Nguyen Thi Binh, returned to the peace table on September 17, 1970, bringing with her an eight-point formula for settlement. The new proposal, like those before it, called for the unilateral withdrawal of all American and allied troops. There were some apparent concessions. Only

the three top men in the Saigon government—Thieu, Ky, and Premier Tran Thien Khiem—were named as unacceptable in a proposed coalition government. The document spoke of a possible cease-fire and of willingness to discuss exchange of prisoners prior to a general settlement. There was a sufficient degree of "give" here, thought the *New York Times,* to warrant exploration through submission of new proposals by the United States.[30]

The new American proposals came in a television broadcast by President Nixon on the night of Wednesday, October 7. The novel features in the President's five-point plan were proposals for a "standstill" cease-fire, immediate exchange of prisoners, a widened peace conference to include Cambodia and Laos (tacit admission that the war had become an "Indochina war"), and a promise to withdraw *all* American troops upon a timetable to be agreed upon as part of an overall settlement. Mr. Nixon rejected emphatically the demand for elimination of Thieu and Ky before elections, and although the actual proposal did not repeat the insistence that withdrawal of troops be mutual, the accompanying briefing made it plain that this demand still stood.[31]

The new formula impressed many of Nixon's former critics at home and abroad (including even Senator Fulbright) as fair and reasonable. The response in the enemy camp, however, was disappointing. Moscow was prompt in describing the offer as "a great fraud," and it was totally rejected by the Hanoi and Viet Cong negotiators in Paris. Hope of an early peace settlement could be found only in the contention of the State Department that the enemy delegations did not mean what they said in public and would prove more conciliatory in secret negotiations.

[29]*New York Times,* July 2, 1970, pp. 1, 14. cf. John Osborne, "Why Cambodia?" *The New Republic,* June 11, 1970, pp. 7–9.

[30]*New York Times,* September 18, 1970, p. 2; September 27, 1970 (sec. 4), p. 14.

[31]*New York Times,* October 8, 1970, pp. 1, 18. *The New Republic,* October 17, 1970, pp. 5, 6.

"Vietnamizing" the War

While still hoping to end the war through negotiations in Paris, President Nixon attempted to quiet criticism of the war at home by a process of "Vietnamization," that is, a gradual withdrawal of U.S. forces and their replacement by South Vietnamese troops with improved training and equipment. An announcement on June 8, 1969, that 25,000 U.S. troops would be withdrawn during July, to be replaced by South Vietnamese, was followed a few days later by an expression of hope that more than 100,000 could be withdrawn before the end of 1970, and a further announcement on September 16 that an additional 35,000 would be brought home by the end of 1969.

The President's first comprehensive exposition of the new policy came in a television address on November 3, 1969. All U.S. combat ground forces, said Mr. Nixon, would be withdrawn from Vietnam and replaced by Vietnamese forces "on an orderly scheduled timetable." He did not announce the timetable, since the rate of withdrawal would depend upon three variables: (1) progress of the peace negotiations, (2) "the level of enemy activity," and (3) progress in training the South Vietnamese forces. The peace negotiations seemed to be at a standstill, but the President spoke hopefully of the other two factors. He warned Hanoi that any increase in violence by North Vietnam would be met with "strong and effective measures," presumably exemplified by a partial renewing of the bombing of North Vietnam in November 1970. He suggested, with logic that seemed not to impress Hanoi, that the latter could make better terms with the United States than with Saigon after U.S. troops departed.[32]

[32]*New York Times,* November 4, 1969, p. 16. The President's address on Vietnamization came nineteen days after a nationwide peaceful demonstration or "moratorium," in which hundreds of thousands of people called generally for an "immediate" pullout of all U.S. forces in Vietnam.

The Vietnamization plan contained a number of ambiguities. It called specifically for the withdrawal of ground combat forces. Other elements—air, logistics, artillery—would presumably remain as long as needed to support Vietnamese ground forces. Furthermore, since the United States was still committed to the preservation of a free South Vietnam, even American ground forces could be expected to remain—in the absence of a peace settlement—until their South Vietnamese counterparts were able to cope with the threat from the North. On the basis of past experience that might take some time— "many years," predicted President Thieu in January 1970.[33]

Nixon's program of Vietnamization, as set forth in the announcements in June and September and in the November address, was further spelled out in a statement of December 15, 1969, that 50,000 additional U.S. troops would be withdrawn by April 15, 1970, and in a television address of April 20, 1970, forecasting that 150,000 more would be brought home by the spring of 1971. This, said Mr. Nixon, would add up to a total reduction of 265,000 (sic) men by the latter period.

In spite of doubts and ambiguities, the President's plan seemed, for the time being, quite effective in quieting the antiwar clamor in the United States. A Gallup poll on the day after his November address showed 77 percent of those questioned supporting the President, 6 percent opposed, and 17 percent undecided. On December 2, the Democratic-controlled House of Representatives adopted by a vote of 333 to 55 a resolution expressing its support of the President "in his efforts to negotiate a just peace in Vietnam." Although there were further antiwar demonstrations in mid November, Nixon's promise to withdraw even a part of the American troops in Vietnam seemed to have taken the steam out of the antiwar

[33]*New York Times,* January 11, 1970, Sec. 4, p. 5.

movement, an effect noted even on the nation's uneasy campuses. Such comparative harmony came to a sudden end with the President's announcement on April 30 that American and South Vietnamese forces were carrying the war into Cambodia.

The Cambodian Adventure

The declared purpose of the intrusion into Cambodia was to destroy Communist bases in areas adjoining South Vietnam which for years had been used as sanctuaries by Viet Cong and North Vietnamese forces with the tacit consent of nominally neutralist Prince Norodom Sihanouk, Cambodian Chief of State. The United States had long tolerated this breach of neutrality rather than take action which might drive Sihanouk into the enemy camp. But a new situation had arisen. Sihanouk had been overthrown in a coup d'état of March 18, led by pro-West Premier General Lon Nol, who now found his rule threatened by thousands of North Vietnamese troops from the sanctuaries. Should they succeed, the President explained, "Cambodia would become a vast enemy staging area and springboard for attacks on South Vietnam along 600 miles of frontier." Faced with these attacks, the government of General Lon Nol had "sent out a call to the United States and a number of other nations for assistance."

Not only was the enemy threatening to take over Cambodia, he was, said Nixon, "concentrating his main forces in the sanctuaries where they are building up to launch massive attacks on our forces and those of South Vietnam." In view of this dual threat to the American program, the President's decision had been

to go to the heart of the trouble. That means cleaning out major North Vietnamese and Viet Cong-occupied sanctuaries which serve as bases for attacks on both Cambodia and

American and South Vietnamese forces in South Vietnam.

Tonight, the President continued, allied units would "attack the headquarters for the entire Communist military operation in South Vietnam"—the "key control center" that had operated for years "in blatant violation of Cambodia's neutrality."

The President insisted that the operation was "not an invasion of Cambodia" but was confined to areas "completely occupied and controlled by North Vietnamese forces, . . . Once enemy forces are driven out of these sanctuaries and their military supplies destroyed, we will withdraw." Success of the operation, the President intimated, would facilitate the previously announced withdrawal from Vietnam of 150,000 men over the next year.[34]

The move into Cambodia, invasion or not, looked to many in America like widening the war. Though the Gallup poll (May 4) showed a small majority favoring the President, the action produced a new round of demonstrations on university campuses, and in the Senate the introduction of several resolutions designed to prevent the President from expanding the area of war without consent of Congress. To conciliate his critics, Mr. Nixon gave assurance that American ground forces would penetrate no farther than 21.7 miles (35 kilometers) into Cambodia and that they and any advisers with South Vietnam forces would be withdrawn no later than June 30. United States aid to Cambodia would be limited to equipment and air support; whether this would be tactical as well as strategic (the bombing of enemy supply routes) was not clear. The Saigon government announced, however, that South Vietnamese troops would not be bound by the United States time-table but might remain to support the Lon Nol government and to assist in training its inexperienced troops.

[34]*New York Times,* May 1, 1970, pp. 1–2.

Upon completion of the sweep through the sanctuaries on June 30, the President issued a long report claiming outstanding success for the operation, even though the "key control center" of the Communist command had not been found. Enemy killed were estimated at over 11,000; enemy captured and detainees at 2,328. But the greatest gain had been in the vast amounts of enemy equipment—weapons, ammunition, vehicles, food (14 million pounds of rice)—and installations captured or destroyed. Enemy operations had been set back many months at least. The concept of sanctuaries in Cambodia had been demolished. The South Vietnamese troops had made an excellent showing, demonstrating the apparent success of Vietnamization.[35]

The Longest War

In the November following the Cambodian invasion, the Nixon administration began increasingly to concern itself with a large build-up of supplies in North Vietnam, the problem being one of how to prevent them from moving southward. To meet the challenge, in February 1971, the United States launched what was to be its last major offensive of the war. Without American advisors but with American air cover, the South Vietnamese were provided with their first real test at fighting alone in the field. It was not very successful. Thereafter, the intensified fighting of 1971 was met with increased United States bombing, albeit within the framework of continued American withdrawals. The bombing, as usual, had marginal results on the battlefields themselves.

What was certain beyond reasonable doubt was that the American public had had enough. According to a Gallup poll

taken in May 1971, six out of ten Americans now thought it had been a mistake for the United States to get involved in the Vietnam war. This was a complete reversal of the position of the public since August 1965. Surprisingly, the poll revealed that Republicans had changed their views of the war almost as drastically as Democrats.[36] Within this climate of opinion, there could be no thought of reintroducing American troops although there seemed to be little constraint on again widening the war.

In 1971 the war also came to embrace Laos. The South Vietnamese army, again supported by American air cover, led the assault. And, not unlike its earlier experience on its own, was badly mauled. To make matters worse, the Viet Cong launched a series of attacks in South Vietnam, and President Thieu demanded that his forces be returned home. In such circumstances, the future of Vietnamization did not bode well.

In the spring of 1972, the Vietnam war witnessed a dramatic turn of events. Perceiving that President Nixon's hands would be tied in an election year and persuaded of the vulnerability of the Thieu regime, Hanoi launched a major offensive in the south, this time abandoning its guerrilla tactics in favor of a conventional alignment led by Soviet-supplied T-54 tanks. Initial results were striking as entire South Vietnamese divisions panicked. In less than a month, Hanoi had captured the northern capital of Quantri and menaced Saigon itself.

Despite his proposed trip to Moscow in May, President Nixon gambled and ordered the heaviest bombing raids of the war

---

[35]*New York Times*, May 31, 1970 (sec. 4), p. 3.

[36]*New York Times*, June 6, 1971. Publication of the so-called "Pentagon Papers" later in the month in the *New York Times* merely reinforced the American public in its belief that the war had indeed been a mistake. *New York Times*, June 13, 1971, pp. 1, 35–38. This was the first in a series of articles.

thus far. Major facilities and installations were struck. Then, in surely what must be rated as the greatest gamble of the war, the President authorized the mining of the entrances of North Vietnamese ports, thus setting the stage for a potentially direct confrontation with either the Soviet Union or Red China or both. But nothing of the sort happened. The war was again stalemated, and all looked forward to a negotiated settlement.

Understandably anxious to secure peace before the coming presidential election in November, Nixon let it be known that he would accept a cease-fire in place rather than the complete withdrawal of North Vietnamese troops from the south. With the American counteroffensive somewhat successful and in the face of a strengthened Thieu government, Hanoi opted for the peace table. Paralleling negotiations taking place at the formal meetings in Paris, preliminary terms of a final agreement were worked out by presidential advisor Henry Kissinger and North Vietnamese representative Le Duc Tho in October. As a sign of American good faith, the bombing of North Vietnam, north of the 20th parallel, was suspended. President Thieu balked, however, when he saw the terms of the agreement and demanded that they be renegotiated. In the end, Nixon issued Thieu an ultimatum and he acquiesced.[37] Meanwhile, when Hanoi began to stall, the President on December 18, resumed the bombing of the north with a vengeance. The North Vietnamese capital and Haiphong were bombed more heavily than at any previous stage of the conflict. In response to worldwide protests, Washington again restricted the bombing on December 30 to the area south of the 20th parallel and on January 15, 1973, ended all bombing of North Vietnam.

[37]President Nixon's letter of proposed postwar support to Thieu came to light after the fall of South Vietnam, *New York Times,* May 1, 1975, pp. 1, 16.

"Peace with Honor"

Consequently, private talks between Kissinger and Le Duc Tho were resumed in Paris on January 8. The talks lasted five days and resulted in the conclusion of the elusive peace agreement. The pact was initialled by the two negotiators on January 23 and signed by Kissinger and the foreign ministers of North and South Vietnam, and the South Vietnamese Provisional Revolutionary Government on January 27.

The Paris cease-fire agreement, as it came to be called, provided, among other things, for a standstill cease-fire to take place immediately; the withdrawal of all U.S. forces from South Vietnam and the release of all American prisoners of war within sixty days; the formation of a four-party joint military commission to enforce these provisions; the establishment of an International Commission on Control and Supervision; the formation by agreement between the South Vietnamese parties of a National Council of National Reconciliation and Concord, which would set about the task of organizing general elections; and the holding of an international conference on Vietnam within thirty days of the signing of the agreement.

American fighting on the ground terminated with the withdrawal of the last United States troops in March 1973, two months after the cease-fire and eight years after the first formal commitment of military forces. Thus ended the longest war in United States history. The costs were staggering in blood and treasure. From 1961 to 1973, American casualties alone reached a figure of 350,000 with approximately 56,000 killed (40,000 in combat). From 1961 to the sudden collapse of the Thieu regime in April 1975, United States expenditures in Indochina amounted to a total in excess of $141 billion. The psychological scars left on the nation were of course incalculable.

The Collapse of American Policy

While the negotiated peace settlement allowed the U.S. an opportunity to extricate itself from Indochina with what the Nixon administration regarded as a semblance of "peace with honor," the reality of the situation was vastly different for those who remained behind. In view of the almost irreconcilable nature of the conflict between President Thieu and his opponents and the potential threat of 150,000 North Vietnamese regulars and Viet Cong poised on South Vietnamese soil, it seemed to most observers that it would be only a matter of time before the South would be overrun, perhaps as few as five years. As it turned out, it only required three years.

Hanoi regarded the peace agreement as a scrap of paper and soon set out to complete its goal of reunifying the two Vietnams by force of arms. Correctly gauging the mood of the American public and taking advantage of the subsequent disgrace and resignation of President Nixon as a result of the Watergate scandal, the North Vietnamese General Staff, according to the most authoritative sources,[38] carefully laid the groundwork for the next offensive. In the spring of 1975 a combined North Vietnamese and Viet Cong attack proved too much for the hapless South Vietnamese army. In March President Thieu abandoned the central highlands region after a number of stunning reverses. The spectacle of thousands of South Vietnamese soldiers trampling civilians in their haste to get to the rear provided a somber moment for even the most sophisticated American observer. Shortly before fleeing to Taiwan, Thieu turned over the reigns of government to Duong van Minh who, in turn, surrendered to the invading Communists. Saigon, renamed Ho Chi Minh City, fell on April 30. The collapse of South Vietnam together with the defeat of the pro-Western forces in Cambodia and subsequently in Laos marked the end of American influence in the area.

[38] Hanoi's Chief of Staff, General Van Tien Dung, candidly recounted these and subsequent events of the war's final battles in two official North Vietnamese newspapers, excerpts of which are found in *New York Times,* April 26, 1976, p. 16.

ADDITIONAL READINGS

BUTTINGER, JOSEPH, *Vietnam: A Dragon Embattled.* 2 vols. New York: Praeger Publishers, Inc., 1967.

COOPER, CHESTER L., *The Lost Crusade: America in Vietnam.* New York: Dodd, Mead & Company, 1970.

FALL, BERNARD B., *The Two Vietnams: A Political and Military Analysis.* New York: Frederick A. Praeger, Inc., 1963.

HALBERSTAM, DAVID, *The Best and the Brightest.* New York: Random House, Inc. 1972.

KEARNS, DORIS, *Lyndon Johnson and the American Dream.* New York: Harper & Row, Publishers, 1976.

KY, NGUYEN CAO, *Twenty Years and Twenty Days.* New York: Stein and Day, 1976.

PIKE, DOUGLAS, *Viet Cong: The Organization and Techniques of the National Liberation Front of South Vietnam.* Cambridge, Mass.: MIT Press, 1966.

ROSE, LISLE, A., *Roots of Tragedy: The United States and the Struggle for Asia.* Westport, Conn.: Greenwood Press, 1976.

The Vietnam War and International Law, ed. Richard A. Falk. Princeton: Princeton University Press, 1968.

25. American Policy in the Middle East

The story of conflict in the Middle East begins in 1917. In the Balfour Declaration of that year (actually a bid for Jewish backing in World War I), the British government promised "the establishment in Palestine of a National Home for the Jewish people." To Britain's later embarrassment, her government had made conflicting promises to the Arabs of the area. The prospect of a Jewish state in a Palestine which had long been predominantly Arab aroused bitter resentment in the Arab world but was embraced with enthusiasm by the influential World Zionist Organization. As holder of a League of Nations mandate for Palestine, Britain found herself trapped by her conflicting promises to these rival forces. Until World War II she blew first hot and then cold upon Jewish aspirations for the National Home, first encouraging, and then attempting to check, Jewish immigration and acquisition of land in Palestine.

By 1947 an exhausted Britain found her position between those angry rivals more than she could bear and announced that she would surrender her mandate on May 15, 1948, yielding responsibility for Palestine to the United Nations. On November 29, 1947, the U.N. General Assembly recommended that Palestine be partitioned between an Arab and a Jewish state, with Jerusalem, containing the holy places of three great religions, to be placed under international administration. Immediately after the vote, the Arab delegates marched out of the Assembly, declaring that they would not be bound by the decision. The Palestine Arabs, with the support of their kinsmen in neighboring states, launched a civil war against the Palestine Jews. The Jews, meanwhile, were not only meeting Arab attacks successfully but were perfecting organs of government for Palestine. On the evening of May 14, 1948 (Washington time), they proclaimed the birth of the independent state of Israel. A few minutes thereafter, President Truman announced United States recognition, *de facto,* of the government of Israel.[1]

Full-scale war now ensued between Israel and its Arab neighbors. The fighting was temporarily halted several times by cease-fire orders issued by the U.N. Security Council and finally ended by a series of armistice agreements negotiated by a United Nations mediator, Dr. Ralph Bunche. The armistice lines, fixed on the basis of territory occupied and held by the antagonists, gave Israel much more territory than the original partition proposal.

The armistice, however, proved to be that and nothing more. Armed clashes occurred from time to time along the border, despite the efforts of a U.N. Truce Supervision Organization. The United Nations resolution calling for an international regime in Jerusalem was unimplemented, and that city was cut in two by the armistice line between Israel and Jordan. The Arab states refused to negotiate peace treaties with Israel or to trade with it. Iraq refused to permit oil to flow through a pipe line to a refinery at Haifa. Egypt refused passage

[1]For two accounts of the difficulties Truman encountered from his own Department of State on this matter, and of the rift between him and Marshall over recognition of Israel, see *New York Times,* November 21, 1976, p. 5; and *Washington Post,* December 29, 1976.

through the Suez Canal to Israeli ships or to ships with Israeli cargoes. Israel was blockaded on all its land frontiers.

A serious obstacle to any Israeli-Arab settlement was the plight of the Palestinian refugees, Arabs who had fled from their homes in Palestine during the war and were quartered in camps just outside the borders of Israel, in Syria, Lebanon, Jordan, and Egypt. Numbering some 800,000 to begin with, they were reported by the U.N. to have increased to 1,500,000 by 1967, and 1,668,205 or 1.6 million in 1977* Their places in Palestine were filled by the great influx of Jews—thousands of them driven from Arab lands—that followed independence. The Arab states would take no steps toward settling the refugees in permanent homes, since to do so would amount to surrendering their claim of right to return to their homes in Israel. The Arab governments would not make peace until Israel repatriated the refugees. Israel, for security reasons and later also because of lack of space, was unwilling to take back more than a token number. Meanwhile, the refugees were fed, clothed, and sheltered in their camps, chiefly through the exertions of the U.N. Relief and Works Agency for Palestine Refugees (UNRWA), established in 1948 and still functioning in 1970. (UNRWA expired on June 30, 1978.) The great majority of the refugees accepted their fate passively, but activists among them organized terrorist bands which waged guerrilla war against Israel from the neighboring states. Their activities and their opposition to any political settlement became a major obstacle to peace.

Aims of the United States

Prior to World War I American interest in the Middle East—the land of the Bible and of the origins of the Christian religion—

*Source: *Basic Facts About the U.N.* (1977), p. 66.

had been chiefly religious and archeological. American traders, too, had early found their way to the eastern Mediterranean and the ports of the Persian Gulf, but such trade had never been large.

In the years just before and during World War I, Americans first became conscious of the importance of the oil of the Middle East. British and French interests were on the ground first. In southern Iran the British, through the Anglo-Iranian Oil Company, attained and held a monopoly; but in Iraq and in the little sheikdom of Kuwait (500,000 people and one-seventh of the world's proved oil reserves!), American companies won a part interest, and in Saudi Arabia and the Bahrain Island field, they secured complete control. World War II, with its terrific drain on the petroleum resources of the United States and Caribbean fields, further emphasized the dependence of Western Europe (and perhaps the future dependence of the United States), on the Middle East, under whose inhospitable surface lies more than half of all the proved oil reserves of the world.

It was the proximity of this vital region to the Soviet Union and the possibility of its subjection to Soviet influence or domination that made it a prime object of American attention in the years of the cold war. Russian desire to penetrate the region was undisguised. It was evident in the prolonged Soviet occupation of northern Iran, in Soviet pressure on Turkey for control of the Dardanelles, in the Russian desire for a trusteeship over former Italian conquests in North Africa. Soviet ambitions had been frustrated at all these points, but no one could suppose that they had been abandoned. Hence exclusion of the Soviet Union from a dominant or influential role in the Middle East became an integral part of the American policy of containment.

The United States pursued its containment policy in the Middle East by three methods: (1) by attempting to compose disputes within the area which might otherwise tempt Soviet interference, especially

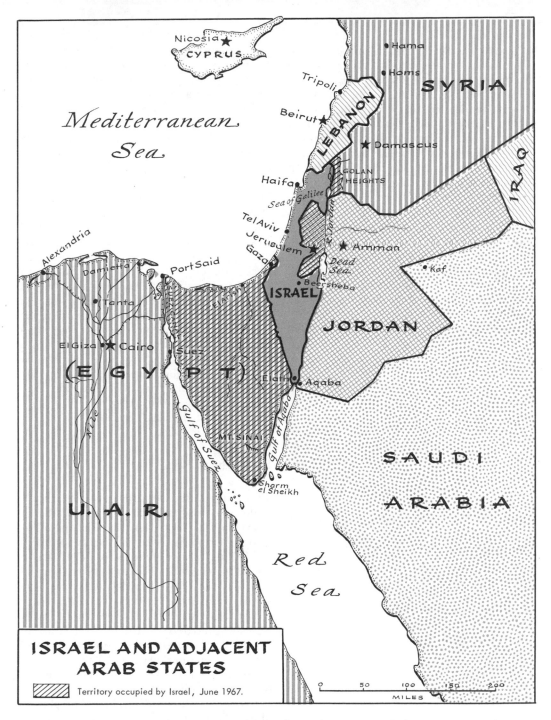

ISRAEL AND ADJACENT ARAB STATES

| | Territory occupied by Israel, June 1967. |

0   50   100   150   200
MILES

Note: In 1950 the Israel Parliament proclaimed Jerusalem the capital of Israel. The United States, however, does not recognize Jerusalem as the capital and maintains its embassy in Tel Aviv, the former capital.

the quarrel between Israel and its neighbors and controversies between Egypt and Iran on the one hand, and Great Britain on the other; (2) by raising living standards through assistance in developing the region's neglected natural resources; (3) by strengthening the area's military potential and its willingness to resist aggression or subversion originating in the Kremlin. In none of these approaches was the United States notably successful.

The United States did play a part, though a minor one, in bringing about two agreements between Britain and Egypt in 1954. By one of these England surrendered her share in the administration of the Anglo-Egyptian Sudan, which thereupon became the independent Republic of the Sudan. By the second agreement Britain agreed to withdraw her armed forces from her base on the Suez Canal over a period of twenty months. The United States also in the same year had a hand in settling a quarrel between Britain and Iran over the terms of Iran's nationalization of the Anglo-Iranian Oil Company.

But in its efforts to settle the Israeli-Arab dispute, the United States fared no better acting alone than through its participation in the U.N.'s Palestine Conciliation Commission. It did join with Britain and France in an attempt to guarantee each party to the controversy against aggression by the other. In a statement of May 25, 1950, the three governments declared that,

> should they find that any of these states was preparing to violate frontiers or armistice lines [they] would, consistent with their obligations as members of the United Nations, immediately take action, both within and outside the United Nations to prevent such violation.[2]

Ironically, on the only occasion when the United States acted under the terms of this

[2]*Documents on American Foreign Relations*, 12: 658–59.

guarantee, in the Israeli-Egyptian war of 1956, it was acting in opposition to the other signatories to the statement, which thus became a dead letter.

In its efforts to raise the standard of living of the peoples of the Middle East (thereby, in theory immunizing them against Communism), the United States achieved little. It signed Technical Assistance agreements with most of the states of the area. It promoted land development and resettlement programs in Egypt and Iraq and assisted the government of Saudi Arabia in modernizing its tariff and customs systems. The most ambitious proposal—development of the water resources of the Jordan River Valley for the benefit of all the people of the area—met an insuperable obstacle in the hostility of Jordan, Lebanon, and Syria to Israel. Any gain in influence that the United States, or the West, might have achieved by such measures was canceled out as the Soviet Union, though ostensibly friendly to Israel in 1948, quickly made itself, from 1956 on, the champion of the Arab states.

The Baghdad Pact

The third American line of approach, the building of military barriers against Soviet aggression in the area, received its principal impetus from Secretary of State John Foster Dulles, whose general policy it was to encircle the Soviet Union with military alliances. NATO (a pre-Dulles creation) reached into the eastern Mediterranean with the inclusion of Greece and Turkey. SEATO guarded Southeast Asia from anticipated Sino-Soviet aggression and, through the membership of Pakistan, came within a few miles of the Soviets' southern boundary. Dulles undertook to fill the gap between Pakistan and Turkey by an alliance of the "northern tier" of states—Turkey and Pakistan (already in NATO and SEATO respectively), linked by Iran and

Iraq. The last-named was lured by the prospect of American military aid to draw apart, for the time being, from other Arab states and to sign a "Pact of Mutual Assistance" with Turkey, on February 24, 1955. Later in the year the pact was signed by Iran and Pakistan and also by the United Kingdom. Headquarters were established at Baghdad, the Iraqi capital, and the alliance was known as the Baghdad Pact.

The United States had promoted the alliance but did not become a member. It sent observers to meetings, participated in certain committees, and gave military aid to the members individually, but what seemed to many its overly cautious abstention from full participation perplexed the British and the friends of the West in the other member states. It also emboldened the Russians and the anti-Western elements in the other Arab countries.[3]

The Baghdad Pact was based on a mistaken conception of the nature of the Russian threat in the Middle East, which lay not in military aggression but in infiltration and subversion. The fruits of these Soviet tactics were quickly apparent. Before the last signatures were appended to the Baghdad Pact, the government of Egypt announced a barter deal, arranged in Moscow, by which Egyptian cotton would be exchanged for arms from Czechoslovakia. Then followed quickly news of an alliance and a joint command agreement between Egypt, Syria, and Saudi Arabia; a Soviet-Syrian trade agreement; and a new treaty of friendship between Yemen and the Soviet Union. The Czech arms began arriving in October, and the next month a group of Egyptian fliers returned from a course of jet training in Czechoslovakia. The Baghdad Pact appeared to have given a sharp

stimulus to Arab nationalism. This, in turn, was cultivated and abetted in Moscow, which felt no qualms about exploiting Arab hatred of Israel. The year of the Baghdad Pact saw impressive Soviet gains in the Middle East and a corresponding deterioration in British, French, and American influence.[4]

The Suez Canal Crisis

The Americans and British attempted to recover their forfeited good will in Egypt by proposing to aid President Gamal Abdel Nasser[5] in financing a new high dam at Aswan on the Nile, a project that would provide hydroelectric power as well as irrigation for thousands of new farms. While Nasser was deliberating whether to accept the offer, British and American officials had second thoughts. Nasser had committed a large slice of Egypt's resources to pay for Czech arms. He seemed a poor risk for a loan such as that proposed. To Secretary of State Dulles, Nasser had not endeared himself by his further dickering with the Russians or his recent recognition of Communist China. Consequently, when Nasser's ambassador made a special trip to Washington in July 1956 to accept the loan, he was told abruptly that the offer was withdrawn. The British, who would have

---

[3]*U.S. in World Affairs, 1954,* p. 319; ibid., *1955,* pp. 154–57; John C. Campbell, *Defense of the Middle East* (New York: Harper & Row, Publishers for Council on Foreign Relations, 1958), pp. 61–62; Anthony Eden, *The Memoirs of Anthony Eden: Full Circle* (Boston: Houghton Mifflin Company, 1960), pp. 71, 374–75.

[4]*U.S. in World Affairs, 1955,* pp. 159–67. France was confronted with rebellion in Algeria and knew that the Egyptian government was giving aid to the rebels. Britain's attempt to include Jordan in the Baghdad Pact touched off anti-Western rioting in Amman, the Jordanian capital, and led soon after to dismissal of the British commander of Jordan's army. Yemen supported anti-British tribesmen in the British protectorate of Aden.

[5]The corrupt and incompetent Egyptian King, Farouk, was overthrown in 1952 by a group of young army officers. The new government was at first headed by General Mohammed Naguib, but in 1954 he was replaced by strong man Col. Gamal Abdel Nasser, who became both Premier and Head of State (later President).

preferred a less spectacular refusal, had not been consulted, though the offer had been a joint one. They were annoyed, but Nasser was infuriated.[6]

Nasser's dramatic response, delivered July 26, was to nationalize the Suez Canal, owned chiefly by British and French stockholders and the vital link between Western Europe and the Middle Eastern oil fields. The Egyptian government, he indicated, would collect the tolls and apply a part of the proceeds to the building of the Aswan Dam. To the British and French this was an intolerable situation; to the United States it was objectionable but less crucial than to Europe. Secretary Dulles flew to London to confer with his British and French colleagues. A conference of twenty-four nations, principal users of the canal, was called to meet in London. A majority, the delegations of eighteen powers, recommended creation of a Suez Canal Board to take over management of the canal. When Nasser promptly rejected this solution, Dulles proposed the formation of a Suez Canal Users Association (SCUA), which might collect the tolls for use of the canal and assure that a proper share of the proceeds was used for maintenance of the canal and compensation to the stockholders of the canal company.

It was clear that Nasser would not accept the new proposal unless compelled to it by the use of force or some form of economic sanctions, such as a boycott of the canal. The British and French were willing to go to any necessary length for this purpose and assumed that Dulles, who had made the proposal, would be ready to back it up. They were chagrined, therefore, when he stated publicly that SCUA had no teeth. They turned for help to the United Nations and obtained from the Security Council, October 13, 1956, approval of a set of six

principles for the management of the canal. These included a declaration of respect for the sovereignty of Eygpt but also assertions that "the operation of the Canal should be insulated from the politics of any country," and that "there should be free and open transit through the Canal without discrimination, overt or covert."[7] Egypt accepted these principles. An attempt by Britain and France to attach an endorsement of the earlier eighteen-power plan and a request that Egypt cooperate with the Users Association was defeated by a Soviet veto. Observance of the six principles was left entirely to the good faith of the Egyptian government.

The British and French had no confidence in Nasser, whose pan-Arab nationalism was abetting rebellion against France in Algeria and denouncing British influence in Iraq and Arabia. They wished to humiliate and if possible to overthrow him. They felt with some reason that they had been led on and then let down by Secretary Dulles. It had become clear that neither he nor President Eisenhower would sanction the use of force or economic pressure against Nasser. Prime Minister Anthony Eden and French Premier Guy Mollet, therefore, planned their next move without taking the United States into their confidence.

The first nation to act, however, was Israel. Israel had been greatly alarmed at Egypt's acquisition of a great variety and profusion of military hardware from behind the Iron Curtain. An announcement in October of the formation by Egypt, Syria, and Jordan of a joint military command, quite encircling the Jewish state, in-

---

[6]Eden, *Memoirs*, p. 470; Richard Goold-Adams, *John Foster Dulles: A Reappraisal* (New York: Appleton-Century-Crofts, 1962), p. 202.

[7]*Documents on American Foreign Relations, 1956*, pp. 342–43. Other documents on the Suez crisis of 1956–57 are printed in ibid., pp. 289–373, and ibid., *1957*, pp. 195–290. Useful accounts are found in *U.S. in World Affairs, 1956*, pp. 251–74, 326–42; ibid., *1957*, pp. 157–74; Campbell, *Defense*, chap. 8; Eden, *Memoirs*, pp. 467–654; Goold-Adams, *Dulles*, pp. 208–33; Herman Finer, *Dulles over Suez: The Theory and Practice of His Diplomacy* (Chicago: Quadrangle Books, Inc., 1964).

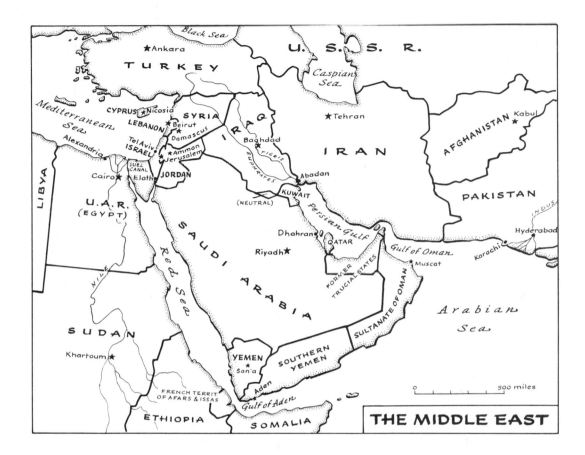

THE MIDDLE EAST

tensified the alarm. Israel's very existence seemed to be at stake. As Israelis saw it, only a preventive war could avert disaster.[8]

On October 29, 1956, therefore, Israeli forces struck without warning at Egyptian positions in the Gaza Strip and the Sinai Peninsula. The Egyptian armies, taken completely by surprise, were overwhelmed. Great stores of arms were captured, the Gaza Strip was overrun, and the invaders pushed on across the Sinai area toward the Suez Canal.

How much collusion there had been between the Israelis and the French and British is unknown. It seems well estab-

[8]Nadav Safran, *The United States and Israel* (Cambridge: Harvard University Press, 1963), pp. 231–42.

lished that the French, at least, knew something of the Israeli plans; France, in fact, supplied a certain amount of air cover for the operation. Officially, the two Western governments on October 30 requested Israel and Egypt to accept a cease-fire, and when Egypt refused, announced that they would occupy positions along the canal to separate the belligerents and keep the canal open. This was the pretext for their intervention. Their real purpose, it would seem, was to restore the canal to international control and clip Colonel Nasser's wings, or, still better, bring him to ground altogether. At any rate, they began, through air attacks, to prepare the way for airborne landings at Ports Said and Fuad.

The United States reacted angrily to

these resorts to force in violation of the U.N. Charter by one friendly state and two allies. In the U.N. Security Council on October 30 both the United States and the U.S.S.R. introduced resolutions calling for a cease-fire in the Israeli-Egyptian war. Both were vetoed by the British and French representatives. The General Assembly, meeting on the night of November 1–2, adopted an American resolution calling for an immediate cease-fire, suspension of military movements into the area, and withdrawal of armed forces behind armistice lines. Significant was the fact that the United States and the Soviet Union stood together against the former's two leading allies. The somewhat moralistic or legalistic position taken by the United States was typified by President Eisenhower in a broadcast of October 31. "There can be no peace without law," the President declared. "And there can be no law if we were to invoke one code of international conduct for those who oppose us and another for our friends." Mr. Eisenhower made plain his awareness of the provocations under which the three offending powers were acting; but he believed their actions had been "taken in error. For we do not accept the use of force as a wise or proper instrument for the settlement of international disputes." The President promised that the United States would not become involved in the existing hostilities and that the government would "do all in its power to localize the fighting and to end the conflict."[9]

On November 5 the General Assembly recommended the creation of the Emergency Force for Palestine, described elsewhere. With this as a face-saving device,

[9]*Documents on American Foreign Relations, 1956,* pp. 49–55. Secretary Dulles was hospitalized for an emergency operation on November 3 and was immobilized for several weeks. When the Soviet Union, November 5, proposed joint action by the U.S. and U.S.S.R. against the three "aggressors," Eisenhower remarked that such action on the part of the United States would be "unthinkable."

under triple pressure from the United States, the U.N., and the U.S.S.R., and subjected to Russia's threats of "volunteers" at the seat of conflict and rockets on their home premises, the British, French, and Israelis agreed next day to a cease-fire. The Israeli campaign had been notably successful, winning virtually all its objectives. The British and French, inadequately prepared for the adventure, had destroyed much of the Egyptian air force but had landed only a few troops near the canal. Far from keeping the canal open, their avowed purpose, they had been unable to prevent Nasser from blocking it so completely with sunken ships that it was not open to normal use for six months.

The French and British had gained nothing from their intervention. A humiliating retreat had impaired their prestige. The Israelis had destroyed a vast quantity of Egyptian war equipment and at least postponed the day of a new Arab offensive. From the stationing of the Emergency Force in the Gaza Strip and at the outlet of the Gulf of Aqaba, they gained protection from Egyptian border raids and access to the high seas from their port of Elath (Eilat). They were still debarred by Egypt from use of the canal. The complete success of their arms had raised their military prestige as it had lowered that of Egypt. Nasser, in spite of a humiliating military defeat, had been saved from complete disaster by the intervention of the U.N. backed by the U.S. and the U.S.S.R. He had had to forgo for a while his attack on Israel, but he had his canal virtually on his own terms. His political prestige in the Arab world was enhanced. Aid for the Aswan Dam, denied him by the West, was provided instead by the Soviet Union.

The United States had made its point, that resort to force should not be allowed to pay. It had failed to show by what alternative means justice could be done. By equating the Anglo-French action at Suez with "colonialism," as both Dulles and Vice President Nixon had done, and by taking a leading part in opposing it, the United States had probably improved its standing in the Asian-African world. But by the same actions and by the equivocal character of Dulles' early support, it had impaired its relations with its two most reliable allies and opened a rift in NATO which required many months to heal.

The Eisenhower Doctrine

Though the Soviet Union had shown that military conquest was not its method of operation in the Middle East, the United States feared that states under Soviet influence might still resort to armed force to extend the boundaries of Communism. The chief objects of this fear were Egypt and Syria, both of which had developed strong economic ties with the Soviet Union and had been supplied with arms by the U.S.S.R. or its satellites. Egypt's losses in equipment in the war of 1956 were promptly restored with Soviet aid, and there was fear that President Nasser, perhaps with Syrian backing, might move to make himself the leader of a united Arab nation which would be, though not Communist, at least under strong Soviet influence.

To guard against such a possibility President Eisenhower secured from Congress (March 9, 1957) a joint resolution setting forth what came to be known as the Eisenhower Doctrine. The resolution empowered the President to use the armed forces of the United States, at the request of any nation of the Middle East, to protect it against overt armed aggression from any nation controlled by international Communism.[10]

[10]*Documents on American Foreign Relations, 1957,* 195–204. In April 1970 the Senate Foreign Relations Committee voted to recommend repeal of the "Eisenhower Doctrine" resolution as well as the Tonkin Gulf Resolution. *New York Times,* April 11, 1970, pp. 1, 4. But the Eisenhower Doctrine was untouched by the rider that repealed the Tonkin Gulf Resolution in Public Law 91–672, January 12, 1971.

Though no nation of the area made the type of request described in the resolution, President Eisenhower found two occasions to act at least in the spirit of it. A few weeks after the passage of the resolution, pro-Western King Hussein of Jordan was threatened by leftist agitators, who, with Egyptian and Syrian backing, called for his overthrow and the alignment of Jordan with Egypt and Syria. This situation brought from Eisenhower an announcement that he considered the independence of Jordan vital to the security of the United States, an order moving the American Sixth Fleet to the Eastern Mediterranean, and the grant to Jordan of $30 million in economic and military aid. These gestures, coupled with assurances of support to Jordan from Iraq and Saudi Arabia, put an end for the time being to the plot against Hussein's rule.

The year 1958 brought a more serious crisis. Early in the year Egypt and Syria merged to form the United Arab Republic (U.A.R.) under Nasser's presidency. This victory of Arab nationalism was a threat to the existing pro-Western regimes in Jordan and Iraq, as well as to Israel. As a countermeasure the kingdoms of Iraq and Jordan federated to form the Arab Union. This course was evidently unpopular in Iraq, where on July 14 a violent revolution overthrew the government. The King, the Crown Prince, and the Premier, all friends of the West, were assassinated. A new government, not Communist but friendly to the Soviet Union, took control. Iraq soon withdrew from the Baghdad Pact. Alliance headquarters were moved to Ankara in Turkey and the name was changed to Central Treaty Organization (CENTO).

The immediate Western reaction to the Iraqi revolution, however, was an assumption (plausible but incorrect) that it had been engineered by Nasser and portended similar moves in Jordan and Lebanon. In Lebanon, in fact, there was already an armed rebellion in progress, with opponents of the regime receiving encouragement and support from the U.A.R., especially its contiguous Syrian branch. The governments of Lebanon and Jordan, on receiving news of the Iraqi revolution, appealed for military protection to the United States and Britain respectively, basing their pleas upon the right of collective self-defense guaranteed by Article 51 of the United Nations Charter.

The appeals met prompt response. The United States landed 14,000 marines and airborne troops in Lebanon, while the British dispatched 3,000 paratroopers to Jordan. While the Soviet Union denounced the intervention as a demonstration of "Western imperialism" and demanded immediate withdrawal of the foreign troops, and the U.N. Security Council was deadlocked, the quarreling Arab states excited general surprise by combining in the General Assembly to sponsor a resolution that broke the impasse. The resolution pledged the Arab states to respect one another's systems of government and to abstain from any action calculated to disturb those systems. It called upon the U.N. Secretary-General to take steps toward seeing that this principle was observed with relation to Lebanon and Jordan and thus to prepare the way for an early withdrawal of foreign troops.[11] The danger of outside interference in Jordan and Lebanon was for the time being removed; the civil strife in Lebanon was terminated through the mediation of American diplomat Robert Murphy; and the foreign troops were withdrawn, the Americans in October, the British in November. Not for nine years did the Middle East see another crisis so serious.

Rifts in the Arab World

Those nine years, however, were by no means quiet or peaceful. They were

[11]*Documents on American Foreign Relations, 1958*, pp. 360–61.

marked, on the Arab side, by agreements made and broken, mutual denunciations, plots, counterplots, coups, and civil wars. The one constant was hatred of Israel, refusal to recognize its existence as a state, and a determination that as a state it must be destroyed. Of all the Arab leaders, only one, Habib Bourguiba of Tunisia, had the realism and courage to urge that the Arabs should accept Israel as a fact and make peace with it on the terms proposed by the U.N. in 1947. For this effrontery Bourguiba's government narrowly missed being expelled from the Arab League; nor did he get much credit from Israel, to which the terms of 1947 were no longer acceptable.

But practical Arab leaders, like Nasser, knew that as yet the Arabs were unprepared to fight another conventional war with Israel with any hope of success. There was, however, the possibility of guerrilla war, and for this purpose a Palestine Liberation Organization was formed among the refugees, spearheaded by a so-called Palestine Liberation Army. By 1966, this and other refugee groups were leading guerrilla raids into Israel from the neighboring states, most often from Syria, though such raiding parties frequently entered Israel from Jordan.

Israel retaliated, sometimes by air, sometimes by ground attack, against the states from which the attacks had come, often inflicting death or injury upon innocent parties, as when the Jordanian village of Es Samu was virtually destroyed by a tank-led Israeli force in November 1966. Such a reprisal was particularly unfortunate because, of all Israel's immediate neighbors, King Hussein of Jordan was most receptive to suggestions for a peaceful settlement, despite serious domestic opposition.

But although the Arab states, with the exception of Tunisia, were in agreement in their uncompromising hostility to Israel, they agreed about little else. They were divided ideologically into two groups. The "progressive" states, led by Egypt, Syria, Iraq, and Algeria (which won its independence from France in 1962), were in theory republican and socialistic and were sympathetic to the Soviet Union, though unwilling to be dominated by it. Saudi Arabia and Jordan, on the other hand, were conservative monarchies and preferred the friendship of the West to that of Moscow. President Gamal Abdel Nasser of the U.A.R., most dynamic of the Arab leaders, not only found his ambition to unite and dominate the Arab world blocked by the monarchies but met with opposition even in Syria and Iraq, where pro-Nasser and anti-Nasser regimes alternated in consequence of a succession of coups. Syria withdrew from the U.A.R. in 1961 (though Nasser retained the name for Egypt alone), and attempts to reconstitute that union with the inclusion of both Syria and Iraq were frustrated by mutual jealousies.

The rift in the Arab world was further deepened by a civil war in Yemen. In 1962 the Imam, the paternalistic sovereign of that backward little state, was ousted at the instigation of Nasser, and a nominally republican regime was set up with Egyptian backing. The Imam, however, refused to bow to the revolution and was aided in his resistance by Saudi Arabia and Jordan. Nasser poured an estimated peak of 70,000 Egyptian troops (accompanied by Russian technicians) into Yemen, but royalist forces, with Saudi Arabian support, continued to resist, and the war dragged on until 1970, in spite of efforts of the U.N. and the U.S. to end it.[12]

Nasser at the same time, looking beyond Yemen, was denouncing British imperialism as exemplified in Aden and the neighboring British-protected South Arabian Federation. In the face of acts of terrorism in this area and armed raids across the border from Yemen, Britain announced that she would withdraw from the

entire area by 1968. Actually, Aden and the South Arabian Federation became independent as the People's Republic of Southern Yemen on November 30, 1967. Rightly or wrongly, Nasser was suspected of scheming to win control of all Arabia, including its petroleum resources and those of the Persian Gulf.[13]

American Preferences

United States policy during these years aimed primarily at keeping the peace in the area—peace for its own sake, and peace as the best means of preventing the growth of Soviet influence. In accord with this policy was President Kennedy's offer of assistance—specifically in resolving "the tragic Palestine refugee problem"—to all the states of the area that were determined to live in peace, maintain their independence, and improve the living standards of their people. Equally a part of this peace policy was the President's warning that, if necessary, the United States would act both through the U.N. and "on our own" to prevent or stop aggression by any state in the area.[14] The United States desired to maintain friendly relations with all states in the area. At the same time, it was fully committed to the right of Israel to exist as a nation, and hence necessarily opposed to the ultimate Arab goal—destruction of Israel; and while it might, in theory, prefer the domestic policies of the "progressive" states to the

---

[12]Egyptian troops were withdrawn during the Six-Day War of 1967, but the civil war continued until April 1970, when the royalist forces abandoned the contest at the instance of Saudi Arabia. *New York Times,* April 15, 1970, p. 11.

[13]Nasser also put pressure on Libya to terminate British and U.S. base rights in that country, due to expire in 1973 and 1971 respectively. Both agreed in 1964 to review their plans. Evacuation of British bases and American Wheelus Field was speeded up after a pro-Nasser military coup overthrew the King on September 1, 1969. The British were out by April 1, 1970; the Americans surrendered their $100 million air base at Wheelus Field in June 1970. *U.S. in World Affairs, 1964,* p. 256; *New York Times,* December 24, 1969, p. 3, June 21, 1970, p. 14.

[14]*Documents on American Foreign Relations, 1961,* pp. 281–84; *New York Times,* May 12, 1963, Sec. 4, p. 2.

paternalism of the monarchies, the affinity of the former group for the Soviet Union automatically aligned the United States with Jordan and Saudi Arabia in any contest between them and the U.A.R.

The peculiar consequence followed that whereas the United States had emphasized its desire to decelerate the arms race in the area, it found itself in 1966 contributing to that race on both sides of the Israeli-Arab contest. To balance Soviet (or satellite) arming of the U.A.R., the United States sold tanks and fighter-bombers to Jordan. To balance this increment to Jordan's tank forces, the United States then provided Israel with Patton tanks; and to balance Egypt's and Jordan's new aircraft (Soviet and American), the United States then found it necessary to sell small Skyhawk jet bombers to Israel. Israel and Saudi Arabia, meanwhile, had both been supplied by the United States with ground-to-air missiles. Such business must have been profitable to American arms manufacturers.

The Six-Day War

The guerrilla attacks on Israel and Israeli counterattacks, which had become flagrant in 1966, intensified in the spring of 1967. Attacks from Syria, May 5 and 6, led the Israeli government to serve notice on the United Nations (which had repeatedly condemned Israeli reprisals with inadequate rebuke for the provocation) that Israel would defend itself. Abdel Nasser, who hitherto had shown a prudent caution, now committed a series of rash and provocative acts, stimulated in part by unfounded Soviet reports that Israel was mobilizing against Syria.[15] On May 18 he

demanded that the U.N. Emergency Force, which had policed the U.A.R.-Israeli border since 1956, be at once withdrawn. Secretary-General U Thant complied; he contended that he had no choice, since the UNEF troops were stationed on Egyptian soil with Egypt's permission. Nasser then moved his armed forces into the Sinai Peninsula, apparently ready to cross the border into Israel. Then, on May 22, Nasser seized Sharm el-Sheikh, guarding the Strait of Tiran (occupied since 1956 by the UNEF), and declared the strait and the Gulf of Aqaba closed to Israeli shipping.

Closing the strait was virtually an act of war, but before resorting to force the Israeli government sought a diplomatic solution. Foreign Minister Abba Eban visited London, Paris, and Washington in a quest for support. From President de Gaulle he got only a warning not to fire the first shot—a warning that was to be invoked as the basis for France's later reversal of her hitherto sympathetic policy to Israel. In London, Prime Minister Wilson encouraged Eban to hope that Britain might act with other powers to keep the strait open. From President Johnson he got a promise to seek international pressure upon Nasser to open the strait, in accord with guarantees given to Israel by the United States in 1957 after the Suez crisis; but Johnson asked for two weeks' time and asked Israel meanwhile not to start the shooting. Thus Israel was left with only vague promises of future support and facing an enemy whose purpose seemed to be its immediate destruction.

The picture darkened on May 30, when King Hussein of Jordan flew to Cairo and signed a mutual defense pact with his former enemy, Nasser. Popular and military pressure for action now led Israeli Premier Levi Eshkol to name General Moshe Dayan, hero of the Suez War, as

---

[15]The Soviet reports were apparently directly responsible for Nasser's determination to mobilize in the Sinai Peninsula, but Moscow was not consulted on his closing of the Strait of Tiran and at the last moment warned him against initiating military action. The Soviets did promise, however, that if Nasser's acts led

to war, they would match for him any aid that the U.S. might give to Israel. See Theodore Draper, *Israel and World Politics; The Roots of the Third Arab-Israeli War* (New York: The Viking Press, Inc., 1968).

Minister of Defense. Early on June 5—claiming that radar screens showed U.A.R. planes approaching to attack—Dayan launched a devastating offense which in a few hours destroyed the air forces of the U.A.R., Jordan, and Syria, and left the way open for an equally invincible land campaign, which carried Israeli troops and tanks to the Suez Canal and Sharm el-Sheikh, to the west bank of the Jordan in Jordanian territory (including complete occupation of the Jordanian section of Jerusalem), and in the north to the summit of the Golan Heights, from which Syrian artillery had harassed Israeli settlements on the shores of the Sea of Galilee. No victory could have been more complete. By June 11, all belligerents had yielded to a series of cease-fire orders issued by the U.N. Security Council, and the Six-Day War was over.

The war had wide international repercussions. It destroyed for the time being any hope of better relations between the "progressive" Arab states and the West (except France). On the false charge that American and British planes had participated in the Israeli campaign, Nasser, who had already severed diplomatic relations with Britain, broke off those with the United States. His example was followed by Syria, Iraq, Algeria, and Yemen, while the oil-producing Arab states agreed to suspend oil shipments to the offending powers. This suspension, however, was short-lived, since it injured the suppliers of oil more than the purchasers. During the fighting Nasser had blocked the Suez Canal with sunken ships. It remained closed. The Israelis, occupying the east bank, would not consent to clearing operations without guarantees of nondiscrimination in its use. For the loss of this principal source of revenue, the U.A.R. was compensated by subsidies from the oil-rich Arab states, Saudi Arabia, Kuwait, and Libya.

On the other side of the board, the Soviet Union and its satellites broke off diplomatic relations with Israel, which they branded as the aggressor. Though President Johnson and Premier Kosygin assured each other on the "hot line," June 5, of their common determination not to become involved in the hostilities, Moscow's uncompromising espousal of the Arab cause—including immediate steps to replace the estimated $1 billion worth of military equipment lost or destroyed—tended to widen the East-West rift. The meeting of the two statesmen at Glassboro, New Jersey, failed to narrow it.

The Search for a Settlement

The cease-fire agreement of June 11, like its predecessors of 1949 and 1956, and like that of 1953 in Korea, ended hostilities for the time being but in no sense restored peaceful relations; in fact, between Israelis and Arabs there had been no peaceful relations to restore. The immediate question, since Israel held important areas of formerly Arab territory, was whether she should surrender these, and if so, upon what conditions? Both the Security Council and the General Assembly of the U.N. had struggled with this question in June and July but had failed to reach agreement. The great powers agreed, in general, that territory seized by force should be handed back. But whereas the U.S.S.R. contended that Israel, the aggressor, should restore the conquered territory at once and unconditionally, the United States and Britain recognized Israel's grievances and held that in return for surrendering her conquests she should receive recognition of her national existence and guarantees of security from attack and of nondiscriminatory treatment in international waterways, specifically in the Suez Canal and the Strait of Tiran.

President Johnson stated the American position in a few words in an address of June 19, 1967:

> Certainly troops must be withdrawn, but there must also be recognized rights of na-

tional life, progress in solving the refugee problem, freedom of innocent maritime passage, limitation of the arms race, and respect for political independence and territorial integrity.[16]

Neither the United States nor the U.S.S.R. was able, during the summer, to secure the necessary votes for the approval of its position in either the Security Council or the General Assembly.

In August there was one hopeful indicator. At an Arab summit meeting in Khartoum, both Nasser and King Hussein of Jordan acknowledged the need for a diplomatic, as distinct from a military, solution of the problem; but such expression meant little in view of the continued insistence by the Arabs that they would not negotiate with the Israelis. Israel, for its part, was, as formerly, quite willing to negotiate, which would mean recognition, but as to the surrender of the Old City of Jerusalem, which had great sentimental value, and such strategically critical spots as Sharm el-Sheikh and the Golan Heights, Israel seemed unlikely to yield.

After months of tension during which the Security Council had several times to rebuke the U.A.R. and Israel for violations of the cease-fire agreement, that body on November 22, 1967, adopted unanimously a resolution, since known as U.N. Resolution 242, proposed by Great Britain, which held some promise as a basis for a compromise solution. The resolution called for the "withdrawal of Israeli armed forces from the territories occupied in the recent conflict"; termination of states of belligerency; "acknowledgement of the sovereignty, territorial integrity and political independence of every State in the area and their right to live in peace within secure and recognized boundaries free from threats or acts of force," and the guarantee of these rights "through measures includ-

ing the establishment of demilitarized zones"; guarantee of "freedom of navigation through international waterways in the area"; and "a just settlement of the refugee problem."

Finally, the Secretary-General was directed to name a special representative to act as mediator and to try to bring about a peaceful settlement based on the principles stated in the resolution.[17]

U Thant designated a Swedish diplomat, Gunnar Jarring, to undertake the delicate task of finding common ground between Arabs and Israelis. Jarring first attempted to bring representatives of the parties secretly to neutral territory in Cyprus, where they could exchange ideas through him as mediator (a technique used in negotiating the truce of 1949). This plan was abandoned when rumors of it leaked out, causing an uproar in Arab lands. The parties then agreed to work through Jarring at U.N. headquarters in New York, where the governments concerned were represented. When no results were achieved there, both U Thant and the French government proposed that the Big Four powers undertake to find a settlement. The proposal was endorsed by the Soviets and finally accepted by Britain and by the new Nixon administration in Washington. To warnings from Israeli Premier Golda Meir (Premier Levi Eshkol died in February 1969) that Israel would not accept an imposed settlement, Secretary of State Rogers responded that the Big Four would rely upon "the force of world opinion" to bring acceptance of a formula on which they might agree.[18]

The Big Four, however, became as deeply divided as the antagonists and along the same lines. Russia, seconded by France, supported the Arabs; the United States and Britain, though somewhat more flexible, supported Israel. The chief issues in dispute were clear. The Arabs would accept

---

[16]*Department of State Bulletin*, 57 (July 10, 1967), 31–34.

[17]*New York Times*, November 23, 1967, pp. 1, 5.
[18]*New York Times*, April 8, 1969, pp. 1, 4.

the U.N. terms of November 1967 but interpreted them to mean that Israel must surrender as a preliminary to negotiation all territory seized in the Six-Day War. The Israelis, on the other hand, would not surrender occupied territory until assured through negotiated treaties of their security against further hostilities and of their right to navigation of the Suez Canal and the Strait of Tiran. It became more and more clear, also, that the Israelis were determined to hold all of Jerusalem and were most unlikely to surrender the Golan Heights and Sharm el-Sheikh. These conflicting views were sufficient to block the road to understanding without facing the complication of what constituted "a just settlement of the refugee problem." By January 1970 the Soviet Union and the United States were accusing each other of supporting demands that made settlement impossible.

In the meantime the cease-fire had largely broken down. Nasser declared it void in April 1969, and U Thant observed in July that a virtual state of war prevailed in the Suez area. Israeli-Egyptian artillery duels roared across the canal. Guerrilla or commando bands—*fedayeen*—had been organized on an enlarged basis among the Palestinian refugees. They staged raids into Israel from Jordan and Syria and resorted to acts of terrorism far from the borders of Israel, attacking or bombing Israeli planes or planes carrying Israeli passengers. Most important, through their politico-military organizations—of which Al Fatah was the most important—they denounced any plan for making peace with Israel and on occasion threatened with assassination any Arab ruler who should venture to negotiate for such a peace. Thus they presented yet a new obstacle to a negotiated peace.

Israel responded to the commando activities by attacks, generally from the air, on the states that harbored them—Egypt, Jordan, Syria, even Lebanon when Palestinian commandos forced their activities on that would-be nonbelligerent little state. Egypt,

however—or the U.A.R.—bore the brunt of the Israeli retaliation. Israeli planes dropped bombs as far within Egypt as the suburbs of Cairo, until Russia came to Egypt's support by deploying SAM-3 (surface-to-air) missiles, manned by Soviet crews, for the defense of the capital. In an even more ominous gesture, the U.S.S.R. sent in Russian pilots to fly Russian-built MIGs of the Egyptian air force, presumably for defense of the missile sites. More alarming than the obvious chance of clashes between Soviet and Israeli personnel was the danger that Russian participation might deprive Israel of its supremacy in the air and doom it to a long war of attrition (3,000,000 Israelis against perhaps 90,000,000 Arabs) or actual destruction by Arab armies.

To offset Russian aid to its enemies, Israel looked to the United States, since France, its chief supplier prior to the Six-Day War, had cut off all planes to Israel and had, in fact, promised one hundred jets to Arab Libya. The United States, anxious not to exacerbate the arms race, delayed action on the Israeli request for 125 jet aircraft (Phantoms and Skyhawks), but in his TV "conversation" of July 1, 1970, President Nixon stated flatly; "We will do what is necessary to maintain Israel's strength vis-à-vis its neighbors. Not because we want Israel to be in a position to wage war—that isn't it—but because that is what will deter its neighbors from attacking it."[19]

Several days before the President's interview, Secretary of State Rogers had submitted to Israel and her neighbors a proposal for a ninety-day cease-fire and a resumption of peace negotiations under U.N. auspices. President Nasser, after a visit to Moscow, accepted the proposal (July 23); King Hussein of Jordan followed suit. The Israeli government also agreed, though with misgivings, after receiving as-

[19]*New York Times,* July 5, 1970, Sec. 4, p. 10; *Buffalo Evening News,* July 2, 1970. Cf. G. W. Ball, "Suez Is the Front to Watch," *New York Times Magazine,* June 28. 1970, pp. 10–11, 58–65.

surances from the United States that the cease-fire would not be used to Israeli's military disadvantage. Syria and Iraq had rejected the proposal, and the Palestinian commando leader, Yasir Arafat, had served notice that his group would accept no cease-fire and no compromise settlement.

The cease-fire became effective on the night of August 7–8, and on August 25 Gunnar Jarring began separate talks with the ambassadors of the three governments at the United Nations. Days earlier, however, Israel had charged that the U.A.R., with Russian assistance, had violated the cease-fire agreement by moving batteries of SAM-2 and SAM-3 missiles into the cease-fire zone west of the Suez Canal. Such reinforcement, the Israelis claimed, endangered Israel's command of the air over the canal and her ability to hold the east bank as her first line of defense. The United States, at first skeptical, became convinced by September 1 that the U.A.R. had broken the truce agreement and two days later called upon Cairo and Moscow to avoid further violations but urged that the peace talks continue. Dissatisfied with this rather bland American posture, the Israeli government, which had already called home its ambassador at the U.N., announced on September 6 that it would not resume negotiations until the newly installed missiles in the cease-fire zone were removed.

On that same day, with the evident purpose of putting a final end to the peace talks, Palestinian commandos hijacked three commercial jet airplanes in flight over Europe. One, a Pan American 747 jumbo jet, was flown to Cairo, where it was blown up after crew and passengers had made a hurried exit. The other two, an American TWA and a Swissair, were landed in the desert near Amman, Jordan, where they were joined three days later by a British BOAC plane, hijacked en route from Bahrain to London. By Friday, September 11, the passengers and crew members, numbering 414, had been removed from the planes. The planes were then blown up, and most of the passengers were moved to hotels in or near Amman, whence they were flown to Cyprus; but some fifty-four (Israelis, Swiss, British, West Germans, and Americans) were separated from the others and held as hostages. The price of their release was to be the freeing of Arab terrorists imprisoned in Switzerland, West Germany, England, and Israel. American Jews, some of whom were reported to have dual U.S.—Israeli citizenship, were to be treated as Israelis.

Negotiations for the return of hostages were under way through the International Red Cross when King Hussein of Jordan installed a military government and on September 17 ordered his Bedouin army to have it out with the Palestinian guerrillas, with whom for weeks there had been intermittent fighting. Ten days of bloody and destructive warfare followed, ending in an apparent victory for Hussein's army and a truce arranged in Cairo September 25, between Hussein and Yasir Arafat under the supervision of the heads of other Arab states. By September 29 all of the hijacked hostages had been released. Thereupon, by agreement, the British, West German, and Swiss governments released their Arab terrorist captives.

The Jordanian civil war had raised new threats of major international involvement. President Nixon had told a private gathering of news editors that the United States might have to intervene if King Hussein's regime should be threatened by interference from Syria or Iraq in behalf of the guerrillas. When Syrian tanks crossed the border on September 18, the President apparently considered direct intervention by the United States. He had already reinforced the Sixth Fleet, which was cruising between Crete and the coast of Israel, and alerted airborne troops in the United States and West Germany. What he had in mind was apparently a bold stroke which would at the same time sustain Hussein's throne and rescue the hostages.

Cautioned by the British ambassador against direct intervention, Mr. Nixon and his advisers concerted with Israel on a contingency plan by which, if it became necessary, Israeli forces would attack the invading Syrians, while the United States would protect the Israeli flanks and rear against possible attack from the U.A.R. or elsewhere. Fortunately, execution of the plan was not necessary. The Syrian tanks withdrew, probably impelled by advice from Moscow as well as by the threat from Israel and vigorous attacks by Hussein's air force and armor.

The challenge to the Soviet Union over control of the Middle East and the Mediterranean, implicit in these events and in promises of increased military aid to both Israel and Jordan, was made more explicit when the President, during a brief trip to Europe (September 27 to October 5, 1970), paid a ceremonial visit to the Sixth Fleet and declared in an address in Rome: "The Mediterranean is the cradle of many great civilizations of the past, and we are determined that it shall not be the starting place of great wars in the future."[20]

There were indications of a Soviet counterchallenge in the Caribbean. On September 25, the White House revealed information (which it had had for some time) of Russian naval activity at Cienfuegos on the south coast of Cuba. The information suggested the possibility that the Russians were preparing to construct a base for nuclear submarines in the Cuban harbor— a development which, the White House warned, the United States would view "with the utmost seriousness."[21] Mr. Nixon's ambition to substitute negotiation with Mos-

cow for confrontation seemed, as James Reston observed, to have been at least temporarily thwarted.[22]

The suspension of fighting in Jordan brought some relief of tension. Then, on September 28, three days after presiding over the signing of the cease-fire agreement, President Gamal Abdel Nasser succumbed to a heart attack. Nasser had so dominated the Middle Eastern scene for the preceding eighteen years that his passing made the future of the area more than ever unpredictable. His immediate successor as President, Anwar el-Sadat, vowed to continue Nasser's policies. His emphatic refusal, supported by Moscow, to remove a single SAM missile from the cease-fire zone made resumption of the peace talks seem at first unlikely. Israel, however, after strengthening her position on the east bank of the canal and receiving assurance of $500 million in military aid from the United States, dropped her insistence upon the removal of the missiles. Urged by the United States to resume negotiations with the Arab states through Gunnar Jarring at the U.N., and given assurances of American support against extreme Arab demands, Israel finally agreed to resume the talks. The U.A.R. had already done so. Unfortunately, little if anything was achieved through negotiation, both sides agreeing only to disagree until the next round of hostilities.

The Yom Kippur War of 1973

The fourth Arab-Israeli war since 1948 broke out on October 6, 1973, on the Day of Atonement—the holiest day in the Jewish calendar. The Arab attack[23] led simultane-

[20]*New York Times*, September 28, 1970, pp. 1, 3.

[21]*New York Times*, September 26, 1970, pp. 1, 8. The charge was vigourously denied by the Soviet Union. Ibid., October 1, 1970, pp. 1, 6; October 14, 1970, pp. 1, 4.

[22]*New York Times*, September 27, 1970, (sec. 4), p. 15.

[23]Other Arab states that contributed military forces to the war effort included Jordan, Iraq, Morocco, and Saudi Arabia.

ously by a powerful Egyptian offensive launched across the Suez Canal and by an equally powerful Syrian offensive on the Golan Heights apparently took the Israeli government of Prime Minister Golda Meir by surprise.[24] On both fronts the Arabs recorded initial successes. Fighting with a spirit and determination that fully redeemed the image of the Arab soldier of 1967, the Egyptians forced the crossing of the Suez with little difficulty; overran the so-called "Bar-lev line," a series of strategic strongholds on the east bank; and plunged deep eastward into the Sinai desert where between October 14 and 19 the world witnessed one of the biggest and bloodiest tank battles since World War II. On the northern front the Syrians, too, met early success. Spearheaded by 1,400 tanks, the Syrian Army drove more than 15 miles into occupied territory, advancing across the Golan Heights to the edge of Israel proper.

Though holding only defensive positions at first, the Israelis soon mounted a counter-offensive both on the Suez and Syrian fronts. In the former the Israelis had achieved a bridgehead on the west bank of the Suez Canal, reaching to within 70 miles of Cairo, and had managed to encircle the Egyptian Third Army of 20,000 men on the east bank. In the latter theatre the Israelis had by October 24, the date of the second and final cease-fire, reconquered the whole of the Golan Heights and had advanced to within 20 miles of Damascus.

The American response to what popularly became known in the United States as the Yom Kippur War was a measured one. At the outset of hostilities President Nixon requested an immediate meeting of the United Nations Security Council to bring an end to the war. After several inconclusive and acrimonious meetings of the Security Council on October 8 and 9, it be-

came obvious that a cease-fire resolution was still in the future. Then, on October 10, the Soviet Union began an airlift to replenish Egyptian and Syrian war stocks, which started out moderately but within days reached, according to Secretary of State Henry Kissinger, disturbing proportions.[25]

At this point the Nixon administration pursued a two-pronged policy of matching Soviet arms on the one hand and persuading the Russians to assist in effecting a U.N. Security Council resolution on the other hand. On October 13 the President decided that the U.S. would have to start resupply efforts of its own; and on October 19 the American Congress approved $2.2 billion in aid for Israel. The Arab response, lasting until March 18, 1974, and having a disastrous effect on the national economy,[26] was to initiate an oil embargo against the United States.

In an effort to bring the Egyptians around, Soviet Prime Minister Kosygin visited Cairo from October 16 to October 19. On the next day, at the request of General Secretary Brezhnev, Kissinger flew to Moscow to work out a joint formula that could be submitted to the Security Council. Before returning the Secretary of State paid a previously unannounced visit to Tel Aviv to persuade the Israelis of the merits of the plan.

On the evening of October 21, and as a matter of extreme urgency, the United States and the Soviet Union convened the Security Council; and in the early hours of October 22 the Council adopted a resolution, presented jointly by the superpowers, calling for an immediate cease-fire in the Middle East. Adopted by a vote of 14–0, the Republic of China abstaining, the resolution called for an immediate cease-fire in place; the immediate implementation of

---

[24]For the U.S. Department of State intelligence estimate of the Middle East situation on the eve of the war consult Ray S. Cline, "Policy without Intelligence," *Foreign Policy,* 17 (Winter, 1974), pp. 131–33.

[25]Transcript of the Secretary of State's News Conference of October 25, 1973, courtesy of the United States Information Service.

[26]During the first quarter of 1974 the gross national product of the U.S. declined 6.3 percent.

U.N. Resolution 242; and for negotiations between the parties concerned under appropriate auspices to bring about a just and durable peace. Thus for the first time were the U.S. and the Soviet Union prepared to offer their assistance, if acceptable to the belligerents.

Egypt and Israel agreed to the cease-fire on the same day and after the truce had been broken, consented again on October 24 to respond to a second U.N. resolution. The Syrians accepted the cease-fire on October 24 as well. What happened next was a crisis with worldwide implications.

In response to certain Israeli territorial gains that took place in the aftermath of the breakdown of the first cease-fire resolution and in response to the anticipated threat of annihilation of the beleaguered Egyptian Third Army, the Soviets proposed the sending of joint U.S. and Soviet military forces to the Middle East to bring about an observance of the cease-fire. The Nixon administration steadfastly opposed the plan on the ground that the superpowers should not impose a military solution on the belligerents.

On October 24 Washington specifically rejected two suggestions of a joint expeditionary force, one from President Anwar el-Sadat of Egypt in the late afternoon, and another from Brezhnev in the early evening, delivered to the White House by Soviet Ambassador Anatoly Dobrynin. The second Soviet note was seen as a Soviet ploy to twist the meaning of the second cease-fire resolution with regard to the dispatch of U.N. observers to supervise the cease-fire. "We strongly urge," the note read, "that we both send forces to enforce the cease-fire and, if you do not, we may be obliged to consider acting alone."[27] This together with the electronic evidence presented caused the President to issue what is known as a Defense Condition #3 alert—troops placed on standby and awaiting or-

ders. Though of a precautionary nature, the alert, in President Nixon's words, "was to indicate to the Soviet Union that we would not accept any unilateral move on their part."[28] The Kremlin understood perfectly, and the crisis dissipated on the night of October 25 when the Security Council adopted another resolution for the creation of a U.N. Emergency Force exclusive of the permanent members of the Council. And so ended what some regarded as the most serious crisis in Soviet-American relations since the Cuban Missile Crisis of 1962. Others were not so sure.

The Search for Peace

At the conclusion of the fighting and the various cease-fire resolutions, there occurred a spate of diplomatic activities aimed at laying the foundation of a more lasting peace in the Middle East. The most important of these, including the visits to Washington by Arab leaders, was Secretary of State Kissinger's mission to the Middle East in November, resulting in not only the resumption of full diplomatic relations with Cairo for the first time since 1967, but also in the signing of an Egyptian-Israeli cease-fire agreement on November 11 at the Kilometre 101 checkpoint on the Cairo-Suez road. The chief provisions of the document required the two nations to agree to observe scrupulously the cease-fire called for by the Security Council and pledged both sides to begin immediately to settle the question of the return to the October 22 positions each held prior to the breakdown of the truce.[29]

The significance of this particular cease-fire was that it was the first major agreement between Israel and an Arab

[27]*New York Times*, November 21, 1973, pp. 1, 17.

[28]Transcript of President Nixon's Press Conference on October 20, 1973, Courtesy of the United States Information Service.

[29]*New York Times*, November 12, 1973, pp. 1, 21.

state since the armistice accord which ended the Palestine war of 1948–1949. And by bringing this about, Kissinger drove a wedge into the Arab ranks that divided the most moderate of the Arab belligerents from the others.[30]

In January 1974 Kissinger achieved an Egyptian-Israeli disengagement understanding whereby Israeli forces were withdrawn into the Sinai desert, leaving only small contingents at the critical Gidi and Mitla passes. For its part, Egypt promised to maintain only a small force on the east bank of the canal. On January 18 the compact was signed by the respective chiefs of staff.

Principally because of Kissinger's so-called "shuttle diplomacy," estimated at keeping the Secretary of State from Washington for the average of approximately one out of every six weeks in 1974 and 1975,[31] other successes followed. On May 31, 1974, Syria and Israel concluded a disengagement pact providing for a demarcation line in the Golan Heights, with U.N. troops in the buffer zone, and Damascus' acceptance of Israeli settlements there in exchange for the return of Queneitra. In September 1975, Egypt and Israel initialed a Sinai disengagement agreement with the novel provision specifying the use of 200 American civilians to monitor the cease-fire between the two opposing forces to forestall surprise attacks.[32]

A comprehensive peace settlement, however, continued to elude the Secretary of State, despite the beginnings made by the ill-fated Geneva conference of December 1973 under the auspices of the United States and the Soviet Union. The problems were the Palestinian question and boundaries. So long as the Palestinian Liberation Organization was committed to the destruction of Israel as a state and so long as Israel refused to deal with the PLO under those terms, it was perhaps at this time inevitable that little could be expected via this course.[33]

By the beginning of 1977, and despite the optimism of the new Carter administration, the American people had grown skeptical of achieving a total settlement in the region. According to a Harris Survey of 1,459 adults, reported in February, a 65 to 22 percent majority did not believe a comprehensive settlement between Arabs and Israelis could be worked out, though no less than 59 to 19 percent still felt it was right for the U.S. to send Israel all the military supplies it needed.[34]

The bitter civil war that wracked Lebanon in 1976 and 1977 demonstrated how difficult it would be to resolve a sectarian-inspired conflict, albeit in this case between Moslems and Christians. The attempt by the Syrian Army to dictate a truce between the warring factions also complicated matters. All things considered, the prospect of peace in the Middle East still seemed distant.

---

[30]One of the dividends to accrue to the American side in 1976 was the Egyptian cancellation of its friendship and cooperation treaty with the Soviet Union. From that time to the present Moscow has taken a dim view of President Sadat's leadership. See for instance, *New York Times,* February 23, 1977, p. 3.

[31]Particularly critical of Kissinger's approach is George W. Ball's "Kissinger's Paper Peace: How Not to Handle the Middle East," *The Atlantic Monthly,* February 1976, pp. 41–49.

[32]The approval to station "civilian technicians" in the Sinai was passed by a vote of 85–9 in the United

States Senate and 341–69 in the House. President Ford signed the measure into law in October.

[33]On January 26, 1976, the U.S. cast its veto in the Security Council on a resolution, which, it was argued, would have affirmed the right of the Palestinians "to establish an independent state in Palestine." It was only the 13th time that the U.S. had used its veto power in the U.N. *New York Times,* January 27, 1976, pp. 1, 4.

[34]*Chicago Tribune,* February 3, 1977.

ADDITIONAL READINGS

DeNovo, John A., *American Interests and Policies in the Middle East, 1900–1939.* Minneapolis: University of Minnesota Press, 1963.

Feis, Herbert, *The Birth of Israel: The Tousled Diplomatic Bed.* New York: W. W. Norton & Company, Inc., 1969.

Ferrell, Robert H., "American Policy in the Middle East," *Review of Politics,* 37 (1975), 3–19.

Fitzsimons, M. A., *Empire by Treaty: Britain and the Middle East in the Twentieth Century.* Notre Dame, Indiana: University of Notre Dame Press, 1964.

Polk, William R., *The United States and the Arab World* (rev. ed.). Cambridge: Harvard University Press, 1969.

Rostow, Eugene V., "The American Stake in Israel," *Commentary,* 63 (April, 1977), pp. 32–46.

Safran, Nadav, *Israel: The Embattled Ally.* Cambridge: Harvard University Press, 1978.

Sheehan, Edward, *The Arabs, Israelis, and Kissinger: A Secret History of American Diplomacy in the Middle East.* New York: Reader's Digest Press, 1976.

Snetsinger, John, *Truman, the Jewish Vote and the Creation of Israel.* Stanford: Stanford University Press, 1974.

Stein, Leonard, *The Balfour Declaration.* New York: Simon & Schuster, Inc., 1961.

Stokey, Robert W., *America and the Arab States: An Uneasy Encounter.* New York: John Wiley and Sons, Inc., 1975.

26. The Western Hemisphere, from Truman to Carter

There was one portion of the world where the threat of Communism seemed insignificant in the early postwar period. The Western Hemisphere appeared dedicated to the ideals of human freedom and free enterprise. The governments of Latin America, too often undemocratic in practice, were still democratic in theory, and the trend, it was hoped, was toward an ever truer democracy. In the United Nations, Latin America habitually voted as a bloc with the United States. Hemispheric relations were still, presumably, governed by the Good Neighbor Policy, and the first three postwar years were marked by an elaboration of cooperative machinery to serve the inter-American system. In reality, however, that elaboration was accompanied by a deterioration in the cooperative spirit and in the degree of cordiality shown to the United States by its southern neighbors. Old-fashioned outcries against "Yankee imperialism" and "dollar diplomacy" were mingled with new complaints that Uncle Sam sent floods of dollars in every direction except southward. Governmental and financial instability, a low standard of living, and an unhealthy distribution of property and income combined to make parts of the region, within fifteen years after the war, a tempting field for exploitation by Communist agitators.

Formalizing the Inter-American System

Franklin Roosevelt's Good Neighbor Policy—essentially a negative policy of nonintervention in Latin American affairs—had exorcised for the time being much of the anti-Yankee prejudice in Latin America and had assured hemisphere support for the United States in World War II, with the exception of Argentina and, to a lesser degree, Chile. Its effect carried over for several years after the war, contributing to the acceptance of an inter-American collective security treaty, sponsored by the United States, and to the formalization of the hitherto loose inter-American system of treaties and understandings in the Charter of the Organization of American States (OAS).

The Inter-American Treaty of Mutual Assistance, signed at a conference at Rio de Janeiro on September 2, 1947, replaced a temporary agreement, the Act of Chapultepec, adopted at a wartime conference in Mexico City, February 15 to March 8, 1945. The delay of two and a half years in converting the act into a treaty was the consequence of an unfortunate quarrel between the United States and Argentina, going back to Argentina's pro-Axis sympathies during the war and culminating in an ill-conceived attempt by the United States to influence a postwar Argentine presidential election. The election was won by Juan D. Perón, the candidate whose alleged pro-Axis activities the State Department had exposed in a "Blue Book." Until the State Department changed hands from James F. Byrnes to George C. Marshall as Secretary, early in 1947, bad feeling between the two governments stood in the way of the proposed inter-American conference.[1]

The Rio Treaty was the first of a number of regional collective security agreements concluded by the United States in conformity with Article 51 of the Charter of the United Nations. It made it the duty of every American state to assist in meeting an armed attack upon another American state until the U.N. Security Council should have taken effective measures to repel the aggression. The nature of the action to be taken by the American states to meet such an armed attack was to be determined by a two-thirds vote of a meeting of Foreign Ministers called for the occasion (parties to the dispute not voting), with the proviso that no state should be required to use armed force without its consent. The treaty, following ratification by two-thirds of the signatories, went into force on December 3, 1948.[2]

The conference at Rio in 1947 was a special one. The next in the regular series, the Ninth International Conference of American States, met at Bogotá, Colombia, March 30 to May 2, 1948. Its principal achievement was to provide the Organization of American States for the first time with a

charter or constitution. The charter restated the "fundamental rights and duties of states" (including nonintervention), formulated and approved at conferences in the 1930's. It named the organs of the organization and defined their powers and duties. As "supreme organ," the Inter-American Conference, meeting theoretically at five-year intervals, was replaced in 1970 by a General Assembly, meeting annually. Meetings of Foreign Ministers occurred as needed. It is these meetings that determined, by a two-thirds vote, the action to be taken to repel aggression against an American state. The Council, consisting of one representative of each state, functioned in Washington as an executive body; it served as a provisional "organ of consultation" pending a meeting of the Foreign Ministers. Operating under the direction of the Council were an Inter-American Council of Jurists, a Cultural Council, and an Economic and Social Council. The old Pan American Union became the Secretariat of the new Organization.[3]

Rifts Between Good Neighbors

The drafting and adoption of this elaborate charter, which was ratified and went into effect in 1951, satisfied an American fondness for committing international agreements to paper, after the manner of the numerous arbitration and conciliation treaties and the Kellogg-Briand Pact, of earlier decades. It was ironic that this paper work peak in inter-American relations came at a time when the spirit of those relations was deteriorating. Symptomatic

---

[1] For the Argentinian side of this story, consult Carlos Moneta, "Argentina and the Cold War," in *The Impact of the Cold War*, ed. by Joseph M. Siracusa and Glen St. John Barclay (Port Washington, N.Y.: Kennikat Press, 1977), pp. 101–24.

[2] Text of treaty in *Documents on American Foreign Relations*, 9: 534–40.

[3] The Charter and a number of other agreements adopted at Bogotá are printed in *Documents on American Foreign Relations*, 10: 484–532. For the 1970 amendment to the Charter providing for General Assembly, see *Department of State Bulletin*, 62 (April 20, 1970), 529–30.

of this trend was the temporary disruption of the Bogotá Conference in its second week by a violent outbreak of rioting in the Colombian capital. Whether or not Communist-inspired, as was charged, the riots were indicative of the widespread breakdown of orderly democratic processes in Latin America.

The Bogotá riots were symptomatic, too, of the revival of anti-Yankeeism which was making its appearance in many areas in Latin America. Never wholly extinguished, this resentment of the "Colossus of the North" had been overshadowed by the cordiality evoked by the Good Neighbor Policy. To Latin Americans, that policy had been identified with President Franklin Roosevelt. But Roosevelt was dead, and the policies followed by his successors, Presidents Truman and Eisenhower, brought many Latin Americans to the conclusion that the Good Neighbor Policy had died with him.

The truth was, not that the Good Neighbor Policy was dead, but that, in its strictly negative character, it no longer sufficed. The Latin Americans, like the peoples of other underdeveloped continents, were experiencing a postwar "revolution of rising expectations." They aspired to narrow the gap between their poverty (collectively speaking) and the affluence of the industrialized areas—Western Europe, North America, and now Japan. But the gap, instead of narrowing, was widening. Wartime prices of Latin America's raw materials—copper, tin, lead, petroleum, coffee—declined, while prices of their imported manufactures rose. Closing by the United States of wartime installations in such countries as Ecuador and Brazil worked economic disruption. Meanwhile, Latin Americans beheld their rich Uncle Sam dispatching billions of dollars in economic and military aid to Europe and the Far East, while they received little or nothing. They were not comforted by being told that the billions in aid were needed to combat the threat of Communism in Europe and Asia—a threat that supposedly did not exist in Latin America.[4]

What Latin Americans now demanded as the substance of good neighborliness was not simply the negative policy of nonintervention, important though that still was, but positive assistance in developing their economies and raising the standard of living of their rapidly growing population. This would involve such items as industrialization, improved transportation and agricultural techniques, and great advances in education in an area where illiteracy on the average was close to 50 percent. All of these things would require money in sums simply not available within the region. The Latin Americans, therefore, demanded two things of their good neighbor to the north: large-scale grants or loans on easy terms, preferably public, not private; and assistance in stabilizing at profitable levels the prices of their chief exports, especially coffee, metals, and petroleum.

To these proposed supplements to the Good Neighbor Policy, the United States reacted at first very negatively. While wholly in sympathy with the desire for industrialization, Washington spokesmen insisted that it should be accomplished chiefly through private investment and that the Latin American governments must attract private capital by offering it improved security—against nationalization, for example. This insistence on the paramount role of private investments as an agent of industrialization ran counter to a widespread Latin American antagonism to foreign private capital as exploitative and "imperialistic"—a prejudice which had some basis in past experience and was now itself exploited by the Communist apparatus, both native and imported. As to

[4]Donald M. Dozer, *Are We Good Neighbors? Three Decades of Inter-American Relations* (Gainesville, Fla.: University of Florida Press, 1959), chaps. 6–10, gives a detailed analysis of the deterioration in the relations of the United States with its neighbors to the south.

stabilization, the United States, itself involved in costly price guarantees to American farmers, was unwilling to extend the operation into the international arena.

Beginning early in the Eisenhower administration (1953–1961), the United States gradually modified its position on both issues and eventually, under Kennedy in 1961, embarked upon an ambitious program of economic development and social reform for Latin America as a whole—the Alliance for Progress. This change in attitude owed something to altruistic humanitarian sentiment but most to a recognition that an unhappy and resentful Latin American brought the threat of Communism to the doorstep of the United States.

The Communist Threat Comes Nearer

In its concern over the threat of Communism in Europe and Asia, the United States government had largely ignored conditions in Latin America which offered a favorable climate for Communist agitators. In a society that comprised a small but powerful upper class, or elite, a middle class insignificant in numbers and influence, and "a horde of uneducated 'have-nots,' a melancholy sea of misery," the need for economic and social reform was imperative. Unless this need could be met within the existing governmental framework, Communism would have a well-nigh irresistible appeal.

In his first year of office (1953), President Eisenhower, aware of the deteriorating relations between the United States and Latin America, sent his brother, Dr. Milton Eisenhower, as head of a mission to the ten republics of South America. The mission recommended certain modest measures for stabilization of prices, expansion of technical assistance (Point IV), encouragement of private investment, and carefully

restricted public loans, but more dramatic happenings were needed to alert this conservative administration to the urgency of the situation.

The first such incident was the adoption of a Communist line, in both domestic policy and in alignment with the Soviet Union in the United Nations, by the administration of President Jacobo Arbenz Guzmán (1951–1954) in Guatemala. Any Communist beachhead in the Americas, no matter how small, seemed to Secretary of State John Foster Dulles, not only a violation of the principles of the Monroe Doctrine, but an actual threat to the security of the United States and its sister republics. At the Tenth International Conference of American States, meeting in Caracas, Venezuela in March 1954, Dulles secured the adoption of a declaration which, without naming Guatemala, condemned "the domination or control of the political institutions of any American state by the international Communist movement," and declared that such a situation would be grounds for a meeting of consultation of Foreign Ministers "to consider the adoption of appropriate action in accordance with existing treaties.[5]

Whether Dulles could have persuaded two-thirds of the American Foreign Ministers to vote for intervention in Guatemala can only be conjectured. Such an effort was made unnecessary when Jacobo Arbenz Guzmán was overthrown in June 1954 by a fellow Guatemalan, Colonel Carlos Castillo Armas, assisted with American arms, and planes, allegedly by the Central Intelligence Agency.

If the brief apparition of Communist power in Guatemala shocked the Eisen-

[5]*Documents on American Foreign Relations, 1954,* pp. 412–14. Many delegations at the Conference were reluctant to adopt a declaration that suggested a policy of intervention in the affairs of a sister republic. The vote was 17 to 1, Guatemala voting no, Mexico and Argentina abstaining. Costa Rica, not represented at the Conference, later indicated its concurrence in the declaration.

hower administration, a perhaps ruder shock was the series of violent demonstrations that assailed Vice President Richard M. Nixon during his tour of South America in the spring of 1958. Nixon departed for South America on April 27, 1958, announcing that the purpose of his trip was to demonstrate "that these countries are not only our neighbors but our best friends." His reception varied from country to country, but in Lima, Peru, and Caracas, Venezuela, he was assailed by angry mobs. In Caracas, his life and that of Mrs. Nixon were in serious danger. Upon his return to Washington, Nixon attributed his hostile reception in part to Communist agitation but in part also to a widespread popular impression that the United States government had shown itself too friendly to dictatorial regimes in Latin America. A relevant instance was the fact that Marcos Pérez Jiménez, the recently ousted dictator of Venezuela, was at that very moment enjoying a safe and comfortable asylum in the United States. As one aspect of its policy of nonintervention, indeed, the United States had customarily made no distinction between dictatorial and democratic governments in its official relations with them. Nixon proposed no abandonment of the nonintervention policy, but he suggested that at least the United States might "have an 'abrazo' [embrace] for democratic leaders, and a formal handshake for dictators." This suggestion was endorsed by Dr. Milton Eisenhower, who in July 1958 made a return good will and fact-finding tour of Central America.[6]

Fidel Castro's Revolution

One of the dictators with whom the United States was thought to have been too friendly was Fulgencio Batista, the one-

[6]*U.S. in World Affairs, 1958,* p. 371; *Documents on American Foreign Relations, 1958,* p. 510.

time army sergeant who had seized power in Cuba in 1933 and had exercised it ever since, whether in or out of the presidential palace. In later years his regime had become "a cruel and corrupt dictatorship" and had grown increasingly unpopular. Consequently, when Fidel Castro, hitherto unknown in politics, launched his armed rebellion against Batista, the so-called 26th of July Movement, he quickly gathered popular support. Whatever may have been Castro's secret purposes, his movement in its days of struggle was neither Communist nor Communist supported, and it elicited considerable friendly unofficial attention in the United States.

The Washington government had maintained friendly relations with Batista and had supplied him, like certain other Latin American governments, with military equipment and advisers under the Mutual Security program. It now adhered to its policy of nonintervention with respect to Cuba. But inasmuch as it was making exertions to prevent clandestine aid from going to Castro, it terminated, in March 1958, the shipment of arms to the Cuban government but did not withdraw a military training mission stationed in Cuba. Castro's rebellion gathered momentum throughout 1958, and on New Year's Day, 1959, Batista boarded a plane for the Dominican Republic, leaving the field to the bearded revolutionist.

Space does not permit a detailed catalogue of the steps by which Castro transformed his revolutionary regime into one frankly Communist and affiliated with the Communist bloc in Europe and Asia. It is enough to say here that early promises of free elections and a free press were repudiated; that foreign property (including United States property approximating $1 billion in value) was nationalized without provision for compensation; that Communists, notably Fidel's brother, Raúl Castro, and Ernesto (Ché) Guevara, gradually replaced moderates in Castro's entourage; and that large-scale economic aid and military equipment and promises of armed support were forthcoming from the Soviet Union and its satellites. Cuba, furthermore, became a center for Communist propaganda directed at the remainder of Latin America and a training school for Latin American revolutionists. Castro, who had based his 26th of July Movement in the Sierra Maestra Mountains of eastern Cuba, boasted that he would cast the Andes in a similar revolutionary role for South America.

In view of the anti-Communist declaration adopted by the OAS at Caracas in 1954, the Eisenhower administration might have expected OAS support in combating Communism in Cuba. But two meetings of American Foreign Ministers, in Santiago, Chile, in August 1959, and in San José, Costa Rica, a year later, produced only inconclusive results. Though the Foreign Ministers at San José did not hesitate to call for a break in relations with the rightist dictatorship of Rafael Trujillo in the Dominican Republic, they refused to mention Castro or Cuba by name, merely condemning intervention in the Americas by an outside power and rejecting any Sino-Soviet attempt to exploit a troubled situation in any American state. In general, at this time and later, the states bordering on the Caribbean were ready for strong action against Castro, while Mexico and the larger South American republics avoided action that would antagonize his regime or offend pro-Castro minorities within their borders.

The United States, therefore, could take only unilateral action against Castro in retaliation for the latter's wholesale confiscation of American property and his continued abuse of the United States in his interminable speeches in Cuba and in his complaints in the United Nations. On July 6, 1960, President Eisenhower canceled about 95 percent of Cuba's remaining quota of sugar imports for the year. Some months later the United States canceled entirely the Cuban sugar quota for the first quarter of 1961; it also placed an embargo on all shipments to Cuba except foodstuffs, medicines, and medical supplies. On January 3, 1961, the President terminated all diplomatic and consular relations with the Cuban government. This was the American reply to a sudden Cuban order limiting the United States embassy staff in Havana to eleven persons and requiring all others to leave the island within forty-eight hours. The Swiss embassy in Havana assumed responsibility for American interests. A few days later, January 20, Eisenhower handed the Cuban problem over to John F. Kennedy.

A "New Deal" for Latin America

Before bowing out, however, the Eisenhower administration had begun to yield to several long cherished desires of the Latin Americans, hoping thereby to restore the atmosphere of good neighborliness and thus to counteract the appeal of *Fidelismo* outside of Cuba. In 1958, following Nixon's ill-fated good will tour, the United States had shown an increased willingness to consider measures for combating fluctuations in the prices of raw materials; it had at long last accepted the proposal for an inter-American lending institution, or bank, to which it would be the principal contributor. It had, indeed, given the impression that it was ready to sponsor a "new deal" for Latin America as a whole; and it had sought to correct the supposition that it showed special consideration to dictators.

The charter for the new Inter-American Development Bank was drawn up and approved during 1959, and the Bank began operations in Washington in October 1960. It would have an eventual lending capacity of $1 billion, of which $450 million would be subscribed by the United States. The United States, meanwhile, was supporting the efforts of the coffee-producing states to stabilize prices by limiting exports; it was looking with favor upon a plan for a free trade area embracing Mexico and several South American states and was lending assistance to a common market already functioning in Central America.

On July 11, 1960, President Eisenhower (who earlier in the year had paid a good will visit to several South American countries) announced a new program of aid for Latin America, which, unlike earlier programs, would emphasize meeting the human needs of the "bulk of the population." A month later he asked Congress to authorize the expenditure for this purpose of $600 million. One hundred million of this sum was intended for Chile, which had suffered a devastating earthquake. The remainder, as Secretary of State Herter explained, would be expended for "projects designed to contribute to opportunities for a better way of life for the individual citizens of the countries of Latin America."[7] Congress promptly (though without enthusiasm) passed the authorization, and this measure gave a sense of reality to a program adopted at Bogotá in September by a Committee of Twenty-one, representing all the American republics. The "Act of Bogotá" envisaged a variety of social reforms, to be undertaken in the respective countries, with United States backing, in such fields as land-tenure and utilization, housing, taxation, education, and public health.[8] The program was termed "Operation Pan America" after a proposal along similar lines recently put forward by President Juscelino Kubitschek of Brazil.

The Alliance for Progress

"Operation Pan America," thus launched in the closing months of the Eisenhower administration, was taken over by President Kennedy and incorporated in his Alliance for Progress (*Alianza para el Progreso*). First suggested in his Inaugural Address, the plan was elaborated in an address to the Latin American diplomatic corps in Washington at a White House reception, March 13, 1961. Referring to the revolutions that had gained independence for the United States and its southern neighbors, the President declared:

> Our hemisphere's mission is not yet completed. *For one unfulfilled task is to demonstrate to the entire world that man's unsatisfied aspiration for economic progress and social justice can best be achieved by free men working within a framework of democratic institutions.*[9]

What the President was proposing was a ten-year plan of economic development and social progress and reform. "Only the most determined efforts of the American nations themselves can bring success to this effort," he commented; but if the Latin American countries would do their part, the United States "should help provide resources of a scope and magnitude sufficient to make this bold development plan a success," as it had done for Europe under the Marshall Plan. He mentioned no figures, but Treasury Secretary Douglas Dillon, speaking at an Inter-American Economic and Social Conference at Punta del Este, Uruguay, in August, estimated that at least $20 billion would be available from outside sources—North America, Europe, Japan—during the next decade, most of it from public agencies. The annual rate of economic growth required to meet the objectives of the Alliance was estimated by Dillon at 2.5 percent per capita, which meant, allowing for Latin America's "popu-

[7]*U.S. in World Affairs, 1960*, pp. 318–19; *Documents on American Foreign Relations, 1960*, pp. 50–51, 528–31.

[8]*U.S. in World Affairs, 1960*, pp. 319–20; *Documents on American Foreign Relations, 1960*, pp. 539–46.

[9]*Documents on American Foreign Relations, 1961*, p. 396. Italics in original. The entire address and the President's message to Congress on March 14 are in ibid., pp. 395–408. See also Milton S. Eisenhower, *The Wine is Bitter: The United States and Latin America* (Garden City, N.Y.: Doubleday & Company, Inc., 1963), pp. 302–9.

lation explosion," a gross annual increase of 5 percent.[10]

The delegations at Punta del Este adopted a Charter defining the aims and procedures of the Alliance for Progress and a "Declaration to the Peoples of America," both signed August 17, 1961. The declaration described the Alliance for Progress as "a vast effort to bring a better life to all the peoples of the Continent." The United States pledged itself to provide "a major part of the twenty billion dollars, principally in public funds," which Latin America would require from external sources over the next decade to supplement its own efforts.[11] Cuba was represented at Punta del Este by its leading Communist theoretician, Ernesto (Ché) Guevara. He did not sign the charter, however, and Secretary Dillon made it clear that Cuba would receive no share of aid from the United States so long as it remained under Communist rule.

After being introduced with much fanfare, the Alliance for Progress got off to a disappointingly slow start. Two years after its inauguration at Punta del Este, the United States had committed a total of $2,180,000,000 to the program and had disbursed over $1,500,000,000. These sums had been expended largely for such items as residential housing, hospitals, water systems, schools, textbooks, agricultural loans, and the like. This was all right as far as it went, but it made small contribution to the self-sustaining economic growth on which the long-run success of the program would depend. Private capital, essential to the success of the program, was being frightened away rather than attracted by threats of nationalization and cancellation of contracts. Reforms in landholding and taxation had been endorsed by a number of governments, but their implementation was encountering powerful opposition.

[10]*Documents on American Foreign Relations, 1961*, pp. 408–16; *U.S. in World Affairs, 1961*, pp. 326–32.

[11]*Documents on American Foreign Relations, 1961*, pp. 416–35.

As a means of promoting political democracy in the Western Hemisphere, the Alliance for Progress had been even more disappointing than in its economic and social role. Between the inauguration of the Alliance and the fall of 1963, six elected governments in Latin America had been overthrown or set aside by military juntas. In two of these countries—Argentina and Peru—the military juntas had permitted fair elections, which had resulted in the choice of reform-minded governments. The crushing defeat of the *Perónistas* in the Argentine election of July 7, 1963, was especially gratifying. But in the Dominican Republic and Honduras the revolutions of September 25 and October 3, 1963, respectively, were very discouraging to the United States. In both, the ousted presidents had been dedicated to the ideals of the Alliance for Progress; and in the Dominican Republic, President Juan Bosch, who had been chosen after the assassination of the longtime dictator, Rafael Trujillo, had become in American eyes a symbol of democratic progress. The United States responded to the revolutions in the Dominican Republic and Honduras by recalling its ambassadors and suspending all foreign aid.

Within less than two months after these events, President Kennedy was dead and direction of the American participation in the Alliance for Progress passed to other hands. The outlook was not promising.

The Bay of Pigs

Between President Kennedy's announcement of the Alliance for Progress and the Conference at Punta del Este, Cuban exiles had made a disastrous attempt to land on the island and spearhead an armed rebellion against Castro's government. Unwilling itself to make war upon Castro, the United States government hoped to see him eliminated by the people of Cuba. Since March 1960 it had supplied training and equipment to several hundred Cuban refugees, some in the United States, more in Guatemala or elsewhere in Central America. Rumors of impending invasion gained credibility when the State Department, April 3, released a pamphlet entitled "Cuba." This document told the story of Castro's betrayal of his own revolution and his conversion of Cuba into a beachhead for Communism, "a fateful challenge to the inter-American system." Questioned at his press conference, April 12, President Kennedy denied categorically that there would be "an intervention in Cuba by United States armed forces."[12]

In the early hours of April 17, 1961, Cuban refugees numbering probably between 1,500 and 2,000 landed at Bahía de Cochinos (Bay of Pigs) on Cuba's southern coast. Here, in the absence of United States air support (which some of the exiles thought they had been promised), they were quickly overwhelmed by Castro's regular troops and militia, and were made prisoners to the number of 1,241. The expected popular uprising on the island had not occurred. The invasion was a fiasco and one very embarrassing to the United States, which had secretly sponsored it.

To a message from Premier Khrushchev, threatening all-out war if the United States should invade Cuba, President Kennedy replied that the United States intended no military invasion of Cuba, but added: "In the event of any military intervention by outside force we will immediately honor our obligations under the inter-American system to protect this hemisphere against external aggression." Speaking a few days later to the American Society of Newspaper Editors, the President declared that the United States did not intend to abandon Cuba to the Communists. He again disclaimed, however,

any intention of unilateral action by the United States. But, alluding to the nonintervention principle accepted by the American republics, he remarked that American restraint was not inexhaustible.

> Should it ever appear [he continued] that the inter-American doctrine of noninterference merely conceals or excuses a policy of non-action—if the nations of this hemisphere should fail to meet their commitments against outside Communist penetration— then I want it clearly understood that this Government will not hesitate in meeting its primary obligations, which are to the security of our Nation.[13]

As for Fidel Castro, he was strengthened and emboldened by his success in crushing the invasion and by the resulting wholesale arrests of Cubans suspected of disloyalty to his regime. He quickly dispelled any doubt that may have remained about his commitment to Communism. On May 1 he proclaimed that Cuba was now a "socialist" state. Some months later he boasted that he was and would always remain a devotee of Marxism-Leninism. In the meantime, he announced that there would be no need of elections in Cuba, merged his 26th of July Movement with the Popular Socialist (Communist) party, thereby making Cuba a one-party state, brought education under full state control, and took steps to curb the activities of the Catholic Church. In the following February (1962) he called for a continental civil war to enthrone Communism in all Latin America.

The earlier of these activities aroused new apprehensions among Cuba's Latin neighbors and led to proposals from Peru and Colombia for a new meeting of American Foreign Ministers. With the reluctant acquiescence of Mexico and the larger South American republics, such a meeting was called, to take place at Punta del Este,

---

[12]The pamphlet, "Cuba," and Kennedy's statement of April 12 are reprinted in *Documents on American Foreign Relations, 1961,* pp. 438–55.

[13]*Documents on American Foreign Relations, 1961,* pp. 456–58, 67.

January 22, 1962. The decisions of this conference were more cheering for the United States than had been those at Santiago and San José. Though the larger Latin states, with their vocal pro-Castro minorities, still resisted drastic action against Cuba, they all joined in unanimous votes (except Cuba's) declaring that the principles of Communism were incompatible with the principles of the inter-American system, and excluding the Communist government of Cuba from membership in the Inter-American Defense Board. By a vote of 16 to 1, with 4 abstentions (Mexico, Ecuador, Brazil, Chile), the conference ordered immediate suspension of trade with Cuba in arms and implements of war. By a vote of 14 to 1, with 6 abstentions (the 4 above plus Argentina and Bolivia), it excluded the Cuban government from participation in any of the organs of the OAS. A beginning had been made toward collective OAS action against Communism in Cuba, but still opposed to any drastic measures were governments representing two-thirds of the area and seven-tenths of the population of Latin America.

Russian Missiles in Cuba

On the evening of Monday, October 22, 1962, President Kennedy made a startling and dramatic disclosure to the American people and to the world. Within the past week, he reported, unmistakable evidence had established the fact that a series of Soviet missile sites were in preparation on the island of Cuba. Their purpose, he explained, could be "none other than to provide a nuclear strike capability against the Western Hemisphere." Some of the sites were designed for medium-range ballistic missiles with a range of over a thousand miles—capable of reaching Washington, D.C., Cape Canaveral, the Panama Canal, or Mexico City. Other sites,

not yet completed, appeared to be designed for intermediate-range missiles with a capability of reaching as far as Hudson's Bay to the north or Lima, Peru, to the south.[14]

Since the previous July, American reconnaissance had noted a heavy flow of traffic into Cuba of Russian ships. Cuban refugee sources and American secret agents in Cuba had reported construction of missile sites, and John A. McCone, Director of the CIA, was convinced that these were designed for missiles of at least medium range. He urged as early as August 10 that this opinion be reported to the President, but during his prolonged absence in Europe his deputy clung to the theory that the sites were designed only for defensive surface-to-air (SAM) missiles, and administration officials repeatedly assured anxious inquirers that such was the case. Lower-level CIA officers became so alarmed at the complacency in the administration that they leaked their telltale information to a trusted reporter, Nat S. Finney of the *Buffalo Evening News,* who published a story on the subject on August 29. Yet not until early October were orders given for high-level aerial photographic inspection of western Cuba, and not until Sunday, October 14, did American cameras obtain clear shots of missile sites near Cristobal in western Cuba; and not until the following Tuesday morning was the processing and analysis of the photographs completed. Then their evidence was convincing.

There followed a week of intense and almost continuous consultations among the President's top-level advisers, with the President himself sitting in from time to time. In order to avoid the appearance of a crisis, the President kept his regular appointments, including several speaking engage-

[14]*Documents on American Foreign Relations, 1962,* pp. 374–80. A blow-by-blow account of the crisis was published in the *New York Times,* November 3, 1962, pp. 1, 6–7.

ments in other cities. He canceled the last of these and returned to Washington on Saturday, October 20, with the fictitious explanation that he was suffering from a respiratory infection and a fever. His advisers—in effect an executive committee of the National Security Council—had meantime discarded proposals for an invasion of Cuba or an air strike against the missile installations, at least until less drastic measures had been tried. They recommended instead a selective blockade of the island, to prevent the importation of further weapons. This recommendation was accepted by the President and by Monday had been determined upon as the policy to be followed. But since it might lead to outright hostilities, air and ground forces as well as naval vessels were mobilized and moved into appropriate strategic locations.

The President had resolved that the United States should act unilaterally, since time was precious and an appeal for collective action by the U.N. or the OAS was certain to lead to prolonged debate. Great care was taken, however, to brief all the allies of the United States, and the unaligned nations as well, upon the proposed action in the last hours before the President's address on Monday night. The response from both European and American allies was gratifying.

In his address, after describing the presence of the missiles as "an explicit threat to the peace and security of the Americas" and denouncing the "cloak of secrecy and deception" under which they had been spirited into Cuba, the President voiced a grave warning to Chairman Khrushchev. The United States, he said, would "regard any nuclear missile launched from Cuba against any nation in the Western Hemisphere as an attack by the Soviet Union on the United States requiring a full retaliatory response upon the Soviet Union." Let Chairman Khrushchev, he urged, "halt and eliminate this clandestine, reckless and provocative threat to world peace and to

stable relations between our two nations." Meanwhile, said the President, he would initiate "a strict quarantine on all offensive military equipment under shipment to Cuba"; he would continue and increase "surveillance of Cuba and its military build-up"; he had already reinforced the United States naval base at Guantanamo and evacuated dependents of personnel stationed there. Finally, both the OAS and the U.N. would be asked to take or support action against this Soviet threat to the peace.

The blockade, or "quarantine," was to go into effect on Wednesday morning. On Tuesday Secretary of State Rusk convened the Council of the OAS and, surprisingly in view of past attitudes, secured a vote of 19 to 0 (the Uruguayan ambassador having no instructions) in support of the American position. The resolution adopted called for "the immediate dismantling and withdrawal from Cuba of all missiles and other weapons with any offensive capability," and recommended that the member states, individually and collectively, take all necessary measures, including use of armed force, to prevent the further arming of Cuba by the Sino-Soviet powers, "and to prevent the missiles in Cuba with offensive capability from ever becoming an active threat to the peace and security of the continent." This unanimous endorsement by the OAS of the blockade of Cuba was given under authority of the Rio Treaty of Reciprocal Assistance of 1947. The State Department's experts on international law maintained that it provided sufficient legal basis for the blockade.[15]

The world now seemed to stand at the brink of nuclear war. The United States, backed by the OAS and its major European allies, had reacted with great firmness to an unexpected threat to its security and that of the hemisphere. It was the Russians who

[15]*Documents on American Foreign Relations, 1962*, pp. 380–83.

retreated, with some assistance from Secretary-General U Thant of the United Nations. They did not challenge the blockade. Some Russian ships en route to Cuba voluntarily turned back. Others, ascertained to carry inoffensive cargoes, were allowed to proceed. In a series of exchanges with the President, lasting until Sunday, October 28, Chairman Khrushchev agreed to withdraw the missiles and also some thirty Russian long-range bombing planes that had been detected in Cuba, and to see to the dismantling of the missile sites. In return for these concessions, whose implementation was to be subject to international inspection, Kennedy promised that the United States would not invade Cuba. But since Castro vetoed any international inspection, it could hardly be argued that Kennedy's promise was binding.[16]

The United States government, however, believed it had satisfactory evidence that the missiles and bombers were removed and the sites dismantled according to promise. It disclaimed, on its part, any intention of invading Cuba and took effective steps to discourage hit-and-run raids from American territory by Cuban refugees.

In any event, Russian troops and technicians remained in Cuba after missiles and bombers had been removed. Their number at the end of March 1963 was estimated at from 13,000 to 40,000. By the end of the year some estimates placed the number as low as 5,000 to 8,000. Cuba continued to remain a Communist state under Soviet protection, and a training center and base for Communists operating elsewhere in the

hemisphere. The situation was precisely of the kind that James Monroe had described in 1823 when he wrote that we should consider any attempt of the European powers "to extend their system to any portion of this hemisphere as dangerous to our peace and safety." Though Khrushchev had backed away from the most provocative aspects of his intervention in Cuba, it was hard to deny that he had successfully defied the Monroe Doctrine.

A New Crisis in Panama

President Lyndon B. Johnson, who succeeded the assassinated John Kennedy in November 1963, had been in office only six weeks when he was confronted with a crisis in relations with the Republic of Panama. Panamanians had long resented the presence of Americans in the Canal Zone, with their high rates of pay, their continental standard of living, and the exercise by the United States of the substance of sovereign rights, as a form of "colonialism." Nasser's nationalization of the Suez Canal had undoubtedly suggested a similar possibility here (though the situations were quite different), but the immediate cause of the trouble was a student quarrel over rival flags at a high school just inside the Zone. Presidents Eisenhower and Kennedy had consented to the flying of the flag of Panama beside that of the United States in the Zone as a symbol of the "residual sovereignty" of Panama. A lowering and alleged defilement of the Panama flag by angry American students (January 9, 1964) led to an attempted invasion of the Zone by a Panamanian mob, their repulse by the American troops, and the death of three Americans and an unknown number of Panamanians in the melée.

It was difficult to place the blame for the brawl and the resulting deaths, but President Roberto Chiari of Panama broke off

---

[16]*Documents on American Foreign Relations, 1962,* pp. 390–403. At one stage in the correspondence, Khrushchev proposed that the United States remove its missiles from Turkey in return for the removal of Russian missiles from Cuba, but did not press the point. The United States did, as a matter of fact, later abandon its missile bases in both Turkey and Italy, substituting Polaris submarines in the Mediterranean, but Kennedy had ordered them abandoned before the crisis.

diplomatic relations with Washington, denounced the United States an an aggressor, and appealed for redress to both the U.N. Security Council and the OAS. A committee of the OAS undertook to mediate the dispute. After a period of semantic difficulty—Johnson would agree to *discuss* all matters in controversy but would not promise to *renegotiate* the existing treaty, as Chiari demanded, under pressure—a formula acceptable to both parties was found, and diplomatic relations were restored on April 4, 1964.

In the following December, President Johnson revealed a plan for a new, sea level canal which might be constructed at any one of four sites, two in Panama, one in Nicaragua, and one in Colombia. The United States, said the President, was ready to negotiate a new treaty with Panama, which would (a) recognize the sovereignty of Panama in the Canal Zone, (b) provide for its own termination upon the opening of the new canal, and (c) provide for the effective discharge by the two states of their common responsibilities for hemisphere defense. Pending the conclusion of such a treaty, the existing treaties would continue in effect.

Negotiations with the government of Panama under the new President, Marco A. Robles, proceeded slowly, but in June 1967, it was reported that three new treaties had been concluded. Though the texts were not made public, for fear of repercussions in a highly charged political atmosphere in Panama, it was understood that the treaties, though recognizing Panama's sovereignty in the Zone and giving her a voice in running the canal, would retain essential control for the United States; also that they provided for retention of United States bases in Panama. Since some of these provisions seemed sure to provoke opposition in Panama (and others, in the U.S. Senate), President Robles apparently thought best not to submit them to the Panama National Assembly until after the next election,

scheduled for May 12, 1968. Before that event, Panamanian politics became chaotic. The coalition of parties that had supported Robles broke apart; the National Assembly impeached Robles and declared him removed from office, but Robles held on, backed by the National Guard. Finally, the opposition candidate, Arnulfo Arias, a critic of the treaties, won the election on May 12, 1968. Inaugurated on October 1, he was overthrown by officers of the National Guard after eleven days in office.

Two National Guard officers formed a junta to serve as the government of Panama. One of them, Brigadier General Omar Torrijos, emerged as the "strong man" after an attempt by his aides to overthrow him in December 1969. He announced that he would name a civilian group to take over the presidential functions.

An earlier intimation from the junta that they would welcome a renegotiation of the new canal treaties had been ignored by Washington, and on September 1, 1970, it was reported that the Panamanian government had notified the United States that the draft treaties were not acceptable even as a basis for renewing negotiation. An apparent impasse had been reached. Meanwhile, the treaty of 1903, as modified in 1936, remained in force, objectionable to Panama though it was. Progress in this area would await further events.

Intervention in the Dominican Republic

Johnson's handling of the Panama crisis had been, on the whole, considerate and tactful and had been well received in Latin America. Quite different was the reception of his intervention in the Dominican Republic in the spring of 1965. Here, it seems certain, he overreacted to a danger that was at least partly imaginary. In doing so, he violated the most basic principle of the

Good Neighbor Policy, now solemnly incorporated in the OAS Charter, and although he extracted perfunctory support from a majority of the Latin American governments, his action produced, in the words of the *New York Times* (July 22, 1965) "a division of opinion between the United States and most of Latin America such as has rarely if ever existed in the last thirty years."

The Kennedy administration, it will be recalled, had deplored the overthrow, in September 1963, of Juan Bosch, the democratically elected President of the Dominican Republic, and had withheld recognition from the military-backed junta that replaced him. Kennedy's successor restored relations with the junta, headed by Donald Reid Cabral, and attempted to strengthen it with liberal grants of economic aid. The Reid Cabral government, nevertheless, soon found itself in economic difficulties. Its austerity measures, especially a cutting of military expenses, provoked a revolt, on April 24, 1965, by a group of young officers. They were promptly joined by the leaders of Bosch's Dominican Revolutionary party. Designating themselves "constitutionalists," they organized a provisional government and proclaimed that their object was to restore Bosch to the presidency.

President Reid resigned, but a group of older officers, headed by Brigadier General Elias Wessin y Wessin, a strong anti-Communist, deployed their tanks and planes in opposition to the revolution. They were encouraged to do so, it seems clear, by local U.S. respresentatives—the chargé d'affaires and military attachés—the U.S. Ambassador being temporarily away from his post. The Embassy also had a hand in organizing a three-man military junta, headed by a Colonel Benoit, which undertook to function as a counterrevolutionary government. When the junta, facing probable defeat, requested U.S. intervention, they were told that the United States would intervene only for the purpose

of protecting the lives of American citizens. Thereupon the Benoit junta made a new request, affirming that it was unable to guarantee protection to American citizens, of whom there were a thousand or more in the country, as well as other foreign nationals.[17]

Upon receiving this revised request, now endorsed by Ambassador W. Tapley Bennett, who had returned to Santo Domingo, President Johnson announced April 28 (with lurid details of the dangers threatening foreigners), that he was landing U.S. marines in the Dominican Republic "to give protection to hundreds of Americans . . . and to escort them safely back to this country."

The 556 marines landed at Santo Domingo at the time of this announcement were quickly reinforced by more marines and by airborne troops to a total of 21,000. In explanation of the sending of this large force, the President explained on April 30 that the revolutionary movement, originally democratic in purpose, had fallen under control of Communists, trained in Cuba and elsewhere, and that intervention alone could prevent the Dominican Republic from becoming another Cuba.

But American intervention was in direct violation of the OAS Charter, which declared: "No State or group of States has the right to intervene, directly or indirectly, for any reason whatever, in the internal or external affairs of any other State." It was Johnson's hope from the beginning to persuade the Latin American states, in spite of this plain language, to participate in an operation which they could regard as essential for hemisphere security. The American Foreign Ministers (actually represented by their deputies) met in formal session in

[17]Interestingly, during the 1964 coup d'état of Brazilian President Joao Goulart, the United States had readied a naval task force to support militarily the armed forces' ouster of what was to be that nation's last civilian government. *Washington Post*, December 29, 1976.

Washington on May 1, but only after five days of persuasion by the United States did they provide the necessary two-thirds vote (14 to 5, with Chile, Ecuador, Mexico, Peru, and Uruguay voting no and Venezuela abstaining) to authorize the creation of an Inter-American Peace Force, including the U.S. troops already there, to assist in restoring normal conditions in the Dominican Republic.

Perhaps more disappointing to Johnson than the barely adequate majority for the resolution was the minimal participation of the Latin Americans in the Peace Force. Compared to the 21,000 U.S. troops on station, Honduras sent 250, Nicaragua 180, Costa Rica 20 policemen. None of the large states participated at all, except Brazil (at the time under military rule), which after some delay sent 1,250 soldiers under a high-ranking general, who was thereupon (May 24) made commander of the entire force, with the American commander as his deputy.

The American invading force, in the meantime, while nominally neutral, appears to have consistently favored the junta, thereby, in the opinion of qualified observers, insuring the defeat of the "constitutionalists." Early in May, United States officials took part in creating a new military-civilian junta, replacing that of Colonel Benoit. Headed by General Antonio Imbert Barreras (one of the assassins of Dictator Trujillo), the new group dubbed itself the Government of National Reconstruction. Fighting between the junta and the "constitutionalists," who had named Colonel Francisco Caamaño Deñó Provisional President, continued sporadically in spite of repeated cease-fire agreements negotiated by OAS representatives and others.

Finally a three-man OAS team, with members from Brazil, El Salvador, and the United States, secured acceptance by both factions of Héctor Garcia Godoy, a businessman and former Foreign Minister, as Provisional President. He was sworn in on September 3, 1965. The Peace Force was to remain until its withdrawal was agreed upon by the provisional government and the OAS.

Such are the bare bones of the story of the intervention in the Dominican Republic by the United States, reluctantly assisted by the OAS. Whether it was justified will long remain in dispute. Was there, as the United States officially contended, a real danger that a "constitutionalist" victory and the restoration of Juan Bosch to the presidency would mean a Communist takeover? No one contended that Bosch was a Communist. Though the Kennedy administration had deplored his downfall, he had not been a strong President and had been more lenient with Communists than his critics thought wise. The American ambassador at Santo Domingo and his staff, military and civilian, were apparently convinced that the return of Bosch to the presidency would be a victory for Communism and must be prevented at all hazards. They impressed Washington with their apprehensions, encouraged resistance by the Wessin group, and guided them in their plea for intervention. They, or the C.I.A., compiled a list of over fifty Communists said to be in the "constitutionalist" camp, thus providing President Johnson with his chief justification for the expanded intervention.

Right or wrong, and subsequent investigation has thrown great doubt upon the seriousness of the Communist threat, the Dominican intervention of 1965 had a happier sequel than might have been expected. Tension did not end, but comparative peace returned under Garcia Godoy, backed by the Peace Force, whose numbers were gradually reduced. In the election of June 1, 1966, generally conceded to have been fair, Joaquín Balaguer defeated Juan Bosch as presidential candidate and was inaugurated on July 1. The last of the Peace Force departed in September. Balaguer included Bosch supporters in his cabinet. Restless military men of both factions were assigned to posts abroad. The United States provided substantial amounts of economic aid, and the country was for the most part peaceful, at least to the end of 1970. Balaguer's insistence upon being a candidate for re-election, with support of the military, led Bosch's Dominican Revolutionary party to boycott the election of May 16, 1970. Bosch himself, who had gone into voluntary exile in Spain in 1967, returned in April, declaring that representative democracy could not solve the problems of the Dominican people. What was needed, he said, was "dictatorship with popular support." He approved his party's boycott of the election but opposed violence. With the chief opposition party holding aloof, Balaguer easily won re-election to another four-year term, but Bosch's repudiation of democratic procedures augured ill for a peaceful Dominican future.

What Policy for the Future?

The question of what policy the United States should follow if the situation of 1965 should be repeated, in the Dominican Republic or elsewhere in Latin America, still remained. Some critics of the policy of 1965, like Senator Fulbright, pointed out the contradiction between that policy and the aims of the Alliance for Progress.

> The direction of the Alliance for Progress is toward social revolution in Latin America [said the Senator in a speech of September 15, 1965]; the direction of our Dominican intervention is toward the suppression of revolutionary movements which are supported by Communists or suspected of being supported by Communists. . . .
>
> We simply cannot have it both ways; we must choose between the Alliance for Progress and a foredoomed effort to sustain the status quo in Latin America. . . .

A few days later, however, the House of Representatives adopted, by a vote in the ratio of 6 to 1, a resolution declaring that any one of the American republics might take any steps necessary "to forestall or combat intervention, domination, control, and colonization in whatever form by the subversive forces known as international communism and its agencies in the Western Hemisphere."[18]

The Johnson administration wished assurance that future threats of Communist takeover in the Hemisphere would be dealt with but without the necessity of unilateral action by the United States. At a Special Inter-American Conference at Rio de Janeiro in November 1965, Secretary of State Rusk tried to promote a plan for a permanent inter-American peace force which could deal with future crises on a multilateral basis. He received some encouragement from Brazil and Argentina, but the more democratic states, especially Mexico, Chile, and Uruguay, were so antagonistic to the concept of intervention, unilateral or multilateral, that Rusk's proposal had to be abandoned. Neither this plan nor any alternative had found favor with a majority of the OAS.

The proposal of Rusk and the House resolution quoted, contemplated safeguards against Communist regimes imposed by outside intervention or internal subversion. But suppose the people of a Latin American state should choose a Communist government in a free election? This problem was raised in Chile in the fall of 1970. In an election on September 4, Dr. Salvador Allende Gossens, a Marxist Socialist, the candidate of a coalition which included the Communist party, won a plurality (36.3 percent) of the popular vote against two rivals. If precedent were followed, the Chilean Congress would choose Allende as the candidate with the highest popular vote.

The prospect of a new Communist-backed government in an important American state created a stir in Washing-

[18]*Congressional Record,* 89 Cong., 1 sess., 1965 (September 15, 20, 1965); 3: 23856, 24347.

ton. Though the State Department remained outwardly calm, "a very high official of the White House," in a briefing of September 16, expressed "dismay" at the prospect and fear that Chile's neighbors, Argentina, Peru, and Bolivia, might follow her down the primrose path. At the same time, however, Washington was said to feel that the United States lacked leverage to change the course of events in Chile even if it desired to do so, while the American corporations with the largest investments in Chile were pictured as believing that their wisest course was to avoid antagonizing the new regime and to hope for fair payment if their properties were nationalized.

Dr. Allende made a course of nonintervention easier by agreeing, before his election by Congress (October 24) to support constitutional amendments which, if observed, would safeguard Chile against a totalitarian regime. Although President Nixon omitted the usual courtesy of congratulating President Allende on his election, he made amends by sending the Assistant Secretary of State for Inter-American Affairs to attend the inaugural ceremonies on November 3.

Once in office, President Allende promptly re-established diplomatic relations with Communist Cuba, breaking with United States and OAS policy on that point. On the other hand, he launched his program for nationalizing the billion-dollar American-owned copper mines through the deliberate and strictly legal process of constitutional amendment and with the promise of compensation for the owners.

Fearful of the implications of yet another Communist bridgehead in the Americas, the Nixon administration adopted a three-pronged strategy for dealing with the Allende regime. First, and in order to deny "the Allende government a handy foreign enemy to use as a domestic and international rallying point," President Nixon took a "cool but correct" overt posture toward the new government; second, and over a

period of three years from 1970–1973, he approved a total of more than $7 million in covert support to opposition groups in Chile; and third, he cut off economic aid, denied credits and, generally, made a number of efforts to exacerbate the already strained Chilean economy.[19]

In the face ·of external and internal opposition—the latter stemming from rampant inflation and attempts to revolutionize the landholding system—Dr. Allende succumbed to a military coup d'état on September 11, 1973, during the course of which he was either murdered or felled by his own hand. Allende was then replaced by a right wing military government led by General Augusto Pinochet. Thus began a reign of terror the repercussions of which were still apparent in 1977.[20] All that could be said in favor of the United States' role in the affair was that there was no hard evidence of direct assistance to the coup. Others would argue, however, that the U.S. must accept some of the responsibility in that the Nixon administration "probably gave the impression that it would not look with disfavor on a military coup."[21]

Cuba after the Missile Crisis

After the dramatic events of October and November 1962, Castro's Cuba was destined to grow, or at least to seem, less formidable as an exporter of Communism to the Western Hemisphere. A year after the missile crisis, in fact, there were undercover negotiations between Havana and Washington, looking to a possible renewal of diplomatic and economic relations.

[19]*Covert Action in Chile, 1963–1973,* Staff Report of the Select Committee to Study Governmental Operations with respect to Intelligence Activities, United States Senate, 94th Congress, 1st Session (Washington: Government Printing Office, 1975), pp. 26–28.

[20]*New York Times,* May 3, 1977, p. 16.

[21]*Covert Action in Chile, 1963–1973,* p. 28.

These negotiations were ended by Kennedy's assassination. Castro continued his efforts to subvert other Latin American governments, but without success. His almost frantic attempt to disrupt by terrorism the elections of 1963 in Venezuela failed completely. Four years later his chief lieutenant, "Ché" Guevara, met his death in an utterly futile attempt to carry Communism to the peasants and tin-miners of Bolivia. Although guerrilla activities with at least Communist coloration continued troublesome in Guatemala, Colombia, and Venezuela, it was evident that the Andes were not ready to become the Sierra Maestra of the Revolution.

Meanwhile Castro had exchanged unpleasant words with both his major patrons, Peking and Moscow. Early in 1966 the Cuban dictator accused the Chinese government of "a display of absolute contempt toward our country" in reducing by 115,000 tons the rice that it had allegedly agreed to exchange for Cuban sugar. Peking replied in kind. The loss in Chinese trade increased Cuba's dependence on Russia, yet in the following year (1967) Castro bitterly denounced the Soviet Union for cultivating diplomatic and cultural relations with the "oligarchic" governments of Latin America—a policy of "peaceful coexistence"—and for opposing Castro's policy of subversion and armed guerrilla tactics in that area.

In 1966 and 1967, Cuba played host to two leftist international gatherings. The first, a "tricontinental conference," attended by delegates from 86 nations of Asia, Africa, and Latin America, met in Havana in January 1966. In speeches and resolutions it stressed the "duty" of giving aid to "national liberation movements," with special emphasis on those said to be operating in Latin American countries.

A follow-up of the "tricontinental conference" was the "First Conference of the Organization of Latin American Solidarity" (OLAS), which met in Havana on July 31,

1967, with delegates from 27 countries or territories. Its declared purpose was "to unite, coordinate and step up the struggle against United States imperialism on the part of all the exploited peoples of Latin America." A novel feature was the presence of Black Power leader Stokely Carmichael from the United States and an effort to equate the contemporary urban riots in the United States with guerrilla activities in Guatemala and Colombia and the Viet Cong struggle in Vietnam. As noted by James Reston of the *New York Times,* however, one thing that the Solidarity Conference lacked was solidarity. The Moscow-oriented Communist parties of Argentina, Brazil, and Venezuela did not attend, and delegations from other Communist parties actually represented splinter groups or factions. The trumpet call for stepping up guerrilla wars in Latin America was in direct contradiction to Soviet policy, and, as a matter of fact, the Conference was followed by a decline rather than an increase in guerrilla activity.

The Organization of American States condemned the program of the OLAS Conference, as it had done that of the conference of the preceeding year, and repeated earlier calls for a tightened quarantine of Cuba. By 1967, all members of the OAS except Mexico had severed diplomatic and commercial relations with Cuba. Mexico kept diplomatic channels open as well as air transport. The United States, which originally had exempted food and medicines from its embargo on exports to Cuba, had in 1964, made these subject to license.

An interesting exception to the ban on United States-Cuban communications was the airlift, arranged in 1965, by means of which Cubans (excepting men of military age) were permitted to emigrate to the United States to the number of from 2,000 to 3,000 per month.

Rumors in 1968–1969 of an impending rapprochement between Havana and

Washington were vehemently denied by a spokesmen for Cuba at a U.N. agency meeting in Lima, Peru. Cuba, he insisted, would remain "an ideological base for violent revolution throughout Latin America." During the next several years, and as Cuban-Soviet relations drew closer, the prospect of normalizing relations between the U.S. and Cuba seemed remote.

Then, in the first official direct contact between Havana and Washington since 1961, Secretary of State Kissinger initiated discussions in the United States with representatives of Castro in late 1974. Meeting sporadically in such places as the coffee shops of the National Airport in Washington and the John F. Kennedy Airport in New York, the emissaries held conversations for over a year. Their purpose was, essentially, to catalogue, clarify, and set about to resolve their nations' outstanding differences. Among these were the U.S. trade embargo against Cuba, the question of compensation for expropriated American property, Cuba's frozen assets in America, political prisoners, and the U.S. naval base at Guantanamo. To facilitate the talks, the Ford administration, among other things, eased travel restrictions on Cuban representatives at the U.N.; voted with a majority in the O.A.S. to abolish that group's embargo on political and economic ties with Cuba; and ended U.S. sanctions against trade with Cuba by American-owned subsidaries in third countries. For his part, Castro handed back the hijacker of one American plane and the $2 million ransom from another.[22]

Unfortunately, Castro's decision to dispatch a 12,000 man expeditionary force to support the ultimately victorious Popular Movement for the Liberation of Angola in the Angolan civil war in December 1975 brought the proceedings to a halt. From that point until the election of President Carter a year later, Kissinger made it plain

[22]*New York Times,* March 29, 1977, pp. 1, 8.

that the U.S. would never again tolerate a Soviet-armed Cuban military adventure anywhere.[23]

Storm over the Panama Canal

The most notable achievement of the Nixon-Ford administrations in Latin American affairs—an area generally overlooked by the preoccupation with the Soviet Union and détente—was the progress made in the renegotiation of an entirely new treaty respecting the Canal Zone. In February 1974, Secretary of State Kissinger and Panamanian Foreign Minister, Juan Antonio Tack, initialed an agreement on the principles of a new treaty. These called for the abrogation of the treaty of 1903 and its amendment; elimination of the concept of perpetuity; and the termination of United States jurisdiction over Panamanian territory to take place promptly in accordance with the terms specified in the treaty.[24]

For the next two years negotiations were under way to implement the principles into a new treaty, which by any reading was designed to yield U.S. sovereignty over the waterway to Panama. Then the storm broke. For the treaty became an important if emotional issue in the hotly-contested Republican Presidential primary race in 1976 between Ronald Reagan and Gerald Ford. Though the canal had lost much of its military and commercial importance, it had come to mean many things to many Americans. As a result negotiations began to drag, and Panamanian strong man General Torrijos grew restless.[25]

Primary considerations such as the duration of the new treaty, which Panama wanted to see end before the year 2000, and defense, which the U.S. wished to retain for

[23]*U.S. News & World Report,* March 15, 1976, p. 26.
[24]*New York Times,* February 8, 1974.
[25]*Chicago Tribune,* December 25, 1976.

twenty years after the treaty lapsed, were still to be worked out.

The Canadian Partner

More intimate than its relationship with its sister republics to the south was the association of the United States with its northern neighbor, Canada. Canada had not been a party to the inter-American conferences, organizations, or treaties. Though a "twenty-second chair" had been reserved for her at the Pan-American Union, it had never been filled, presumably because Canada was not a republic but a constitutional monarchy and a member of the British Commonwealth of Nations. The Mexico City Conference of 1945 expressed a hope for closer collaboration with Canada, and the Bogotá Charter of 1948 set up an Organization of American *States,* rather than *republics,* in order to include Canada if she so desired.

Many Canadians, after World War II, urged that Canada accept the invitation, but the opposition arguments prevailed. Prominent among these was the realization that, as a member of the OAS, Canada would often have to take sides in controversies between the United States and Latin America, perhaps incurring the ill will of one or both. This argument gained force with growing Canadian disapproval of United States policy in Cuba and the Dominican Republic. American foreign policy, Canadians felt, tended to use the OAS when it could and to ignore it when it could not. Membership in such an organization would at times be frustrating. Canadian divergence from United States policy elsewhere, notably in China and Vietnam, lessened still further the attractions of OAS membership.[26]

[26]Gerald M. Craig, *The United States and Canada* (Cambridge: Harvard University Press, 1968), pp. 326–32.

But though Canada held aloof from the OAS and was unsympathetic to certain features of American foreign policy, similarity in race, language, culture, economic and political principles, and the need for a common defense system bound the two nations in a close, if not always comfortable, partnership. Before World War II, President Roosevelt and Prime Minister King had exchanged pledges of cooperation for mutual defense against the Axis powers. In 1940, the two nations had established a Joint Board on Defense and meshed together their production and defense mechanisms in the war that followed. The cold war found them again facing a common enemy. The prospect that hostilities might see long-range bombers, armed with nuclear weapons, striking across the north polar regions, heightened the military dependence of Canada and the United States on one another.

It was in the interest of both nations, therefore, to maintain the Joint Board on Defense as a permanent body, and this was supplemented in 1958 by the establishment at cabinet level of a Canada-United States Committee on Joint Defense.

Another important step had been taken in the preceding year (1957) with the creation of the North American Air Defense Command (NORAD), combining elements of both Air Forces. NORAD headquarters were established at Colorado Springs with an American commander in chief and a Canadian deputy commander. The purpose was the integrated use of the facilities of the two nations for the defense of the United States, including Alaska and Canada, against possible air attack from the Soviet Union. Another measure for the same purpose, the construction of a triple screen of radar warning stations drawn across Canada from ocean to ocean, was also complete and in operation by 1957.

It was ironic that the year of the completion of this screen and the creation of NORAD, both designed to safeguard the continent against attack by long-range bombing planes, was also the year of Sputnik; for Sputnik introduced the missile age, which would soon make bombers and defenses against them obsolete.

The transition from the bomber to the ICBM, had, in fact, signalled a decline in U.S.-Canadian cooperation for defense. Canadian disapproval of the use of nuclear weapons asserted itself. Though the two governments had reached a tentative agreement for the arming of Canadian interceptor planes and short-range missiles with nuclear warheads, Conservative Prime Minister John Diefenbaker (1957–1963) refused to permit the stockpiling of the warheads in Canada, on the ground that they would be useless against ICBMs and would only expose Canada to nuclear attack. He also, during the Cuban missile crisis in 1962, refused to authorize what the United States command considered an adequate number of precautionary flights over Canada by nuclear-armed American planes.

Diefenbaker's uncooperative defense policy met criticism in both the United States and Canada and contributed to the fall of his government in February 1963 and the return to power of the Liberals. Lester Pearson, the Liberal Prime Minister, was less critical of the United States than was Diefenbaker but, like Diefenbaker, was unhappy over the agreement which committed Canada to arming with nuclear weapons.

After 1963, the two nations diverged somewhat in their defense policies, though the official structure of alliance remained. "Canadians," wrote Gerald Craig, "are increasingly doubtful that their country plays, or can play, any real role in making the decisions at NORAD headquarters," and many feel that Canada's limited military resources should be used for other purposes than continental (or NATO) defense; such, for example, as the U.N. peacekeeping activities in which Canada

has played an active role. The United States, on its part, thought it unnecessary to consult Canada in advance about installation of the now dismantled Safeguard ABM stations in North Dakota and Montana, though the interception missiles fired from those stations would presumably explode in Canadian airspace.[27]

Canada's sense of inequality with its giant neighbor in matters of defense was symptomatic of Canadian—U.S. relations in general. Canada, with its 21,000,000 inhabitants, vast territory, and rich resources, was an important "middle power," jealous of its independence and proud of its distinctive character and traditions. It was sensitive to what at times seemed a patronizing attitude on the part of the United States and resentful at having its goodwill and cooperation taken for granted, as they sometimes were. Economically, Canadians were unhappy at the steadily unfavorable balance—around $1 billion annually—in their trade with the United States and at the imposition of quotas or other restrictions upon imports to the United States of Canadian lead, zinc, and petroleum. They regarded as unfair the disposal abroad of American surplus wheat at less than world prices, undercutting the market for Canadian wheat. They were disturbed by the growing extent to which their industry and business were owned and controlled in the United States. Sixty percent of Canada's principal manufacturing industries, complained the Canadian Prime Minister in 1957, and a larger proportion of its mine and oil production, were owned and controlled by United States corporations or their Canadian subsidiaries, and few of these offered their stock to Canadian investors. Policies of the Canadian subsidiaries were apt to be determined on the basis of United States, rather than Canadian, interests and national policies. Canadians

[27]Craig, *The U.S. and Canada,* p. 316; *New York Times,* March 20, 1969, p. 11.

feared an impairment of their independence, both economic and political. They were further disturbed by the dominant position in the Canadian market of books, magazines, radio and television programs from south of the border. They did not admire all manifestations of the "American way of life" nor wish to make it theirs.[28]

The United States, with a population almost ten times that of Canada and with a growing drain upon its natural resources, was coming, in the late 1960's, to the view that Canada's minerals, petroleum, natural gas, and abundant fresh water should be treated as "continental resources," to be disposed of, in other words, by joint agreement between the two governments. Not surprisingly, this view was not welcomed in Canada. As applied particularly to fuels, it brought from J. J. Greene, Canadian Minister of Energy, Mines, and Resources, in May 1970, the declaration that any bargaining with the United States on the subject of continental resources "must lead to Canadian solutions in a Canadian interest."[29]

Another Canadian worry arose from the discovery of oil on the Arctic slope of Alaska and the voyage, in the summer of 1969, of the giant icebreaking tanker *Manhattan* through the legendary Northwest Passage, in the effort to demonstrate that the oil could be transported by sea to East Coast ports. A natural fear of pollution from such traffic led Canadian Prime Minister Pierre Elliott Trudeau (1968–   ) to introduce in Parliament legislation to extend Canadian control of shipping over an area up to 100 nautical miles from Canada's shore line. Thus the Canadian government would be able to regulate oil transport and oil drilling in the waters of the Northwest Passage and to preserve what the Prime Minister called "the

world's last big natural reserve." The United States took prompt exception to Canada's unilateral action and called for international talks to pass upon the Canadian claim to jurisdiction over what had hitherto been considered international waters.[30]

Such complaints as the United States had against Canada were chiefly, like this one, in the field of foreign policy. Canada's anti-Communist position was in general less rigid than that of the United States. Canada refused to accept Washington's view of Castro's Cuba. Canada maintained normal diplomatic and commercial relations with Cuba after the United States had broken them off, and, as said before, gave the United States less than complete cooperation in the Cuban missile crisis of 1962. Like the United States but unlike Great Britain, Canada until 1970 withheld recognition from Communist China. Canada refused, however, over a twenty-year period, to join the United States in a complete embargo on trade with China. In 1961, indeed, it granted a credit of $300 million to that famine-stricken country for the purchase of Canadian wheat, other grains, and flour. At last, Pierre Trudeau, the "swinging" young Liberal who became Prime Minister upon Pearson's retirement in 1968, announced that he would seek to establish normal relations with Peking as a step toward ending China's isolation from the non-Communist world. The establishment of diplomatic relations was announced in Ottawa and Peking on October 13, 1970, and at the same time Canada severed relations with the Chinese Nationalist government at Taipei. Canada made it plain, however, that she was not taking sides in Communist China's claim to sovereignty over Taiwan. In Washington the State Department took no issue with the Canadian decision, merely expressing con-

[28]Joseph Barber, *Good Fences Make Good Neighbors: Why the U.S. Provokes Canadians* (Indianapolis: The Bobbs-Merrill Company, Inc., 1958), is a comprehensive treatment.

[29]*New York Times,* May 31, 1970, p. 2.

[30]*New York Times,* April 10, 1970, p. 13. *Ibid.,* April 16, 1970, p. 6. *Ibid.,* April 20, 1978 (editorial), p. 38.

cern for the adverse effect it might have on the international position of Nationalist China. The action would not, it was said, affect United States opposition to Red China's admission to the United Nations.

Whatever the bickerings between the two neighbors, each was vitally essential to the other in economics and defense. They shared, moreover, the same world view. Both were democratic and freedom-loving; both had stable governments that derived along different channels from British origins; both, as allies in NATO and the U.N., were dedicated to the preservation of order and peace in the world and against the spread of Communism. Responsible statesmen on both sides knew that cooperation was imperative.

These facts were recognized in a White Paper on foreign policy issued by the Trudeau government in June 1970. "The United States," declared this important document, "is Canada's closest friend and ally and will remain so." Recognizing at the same time the "constant danger that sovereignty, independence and cultural identity may be impaired" by this close relationship, the White Paper observed that "active pursuit of trade diversification and technological cooperation with European and other developed countries will be needed to provide countervailing factors." This broadening of Canada's external relations should be extended to Latin America, without, for the present, its becoming a member of the OAS—though this was suggested for some future time—and to the Far East, where Canada might assist in "bringing Communist China into a more constructive relationship with the world community." Canada would continue an active member of the United Nations and of NATO, though with reservations as to the extent of its military contribution to the latter. In contrast to the contemporary

trend in the United States, Canada should "steadily increase its foreign aid contributions." In all this program, as the *New York Times* remarked editorially, there was "nothing to which Americans can legitimately object."[31]

More than a year later, in December 1971, after a visit with President Nixon in Washington, Trudeau received American assurance that a more independent Canada was in the interest of all concerned. Or, as the Prime Minister observed on the floor of the Canadian Parliament: "He [the President] assured me that it was in the clear interests of the United States to have a Canadian neighbor, not only independent both politically and economically but also one which was confident that the decisions and policies in each of these sectors would be taken by Canadians in their own interests, in defense of their own values, and in pursuit of their own goals."[32]

To be sure, not all of Trudeau's foreign policy actions were to Washington's liking nor perhaps even to the majority of Canadians themselves.[33] What was significant was that he managed to restrain the latest surge of Canadian nationalism from becoming an issue of great contention, especially as it affected the public media in Canada with its high American content. Whether or not Trudeau's ability to manage the seemingly unmanageable could be applied to the civil strife threatening the separatist-minded Quebec Province was a question that could only be answered with time. If he could not, it would then undoubtedly draw America directly into the internal affairs of Canada.[34]

[31]*New York Times,* June 26, pp. 6–7; July 4, 1970 (editorial), p. 20.

[32]Quoted in Abraham Rotstein, "Canada: The New Nationalism," *Foreign Affairs,* 55 (1976), p. 110.

[33]*New York Times,* September 5, 1976, p. 18.

[34]*New York Times,* December 27, 1976, pp. 1, 9.

ADDITIONAL READINGS

DOMINGUEZ, J. I., "Taming the Cuban Shrew," *Foreign Policy,* 10 (Spring, 1973), pp. 94–116.

DRAPER, THEODORE, *The Dominican Revolt: A Case Study in American Policy.* New York: Commentary, 1968.

HILSMAN, ROGER, *To Move a Nation: The Politics of Foreign Policy in the Administration of John F. Kennedy.* Garden City, N.Y.: Doubleday & Company, In., 1967.

KENNEDY, R. F., *Thirteen Days: A Memoir of the Cuban Missile Crisis.* New York: W. W. Norton and Company, Inc. 1969.

MARTIN, JOHN B., *Overtaken by Events: The Dominican Crisis from the Fall of Trujillo to the Civil War* Garden City, N.Y.: Doubleday & Company, Inc. 1966.

ROGERS, WILLIAM D., *The Twilight Struggle: The Alliance for Progress and the Politics of Development in Latin America.* New York: Random House, Inc., 1967.

SCHLESINGER, A.M., JR., *A Thousand Days: John F. Kennedy in the White House.* Boston: Houghton Mifflin Co., 1965.

TAMBS, LEWIS A., ed., *United States Policy toward Latin America: Antecedents and Alternatives.* Tempe, Arizona: Arizona State University, 1976.

TAYLOR, PHILIP B., JR., "The Guatemalan Affair: A Critique of United States Foreign Policy," *American Political Science Review,* 50 (1956), 787–806.

WHITAKER, ARTHUR, P., *The United States and the Southern Cone: Argentina, Uruguay, and Chile.* Cambridge: Harvard University Press, 1977.

27. New Directions: The Foreign Policy of Jimmy Carter

President Jimmy Carter's administration, despite the great expectations accompanying change in the White House and the flurry of diplomatic activity marking most of 1977, produced little of substance in the field of foreign policy. To be sure, the personnel, style, and emphasis of President Carter differed from those of his predecessor. The so-called "Lone Ranger" concept of American foreign policy, as supposedly practiced by Henry Kissinger, was replaced by a more open team-player concept led by Secretary of State Cyrus R. Vance. Other "new faces" included national security adviser Zbigniew Brzezinski, a Polish-born Columbia University professor specializing in Russian and Soviet history, and U.S. Ambassador to the U.N. Andrew Young, former Georgia Congressman and civil-rights activist.[1] More significantly, the President's commitment to the issue of human rights in nations ruled by authoritarian governments, both left and right, together with his apparent determination to press them at the expense of détente with the Soviet Union and bilateral military relations with a number of Latin American nations, set him apart from the "power politics" emphasis of the preceding Nixon and Ford administrations. For example, Carter's communicating with the well-known

Soviet dissident Andrei D. Sakharov against the wishes of the Kremlin was an act that would have been unthinkable for President Nixon. The new administration's reasoning that such defense of basic human rights[2]—life, liberty, and pursuit of happiness—did not constitute interference in the internal affairs of other nations was perhaps too subtle for the Soviets.[3]

The Soviet Union and the Arms Race

Despite campaign criticism of Secretary Kissinger's preoccupation with the Soviet Union in general and arms controls in particular, the Carter administration devoted considerable time and energy to these same matters in 1977. Shortly after the Senate confirmation of the controversial Paul C. Warnke as the nation's chief arms negotiator, Secretary of State Vance headed a delegation to Moscow in late March to work out the second phase of the Strategic Arms Limitation Talks (SALT II), presumably along guidelines laid out by former President Ford and General Secretary Leonid I. Brezhnev at Vladivostock in

---

[1]*U.S. News and World Report,* February 21, 1977, pp. 27–31.

[2]For the President's own definition of human rights, see Jimmy Carter, Letter to Op-Ed Page, *Baltimore Sun,* September 19, 1977.

[3]Interestingly, Carter failed to respond to a second letter from Sakharov several months later, *New York Times,* May 11, 1977, pp. 1, 15.

November 1974. At that time, it will be recalled, the two leaders had tentatively agreed to limit each side to 2,400 strategic missiles or bombers, with no more than 1,320 of the missiles armed with multiple warheads. The Secretary of State approached the Soviets with two proposals. One was simply to ratify the Vladivostok guidelines, postponing discussion of the American cruise missile—a winged low-flying missile—and the U.S.S.R.'s recently developed supersonic bomber, code-named Backfire by NATO.[4]

Another, called by one influential commentator the most revolutionary arms proposal since the beginning of the Cold War,[5] was an offer to effect joint and substantial reductions in the level of deployment of missile launchers and multiple warheads missiles well below the 2,400 and 1,320 levels established at Vladivostok; to stop the development and deployment of new weapons systems; and to freeze at the present level about 550 intercontinental ballistic missiles, specifically the American Minuteman and Soviet missiles known as SS-17, –18, and –19. Other important aspects of what came to be called the "comprehensive" proposal included a ban on the deployment of all mobile missiles; a strict limit on the deployment of the Backfire bomber, as well as on the range of cruise missiles; and a limit on the number of test firings of missiles to six firings per year on the intercontinental range and six on the medium range missiles.[6]

The Soviet Union summarily rejected both proposals and offered none in their place, asserting that the Vladivostok accords constituted the only acceptable basis for a strategic arms agreement. In a rare televised news conference following the talks, Soviet Foreign Minister Andrei A. Gromyko charged that the Americans'

"comprehensive plan," calling, as he held, for eliminating half of the Soviets' "heavy" missiles, was grossly unfair to the Soviet Union. Furthermore, he complained, the Carter administration, had misrepresented the Soviet position to the American people.[7] That the harsh Soviet response might have been induced in part by the President's stand on human rights was possible, but, as some American commentators pointed out, neither the substance of the American proposal nor the manner in which it was made could have been expected to win ready Soviet approval.

The Vance mission was not a total loss, however, as both sides agreed to set up working groups to deal with such issues as a ban on underground nuclear tests; a ban on chemical weapons; prior notification of missile tests; anti-satellite weapons; civil defense; military installations in the Indian Ocean; radiological weapons; conventional weapons; and nuclear proliferation.

During the remainder of 1977, both sides continued to search for a common ground. By October, the outlines of the proposed SALT II were known, although the actual conclusion of a new treaty still appeared in the distance.[8] According to the best estimates, the U.S. and the U.S.S.R. had each agreed to restrictions of about 2,200 long-range missiles and bombers; and of these, it was further agreed, no more than 1,320 could carry multiple warheads or cruise missiles. A further breakdown of the 1,320 multiple weapons specified that no more than 1,200 could be ballistic missiles, of which only 800 could be land-based. These limitations would be effective until 1985.[9] A separate protocol, envisaged

[4]*New York Times,* April 24, 1977, p. 13.

[5]James Reston, "Why Moscow Failed," *New York Times,* April 1, 1977, p. 29.

[6]*New York Times,* March 31, 1977, pp. 1, 12.

[7]*New York Times,* April 1, 1977, pp. 1, 8; April 2, 1977, pp. 1, 2; May 11, 1977, p. 23.

[8]Although SALT I expired in October 1977, both sides voluntarily agreed to keep it in force pending SALT II which was expected to come into force in early 1979.

[9]See *New York Times,* October 16, 1977 (sec. 4), p. 14; October 23, 1977, pp. 1, 13.

for a period of three years, would deal with, among other things, limits on the range of permissible cruise missiles and the number of "heavy" missiles.[10]

Western Europe and Japan-Trilateralism

True to his campaign promises, and despite disagreements with France and West Germany over their proposed sales of nuclear technology to third world countries, President Carter took pains to reassure America's traditional allies of the steadfastness of American support. Even before his nomination for the presidency, Mr. Carter had been a member of the Trilateral Commission, an international group of political, business, and academic leaders who advocated an alignment of the industrialized democracies—primarily Western Europe, North America, and Japan—to promote by joint action their own economic and social well-being and eventually that of developing countries of the third world. It was in keeping with this point of view that Carter named Professor Brzezinski as his national security adviser and other Trilateralists to influential posts in the State, Treasury, and Defense Departments.[11] Consistent also with this philosophy was his dispatching of Vice President Mondale, three days after his inauguration, on a goodwill tour of the principal capitals of Western Europe and also Tokyo.

In May Carter himself attended the London economic summit parley of seven industrialized nations (including Japan and Canada) and the following NATO meeting.

In both instances the President assured America's alliance partners of the nation's resolve to contribute to the solution of the free world's economic and defense problems.

At the economic summit, the leaders of the U.S., the United Kingdom, France, Italy, West Germany, Canada and Japan agreed to address themselves to the urgent task of creating more jobs while continuing to combat inflation. Significantly, the seven countries committed their governments, in the words of the communiqué, "to state economic growth targets or to stabilization prices which, taken as a whole, should provide a basis for sustained noninflationary growth in our own countries and worldwide and for the reduction of imbalances in international payments." They also agreed to seek means of stabilizing the prices of raw materials supplied by the poorer countries and better methods of financing the development needs of those countries.[12]

At the NATO proceedings, President Carter asserted that the U.S. would continue to make the alliance the heart of the nation's foreign policy. He also stated that the U.S., while supporting the existing strategy of flexible response and forward defense, would continue to provide its share of the forces necessary to carry through such a strategy, maintaining both an effective strategic and conventional deterrent.[13]

In much of what he said the President confirmed recent analyses of the offensive character of the Soviet military build-up in Eastern Europe.[14] This together with the recognition that, according to the President, the Soviet Union had achieved essential nuclear equivalence, made the lesson clear to the West. Failing early agreement with the Warsaw Pact nations on mutual

---

[10]Also see G. B. Kistiakowsky, "The Arms Race: Is Paranoia Necessary for Security?" *New York Times Magazine,* November 27, 1977, pp. 52 ff.

[11]Richard H. Ullman, "Trilateralism: Partnership for What?" *Foreign Affairs,* 56 (1976), pp. 1–19; and Jeremiah Novak, "The Trilateral Connection," *Atlantic Monthly,* July 1977, pp. 57–59.

[12]*New York Times,* May 9, 1977, p. 12.

[13]*New York Times,* May 11, 1977, pp. 1, 14.

[14]For example, see *Des Moines Register,* January 3, 1977; and *Wall Street Journal,* January 25, 1977, p. 3.

and balanced force reductions in Europe, negotiations stalled since April, NATO military strength must continue to be maintained. In practical terms, and to increase the combat readiness of NATO forces, there was general agreement on two major military efforts: U.S., Dutch, and Belgium troops would have to be moved closer to the frontier between West and East Germany, the potential battlefield; and there would have to be additional expenditures for such items as barracks, communications, and highways,[15] The predictable Soviet response accused the West of aggressive behavior.

Again, in Brussels, in January 1978, toward the end of his first extended trip abroad, taking him to six countries in nine days,[16] President Carter reaffirmed his intention to make NATO the centerpiece of his administration's foreign policy. "We will work with you," he added, "to maintain deterrents across the entire spectrum of strategic, nuclear and conventional forces so that the Warsaw Pact forces will know that all of us are united in commitment to defense of all territories of NATO members." Carter also reminded his allies that the presence of American troops in Western Europe was scheduled to be increased by more than 8,000 over the next year and a half, and that in Carter's words, "We will substantially improve our reinforcement capability."[17] The President's proposed record defense budget of $126 billion for 1979 gave his pledge to NATO special meaning.

[15]*New York Times*, April 16, p. 3; May 12, 1977, p. 16.

[16]Beginning in late December 1977, over a period of six days, President Carter travelled to Poland, Iran, India, Saudi Arabia, France, and Belgium. He also met with President Sadat of Egypt at Aswan airport en route to Paris. The second part of this trip was completed in March and April 1978 and included Venezuela, Brazil, Nigeria (the first state visit of a President to Africa south of the Sahara), and Liberia.

[17]*Times* (London), January 7, 1978, pp. 1, 4.

Latin America

In his first major statement on Latin America, an address before the Permanent Council of the Organization of American States in April 1977, President Carter observed that it was no longer in the interest of the U.S. to pursue a single policy toward Latin America and the Caribbean. What was needed was a wider and more flexible approach, and one that could be worked out in consultation with the respective states involved. The new American approach, according to this view, would be based on three elements: "a high regard for the individuality and sovereignty of each Latin American and Caribbean nation"; "respect for human rights"; and "our desire to press forward on the great issues which affect the relations between the developed and developing nations." With respect to the latter, Carter promised to take a more positive attitude toward the negotiation of agreements to stabilize commodity prices, liberalize trade and economic assistance, and to meet in full, U.S. pledges to the American Development Bank and other multilateral lending institutions, though the administration's proposal a month later for a 25 per cent cut in the $40 million annual U.S. contribution to the O.A.S. doubtless gave pause to these same delegates.[18]

The two most controversial problems the new administration had to face, the Panama Canal treaty negotiations and the normalization of relations with Castro's Cuba, were met head on.

With respect to the Panama Canal impasse, President Carter not only directed what he regarded as a new approach to the problem but also underscored his commitment, in his words, "to negotiating in as timely a fashion as possible a new treaty which will take into account Panama's legitimate needs as a sovereign nation and

[18]*New York Times*, April 15, p. 10; May 15, 1977, p. 8.

our interests in the efficient operations of a neutral canal, open on a nondiscriminatory basis to all users."[19] After prolonged and intense debate throughout much of 1977, two new treaties ultimately emerged from the negotiations. The first of these, the Panama Canal Treaty, gave to the U.S. the continued primary responsibility for the operation and defense of the canal until the year 2000 and the right to use all land and water areas necessary for this purpose; at the expiration of the treaty, Panama was to assume these responsibilities, as well as full territorial and criminal jurisdiction over the Canal Zone. The second treaty, the Treaty Concerning the Permanent Neutrality and Operation of the Panama Canal, pledged Panama to maintain the permanent neutrality of the canal "in order that both in time of peace and time of war it shall remain secure and open to peaceful transit by the vessels of all nations on terms of entire equality, so that there will be no discrimination against any nation, or its citizens or subjects, concerning the conditions or charges of transit, or for any other reason." Added for clarification was a statement of understanding following a meeting of President Carter and Panamanian dictator General Torrijos on October 14, 1977, in which the U.S. underscored its right after the year 2000 to "defend the canal against any threat to the regime of neutrality," as well as the right of its vessels of war to transit the canal expeditiously.[20] The Senate on March 16, 1978 approved the neutrality treaty with an amendment giving the United States the independent right to use military force to reopen the Canal at the end of the century. On April 18, 1978 the Senate approved the first trea-

ty agreeing to turn over the Panama Canal on December 31, 1999.[21] Thus, the President had scored his first major foreign policy success.[22]

Despite the Carter administration's warnings to Fidel Castro that the normalization of relations between Cuba and the U.S. would depend, in the first instance, on the Cuban leader's willingness to restore basic human rights in his own land and his attitude toward overseas adventures such as the dispatching of Cuban troops to Angola and, subsequently, to Ethiopia, some progress was made in this area. To begin with, a high ranking American delegation met with government representatives in Havana in April, 1977. Meeting ostensibly to regulate fishing rights in the waters between their countries—both countries promulgated 200-mile fishing zones off their coasts—the two sides set the stage for the establishment of "diplomatic interest sections" in Washington and Havana with a view to resolving outstanding issues.[23] This was accomplished in June. Preceding the April meeting, President Carter removed all restrictions on Americans who wished to travel to Cuba; and the Department of the Treasury ended the ban on the spending of United States dollars by American tourists in Cuba. Later, in an effort to ease the trade embargo against Cuba, the Senate Foreign Relations Committee voted to allow Cuba to purchase medicine, medical supplies, and a limited number of agricultural products, a proposal later rejected by the Senate as a whole. For his part, Castro assured the U.S. that Cuba still intended to observe its bilateral anti-hijacking agreement even though it had lapsed in 1976. Nonetheless, the trade embargo together with the introduc-

[19]*New York Times,* April 15, 1977, p. 10.

[20]Transcript of testimony of Secretary of State Cyrus R. Vance before the House Committee on International Relations, October 20, 1977, and text of statement of understanding issued by the White House, October 14, 1977. Courtesy of the United States Information Service.

[21]*New York Times,* March 17, 1978, pp. 1, 17; April 19, 1978, p. 1.

[22]For a vigorous critique of the American position, see Charles Maechling, Jr., "The Panama Canal: A Fresh Start," *Orbis,* 20 (Winter, 1977), pp. 1007–1023.

[23]*Washington Post,* April 26, 1977.

tion of Cuban soldiers in the sensitive African war theater continued to remain the major obstacles in further steps towards normalization of relations at the beginning of 1978.

The Middle East

The initial thrust of the Carter administration's Middle East policy, beginning with Secretary of State Vance's mission to the area in February 1977, was, in the President's words, "to mount a major effort in our Government in 1977 to bring the parties to Geneva." None could doubt Vance's conclusion at the time that the road ahead would be hard.

At a news conference in March, and in what amounted to the first publicized American concept of a comprehensive settlement of the Middle East problem since the Arab-Israeli War of 1973, the President noted three basic elements to any solution of the Middle East question: an ultimate commitment to complete peace in the region, border determinations, and a resolution of the Palestinian issue. Carter argued that the Arab nations and Israel would have to agree on permanent and recognized borders. Furthermore, he suggested, defense lines might not have to conform in the near future to those borders, a prospect meaning the possible extension of Israeli defense capabilities beyond the permanent and recognized borders. Within this framework there would only be "minor adjustment" of the pre-1967 borders. Finally, there remained the Palestinian question. Much to the dismay of the newly-elected Israeli government (the right-wing Likud party, headed by Menahem Begin, May, 1977), President Carter, throughout his first year in office, stressed the necessity of resolving the Palestinian problem, and of finding a homeland for the Palestinians. His endorsement of a "homeland" for the

Palestinians, a point not mentioned in the relevant U.N. Security Council Resolutions, was particularly alarming to the Israelis. Vice President Walter Mondale emphasized the President's concern in a major address delivered in June when he noted "that in the context of a peace settlement we believe the Palestinians should be given a chance to shed their status as homeless refugees and to partake fully of the benefits of peace in the Middle East including the possibility of some arrangement for a Palestinian homeland or entity—preferably in association with Jordan."[24] In October, in a joint Soviet-American statement on the Middle East aimed at assisting the resumption of the Geneva Conference by the end of the year, the two superpowers concurred that a peace settlement should include "insuring the legitimate rights of the Palestinian people."[25] Nonetheless, despite the many visits of Arabs and Israelis alike to Washington and the Secretary of State's reciprocal visits to the region, little was accomplished until the spectacular diplomatic initiative undertaken by President Anwar el-Sadat of Egypt.

On November 19, President Sadat stepped aground at Jerusalem's Ben-Gurion International airport, becoming the first Arab leader to touch Israeli soil since Israel's founding in 1948.[26] At the expense of Arab solidarity,[27] Sadat went before the Israeli Parliament with his own peace proposals and exchanged vows with Prime Minister Begin to seek peace in the Middle East. Though no startling new offers emerged, the Egyptian President succeeded in capturing the world's imagination. One month later Begin reciprocated

[24]*New York Times*, June 18, 1977, p. 5. There were approximately 2.2 million Palestinians scattered abroad with an estimated 1.5 million under Israel control. *New York Times*, September 25, 1977 (sec. 4), p. 2.

[25]*New York Times*, October 2, 1977, p. 16.

[26]*New York Times*, November 20, 1977, p. 1.

[27]For example, see Syrian President Hafez Assad's comments in *Newsweek*, January 16, 1978, pp. 41–47.

with a similar unprecedented visit to Is-malia, Egypt, and put forth his own peace proposals. In reply to Egyptian demands for a total and unqualified withdrawal from Arab territories occupied during the 1967 Middle East War and the creation of a Palestinian state carved out of the West Bank of the Jordan River and the Gaza Strip, Begin offered the demilitarization of most of Sinai, gradual withdrawal of occupied territory, and limited self-rule for Palestinian Arabs in what he regarded as Judea and Samaria (biblical references to the West Bank) and the Gaza Strip.[28] By the end of January 1978, in the face of stalled peace talks in Cairo[29] and Jerusalem, Egypt and Israel were deadlocked over an agreement of principles that would govern the still-hoped for Geneva Conference, the favored course of the Soviet Union and most of the Arab world, especially, Syria and the Palestinian Liberation Organization.

In an equally dramatic development, President Carter met with President Sadat and Prime Minister Begin at Camp David, from September 5 to September 17, in order to compose their differences. The outcome resulted in two major agreements: A Framework for Peace in the Middle East and A Framework for the Conclusion of a Peace Treaty between Egypt and Israel. At the time, it was hoped that the final peace treaty would be signed within three months, that is, by December 17, 1978.[30] By early 1979, the treaty had yet to be signed, owing principally to the Egyptian leader's demand for a timetable linking the treaty itself with graduated steps toward Palestinian autonomy in the West Bank of the

Jordan River and the Gaza Strip.[31] It has been suggested that the President may once again have to intervene in pushing Cairo and Jerusalem down the road to peace.

Asia and Africa

Asia, apart from Japan, received relatively low priority on the Carter White House agenda, but Africa attained unprecedented prominence. With regard to the People's Republic of China, the United States began unpublicized negotiations in the spring of 1977 to settle outstanding financial claims, a move preparatory to the resumption of normal trade relations. An April visit of a Congressional delegation, accompanied by the President's son, underscored the administration's desire for increased trade and political exchanges. In late August, Secretary of State Vance travelled to Peking for several days to meet with the Chinese leadership. These talks were described by Vance as "very useful," despite the lack of progress on the question of normalization of relations between the two countries. The problem of how to effect the resumption of diplomatic relations with Peking without unduly undermining the Taiwan regime, was resolved on the evening of December 15, 1978, when the President announced on national television, that the United States and the People's Republic of China, had agreed to recognize each other and establish diplomatic relations as of January 1, 1979. In return for placing relations with Peking on an official footing, Washington agreed to break diplomatic relations with Taiwan, withdraw its remaining troops (700) and abrogate its 1954 defense treaty with Taipei.[32] The implications of such a

---

[28]*Sydney Morning Herald,* December 26, 30, 1977, p. 5.

[29]On November 26, 1977, President Sadat invited all parties involved in the Middle East—including the U.S. and the Soviet Union—to Cairo for a pre-Geneva meeting aimed at establishing a conference agenda. Only Israel and the U.S. agreed to send representatives. *New York Times,* November 27, 1977, p. 1.

[30]Texts of all the agreements are found in *The Camp David Summit, September 1978,* Department of State Publication 8954.

[31]Also see, *New York Times,* December 10, 1978, p. 3.

[32]*New York Times,* December 18, 1978, p. 1. President Nixon had apparently intended to establish complete diplomatic ties with Peking in his second term. *New York Times,* April 11, 1977, pp. 1, 5.

move, which did not secure a pledge from the PRC not to use force in the ultimate reabsorption of Taiwan into China, were bound to be felt for a long time.[33]

On the Korean front, the President promptly undertook to make good his campaign pledge in regard to the gradual withdrawal of American ground troops from South Korea. Carter asserted that the withdrawal, to be carried out in close cooperation and consultation with both Seoul and Tokyo, would take place over a four– or five–year period.[34] In May, the President dispatched General George S. Brown, Chairman of the Joint Chiefs of Staff, and Philip C. Habib, Under Secretary of State for Political Affairs, to the Korean capital to commence talks on fulfilling the decision. According to the plan, which met some opposition in Congress and among members of the American command on the peninsula,[35] the United States ultimately expected to withdraw 33,000 American ground troops, leaving behind 11,000 to 13,000 Air Force personnel and support troops. In the first phase 6,000 U.S. soldiers were scheduled to depart in 1978. Then, in July, in response to a plea by Seoul, the administration announced that the bulk of the American combat troops—the key unit being the highly-trained Second Infantry Division deployed in the corridor leading from the demilitarized zone toward the South Korean capital—would remain there until the final year of the proposed planned troop withdrawal.[36]

To assuage South Korean fears that withdrawal would encourage North Korea to attack, President Carter reassured President Park that the United States remained fully committed to the security of South Korea. "The mutual defense treaty between our two countries," Carter pledged, "remains fully in force, and our determination to provide prompt support to help the Republic of Korea defend against armed attack, in accordance with the treaty, remains firm and undiminished."[37] In the meantime, the President promised to assist in the development of modernizing the South Korean armed forces, a move that was hampered by a Congressional inquiry into South Korean bribes to numerous members of Congress in exchange for their support.

Slight progress was made toward the reestablishment of normal relations with Vietnam. In the wake of a fact-finding commission that had gone to Hanoi in March in search of additional information concerning the whereabouts of 2,500 American servicemen still unaccounted for since the conclusion of the Vietnam War, delegates of the U.S. and Vietnam met in Paris to discuss outstanding issues between their nations. As a result, the United States pledged not to veto Vietnam's admission to the U.N., which became its 149th member in September, and to lift its trade embargo after the establishment of diplomatic relations, which did not happen. For its part, Vietnam promised to intensify efforts to provide information on the missing Americans, all of whom were presumed dead. The issue of aid to Vietnam, which Hanoi claimed stemmed from the Paris cease-fire agreement of 1973 and which the Americans, in turn, claimed was invalidated by the invasion of South Vietnam by North Vietnam, was left unsettled.[38] Against the background of these and subsequent negotiations, the Southeast Asia Treaty Organization dissolved itself officially on June 30, 1977.

Africa, except for its Mediterranean

[33]*New York Times,* December 18, 1978, p. 12.

[34]*New York Times,* March 10, p. 9; May 27, 1977, pp. 1, 3.

[35]*New York Times,* May 26, 1977, p. 3. *U.S. News and World Report,* June 20, 1977, pp. 27–28.

[36]*New York Times,* July 27, 1977, pp. 1, 6.

[37]Also see Donald S. Zagoria, "Why We Can't Leave Korea," *New York Times Magazine,* October 2, 1977, pp. 17 ff.

[38]*New York Times,* March 13, p. 8; May 5, 1977, pp. 1, 12.

frontage (once the home of Barbary pirates and scene of crucial military campaigns in World War II), had never loomed large in American foreign policy. Emergence of a major portion of the continent from colonialism to independence in the 1960s and early 1970s produced two conflicts, both of serious concern to the United States. The first was a three-cornered contest between the Soviet Union, Communist China, and the West for influence in the newly independent states. China's success in building a much-needed railroad between Tanzania and Zambia won friends, particularly in that area of East Africa. Of far greater concern to the U.S. and Europe were footholds won by the Soviet Union in Somalia[39] and, through her surrogate Cuba, in Angola and Ethiopia. Were the Soviets to establish naval or air bases in these sites in East and West Africa, they could threaten the vital flow of oil from the Persian Gulf to America and Western Europe.

The second conflict was between white and black for control of Rhodesia and South Africa, where white minorities (miniscule in Rhodesia) enjoyed a monopoly of political and economic power, and in Southwest Africa, or Namibia, which South Africa ruled under an expired mandate from the League of Nations despite repeated efforts by the U.N. to oust her from control. In all three the black majorities had the support of the independent black African nations and of the Soviet bloc. The interest of the U.S. lay in promoting a transition to majority rule in the three areas by peaceful means. Race war, horrible in itself, might bring in the Soviet Union on the side of the black majority with incalculable consequences.

Under the Kennedy and Johnson administrations the U.S. had made clear, through its spokesman at the U.N., its dis-

approval of white minority rule in Rhodesia and South Africa ("apartheid", separateness, was the term used in the latter) and of South Africa's rule in Namibia but also its opposition to the use of force or expulsion from the U.N. to induce change. Over the opposition of President Johnson, Congress had undercut U.N. sanctions against the white Rhodesian government by adoption of the Byrd amendment, permitting the importation of Rhodesian chrome in violation of a U.N. resolution the U.S. had supported.

The Nixon administration had quietly adopted an attitude more tolerant of the white minority governments on a calculation that they were destined for long survival.[40] President Carter completely reversed that attitude. His position was dramatically symbolized by the appointment of Andrew Young, a black, to be U.S. ambassador to the U.N. While the free-wheeling Young was visiting black governments in Africa and making forceful and often indiscreet statements on racism,[41] Carter persuaded Congress to repeal the Byrd amendment, thus closing the American market to Rhodesian chrome, and was working with the British government to induce Premier Ian D. Smith of Rhodesia to accept a plan for transition to majority rule. Vice President Walter Mondale, meanwhile, in a conference with Prime Minister John Vorster of South Africa, warned that official that continuance of cordial relations with the U.S. would depend upon South Africa's willingness to abandon apartheid and to agree to eventual majority rule.[42] All in all, in spite of continued civil war in Rhodesia

---

[39]Somalia expelled its Soviet community of technicians in late 1977 in response to the Kremlin's support of Ethiopia over regional conflict.

[40]See *The Kissinger Study of Southern Africa: National Security Study Memorandum 39 (Secret)*, eds. Mohamed A. El-Khwas and Barry Cohen (Westport, Conn.: Lawrence Hill, 1976).

[41]*New York Times*, May 20, May 22, 1977.

[42]*New York Times*, May 21, 1977; for Vorster's assessment of Carter's African policy, see *New York Times*, August 7, 1977.

and suppression of opposing views in South Africa, none could doubt the Carter administration's commitment to the principle of political equality of black and white, whatever the consequences, in all of Southern Africa.

ADDITIONAL READINGS

BALL, GEORGE W., "How to Save Israel in Spite of Herself," *Foreign Affairs,* 55 (1977), 45–71.

BARNETT, A. DOAK, "Military-Security Relations between China and the United States," *Foreign Affairs,* 55 (1977), 584–97.

GIBNEY, FRANK, "The Ripple Effect in Korea," *Foreign Affairs,* 56 (1977), 160–74.

GONZALEZ, EDWARD, "Complexities of Cuban Foreign Policy," *Problems of Communism,* 27 (November–December 1977), pp. 1–15.

HOFFMAN, STANLEY, "The Hell of Good Intentions," *Foreign Policy,* (Winter, 1977–78), pp. 3–26.

JOHNSON, WHITTLE, "The New Diplomacy of President Carter," *Australian Journal of Politics and History,* 24 (1978), 159–73.

NITZE, PAUL H., "Deterring our Deterrent," *Foreign Policy,* 25 (Winter, 1976–77), pp. 195–210.

SMITH, GERARD C., "Negotiating with the Soviets," *New York Times Magazine,* February 27, 1977, pp. 18ff.

SZULC, TAD, "Washington Dateline: Springtime for Carter," *Foreign Policy,* 27 (Summer, 1977), pp. 178–91.

Index

ABC powers, 205
Aberdeen, Lord, 77, 85, 86, 88–89, 91, 100
Acheson, Dean, 299, 404, 405, 430
  Korea and, 431, 433
Adams, Brooks, 170
Adams, Charles Francis, 141
  Alabama Case and, 141
Adams, John, 15, 16, 17, 27
  Cuba and, 130
  peace negotiations and, 16, 17–19
  President, 36–38
Adams, John Quincy, 51, 52, 56, 57, 71, 130
  Monroe Doctrine and, 62–64, 65–67, 68, 69, 71
  Texas and, 89, 90
Adenauer, Konrad, 402
Agreements. See specific agreements; Executive agreements; Treaties.
Aguinaldo, Emilio, 183, 185, 188
Aichi, Kiichi, 445
Aigun, Treaty of (1858), 122
Alabama (cruiser), 53, 140–41, 142, 143
  claims from, 141–44
Alaska, 6, 126
  purchase of, 146–47
  boundary dispute over (1903), 224–26
Albania, 338
Alexander I, Czar of Russia, 64
Al Fatah, 495
Algeciras Conference (1906), 229, 230, 231
Algeria, 490, 493
Alliance for Progress, 505, 508–9, 517
Allied Control Committee for Germany, 381
Allied Council for Japan, 426
"All-Mexico" movements, 110–11, 112
Alsace-Lorraine, 251, 257
Alverstone, Lord, 226
Ambassador, rank of, 2
Ambrister, Robert, 57
Amelia Island, 56
America First Committee, 341
American Peace Society, 221
American Revolution, 11–26
  causes of, 11–12
  quest for foreign aid in, 12
  Spain and, 12, 13, 14–15
  alliance with France, 12–14
  peace negotiations, 16–19
  Paris, Treaty of (1782), 19–21
Amiens, Peace of (1802), 39, 45
Ampudia, General Pedro de, 104
Angell, Norman, 222
Anglo-Japanese Alliance (1911), 281–82
  terminated, 284
Anglo-Spanish Nootka Sound Convention of 1790, 81
Anti-ballistics missiles (ABMs), 417

Anticolonialism, 425
Antietam, battle of, 135
Anti-Imperialist League, 184, 187–88
Anti-Semitism, 309, 310
Apartheid, 534
Arab-Israeli conflict, 416, 495, 531–32
  causes of, 481
  Palestinian refugees and, 482, 491
  Suez crisis, 485–89
  Six-Day War, 492–97
  Yom Kippur War, 497–500
Arab League, 490
Arab Union, 489
Arafat, Yasir, 496
Aranjuez Convention (1779), 14, 15
Arbitration
  (post-1814), 53–54
  (post-1898), 223–31
  Taft treaty (1911), 281
Arbuthnot, Alexander, 57
Argentina, 65, 67, 71, 368, 369, 502–3
Argol agreements, 166
Arias, Arnulfo, 514
Arias, Desiderio, 202
Arkansas River, 59
Armas, Carlos Castillo, 505
Armstrong, Hamilton Fish, 384
Arthur, Chester A., 156–57
Articles of Confederation, 21, 23, 25, 32
Ashburton, Lord, 73, 74, 75, 83, 100
Astor, John Jacob, 55
Atlantic Charter, 366, 372
  framed, 345
  principles of, 372, 385
Atocha, A. J., 103, 108
Atomic bomb, exploded, 382
Atomic Energy Act, 407
Attlee, Clement, 382, 394
  at Potsdam, 394–96
Aury, Luis, 56
Austin, Moses, 89
Austin, Stephen F., 89
Austria, 249. See also Austria-Hungary
  Germany and, 294
  invaded by Germany, 336–37
  regains independence, 397
  occupation ends, 410
Austria-Hungary, 229, 231, 232. See also Austria
  peace (1917) and, 248
Autobiography (Roosevelt, T.), 193

Baez, Buenaventura, 145
Baghdad Pact (1955), 484–85. See also Central Treaty Organization
  Iraq withdraws from, 489
Bagot, Charles, 53
Bagota, Act of (1960), 508
Baker Island, 126
Balaguer, Joaquin, 516
Bale, Treaty of (1795), 33, 39

Balfour, Arthur James, 284
Balfour Declaration (1917), 481
Balkan Wars (1812–1913), 230
Ballistic missiles. See specific types
Bancroft, Edward, 12
Bancroft, George, 98, 104
Bank for International Settlements, 295
Bankhead, Charles, 109
Bao Dai, 457, 458–59, 462
Barbé-Marbois, Francois, 41
Barclay, Anthony, 76
Barlow, Joel, 50
Barreras, Imbert, 516
Baruch, Bernard, 391
Baruch Plan, 391
Batista, Fulgencio, 506
Bay of Pigs, invasion, 509–11
Bayard, James A., 51
Bayard, Thomas F., 148, 157
Bear Flag revolt, 107
Beaumarchais, Caron de, 12
Beer, G. L., 256
Begin, Menahem, 531–32
Belgium, 257, 342
Bemis, Samuel F., 32, 33
Bennett, W. Tapley, 515
Bennington, U. S. S., 186
Benton, Thomas Hart, 81, 92–93, 107
Bering, Vitus, 63
Berlin, Treaty of (1889), 149
Berlin and Milan decrees, 47, 48, 50
Berlin Wall, 415
Bermuda (ship), 138
Bernstorff, Count Johann H. von, 239, 242, 243
Bethmann-Hollweg, Chancellor Theobald von, 233, 241
Bevin, Ernest, 394
Bidlack, Benjamin, 129
Biglow Papers (Lowell), 110
Bizonia, 398
Black Warrior incident, 131–32
Blaine, James G., 148, 165, 171
  Pan Americanism and, 156–57
Blaine, John J., 277
Bliss, Tasker H., 249
Blockades, 27, 33, 47, 52, 137
  paper, 45, 47–48
  In U. S. Civil War, 136, 137–38
  (1915), 240
  Cuba (1962), 512–13
Blount, James H., 151
Bogotá Charter (1948), 521
Bolivar, Simon, 156
Bolivia, 326
Bonaparte, Joseph, 37, 43
Bonaparte, Napoleon. See Napoleon Bonaparte
Bonin Islands, 121, 444
Borah, William, 260, 261, 262, 270, 273, 274, 282, 305, 339
Borg, Dorothy, 307

Bosch, Juan, 515, 516, 517
Boston, U.S.S., 151
Boun Oum, Prince, 463
Boundaries, U. S. *See also individual states*
  as specified by Congress (1779), 16
  proposed by John Adams, 17
  peace negotiations and, 17–19, 23, 24
  treaty of 1783 and, 23, 55
  Western, 24, 25
  Pinckney's Treaty and, 34–35
  and Ghent, 54, 55
  northeastern, 54, 71–76, 81–83
  treaty of 1818 and, 55
  northern, 55–56
  treaty of 1819 and, 56
  with Mexico, 112–13, 126–27
Boundary Treaty (1818), 55–56
Bourguiba, Habib, 490
Bowman, Isaiah, 384
Boxer Rebellion, 209–12
Bradley, Omar N., 433
Brandt, Willy, 422
Brazil, 71, 78, 154
Brezhnev, Leonid I., 416, 418, 498, 499, 526
  seeks détente with U. S., 416–19
  Czechoslovakia and, 421
Brezhnev Doctrine, 421, 452
Briand, Aristide, 275–76
Bricker, John W., 8
  Bricker Amendment, 8
Bright, John, 135
British Aggressions in Venezuela, or the Monroe Doctrine on Trial (Scruggs), 159
British Guiana, 158–62
Brockdorff-Rantzau, Count Ulrich von, 259
Broken voyage, doctrine of, 47, 137–38, 236
Brown, George S., 533
Brown, Jacob, 51
Bruce, David K. E., 475
Brussels Conference (1937), 334–35
Bryan, William Jennings, 199, 200, 203, 207, 221, 234, 235, 238, 266, 277, 304
  imperialism and, 185, 187–88
  dollar diplomacy and, 199, 200, 207
  World War I and, 224, 234–35, 238
Bryan-Chamorro Treaty (1914), 199
Bryant, Irving, 49
Brzezinski, Zbigniew, 526
Bucareli agreement, 328
Buchanan, James, 84, 100, 102, 103, 105–6, 108, 110, 121, 124, 126, 127, 129, 132
  Oregon and, 84–89
  Clayton-Bulwer Treaty and, 129–30
Buena Vista, battle of, 108
Bulganin, Nikolai A., 410
Bulgaria, 392, 393, 396
Bullitt, William C., 252, 262–63
Bulloch, James D., 140

Bulwer, Henry, 129
Bunau-Varilla, Philippe, 192, 193
Bunche, Ralph, 481
Bunker, Ellsworth, 471
Burgess, John W., 168–69
Burgoyne, John, 13
Burlingame, Anson, 122, 123, 162
Burlingame Treaty (1868), 162
Burma, 368, 426, 460
Butler, Anthony, 89
Byrd amendment, 534
Byrnes, James F., 382, 392, 396, 398, 503

Cabral, Donald Reid, 515
Cáceres, Ramón, 201
Cairo Conference (1943), 375–76
Calhoun, John C., 49, 57, 86, 92, 93, 110, 111, 112
  Texas and, 91, 92, 93, 96
California, 96
  desired by Polk, 96, 98
  exploration of, 99
  settled by Americans, 99
  Monroe Doctrine and, 101–2
  Mexican War and, 105–7
  occupied by U. S., 106–7
  Japanese in, 216, 218
Calles, Plutarco Elias, 328
Calvo Doctrine, 206
Camacho, Manuel Avila, 330
Cambodia, 9, 458, 459, 460, 461, 462, 471, 475, 477–78
  U. S. invasion of, 477–78
Campbell, Archibald, 32
Canada, 419
  War of 1812 and, 49–50
  McCleod incident and, 78–80
  Maine boundary and, 72–76
  reciprocity treaty with, 125
  Alabama claims and, 142
  Alaska boundary and, 224–26
  northeast fisheries dispute, 226–28
  U. S. and, in World War II, 345
  Latin America and, 521
  U. S. and (post-1945), 521–24
  oil in, 523
Canada-United States Committee on Joint Defense, 521
Canning, George, 47, 67
  Monroe Doctrine and, 67–79
Carden, Lionel, 205
Caribbean. *See* Latin America
Carlisle, Lord, 13
  Commission, 13
Carmichael, Stokley, 519
Carnegie, Andrew, 221, 222
Carnegie Endowment for International Peace, 221
Caroline (ship), 78–80
Carranza, Venustiano, 205–6, 327
Carter, Jimmy, 416
  Korea and, 438
  human rights and, 526

Carter, Jimmy (*cont.*)
  arms limitation and, 526–28
  U. S. foreign policy and, 526–35
  trilateralism and, 528–29
  Latin America and, 529–31
  Middle East and, 531–32
  Far East, 532–33
  Africa and, 533–35
Casablanca Conference (1943), 373
Cass, Lewis, 77, 78
Castlereagh, Lord, 55
Castro, Cipiano, 196
Castro, Fidel, 506–7, 509–13, 518–20, 530–31
Castro, Raúl, 506
Catherine II, Empress of Russia, 15
Cavell, Edith, 234
Cazneau, William L., 130
Central American Court of Justice, 199
Central Intelligence Agency, U. S. (CIA), 5, 505
Central Treaty Organization (CENTO), 489. *See also* Baghdad Pact
Ceylon, 426, 460
Chamberlain, Austen, 276
Chamberlain, Neville, 337, 338
Chamberlin, William Henry, 379
Chang, Hsüeh-liang, 301, 303
Chang, John M., 435
Chang, Tso-lin, 301
Chapultepec
  conference (1945), 388
  Act of, 388–89, 502
Chargé d'affaires, rank of, 2–3
Charles IV, King of Spain, 40
Charleston, U.S.S., 179
Chattahoochee, 35
Chennault, Claire L., 367, 368
Chiang Kai-shek, 6, 301, 335, 351, 362, 368, 373, 382, 383, 427, 428
  united front with Communists against Japan, 309
  at Cairo, 375
  Yalta agreement and, 379–80
  overthrown, 429
  regime on Taiwan, 447–48
Chiari, Roberto, 513
Chicago Tribune, 260, 341
Chile, 65, 67, 71, 368, 369, 502, 517–18
  revolution in, 517–18
China
  early contacts with, 115, 117
  Open Door Policy and, 116, 122, 164–65, 208–9, 278, 281, 283, 307–9
  Opium War and, 117
  Treaty of Nanking and, 117, 119
  Wanghia Treaty and, 118–19
  grants extraterritoriality, 119
  Taiping Rebellion, 119, 122
  Tientsin treaties, 121–22
  Anglo-French wars, 122
  Russia and, 122, 427–28, 451
  immigration from, 162–63, 367

China (*cont.*)
fights Japan, 163
Korea and, 163–64
Open Door diplomacy and, 164–65
market for U. S. surplus, 165–66
Boxer Rebellion, 209–12
revolution in (1911), 219
Washington Conference
(1921–1922), and, 277–78
Nine-Power Treaty (1922) and,
283
Manchuria and, 300–9
attacked by Japan, 332–34, 335–36
in World War II, 348, 350, 351
U.S. and World War II, 367–68
communist victory in, 405, 429–30
post-1945, 425, 427–30, 446–53
Korean War and, 432–33
Japan and, 442
Nixon visits, 445, 452–55
U.S. and, 446–48, 451–55
Formosa and, 447, 455
cultural revolution in, 450
admitted to U.N., 450–51, 454
becomes a nuclear power, 451–52
Cuba and, 519
in Africa, 534
U.S. recognition of, 532–33
Chinese Eastern Railway, 213
Chou En-lai, 429, 447, 450, 453
meets Kissinger, 454
Churchill, Winston, 286, 343, 345,
352, 362, 366, 385, 392, 393, 394,
399
Atlantic Charter and, 345
plans war strategy with Roosevelt,
362–64
war and post-war aims of, 371–80
"iron curtain" speech, 399
Civil War, American, 134–44. *See also*
Confederate States of America;
Slavery
Claiborne, W. C. C., 43
Clark, Champ, 293
Clark, George Rogers, 16, 19
Clark, J. Reuben, 322
Clay, Henry, 49, 51, 66, 92, 130, 152,
156
Monroe Doctrine and, 65–67, 71
Texas and, 91
Cuba and, 130
Clayton, John M., 129
Clayton-Bulwer Treaty (1850), 6, 7,
127–30, 148, 191. *See also*
Hay-Pauncefote Treaty (1901)
Clemenceau, Georges, 249, 251, 252,
253, 256, 259, 260
Cleveland, Grover, 148, 151, 157, 158,
175
Hawaii and, 151–52
Latin America and, 157, 158–62
Clifford, Clark M., 473
Cochin China, 457, 458. *See also* South
Vietnam
Cockburn, Alexander, 143
Co-hong system, 117

Cold War
causes of, 391–93
U.S. and, 391–408
Germany and, 393–96, 397–98,
401–3, 406
escalates into arms race, 406–8
Colombia, 65, 67, 71
Panama dispute and, 193–94
Columbia River, 54, 55
Cominform. *See* Communist
Information Bureau
Comintern, 366
Commerce, colonial, 21–22
Commerce, U.S.
neutral rights and, 27–28, 46–48,
234–39
with Far East, 115, 117, 118–19,
165–66
with Canada, 124–25
Manifest Destiny and, 170
World War I and, 234–35
Commission on Organization of the
Executive Branch of the
Government. *See* Hoover
Commission
Committee to Defend America by
Aiding the Allies, 341
Common Sense (Paine), 11
Communism, 252–53, 332, 392, 400,
401, 425, 502
Russian vs. Chinese, 451
in Latin America, 502, 504, 505–7
Communist Information Bureau
(Cominform), 403
Conciliation Treaties (Bryan's), 224
Confederate States of America, 134.
See also Civil War; Slavery
Conference on Security and
Cooperation in Europe. *See*
Helsinki Conference
Congress (of the Confederation),
foreign affairs and, 1
Congress, Continental. *See*
Continental Congress
Congress, U.S.
powers of, in foreign affairs under
Constitution, 1, 7, 9–10
Senate, 7
Congressional Record, 260
Constitution (U.S.), 9, 21, 25, 28
division of powers in foreign affairs
under, 1
Consul, rank of, 3
Containment, policy of, 391, 399–400,
446–47, 482, 484
Contiguity, principle of, 81
Continental Congress
Committee of Foreign Affairs, 1
Committee of Secret
Correspondence, 1
Contraband, 30, 47, 139, 236
persons as, 139–40
Conventions. *See also* Treaties
Aranjuez (1779), 14, 15
(1824), 76–77
(1827), 81

Conventions (*cont.*)
with Japan (1857), 123
Johnson-Clarendon (1869), 142
Montevideo Conference (1933), 323
Inter-American conference (1936),
326
Havana (1942), 369
Coolidge, Calvin, 277, 286, 289, 300
Latin America and, 320–21
Mexican crisis and, 329
Corinto incident, 160
Cornwallis, Lord, 14, 15
Costa Rica, 199
Council on Foreign Relations, 384
Cox, James M., 270
Craig, Gerald, 522
Creek Indians, 52, 56
Cromwell, William Nelson, 192
Cuba, 67, 68, 78
Isthmian canal and, 130–31
U.S. interest in, 130–32
revolt in (1895), 172–74
U.S. invades, 174–78
U.S. protectorate, 194–95
Platt Amendment and, 195–96
protectorate ended, 196, 325
Castro and, 506–7, 509–13, 518–20,
530–31
Russia and, 510, 511–13, 519–20
China and, 519
Cushing, Caleb, 117–18
Cyprus, 419
Czechoslovakia, 248, 253, 257, 400
Sudetenland ceded to Germany,
337–38
Communist coup in (1948), 402
invaded by Russia, 421

Dairen, 427
Daladier, Edouard, 338
Daniels, Josephus, 330
Danzig, 338
Darlan, Jean Francois, 370
Darwin, Charles, 168
Davie, William R., 37
Davis, Jefferson, 126
Davis, Norman H., 311
Dawes, Charles G., 290, 303–4
Dawes Plan (1924), 290–91
Dawson, Thomas C., 198
Day, William R., 182, 208
Dayan, Moshe, 492–93
Deane, Silas, 12
Declaration(s)
of London (1909), 223, 241
of Buenos Aires (1936), 326
Panama (1939), 368
Rio de Janeiro (1942), 369
Moscow (1943), 368, 385
on Austria (1943), 374
on Italy (1943), 374
Cairo (1943), 375–76, 382
of Four Nations on General Security
(1943), 374
on German atrocities (1943), 375
Potsdam (1945), 381–82

Declaration of Independence, 12, 13
of the United Nations, 361, 366,
369, 372, 377
Declaration of Paris (1856), 52, 136
de Gaulle, Charles, 362, 370, 371, 469,
492
NATO and, 419–21
on U.S. in Vietnam, 469
Delafield, Joseph, 76
Democratic Party
expansion and, 84, 110–11, 112
Texas and, 91, 92
Panama Canal tolls and, 228
Democratic Review, 86, 111, 112
Denmark, 257, 342, 388
in Armed Neutrality, 15
Dennett, Tyler, 117
Denó, Francisco Caamaño, 516
Detroit, 31
Dewey, George, 179
Diaz, Adolfo, 199, 320–21
Diaz, Portfirio, 202, 327
Diefenbaker, John, 419, 522
Diem, Ngo Dinh, 465
Dienbienphu, 459
Dillon, Douglas, 508, 509
Dingley tariff (1897), 165, 166, 292
Disarmament
(pre-1914), 231
Fourteen Points and, 255
at Washington (1921–1922), 277–78
World Conference (1932–1933),
310–11
at Geneva (1955), 411
Khrushchev proposal for, 413
(post-1943), 526–28
Dobrynin, Anatoly, 499
Dodd, William E., 312
Doenitz, Karl, 381
Dole, Sanford B., 152
Dollar Diplomacy
Taft's, 198–99, 218–20
Wilson's, 199, 200–7
Dollfuss, Chancellor, 332
Dominican Republic. *See* Santo
Domingo
Donelson, Andrew Jackson, 93–94
Doniphan, A. W., 106
Dorchester, Lord, 31
Douglas, Stephen A., 132
Drago Doctrine, 206, 326
Drought, James M., 351
Dual Alliance, 228, 229
Dudley, Thomas H., 141
Dulles, John Foster, 406, 412, 440,
448, 449, 459
Quemoy and, 448
Communist China and, 449–51
Indochina and, 459
SEATO and, 460–62
Baghdad Pact (1955) and, 484
Suez Canal crisis and, 485
Communism in Latin America and,
505
Dumbarton Oaks Conference (1944),
385–86

Duong Van Minh, General, 467, 468,
480
Du Pont, Pierre Samuel, 40, 41
Durdin, Tilman, 453
Durfee, Amos, 79

East Germany. *See* Germany
East India Company, 115
Eban, Abba, 492
Economic Cooperation
Administration, U.S., 401
Ecuador, 67
Eden, Anthony, 315, 372, 374, 410,
486
Egypt, 481, 482, 485, 490
nationalizes Suez Canal, 485–89
conflict with Yemen, 491
Six-Day War and, 492–93
Eisenhower, Dwight D., 299, 394, 410,
508
at Geneva, 411
Hungary and, 412
Khrushchev visit and, 413
U-2 incident and, 414
in Korea, 434
Indochina and, 459
Suez Canal crisis and, 488
Communism in Latin America and,
505, 507
Eisenhower, Milton, 505, 506
Eisenhower Doctrine, 489–500
El Salvador, 199
Elgin, Lord, 125
Elliot, Charles, 94–95
Ellsworth, Oliver, 37
Embargo(es), 31
(1794), 31
(1807), 48
Italo-Ethiopian War, 315–16
World War II and, 340, 342, 350
Empress of China (ship), 117
England. *See* Great Britain
Entente Cordiale, 229
Erhard, Ludwig, 422
Eritrea, 396
Eshkol, Levi, 492
Essex (ship), 47, 137
Estaing, Compte de, 14
Estonia, 365
Ethiopia, 396
Italy and, 312, 314, 315–16
European Advisory Commission
(EAC), 374, 393
European Common Market, 299
European Recovery Program. *See*
Marshall Plan
Everett, Edward, 131
Executive agreements. *See* Treaties
Extraterritoriality, principle of, 119
China and, 119, 367
Japan and, 123

Facism, 309–10
Fallen Timbers, battle of, 32, 34

Far East. *See also specific countries.*
early contacts with, 115–17
U.S. commerce with, 115, 117,
118–19
(1898–1914), 207–20
dollar diplomacy in, 218–20
U.S. policy towards (post-1914),
278–86
World War II, 348–60, 367–68,
378–79, 381–82
(post-1945), 425–30, 441–65,
532–33
Korean War, 430–38
Vietnam War, 465–80
Faure, Edgar, 410
Federal Council of Churches of Christ
in America, 384
Federalist party, 32
Federalists, 40
Ferdinand, Francis, 230, 231
Ferdinand VII, King of Spain, 59, 64,
65
Fidelismo, 507
Fight for Freedom Committee, 341
Fillmore, Millard, 120, 124
Finland, 365, 400
Finney, Nat S., 511
First Neutrality Act (1935), 314
Fish, Hamilton, 142, 143, 145
Fisheries
in 1783, 55
in 1818, 55–56
in 1909, 226–28
in 1970's, 530
Fiske, John, 168
Fiume, 254, 257, 258
Five-Power Treaty (1922), 282, 288,
306
Fletcher, Henry P., 206
Florida, 6, 15, 21, 39, 40, 41, 50, 52, 56,
57, 59
acquisition of, 15, 42–44, 57
Florida (ship), 140, 141, 142
Floyd, John, 81
Foch, Ferdinand, 245
Foch, Marshal, 249
Food and Agricultural Organization,
389
Ford, Gerald R., 416, 520
at Vladivostok, 418
Korea and, 438
visits China, 455
Fordney-McCumber tariff (1922),
293
Foreign Affaires (periodical), 384
Foreign Affairs, Committee of, U.S.,
1
Foreign Affairs, Department of, U.S
(1781–1789), 1
Foreign Assistance Act (1948), 9
Foreign Enlistment Act (1819), 140
Foreign Operations Administration
(FOA), U.S., 401
Foreign policy, U.S.
Congress and, 1
President and, 1

Foreign Policy, U.S. (*cont.*)
  instruments and procedures of,
    1–10, *See also specific departments
    and agencies*
  (post-1783), 28–38
  Far Eastern (pre-1900), 116–24
  (post-1919), 288–99
  (post-1945), 425–26
Foreign Service, U.S., 2–3
  history of, 3–5
  integration of State Department
    and, 4–5
Foreign Service Act (1946), 4
Formosa, 121, 163, 429
  U.S. and, 430, 431, 447
  China and, 447–55
  U.S. withdraws recognition of, 532
Forsyth, John, 77
Fort Montgomery, 74
Fort Ross, 63
Fort Sumter, 134
Foster, A. J., 48–49
Foster, John W., 165, 171
Four Freedoms, 372
Four-Power Treaty (1921), 284
Fourteen Points, 246–48, 250
  Versailles Treaty and, 255–59
France, 229
  colonial revolt and, 12
  U.S. alliance with, 12–14
  Spain, alliance with, 14
  revolution in, 28
  war with Great Britain (1793), 28
  friction with U.S., 35–38
  trade problems of, 47–48
  Latin America and, 66, 67, 69
  U.S. Civil War and, 134
  Mexico and, 153–56
  Open Door and, 164
  Morocco and, 229
  League of Nations and, 254
  German rearmament and, 311
  Munich crisis and, 338
  in World War II, 342, 370–71
  Algerian revolt and, 407
  leaves NATO, 419–21
  in Indochina, 457–59
  Suez Canal crisis and, 485–89
Franco, Francisco, 317, 332, 371
Franklin, Benjamin, 3, 12, 16, 17
  American Joint Commission and,
    12–13
  peace negotiations and, 16–19
Freedom of the seas. *See* Blockade;
  Neutral rights; Neutrality
Frelinghuysen, Frederick T., 148, 157
Frémont, John C., 99, 107–8
French and Indian War, 11, 38
Frick, Henry Clay, 261
Fulbright, William J., 469, 470, 517

Gadsden, James, 124, 126–27
Gadsden Purchase, 126–27
Gallatin, Albert, 51, 55, 56, 87
Galvez, Bernardo de, 14, 25

Gardoqui, Don Diego de, 21, 25
Garfield, James A., 157
Gates, Horatio, 13
General Agreement on Tariffs and
  Trade (GATT), 298, 442
General Disarmament Conference
  (1932–1933), 310–11
Genêt, Edmond, 28–30, 34, 36
Geneva Conferences
  (1927), 286
  (1954), 459–60, 463
  (1955), 411
  (1962), 463
Gentlemen's Agreement (1907–1908),
  215–16
George, David Lloyd, 241–42
George, Lloyd, 249, 251, 252, 253,
  256, 258, 266, 267, 282
Germany
  Open Door and, 164
  Philippines and, 183
  Morocco and, 228–29
  pre-World War I, 228–30
  uses submarine warfare, 237–39,
    242–43
  peace negotiations, World War I,
    248–60
  reparations from, 249, 258–59,
    289–92, 294–96
  accepts Versailles Treaty, 259–60
  Austria and, 294
  Nazism in, 309–10
  repudiates disarmament, 311
  Rome-Berlin-Tokyo Axis, 332
  Great Britain and, 337–38
  seizes Austria and Sudetenland,
    337–38
  threatens Poland, 338–39
  invades Poland, 340
  makes pact with Russia, 340
  invades Russia, 345
  anti-Semitism in, 375
  postwar planning for, 377–78,
    393–96, 396–98, 401–3
  reparations from (World War II),
    378, 380, 396, 398
  surrenders (1945), 381
  reunification of, 398, 411, 412–13
  Berlin airlift, 402–3
  divided, 402–3
  Berlin crisis, 412–13, 414–15
  Cold War and, 393–96, 397–98,
    401–3
  (post-1945), 393–96, 397–98, 401–3,
    406
Gerry, Elbridge, 36
Ghent, Treaty of, 51–53, 54, 55, 76
Gibraltar, 371
Gilbert, Prentiss, 303
Gillespie, Archibald H., 101
Ginn, Edward, 221
Giraud, Henri, H., 370
Godoy, Héctor Garcia, 516
Godoy, Manuel de, 35
Goebbels, Joseph, 374
Gold standard, 296

Goldberg, Arthur, 472, 473
Goldwater, Barry, 469
Goluchowski, Count
  (Austria-Hungary), 165, 166
Gomulka, Wladyslaw, 411
Good Neighbor Policy
  basis of, 321–22
  Haiti and, 324
  Cuba and, 325
  Panama and, 325
  Mexico and, 327–31
  World War II and, 368–69
  deteriorates, 502, 503–5
Gossens, Salvador Allende, 517–18
Grant, Ulysses S., 142, 145
  Santo Domingo and, 145–46
  appoints Interoceanic Canal
    Commission, 147
Grasse, Compte Francois J. P. de, 14
Graves, William S., 280
Gray, Robert, 54
Great Britain
  American Revolution and, 11–12
  colonies and, 11
  relations with other powers during
    American Revolution, 15
  war with France (1793), 28
  relations with U.S. (post-1783),
    21–22; (post-1794), 30–34
  Jay Treaty and, 32–34, 36
  renewed war and, 45
  and War of 1812, causes, 45–50
  in War of 1812, 50–51
  Ghent negotiations, 51–53
  claims Oregon, 55
  treaty with (1818), 55–56
  Monroe Doctrine and, 65, 66, 67–71
  Ashburton negotiations, 72–80
  convention of 1824, 76–77
  Caroline incident and, 78–80
  convention of 1827, 81
  Oregon and, 81–89
  Texas and, 91, 93–94
  California and, 100, 101
  Opium War and, 117
  Bulwer negotiations and, 129–30
  in Caribbean, 129
  U.S. Civil War and, 135
  proclaims neutrality, 136
  bans privateers, 136–37
  Declaration of Paris (1856), 136–37
  in *Trent* affair, 138–40
  Alabama claims and, 141–44
  Samoa and, 149
  Mexico and, 153
  Venezuela and, 158–62
  Open Door and, 164, 208, 213
  Spanish-American War, 177
  Japan and, 213
  Alaska boundary and, 224–26
  fisheries dispute and, 227
  Panama Canal tolls dispute, 228
  in World War I, 235–37
  Wilson's leadership and, 240–41
  Fourteen Points and, 258–59
  Yap Island mandate and, 280

Great Britain (*cont.*)
alliance with Japan, 281–82, 284
Middle East oil and, 281
naval rivalry with U.S., 281–83, 286–88
London Naval Conference (1930), 286–87
Far East crisis and, 305
Italo-Ethiopian War and, 315–16
appeases Germany, 337
Munich crisis and, 338
destroyer deal with, 343
and U.S. in World War II, 362–64
Russia and (World War II), 376–77, 392
Berlin airlift and, 402–3
grants independence to colonies, 426
recognizes Communist China, 429
Middle East and, 481, 484
Suez Canal crisis and, 485–89
Six-Day War and, 493
Great Illusion, The (Angell), 222
Greece, 338, 392, 399, 404, 419
Greene, J. J., 523
Greenland, occupied, 346
Greenville, Indian Treaty of (1795), 34
Greer, U.S.S., 346
Grenville, Lord, 33–34
Gresham, Walter Q., 159
Grew, Joseph, 308, 333, 334, 336, 348, 353, 357, 358, 359, 382
Grey, Edward, 237, 240, 266
Gromyko, Andrei A., 527
Guadalupe Hidalgo, Treaty of (1848), 111–14, 127
Guam, 179, 180, 186
Guano Law (1856), 126
Guatemala, 505
Guevara, Ernesto (Ché), 506, 509, 519
Guizot, Francois Pierre G., 102, 154
Gulf of Tonkin, 9
Guzmán, Jacobo Arbenz, 505

Habib, Philip C., 533
Hague Court. *See* Permanent Court of Arbitration
Hague Peace Conferences (1899, 1907), 222–23
Haiti
U.S. protectorate, 194–95, 200–201
dollar diplomacy in, 200–201
withdrawal from, 324–25
Hamaguchi, Yuko, 301
Hamilton, Alexander, 28, 32, 33, 36, 37
pro-British sympathies of, 28–29
Hammond, George, 33
Hanihara, Masanao, 300
Hanna, Mark, 172, 192
Hannegan, E. A., 86, 87
Harding, Warren G., 262, 273, 282, 289, 293
League of Nations and, 269–70
Latin America and, 320
Harmar, Joseph, 31

Harper, John A., 49
Harriman, E. H., 218
Harriman, W. Averell, 365, 378, 388, 472, 473
Harris, Townsend, 120, 122–23
Harrison, Benjamin, 157, 171
Hawaii and, 151
Harrison, William Henry, 49
Harvey, George, 271
Havana, Act of (1940), 369
Hawaii
early contacts with, 125
U.S. interest in, 125–26, 149–52
reciprocity treaty with, 150
revolution in, 150–52
annexation proposed, 172
annexed, 186–87
Hawley-Smoot tariff (1930), 294, 298
Hawthorne, Nathaniel, 3
Hay, John, 183, 191, 971
Open Door in China and, 208–9, 211–12
Boxer Rebellion and, 209–11
arbitration and, 223
Hay-Pauncefote Treaty (1901), 191, 228. *See also* Clayton-Bulwer Treaty (1850)
Hayes, Rutherford B., 162
in isthmian canal, 148
Hearst, William R., 173
Helsinki Conference (1975), 423
Henlein, Konrad, 337
Herrera, Jose, 97, 102, 103
Herter, Christian A., 414, 508
Hindenburg, Paul von, 310
Hippisley, Alfred E., 208
Hirohito, Emperor of Japan, 445
Hiroshima, bombed, 382
Hirota, Koki, 308
Hispanic America. *See* Latin America
Hitchcock, Gilbert M., 265
Hitler, Adolf, 309, 310, 338
repudiates Versailles, 311–12
forms axis, 332
Austria and, 336–37
Czech crisis and, 337
precipitates war, 340
refrains from war with U.S., 347–48
death of, 381
Hoar, George F., 184–85
Hoare, Samuel, 315
Ho Chi Min, 457, 458, 464, 475
Hofstadter, Richard, 170
Holy Alliance, 64
Hong Kong, 117, 121
Hoover, Herbert, 6, 211, 267, 270, 286, 304, 311
tariff and, 294
war debts and reparations, 294–96
Hoover Commission, 4, 5
Hoover-Stimson Doctrine, 304–5, 306, 321
Hopkins, Harry, 6, 365, 385, 388
Horseshoe Bend, battle of, 52
House, Edward M., 6, 231, 233, 240, 249, 252, 254

Houston, Sam, 90, 91, 93, 94, 130
Hudson's Bay Company, 33, 81, 88
Huerta, Victoriano, 202–3, 205
Hughes, Charles Evans, 250, 272, 273, 280, 282, 283, 284, 285
League of Nations and, 270–71
Dawes Plan and, 290
Japan and, 300
Hull, Cordell, 307, 314, 372, 373, 374
London Economic Conference and, 296, 297
favors reciprocity, 297–99
Good Neighbor Policy and, 323–24
Japan and, 335–36, 351, 352, 353, 355, 356, 357, 358
Russia and, 365
China and, 367
post-war planning of, 384–87
Humphrey, Hubert H., 479
Hungary, 253, 377, 392, 396
revolt (1848), 124
revolt (1956), 411–12
Hussein, Ibn Talal, 489, 490, 492, 495

Iberville River, 56
Iceland, occupied, 346
Ikeda, Hayato, 443
Immigration
Chinese, 162–63, 367
Japanese, 215–16
Imperialism
beginnings of, 146–47
Spanish-American War and, 170, 184–86
Monroe Doctrine vs., 185, 187
Impressment, 45–46, 47, 53, 77
India, 426, 460
Indians (American). *See also specific tribes*
British incitement of, 31
treaties with (1784), 31; (1795), 34
Greenville Treaty with, 34
incited by the French, 39
Indochina. *See also* Cambodia; Laos; Vietnam
Japan and, 352, 356
France and, 457–59
U.S. and, 460–62
Indonesia, 426, 460
Influence of Sea Power upon History, 1660–1783, The (Mahan), 169, 171
Inter-American Conference (1933), 297
(1936), 326
Mexico City (1945), 502
Bogota (1948), 503
Caracas (1954), 505
Santiago (1959), 507
San José (1960), 507
Punta del Este (1961), 508–9; (1962), 510–11
Rio de Janeiro (1965), 517
Inter-American Council of Jurists, 503
Inter-American Defense Board, 511

Inter-American Development Bank,
    507
Inter-American Peace Force, 516
Inter-American Treaty of Mutual
    Assistance (1947), 502, 503
Intercontinental ballistic missile
    (ICBM), 408, 418, 522
Interim Agreement on Strategic
    Offensive Missiles (1972), 418
Intermediate-range ballistic missile
    (IRBM), 408
Internal Court of Justice, 386, 390
International Bank and Monetary
    Fund, 389
International Court of Justice, 389
International Labor Organization,
    271, 389
Interoceanic Canal Commission, 147
Iran, 484
Iraq, 481, 482, 485, 489, 490, 493
Ireland, 261
Irving, Washington, 3
Ishii, Viscount Kikujiro, 278
Isolationism. See also Neutrality;
    Nonentanglement,
    nonintervention
    Washington's Farewell Address and,
        36
    Open Door and, 116–17
    League of Nations and, 261, 269–70
    Permanent Court of International
        Justice and, 272–74
    "quarantine" speech, 334
    Hitler and, 339–40, 341
    United Nations and, 385
Israel, 490. See also Palestine
    Six-Day War (1967), 416, 492–97
    Yom Kippur War (1973), 416, 419,
        497–500
    Created by U.N., 481
    U.S. and, 481, 483, 491, 495
    Suez crisis and, 485–89
    Suez Canal crisis and, 486–89
Israeli-Egyptian War (1956), 484,
    486–89
Isthmian Canal, 147–48. See also
    Panama Canal.
    Nicaragua and, 129
    U.S. negotiates with Colombia, 129
    Cuba and, 130–31
Isthmian Canal Act (1902), 192
Italo-Ethiopian War, American
    neutrality and, 315–16
Italy, 229, 419
    facism, in, 309–10
    invades Ethiopia, 312, 314, 315–16
    Rome-Berlin-Tokyo Axis, 332
    attacks France, 342
    surrenders (1943), 374
    peace treaty and, 396

Jackson, Andrew, 51, 52, 57, 89
    Florida and, 57
    Texas and, 89, 90, 93–94
    California and, 100

Jackson, Robert, 343
Jameson raid, 160
Japan, 162
    early contacts with, 116, 119–20
    increasing U.S. interest in, 120
    Perry in, 120
    Perry's treaty, 120–21
    treaties with other powers, 121
    Townsend Harris in, 122–23
    isolation ended, 123–24
    Meiji Restoration in, 124
    fights China, 163
    Korea and, 163–64, 215
    Philippines and, 183
    fights Russia, 212–16
    Gentlemen's agreement, 215–16
    U.S. immigration and, 215–18
    Root-Takahira agreement and,
        217–18
    Manchuria and, 229, 277, 287,
        300–309
    German islands and, 251, 256,
        278–80, 285
    pressures China, 277–78, 280–81
    Washington Conference
        (1921–1922), 277, 278
    Yap and, 278–80
    naval rivalry with U.S., 280–83, 284,
        286–88
    in Siberia, 280, 285
    alliance with Great Britain, 281–82,
        284
    leaves Shantung, 284
    London Naval Conference (1930)
        and, 286–87, 301
    immigration from, 300
    Open Door and, 307–9
    China incident and, 332–34
    "New Order" and, 335–36
    Panay incident, 335
    in prelude to Pearl Harbor, 348–49
    joins Germany and Italy, 349–60
    attacks Pearl Harbor, 357–60
    surrenders (1945), 381–82
    (post-1945), 425, 426–27, 441–46
    peace treaty, 440–41
    admitted to U.N., 441
    Russia and, 441–42
    U.S. policy towards, 441–46
    China and, 442
    signs nuclear nonproliferation
        treaty, 445
Jarring, Gunnar, 494, 496, 497
Jarvis Island, 126
Jay, John, 14, 16, 25, 28, 32, 35
    peace negotiations and, 17–19
Jay Treaty (1794), 6, 32–34, 36
Jefferson, Thomas, 16, 28, 29, 30, 47,
    61, 66, 68, 130
    plans Louisiana Purchase, 38, 40–42
    and British friction, 48–49
    policy toward revolutionary France,
        66
    Cuba and, 130
Jews, in Germany, 309, 310, 375
Jiménez, Marcos Perez, 506

Johnson, Andrew, 145, 152
Johnson, Hiram, 262, 270, 296
Johnson, Lyndon B., 9, 416, 465
    seeks détente with Russia, 416
    Vietnam and, 465, 468–73
    Six-Day War and, 492, 493–94
    Panama riots and, 513–14
    Santo Domingo and, 514–17
Johnson Act (1934), 296, 300
Johnson-Clarendon convention
    (1869), 142
Joint Commissions in arbitration,
    53–54
Joint U.S.-Japan Committee on Trade
    and Economic Affairs, 442
Jones, Anson, 93, 94–95
Jordan, 482, 489–90, 491, 492, 493
    Six-Day War and, 493
    expels Palestinian terrorists, 496–97
Joseph II, of Austria, 15
Journal of Commerce, 174, 181
Juarez, Benito, 127, 153, 154
Jusserand, J. J., 235

Kádar, János, 411
Kalakaua, David, 150
Kansas-Nebraska Act, 132
Katsura, Taro, 215
Kearny, Stephen W., 107
Kearny, U.S.S., 346
Kellogg, Frank, 275–76
Kellogg-Briand Pact (1928), 274–77,
    286, 287, 302
Kennan, George F., 212, 470
Kennedy, John, F.
    Berlin crisis and, 414–15
    Laos and, 463
    Vietnam and, 465, 466–67
    Alliance for Progress and, 505,
        508–9
    Bay of Pigs invasion and, 509–11
    Cuban crisis and, 511–13
Kennedy, Robert F., 473
Kerrsarge, U.S.S., 140
Khrushchev, Nikita S.
    "peaceful coexistence," policy of,
        410
    Berlin crisis and, 412–13, 414–15
    proposes disarmament, 413
    Kennedy and, 414–15
    U-2 incident and, 414
    Berlin Wall and, 415
    seeks détente with U.S., 416
    Laos and, 463
    Cuban crisis and, 510, 511–13
Kiesinger, Kurt Georg, 422
Kim Il Sung, 430, 435, 437, 438
Kimmel, Husband E., 358, 359
King, E. J., 346
King, Mackenzie, 345
King George's War, 11
King William's War, 11
Kipling, Rudyard, 293
Kishi, Nobusuke, 443

Kissinger, Henry, 418, 437–38, 520, 526
  meets Chou En-lai, 454
  negotiates peace treaty with North Vietnam, 479
  Yom Kippur War and, 498, 499, 500
Knox, Frank, 343
Knox, Henry, 28
Knox, Philander C., 218, 223, 260, 262
  dollar diplomacy and, 198–99, 218–20
Komura, Jutaro, 217
Konoye, Fumimaro, 349, 353–54
Korea, 425
  early contacts with, 116, 163–64
  Japan and, 215
  war in, 404, 430–38
  (post-1945), 430–38
  U.S. withdrawal of troops from, 533
Korean War, 9, 404, 405, 430–38
Kossuth, Louis, 124
Kosygin, Alexy, 416, 451, 493, 498
Kruger, Paul, 160
Kuang Hsü, Emperor of China, 209
Kubitschek, Juscelino, 508
Kun, Béla, 253
Kurusua, Saburo, 355, 356
Kuwait, 482
Ky, Nguyen Cao, 468, 475

Lackawanna, U.S.S., 147
Laconia, S.S. 243–44
Lagoda (ship), 120
Laird rams, 141
Lake Champlain, 53
  battle of, 51
Lake Huron, 54, 74
Lake of the Woods, 33, 54, 55, 56, 71, 74, 75, 76
Lake Superior, 56, 76
La Luzerne, Franch Minister, 15
Lamas, Carlos Saavedra, 323–24
Lansing, Robert, 200, 232, 235, 238, 249, 251, 262–63, 277
Lansing-Ishii agreement, 284
Laos, 458, 460, 461, 462–64, 471, 475
Larkin, Thomas O., 99, 100–101, 106
Latin America. *See also* Dollar diplomacy; Inter-American Conferences; Pan-Americanism
  Communism in, 502, 504, 505–7, 509–20
  (post-1945), 502–24, 529–31
  U.S. economic aid to, 507–9
  U.S. Pan Americanism and, 156–57, 161
  Venezuela crisis (1895), 158–62
  revolutions in, 65
  recognized, 65–66
  (in the 1920's), 320–22
  in World War II, 346, 368–69
Latvia, 365
Laurens, Henry, 16
Laurier, Wilfrid, 293

Laval, Pierre, 315, 370
League of Armed Neutrality, 15
League of Nations, 61, 253–55
  Senate opposes, 260–68
  U.S. isolationism and, 261, 269–70
  defeated by Congress, 265–68
  campaign of 1920 and, 269–70
  U.S. relations with, 270–71
  Japan and, 302–7
  disarmament and, 310
  Italy's invasion of Ethiopia and, 315–16
  condemns Japan, 334
League to Enforce Peace, 272
Leahy, William D., 370
Lebanon, 482, 489–90, 500
Leclerc, Victor E., 39
Le Duc Tho, 479
Lee, Arthur, 12
Lee, Robert E., 108
Lend-Lease Act (1941), 9, 344
Lenin, Nikolai, 252
Leopard (frigate), 46
Lesseps, Ferdinand de, 147
Levinson, Salmon O., 274
Lewis and Clark expedition, 54, 81
Lexington, U.S.S., 283
Li Hung-Chang, 163
Liaotung peninsula, 163, 164, 301
Libya, 396
Life (periodical), 416
Liliuokalani, Lydia, 151–52
Lincoln, Abraham, 134, 136, 152
  British neutrality and, 136
  privateering and, 136–37
  Trent affair and, 139
Lindbergh, Charles A., 341
Linn, Lewis F., 83
Lippmann, Walter, 470
Lithuania, 365
Litvinov, Maxim, 340, 365
Liverpool, Lord, 68
Livingston, Robert R., 40, 41, 42
Locarno Pact of 1925, 312
Lodge, Henry Cabot, 169, 170–71, 174, 180, 260, 261, 273
  Alaska boundary and, 226
  not sent to Paris, 250
  Round Robin and, 254
  opposes Versailles Treaty, 254–55, 260–68
  Fourteen Points of, 263–65
Lodge, Henry Cabot, Jr., 454, 467, 474
Logan, George, 37
Logan Act (1799), 37
Lôme, Dupuy de, 175
Lon Nol, General, 477
London Economic Conference (1933), 296–97
London Naval Conference
  (1908–1909), 235
  (1930), 286–87, 301
  (1935), 287
London Naval Treaty (1930), 301
London *Times,* 140
Long, Breckinridge, 385

Lopez, Narciso, 131
Louisiana, 56
Louisiana Purchase, 6, 37, 38–44
Louis XVI, King of France, 12, 21, 28, 29
Louis XVIII, King of France, 64
L'Ouverture, Toussaint, 39, 200
Lowell, Abbott Lawrence, 270
Lowell, James Russell, 3, 110
Loyalists, 34
Lusitania, S.S., 239
Lyons, Lord, 139
Lytton Commission, and Japan, 304, 305, 306–7

McAdoo, William G., 235
MacArthur, Douglas, 362, 431
  in Japan, 426
  Korean War and, 431–32
  recalled, 433
McCarthy, Eugene, 473
McCone, John A., 511
McCoy, Frank R., 306
Mac Donald, Ramsay, 6, 287
Machado, Gerardo, 325
Mackenzie, Alexander Slidell, 105, 108
McKinley, William, 179, 249
  Hawaii and, 172
  shuns war with Spain, 175
  seeks peaceful settlement, 177
  taxes Philippines, 180–86
  re-elected, 188
  on Cuba, 195
McLane, Louis, 85, 86, 87
McLane, R. M., 127
McNamara, Robert S., 472
Macon's Bill No. 2 (1810), 48
Madero, Francisco I., 202
Madison, James, 42, 43, 48, 50, 68
Magsaysay, Ramón, 460
Mahan, Alfred Thayer, 168, 169, 170, 172, 180
Maine, 15, 71
  boundaries of, 54, 71–76
Maine, U.S.S., 175–76, 177
Malaya, 426
Malaysia, 426
Malenkov, Georgi M., 410
Malik, Yakov A., 431, 433
Manchuria, 278, 380, 427, 428, 433
  Japan and, 229, 277, 287, 300–309
Mandates
  and Fourteen Points, 255–56
  for Yap, 278–80
Manifest destiny, 86, 124, 147
  Mexican War and, 109–11
  Cuba and, 131
  (post-1890), 168–71
  racism and, 168–69
Mansfield, Mike, 421, 470
Mao Tse-tung, 393, 428, 429, 450
Marcy, William L., 125, 126, 131–32, 136
Marcy-Elgin Treaty (1854), 125

Maritime Canal Company, 148, 191
Marshall, George C., 362, 398, 400, 503
in China, 428
Marshall, Humphrey, 122
Marshall, John, 36
Marshall Plan, 9, 400–401, 402
Point Four and, 401
Mason, James M., 138, 139, 141
Mason, John Y., 132
Matsu, 447–48
Matsuoka, Yosuke, 349–50, 352, 354
Maximilian, Emperor (Mexico), 127, 154–56
Meighen, Arthur, 281
Mein Kampf (My Struggle) (Hitler), 310
Meir, Golda, 494
Mellon, Andrew W., 261
Memorandum on the Monroe Doctrine (Clark), 322, 323
Merritt, Wesley, 179
Mesabi range, 76
Metternich, Klemens Wenzel N. L. von, 64, 70
Mexican War
causes, 96–98
outbreak of, 104–5
battles of, 106, 107–9
U.S. objectives of, 106–7
peace negotiations, 105, 108–9
Manifest Destiny and, 109–11
slavery and, 110–11
peace treaty, 111–14
Mexico, 65, 67, 71, 86
Texas and, 89
Texas revolt, 89–90
recognizes Texan independence, 94–95
resents annexation of Texas, 96, 97
U.S. claims on, 96, 98, 102
terminates relations with U.S., 97
California and, 99
fights U.S., 104–5
Napoleon III and, 153–56
Maximilian in, 154
Wilson's troubles with, 202–7
Pious Fund controversy (1902), 224
expropriation of foreign holdings in, 327–31
Middle East. *See also individual countries;* Arab-Israeli conflict
oil, 281, 482
Arab-Israeli conflict, 416
U.S. and, 416
Great Britain and, 481, 484
Russia and, 482, 485, 489, 490
U.S. policy in, 482–501
Suez Canal crisis, 485–89
(post-1945), 531–32
Middleton, Henry, 63
Midway Island, 147
Miki, Takeo, 443
Mikolajczyk, Stanislaw, 377, 380
Miller, Douglas, 312
Minister, rank of, 2
Minnesota, 76

Missiles, rocket-propelled. *See specific types*
Mississippi River, 23, 35
navigation rights on, 14, 25, 32, 33, 35
Missouri, U.S.S., 382
Missouri Compromise, 93
Mollet, Guy, 486
Molotov, Vyacheslav M., 340, 366, 372, 374, 396
Moncada, Francisco de, 321
Mondale, Walter, 528, 531, 534
Monroe, James, 50, 56, 57, 59, 61
minister in France, 35-36
Louisiana Purchase and, 41–42
neutral rights treaty and, 48–49
issues Monroe Doctrine, 62
Latin America and, 65–67, 68–69
Monroe Doctrine, 61–62, 129, 195, 200, 316, 369. *See also* Roosevelt Corollary to Monroe Doctrine
proclaimed, 62
reaction to, 69–71
California and, 101–2
invoked by Polk in Mexican dispute, 101–2
Clayton-Bulwer Treaty and, 129, 130
canal schemes and, 148
Pan Americanism and, 152–62
imperialism vs., 185, 187
League of Nations and, 254
Kellogg-Briand Pact and, 277
Roosevelt corollary reversed, 321–22
Clark memorandum and, 322
continentalized, 325–27
United Nations Charter and, 389
communism in Latin America and, 505, 513
Montevideo Conference (1933), 323, 325–37
Morales, Spanish intendant at New Orleans, 40
Morgan, J. P., and Company, 234, 288
Morgan, John T., 191
Morgenthau, Hans J., 407, 470
Morgenthau, Henry, Jr., 373, 375
Morgenthau Plan, 373–74
Morocco
U.S. treaties with, 21, 28
crises (pre-1914), 229–30
U.S. and, 230–31
Morrow, Dwight W., 329
Moscow Conference (1943), 374
Moscow Declaration on General Security (1943), 368
Most favored nation principle, 34
Multiple independently targetable reentry vehicle (MIRV), 417
Murphy, Robert, 490
Murphy-Weygand agreement, 370
Murray, William Vans, 37
Mussolini, Benito, 309–10, 312, 316, 338

Mussolini, Benito (*cont.*)
forms axis, 332
attacks France, 342

Nagumo, Admiral, 357, 359
Nagy, Imre, 411–12
Namibia, 534
Nanking, Treaty of (1842), 117, 119
Napoleon Bonaparte, 37, 38, 42, 43, 52, 64, 65
covets Louisiana, 39–40
sells Louisiana, 41
"Continental System" of, 47
Napoleon III
and U.S. Civil War, 134
Mexico and, 153–56
Nasser, Gamal Abdel, 485–89, 491, 492, 495
National Liberation Front (NLF), of South Vietnam, 465, 473, 474, 475
National Munitions Control Board, U.S., 315
National Security Act (1947), 5
National Security Council, U.S., 5
Naturalization, 46
Navy, U.S.
expansion of, 169–70, 171, 190
World cruise of, 217
in World War I, 241
(post-1919), 280–81, 282–83
Nazism, anti-Semitism and, 309, 310
Neebish Rapids, 71, 75
Netherlands, 342
U.S. treaties with, 21, 28
Neutral rights, 32, 35, 52
during Napoleonic wars, 28–30, 37–38
War of 1812 and, 45–53
and duties, 47
Civil War and, 134, 136, 140–41
World War I, 234–39
Fourteen Points and, 255
in the 1930's, 314–18
Neutral trade, 37
Neutrality, 61. *See also* Isolationism; Nonentanglement, nonintervention
armed, 15
(1793), 27–33
(1905), 230
(1914), 233
World War I, 234–39
(post-1919), 313–14
in the 1930's, 314–18
U.S. abandons, 339–47
Latin America and, 346
World War II and, 346–47
Neutrality Acts
(1794), 30
(1939), 342, 368
modified, 346–47
New Orleans, 40, 41
New Orleans *Picayune,* 111
New Panama Canal Company, 192, 193

New York City, 15
New York *Evening Post,* 111
New York *Herald,* 111
New York *Journal,* 173, 174, 175, 176
New York *Morning News,* 86
New York Peace Congress (1907), 221
New York Peace Society, 221
New York *Sun,* 111, 174
New York Times, 241, 275, 321, 428, 470, 471, 474, 475, 515
New York *Tribune,* 174, 181
New York *World,* 173, 174
Ngo Dinh Diem, 458, 460, 462, 464, 466–68
Ngo Dinh Nhu, 462, 466
Nguyen Thi Binh, Mme, 475
Nicaragua
    canal route and, 129, 147, 148, 191, 192, 199
    U.S. protectorate, 194–95, 198–200
    dollar diplomacy in, 198–200
    U.S. intervenes in, 320–21
Niles' Register, 111
Nine-Power Treaty (1922), 283, 302, 306, 308, 334
Nixon, Richard M., 9, 416, 437
    seeks détente with Russia, 416–18, 424
    Okinawa and, 445
    visits China, 445, 452–55
    recognition of China and, 453, 455
    Vietnam War and, 474–80
    orders invasion of Cambodia, 477–78
    Yom Kippur War and, 498
    in Latin America, 506
    Chile and, 518
Nomura, Kichisaburo, 351
Nonbeligerency, 341
Noncolonization, principles of, 62–64, 70, 101
Nonentanglement, nonintervention.
    See also Isolationism; Neutrality
    Washington's Farewell Address and, 36
    Monroe Doctrine and, 64–65, 69, 70
    in World War I, 245
    Spanish civil war and, 317–18
    in Latin America (post-1945), 504, 506, 517
Nonintervention. *See*
    Nonentanglement,
    nonintervention
Nonrecognition, Hoover-Stimson
    Doctrine and, 305, 306
Norstad, General Lauris, NATO
    Supreme Commander, 415
North, Lord, 16
North American Air Defense
    Command (NORAD), 521
North Atlantic Treaty Organization
    (NATO), 389, 403–6, 529
    de Gaulle and, 419–24
North Vietnam, 426. *See also* Vietnam
North West Company (Montreal), 55, 81

Northeast Fisheries Dispute (1909), 226–28
Northwest Territory, 31, 34
Norway, 342
Nuclear Nonproliferation Treaty (1969), 417
Nuclear Test Ban Treaty (1963), 408, 416–17
Nye, Gerald P., 314

Obregón, Álvaro, 205, 328
Okinawa, 444–45
Olney, Richard, 158, 159–62
Olney-Pauncefote Treaty (1897), 161
Onis, Luis de, 56
Open Door, 122
    colonial origins of, 116, 122
    threatened, 164–65
    Japan menaces, 350
    (post-1945), 427
Operation Pan America, 508
Opium War (1839–1842), 117
Ordinance of, 1787, 31
Oregon, 63, 70
    conflicting claims to, 54
    Asiatic trade and, 81
    colonized by Americans, 81, 83
    crisis with Great Britain over, 81–89
Oregon, U.S.S., 172, 191
Oregon Trail, 99
Oregon Treaty (1818), 7–8; (1827), 8
Organization of American States
    (OAS), 502, 503, 507, 515, 516, 519, 521
Organization of Latin American
    Solidarity (OLAS), 519
Orlando, Vittorio, 251, 253, 257
Ostend Manifesto, 132
O'Sullivan, John L., 86, 131
Oswald, Richard, 16, 17, 18, 19

Pacific Charter (SEATO), 460
Page, Walter Hines, 231, 233
Paine, Thomas, 11
Pakenham, Richard, 84
Pakistan, 426, 460, 484
Palestine. *See also* Israel
    partitioned by U.N., 481
Palestine Liberation Organization
    (PLO), 490, 500
Palmerston, Lord, 77, 79, 88, 135
Pan American Union, 158, 503, 521
Pan Americanism. *See also*
    Inter-American Conferences;
    Latin America.
    Monroe Doctrine and, 152–62
    beginnings of, 156–58
Panama
    favored for canal, 191–93
    U.S. leases zone, 191–94
    U.S. protectorate, 194–95
    protectorate ended, 325
    riots in, 513–14

Panama Canal. *See also* Isthmian Canal
    begun, 148
    planned, 191
    opened, 194
    tolls problem, 228
    termination of U.S. jurisdiction over, 520, 529–30
Panama Canal Company, 191
Panama Canal Treaty (1978), 530
Panama Congress of 1826, 156
Panay, U.S.S., 335
Paper blockades, 45, 47–48
Paraguay, 326
Paredes, Mariano, President of
    Mexico, 97, 103, 104
Paris, Treaty of (1763), 11, 13
    (1782), 19–21
Paris Peace Conference (1919), 6
Park, Chung Hee, 435, 533
Parker, Peter, 119, 121, 125
Pauncefote, Julian, 191
Payne-Aldrich tariff (1909), 292
Peace conferences. *See specific*
    conferences; Arbitration;
    Inter-American conferences;
    Treaties
Peace of Tipitapa, 321
Pearl Harbor, attacked by Japan, 357–60
Pearson, Lester, 522
Pena y Peña, Mexican Foreign
    Minister, 102, 103, 109
Perdido River, 42, 56, 59
Perkins, Dexter, 64, 70, 154
Permanent Court of Arbitration, 222, 224, 226–28, 272
Permanent Court of International
    Justice, 271–73
    U.S. and, 273–74
Perón, Juan D., 503
Perry, Matthew Calbraith, 120–21, 125
Pershing, John J., 205, 206, 245
Pescadores Islands, 163, 447
Pétain, Marshal, 370
Peterhoff (ship), 138
Philippines, 179, 200, 460
    U.S. acquires, 179, 180–84
Phoumi Nosavan, Prince, 463
Pickering, Timothy, 37
Pierce, Franklin, 124, 126, 130
    Perry and, 120
    Hawaii and, 126
    Gadsden Purchase and, 126–27
    Cuba and, 131–32
Pickney, C. C., 36
Pickney, Thomas, 34–35
Pickney's Treaty (1795), 34–35, 40
Pinkney, William, 47
Pinochet, Augusto, 518
Pious Fund controversy, 224
Pitt, William, the Younger, 22
Plan of 1776, 13, 27, 28, 30, 32, 37
Platt Amendment, 195–96, 199, 201
    abrogated, 325
Platt, Orville H., 179, 185, 195
Poinsett, Joel R., 89

Point Four Program, 401
Poland, 253, 257, 376, 378, 392, 400
    threatened by Germany, 338–39
    invaded by Germany, 340
    London exile regime, 377
    boundaries, 377, 380, 396
    rejects Marshall Plan, 400
    revolt in, 410
Polignac, Prince de, French
        Ambassador in London, 69
Polk, James K., 91, 92, 96, 129, 130,
        160
    Oregon and, 84–89
    Texas and, 92–93, 95, 96, 98
    California and, 96, 98–105
    limits Monroe Doctrine to North
        America, 101–2
    sends envoy to Mexico, 102–3
    prepares for war, 103–4
    declares war, 104–5
    peace negotiations and, 105, 108–11
    Cuba and, 130, 131
Popular Movement for the Liberation
        of Angola, 520
Port Arthur, 427
Porter, Peter B., 49, 76
Portsmouth Conference (1905),
        214–15
Portugal, 419
Potsdam
    Declaration, 381–82
    Conference (1945), 394–96
Powers, Francis Gary, 414
Pravda, 454
President, U.S., powers of, in foreign
        affairs under Constitution, 1, 7,
        9–10
Prevention of Nuclear War (1973), 418
Privateers, 27, 30, 33, 37, 66
    during American Revolution, 22
    in U.S. Civil War, 136–37
Proctor, Redfield, 176
Propaganda, World War I, 233–34
Protectorates. *See* Cuba; Haiti;
        Nicaragua; Panama; Santo
        Domingo.
Prussia, U.S., treaties with, 21
Public opinion, U.S.
    (post-1783), 28
    in Venezuela crisis (1895), 160
    (post-1890), 168–71
    on war with Spain, 173–77
    anti-Japanese (1906–1907), 216–17
    on World War I, 232–34
    World War II and, 347
    Vietnam War, 469–71, 473, 476–77,
        478
    Arab-Israeli conflict and, 500
Pueblo, U.S.S., 435, 437
Puerto Rico, 78, 180, 181, 182, 200
    ceded to U.S., 184
Pulitzer, Joseph, 173

Quadripartite treaty (1970), 423
Quadruple Alliance, 64, 65, 69, 71

Quebec Conference (1943), 373
Queen Anne's War, 11
Quemoy, 447–48
Quitman, John A., 131

Raccoon (ship), 55
Racism
    Manifest Destiny and, 168–69
    League of Nations and, 261
Randolph, Edmund, 28, 29, 32
Regan, Ronald, 520
Reciprocal Trade Agreements Act
        (1934), 8, 298
Reciprocity. *See also* Tariff
    treaty with Canada, 125
    treaty with Hawaii, 150
    Taft's with Canada, 293
    Trade Agreements Act (1934),
        297–99
Reid, Whitelaw, 182
Reparations
    demanded by Allies, 249, 289–92
    at Paris, 258–59
    commission, 259, 264, 271, 290, 291
    war debts and, 288–89, 291, 294–95
    suspended, 295–96
    Germany (World War II), 378, 380,
        396, 398
Republican Party, expansionism and,
        171–72
Resolution 242 (1967), 494, 499
Reston, James, 519
Restook War (1838–1839), 72
Reuben James, U.S.S., 346
Revolution. *See* American Revolution
Reynolds, William, 147
Rhee, Syngman, 430, 434, 435
Rhineland, 258
Rhineland occupied, 312
Rhodesia, 534
Ribbentrop, Joachim von, 340
Richardson, James O., 359
Right of deposit at New Orleans, 35,
        38, 40, 56
Rio Grande, 56, 97–98, 108
Rio Pact (1947), 403
River Nueces, 97
Robinson, Joseph T., 329
Robles, Marco A., 514
Rochambeau, Comte de, 14, 15
Rockefeller, Nelson, 389
Rockhill, W. W., 208
Rockingham, Marquis of, 16
Rodrigue Hortalez et Compagnie, 12
Rogers, William, 494, 495
Rogers Act (1924), 3
    as amended, 1963, 3–4
Rome-Berlin-Tokyo-Axis, 332,
        349–50
Roosevelt, Franklin D., 6, 8, 311, 394
    London Economic Conference and,
        296–97
    trade agreements and, 297–99
    Japan and, 307
    disarmament and, 311

Roosevelt, Franklin D. (*cont.*)
    neutrality revision and, 314–16, 318,
        339–47
    Good Neighbor Policy of, 322–31
    China incident and, 333–34
    "Quarantine" speech of, 334
    Munich crisis and, 338
    for intervention, 340–41, 347
    Neutrality Act (1939) and, 342
    re-elected, 343
    lend-lease and, 343–44
    Atlantic Charter and, 345
    wins third term, 350
    global strategy of, 350, 355
    places embargo on Japan, 350
    Konoye conference and, 355–56
    Hitler-first strategy, 362–63, 368
    plans war strategy with Churchill,
        362–64
    Russia and, 365
    war and post-war aims of, 371–80
    Four Freedoms of, 372
    German anti-Semitism and, 375
    wins fourth term, 377
    Yalta Conference and, 378–80, 387
    United Nations and, 384–85
    Indochina and, 457–58
Roosevelt, Theodore, 130, 169, 187,
        195, 224, 251
    Spanish-American War and, 169,
        172, 179, 180–81
    proclaims corollary to Monroe
        Doctrine, 195
    international police power, doctrine
        of, 202
    Russo-Japanese War and, 214–16
    Pious Fund dispute, 224
    Alaska boundary dispute, 224–26
    Moroccan question and, 230–31
Roosevelt Corollary of Monroe
        Doctrine, 195, 196–97, 199,
        321–22
Root, Elihu, 195, 196, 217–18, 226,
        232, 250, 270, 273
    arbitration and, 223
Root-Takahira agreement (1908),
        217–18
Round Robin (1919), 254
Rule of 1756, 30–31, 33, 47, 52, 137
Rumania, 253, 257, 338, 377, 392, 393,
        396
Rush, Richard, 53, 55, 56, 63, 67, 68,
        69, 70
Rush-Bagot Agreement (1817), 53
Rusk, Dean, 449, 517
Russell, Jonathan, 51
Russell, Lord, 135, 136, 137, 139, 140,
        141
Russia, 229
    in Armed Neutrality, 15
    Monroe Doctrine, 63–64, 66–69
    China and, 122
    sells Alaska, 146–47
    Korea and, 163, 164, 430
    Open Door and, 208–9
    fights Japan, 212–16

Russia (*cont.*)
  revolution (1917), 247
  World War I and, 249–48
  peace negotiations, World War I
    and, 252–53
  signs pact with Germany, 340
  Germany invades, 345
  attacked by Germany, 352
  signs pact with Japan, 352
  U.S. and, before and during World
    War II, 364–67
  expelled from League of Nations,
    365
  lend-lease for, 365
  recognized by U.S., 365
  Atlantic Charter and, 372
  Great Britain (World War II),
    376–77, 392
  enters war against Japan, 382
  vs. U.S. in United Nations, 390–93
  Cold War and, 391–408
  German policy, 393–96, 397–98,
    401–3
  German reparations and, 398
  Marshall Plan and, 400, 402
  Berlin blockade, 402–3
  explodes first atomic bomb, 405
  begins arms race with U.S., 406–8
  first hydrogen bomb, 408
  first rocket-propelled satellites, 408
  ends Austrian occupation, 410
  post-Stalin internal changes in, 410
  suppresses Hungary, 411–12
  Berlin crisis and, 412–13, 414–15
  U-2 incident, 414
  détente with U.S., 415–19
  in Middle East, 416
  Vietnam War and, 416
  suppresses Czechoslovakia, 421
  China and, 427–28, 429, 451
  Japan and, 441, 442
  Vietnam War and, 475
  Middle East and, 482, 485, 489, 490,
    497
  Six-Day War and, 493–97
  Yom Kippur War and, 499–500
  Cuban crisis and, 511–13
  Arab-Israeli conflict and, 531
  in Africa, 534
Russian American Company, 63
Russo-Japanese War, 212–16
Ryukyu Island, 444–46

Saar Valley, 251
Sabine River, 59
Sacasa, Juan B., 320, 321, 328, 329
Sadat, Anwar el, 497, 499, 531–32
St. Clair, Arthur, 31
St. Croix River, 33, 53, 54, 72
St. John River, 72, 74
St. Lawrence River, 23, 54, 72, 75, 125
St. Louis River, 76
St. Mary's River, 76
Saito, Hiroshi, 308
Sakharov, Andrei D., 526

Salisbury, Lord, 159, 160, 161, 177
Sam, Guillaume, 201
Samoa (Tutuila), 187
  controversy over, 148–49
San Antonio formula, 473
San Francisco Conference (1945),
    387–88
San Ildefonso, Treaty of (1800), 38,
    39, 42
San Jacinto (warship), 138
San Jacinto, battle of, 90
San Lorenzo. *See* Pinckney's Treaty.
Sandino, Augusto Cesar, 321
Santa Anna, Antonio Lopez de, 89, 97,
    103, 105, 107–9, 112, 126–27
Santo Domingo, 39, 130, 145, 152
  Grant's scheme for, 145–46
  Seward and, 145, 152–153
  U.S. protectorate, 194–95, 197–98,
    201–2
  U.S. intervenes in, 197–98, 320
  U.S. invades, 201–2, 514–17
Saratoga, U.S.S., 283
Sato, Eisaku, 443–44, 445, 454
Saudi Arabia, 482, 485, 489, 491, 492
Schomburgk, Robert, 158
Schurz, Carl, 172
Schuschnigg, Kurt von, 336, 337
Scott, Winfield, 51, 72, 107–9, 111
Scruggs, William L., 159
Second Neutrality Act (1936), 316
Secret Correspondence, Committee
    of, U.S., 1
Self-Determination
  Fourteen Points and, 256–58
  Yalta Conference and, 392–93
Seminole Indians, 56
Serbia, 229–30, 232
Seven Years' War, 31
Seward, William H., 79, 134, 136, 145,
    152
  foreign war scheme of, 134, 152
  privateering and, 136
  British neutrality and, 136–37
  Trent affair and, 139–40
  purchases Alaska, 146–47
  treaty with Nicaragua on transit
    rights, 147
  and Spain in Santo Domingo,
    152–53
  Maximilian and, 154–56
Seyss-Inquart, 337
Shanghai Communiqué (1971), 455
Shantung, 251, 256, 277, 278, 284
Shelburne, Lord, 16, 18, 19
Shenandoah (ship), 140, 141, 142, 143
Sherman, John, 172, 208
Shidehara, Kijuro, 285, 301, 303
Shih-k'ai, Yüan, 277
Shimonoseki, Treaty of (1895), 163
Shipping, 37
Shipping, U.S.
  neutral rights of, 27–28, 37–38,
    46–48
  Confederate, 137–38, 140–41
  World War I and, 234–39

Short, Walter C., 358, 359
Shotwell, James T., 275
Shufeldt, R. W., 163
Siberia, Japan and, 280, 285
Sihanouk, Norodom, Prince, 477
Simcoe, John Graves, 31
Simpson, George, 99
Singapore, 426
Sino-Japanese War (1894), 163–64
Six-Day War (1967), 416, 492–93
  settlement of, 493–97
Six-Power Consortium, 219
Slave trade
  abolished by U.S., 76
  right of search and, 76–78
Slavery, 124. *See also* Civil War;
    Confederate States of America
  Texas and, 90, 91, 92, 93
  Mexican War and, 110–11
Slaves, 34
Slidell, John, 102–3, 138, 139
Sloat, John D., 107
Smith, Ian D., 534
Smith, Walter Bedell, 459
Smuts, Jan Christiaan, 256
Somalia, 534
Soong, T. V., 427
Soulé, Pierre, 132
Souphanouvong, Prince, 463
South Africa, 534, 535
South Vietnam, 426. *See also* Cochin
    China; Vietnam
South-east Asia Collective Defense
    Treaty (1954), 460–62, 470
Southeast Asia Treaty Organization
    (SEATO), 460–62, 533
Southern Confederacy. *See*
    Confederate States of America
Souvanna Phouma, 463
Soviet Union. *See* Russia
Spain, 370, 371
  aids U.S., 12, 13, 14–15
  France, alliance with, 14
  and Mississippi navigation, 14, 25,
    32, 35
  recognizes U.S. independence, 21
  and Peace Treaty (1783), 23, 25
  Pinckney's Treaty with, 34–35
  Louisiana and, 38–40
  Jackson's raid and, 57
  cedes Florida, 57, 59
  Latin America and, 64–65, 66
  claims to Oregon, 81
  Cuba and, 131, 172–74
  Santo Domingo and, 152–53
  Mexico and, 153
  U.S. fights, 174–80
  loses Philippines, 180–84
  loses Puerto Rico, 184
  Morocco and, 229
  civil war in, 317–18
  in World War II, 370, 371
Spanish America. *See* Latin America
Spanish-American War
  causes, 170, 172–74
  armistice, 177

Spanish-American War (*cont.*)
  battles, 178–80
  end of, 180
  peace treaty, 184–86
Springbok (ship), 138
Sputnik, 522
Stalin, Joseph, 6, 364, 365, 366, 392,
    393, 394, 399
  war and post-war aims, 371–80
  Yalta Conference and, 378–80, 393
  at Potsdam, 394–96
  denounced, 410
  dies, 410
State, Department of, U.S., 1–5
  creation and growth of, 1–2
  functions, 1–2
  under George Washington, 2
  Foreign Service and, 4–5
State, Secretary of, U.S., 6
Stettinius, Edward R., 387
Stevens, John L., 151
Stevenson, Andrew, 77
Stilwell, Joseph W., 368, 428
Stimson, Henry L., 270, 287, 321, 343,
    355, 373, 382
  Japan crisis and, 302–5, 306
Stockton, Robert F., 107
Stoeckl, Edouard, 146
Stoph, Willi, 422
Straight, Willard, 218, 219
Strategic Arms Limitation Talks
    (SALT), 418
  SALT II, 526
Strong, Josiah, 168
Submarine-launched ballistic missiles
    (SLBMs), 418
Sudan, 484
Suez Canal, 484
  nationalized by Egypt, 485–89
Sugar Island, 75
Sukarno, 426
Sumner, Charles, 143, 146
  Alabama claims and, 142
Sun Yat Sen, 448
Suñer, Serrano, 371
Supreme Allied Commander, Europe
    (SACEUR), 406
Supreme Headquarters, Allied Powers
    in Europe (SHAPE), 405
Sussex (ship), 240, 242, 243
Suzuki, Kantaro, 381, 382
Sweden, 370
  in Armed Neutrality, 15
  U.S. treaties with, 21, 28
Switzerland, 370
Syria, 482, 485, 490, 492
  Six-Day War and, 493

Tack, Juan Antonio, 520
Taft, William H., 6, 9, 203, 215, 218,
    250, 266, 293
  Caribbean and, 198–200
  Far East and, 218–20
  arbitration treaties, 223–24

Taiping Rebellion (1851–1865), 119,
    122
Taiwan. *See* Formosa
Takahira, Kogoro, 217–18
Talleyrand, Charles M., 36, 37, 41, 42
Tariff, U.S., *See also specific tariffs:*
    Reciprocity
  (of 1890), 165
  (of 1894), 165
  (of 1897), 165, 292
  (post-1900), 292–94, 297–99
Taussig, E. D., 186
Taylor, Maxwell D., 465
Taylor, Zachary, 98, 103, 104, 106,
    107
Tecumseh, 49, 52
Teheran Conference (1943), 372–73,
    375, 376, 380
Teller, Henry M., 178
Teller Amendment, 178, 180, 181
Ten Years' War (1868–1878), 173
Texas, 56, 57, 59
  U.S. settlers in, 89
  independent, 89–90
  recognition of, 90
  annexation of, 90–95
  boundary dispute, 97
Thailand, 426, 460, 463
Thant, U, 469, 472, 492, 513
Théophile Declassé, 229
Thieu, Nguyen Van, 468, 474, 475,
    476, 478, 479, 480
Third Neutrality Act (1937), 318
Thornton, Edward, 111
Thoughts of Mao Tse-tung, The, 450
Thurston, Lorrin A., 151
Tientsin treaties (1858), 121–22
Tippecanoe, battle of (1811), 49
Tito, Marshal, 376, 411
Tojo, Hideki (Eiki), 354–55, 426
Tonkin Gulf Resolution, 9, 468–69,
    470
Torrijos, Omar, 514, 530
Tracy, Benjamin F., 171
Trade Expansion Act (1962), 299
Tran Thien Khiem, 475
Transcontinental Treaty (1819),
    56–59
Trans-Siberian Railway, 213
Treaties (Agreements, Conventions),
    U.S. *See also specific agreements,*
    conventions and treaties.
  general, 1, 6–9
  with France (1778), 13–14, 21, 27,
    29, 37, 38; (1800), 37–38
  with the Netherlands (1782), 21, 28
  with Sweden (1783), 21, 28
  with Indians (1784), 31; (1795), 34
  with Prussia (1785), 21
  with Morocco (1786), 21, 28; (1880),
    230
  with Great Britain (1794), 6, 32–34,
    36, 53; (1782), 19–21; (1783), 23,
    28, 31, 71–72; (1806), 47; (1814),
    5–53, 54, 55, 76; (1817), 53;
    (1818), 7, 55–56, 72–76, 78–80;

Treaties (*cont.*)
  with Great Britain (*Cont.*)
    (1827), 8; (1842), 54; (1846),
    88–89; (1850), 6, 7, 34, 38, 55,
    127–30, 148; (1871), 142–43;
    (1897), 161; (1901), 191, 228
  with Spain (1795), 34–35; (1819),
    56–59; (1898), 184–86
  with Mexico (1828), 89; (1848),
    111–14, 127; (1854), 126–27
  with China (1844), 118–19; (1858),
    122; (1868), 162; (1880), 162;
    (1943), 367
  with Colombia (1846), 129; (1903),
    193
  with Japan, (1854), 120–21; (1858),
    123; (1922), 284–85; (1951),
    440–41, 442; (1960), 443, 445
  with Canada (1854), 125
  with Russia (1867), 146–47; (1972),
    418; (1973), 418; (1976), 418
  with Nicaragua (1867), 147; (1884),
    148; (1914), 199
  with Hawaii (1875), 150
  with Samoa (1878), 148
  with Great Britain and Germany
    (1889), 149
  in 1880s, 161–62
  with Santo Domingo (1907), 198,
    320
  with Haiti (1915), 201
  Versailles (1919), 252
  with Austria (1921), 269
  Four Power (1921), 284
  with Germany (1921), 269
  with Hungary (1921), 269; (1947),
    397
  Five Power (1922), 282, 288, 306
  Nine Power (1922), 283, 302, 306,
    308 334
  Kellogg-Briand (1928), 274–77, 286,
    287, 302
  with Cuba (1934), 325
  with Panama (1936), 325; (1978),
    530
  Act of Chapultepec (1945), 502
  with Bulgaria (1947), 397
  Inter American Treaty of Mutual
    Assistance (1947), 502, 503
  with Italy (1947), 397
  Rio Treaty of Reciprocal Assistance
    (1947), 512
  with Rumania (1947), 397
  North Atlantic Pact (1949), 407
  with Austria and New Zealand
    (1951), 441
  with Philippines (1951), 441
  with South Korea (1953), 435;
    (1954), 437
  with Formosa (1954), 447
  South-east Asia Collective Defense
    (1954), 460–62, 470
  Nuclear Test Ban (1963), 408,
    416–17
  peaceful uses of outer space (1967),
    417

Treaties (*cont.*)
  Nuclear Nonproliferation (1969), 417
  Quadripartite (1970), 423
  with North Vietnam (1973), 416
Treaty concerning the Permanent Neutrality of the Panama Canal (1978), 530
Treaty of Reciprocal Assistance (1947), 512
Treaty on the Limitation of ABMs (1972), 418
Trent affair, 138–40
Trieste, 397
Trilateral Commission, 528
Tripartite Pact. *See* Rome-Berlin-Tokyo-Axis
Triple Alliance, 228
Triple Entente, 229
Trist, Nicholas P., 108
Trotsky, Leon, 364
Trudeau, Pierre Elliott, 419, 523, 524
Trujillo, Rafael, 507
Truman, Harry S 6, 9, 381, 382, 392, 394
  Cold War and, 392
  at Potsdam, 394–96
  aid to Greece and Turkey, 400
  Marshall Plan and, 400–401
  issues Truman Doctrine, 400
  Point Four and, 401
  Berlin airlift and, 402–3
  North Atlantic Treaty Organization and, 404–5
  sends Marshall to China, 428
  Formosa and, 430
  Korea and, 431–32
Truman Doctrine, 400
Tumulty, Joseph P., 266
Tunisia, 490
Turkey, 229–30, 399, 400, 404, 419, 484
Turner, Frederick Jackson, 170
Turner, George, 226
Tuyll, Baron, Russian minister to U.S., 63, 64
Twenty-One Demands on China, 256
Tyler, John, 74, 92, 125
  Oregon and, 83
  Texas and, 91, 92–93, 96, 97
  California and, 100
  China and, 118
Tzu Hsi, Dowager Empress, 209–10

U-2 incident, 414
Ulam, Adam, 407
Underwood Tariff (1913), 293
Union Pacific Railroad, 145
United Arab Republic (U.A.R.), 489
United Nations (UN). *See also specialized agencies.*
  Declaration, 361, 366, 369, 372
  San Francisco Conference, 368, 387–88
  planning for, 377, 384–87

Charter, 6, 385–86, 388–90
  Economic and Social Council, 386–88, 389
  General Assembly, 386, 388, 412
  Secretariat, 386, 388
  Security Council, 386, 387, 388, 389, 390, 391
  Yalta Conference and, 386–87
  Trusteeship Council, 388, 389–90
  veto power in, 388
  accepted by U.S., 390
  U.S. vs. Russia in, 390–93
  Atomic Energy Commission, 391
  U.S. opposes admission of China to, 429, 449–50
  Korean War, 430, 431–33
  partitions Palestine, 481
  Palestine Conciliation Commission, 484
  Relief and Works Agency for Palestine Refugees (UNRWA), 482
  Suez Canal crisis and, 486, 488
  Emergency Force for Palestine, 488
  Emergency Force (UNEF), 492, 499
  Six-Day War and, 493–97
  Resolution 242 (1967), 494, 499
  Yom Kippur War and, 499–500
United Nations Educational, Scientific and Cultural Organization (UNESCO), 389
Upshur, Abel P., 90

Van Buren, Martin
  Canadian revolt and, 78–80
  Texas and, 90, 91
Vance, Cyrus R., 526, 532
Vandenberg, A. H., 387, 388
Vanderbilt, Cornelius, 129
Venezuela, 67
  Great Britain and, 158–62
  1902 dispute, 196–97
Vergennes, Charles Gravier, 12, 13, 15, 16, 17
  favors Americans, 13
  discussions with Adams, 15
  on U.S. boundaries, 16, 17
Versailles, Treaty of, 7, 252
  debated in U.S., 254–55, 260–63
  Fourteen Points, 255–59
  accepted by Germany, 259–60
  repudiated by Germany, 311–12
Vichy, puppet government, 370–71
Viet Cong, 465, 468, 469, 471, 475, 478, 480
Viet Minh, 459, 462
Vietnam, 9, 459, 460, 462, 464
  divided, 459–60
  civil war in, 464–65
  U.S. and, 533
Vietnam War, 416
  prelude to, 457–65
  U.S. and, 465–80
  stalemated, 471
  peace negotiations, 472–75

Vietnam War (*cont.*)
  "Vietnamizing," 476–77
  peace treaty signed, 479
  U.S. costs for, 479
Villa, Francisco, 205
Virgin Islands, 145
Vorster, John, 534

Wachusett, U.S.S., 140
Wakatsuki, Premier, 301, 303
Wake Island, 186
Walker, Robert J., 110
Walker, William, 129
Wall Street Journal, 176
Walsh, James E., 351
Wang, Ching-wei, 336
Wanghia, Treaty of (1844), 118–19
War hawks (1812), 49
War of 1812
  causes, 45–50
  declared, 50
  course and results, 50–53
War Industries Board, U.S., 245
War Powers Act (1973), 9
War Refugee Board, U.S. 375
Warnke, Paul C., 526
Warsaw Pact, 410, 411
Washington, George, 12, 15, 31, 35
  proclaims neutrality, 28–29
  Jay's Treaty and, 32
  Farewell Address, 61
Washington, Treaty of (1871), 142
Washington, U.S.S., 201
Washington Disarmament Conference (1921–1922), 277–78, 285–86
Washington Pòst, 470
Wayne, "Mad" Anthony, 31, 32, 34
Webster, Daniel, 74, 91, 112, 118, 120, 124, 125
  Ashburton negotiations and, 74–76
  Caroline affair and, 79–80
  Oregon and, 83, 87
  Hawaii and, 125
Webster-Ashburton Treaty (1842), 54, 72–76, 78–80
Welles, Sumner, 323, 325, 386
Wellington, Duke of, 52
Wessin y Wessin, Elias, 515
West, the, 33
  controlling, after independence, 22–25
  boundaries, 23–25
  Jay's Treaty and, 33–34
  Pinckney's Treaty and, 34–35
  Indian problem in, 49
  transportation to, 126
Western European Union (W.E.U.), 406, 410
West Germany, *See* Germany
Westmoreland, William C., 471
Weyler, Valeriano, 173, 175
Whig Party
  Oregon and, 84, 87
  Texas and, 91–92

Whig Party (*cont.*)
　Mexican War and, 105
　Cuba and, 131
White, Andrew D., 183
White, Henry, 249, 250, 260
White, William Allen, 341
Wilkes, Charles, 99, 138–39, 186
Wilkie, Wendell L., 343
Wilkinson, James, 25
Willis, Albert S., 152
Wilmot Proviso, 110
Wilson, Henry Lane, 203
Wilson, Woodrow, 6, 7, 62, 221, 228,
　289, 384
　Caribbean and, 199, 200–207
　intervenes in Mexico, 202–7
　Latin American policies of, 206–7
　Panama Canal tolls and, 228
　proclaims U.S. neutrality in World
　　War I, 233
　turns pro-ally, 235, 241
　peace efforts, 240–41
　Fourteen Points, 246–48, 250
　negotiates armistice, 248–49
　goes to Paris, 249–50
　names peace commission, 249–50
　negotiates peace, 250–51
　at Paris Conference, 250–53
　League of Nations and, 253–68
　appeals to people, 263
　compromises, 265
　vetoes separate peace, 269
　election of 1920 and, 269–70
Wilson-Gorman tariff (1894), 165, 173
Wohlstetter, Roberta, 358
Wood, Leonard, 195

Wood, Robert E., 341
Woodford, Stewart L., 177
World Court. *See* Permanent Court of
　International Justice.
World Health Organization, 389
World War Foreign Debt Commission,
　289, 295
World War I
　events leading to, 228–30
　efforts at prevention of, 231
　American opinion and, 232–34
　beginning of, 232
　U.S. neutrality in, 233
　U.S. economy and, 234–35
　submarine warfare in, 237–39,
　　242–43
　Lusitania crisis, 239
　U.S. peace efforts in, 240–41, 242
　U.S. enters, 243–44
　armistice, 248–49
　peace negotiations, 248–60
　Treaty of Versailles, 252
　U.S. adopts peace treaties, 269
World War II
　outbreak of, 340
　Italy attacks France, 342
　France surrenders, 342
　U.S. rearms, 342–43
　U.S. enters, 342–47
　Germany attacks Russia, 345
　Germany invades Russia, 352
　Germany and Italy declare war on
　　U.S., 357
　Japan attacks Pearl Harbor, 357–60
　post-war planning, 371–80
　Italy surrenders, 374

World War II (*cont.*)
　Germany surrenders, 381
　Japan surrenders, 381–82
World Zionist Organization, 481
Wriston, Henry M., 5

X, Y, Z affair, 36
Xuan Thuy, 473

Yalta Conference (1945), 376
　Germany, treatment of, 377–78
　Poland and Liberated Europe, 378
　Far East War and, 378–79
　critique of, 379–80
　Cold War and, 392–93
　Germany and, 393
Yap Island, 278–80
Yemen, 485, 491, 493
Yom Kippur War (1973), 416, 497–99
　settlement, 499–500
Young, Andrew, 526, 534
Young, Owen, D., 291
Young Plan (1930), 291
Yucatán, 130
Yugoslavia, 257, 376, 377, 392, 393
　breaks with Russia, 402

Zacharias, Ellis M., 381
Zapata, Emiliano, 205
Zelaya, José Santos, 199
Zimmerman, Arthur, 243

327.73
P   1980

A HISTORY OF UNITED STATES FOREIGN

POLICY   4th ED

CA
BALTIMORE COUNTY
PUBLIC LIBRARY
CATONSVILLE AREA BRANCH

WITHDRAWN